A History of the Human Community

Volume I

FIFTH EDITION

A History of the Human Community

Volume I: Prehistory to 1500

William H. McNeill

Professor of History Emeritus
University of Chicago

PRENTICE HALL, Upper Saddle River, New Jersey 07458

Library of Congress Cataloging-in-Publication Data

MCNEILL, WILLIAM HARDY,
    A history of the human community : prehistory to the present /
William McNeill. — 5th ed.
        p.   cm.
    Includes bibliographical references and index.
    ISBN 0-13-266289-2
    1. World history.   I. Title.
D20.M485 1996
909—dc20   96-19658
                                                 CIP

Acquisitions editor: Sally Constable
Editorial/production supervision and
    interior design: Judith Winthrop
Manufacturing buyer: Lynn Pearlman
Copy editor: Kristen Cassereau
Photo editor: Lorinda Morris-Nantz
Cover design: Kiwi Design
Cover art: Illustrated Handscroll of Minister Kibi's Trip
    to China (Kibi dajin nitto emaki). 12th c.
    Museum of Fine Arts, Boston.

This book was set in 10/12 Aster by Compset, Inc.
and was printed and bound by Courier-Westford, Inc.
The cover was printed by Phoenix Color Corp.

©1997, 1993, 1990, 1987, 1963 by William H. McNeill.
Simon & Schuster/A Viacom Company
Upper Saddle River, New Jersey 07458

Printed in the United States of America

10 9 8 7 6 5 4 3 2 1

ISBN 0-13-266289-2

Prentice-Hall International (UK) Limited, *London*
Prentice-Hall of Australia Pty. Limited, *Sydney*
Prentice-Hall Canada Inc., *Toronto*
Prentice-Hall Hispanoamericana, S.A., *Mexico*
Prentice-Hall of India Private Limited, *New Delhi*
Prentice-Hall of Japan, Inc., *Tokyo*
Simon & Schuster Asia Pte. Ltd., *Singapore*
Editora Prentice-Hall do Brasil, Ltda., *Rio de Janeiro*

Contents

Epilogue: Part I
The State of the World: 500 B.C.E. 163

Part II
EURASIAN CULTURAL BALANCE
500 B.C.E. TO A.D. 1500
---

14 *Western Europe 1200 to 1500*   *330*

Epilogue: Part II
The State of the World: 1500   *353*

Index   *I-1*

Map List

Preface

This book is built around a simple idea: People change their ways mainly because some kind of stranger has brought a new thing to their attention. The new thing may be frightening; it may be delightful; but whatever it is, it has the power to convince key persons in the community of the need to do things differently.

If this is true, then contacts between strangers with different cultures become the main drive wheel of history, because such contacts start or keep important changes going. The central theme of human history, after all, is change—how people did new things in new ways, meeting new situations as best they could.

It follows that world history can and should be written to show how in succeeding ages different human groups achieved unusual creativity and then impelled or compelled those around them (and, in time, across long distances) to alter their accustomed style of life to take account of the new things that had come to their attention by what anthropologists call "cultural diffusion" from the center of creativity. There remains a central mystery: How does important creativity occur? Accident, genius, and breakdown of old habit patterns all play a part in provoking inventions. Even more important (because it is commoner) is the need to readjust other elements in daily life after borrowing something from an outsider. So here, too, I am inclined to emphasize contacts between strangers as a basic force in increasing the variety and multiplying the openings for all kinds of creative inventions.

This angle of vision upon human affairs came to me from anthropology. In the 1930s anthropologists studied simple, isolated societies; only a few of them tried to think about relations between such "primitive" peoples and the more complicated civilized societies that occupied so much more of the face of the earth. One of the men who did wonder about the relationships between simple and complex societies was Robert Redfield. My most fundamental ideas took form while sitting in his classroom at the University of Chicago in the summer of 1936.

But even very simple general ideas have to be applied to the data of history with some care before we can really be sure whether they are much use. This took me about twenty-five years. Not till I had written *The Rise of the West: A History of the Human Community* (published in 1963) could I know how the history of humankind, insofar as modern scholars have been able to find out about it, would fit into this sort of anthropological framework.

Since then much new research has improved historical understanding. Most research corrects small details, and enough details can add up to give us, for example, a much enlarged and corrected view of the history of Africa, about which little was known a generation ago. But the greatest change in overall perspective on world history came when scholars pointed out the leading role of China in developing a trading network that bound all of the civilizations of Eurasia together after about A.D. 1000. This meant that before western Europe took over world leadership, there was a period of about 500 years when China played the same sort of role, though on a more restricted geographical scale, since, of course, the Americas remained unknown to them.

This and many other corrections of understanding are incorporated into this book. Intended for students, this book differs from *The Rise of the West* not just in being more up to date but also by spelling out more fully some of the basic information upon which the study of history is based. This risks overloading you, the student, with new names and unfamiliar technical terms. Keeping a balance between overall structure and local detail is *the* central challenge of world history, and I have tried to highlight the framework with just enough detail to give that framework meaning and substance. If you try to focus always on the question of how each part of the world fitted into the overall balance in each successive age, the burden of detail will prove bearable. For as details fit into place in your mind, this book can satisfy your natural curiosity about how we got to be the way we are. It is a curiosity everyone shares to some degree. I invite you to try and see.

William H. McNeill

Photo Credits

Fotographico; (*right*) Art Resource, New York. **195** Art Resource, New York.

Chapter 9: **198** Giraudon/Art Resource, New York. **204** (*top left*) Yale University Art Gallery, anonymous gift through Alfred R. Bellinger; (*top right*) Art Resource, New York; (*bottom left*) Art Resource, New York; (*bottom right*) Giraudon/Art Resource, New York. **210** (*top left*) Art Resource, New York; (*top right*) Scala/Art Resource, New York; (*bottom left*) Erich Lessing/Magnum Photos; (*bottom right*) William H. McNeill slide collection **221** (*left and right*) *A Pictorial Encyclopedia of the Oriental Arts: Japan,* Crown Publishers, New York.

Chapter 10: **226** Freer Gallery of Art, Smithsonian Institution, Washington, D.C. **231** William H. McNeill slide collection. **238** (*top*) William H. McNeill slide collection; (*bottom*) Omikron/Photo Researchers. **239** (*top*) Omikron/Photo Researchers; (*bottom*) Art Resource, New York. **242** Lawrence L. Smith/Photo Researchers. **243** (*top*) Archaeological Survey of India, New Delhi; (*bottom*) Columbo Museum, Ceylon. **246** Walters Art Gallery, Baltimore.

Chapter 11: **250** Giraudon/Art Resource, New York. **254** (*left*) Courtesy Museum of Fine Arts, Boston, Ross Collection Fund; (*right*) Art Resource, New York. **256** William H. McNeill slide collection. **257** University of Chicago, Department of Art. **260** (*top*) William H. McNeill slide collection; (*bottom*) Art Resource, New York. **266** (*left*) William H. McNeill slide collection; (*right*) Asukaen, Nara. **269** (*top and bottom*) Art Resource, New York.

Chapter 12: **273** Foto Marburg/Art Resource, New York. **277** (*top*) William H. McNeill slide collection; (*bottom*) Urania-Verlag, Leipzig. **282** (*top*) Josephine Powell; (*bottom*) Ann Munchow. **284** Universitets Oldsaksamling, Oslo. **287** (*top*) Paolo Koch/Rapho, Photo Reseachers; (*bottom*) Art Resource, New York. **295** (*top and bottom*) Art Resource, New York.

Illustrated Essay 2: **302** (*top*) Bettmann Archive; (*bottom*) American Museum of Natural History. **303** (*left*) Bettmann Archive; (*right*) Library of Congress.

Chapter 13: **304** Maurice Babey, Basel. **307** William H. McNeill slide collection. **308** University of Chicago, Department of Art. **310** William H. McNeill slide collection. **316** Bettman Archive. **322** (*top*) William H. McNeill slide collection; (*bottom*) George Holton/Photo Researchers. **323** (*left*) Mary M. Thacher/Photo Researchers; (*right*) Art Resource, New York.

Chapter 14: **330** Alinari/Art Resource, New York. **332** Art Resource, New York. **335** Art Resource, New York. **339** Giraudon/Art Resource, New York. **349** National Gallery, London. **350** (*left and right*) Art Resource, New York. **351** New York Public Library Picture Collection.

Epilogue II: **354** Art Resource, New York. **357** Carl Frank/Photo Researchers. **359** Art Resource, New York.

In the Beginning

1

Magdalenian Cave Art from France   The people who painted animal figures about 15,000 years ago in a cave in southern France were probably trying to make sure that the animals they hunted would continue to flourish on the face of the earth. By going deep inside the caves, they may have hoped to plant animal seeds in the womb of Mother Earth.

From the careful study of rocks, geologists know that the face of the earth has changed repeatedly. The earth itself may be about 4.5 billion years old—an unimaginably long time when measured against a human lifetime. During long ages of that past, changes in the earth's surface went very, very slowly. Yet across hundreds of millions of years, mountain ranges rose and then were cut down again by the slow action of wind and water on rock; seas spread their waters where dry land had been, and then withdrew as the land emerged once more into the atmosphere. Ice ages have come and gone; climates have altered. New forms of life evolved and old ones disappeared; even the chemical composition of sea and air changed.

The Emergence of Humans upon the Changing Face of the Earth

Deep in the geologic past, conditions on earth appear to have remained stable for quite long periods—50 to 100 millions of years. But such periods of stability were separated from one another by other times of comparatively rapid and dramatic change. The most recent million years, which constitute the Pleistocene epoch (Ice Age) of geologic time, was a period of relatively sharp and sudden change—though by our human standards of time even these changes went so slowly that we may be living amidst them still without really being much aware of the fact.

Four times during the Pleistocene epoch, great ice sheets, thousands of feet thick, formed in Europe and North America and advanced southward. Four times these glaciers melted back. The most recent melting time began about 25,000 years ago and is probably still going on in places like Greenland and Antarctica, where thick ice caps continue to cover the land.

The coming and going of the ice meant sharp and serious changes in the conditions of life for all kinds of plants and animals. Only those able to adapt themselves to such changes could survive, and, in fact, many creatures disappeared. Saber-toothed tigers and mastodons, for example, no longer exist. Other animals such as horses once galloped across the grasslands of both Europe and North America, but they disappeared in America a few thousand years before the Spaniards again introduced them from the Old World, where they had never died out.

Changes such as these were dramatic in themselves. But the rise of humankind, which took place during the same million-odd years when the ice advanced and retreated, also changed conditions of life in remarkable and far-reaching ways. For human beings learned how to alter the biological balance of the earth by making specially selected and domesticated plants and animals flourish in the fields and pastures of the world, thereby displacing wild species.

Such achievements often have unexpected and undesired results. Diseases and pests, for example, infested barns and fields; and erosion sometimes stripped the topsoil from whole regions where farmers had destroyed the natural vegetation in order to plant grain or other crops. In recent times we have even begun to alter the earth's physical geography, not only by building cities, highways, dams, pipelines, and canals, but also by polluting the air and water with all kinds of wastes.

In all these ways, human activity began to change the face of the earth far more rapidly than ever before. The slow-acting forces of unconscious nature were no match for conscious and cooperative human efforts to make over the environment.

Charles Darwin in 1859, after studying geological fossils as well as the differences among forms of life that existed in his own day in different parts of the world, proposed the theory of organic evolution in his book *On the Origin of Species*. He later wrote *The Descent of Man* (1871), in which he suggested that human beings, too, had evolved from other forms of life. Such an idea was shocking to most of Darwin's contemporaries. But more and more evidence has been found since then to support his theory, even though some of Darwin's ideas about how one species turned into another were later disproved.

Scientific thought is always subject to correction when new evidence turns up. Current ideas about human origins are especially uncertain, for the gaps in the evidence are still great. Nevertheless, most experts on human evolution now agree that creatures enough like ourselves to count as prehumans began to walk the earth more than a million years ago.

Little is yet known about these prehumans or how they came into existence. Bits of skeletons have been found in many parts of the world, from England to China and from Java to Africa. Much uncertainty remains, but the bones that have been discovered tell us something. For instance, a half-million years ago the various kinds of humanlike creatures differed from one another much more than human races differ today. There were both giants and pygmies, with teeth and skulls combining characteristics of modern apes and humans in different ways.

From Prehuman to Human

Prehuman communities presumably evolved biologically; that is, changes in genes were more important than changes in learned behavior. No one can say when evolution by learning to do things in a new way became more important than genetic changes. We can be fairly certain that prehumans had to be able to talk before learning could attain decisive importance. Our prehuman ancestors also had to be able to handle sticks and stones as weapons and tools.

But definite biological changes had to come before the legs and feet of our prehuman ancestors became strong enough to walk on, leaving their hands and arms free to explore the world, with the help of eyes and tongue. Other changes were needed to give the tongue free play for articulate (distinctly spoken) speech. Connected with these biological changes was an increase in the size of the brain. These changes did not come all at once. Nor can we tell whether humanlike creatures finally became fully human at a single place and time, or whether genetic strands combined and recombined to bring different groups, in different parts of the world, across the threshold of humanity at different times.

Tool-using is not exclusively human. Traces of fire and stones that had been chipped to make crude tools have been found in association with skeletons that are very different from those of modern humans; in fact, chimpanzees and other animals have been known to use simple tools.

The critical difference, perhaps, was first dance, then speech. Dancing together created warm feelings that allowed larger numbers to cooperate; and speech made their cooperation more effective and precise. With language a plan could be worked out ahead of time, assigning one person here and another there to take the victim by surprise or to drive the game into a prearranged trap. Enormous improvement in the food supply must have resulted from the use of language for hunting. In particular, language allowed our earliest ancestors to kill larger and larger animals, instead of having to depend only on small game.

As this change occurred, prehuman hunters could become fully human, because, for the first time, they could afford to support and train children for months and even years after birth. Thus the period in which children learned the arts of life and how to behave could be prolonged. And it was by learning more and inheriting less that prehumans became humans.

In the second place, language allowed people to refine and improve their reactions to the world around them. Different kinds of animals and plants, stones, and even actions were given names, and having names, could then be recognized more easily; and their possibilities for good or evil could be learned ahead of time. Such words allowed our distant ancestors to organize their world according to general categories or classifications into which particular sights and sounds could be made to fit. Knowing what to expect from each category, they could then act more efficiently in a particular case.

There is yet a third sense in which words and language made prehumans into human beings. Words can be combined and recombined in much the same way that people can use their hands to play with small objects and combine them or recombine them into new devices, patterns, and forms. As playing with things may inspire someone to invent new weapons, tools, and works of art, so playing with words can provoke new ideas and feelings. Thus reason and invention were let loose by the power of speech to classify things and by the capacity of hands to handle them. From the interplay between these two distinctive abilities, the human species finally and fully emerged, probably in Africa sometime between 500,000 and 50,000 years ago.

The Origins of Race

Modern races presumably descend from various mixtures of ancestral types. Some of the most obvious differences, such as skin color, which divide us today are a result of adaptation to different climates. For example, Mongolian features and skin color are well adapted for survival in cold climates; African and Indian populations have dark skins that protect them from tropical ultraviolet rays; and the pale skins of Europeans are adapted to the scarcity of sunlight in a cloudy climate.

Race has become an issue in politics and social life not only in the United States but also in many other parts of the world. Skin color is obvious; hence our sensitivity to the shade of a person's complexion. But classification by skin color distorts and confuses the genetic facts of human variation, which are much more complicated than any difference indicated by skin color alone. Human beings cannot be divided into clearly separate races, for they show many kinds of intermediate types, involving every sort of variable characteristic. Moreover, variations in one physical characteristic, such as skin color, do not necessarily match variations in other characteristics, such as hair texture or head shape.

No satisfactory classification of humanity according to physical type has ever been devised. A common system recognizes white, yellow, and black races; but it is not really helpful, because each of these races includes many subtypes and local populations that differ from one another in important ways. The Ainu peoples of Japan, for example, have white skins but in other respects do not physically resemble Euro-

pean populations; and the Australian aborigines are certainly black, but they still are very different in their bodily form from black-skinned peoples elsewhere.

Small, isolated communities may at times have been able to establish a nearly uniform genetic pattern among a few hundred or a few thousand human beings. But such communities never kept themselves apart from the rest of humankind long enough to become a different biological species; or rather, if any communities did so, they were later destroyed when they came into contact with a human population more open to the outside world.

When two or more different races live side by side for a few generations, biological boundaries blur. As time passes, more and more people of mixed blood combine features from the different races. This is as true in the United States, where whites and blacks have lived together for about 300 years, as it is in India, where light-skinned and darker-skinned populations have lived side by side for about 4500 years.

Wherever people mingle and move about, as has been happening more and more frequently in recent centuries, all sorts of intermediate mixed racial types come into existence. Until a few hundred years ago, most human beings were grouped in small village or tribal communities whose relations with the outside world were quite limited. As a result, ten or fifteen generations back, our ancestors seldom saw anyone who did not fall within a well-defined local range of physical variation. This ceased to be true as ships and trains and airplanes made it easier to move about, so that all the different types of human beings began to mix more rapidly than before.

Racial purity among large and flourishing human communities never existed. Variations in physical appearance of course occur, and people react to such variations, thinking some persons beautiful or desirable and others ugly. But these opinions vary from time to time and from place to place.

The breakdown of age-old isolation is what created the conditions for modern race feeling. In more and more parts of the world, people of different appearance find themselves living side by side. However unreasonable, it is sometimes

THE OLDUVAI GORGE IN AFRICA

The Olduvai Gorge in Tanzania, located a little southeast of Lake Victoria, has recently become the most important site in the world for finding out about human origins. The gorge itself is a narrow slash cut some 300 feet deep into the African landscape by the Olduvai River that runs through its bottom in the rainy season and then almost dries up for most of the year. The walls of the gorge expose layers of soft sediments that formed at the bottom of an old lake during the past million or so years.

Geologically, the gorge is remarkable because its walls are so soft. The change in earth levels that drained the former lake and allowed the Olduvai River to begin cutting through its bottom is very recent, as geological time goes, being measured in thousands rather than in millions of years. And because the change is so recent, the steep, soft sides of the gorge now stand almost bare under the African sun; they can easily be examined by human eyes and can be scratched with pick or dug with spades.

When Dr. Louis Leakey and his wife, Mary, began to examine the gorge in the early 1950s, they quickly found vast numbers of chipped stones that had presumably been shaped by humans or by humanlike creatures. Such a complete and lengthy series of tools was unmatched elsewhere in the world. The most dramatic find, however, fell to Mary Leakey in 1959, when, at the very lowest level of the Olduvai deposits, she discovered the shattered fragments of a skull that had once belonged to a humanlike creature. She named her find *Zinjanthropus*, though some experts denied that the skull really belonged to a creature enough like humans to deserve the name *anthropos* (Greek for "man"). From the position where she found the skull fragments, Mary Leakey argued that they must be about a million years old. Here, it seemed clear, was what remained of one of the makers of the earliest, crudest type of stone tools found in the lowest layers of the Olduvai Gorge.

At other levels in the Olduvai Gorge, other similar bones have been found. They differ from one another in important details. In addition, the types of stone tools changed with the levels from which they came. With so many finds in hand, the Leakeys were able to prove that with the passage of time the designs and workmanship of the chipped stones consistently improved; but relationships between the different kinds of skeletal remains are not yet clear.

These discoveries in the Olduvai Gorge may show that humans first came into existence on the high plateau region of Africa in the neighborhood of Lake Victoria. This is what the Leakeys believe, and many others are inclined to agree with them. On the other hand, the finds at Olduvai, dramatic and important as they are, also prove how very little we yet know about human origins. The discovery of a single new skeleton in some other part of the world can still change the whole picture, just as the Leakeys' discoveries in the Olduvai Gorge have done.

hard not to fear and distrust people who seem strange, or whose forebears have run afoul of yours—even (or especially) when they live next door or just a few blocks away. But the fact that differing human types are now living side by side more often than ever before means that the age-old process of biological and social mixture is going ahead more rapidly than in times past. If new barriers to movement do not arise, the physical differences among people will eventually become less than they are today, just as the differences today are less than they were when widely different prehuman types walked the earth.

The Age of the Hunters— Old Stone Age

The first humans were gatherers and big game hunters. They lived in small groups, probably averaging no more than twenty to sixty people most of the time. Leadership rested with bold and experienced men who knew the habits of game and how to kill. Each group hunted within a fairly well-defined territory and rarely encountered strangers. Such communities probably had more or less settled campsites to which everyone came back at night; but from time to time, if food became scarce, the whole group might move to another hunting ground.

There were deep satisfactions in such a life, but hunger and fear were never far away. A wound or a broken leg was likely to be fatal. At almost any moment, a sudden encounter with some fierce animal might end even the bravest hunter's life. Or strangers might suddenly try to take hunting grounds away, forcing the group to make a choice between fighting back, withdrawing, or trying to make peace.

Community Activity

Women's life consisted of steady work. Searching for food—seeds, berries, roots, grubs, insects, and other edibles—was a main part of their task. In addition, women made baskets out of twigs and grass, guarded the campsite, cared for infants, taught small children how to behave, and all the while kept a sharp eye out for any danger that might threaten.

Men undertook tasks that required muscular strength and endurance. Preparation for the hunt involved making or repairing spears, knives, and similar tools by joining sharpened rocks to wooden handles. Stalking animals that could run much faster than their pursuers—and that sometimes were far stronger and better equipped for combat than human beings—took much patience and prolonged cooperation. To strike an animal in an exposed vital part with sudden, sharp exertion required courage as well as precise muscular coordination.

After the kill came joy and a time for boasting, living over again the stages of the expedition, praising or blaming each hunter's actions, and reasserting the group's solidarity by dividing the flesh of the victim among the hunters and their families. After the meal, came dancing and singing around the fire. Rhythmic movements expressed and reinforced the solidarity of the group, healed any individual frictions or frustrations the day might have brought, and prepared everyone for a sound sleep. Within a day or two the cycle began over again, when nothing but well-gnawed bones remained from the last kill.

Prehistoric Beliefs   Ancient hunters probably believed the world was full of spirits. How people first got the idea that spirits existed we do not know; and how they tried to deal with them we can only guess by studying how contemporary hunting peoples behave, and by taking note of the bits of evidence ancient hunters left behind them.

By far, the most impressive prehistoric evidence can be seen in the famous cave paintings located in south-central France and in northern Spain. Here, about 15,000 years ago, artists painted beautiful and amazingly lifelike portraits of the animals they hunted and killed. These paintings are located deep in the earth, as much as a half-mile from daylight. They may have been intended to appease the spirits of the animals portrayed. Or perhaps the paintings were meant to persuade the "Earth Mother" to give birth to deer, bison, woolly mammoth, and other beasts for men to kill and eat.

Everywhere, we may guess, humans felt a sense of mystery as they watched the change of seasons, the migration of game, the waxing and waning of the moon, and the growth and decay of their own bodily strength and skill with the passage of years.

Tools of the Old Stone Age   The cave paintings of France and Spain are, so far as we know, unique. From most of the world all we have is enormous numbers of shaped and sharpened stones dropped around old campsites or in caves. Experts have classified those tools into sequences by determining that certain kinds of harpoon heads or fishhooks, found near the surface of a cave floor, were made by people who came after others who had used spearheads and knives of a different design, found further down in the earth. By digging still deeper, cruder tools made by still earlier humans sometimes turn up.

Precise sequences of this kind were first worked out by arachaeologists comparing the remains from caves of the Dordogne Valley of south-central France, near the site where the cave paintings were found. Elsewhere not nearly so much is known, and we should not assume that the succession of tool types discovered in France corresponds to what happened in other parts of the world.

Still, scholars now know enough to say that in general, and all over the world, hunting bands developed more and better kinds of tools as time passed. This was particularly true when new materials like bone, antler, and rawhide came into use. But throughout the age of the hunters, the fundamental tool remained a cutting edge, which was made by chipping bits away from a piece of brittle stone until the right shape and size had been achieved. In Europe and western Asia, such tools were made by knocking a large flake from a larger block of stone and then improving its shape by taking a lot of smaller chips from the large flake. In eastern Asia people preferred to keep on knocking chips from a core and shape the core into the final form. This difference of technique lasted for hundreds of thousands of years and is almost all that can be

said for sure about the earliest differences in human ways of doing things.

But whether the ancient hunters worked from a flake or from a core, the end product was much the same. Sharp and serviceable spearheads, arrow points, and knife blades could be made quite easily—as is shown by the incredible numbers of such remains that still can be picked up. With the right kind of stone to work with, it took a skillful hunter only a few minutes to make a new blade when an old one had been lost or damaged.

People later learned to grind stones into smooth shapes. This very obvious difference led the scholars who first studied early tools to divide them into Old Stone, or Paleolithic, and New Stone, or Neolithic, types. The difference was important, for, as we shall see, people began to polish stone tools only when they needed them for new purposes. But the rough, quickly made chipped blades of the Old Stone Age were, in fact, very well suited to the ancient hunters' needs, so changes in design came very slowly indeed.

If we assume that human communities developed more than a million years ago, then human beings lived more or less according to the patterns we have just described for approximately 99 percent of their time on earth. Even if we make a much more recent estimate of the date at which human beings emerged, we still must assign at least four-fifths of humanity's earthly career to this sort of life. During most of that long time, there is little trace of any alteration in the way people did things. Indeed, insofar as we have instincts and inborn traits of behavior, they are surely attuned to the routines of small hunting and gathering bands. One of the problems civilized populations have always had to face is how to reconcile the aptitude for violence so necessary for the ancient hunter with the requirements of peace and order within large, complicated communities.

The Appearance of Modern Human Types

By the fourth period of glaciation of the Pleistocene epoch, humans had already come a long way. As climates changed and became cooler, some bands of hunters responded by learning how to sew animal skins together, thus making clothes to keep themselves warm. With clothing, almost hairless humans could live in climates where temperatures went below freezing for part of the year. The cold also required more elaborate shelters, either caves, tents made of animal skins, or houses built of mud and wood.

The climatic change may also have stimulated considerable human migration. With better tools and the skills and knowledge needed to build warm houses and to make warm clothes, people were able to spread into new regions of the earth. In particular, the part of Eurasia that lies north of the great mountain backbone of that land mass opened for human settlement, up to the limit set by the glaciers. The Americans also appear to have been populated for the first time by people who walked across the ice that covered Bering Strait. Less is known about changes in human distribution in the Southern Hemisphere. Boats or rafts carried people to Australia and Tasmania at an early date, perhaps at a time when so much sea water was locked up in the glaciers that the gap between Australia and southeast Asia was narrower than it is today.

New physical types appeared during this period in Europe and other parts of the Old World. The most famous of these were Neanderthalers, named for a valley in Germany where this sort of skeleton was first discovered. Neanderthalers were short and stocky, stoop-shouldered and low-browed, and may have been very hairy. They lived in caves, which helped them to endure the glacial cold.

As the glaciers began to melt, "modern" kinds of humans moved into Europe, and Neanderthalers disappeared. The newcomers may have hunted the older type to death, or the two kinds of humans may have intermingled, but if so their descendants' bones showed practically no trace of Neanderthal traits.

As modern kinds of people spread across the earth some 300 generations ago, hunting bands learned to live in many different climates and to hunt many different kinds of animals. Yet they remained relatively rare in the balance of nature. Populations were thinly spread, and groups remained small because the food they needed was scarce and hard to come by. Too many hunters soon meant too little to eat. Human beings, in other words, were still at the mercy of the natural balances that defined the kind and numbers of plants and animals that could grow in a given region.

For many thousands of years, this natural balance set limits that seemed to be fixed and absolute. Yet the next great stage in human development allowed people to escape from this limitation. They learned how to change the balance of nature deliberately by planting crops and domesticating animals. By doing so, they vastly increased the food supply at their disposal, allowing their number to increase, and creating the basis upon which all later civilizations depended.

The Age of the Food Producers— New Stone Age

No one knows for certain when and where human communities first learned to cultivate the ground and plant crops. Women probably took the important first steps. They were the ones who picked seeds and berries while the men hunted. And women may have known for a very long time how to pull out useless plants to make more room for those that produced good seeds or fruits. But as long as bands of humans moved to and fro across miles of country, always looking for the best hunting grounds, the women could do only a little to encourage the growth of edible berries, seed grasses, or roots.

Grain Farming and Herding

Not long before 7000 B.C.E., however, a basic change began to affect the part of the world now called the Middle East. We can tell well enough what came out of the change: small, simple villages of farmers. But no one knows just how or exactly where the change occurred.

The most favorable ground for the invention of agriculture lay on the western side of the numerous hills and mountains that lie east of the Mediterranean Sea but to the west of what is now the central desert region of Iran. In this region, hillsides facing westerly winds caught enough rain to support a fairly heavy growth of trees. The plains were usually too dry for trees and could only support grasses, with occasional clumps of trees along watercourses or where underground water came near the surface. Toward the south, the land became drier and shaded off into harsh desert in southern Iraq and northern Arabia.

As to how farming was invented, we have to guess. The real breakthrough was the discovery of how to make seed-bearing grasses—ancestors of our wheat and barley—grow in places where they did not grow naturally. By preparing fields in forested land, where grasses did not ordinar-

ily grow at all, people could plant suitable kinds of seeds and be sure that only food crops would grow. In such locations natural competitors (weeds) could not mix with and partly crowd out the seed-bearing wheat and barley, because weed seeds could not easily pass through the forest barrier and establish themselves on the artificially cleared land.

The trick, then, was to be able to create at will special environments where useful plants could thrive. Men did this by cutting a ring of bark around trees of the forest. Slashing the bark killed the trees and opened the forest floor to sunlight. In such a specially prepared place, wheat and barley could grow very well indeed.

But before agriculture could flourish, still another change had to take place. When shaken by the wind or by some passing animal, wild wheat and barley scattered their ripe seeds on the ground. This made harvesting difficult. But human action soon selected strains with tougher stems, so that seed no longer shook out of the ripened ears, even when the stalks were grasped by human hands and cut with a sickle. After all, only those seeds that stayed in the ear could be carried home by the farmers, and only seeds that had been safely harvested could be planted the next year. Rapid selection therefore took place in favor of varieties that suited human needs.

After forest clearings had been cultivated for two or three years, the cultivators found it helpful to burn the dead tree trunks and scatter the ashes over the soil. This fertilized the ground for one or two more crops. But after five or six years, such fields usually became choked with thistles and other weeds (whose seeds had come in on the wind), so that the soil was no longer worth cultivating. Instead, the early farmers killed the trees somewhere else in the forest and started the cycle of slash-and-burn cultivation all over again. Their old fields, abandoned, soon filled with trees again.

Tools of the New Stone Age   The soft soil of the forest floor scarcely needed to be dug. A pointed stick to stir up the leaf mold and make sure the seeds were in contact with moist ground beneath was all that was necessary to make the seeds grow. Special sickles for cutting

Slash-and-Burn Cultivation   Early farmers knew how to make grain grow in places where it did not grow naturally. By cutting the bark around trees, thus killing them, and letting sunlight reach the ground, farmers could make grain grow abundantly. After a year or two, farmers burned the dead trees so the ashes could improve the fertility of the soil. But in time, airborne seeds arrived to share the space farmers had opened up, and eventually weeds crowded out the grain. When that happened, farmers moved on, cleared a new plot in the forest, and repeated the cycle. This sort of slash-and-burn agriculture still exists in Borneo and a few other remote regions of the earth.

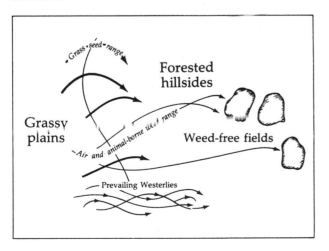

grain stalks had already been invented to aid in harvesting wild-growing grain. None of these implements required any fundamental change in tool types.

But cutting the bark around tree trunks was a different matter. An ax sharp enough to bite through into the wood, and tough enough not to shatter on impact against the tree trunk, demanded a different kind of stone from that used in making hunting tools. Arrowheads, knives, and spears could be made of brittle stone, for they were designed to cut soft animal tissues. They needed to be sharp, and even pre-humans had discovered how to shatter a stone in such a way as to produce suitable cutting edges. But the techniques for shaping brittle stone would not do for an ax. Tough, unchippable kinds of stones were needed to withstand the

Paleolithic and Neolithic Axes These axes were made differently because they were used for different purposes. The chipped ax (above) was intended to cut soft animal tissues. It was shaped by tapping one end of a hard stick while holding the other end tightly against the stone's surface. With practice, chips of the right size and shape could be knocked off quickly and easily to make a sharp cutting tool.

The smooth ax (below) was made by polishing a tough-grained kind of stone that would not shatter when struck against wood. Attached to a handle, it was used to cut down trees in order to clear fields for grain. Polishing stone took a long time and was much harder work than chipping away at brittle stones. In general, farmers had to work a lot more than hunters, and the different way in which they made their axes illustrates this fact.

impact against a tree trunk. The problem was solved by grinding and polishing basalt and similar varieties of hard, dense stone.

Tools produced by this method look very different from those made by chipping brittle pieces of flint. Slow, patient work of grinding and polishing the natural surfaces of the stone produced smooth, keen cutting edges. Obviously, this took much longer than chipping tools into shape; but a well-made stone ax might last a lifetime and could be resharpened over and over again in exactly the same way that it had been made in the first place. Such axes were quite efficient. Modern experiments have shown that, when put onto a proper handle, ancient stone axes can cut down a tree almost as fast as a modern steel-bladed ax.

Needless to say, people did not cease to be hunters when they discovered how to make little fields in the forests and plant grain in them. Moreover, in places far away from the forest slopes of the Middle East, life went on quite unchanged by the fact that a few human communities had made this discovery. All the same, the balance of nature was seriously upset, for as food from the forest grainfields became more and more abundant, larger numbers of human beings could survive. Soon there were far too many hunters, fed partly by grain from the new fields. Wild game animals within range of the farming communities were nearly exterminated.

The Domestication of Animals This imbalance presented hunters with a great crisis. Some of them met it by domesticating a few of the kinds of animals they had been accustomed to chase and kill. At first these animals were only used for meat. But by or before 4000 B.C.E., some communities in and around the Middle East had worked out other ways to exploit their flocks and herds. In particular, animal milk became an important new food; animal hair and wool was sheared and made into cloth; and animal strength was harnessed to carry and pull heavy loads. On the grasslands north of the Black Sea, horse breeders may have learned to ride, but for a long time no one dared to drop the reins in order to shoot with a bow, so the military significance of riding horseback was delayed for more than two millennia.

Nonetheless, these new ways of using domestic animals gave farm communities valuable new resources. Milk and milk products (cheese, butter, yogurt) added fat and protein to a mainly cereal diet, and woolen cloth could be tailored to fit local climates as tanned animal skins—the older sort of clothes—could not be.

Animals selected for their readiness to submit to human exploitation quickly diverged from their wild ancestors. Their skeletons changed, and so experts can usually tell whether a particular pile of bones scattered around some ancient dwelling place came from wild or domesticated stock.

The fact is that as humans became dependent on food coming from domesticated plants and animals, domesticated plants and animals also became dependent on human beings. Wheat and barley that did not scatter its seeds naturally on the ground could not grow unless planted by hand. Domesticated animals, lacking the fierceness of their wild relatives, could not survive without human protection.

Humans, of course, became even more immediately dependent on their crops and herds. They paid another price in the form of less free time than hunters and gatherers enjoyed; and settling down in one place had the effect of intensifying exposure to various infectious diseases.

All the same, when the new kinds of plants and animals had come into existence and when men and women had learned how to manage them skillfully, the scene was set for comparatively rapid expansion of a radically new style of human living. Wherever suitable broad-leaved forests could be found, it was easy to carve out the fields upon which these little farming communities depended. Wherever grasses or leafy plants grew wild, people could drive their flocks and herds to pasture. Northern cold and desert dryness set limits to this kind of life, but within the wide zone that lay between these extremes, the whole world lay open to the first Neolithic farmers and herders.

As grainfields became more and more important, bands of people settled down to live in one spot for several years at a time. A prolonged stay made it worthwhile to build solid houses, often of mud or mud-brick, perhaps with some kind of thatched roof. It was also possible to furnish the house with breakables, such as pottery; and since grain had to be stored in a dry place to prevent premature sprouting, large storage pots became important.

From the time pottery first appeared, different communities shaped and decorated pots and other objects in different ways. And since baked clay lasts a long time, and styles of decoration changed with time as well as with place, pottery provides the experts with their principal evidence of cultural traditions and connections between archaeological sites.

Three Major Problems of the Early Farmers

The earliest farmers probably led peaceful lives, but not for long. While some human communities learned how to farm, others lived in drier, grassy areas where slash-and-burn cultivation would not work. But such communities could domesticate animals and pasture them on the wide grasslands that lay both north and south of the forested zones of the Middle East. Communities that specialized as shepherds and herders remained footloose, moving from place to place in search of pasture. The men in such communities kept much of the spirit and organization of the early hunting bands, for their daily task was to defend their animals against wild beasts and against other men. Warlike habits and the discipline of cooperation in combat naturally arose from such daily experience.

Relations with Herders   Farmers' daily experience, on the contrary, required each family to scatter for work in the fields. Warlike habits did not find much scope when the daily tasks were to chop the trees, dig the ground, and cut the grain. As a result, herders soon discovered that they could attack and defeat farmers and then force them to part with their precious grain or other useful goods.

The balance between farmers and herders was by no means simple. Usually, farmers were more numerous but not so well organized for fighting. Walls could be built, as in China, and guards assigned to protect farming villages from surprise, but it was difficult to combine constant readiness for attack with the tasks of cultivation.

Contact between herders and farmers was not always hostile, however. Instead of seizing grain and others goods by force, the herders might come as bargainers, offering cheese or wool or animals in exchange for cereal food or some other product of the farmers' skills. Herders were sometimes able to offer the farmers special stones or shells, or some other rare commodity that they had found in the course of their wanderings. In this way, rarities that were particularly valued, such as jade, often traveled long distances, passing from hand to hand several times en route.

Accurate Measurement of Time   Another critical problem for early farmers was deciding when to plant. In the Middle East, rains fall only in the winter months. Grain must be planted in the fall and ripens in early summer after the drought sets in. If, however, the seed grain is planted too soon, a chance shower might cause the seed to sprout, only to wither in the sun's pitiless rays. If, on the other hand, the seed grain is planted too late, the plants might not ripen fully before summer drought sets in again.

Such errors were disastrous; how could they be avoided? The answer was to watch the moon and count the months marked out by the moon's phases. But, of course, the waxing and waning of the moon does not exactly fit into the solar year, which determines the seasons. Every so often, communities that counted by the moon had to put an extra month in their calendar to adjust to the track of the sun.

Exactly how to do this in order to keep an accurate calendar was never solved satisfactorily by the early farmers. But, compared to what hunters had to know about time, the first farmers had a far greater need for accurate timekeeping, and they made great advances. In the hunter's life, one day was much like the other. Whether it was sunny or rainy, hot or cold, made small difference in what had to be done. The farmer, on the other hand, had to look forward and learn to count and calculate. How much grain could a family afford to eat, and how much

should be set aside for planting? Farmers had to ration consumption so as to make the grain last until the new harvest. The year, instead of the day, became the fundamental unit of human time, and the annual measurement of time became vital.

Very likely certain individuals in the early farming communities became ritual experts—the earliest priests—and decided under which

---

Neolithic Fertility Goddess   This crude figure from southern France probably symbolized Mother Earth. It was carved by Neolithic farmers who depended on crops of grain that they planted each year. The object in the goddess's left hand looks both like a horn and a crescent moon. Perhaps it is both. The horn of plenty, filled to overflowing with the fruits of the harvest, was a commonplace image in the art of later ages and may date all the way back to Neolithic times. The moon was important to early farmers as a marker of time. They knew when to plant their crops by counting months marked off by the phases of the moon.

moon to plant the grain. But we have no certain information about this. We do know that the farmers' concern about planting and harvesting crops found expression in religion. Sun and moon, particularly the latter, were worshiped as gods or spirits with power over fertility. The earth, too, was thought of as a great mother, giving birth to the food people needed.

The parallel between the patterns of human life and plant life impressed itself on early farmers' minds. If seed, when planted, sprang again to life, only to die and then be planted once again, what of humans? If buried in a grave, would a person not rise again? Since dead relatives and friends often appeared in dreams, it seemed logical to answer yes. After death a person's lot must be a shadowy life, perhaps in a dark underworld. Old Stone Age hunters, too, probably believed in life after death and may have conceived of the earth as a mother. Differences, therefore, were more of emphasis than of kind.

Shortage of Suitable Land   The third great practical problem the early farmers confronted was a growing shortage of suitable forest land. As the population grew, virgin timber became scarcer and scarcer. It became necessary after a while to use abandoned fields over again, and at shorter and shorter intervals. This meant less abundant crops, since the soil was less fertile. It also became increasingly difficult to keep weeds under control: The closer together fields got to be, the more easily could weed seeds pass from one open sun-soaked patch of ground to another. Less-fertile soils and weed-choked fields meant less food for the same effort. Each family therefore had to cultivate more land, but this only made the problem worse.

Not very long before 3000 B.C.E., a brilliant solution to the problem of land shortage was discovered—the invention of the plow. Probably it was not in the forested regions but in more open land along river banks that plows were invented. After all, the first fields were full of stumps. How could a plow do much good in such a place? But when men began to use animal strength to drag a spade or hoe through the ground, new possibilities opened up. Plowing could keep down the weeds. This, indeed, was its most important function. Plowing could also allow a single family to cultivate a far greater area than was possible with digging sticks. Finally, plowing allowed farmers to keep the same fields under cultivation indefinitely, for they soon discovered that a field left fallow (that is, unseeded) and plowed once or twice during the growing season—to kill the weeds before they could go to seed—would yield a satisfactory harvest next year. A simple rotation between fallowing one year and planting the next thus developed. And a single family, with a suitable plow and team of oxen or donkeys, could keep enough land in tillage to feed themselves and have something left over—on most soils and in most seasons.

The invention of the plow was fundamental to all subsequent Middle Eastern, Indian, and European civilizations. The plow was unknown in the Americas and never became as important in China as in western Eurasia. It brought animal husbandry (care and breeding) and grain farming together in a new way. It made men instead of women the main cultivators, for men followed their beasts into the fields and drove the plow, whereas before the invention of the plow women had probably done most of the work in the fields.

The plow also created the sort of field we know today. When the same ground was kept in cultivation, after a few years stumps rotted away, and the plow soon evened off the small hummocks that nature creates in any forest floor. Such fields could then become the smooth, open-land surfaces, one adjacent to the next, often laid out in a more or less regular geometric pattern that we think of when we use the word "field."

Finally, the plow enabled grain farmers to settle down permanently. Once plowed fields had been laid out and brought into cultivation there was no reason to move on. Permanent village sites, fixed patterns of ownership of particular fields, and a structure of village life that has lasted to the present day in Europe and western Asia thus came into existence. At the same time, the possibility of empire dawned. Farmers who could not afford to move away could be taxed; and taxes could support courts, rulers, armies, and cities. Civilization, in short, became a possibility.

The Root Farmers

Before the Middle Eastern style of grain farming and herding had spread very far, people in other parts of the world began a different kind of cultivation. In fact, cultivation of roots for food in the tropical regions of southeast Asia may be older than the grain farming of the Middle East. No one can be sure.

We know far less about how root farming began than about the beginnings of grain farming. It is a good guess—but only a guess—that this kind of farming started among fishermen who lived along the river edges and seacoasts of southeast Asia. The reason for thinking this may have been the case is that fishermen who use boats must come back to the land frequently, and they must come back to sheltered places where their boats are not likely to be damaged by a storm. Hunters were always moving on, but fishing communities tended to settle permanently around suitable harbors. When this happened, the women could concentrate on finding good food crops and planting them near the boat landings.

The addition of root crops—manioc, taro, cassava, yams, and many more—to the food supply of fishing communities presumably increased the number of fishermen. If they became so numerous that there were fewer fish per fisherman to catch, then they had to eat more of the starchy roots, but they could not domesticate fish in the way hunters in the Middle East domesticated animals.

Contrast with Grain Farming   The differences between grain farming and root growing are simple but important. Grain farmers harvested seed and planted some of their last year's harvest to get the next crop. Root farmers planted a live shoot from the parent plant in a new place and waited for the shoot to grow new roots. When the roots were big enough, they were dug up and eaten. In the same patch of cultivated ground, therefore, plants at all stages of growth could usually be found—some freshly transplanted, some almost ready to be used, and others at various stages in between.

This kind of farming can flourish only where the difference between summer and winter is slight and plants grow all through the year. Grain farming, on the other hand, assumes a time in the year when plants do not grow, for only in such a climate will plants develop food-rich seeds to carry on the germ of life from one season to the next. Hence, root cultivation fitted the tropics and must have started there, whereas seed farming started in the temperate zone.

Because the beginnings of root cultivation probably did not make very much difference in the way people lived, there is little indication of when it happened. There is no sign that population started to grow massively, as happened in the Middle East when grain cultivation got established. The east Asian root crops never supplied the basic foods for civilized societies in Eurasia. The development of root cultivation, therefore, was not nearly so world-shaking as the changes brought by the first farmers of the Middle East.

Rice Paddy Farming

At a later stage, however, the farming of the monsoon region of Asia achieved a much greater life-transforming power. This happened when Asian root growers discovered that rice, a kind of water-loving plant that invaded their fields when river floods put them temporarily underwater, had a seed that was good to eat and worth raising for its own sake. They used the methods of planting they already knew; that is, they transplanted a growing rice seedling into the fields or paddies, instead of sowing the grain by throwing it broadcast on the ground.

To this day, the rice of Asia is first set out to sprout in special seed beds, and then each plant is separately put into the ground to grow to maturity in fields that are flooded by water brought from some nearby stream. Rice paddy farming feeds a third or more of the people on earth today. It provided the main agricultural basis of the Chinese and Japanese civilizations.

Its success rested on two technical facts. First, by creating artificially flooded fields in places where such flooding did not normally occur, the rice paddy farmers made an environment in which the rice plants, which naturally grow in shallow, fresh water, had no competition. Most weeds were eliminated by drowning. This method is comparable to the way that slash-and-burn farmers of the Middle East eliminated competing grasses by creating an artifial environment for their wheat and barley in isolated forest clearings. Second, the steady flow of fresh water into the paddies and out again brought dissolved minerals to the fields. The slow flow of water also provided an environment in which complicated interactions of light, water, and innumerable microorganisms kept up the fertility of the paddies year after year. Once the fields had been laid out, farmers could expect a good crop each year. Unlike slash-and-burn grain cultivators, who had to move on from time to time, rice cultivators had absolutely no incentive to move away and leave their carefully leveled fields behind.

People thus discovered how to change the natural balance of plants and animals in thoroughgoing and drastic ways. In the Middle East, human communities invented grain cultivation and the domestication of animals between about 8000 and 6000 B.C.E. In southeast Asia, root cultivation developed, beginning no one knows when. But rice paddy farming was probably perfected not long before 2400 B.C.E., when the earliest definite evidence of rice cultivation comes from China.

The Spread of Farming Techniques

In other parts of the world, farming became important still later—often, and perhaps always, after people had heard from strangers how it was possible to plant and harvest seeds or roots. Rice paddy agriculture spread more slowly than slash-and-burn grain farming. It also spread less far, but where it established itself, it took over the landscape in a much more thoroughgoing way than the early grain farming did.

By the standards of our day, life in tiny farming settlements of 200 to 300 people changed very slowly. When experts compare the bits and pieces left from Neolithic villages, they do find small differences from one layer to the next, or from one site to another, but the general impression is of a great sameness. This presumably reflects the fact that once the skills and tools needed for a farmer's life had been invented, nothing much more was needed. Year after year the same tasks had to be done: grain planted and harvested, new fields broken in, houses repaired or rebuilt; from time to time the whole community might have to move a few miles to some place where fresh forest land lay at hand.

But however unchanging Neolithic village routines may have been, the rise and spread of this new way of life worked great changes in the landscape. Slash-and-burn methods of cultivation required frequent relocation. A single community might move several times in a person's lifetime, perhaps twenty or more miles at a time. By comparison with any earlier changes that we know of, this meant a tremendously rapid transformation of the natural environment. Moreover, the new techniques could easily be imitated by neighboring bands of hunters. Grain farming therefore spread in every direction from its Middle Eastern place of origin. Farmers arrived in south Russia and the Balkans soon after 4500 B.C.E., and slash-and-burn cultivation reached the Atlantic coast of Europe about a thousand years later. A similar movement carried farmers across north Africa and into western Europe, where they met and mingled with those who came by the more northerly route.

We know less about migrations eastward and southward. Communities of Neolithic farmers drifted into northwestern India at an early date, but the record is still spotty, and no exact time can yet be assigned to the earliest village sites in that part of the world. Traces of Neolithic farming, similar to that long established in the Middle East, have also been found in China. But the earliest Chinese farmers cultivated millet, a crop unknown in the ancient Near East, so agriculture may have been invented independently there. By about 2400

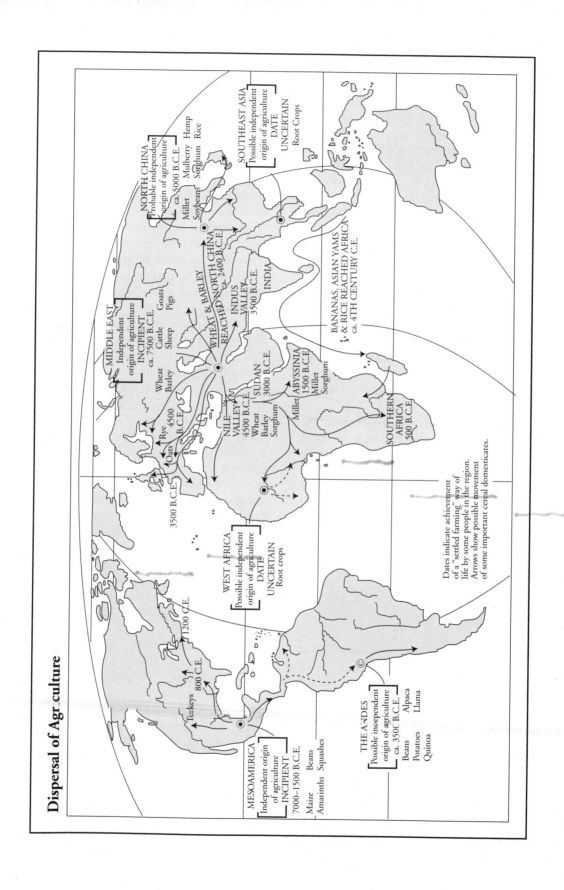

Dispersal of Agriculture

NORTH CHINA Probable independent origin of agriculture ca. 5000 B.C.E.
Millet Mulberry Hemp
Soybeans Sorghum Rice

SOUTHEAST ASIA Possible independent origin of agriculture DATE UNCERTAIN
Root Crops

MIDDLE EAST Independent origin of agriculture INCIPIENT ca. 7500 B.C.E.
Wheat Cattle Goats
Barley Sheep Pigs

WHEAT & BARLEY REACHED NORTH CHINA ca. 2400 B.C.E.

INDUS VALLEY 3500 B.C.E.

INDIA

Rye 4500 B.C.E.
Oats

3500 B.C.E.

NILE VALLEY 4500 B.C.E.
Wheat Barley Sorghum

SUDAN 3000 B.C.E.

ABYSSINIA 1500 B.C.E.
Millet Sorghum

Millet Sorghum

BANANAS, ASIAN YAMS & RICE REACHED AFRICA ca. 4TH CENTURY C.E.

SOUTHERN AFRICA 500 B.C.E.

WEST AFRICA Possible independent origin of agriculture DATE UNCERTAIN
Root crops

Dates indicate achievement of a "settled farming" way of life by some people in the region. Arrows show possible movement of some important cereal domesticates.

1200 C.E.

Turkeys 800 C.E.

MESOAMERICA Independent origin of agriculture INCIPIENT 7000–1500 B.C.E.
Maize Beans
Amaranths Squashes

THE ANDES Possible independent origin of agriculture ca. 3500 B.C.E.
Beans Alpaca
Potatoes Llama
Quinoa

16

B.C.E., wheat and barley also appeared in China; these crops came, presumably, from western Asia. But the few scattered discoveries in central Asia do not yet allow us to put the whole story together.

In the Americas and Africa, people probably invented agriculture independently. When Columbus discovered America, the Indians in Mexico, and in part of what is now the United States and Canada, planted corn (maize), squash, and beans. This was a seed agriculture, rather like that of the Middle East. But the plants were completely different. In the Caribbean Islands and South America, root cultivation also existed. Sweet potatoes were the most important crop; but in the high uplands of Peru, the plant we call potato also flourished.

Most of the scholars who have studied the question think that American Indians invented agriculture for themselves, without any stimulus from Eurasia. Some, however, disagree. They argue that boats from southeast Asia (perhaps also from Africa) drifted onto American shores from very early times; and storm-tossed castaways who knew how to raise root crops would have found it perfectly natural to try out local plants until they discovered new and valuable foods.

The domestication of corn, however, was complicated and took a long time, since the wild plant had to be profoundly transformed before it could support large human populations. Yet the *idea* of seed farming, too, may have been carried from Asia to America, either by land or across the ocean by some boat's crew, driven before the winds to an unknown land. In the nature of the case, we can never expect to know, for such an event would leave no evidence behind.

In other places, too, scholars have thought that farming may have started independently. In west Africa, for example, there are several crops, both roots and seed-bearing plants, not found extensively elsewhere. Does this indicate another center of agricultural invention? Or was it a matter of applying the idea of farming in a new environment, where new kinds of plants offered themselves and the staple grains of the Middle East did not grow well? Scholarly opinion is divided, and the only way to settle the question would be to learn much more than is yet known about what happened before and after west African agriculture began.

Neolithic Pot from China This handsome pot was made in China about 1500 B.C.E. It was probably meant for liquids, but its swirling decoration shows that its maker also aimed at beauty. Neolithic farmers lived in one place for years at a time and needed pots in which to store things. The skill of shaping clay and then baking it in an oven to make it hard and waterproof spread with farming all across Eurasia. This particular pot looks quite similar to those made in southern Russia. Patterns of decoration along with other skills and ideas traveled far and wide with the early farmers, who migrated every few years to clear new fields when weeds got too thick in their old ones.

The Beginnings of History

With the development of communities whose ways of life differed as radically as the lives of farmers differed from the lives of herders, and both differed from the lives of hunters and gatherers, human society became much more varied. Interaction between different human groups could and did become a powerful stimulus to further invention and borrowing.

Usually strangers' ways seemed silly or useless; but every so often some new tool or idea, new style of art or new sound of music, new food or new pastime, caught on. Anything borrowed had to fit in with all the things already known and done in the community. This frequently required numerous readjustments before whatever had been borrowed could work smoothly in its new setting. Sometimes the setting itself had to change; and all such changes provoked the possibility of brand-new inventions because each new situation made people more conscious of what they were doing and forced them to make deliberate choices.

Neolithic Portrait Head, Jericho ca. 6000 B.C.E.
This head was made by adding plaster to a skull to represent the fleshy parts of the face. We do not know why it was made. Death and rebirth were important for neolithic farmers because their grain plants died but buried seeds grew green again. It was easy to hope that humans, too, might have life after death. This portrait head may have been intended to assure that result.

Earlier, when one band of humans lived in almost the same way as every other band, contacts and collisions between such groups could do little to cause either party to change its ways. But when important differences began to appear, contacts and collisions between different human groups then assumed a new importance. People could and did begin to take advantage of what others knew, and they were forced to invent new ways to protect themselves or to seek more effective modes of attack. A self-sustaining process of action and reaction thus set in, keeping human societies from settling back to an unchanging routine. Historical change, in other words, assumed a new velocity; history, in the narrow sense of written records left by civilized communities, lay just around the corner.

People did not wait long before realizing the possibility of creating the first civilizations. How they did so will be the theme of the next chapter.

Conclusion

Prehumans became fully and finally human when cooperation, based first on dance and then also on language, improved the food supply so that it became easy to support children for several years before they became able to feed themselves. This gave children a prolonged time to learn the arts of life with a minimum of reliance on inherited instincts. Learning, in turn, allowed for flexibility and change, but at first changes came very slowly indeed. Hunters and gatherers knew what plants were good to eat, how to stalk their prey, and how to make baskets and sharp-edged tools. In other words, they knew all they needed to know and taught their children exactly what they themselves had been taught.

The first great change in this pattern came when people in the forested hill country of the Middle East discovered how they could make grain grow luxuriantly in the heart of the forest. More food meant more hunters; more hunters soon destroyed most of the game. Then people discovered how to domesticate some of the animals they had formerly hunted. This allowed certain communities to specialize as herders. They followed flocks and herds onto the grasslands that lay north and south of the hill regions of the Middle East.

Farmers soon had to deal with herders, either peacefully through trade or by taking defensive measures to guard against sudden raids. They faced other problems: how to know when to plant, and, as population continued to grow, how to find enough good land for next year's harvest. Accurate time reckoning was not achieved until the first civilized societies emerged; but the problem of land shortage was met before that time by the invention of the plow. Plowing kept back weeds and greatly extended the amount of land a single family could cultivate. By planting only half of what they plowed, farmers could raise a crop every second year on the same piece of land. Regular fields, settled village life, and the patterns of rural life that have lasted to the present in most of Europe and western Asia thus emerged before 3000 B.C.E.

In eastern Asia a different kind of agriculture arose, based on root crops. Later, these Asian farmers discovered rice and developed the style of paddy cultivation that supports the dense populations of that region today.

Agriculture also developed in other parts of the earth, perhaps by independent invention or perhaps by borrowing from either the Middle East or the east Asian style of cultivation, with suitable adjustments to local climates and the array of food plants available in the region.

The net effect of the development of agriculture was an enormous increase in human numbers. Our ancestors first became the best hunters, lords of beasts; then people began to transform the natural balance by planting crops and domesticating animals, increasing their own numbers many times over.

From this time onward, relations between different human communities became more important than interaction with the natural environment. Human history, as opposed to the natural history of *homo sapiens*, thus commenced.

Bibliography

The discovery of prehistory counts among the intellectual triumphs of the past two centuries. For a vivid account of how it was done, C. W. Ceram, *Gods, Graves and Scholars* (1951), is a good starting place. Glyn Daniel, *A Hundred and Fifty Years of Archeology* (2nd ed., 1975), offers a more formal account. The important discoveries about human evolution made in Africa during the past generations are described in thumbnail fashion in Richard E. Leaky, *Human Origins* (1982), and at greater length in his *The Making of Mankind* (1981). For still more recent surveys of human evolution, see Roger Lewin, *Human Evolution: An Illustrated Introduction* (3rd ed. 1993), and Richard G. Klein, *The Human Career* (1989).

Books about human behavior in prehistoric times depend partly on observation of contemporary subsistence farmers and hunting and gathering peoples and partly on deduction from archaeological remains. Useful surveys along these lines include Richard B. Lee and Irwen De Vore, eds., *Man the Hunter* (1963); Robert J. Braidwood, *Prehistoric Men* (8th ed., 1975); and Brian M. Fagen, *People of the Earth: An Introduction to Prehistory* (7th ed., 1992). On the peculiar human capacity for dance and language, see William H. McNeill, *Keeping Together in Time: Dance and Drill in Human History* (1995), and Derek Bickerton, *Language and Species* (1990). Even though some older books miss some of the most recent discoveries, they are so readable as to deserve attention still. Carlton S. Coon, *The Story of Man* (1954); Carol O. Sauer, *Agricultural Origins and Dispersals* (1952); and Kenneth P. Oakley, *Man the Toolmaker* (6th ed., 1972), belong in this category. Encyclopedic but authoritative is another older work: J. G. D. Clark, *World Prehistory: An Outline* (1961). Margaret Ehrenberg, *Women in Prehistory* (1989), deals with the much-debated issue of gender roles in early human history.

Art, especially cave paintings, permits direct encounter with a small part of prehistoric human thought and feeling. Henry Breuil, *Four Hundred Years of Cave Art* (1952), describes how these paintings were discovered and interpreted up to his own time. More general surveys of the known dimensions of the earliest human works of art are Andre Leroi-Gourhan, *The Dawn of European Art: An Introduction to Paleolithic Cave Painting* (1980), and Ann Powell, *The Origins of Western Art* (1973).

Evolution of Human Societies

PART I: TO 500 B.C.E.

| 200,000 B.C.E. | 175,000 | 150,000 | 125,000 | 100,000 | 75,000 | 50,000 | 25,000 | 8500 | 7500 | 6500 | 5500 |

Homo sapiens emerges

Hunting and gathering bands

Language [?] Rapid development of tool types; human dispersal to Australia and America

Food production in villages of Middle East

River valley civilizations: Sumer, Egypt, and Indus

Civilization in America: Olmecs

Food production in settled villages

Present

| 500 B.C.E. | 1500 | 2500 | 3500 | 4500 |

Definition of four major Eurasian civilizations: Middle Eastern, Indian, Chinese, and European

Rise of cities and civilization in river valleys of Middle East and India

Civilizations on rain-watered land: China, Middle East, and Crete

Pastoralism became an alternate way of life: exploitation of animals for milk, wool, and traction in Middle East and western Steppelands. Raid and trade between pastoralists and agriculturalists set in.

River Valley Civilizations
3500 to 1500 B.C.E.

2

Sumerian Priests at Prayer   These figurines show how anxious Sumerians were about the good will of the gods, who sometimes sent prosperity and sometimes sent disaster. To win the favor of the gods, elaborate public ceremonies and prayers were necessary. That was the priests' supremely important job.

The earliest farmers were not civilized and could not be. To build a civilization required far larger communities than could be sustained on the basis of slash-and-burn cultivation. Thousands of persons had to work together to build the monumental temples, tombs, and palaces that dominated the earliest centers of civilization. Only in large communities could specialists arise and develop the skills and knowledge that distinguished civilized from uncivilized peoples.

At first such sizable communities could arise only in geographical environments of unusual fertility. In the Middle East, where grain farming had first become important, the floodplains of large rivers provided such environments. Near the rivers, irrigation was easy and assured large and abundant crops.

Consequently, it was not by accident that the earliest societies we recognize as civilized arose in three large river floodplains within the general region of the Middle East: the Tigris and Euphrates rivers in present-day Iraq; the Nile River in what is now the Arab Republic of Egypt; and the Indus River in present-day Pakistan.

Each of the ancient river valley civilizations had its own way of doing things, its own ideas, its own art. Yet ships carried people and goods back and forth, apparently from the earliest times, so that key ideas and skills were able to pass from one civilized society to another, even across the hundreds of miles that separated them. This kind of contact explains, in part, why the rise of these three civilizations took place at nearly the same time: about 3500 to 3000 B.C.E. in the Tigris-Euphrates Valley and between 3000 and 2500 B.C.E. in the Nile and Indus valleys.

Sumerian Civilization

The first known civilization arose in the lower Tigris and Euphrates valleys, in the land of Sumer, which lies a few miles inland from the present coastline of Iraq on the Persian Gulf. This whole region is often called Mesopotamia, the name given to it by the ancient Greeks. (*Mesopotamia* in Greek means "the country between the rivers," and the term refers not only to Sumer in the south but also to Akkad, Babylonia, and Assyria strung out to the north. All these lands were bounded by the Tigris River on the east and the Euphrates River on the west.)

Before people began to change the natural landscape, the Tigris and Euphrates flowed to the sea through swamps. On either side of the swamps lay dry, harsh desert. Plant life was confined to the swamps and the regions near their edges where there was enough groundwater to make up for the almost complete absence of rain. The swamps were made by river floods, which came each spring when the snows in the mountains melted. Later, when the summer drought set in up north, the rivers dwindled

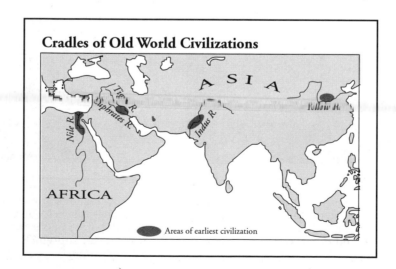

Cradles of Old World Civilizations

ASIA

AFRICA

Tigris R.

Euphrates R.

Nile R.

Indus R.

Yellow R.

Areas of earliest civilization

away until the rains of autumn and winter began to swell them once again.

When the rivers were in flood, the waters spread out from the usual channels. As the water left the main stream, its flow became much slower, so that silt and sand sank quickly to the bottom. The effect was to build up a natural levee (or embankment) of higher ground close beside the main river stream. The levees, in turn, created natural basins on either side of the riverbed, where swamp waters got trapped after each flood.

This was not the only peculiarity of the floodplain, for since the rivers flowed more slowly across the flat landscape than they did in the mountains, the heavier bits of sand and gravel carried down from the mountains by the waters came to rest along the bottom of the

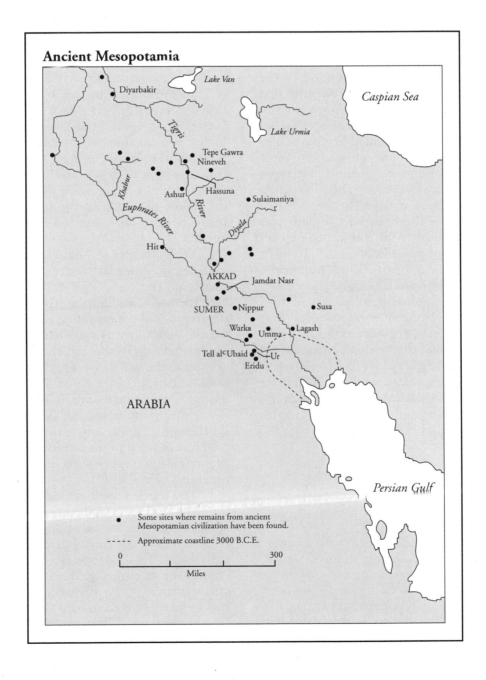

Ancient Mesopotamia

Lake Van

Caspian Sea

Diyarbakir

Tigris

Lake Urmia

Tepe Gawra
Nineveh

Khabur

Ashur   Hassuna

River

Sulaimaniya

Euphrates River

Diyala

Hit

AKKAD — Jamdat Nasr

SUMER • Nippur   • Susa

Warka
Umma — • Lagash

Tell al ͨUbaid   Ur
Eridu

ARABIA

Persian Gulf

• Some sites where remains from ancient Mesopotamian civilization have been found.

- - - - Approximate coastline 3000 B.C.E.

0   300

Miles

main stream itself. The Euphrates in particular tended to build up its bed in this way until the river might actually flow, between its natural levees, slightly above the level of the surrounding plain. Then every so often, when a particularly powerful flood occurred, the river would break through the levee on one side or the other and make a new bed for itself, leaving only a few stagnant pools to show where the river water formerly had flowed to the sea.

Such an environment presented human beings with some useful resources. Fish were abundant and so were waterfowl. Date palms grew naturally along the levees and offered a richly nutritious fruit. Reeds abounded in the swamps and provided materials for constructing simple huts. Floods were a serious problem, but families with a boat had little to fear because no matter how high the waters rolled in a particular year, they would soon subside again, and in most years a few bits of higher ground remained above flood level all the time. The first thing needed, therefore, was a boat; hence, we can guess that the Tigris-Euphrates floodplain was occupied for the first time by human communities that knew how to make boats.

Unfortunately, reed huts leave practically no traces for modern archaeologists to detect. The boats and nets upon which fishers and bird snarers depended were perishable too. The first settlers needed little in the way of stone tools, and any that may have survived are scattered far and wide underneath many feet of silt. Hence, it is only by interpreting religious symbolism from later ages that modern scholars can guess at the existence of such communities in the very beginning of the floodplain's history.

Beginnings of the Sumerian Civilization

About 4000 B.C.E. the scene began to change. Large villages of mud-brick houses arose. Within a thousand years communities large enough to be called cities, and guarded by massive walls and gates, had come into existence in the land of Sumer. By that time, too, there had evolved a system of writing that modern schol-

ars can read, thus opening up another path for the understanding of an ancient way of life which we can begin to call a civilization.

Breakthrough to Irrigation Farming   Irrigation was the key to this entire development. Crop raising was impossible without irrigation. Fresh-sprouted grain would wither and die under the fierce sun unless lifesaving water could be brought to the fields often enough to allow the crop to ripen. But as soon as men learned to water their fields at will, they could count on regular and abundant harvests: With enough moisture, the soil of Sumer, which had been built up from river silt, was extremely fertile.

In the beginning, we may imagine, irrigation was practiced on a very small scale. The peculiar landscape of the lower Tigris-Euphrates Valley made this easy. By digging a ditch through the levee, farmers could allow water from the river to flow onto the lower levels of the adjacent plain. When enough water had reached the fields, the ditch in the levee could be filled in, to be dug out again when more water was needed.

When, however, farmers became more numerous, they needed to irrigate land lying farther from the river. This called for more elaborate methods. By tapping the river a few miles upstream and constructing an artificial channel for the water, it was possible to irrigate land lying farther and farther from the river. The higher upstream the canals began, the wider the area of land that could be irrigated. But with the lengthening of every new canal and dike, the task of maintaining the irrigation system became more burdensome. Soon it required the cooperation of thousands upon thousands of people to clean the irrigation channels each year and to inspect and repair the dikes.

The harder communities worked to extend the irrigation system, the greater the risks. Every spring flood threatened sudden destruction. The river might wash out vital dikes or obstruct a canal with fresh deposits of sand. Or if perchance the river changed course somewhere upstream, then every available man and woman had to be mobilized to turn the stream back into its old channel; otherwise, the entire irrigation system would have to be redesigned—old canals

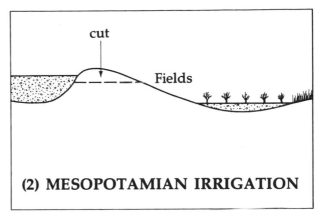

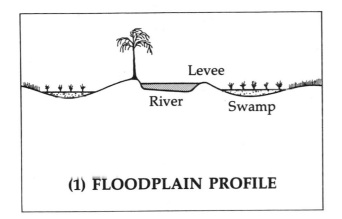

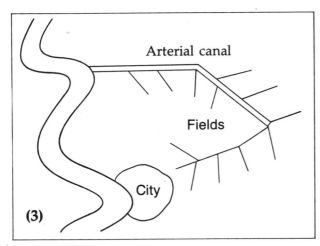

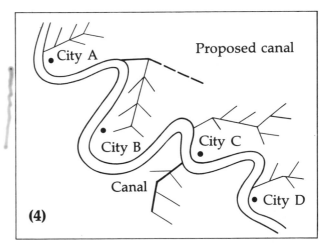

Mesopotamian Irrigation These schematic drawings show how irrigation developed in Mesopotamia. (1) Natural dikes at the rivers' edges were built up by annual flooding. Swamps remained behind the dikes each season as the waters receded, drying up entirely before summer was over. (2) By cutting a channel through the dike, water could be brought to the land after the flood had receded and when grain needed extra water to ripen. (3) As the canals became progressively larger and began branching out, it eventually got to the point where building a new canal upstream threatened the supply of water for those downstream. (4) When this happened, wars between adjacent cities in Sumer became serious, and military leaders arose alongside the priests who had been the managers of society when irrigation first began.

abandoned and new ones dug—a task that might take years.

When everything went right, the practical rewards were spectacular. Enough water, supplied at the right time, assured better yields than could be obtained from ordinary rain-watered fields. Irrigation agriculture, therefore, could support comparatively large and dense populations in the same place, year after year. Not only

this: River silt was perfectly suited to the plow, so that a single family with a team of oxen could easily produce more grain than was needed for its own consumption. Farmers had to be able to produce a food surplus for civilization to get started. Only then could a substantial number of persons begin to spend their time doing other things. This, in turn, allowed specialized skills and new ideas to multiply until society as a whole became sufficiently complex, wealthy, and powerful to be called civilized.

Sumerian Achievements of the Bronze Age

These factors all came together for the first time in Sumer between 3500 and 3000 B.C.E. During that 500-year period, the ancient Sumerians rapidly developed new skills and knowledge. Individuals who specialized in serving the gods, in laying out canal systems, or simply in making clay pots had time to invent better ways of doing the job when they became full-time specialists. New crafts soon emerged: wheelwrights to make round, strong wooden wheels; boatbuilders and sailmakers; jewel engravers; scribes who kept written records; gold and silver smiths; and (perhaps most important of all) bronze founders, who poured hot liquid metal into clay molds to make a great variety of tools and weapons.

Like the stone tools and weapons that had been used in earlier ages, bronze does not easily decay. Hence the first modern scholars who studied human beginnings invented the term "Bronze Age" to describe the period when people made their most important tools and weapons out of bronze instead of stone, or, as in still later time, iron. Recently, however, experts have played down the contrast between the Bronze Age and the Stone Age. Stone tools continued to be used in the fields long after warriors and kings began to use bronze swords and axes. Moreover, the use of metals did not begin with the birth of civilization, as scholars once thought.

Long before the first Sumerian cities took shape, various small communities of Neolithic villagers in the Middle East had learned that when some kinds of rocks were put into a hot fire, shiny metal would ooze out. In this way, copper, tin, lead, and silver could be produced from the right kinds of ore. Nuggets of pure gold could also be picked up in stream beds. The shiny stuff was good for jewelry, but it was too soft for tools or weapons.

Not long before 3000 B.C.E., however, Middle Eastern smiths found out that a much harder material, bronze, could be made by combining copper and tin in a proportion of about 9 to 1. By pouring the hot liquid bronze into molds, it could be made to harden into almost any shape. And such objects were so tough that even strong blows would not damage them.

Here was a material ideally suited for weapons. Soon, the Sumerians began to make bronze axes, spearheads and swords for offense, and helmets, shields, and body armor for defense. As war became more important, a never-ending quest for tin and copper ores began. This quest drove civilized and semicivilized merchants far afield into the mountains north, west, and east of Mesopotamia, and, before long, to even more distant places, such as Cyprus, Sardinia, and up the Danube River to the Carpathian Mountains in modern Romania.

With these and similar improvements in technique went an accumulation of new kinds of knowledge, organized more systematically than ever before. The key breakthrough was the development of a body of full-time priests, who passed on their wisdom to their successors by formal patterns of teaching and apprenticeship.

The priests' main concern was how to deal with the gods. In addition to this, however, the priests accumulated many other kinds of knowledge. They employed the first scribes, keeping records of temple income and expenses. They learned how to measure space and time far more accurately than before. Without precise measurement of space it was impossible to build the great temple structures that came to dominate each Sumerian city; it was also impossible to construct really elaborate canal systems without being able to measure ground levels and slopes too gradual to be sensed accurately by the eye. As for the measurement of time, it was tied in with the calculation of the seasons and with the art of interpreting what the movements of the heavenly bodies signified for the future.

By acquiring and preserving such skills and knowledge, the ancient Sumerians achieved the essentials of civilization by 3000 B.C.E. Instead of small, isolated villages, in which everyone did almost the same things and had about the same abilities as everyone else in the community, Sumerian cities had become far more complicated. Experts and professionals knew how to do things that others did not. Most people continued to farm and dig and perform other kinds of heavy labor, and they needed to know nothing their Neolithic predecessors had not already known. But a minority of experts and specialists had added a whole dimension to human capability. Their skills and knowledge opened the door upon a new epoch of human history: the era of civilization.

Problems of Civilization

The success with which the Sumerians solved the problems of irrigation farming in the Tigris-Euphrates floodplain between 3500 and 3000 B.C.E. quickly created a whole new set of problems. Relationships between people doing different things and living in different environments became critical. The emergence of different social classes within the cities presented an obvious challenge: How could their different interests and outlooks be made to harmonize so that cooperation instead of quarreling would prevail? No less difficult was the relation between civilized society and the peoples round about. How, for example, could the Sumerians acquire such necessary things as timber, building stone, and metal ores that could not be found in the floodplain? Simple seizure was one solution; trade with local inhabitants of the hill zones to the north and west, where trees and rock abounded, was another. Nor did initiative always rest with the city folk. Hillsmen from afar could raid the floodplains or might prefer to trade peaceably if the cities were prepared to defend themselves.

But no matter how significant the new specialized products of city skills were for human history as a whole, it is worth remembering that nearly all of the inhabitants of the floodplain remained farmers. Basic to everything else was the fact that with irrigation farming, as long as the rivers were normal and enemies did not strike, more people got more food from a smaller area

of ground than ever before, and they did so by working harder and submitting to someone else's orders about how to do what needed to be done.

Sumerian Social Structure and Technical Advances

By themselves, the techniques of irrigation would not have made much difference if the Sumerians had not been willing to remodel the social structure to take full advantage of the new possibilities. Among slash-and-burn farmers, scattered plots of cultivated land, each cleared and tended by the members of a single family, worked very well. Each family controlled the grain harvested from the plots that its own members cultivated and saved the necessary seed for next year, or else it faced the consequences. But when the same irrigation channel had to supply many families, irrigation farmers had to invent new patterns of cooperation and control. When everyone needed water, how much each could take had to be settled somehow. Means also had to be found to make each family do its share to maintain and repair the canals and dikes upon which all the fields depended. And the new skills and specialized occupations that made Sumer civilized could never have come into existence if ways had not been found to transfer grain and other food from those who raised it to those who no longer spent their time working in the fields.

Exactly how the Sumarians achieved the new patterns of living is not known. During the thousand years from 4000 to 3000 B.C.E., when the new type of society slowly took shape, no one had yet learned to write. Without texts that can tell us what people thought and did, we cannot know anything definite about Sumerian customs and the ideas of property, duty, law, or prudence that defined their social relationships. Religious myths, which were recorded many centuries later, provide some hints as to how Sumerians may have looked upon the world in the formative centuries when they were learning how to construct bigger and bigger canals and how to construct a complex, civilized society that would both hold together and be able to defend itself from outside attack. But the myths only hint at what happened, and modern scholars do not agree on how to interpret them.

Origins of the Sumerians

One theory holds that the Sumerians were invaders who came by sea from somewhere along the shores of the Persian Gulf or even farther away. Having better and more seaworthy boats than the older inhabitants, they may have been able to control movement by water. This would allow an easy concentration of force against the older inhabitants—whoever they were—who then were compelled to work for the Sumerian newcomers as farmers and servants. A few references in myths to arrival by sea from south support such an idea, as well as the fact that mountains and domesticated animals play a much larger part in Sumerian religious symbolism than one would expect from a people who had always lived in the flat floodplains.

Other scholars think that the Sumerians lived amid the swamps for a long time before they became irrigation farmers. After they learned to irrigate, according to this view, they developed their civilization under the leadership of priests who persuaded the people that unless they brought part or all of the harvest to the temple and gave it as a gift to the god, some sort of divine punishment would surely follow.

The question, then, is whether the farmers of ancient Sumer transferred part of the grain they raised to others because some conquering strangers forced them to do so, or whether they acted mainly from fear of the gods' displeasure.

There is simply not enough evidence to prove which of these theories is right. The important fact is that somehow the Sumerian farmers became accustomed to seeing a large part of their crop taken away to be used by others. And instead of reacting to this experience by planting and harvesting less grain than before, these ancient peasants kept on working hard, year after year. Only with such an arrangement could enough grain be raised so that the society could sustain the specialized skills and distinct occupations—that is, different social classes—that are a hallmark of civilization.

The Status of the Peasants

The Sumarian peasants received little tangible in return for their work. They may have been able to watch magnificent temple ceremonies from a distance, but the precious goods produced in temple workshops were for the gods (and their chief servants, the priests)—not for ordinary mortals. Peasants usually made their own tools and household articles, just as the earliest farmers of Neolithic villages had done. Wood for plows and sharp flints to put teeth in sickles had to come from afar, and farmers may have traded extra grain for such necessary supplies. They may sometimes have had enough grain to barter some of it for trinkets from town, but such exchanges were unimportant. In general, what the peasants received in return for the grain they handed over to their superiors was protection from the wrath of both gods and men.

The Role of the Priests

Sumerian religious ideas go far to explain how the system worked. According to myths, mentioned earlier, the world was ruled by a handful of gods. These gods behaved very much like human beings but were more powerful and lived forever. Individual gods personified the great natural forces that mattered: earth, sky, sun, moon, storm, fresh and salt water. Each had his or her own temple. Here the god lived, inhabiting the statue that resided there, in the same way that human souls inhabited human bodies. Like ordinary mortals, the god had to be fed, clothed, and amused. Indeed, the gods had created humans precisely to perform these services. Accordingly, Sumerian cities arose around the house (or temple) of a god. If the people of the city served him or her well, the god might be pleased and would protect his or her faithful servants from danger. If for any reason a god was not pleased, then woe betide! Flood or famine or enemy attack would surely come, unless extraordinary prayer and supplication could persuade the god to withhold punishment.

The Sumerians believed that the gods were very powerful and were liable to take sudden likes and dislikes, just as powerful persons might do. It was therefore important to keep track from day to day of just how the local god or gods felt. Special servants—the god's household staff—not only looked after each god's daily wants, but made it their business to watch carefully for any and all signs of their god's intentions. Only in this way could communities hope to head off possible disasters. These "special servants" were, of course, the priests.

They used several methods to discover the god's will. A priest might sleep in the god's house—the temple—and wait for the god to come in a dream and instruct him directly. Another method was to study the shape of the livers of sheep that had been sacrificed to the god. Still a third method was to watch the way the planets moved in the sky. Careful records of what these different signs had foretold on previous occasions allowed the priests to predict what the god intended by sending the same sign again. And they could also take preventive measures to ward off danger.

Granted the basic assumption that the Sumerians made about the world, the system was foolproof. If what had been predicted actually happened, this proved that the sign had been interpreted correctly. In such instances, any human efforts to change the god's plans had obviously been inadequate—too late or too weak to affect the divine will. If, on the other hand, what had been predicted failed to take place, the priests could claim credit for having warded off

danger by acting quickly in the light of their special knowledge. Such doctrines obviously magnified the power and importance of priests.

Archaeological discovery shows that, under the stimulus of their religious ideas, Sumerians built and rebuilt the temples ever more elaborately. From rather simple beginnings—a mud-brick house set on a low platform—the temples grew higher and higher, until they became the fabled seven-storied *ziggurats*, reaching hundreds of feet into the sky. Around the temple clustered storehouses. Here the priests gathered everything needed for running the temple household. Skilled artisans manufactured precious and semiprecious articles for the god's own use. They might also produce goods that could be bartered with distant peoples for the gems, metals, incense, lapis lazuli, mother-of-pearl, dyestuffs, and other luxuries that were needed to humor the god.

The Emergence of New Artisan Skills

Temple storehouses played a central role, therefore, in fostering new skills. Artisans who did nothing but carve gems, for example, quickly learned how to do so very skillfully. As a matter of fact, the Sumerians soon found a use for this skill that made the jeweler's trade an important one in all later Mesopotamian history. By cutting

Sumerian Cylinder Seal
Sumerians were traders and needed a way to mark property belonging to a particular person or temple. They did this by imprinting a mark on soft clay with a specially cut seal. Since each seal was different, it left a mark that was unique and could be used to prove ownership. Sumerian seals were made by cutting scenes in reverse into small cylinders, as shown on the right. When rolled across soft clay, this seal leaves the imprint shown on the left. The scene depicts suppliants before a seated god; the marks on the side are cuneiform writing, thus identifying the seal's owner in yet another way.

patterns into the sides of a cylinder, attached to a handle that allowed it to rotate freely, a pattern could be reproduced on soft wet clay by simply running the "seal" across it. When the clay dried, it formed a nearly indestructible record of ownership. Since no two cylinder seals were exactly alike, an owner could always prove his rights by running off a matching set of prints from the seal he carried with him. Everyone who had any property obviously needed such a proof of ownership. Hence it is not surprising that thousands upon thousands of these carved cylinders have been discovered. Some of them, their designs skillfully cut in reverse into the hard stone, produce an amazingly beautiful imprint even today.

We have far less information about other artisan skills developed in the ancient temple households. Weaving and dyeing were important; cloth seems to have been a major Sumerian export. A few examples of goldsmiths' art as well as some statues carved of stone have survived. But to our eyes, these two products of Sumerian skill are not particularly pleasing. Cult statues (statues inhabited by the gods) in the temples were probably made of precious materials, and none of them has survived. Hence the masterpieces of Sumerian art have been irreparably destroyed. This makes it unfair to compare Sumerian art with that of Egypt, where stone played a much larger role and nearly undamaged masterworks still exist.

The Development of Writing

As the size and wealth of the Sumerian temples increased, the priests had to keep track of what was delivered to and taken from the storehouses. To do this systematically, they invented the world's earliest writing. It was not too difficult to prepare a tablet of moist clay and then make marks in it with a chopped-off reed stem whenever a basket of barley came in or out. Nor was it difficult to develop a set of signs to stand for barley, for basket, and for all other things that came in and went out. But how could marks on the clay tablet identify the person who was making a payment or being paid? He had a name of course, but how could this name be written down? How could the chief priest know who had and who had not paid his dues?

Unless this sort of record could be accurately kept, as soon as the number of taxpayers got too large for a single person to remember who owed what and who had paid what, the whole system threatened to break down. If a farmer could get away without paying, others would surely try to do the same. Temple income would shrink; the god would get angry; disaster would ensue.

The problem was solved by drawing pictures of signs to represent sounds. A person's name could be broken down into separate sounds, and each sound (or sound cluster) indicated by a symbol. To illustrate this in English, take the name "Mitchell." This might be portrayed as a baseball mitt followed by a sea shell. Using this method (along with some bad puns), ancient Sumerian scribes were able to write down the names of individual persons and draw pictures of concrete objects.

The next step was to find ways to express ideas and whole sentences. This they achieved by generalizing some of the picture signs as syllables—the pronounced sound—in any kind of word. To go back to our example, the picture sign for baseball mitt could be used for a lot of different words in English, wherever the sounds we symbolize as "mit" are spoken. Thus: ad-*mit*, per-*mit*, inter-*mitt*-ent, and so forth. And if such a sign were used often enough, it might lose its original meaning entirely. This happened when the scribes simplified the original picture by altering or leaving out some of the strokes, until the sign no longer looked like a picture of anything other than itself.

When a few hundred signs achieved this kind of flexibility, scribes could begin to write ordinary sentences, combining the syllable-signs with one another and with an indefinite number of picture-signs that stood for particular, concrete objects.

This kind of writing was well worked out by about 3000 B.C.E. Since the total number of signs that could be used was very large, it took special effort to learn how to write and how to read. Scribal schools were established where young boys learned the art of writing by copying old clay tablets. As writing became an everyday skill,

Original pictograph	Pictograph in position of later cuneiform	Early Babylonian	Assyrian	Original or derived meaning
				bird
				fish
				donkey
				ox
				sun day
				grain
				orchard
				to plow to till
				boomerang to throw to throw down
				to stand to go

THE ORIGIN AND DEVELOPMENT OF A FEW CUNEIFORM CHARACTERS

The First Writing The invention of writing allowed Sumerian priests to keep track of what went in and out of temple storehouses, even when many thousands of items were involved. These diagrams show how writing began. First there were little pictures; then the drawing was simplified and eventually reduced to patterns of three different sorts of marks—vertical, horizontal, and slanted—made in soft clay by the end of a reed. When conventions for writing were fixed, it became possible to write any word—even those that had no definite picture from which to start. Several thousand signs were needed, and learning them all was a big job. This meant that very few scribes and priests were able to read and write. They had special power and privilege because of what they knew.

recognizable pictures disappeared. Written symbols were reduced to a few standard, simple strokes and imprints left by the reed stems that the Sumerians used to mark up the moist clay. Because the reed end made a triangular or wedge-shaped imprint, this kind of writing is called cuneiform (from Latin *cuneus*, meaning "wedge").

The cuneiform script could be used to write any language, but unless the readers were well acquainted with the proper pronunciation and names to give to the picture-elements in the script, it was difficult to read. For this reason, at a later period, when Akkadian had replaced Sumerian as the standard literary language of Mesopotamia, the priests needed help in reciting sacred songs in the original tongue. Akkadian-speaking priests had to learn Sumerian with the help of dictionaries and bilingual texts, in which the words of their own language paralleled the Sumerian words. Recovery of such tablets enabled modern scholars to figure out how to read Sumerian. Of course, they first had to learn to read Akkadian. This was done partly by comparing it with Hebrew and Arabic—for Akkadian, like these modern languages, is a Semitic speech—and partly with the help of a few inscriptions that contained parallel texts in Persian and Akkadian.

The invention of writing marks the boundary between prehistory and history. Being able to read the ancient tablets enables modern scholars to know a good deal about the thoughts, customs, and actions of the Sumerians. However, we should keep in mind that written records developed initially in the temples. It is therefore possible that surviving texts overemphasize the role of temples in that ancient society. Temples and the service of the gods were important; we can be sure of that. But we cannot be sure that other groups and social classes did not also play an important, unrecorded role in early Sumer.

Despite this sort of uncertainty, it is clear that between 3500 and 3000 B.C.E. the ancient Sumerian cities established a social system that allowed for specialization. With specialization came a rapid improvement in skills and some basic new inventions. Wheeled wagons, for example, allowed people to carry heavy loads overland as never before and to get the grain harvest into the temple storehouses. Sails allowed boats to travel with unexcelled ease downwind, while the addition of a keel and steering oar allowed sailing ships to travel across the wind and make port more or less at will. Improved ships and wagons made it easier to bring timber and metal from distant parts. This in turn meant larger buildings and better tools and weapons.

The Problem of Peace and Order—The Rise of Kingship

In early times, so myths and stories tell us, each year, on New Year's Day, the gods met in council to "decide fate" for the year ahead. Perhaps such stories go back to a time when the priests of each temple gathered together annually at Nip-pur—seat of the important storm-god Enlil—to talk things over, exchange ideas, and make necessary decisions. As long as each of the cities was separated from its neighbors by stretches of swamp and open desert country, this sort of informal association probably worked well. But bitter quarrels broke out when most of the land near the river came under cultivation so that the irrigation works of one city interfered with the water supply needed by another. Such disputes were matched by mounting foreign dangers, for the larger and richer the cities got to be, the more tempting they became to barbarian raiders.

The Rise of Military Chiefs   Tensions such as these opened the way for complicated diplo-

---

The Standard of Ur: Peace   Here Sumerian craftsmen, using inlays of lapis lazuli, show us the Sumerian world view. At the top of the panel sit the seven great gods who rule the universe—storm, sky, earth, fresh water, salt water, sun, and moon. They are meeting to decide the fate for the coming year, while attendants play music to soothe them and ply them with drink. In the two bottom rows is a procession bringing gifts to the gods. According to the Sumerians, the gods had created human beings to have servants who would supply their every desire. Thus it was everyone's duty to help the priests try to keep the gods happy. Otherwise, the angry gods might decree an evil fate for the coming year and bring death and destruction to disobedient humanity.

matic intrigue. A city at feud with its neighbor naturally looked for allies and might find them among barbarians as well as within the circle of Sumerian cities. Old-fashioned priestly consultation at Nippur could not cope with such situations. Strong, violent men, able to lead the citizens in battle, were needed to seize and hold access to the life-giving water. Such leaders may at first have been appointed only for a particular campaign or for a limited period of emergency. But soon they were needed all the time. Indeed, a successful captain might build up a personal household like the temple household itself. And when plunder from defeated enemies fell short, the great man might use his slaves, servants, and armed retainers to compel the citizens he was supposed to protect to supply his household from their own resources.

When a war leader or king fastened his power on a single city, he did not need to invent new forms of government. The revenue required to keep his personal household well supplied came by diverting grain and other forms of income from the temple. This risked the anger of the priests and, no doubt, of the god; but it saved the war leaders from having to invent a tax-collecting system of their own. Moreover, priests were not always against the kings. Sometimes they interpreted the signs from the gods as requiring the people to follow their king into

The Standard of Ur: War   On the back of the same work of art that showed the great gods deliberating about fate for the new year, we see another side of Sumerian civilization. At the top, an army goes to war, with the king standing taller than his followers. He confronts some foreigners, perhaps captives. In the middle row, infantry soldiers are moving forward with spears ready against an enemy on the right. In the bottom row, charging chariots roll over the defeated foe. The authority of battle leaders rivaled priestly leadership in Sumer. As time passed, the military element gained in importance because adjacent cities fought one another, probably over water rights needed for the irrigation on which everything depended.

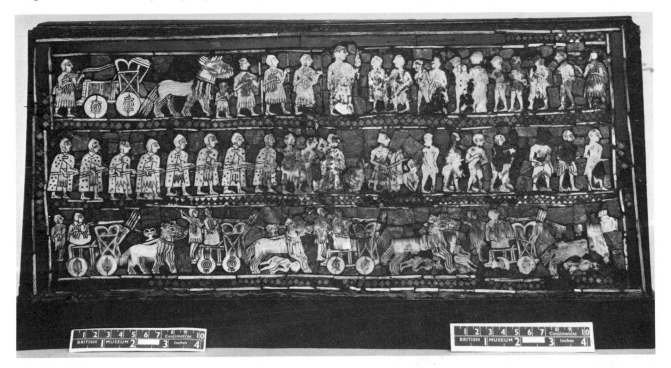

battle against some threatening foe. In other words, among the ancient Sumerians, warlike and priestly forms of leadership often worked together. Only sometimes did priests and kings quarrel over how to use the resources of the city—whether for war or for the temple services.

But the rise of kingship within each city did nothing to solve the larger problem of establishing harmonious relationships among the separate cities of Sumer. Early kings sometimes defeated a rival city and compelled its citizens to hand over grain or other valuable things. But after a few weeks a king had either to return home or else set up his headquarters permanently in the conquered city. In either case the king's household could control only the community immediately at hand. To divide forces was to invite defeat. Furthermore, if any army stayed in a conquered city for very long, food supplies were likely to run short. No less important, the god of the defeated city might not like to see a stranger encamped among his people. And the conqueror's god, who lived in another city, was, after all, far away and might not be able to protect him.

The Beginnings of Empire

King Sargon I of Akkad   About 2350 B.C.E. the first imperial conqueror appeared. His name was Sargon and he came from Akkad, the region immediately upriver from Sumer. At one time or another he subdued all the cities of the floodplain and penetrated deep into neighboring lands. His soldiers may have reached the seacoast of the Mediterranean and the coast of the Black Sea. In Mesopotamia proper, they met no equal.

The secret of Sargon's success was partly the size of his army. He had more soldiers than any opponent could gather against him. Since they campaigned every year, Sargon's followers soon became veterans, more resolute, disci plined, and experienced than any enemy they had to face. In other words, Sargon's household became a standing professional army. Yet there was a serious flaw in Sargon's power. He could not feed his household for long in any one place, and he could not bring enough supplies to an imperial capital to sustain his army year in and

year out. As a result, the great conqueror had always to be on the move, taking his troops to where plunder and food could be found.

As long as he lived, however, Sargon's power over the lands of Sumer and Akkad was never successfully challenged. But after he died, his successors found it impossible to maintain supremacy. Mesopotamia soon broke up again into smaller political-military units. Some of these were tribal; some centered upon a city-state (composed of an independent city and the land around it); about others we cannot tell. The secret of an enduring empire had yet to be discovered.

By Sargon's time, however, important changes in the structure of civilized society in Mesopotamia had begun—changes that were to pave the way for more firmly established empires. What happened was that when the formerly barbarian Akkadians began to share, more or less as equals, in the Sumerian style of civilized life, they brought new principles of social order with them. The Akkadians spoke a Semitic tongue and had been herders before they settled in the river valleys. Probably they were organized into tribal groups, led by chiefs.

Irrigation agriculture penetrated Akkad before and during Sargon's time. In Akkad, the farmers usually did not deliver their harvest to a temple. Instead, local warring chiefs put slaves and their other human servants to work in the fields and took a share of what they produced as rent or tribute. For the families that sweated in the fields, it made little difference whether their surplus grain went into a temple storehouse or into the hands of some strong-armed master.

For society at large, however, the Akkadian pattern meant that more resources were earmarked for military purposes and less for religious uses. Warriors needed craft specialists too: metal-workers, especially, to produce weapons and armor on an ever-expanding scale. They also enjoyed luxuries of the sort the priests had once reserved for the gods. Hence the rise of a secular, military class of landlords and agricultural rent takers did not make much difference to the artisans either.

For a would-be ruler of all the land, however, the development of a more or less professional military class made the task of unifying the irrigated land a little easier. Individual landlords were not strong enough to resist the king's demands for military service and tax payments. They did not resist such demands in the way temple communities, dedicated to serving a local god, usually did. And if perchance a landowner refused to obey, he could easily be replaced, for many men were ready and eager to receive rent in return for serving the king as a soldier. But how could a king make sure of the obedience of landlords and cities scattered far away from the royal person?

The Ur III Dynasty　　The first systematic steps toward solving the problem of ruling distant subjects seem to have been taken under a line of rulers who governed from the ancient Sumerian city of Ur.* This dynasty, usually referred to as Ur III, ruled from about 2050 to 1950 B.C.E. The Ur III kings claimed to rule over all of Sumer and Akkad. They made their power effective by appointing officials to represent them in all important cities. Such appointees held office at the king's pleasure. They had standing orders and instructions, that is, a set of rules to enforce. In addition, letters passed regularly between the monarch and his officials. This allowed the king to make his will known in particular cases of unusual importance, even at a distance, and applying, perhaps, to persons he had never actually seen.

The kings of Ur III, in other words, ruled by means of an elementary *bureaucracy*. The bureaucratic principle is fundamental to all modern government. According to this idea, an official acquires certain powers by virtue of appointment to an office and can command others to obey simply because of holding the office. Who the individual may be apart from the office is irrelevant. In other words, the official plays a role, and ordinary people respond appropriately to that role. In this way the complicated relations of a vast and impersonal society may be

regularized, peace can be maintained, and a degree of predictability can be achieved even among strangers who may never have seen one another before and may never meet again.

The delegation of authority from some central authority to officials stationed far from the capital may seem obvious today. It was far from obvious when rulers fumblingly first began to try to use the principle. It was not easy to convince everyone that some unknown individual could and should be allowed to exercise the king's delegated powers. Revolt, of course, was always a possibility. Officials might be disloyal or incompetent. Even at best, effective central control over distant cities was hard to maintain when communications depended on messengers who might be intercepted or delayed by rebellious subjects or by some other unusual occurrence. Nevertheless, most of the time the system worked.

Hammurabi, King of Babylonia　　Several centuries later, another famous ruler, Hammurabi of Babylon (ruled ca. 1700 B.C.E.), found it possible to disperse his soldiers over the Mesopotamian countryside without losing track of where each captain was and how many fighting men he had with him. Hammurabi did this by keeping records. Each captain was granted the right to collect what he could from the inhabitants of a particular district; in return he promised to supply a certain number of fighting men, equipped for war, when called upon to do so by the king or by the king's local official representative. On the basis of such records, the king could then summon part or all of his army whenever a campaign seemed necessary.

In this way Hammurabi overcame a problem that had been beyond the ability of Sargon of Akkad to solve. Instead of holding a large force around his own person and then having to keep forever on the move to find enough supplies to maintain such a horde, Hammurabi sent his soldiers to the places where food was available to support them. If one of his captains failed to come when called, his absence from the army could be detected at once. Drastic punishment would follow. Knowing this, everyone—at least in principle—obeyed the king's summons when it came.

---

*A government that rules over a number of different lands and peoples is referred to as an "empire," and a line of rulers who belong to the same family is known as a "dynasty."

From the point of view of the farmers and townsmen who had to support the king's soldiers, Hammurabi's system was preferable to Sargon's. The arrival of Sargon's army was like a plague of locusts—unpredictable and all but ruinous. Under Hammurabi's system, the soldiers were on the spot most of the time. Even if over a period of years the demands for goods and services made by Hammurabi's troops exceeded the ravages made by Sargon's occasional visits, regular burdens were easier to bear and did less damage to ordinary civilian life and property.

Law, codified or systematized by Hammurabi and other monarchs, provided another important means of making human relations, even among strangers, more predictable. A rudimentary market whereby merchants organized interregional exchange of goods also emerged by Hammurabi's time. This was another way to coordinate human effort across long distances, often to mutual advantage. It is, however, difficult to tell just how effective these two devices really were. Recorded lawsuits, for example, do not seem to have been decided according to the provisions of Hammurabi's famous law code; and anything like free-market exchanges may have been rare.

Despite these advances in administration, military organization, and trade, the balance of strength between inhabitants of the floodplains and the neighboring barbarians was very unstable. Barbarians learned much from living within range of Mesopotamian civilization. Many of them were especially interested in getting hold of better arms and armor so as to raid the rich, irrigated countryside.

Other factors also changed the balance of strength between Sumer and its neighbors. Sumerian methods of irrigation allowed the river water to evaporate from the cultivated fields. As a result, each year the water left small quantities of salt behind. Salt is present in most soils and is very easily dissolved in water. Hence rain picks salt up from the earth and carries it, in weak solution, via streams and rivers to the sea. But when the water evaporates into the air, salt remains behind. In the ocean, the result is that the seas are slowly becoming saltier. On the irrigated land of Sumer, too, salt slowly accumulated. Century after century these deposits in-

creased until the soil, once so fertile, became too salty to grow anything. In this way the cradleland of civilization slowly became desolate. Wealth and power moved steadily north: first to Akkad; then, by Hammurabi's time, to Babylonia.

But as the center of civilization moved north, it approached a region where rain falls often enough to allow cultivation without benefit of irrigation. In such country the boundaries between irrigated and nonirrigated land became less sharp: The gap between what could be done with irrigation and what could be done without it narrowed. Little by little civilized social structures that had at first been possible only on irrigated land developed also on rain-watered land. The transition was gradual and extended from about 2500 to 1500 B.C.E. We shall consider its nature and consequence in the next chapter. Before examining that breakthrough, however, we must first look at two other river valley civilizations based, like the civilization of Sumer and Akkad, on irrigation, and like it, very old.

Egyptian Civilization

Several small rivers with floodplains that could be irrigated lay within easy range of Mesopotamia. But these were not big enough to become the seats of independent new civilizations. Instead, settled life in the Jordan Valley, for example, although very old, was strongly influenced by the Mesopotamian style of civilization when the farmers of the Jordan became acquainted with Sumerian achievements and ideas.

The Nile and Indus rivers, however, were farther away from the Sumerian center of civilization. Their valleys were spacious and their waters abundant. Here, to the southeast and southwest of Mesopotamia, two other ancient river valley civilizations arose not long after the Sumerians pioneered the way. Contact by sea with Sumer helped. In Egypt, for example, the idea of how to make large buildings clearly came from the Sumerians. We know this because Egypt's earliest monumental structures imitated the mud-brick buildings of Mesopotamia. But

THE DECIPHERMENT OF HIEROGLYPHICS AND CUNEIFORM WRITING

Jean Francois Champollion (1790–1832) was a prodigy. At the age of sixteen he read a paper to a learned society in Grenoble, France, in which he argued that the ancient Egyptians had spoken a tongue ancestral to the Coptic language used by Egyptian Christians in their church services. Fifteen years later he proved that this theory was correct by deciphering hieroglyphic writing, after nearly 2000 years during which no one had been able to read that ancient script.

Champollion performed this feat by studying the Rosetta Stone, found in 1799 near the Rosetta mouth of the Nile River. It carried inscriptions in three languages: Greek (which scholars had no trouble reading), demotic (that is, common) Egyptian, and hieroglyphic. Champollion assumed that the two Egyptian texts were translations from the Greek. He also guessed that in hieroglyphic the names of rulers were enclosed within oval figures called cartouches. Then he simply assigned sound values to each hieroglyph inside the cartouches by comparing its position in the royal name with the corresponding Greek letters. The next step was to test the result on the rest of the inscription to see whether anything like a pronounceable text came out. It did, and sure enough the language of the hieroglyphs was enough like Coptic to prove Champollion's theory.

The meaning of the Rosetta Stone's hieroglyphic words could, of course, be established by comparing them with the words of the Greek text. But this did not solve all problems. Further difficulty arose from the fact that hieroglyphs sometimes used a single symbol to stand for a whole word or idea—like our use of "5" for *five* or "&" for *and*. But Champollion's key to the sound value of some of the hieroglyphs allowed him and other scholars to make guesses about the meanings of additional characters. Then what had to be done was to check the context in which the ideograph occurred elsewhere, to make sure that everything fitted and made sense. Within about fifty years, therefore, European scholars learned to read the ancient Egyptian writing very accurately and sometimes could even correct the grammar or point out a spelling error the ancient stonecutters had made.

Roughly a generation later, other European scholars cracked the coded meanings of Mesopotamian cuneiform. They did so in fundamentally the same way. The key breakthrough began in 1835, when Henry Creswicke Rawlinson, a young English army officer, arranged an expedition to copy a long inscription cut into a roadside cliff at Behistun, Persia. At Behistun there were three kinds of writing: ancient Persian, ancient Elamitic, and ancient Babylonian. The carvings loomed some 300 feet over the heads of passers-by. Part of the time Rawlinson had to dangle from ropes let down from the top of the cliff, about 1200 feet above, in order to be able to copy everything carefully.

It took him eleven years to figure out how to read the Persian part of the Behistun inscription. He worked by comparing the words and spellings of the inscription with modern and medieval Persian words, and then guessing at the forms and meanings the same words might have had in earlier times. The method was perfectly OK, and Rawlinson proved that the inscription had been made by King Darius (reigned 521–486 B.C.E.) to justify his usurpation of the throne.

On the assumption that the Behistun inscription repeated Darius' account in the Elamitic and Babylonian languages, Rawlinson and others set to work to decipher these languages too. But there are not enough Elamitic texts to compare usages, so that its decipherment remains imperfect. Not so with Babylonian cuneiform, however. Vast numbers of baked clay tablets with cuneiform writing on them have survived; and with the key to cuneiform meanings that the Behistun inscription provided, it became possible to refine and correct first guesses by comparison with other texts, just as the Egyptologists had done with hieroglyphic. As a result, by about 1900, experts could read cuneiform almost as well as other experts could read Egyptian hieroglyphics.

Scholarly exchanges through learned journals allowed hundreds of individuals from many different countries to work together on each of these discoveries. Brilliant pioneering by Champollion and Rawlinson showed the way, but deciphering details correctly required systematic mutual checking among the entire company of scholars who engaged in the task. This kind of international collaboration, more than the genius of any individual, was what made the dramatic recovery of knowledge about the world's early civilizations possible.

whatever Egyptians may have borrowed, they soon developed a civilization specifically and uniquely their own. The same was true of the Indus peoples and civilization.

Valley of the Nile

The lower Nile Valley differed significantly from the Tigris-Euphrates floodplain. The river flowed more gently; its floods were regular and slow. The Nile's narrow floodplain lay between high rock walls. Beyond the cliffs lay desert, even more barren than the deserts of southern Mesopotamia. Thus the Nile Valley was enclosed and protected, so that raids of the sort that constantly troubled Mesopotamia were of little or no importance for the early farmers of the Nile Valley.

Another peculiarity of the Nile made political unification remarkably easy. The Nile flows north and, unlike the Tigris and Euphrates, was navigable to the First Cataract—which marked the traditional boundary of ancient Egypt. The country lies in the tradewind zone, which means that a gentle, even breeze blows almost constantly from the northeast. By hoisting a sail, therefore, a boat may easily quarter across the wind and go upstream; by lowering the sail and allowing the vessel to drift, it can go downstream with equal ease. Since the valley is only a few miles wide, anyone who controls shipping on the Nile controls the land of Egypt. Gathering the fruits of the soil into a single storehouse presented no difficulties for ancient Egyptians. Boats could easily move vast quantities of barley and other commodities up and down the Nile.

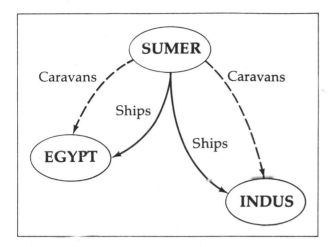

Early Civilizations of the Middle East   This diagram shows contacts between the earliest river valley civilizations of the Middle East. Sumer developed first and gave Egypt and the Indus peoples some useful hints about how to organize city life. But contacts were always few and infrequent, so once started, each civilization went its own way with different art, religion, and forms of government.

Egypt, Gift of the Nile   Egypt depended on the Nile for water to irrigate its fields. The river also provided the country with a cheap and efficient system of transport and communications. The placid river flows north, so vessels drift northward with the current. The wind almost always blows from the northeast, since Egypt lies in the tradewind zone. Hence, by hoisting a tall sail like those in the photograph, a ship can travel south against the gentle current with perfect ease. With this kind of transport at his disposal, the Pharaoh could govern the whole country simply by making sure he controlled all the vessels that plied the Nile. Egypt's precocious unification became possible as a result.

Even in flood, the Nile waters moved too slowly to damage dikes and canals. In fact, the ancient Egyptians never had to develop elaborate canal systems like those of the Mesopotamians. Instead, they relied on basin irrigation. This meant that they built low dikes all around a field and opened the dikes to let the Nile River flow into the field at flood time. When enough water had soaked into the earth, gaps were opened in the dikes to let the extra water run off onto a neighboring field that lay slightly lower because it was further down the valley slope. This method of irrigation prevented the accumulation of salt by evaporation—a fatal flaw in the Sumerian technique of irrigation, as we saw. Thus Egypt remains fertile today, whereas the land of Sumer has become a salty wilderness of sun-baked mud and sand.

The Egyptian cultivator seeded his fields before the flood. Later in the season, when the seed had sprouted and the level of the river had gone down, additional water had to be lifted onto the fields by hand. This water evaporated, but the floodwaters of the following year flushed away whatever salt was left behind by the comparatively small amounts of water that even the hardest-working farmer could lift onto his fields.

The Old Kingdom

Largely because of these environmental differences, early Egyptian history differed sharply from that of Sumer and Akkad. First of all, the land of Egypt was united by conquest before it became fully civilized. The name of the conqueror was Menes. His victory established what is called the Old Kingdom, lasting from about 3100 to 2200 B.C.E. During all that time Egypt remained politically united, with only trifling periods of upheaval as power passed from one dynasty to another. The capital was at Memphis, near modern Cairo.

Egypt's civilized styles of life and art developed far more quickly than had been the case in Sumer. About 2650 B.C.E. the kings of the Fourth Dynasty began to build the great pyramids, which ever since have symbolized ancient Egypt. By that time, Egyptian civilization had achieved a perfection that later generations always took as a model.

The Role of the Pharaoh   In Egypt the king, or Pharaoh, played the role reserved for the gods in Sumer. Indeed, the Egyptians believed he *was* a god—owner and ruler of all the land. As such he was immortal, and when he died his soul went to inhabit a blissful after-

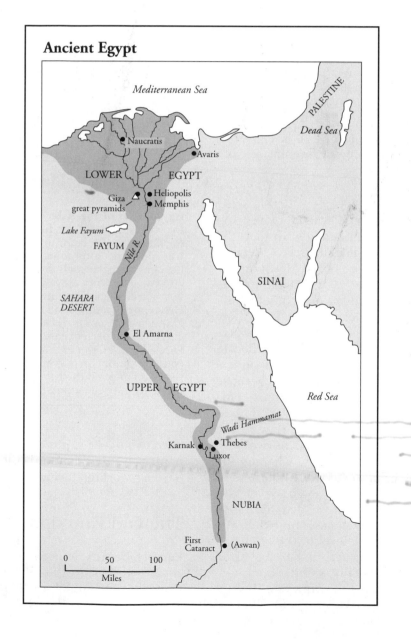

Ancient Egypt

Pharaoh Khafre This statue portrays Pharaoh Khafre, who built the second largest of the great pyramids as his tomb about 2500 B.C.E. The Pharaoh was both man and god according to the ancient Egyptians. This statue portrays the man-god by putting the human figure of Khafre under the protective wings of the god Horus, the falcon. The way the two blend into one is a supremely effective device for proclaiming the Pharaoh's double role as both man and god. As long as Egyptian civilization lasted, Pharaonic portraits followed the pattern established in the pyramid age by this statue and others like it.

world. The mighty pyramids were intended to preserve the Pharaoh's body, on the theory that his soul would wish to return from time to time to pay a visit to its former earthly home. The Egyptians also believed that the departed Pharaoh would continue to need servants just as he did on the earth. Persons who had served him well were therefore allowed to build their own tombs nearby so that they might join the Pharaoh in the afterworld and enjoy eternal life in his service. This obviously encouraged strict obedience to the Pharaoh's commands and helped strengthen the political unification of Egypt.

The Pharaoh's court was like one of the Sumerian temple households. As irrigated agriculture spread, Egyptian peasants delivered vast quantities of grain to the Pharaoh's storehouses. Part of the grain was used to support skilled artisans and courtiers of every sort who ministered to the Pharaoh's wants and ran the country, much as the priests and temple servitors of Sumer ministered to their gods' wants and managed the local temple community.

In Egypt work on dikes did not take nearly as much time as maintaining canals did in Sumer. Hence the labor power of the entire country could be mobilized to work on pyramids during the seasons of the year when the Nile was low and there was nothing to do in the fields. Barley sent to the Pharaoh's storehouses was paid back to the peasants who labored to cut and transport the great stones to make the pyramids. Then, when it was time to begin plowing and planting again, work on the pyramids stopped (or at least slacked off) until the next harvest was in, after which the laborers reassembled to carry on their enormous task.

By concentrating wealth and skill so completely in the Pharaoh's household, the Old Kingdom was able to achieve amazing artistic perfection. From sculpture and wall painting, of which many examples survive, we can appreciate the extraordinary skill attained by Egyptian artists.

Hieroglyphic Writing The so-called hieroglyphic style of writing has the same high artistic quality as Egyptian art. Although hieroglyphic symbols were completely different from those used in Mesopotamia, the principles were the same. Signs for syllables and signs for whole words were confusingly mingled. Yet modern scholars can read hieroglyphic inscriptions quite accurately thanks to the famous Rosetta Stone, discovered by the French when they invaded Egypt in 1799 (see page 37).

Ancient inscriptions tell modern scholars a good deal about Egyptian religion. Besides the Pharaoh, many gods were honored. Some of them had animal shapes; others were conceived in human form. Only a few gods had great temples like those of Sumer. As long as the Pharaoh, god and king, ruled the land of Egypt, the priests who served local gods could not obtain a large enough income to support elaborate temples. But after the Old Kingdom came to an end, local temples and priests sought more power and income—and got them.

The Middle Kingdom

The increase of local and priestly power brought many troubles to Egypt. Priests and nobles began violent struggles among themselves. Egypt became a divided country, and art and artisan skills suffered a decline. The struggle for power lasted from about 2200 to 2050 B.C.E. Then Egypt was again united under a new Pharaoh, who founded what is called the Middle Kingdom. The new capital was at Thebes, in Upper Egypt, instead of at Memphis.

Pharaohs of the Middle Kingdom tried to imitate their predecessors of the Old Kingdom and claimed to be gods just as before. But in spite of the outward show, the Pharaohs of the Middle Kingdom were no longer absolute. They had to share revenue and power with the priests and with new-sprung local lords of the Egyptian countryside. As a result, control of Egypt under a single central authority was never restored. No new pyramids were constructed. The Pharaoh could no longer command the entire labor force of Egypt. Peasants had to stay home and work for their local lords and masters, each of whom, as best he could, tried to keep up some part of the artistic and other cultural traditions that had been established by the Pharaoh's household in the time of the Old Kingdom.

This political order lasted for about 250 years (2050–1800 B.C.E.). Then, for a second time, local upstarts refused to submit to the Pharaoh's authority, and Egypt divided again into rival principalities. Something new to Egyptian experience then happened; about 1730 B.C.E., foreigners, called Hyksos, crossed the Sinai desert and conquered the land. They brought unfamiliar ways and ideas with them influenced, perhaps, by Mesopotamian civilization. The Egyptians hated their conquerors' for-

Keeping Records   Egyptians invented a different way of writing from what was known in Mesopotamia. Instead of making marks in soft clay and baking it hard afterwards, as the Sumerians did, in Egypt artisans wove papyrus reeds together to produce a paperlike material on which scribes could write with pen and ink. The scribe portrayed here was perhaps awaiting dictation from his master. His self-assured manner suggests how vital record keeping and letter writing was in ancient times. Governments and priesthoods could also keep track of daily transactions and send instructions to people living at a distance. Writing in the form we call hieroglyphics was as important as Nile navigation in keeping ancient Egypt united under the Pharaohs for so much of its history.

eign ways and, about 1570 B.C.E., were able to drive them back into Asia. Egypt was thus again united under the so-called New Kingdom.

The Indus Civilization

We know far less about what happened in the Indus River valley. The Indus River, like the Tigris and Euphrates rivers, flows from high mountains through desert to the sea. In its lower reaches, it behaves like the two rivers that cradled Sumerian civilization. The spring flood on the Indus was strong but irregular, and from time to time the main stream changed course by breaking through natural levees, created in the same way as those along the lower Euphrates River. As a result, the remains of the ancient city of Mohenjo-Daro, discovered in the 1920s, are located in a barren desert, several miles from where the Indus River now flows. A twin city, Harappa, lay some 600 miles upstream, near the bank of one of the main tributaries of the Indus.

Two obstacles prevent modern scholars from learning very much about the civilization that once flourished in these cities. First, groundwater has made it impossible for archaeologists to dig to the bottom at either Mohenjo-Daro or Harappa. Expensive engineering work would be required to drain the water and permit further digging. Thus physical remains dating

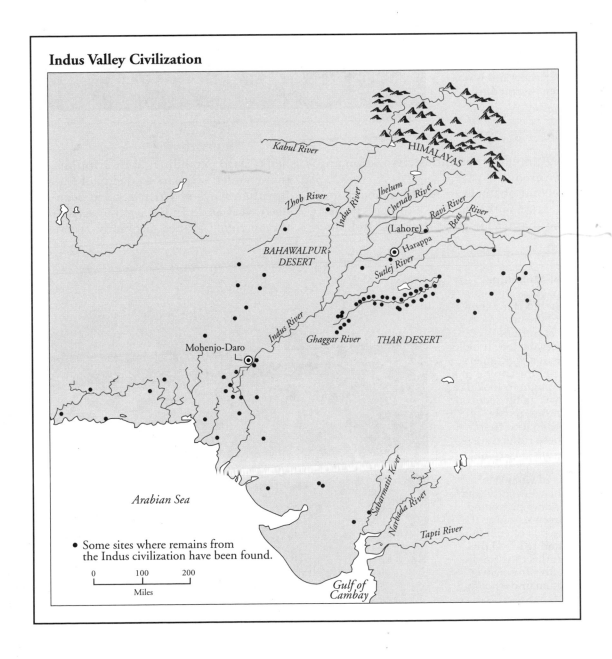

Indus Valley Civilization

Kabul River

HIMALAYAS

Zhob River

Indus River

Jhelum

Chenab River

Ravi River

Beas River

(Lahore)

BAHAWALPUR DESERT

Harappa

Sutlej River

Indus River

Mohenjo-Daro

Ghaggar River

THAR DESERT

Arabian Sea

Sabarmatir River

Narbada River

Tapti River

• Some sites where remains from the Indus civilization have been found.

0   100   200

Miles

Gulf of Cambay

Women's Work Division of labor between the sexes was sharp and clear in ancient times. The woman shown here is bending over a stone on which each day's ration had to be prepared for consumption by rubbing a smaller stone over the grains of wheat or barley until they turned into flour. Grinding was only a beginning, for the flour had to be kneaded into loaves and then baked into bread. These were time-consuming tasks and, together with other household chores, meant that a woman's work was never done. This remained true long after wind and water mills had been invented to grind flour.

from the beginnings of the Indus civilization are still undiscovered.

The second obstacle to learning about the Indus civilization is that no one can read the ancient writing that was used at Harappa and Mo-

henjo-Daro. No bilingual inscriptions, like those that enabled scholars to decipher Sumerian and Egyptian ways of writing, have been found. Indeed, very little Indus writing has survived, for the ancient scribes probably wrote on palm

The Ruins of Mohenjo-Daro This view of the main street of Mohenjo-Daro shows how regularly the brick foundations of ancient buildings were aligned. It looks like the work of city planners who knew what the capital of a great empire ought to look like. Not much else can be deduced from the remains, partly because the men who first uncovered these ruins were looking for works of art and other treasures and did not keep exact records of what they found. Another difficulty was that ground water prevented the diggers from reaching the bottom of the pile of rubble to which time had reduced this once proud Indus city. No one has yet been able to uncover what lies hidden underneath.

leaves or some other perishable material. Only a handful of inscriptions, cut into cylinder seals like those the Sumerians used, prove that the Indus people did have their own kind of writing. Without more material to work with, even the most skillful cryptographic (deciphering) methods are unlikely to unlock the secret of how to read the ancient Indus script.

Several Mesopotamian cylinder seals have been discovered at the Indus sites, and a few Indus seals have also turned up in Mesopotamia. Evidently, merchants traveled from one region to the other, carrying their seals with them to prove their ownership of goods stashed away in a ship's hold. Since the style of Sumerian seals changed from century to century, it is possible to tell roughly when a particular seal was made. In addition, the archaeological level at which an Indus seal was found in Sumer can help identify its approximate date. This sort of cross-dating shows that the two great Indus cities were well established by about 2500 B.C.E. and were destroyed about a thousand years later. Their destruction may have been caused by invasions from beyond the Himalayan Mountains that brought Aryan-speaking barbarians into India for the first time.

Harappa and Mohenjo-Daro were well-planned cities. Their exact geometrical layout and skillfully organized sanitation systems suggest that there was a strong central authority. Very likely the rulers were priests or priest-kings. But the doctrines of their religion and the methods by which they controlled and directed the common people are not known.

A surprising thing about Mohenjo-Daro and Harappa was that the archaeologists who dug them up were not able to notice much difference between successive layers. In Mesopotamia and elsewhere, changes in the ways things were made allow experts to date miscellaneous objects—even odd bits of broken pottery—quite accurately. Nothing similar was done at the Indus sites, partly because the men in charge of the excavation were in a hurry and did not record very carefully where they found things, but also because everything about the two cities seems to have remained about the same for centuries. To be sure, floods often undermined the buildings; but, time and again, each damaged structure was carefully restored on exactly the same ground plan as before. Only toward the end did changes appear. Jerry-built structures replaced older buildings, perhaps because the rulers no longer had the means to keep the old traditions alive.

A few small statues were discovered amid the rubble of brick at the two Indus sites. No other works of high art were found. Other traces of ancient artisan skills had nearly all disappeared, so that we have scant material with which to judge the style and quality of ancient Indus workmanship. The statues were oddly different from one another but full of charm and grace. Indus seal engraving was up to Mesopotamian standards. Indeed, the skills and knowledge attained by the Indus civilization were probably very similar to those familiar to the Egyptians and Mesopotamians of the same age. But we have too little information to be sure.

Numerous village sites dating from the Indus period have been uncovered. Several small

The Indus Civilization in Art This object comes from an Indus site. It is an imprint from a seal used to establish ownership of commodities, just as in Sumer. The writing that accompanies the image of the bull cannot now be read, so we know far less about Indus civilization than about ancient Egypt and Sumer.

towns along the seacoast are also known to have existed. Whether such communities were subordinated to the two main cities, and what was the nature and importance of relationships between the Indus peoples and their various neighbors, remain completely obscure. A civilization as complex and wonderful in its own way as anything that the Egyptians or Mesopotamians achieved probably lies behind these puzzling traces. But without readable records, we cannot understand the ideas and institutions that held it together.

tween 1750 and 1500 B.C.E., both were conquered (the Indus civilization was destroyed) by warrior tribes whose style of fighting and military equipment had been developed through border warfare between the civilized cultivators of the Mesopotamian floodplain and the dry-land farmers and herders of the hills and steppelands surrounding the Tigris-Euphrates Valley. In the next chapter, therefore, we shall take up the interaction between civilized and neighboring peoples that resulted not only in these conquests but also in the transfer of civilized skills and social organization to rain-watered land.

Conclusion

The ancient Mesopotamians, Egyptians, and Indus peoples created the world's earliest civilizations. In the special environment of river floodplains, they constructed societies rich enough to free a few persons from the task of producing their own food. Individuals set free from the need to spend their time producing food became specialists and developed a substantial range of new skills: writing, bronze-making, seal engraving, large-scale building, and many more.

To begin with, such skills were largely directed toward the service of the gods, conceived in Mesopotamia as invisible and immortal but in other respects very much like humans, whereas in Egypt the most important god was the Pharaoh. As for the Indus civilization, we do not know what kinds of gods they may have worshiped; we do not even know for certain that the organizers and leaders of that society were priests, although archaeologists' discoveries do not contradict such an idea.

In Mesopotamia, from soon after 3000 B.C.E., when written records began, warfare became a second major consumer of the products of special skills mentioned above. This was not true in Egypt, where natural barriers to invasion were much greater than in Mesopotamia. Nothing in the remains from the Indus cultivation suggests that military enterprise was particularly important there either. Yet these two civilizations did not escape militarization. Be-

Bibliography

For a general overview of the earliest beginnings of civilization, try William H. Hallo and William Kelly Simpson, *The Ancient Near East: A History* (1971). V. Gordon Childe, *What Happened in History* (1954), offers an older, brief, and very readable account. Authoritative recent books about early Mesopotamian civilization are A. Leo Oppenheim, *Ancient Mesopotamia: Portrait of a Dead Civilization* (1964), and I. M. Diakanoff, ed., *Ancient Mesopotamia: Socio-Economic History* (1969). On Egypt, see B. J. Kemp, *Ancient Egypt: Anatomy of a Civilization,* (1989); John A. Wilson, *The Burden of Egypt* (1951); Cyril Aldred, *The Egyptians* (rev. ed., 1984). For the Indus civilization, Mortimer Wheeler, *The Indus Civilization* (3rd ed., 1968), is standard.

Decipherable writing opens a new avenue for understanding the way people thought and lived and marks the horizon between prehistory and history proper. Ignace J. Gelb, *A Study of Writing* (1954), explains how systems of writing arose and spread. The most entrancing literary monument from ancient times is the *Epic of Gilgamesh*, available in several translations, and reproduced conveniently in James B. Pritchard, *Ancient Near Eastern Texts Relating to the Old Testament* (3rd ed., 1969), along with many other important ancient Mesopotamian and Egyptian writings. Miriam Lichtheim, *Ancient Egyptian Literature: A Book of Readings* (3 vols., 1973–80), is a more exhaustive collection

Two old but notable books seek to interpret ancient thought and science: Henri Frankfort et al., *Before Philosophy* (1941); and Otto Neugebauer, *The Exact Sciences in Antiquity* (1952). Other special topics of critical importance for ancient river valley civilizations are dealt with by W. F. Leemans, *The Old Babylonian Merchant: His Business and Social Position* (1950); Yigael Yadin, *The Art of Warfare in Biblical*

Lands in the Light of Archaeological Study (1963); and Karl W. Butzer, *Early Hydraulic Civilization in Egypt: A Study in Cultural Ecology* (1976).

On the roles of women, see Barbara S. Lesko, ed., *Women's Earliest Records from Ancient Egypt and Western Asia: Proceedings of the Conference on Women in the Ancient Near East* (1989).

Art constitutes another avenue of approach to antiquity. Cyril Aldred, *Egyptian Art in the Days of the Pharoahs, 3100–320* B.C. (1980) is recent and authoritative, and L. E. S. Edwards, *The Pyramids of Egypt* (rev. ed., 1986), describes in detail the most famous of all ancient monuments. Henri Frankfort, *The Art and Architecture of the Ancient Orient* (1955), surveys Mesopotamian as well as Egyptian art; C. Leonard Woolley, *The Development of Sumerian Art* (1935), summarizes his own and others' archaeological discoveries.

Emergence of Civilizations; 3500 B.C.E. to 1250 B.C.E.

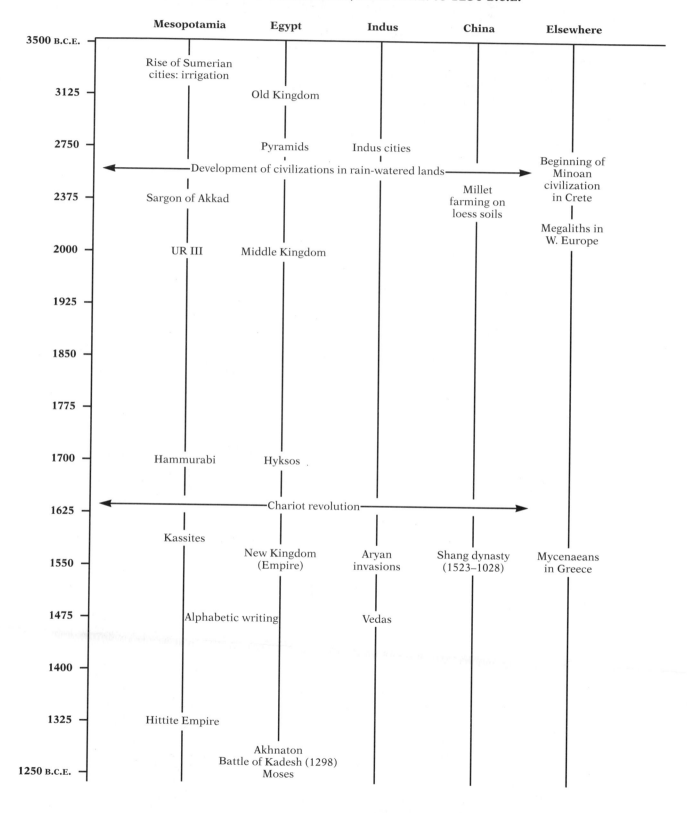

The Rise of Civilizations on Rain-Watered Land

2000 to 1200 B.C.E.

3

Palace of Knossos, Crete   The throne room of the Palace of Minos, Crete, as somewhat restored by its discoverer, Sir Arthur Evans. It was once a temple-palace, and the columns may be compared with the mightier columns of the Temple at Karnak (p. 66). Cretan civilization arose through contacts with Egypt and other lands across the Mediterranean Sea. The rulers of the island gathered the profits of sea trade as much as or more than they took rents from local farmers. This made Cretan civilization fundamentally different from the more militaristic Hittite civilization.

Initially, the complex kinds of societies which we call civilized could arise only on irrigated land in river floodplains. Elsewhere, farmers did not produce enough food, over and above what they needed for themselves, to be able to support specialists—whether soldiers, artisans, priests, or landlords. Then, not long before 3000 B.C.E., the invention of the plow changed things. By using a plow and a team of oxen, a family could raise more than enough grain for its needs on ordinary soil, as long as there was sufficient rainfall and a warm enough temperature to encourage plant growth. Hence, the special environment of river floodplains was no longer necessary for the support of civilized society.

This opened broad expanses of land in the temperate zones of the earth to civilization— but only potentially. The acquisition of special skills and far-reaching changes in social structure were needed before simple Neolithic village communities could become civilized. By 2000 B.C.E., these changes had been made throughout most of what we call the Middle East. During the following 500 years—between 2000 and 1500 B.C.E.—a series of dependent and derivative civilizations grew up on every side of the old centers of Mesopotamia. The ones we know most about are the Hittite society of Asia Minor and the Canaanite communities of Syria and Palestine, but others also arose to the east in Iran and in Armenia to the north of the Tigris-Euphrates Valley.

Civilization, Barbarism, and Cultural Diffusion

How did civilization make the transition from irrigated to nonirrigated land? In a general way, the answer is obvious enough. Some persons set themselves up over ordinary farming folk and made them plow and harvest more land than was needed for their own support. The surplus food was then used to support soldiers, priests, artisans, sailors, caravan folk, miners, loggers, and other specialists. As the skill and numbers of such groups increased, a society we recognize as civilized emerged.

To understand fully how simple villages— in which everybody did the same kind of work and lived very nearly in the same way—could give birth to the more complicated structure of civilized communities, we have to consider the nature of relationships between civilized and uncivilized peoples.

How Barbarians and Civilized Communities Differ

We may assume that most people wish to be able to enjoy or use anything new that seems better than what they already have. Hence, civilized goods, produced by skillful artisans, and civilized ideas, worked out by full-time experts, usually impress neighboring peoples as superior. When a whole people comes to realize that some neighbor is superior to themselves in important respects, they may appropriately be called *barbarians*.

The word "barbarian" was invented by the Greeks to describe people who spoke any language they could not understand, and who therefore seemed to utter mere nonsense syllables—"barbarbar." In Roman times the word was applied mainly to Germans and Slavs living beyond the borders of the empire, and that was the meaning that entered English. If we generalize from this relationship between Germans and Romans in the early Christian centuries and use the word *barbarian* to mean peoples who were in touch with a center of civilization (as the Germans were) but whose own skills fell short of those of their civilized neighbors, then the term can be used to describe a relationship that appears very frequently through recorded history.

Indeed, if we accept this definition, the development of every civilization created barbarisms by opening a gap between the skills of the people at the civilized center and those others living outside it. It also established a difficult love-hate relationship. Barbarians wanted to enjoy the fruits of civilization, but at the same time, they did not like to admit inferiority. They often reacted by calling civilized ways corrupt. Civilized people, on the other hand, usually feared and despised their barbarian neighbors. Yet they sometimes admired barbarian hardihood, courage, and liberty, especially since civilized people were liable to lose faith in their own way of life whenever the injustices arising from social inequality became too sharp. In ancient times, all civilized societies were built upon social as well as economic inequality. Most of the people labored in the fields and were very poor. A few were rich, and some lived in luxury. By comparison, barbarian societies were simpler and often more united, as well as poorer and less skilled.

Trade Relations with Barbarian Communities

In the ancient Middle East, as elsewhere, the relationship between civilized and barbarian communities was always uneasy. Yet they could never leave one another alone for long. The cities of the floodplain needed to import timber, stone, and metal ores from barbarian areas. They could—and sometimes did—seize such commodities by force. More often they found it convenient to trade. Merchants and diplomatic agents from the Mesopotamian cities were usually eager to exchange artisan products— tools, cloth, trinkets—for raw materials that could not be found in the floodplain. But the task of gathering whatever civilized peoples wanted and preparing them for transport required changes in barbarian habits. Specialists inevitably arose whenever trade became regular and important. And such specialization within the barbarian community meant the beginning of inequality.

The new inequality arose between as well as within barbarian villages. Thus, for example, by 2000 B.C.E., trade relations had created a series of mining and logging communities in the higher hills of the Middle East. Such communities often had to import food. The livelihood of producers of raw material who lived high in the hills depended on delicate relations with both distant cities and nearby villages that supplied their food. If war or natural disaster interrupted these relationships, miners and loggers faced starvation. They responded by raiding the villages at the foot of their hills and seizing the food they could not raise for themselves.

The result was that peaceful farmers of the Middle East increasingly found themselves boxed in between warlike pastoral nomads from the desert fringe to the south and raiding hillsmen from the north. Professional "protectors"— men who specialized in war and violence— wanted heavy rents and labor services in return for standing guard. But it might be safer and easier to pay such exactions regularly than to risk utter and unpredictable devastation. Between 3000 and 2000 B.C.E., this unpalatable choice confronted villages of the Middle Eastern plains more and more often.

War Between Civilized and Barbarian Communities

War and violence also played a big role in the relations between civilized and barbarian peoples. Organized armies, like those of Sargon of Akkad, could penetrate deep into barbarian territory. Everywhere civilized soldiers went, they seized anything of value they could lay hands on. But barbarian countrysides offered rather slim pickings for such forces. Food supplies were scarce. Locally manufactured products hardly compared with civilized goods. Only new access to raw materials—which might better come by persuading resident barbarians to dig the ore or prepare the timber for export—made raiding by civilized armies worthwhile.

Barbarian war bands, however, had much to gain by penetrating civilized territory. They could seize new and precious articles otherwise beyond their reach. If it was food they needed, civilized storehouses were likely to be better stocked than anything in their own country.

Barbarian raids had much the same effect on barbarian society as did trade. Whenever raiding became successful and profitable, members of barbarian war bands made plunder a way of life. Civilized products spread. New tastes arose, and new knowledge about civilized customs seeped into barbarian society. The overall effect was to link the raiding and raided communities more closely than before; and as specialization and social differences spread among the barbarians, their own societies edged their way toward civilized complexity.

Frequently, of course, civilized rulers failed to check barbarian raids. In such cases, the raiders began to live among their victims and soon became a ruling class, extracting rents and services from everyone in sight. In return, such conquerors could be expected to try to defend the people under their control from further harassment. The most famous rulers of Mesopotamia, in fact, were often barbarians (or semibarbarian) conquerors of this kind. Sargon of Akkad, for example, started his ever-victorious career as an Akkadian chief on the borders of Sumer. Some 500 years later, Hammurabi consolidated his rule (ca. 1700 B.C.E.) by leading a new people, the Amorites, from the desert fringes of the northwest into the heartland of Mesopotamia. Soon after Hammurabi's death, still another barbarian conquest took place,

coming this time from the northeast and led by the people known as Kassites.

A definite political cycle thus established itself. One barbarian group after another conquered civilized peoples, but such rulers found it impossible to maintain themselves in power for more than a few generations. Either revolt, organized by heirs of the older civilization, overthrew them from within, or new borderland barbarians started raiding anew and worked up to a fresh takeover.

The dynasty of Ur III was the result of a successful revolt on the part of the old civilized population, as were the empires of Babylonia and Assyria that came after the Kassites. But civilized reactions against barbarian rulers were hard to organize, whereas barbarian war bands always had strong incentives to attack. The political history of the ancient Middle East was therefore dominated by successive waves of invasion from the barbarian fringe lands.

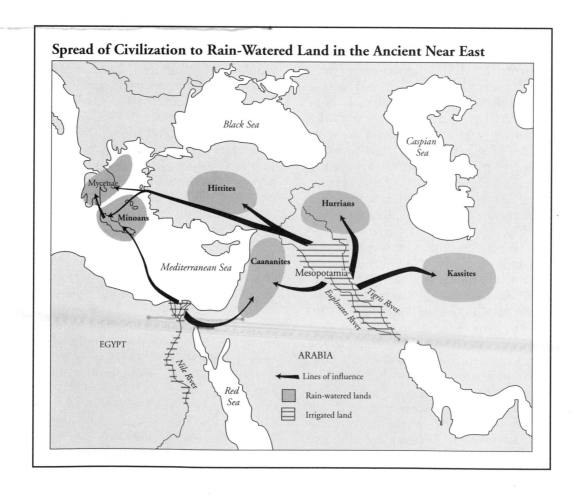

Spread of Civilization to Rain-Watered Land in the Ancient Near East

It is worth noting, however, that with the passage of time, those fringe lands got farther and farther away from the central heartland of Mesopotamian civilization, which always remained somewhere between the Tigris and Euphrates rivers. This reflects the fundamental fact that the complicated interactions between civilized and barbarian peoples steadily tended to spread civilized patterns of society to new ground. This is another way of saying that, in barbarian societies, specialization and a widening division between rich and poor were the usual consequences both of raiding and of trading with civilized communities.

The spread of civilization suffered many setbacks. Sometimes whole civilizations were wiped out, as we shall shortly see. But taking human history as a whole, it is clear that civilizations have always tended to spread to new ground, and did so from their earliest beginnings. There is nothing mysterious about such an overall trend. Civilized specialization and social inequality allowed people to command greater wealth and power than could be created by a simpler, less-structured society. In ancient civilized communities, farmers and artisans often suffered cruel exploitation, while rulers and priests always profited from work done for them by others. But civilized society as a whole exerted greater control over the environment than any simpler community could and extracted greater resources from it.

When given a choice, most barbarians therefore preferred the way of civilization. Consequently, the net result of contact between civilized and barbarian peoples was the borrowing of as much civilized skill and knowledge as the uncivilized partner was able to put to use in his particular social and physical environment. This meant an unending remodeling of barbarian societies along civilized lines, or, to look at the process from the other side, a persistent spread of civilization.

The Mesopotamian Sphere of Influence

We have already seen this process at work within the Tigris-Euphrates floodplain. Civilization began in the extreme south in Sumer. It moved upstream, first to include Akkad, then Babylonia, and last of all, Assyria. Each time a new region or people entered into the circle of Mesopotamian civilization, minor changes were made in older styles of life. For example, when the center of political power shifted to Babylon in the time of Hammurabi, patriotic local priests revised the old Sumerian epic of creation to make their god, Marduk, the most important actor in the story. Marduk simply took over the role previously assigned to Enlil, god of storm and thunder.

At about the same time, Babylonian priests also made important improvements in mathematics and astronomy. They learned how to measure and record the positions of the planets and of the sun and moon quite accurately using the same spherical grid (degrees, minutes, and seconds) used today. Accurate records of the movements of the sun, moon, and planets, in turn, allowed them to predict the location of these "moveable lights of the firmament" at any particular time, whether in the future or in the past. Priest-astronomers also learned how to predict eclipses with considerable accuracy. All this required lengthy, complicated figuring, but the effort seemed worthwhile because everyone believed that the movements of the heavens foretold what would happen on earth. Careful observation of the positions of the sun, moon, and planets therefore allowed rulers to know the best times to start a war, build a palace, or sign a treaty. The mathematical breakthrough in Hammurabi's time permitted the priests to make more accurate and impressive predictions than their predecessors had been able to, but it did not lead to any fundamentally new concepts.

This illustrates the general fact that as long as irrigation agriculture remained the basis of life for the population of Mesopotamia, the ideas and techniques that had been first worked out by the ancient Sumerians remained generally satisfactory and were faithfully preserved as the center of political power moved northward. Akkadians, Babylonians, and then Assyrians, one after the other, gladly borrowed nearly everything they required from age-old temple rituals and traditional knowledge. They changed and elaborated only a few details.

Hammurabi before the Sun-God, Shamash   This carving stands atop a tall stone on which Hammurabi's famous Code of Laws was carved. It shows the King greeting the sun-god, Shamash, reverently. Shamash returns the greeting, extending a scepter toward the King. This was probably meant to show that Shamash gave Hammurabi the right to rule in accordance with the laws inscribed below. By Hammurabi's time, Mesopotamian rulers had learned how to govern at a distance through laws and officials appointed to enforce the laws. Consequently, a bureaucratic empire made everyday life safer and more predictable for all concerned. Perfect strangers knew what to expect—more or less—even when meeting for the first time.

The Search for New Metals   The influence of Mesopotamian civilization had never been limited to the floodplain. Even in early times, expeditions went into the mountains to cut timber, dig ores, and quarry building stone. The *Epic of Gilgamesh** describes such a venture, and we may be sure that trade in metals existed from the earliest beginning of Sumerian civilization. Civilized armies and military operations created an insatiable demand for tin and copper, from which bronze, the best metal for both weapons and armor, was made. To meet this demand, prospectors, miners, and smelters gradually be-

came a distinct professional and social group, possessing craft secrets that separated them from others. Such specialists operated throughout the mountain zone that lies in a great arc to the north of Mesopotamia. Soon sources of copper and tin were discovered farther afield, in the island of Cyprus, for example. Not long after 2000 B.C.E., copper was mined in Sardinia. The famous tin mines of Cornwall in England may have begun to feed tin into the Mediterranean market at about the same time.

Whenever the search for metals proved successful, links with the Mesopotamian market were established. Such links sometimes crossed long distances and involved several different intermediaries. And interesting proof of how far away the presence of Sumer made itself felt is provided by the shape of the favorite weapon

---

*A long poem tells the story of an early Sumerian king, Gilgamesh, and his heroic adventures in search of wealth and eternal life.

used by a warrior people who lived (ca. 2500 B.C.E.) in what is now southern Russia. Their distinctive stone battle ax was modeled on a Sumerian bronze pattern!

Syria and Palestine

Closer to the Tigris-Euphrates Valley, the influence of Mesopotamian models was stronger. Generally speaking, all of the peoples who lived in Syria and Palestine, together with people of the desert fringes of northern Arabia, fell under Mesopotamian influence to some degree. Nomad herders, to be sure, could not do much with civilized ways, although Babylonian stories about the beginning of the world, the great flood, and naive descriptions of Mesopotamian temples—so high they seemed to touch the sky—were certainly told around the nomads' campfires. The Bible preserves some of these tales as they were known among the Hebrews. Comparison with written Mesopotamian versions shows how persuasive the civilized myths seemed. The Hebrew story of Noah and the flood, for example, bears a close resemblance to the flood story in the *Epic of Gilgamesh.*

Where farming was established, it was possible to introduce far more of the Mesopotamian way of life. Local chieftains, kings, or priests imitated the pomp and refinement of Mesopotamian courts and temples insofar as their resources allowed. Even a port like Byblos on the Mediterranean (near modern Beirut), where contact with Egypt by sea counterbalanced contact with Mesopotamia by land, took its style of writing and elements of religious myths from the land of the Two Rivers. Linguistic affinity was one reason for the influence Mesopotamian models of civilization exerted in all this region. The people of Syria and Palestine all spoke Semitic tongues, like the Akkadian that supplanted Sumerian to become the ordinary language of Mesopotamia by the time of Hammurabi.

Iran, Anatolia, and the Western Steppe

Farther afield, Mesopotamian culture lacked the advantage of similarity of language. In Elam, and on the Plateau of Iran, different kinds of languages prevailed. But here, too, the Mesopotamian model of civilization colored the lives of all the peoples who settled down to an agricultural life. As we shall soon see, even distant herders of the Eurasian steppe, keepers of horses and cattle, borrowed and improved upon certain Mesopotamian skills. The same was true in Anatolia (modern Turkey). Archaeologists happen to have discovered a number of interesting letters written (ca. 1900 B.C.E.) by merchants residing in small towns of Anatolia and addressed to their home base in the city of Ashur (later the capital of the Assyrian Empire) in northern Mesopotamia. These letters show that Anatolia was politically divided among a number of local princes, each of them eager for trade with Mesopotamia.

Soldiers, priests, and artisans gathered at these rulers' courts. They took the superiority of Mesopotamian goods, styles, and ideas for granted. As a result, no truly independent artistic or intellectual style took root among them. Even when a Hittite Empire arose and took control of most of Anatolia (ca. 1800 B.C.E.), the court and capital at Hattusas remained a small town by Mesopotamian standards. Hittite art, too, never rose above the level of a somewhat clumsy variation upon Mesopotamian styles. Local languages and local gods, different from those of Mesopotamia, persisted; but when it came to writing, even in that remote region scribes used cuneiform.

Farther away we have only indirect evidence of the influence of Mesopotamia. The same barbarians of the Russian steppe who shaped their battle axes to Sumerian patterns also remodeled their ideas about how the universe was governed when they heard the Sumerian account of the way the gods managed things. Since these barbarians later overran Europe and gave their Indo-European languages to nearly all of that continent (as well as to most of India), the diffusion of Sumerian religious ideas among them had lasting consequences. Most of the pagan gods worshiped by the Greeks, Romans, Celts, and Germans, whose names and attributes enter into literary speech even today, had a distant connection with the Sumerian pantheon. (*Pantheon* comes from Greek and means "all the gods.") Thus, for example, Thor from Scandinavia, Zeus from Greece,

Jupiter from Rome, as well as Indra from India, all began as country cousins of the ancient Sumerian Enlil, god of storm and thunder.

The Egyptian and Indus Spheres of Influence

Egypt's protective deserts reduced contacts between Egypt and barbarians. For that reason, Egypt did not develop as large a sphere of influence as ancient Mesopotamia did. But the Egyptian civilization was by no means without impact on outsiders. Westward along the Mediterranean coast lay Libya. That country, then as now only thinly inhabited, fell thoroughly under the spell of Egyptian culture; but the harsh desert environment did not permit much to be achieved.

We know far less about Egyptian influence upon peoples to the south. Fully developed Egyptian civilization never penetrated above the First Cataract of the Nile because the rapids stopped shipping. Yet chieftainship in the Great Lakes region of central Africa and in west Africa resembled the Pharaoh's role in Egypt. The question is: Did the Africans borrow ideas of divine kingship from ancient Egypt, or did the Egyptians, when they first began to farm the Nile Valley, bring the idea with them from an African hunting background which they shared with the peoples of central and west Africa? No one knows the answer.

Minoan Courtly Elegance   This fragment from a wall painting in the palace of Knossos reflects a court life in which the arts of peace mattered more than warfare. Control of the seas surrounding Crete gave the rulers of Knossos far greater security than the Hittite kings could attain behind their heavy fortifications. Minoan society could therefore become more peaceful and playful than was possible when enemies were close at hand.

Minoan Civilization   Egypt's relation with the island of Crete to the north is much clearer. Trade between the two countries began very early. Precious objects made in Egypt have been found in Crete, dating from about 2500 B.C.E. But Cretan society also carried a Mesopotamian imprint. Invaders from Asia Minor, who were indirectly in touch with the ideas and techniques of Mesopotamian civilization, seem to have reached the island before sea contact with Egypt opened up.

Encounter with two distant, different civilizations stimulated the Cretans to create their own distinctive type of civilization. The chief center was at Knossos on the north coast of the island. Here a vast palace-temple began to arise about 2100 B.C.E. The Cretans also invented a charming art style of their own, as well as a unique form of writing. We call their civilization Minoan because, according to later Greek legends, King Minos ruled Crete and the surrounding seas before the Greeks themselves came on the scene. Like "Pharaoh," the term "Minos" probably referred to an office and was not a name.

The royal palace-temple at Knossos was several times rebuilt before suffering final destruction about 1400 B.C.E. Wall paintings of youths and maidens in ceremonial procession still survive, and they show how elegant Minoan court life became. Artisan skills also reached a very high level. Minoan painted pottery was delicate and lovely, and the naturalistic portrayal of octopi and other marine creatures reminds us of the importance of the sea to Cretan civilization.

The wealth that sustained the great palace-temple of Knossos probably did not come from rents and labor services extracted from peasants living in the immediate environs of the court. This was the only way the Hittite rulers and other inland monarchs could accumulate enough wealth to support soldiers, artisans, and other kinds of specialists. But the ruler of an island like Crete did not need many soldiers, nor did Minos need to hide behind heavy walls. Instead, he controlled the sea and profited from trade.

It is likely that Minoan Crete exported wine and olive oil, since grapevines and olive trees grew well in the climate of the island. Olive oil had many uses. As an element in the diet it supplied fats, which people who depended mainly on cereals often lacked. It could also be burned by means of a wick to provide artificial light at night. Finally, oil took the place of soap: Small quantities rubbed on the skin helped to clean away sweat and grime.

Wine was precious, too. Drunken conviviality was an attraction no doubt. This, however, does not account for the importance of wine (and of beer) in ancient times. Most people were far too poor to be able to get drunk. But anyone who could possibly afford it put a little wine in his drinking water—and kept healthy as a result. The reason for this was that alcohol from the wine poisoned many of the disease bacteria lurking in polluted water. Men in the ancient Mediterranean world did not, of course, know that alcohol destroyed bacteria. But they did know that drinking plain water, unmixed with wine, was often dangerous, to be avoided whenever possible.

The cultivation of grapes and olives required special skill; it also required farmers to wait several years between the time they planted and began to cultivate the vines and trees and the time of the first harvest. As a result, the cultivation of olive trees and grapes spread rather slowly, and in Minoan times the Cretans may

have had something close to a monopoly on these specially valued products. Almost anywhere along the Mediterranean coast they were therefore able to exchange them on very advantageous terms for grain or metal or any other valuable local product. Consequently, as long as Cretan soil produced oil and wine, Minoan ships could sail east or west and expect to return home laden with the assorted goods needed to keep the luxurious life of the palace-temple at Knossos well supplied. Such voyaging was aided by the establishment of more or less permanent shore stations on several of the Aegean Islands, on the Greek mainland, and as far away as Sardinia in the west and Syria in the east. Such trading posts extended the imprint of Minoan civilization over a very large part of the entire Mediterranean shoreline.

The relation between Minoan and Egyptian civilization is like that between the earliest Egyptians and the Sumerians. When each civilization was beginning to develop, important ideas and new skills came by way of the sea. But the early Egyptians soon struck out on their own and began deliberately to reject borrowings from Sumer. Much the same occurred in Crete. Stimulus from Egypt, important though it was, lasted only until the Minoans established their own style of life.

In both these cases, contacts by sea encouraged independent responses, whereas overland contacts between Mesopotamia and its neighbors failed to do so. It is worth asking why this was so. Communication by sea between civilized and barbarian peoples was sporadic. Every time a ship sailed away, contact was broken off, sometimes for years and nearly always for months at a time. This left lots of time for the weaker parties to think about what they had seen during the ship's visit to their shores. Ingenious local tinkerers might feel challenged to try to make for themselves some of the things that had been brought so dramatically to their attention by the visiting crew.

Overland contacts were different. Ordinarily it was rude frontier types, only semicivilized themselves, who took the risks of opening up communication with a previously isolated society. Such persons were often not much more skilled than the people they encountered. Moreover, they were more likely to rely on superior force than on superior goods. It was difficult for the weaker community to borrow from people they feared and hated. Often they did not have time to think and experiment for themselves, because the rude intruders refused to go away; instead, they tried to collect rents or taxes, command labor for gathering raw materials, or in some other way alter old habits and customs by issuing orders and making threats. Improvements in local skill that came in this way from an outsider's initiative obviously lacked spontaneous creativity.

The barbarian peoples who entered into the circle of civilization along this path only had to do what they were told, that is, to imitate, as best they could, the patterns of civilized craftsmanship and technique. The chance for sudden creative response under such circumstances was far smaller than when contact with civilized ways first started by means of ships. Throughout history, therefore, seaborne contacts among peoples of varying cultures have played a different and more creative role than collisions across land frontiers.

Megalithic Culture   The special character of cultural stimuli that travel by the sea was well illustrated by the history of another high culture that spread through the western Mediterranean and along the Atlantic coast of Europe and Africa between about 2500 and 2000 B.C.E. We know of its existence because of stone graves and other structures, often called megaliths (Greek for "great stones"). Presumably what happened was that holy men, teaching a doctrine of life after death that probably derived from Egyptian ideas, traveled by sea and found welcome among local farmers and fisherfolk. The doctrine must have been powerful enough to persuade thousands of people to shape great hunks of stone and drag them into position to form the monumental graves that seem to have been essential to the faith.

Thus, just as Sumerian religious ideas were finding lodgment among the barbarians of the Russian steppe (as we saw earlier in this chapter), Egyptian—or at least partly Egyptian—religious ideas were also spreading among the peoples of westernmost Europe and north Africa. Soon after 2000 B.C.E. the two encountered each other. Warriors, whose ancestors had come from the steppe, reached the Atlantic coast of Europe and conquered the megalithic farmers and fisherfolk who lived there. The conquerors then put their new subjects' skill in handling big stones to use by compelling them to erect standing stone circles. Stonehenge in England is the most famous specimen of this kind of monument. These were versions in stone of tree-trunk circles which had presumably been the sort of sacred architecture the conquerors had previously known. The exact position of the stones was related to the rising and setting of the sun in such a way that sight lines from one pair of stones to another allowed the priests to keep an accurate calendar by checking the exact day when the sun and certain clock stars reached key points in their annual sweep through the skies.

Such precision is suggestive of Mesopotamian astronomical achievements, but the skill that quarried and carried the great stones to their resting places derived just as clearly from Egypt. In this remarkable way, the Egyptian and Mesopotamian spheres of influence met and mingled at Stonehenge (and similar structures existing elsewhere in the remote reaches of western Europe) about 1900 B.C.E..

Indian Cultures   Many uncertainties arise when we try to trace the impact of Mesopotamian and Egyptian civilizations on surrounding peoples. But these are as nothing when compared to our ignorance about what sort of impact Indus civilization had upon its neighbors in India or elsewhere—for example, along the east coast of Africa. Without better archaeological evidence, it is foolish even to guess. Yet the impressiveness of the Indus cities at their height must have been borne in upon barbarian neighbors, just as much as the greatness of Mesopotamian cities impressed itself upon the neighbors of Sumer and Akkad. And since the Indus Valley lies open to overload contacts in much the same way that the Tigris-Euphrates Valley does, satellite communities of one sort or another presumably came into existence. There are scores of sites in southern and central India where traces of Indus civilization have been discovered. Careful study is only beginning, however, and until it has been carried through no one can say anything definite about how Indus civilization spread.

The Chariot Revolution

Soon after 1700 B.C.E., a really basic change upset the balance of power between barbarians and civilized peoples. Barbarians, living on the distant flank of the Mesopotamian sphere of influence, invented or perfected a new instrument of war—the light, two-wheeled chariot.

How to Combine Speed and Firepower

The invention of the war chariot was a brilliant breakthrough in design. Four-wheeled wagons had been known in Sumer from before 3000 B.C.E. Wheels were fixed to the axle, which was strapped to the bottom of the wagon so that it turned against the wagon floor. Resulting friction created a clumsy, slow-moving vehicle for carrying heavy loads overland. Turning was difficult, since the wagon could change direction only by slipping its wheels sideways.

War chariots differed from their clumsy predecessors in having only two wheels. This solved the problem of turning; a two-wheeled cart can turn easily and sharply by backing one wheel while the other rolls forward. In addi-

Hunting from a Chariot This scene came from the walls of a palace built for the Assyrian king, Ashurnasirpal II (reigned 883–859 B.C.E.). Killing lions was meant to show the king's greatness and courage. More interesting for us are the details of how ancient war chariots worked, shown here with unusual clarity. Mobility came from a galloping team of horses, controlled by separate reins clutched in the driver's two hands, as he stood beside the king in the body of the chariot. This freed the archer to turn to face the foe, whether human or an attacking lion. The spoked wheel, axle, and the low protecting framework of the chariot body are clearly visible, but what is not clear is how the horses were harnessed. The fabric around their chest and shoulders was somehow attached to a tongue of wood projecting from the chariot (which can barely be seen under the near horse's tail). (See Chinese chariot, p. 257, for a view of the tongue.) This did not allow much pulling power, but chariots were light and built for speed, so the inefficient method of harnessing did not matter.

tion to this, a radically new wheel design gave strength and lightness to the chariot. Instead of being thick and solid, chariot wheels were constructed by combining separate pieces—hub, rim, and spokes. The axle was fixed to the chariot body, and the hubs of the wheels turned around the ends of the axle, thus greatly reducing friction and making these vehicles comparatively easy to pull.

Once chariots had been perfected, two factors limited their use in warfare. The skills and materials needed for chariot construction made them very expensive; only a rich man could afford to have one. In particular, making good spoked wheels was difficult. Exact fitting of part to part was essential; and the problem of making a rim that was round and at the same time strong enough to stand up to the jounces and jolts that came from rolling rapidly across open country could only be solved by highly skilled, professional wheelwrights who knew how to steam wood, bend it into smoothly curving shapes, and then bind all the pieces together with a tight-fitting tire made of hide or metal.

Horses, too, were costly. These animals probably had not been domesticated much before 4000 B.C.E., and for a long time did not spread beyond the grasslands of the northern steppe where their wild ancestors had lived.

Perhaps it was on the Iranian Plateau, not long after 1700 B.C.E., that the critical combination took place: Barbarians who had long been accustomed to herding horses met artisans who could make light, strong wheels. As a result, the first war chariots were designed and built. When that happened, barbarian horseherders suddenly found themselves in possession of a new master weapon.

Tactics of Chariot Warfare   It may have taken some time for the first charioteers to realize what they could do with the mobility and firepower their chariots afforded. When tactics developed fully, each chariot carried a driver and an archer. As the array of chariots charged, archers launched arrows at the enemy. If the foe gave no signs of panic, the drivers made the chariots swerve sharply, as close as possible to the enemy front line. The archers continued to shoot while passing rapidly along the enemy front. Then the

chariots would withdraw to a safe distance to give their horses a breather and to permit the archers to replenish their emptied quivers. The charge could then be repeated, or perhaps there would be a maneuver to take the foe from the rear. Under such harassment, sooner or later every enemy broke and fled. The charioteers could then pursue and hunt them down.

This tactic proved literally irresistible. Soldiers unfamiliar with horses were usually terrified at the mere sight of the charge, and the speed with which the chariots raced across the battlefield made it very difficult for foot soldiers to injure horse or charioteer. Walled cities were, of course, proof against chariot tactics. But if the countryside fell into the hands of an invading body of chariot warriors, even the strongest city would have to open its gates before long, since food had to come from outside the walls.

When dismounted, charioteers were vulnerable. To guard against surprise attack, they soon learned to establish fortified camps, laid out on a regular quadrilateral plan with entry points in the middle of each side. This layout was used much later by Roman legions; it also provided the pattern for the ground plan of the city of Anyang, the Shang capital in China (ca. 1300 B.C.E.). Such a range, all the way from China to Europe, reflects the chariot's power. Since no preexisting armies could resist the new tactics successfully, warriors with chariots could conquer whomever they chose. Wherever a sufficiently dense and skilled population tilled the soil, it was worth their while to make the cultivators into peasants by requiring them to pay rents and taxes. Where local resistance was more effective, as in most of northern and western Europe, the chariot was used more for prestige than as a practical weapon of war. Yet so high did the chariot's prestige become that remote chieftains in Sweden were buried with them (ca. 1200 B.C.E.).

The Political Impact of Chariot Invasions

In different parts of the world the effect of the chariot invasions was very different. In far-off China, for example, chariot fighters of the

Shang Dynasty (ca. 1523–1028 B.C.E.) built the first Chinese empire along the middle reaches of the Yellow River (Hwang Ho) and established Chinese civilization by forcing the local farmers to support them in style. In India, on the contrary, the arrival of Aryan-speaking charioteers from the Iranian steppes (ca. 1500 B.C.E.) was probably the blow that finally destroyed the Indus cities and inaugurated a "dark age" in India.

Effect on Minoan and Mycenaean Civilizations   In Crete the ancient Minoan civilization was snuffed out (ca. 1400 B.C.E.) when an enormous volcanic explosion on nearby Thera (an island in the Aegean) created a devastating tidal wave and ash-fall. Perhaps invaders from the Greek mainland finished what nature had begun, leaving the palace-temple of Knossos plundered and abandoned. At any rate, control of the sea passed to Mycenae on the Greek mainland.

The fall of Knossos and the rise of Mycenae closely coincided with the appearance of charioteers in Greece. Indeed, the power of the piratical kings of Mycenae may have rested almost as much on their horses and chariots as on their ships, although Homer's poems seem to show that Mycenaeans did not know how to use their chariots effectively in battle. For, according to Homer, Mycenaean warriors rode their chariots

Lion Gate, Mycenae   Here is a well-preserved example of the heavy fortification a capital city needed in the Chariot Age. As at Hattusas, lions guarding the gate symbolized the power and ferocity of the king who ruled most of Greece. In later ages, Greeks marveled at the large stones used in Myceneaen fortifications and said it was the work of giants. But in fact these big blocks (like those used in the pyramids) saved time and effort. The difficulty of transporting and lifting them into place was more than made up for by the fact that they needed less squaring and trimming than smaller blocks would have required.

Death Mask from Mycenae When Heinrich Schliemann discovered this paper-thin golden death mask in a royal grave outside the walls of Mycenae, he at once decided that he was looking at an imprint from the face of Agamemnon, whose fame had been perpetuated by Homer's *Iliad*. Schliemann may have been right, but in fact no one really knows what king's visage was imprinted on the gold leaf to make this mask.

done by Cretan workmen. Perhaps the artists were enslaved or captured in raids.

The great difference between Minoan and Mycenaean civilization was the increased importance of war. Heavy fortifications surrounded the palace at Mycenae; Knossos, by contrast, had no protective walls at all. We catch a glimpse of the warlikeness of Mycenaean society through Homer's poems. To be sure, Homer lived several centuries afterward and got a good many things about Mycenae mixed up. Still, the poet did build upon an unbroken oral tradition coming down from the days when the high king, Agamemnon, sat in state at Mycenae and planned raids far and wide across the seas. There is no reason to doubt that a raiding expedition attacked Troy, as Homer says. Even the traditional date, 1184 B.C.E., fits everything modern scholars know. Troy was sacked and burned at about that time, but Homer's say-so is all that proves who did it. Mycenae's turn came soon afterward. Greeks speaking Dorian dialects came down from the north and destroyed Mycenae (ca. 1100 B.C.E.). They brought a "dark age" to Greece like the Dark Age the Aryans had brought to India several centuries earlier.

to the field of battle but then dismounted and fought on foot with spears. Perhaps the lords of Mycenae had developed their own style of spear fighting before they ever heard of chariots, and when they imported the new master weapon of the age—probably from Syria—refused to change over to bows because killing from a distance seemed cowardly and unworthy of a hero, just as Homer says it was.

The civilization of Mycenae was closely akin to the Minoan. Greek-speaking rulers controlled Knossos in its last days, as we know from the decipherment of one of the two forms of writing used in ancient Crete. The rulers of Mycenae were also Greek-speaking, using the Achaean dialect. Art styles were very similar—so similar, in fact, that experts believe the decoration of the Mycenaean palaces was probably

The Chariot Empires of the Near East Where the older and more massive Mesopotamian and Egyptian civilization held the ground, chariot conquerors did not inflict nearly so much damage. Kassite invaders brought the chariot into Mesopotamia soon after 1700 B.C.E. and ruled from Babylonia as Hammurabi had done before them. A little farther north, a people called Mitanni ruled over Assyria and Syria. From them the Hittites in Anatolia (and, probably, the Mycenaeans in Greece, too) learned how to build and use chariots. With the stronger striking force chariots gave them, the Hittites soon created a large empire in Anatolia.

Egypt was ruled from 1730 to 1570 B.C.E. by another warrior band, known as Hyksos, who incorporated several different language groups into their ranks. During the latter part of their lordship over Egypt (and perhaps from the first) they, too, used chariots to overawe their restless subjects.

HEINRICH SCHLIEMANN'S SUCCESS STORY

Heinrich Schliemann was the son of a German Lutheran pastor, so poor that he had to apprentice his son to a grocer. But young Heinrich was not willing to settle down to keeping shop and decided to seek his fortune overseas by signing on as a cabin boy on a ship bound for Venezuela. The venture had scarcely started when he suffered a shipwreck off the coast of Holland. He then got a job with a Dutch merchant and did so well that at the age of twenty-four he was sent to St. Petersburg to act as the firm's agent in the Russian capital. Soon Schliemann set up an export-import business for himself and quickly made a fortune.

By the time he was forty-one, Schliemann had made enough money to retire from business and do what he had dreamed of doing since he was a boy. In school he had studied Greek, and he memorized the whole text of the *Iliad* and *Odyssey*. He found Homer intoxicating. From that time on he dreamed of going to the places Homer had described in order to find whatever might remain from the times that Homer celebrated.

Such an idea seemed silly to the learned professors of the day. For fifty years they had argued about just how the Homeric poems had been put together out of earlier songs and stories. Most experts agreed that no one man had composed the Homeric poems. Absolutely no one supposed that the siege of Troy had really happened the way Homer said it did. To treat Homer as though he knew what he was talking about struck them as naive and foolish.

But Schliemann had enough money to make a fool of himself in his own way if he wanted to, so he proceeded to search for Troy, taking Homer's lines as his guide. By 1879 he decided that a mound of rubble, known locally as Hissarlik (situated in modern Turkey, about four miles southeast of the mouth of the Dardanelles), fitted Homer's description. So he started to dig, finding Troy just where he said he would. Near the bottom of the mound, Schliemann discovered a hoard of buried treasure, and since Homer described Troy as rich in gold, Schliemann decided that this must be the level that corresponded to the city of which Homer had sung.

Schliemann dug at Hissarlik for three years. Then he moved to Greece and began digging at Mycenae, where, according to Homer, Agamemnon once had ruled. There he found a series of royal graves that had never been plundered and contained great amounts of gold and other precious objects. The richest, he decided, belonged to Agamemnon. It contained a death mask of thin gold, which allowed Schliemann to see, or at least so he thought, the actual features of Agamemnon's face.

Great was the confusion among the learned professors when Schliemann, by defying all their rules, found such treasures. Perhaps Homer's poems were not so unreliable as they had supposed. But how could a man like Schliemann—self-made, self-educated, and self-important—be right? In fact, as we now know, he picked the wrong level at Troy for Homer's city. Yet in a larger sense Schliemann was right for survey of local landscapes and digging, as Schliemann proved, may bring important new information and fresh understandings that could never come from study of the ancient texts themselves.

Yet in spite of their chariots, the Kassite, Mitanni, and Hyksos empires turned out to be fragile. The conquerors were few. They scattered out across the lands they seized, living as land-owners. The income from each estate had to be large enough to allow its owner to maintain a chariot. But that kind of an income also allowed him to enjoy most of the luxuries of civilized life as well. After a few generations, descendants of the conquerors much preferred the comforts of their homes to the harshness of camp life and the risks of battle.

This made successful revolt easier to orga-nize. Thus, for example, native Egyptians drove the Hyksos from their land about 1570 B.C.E. and founded the New Kingdom. The Pharaoh was no longer content to rule only Egypt. Perhaps it did not seem safe to leave Palestine and Syria, where the Hyksos had come from, in foreign hands. At any rate, Egyptian chariots and armies crossed the desert and conquered the whole Mediter-ranean coastland as far north as the Taurus Mountains. Egypt's new imperial power also stretched southward, beyond the Nile cataracts, into Nubia. This was important because the Pharaoh got gold from Nubia in rather large amounts and used that gold to pay professional charioteers—mostly foreigners—who made up a standing army, ready at a moment's notice to sally out against an enemy. No other ruler had so much gold to keep so many soldiers at the ready. For a while, therefore, Egypt enjoyed mil-itary supremacy. Eventually, the Hittites far in the north became interested in Syria. In 1298 B.C.E., they fought a spectacular chariot battle against the Egyptians at Kadesh in northern Syria. After the battle the Egyptians had to with-draw, although Pharaoh Ramses II, upon his re-turn home, put up an inscription claiming vic-tory.

A little before the Battle of Kadesh, the Mi-tanni were overthrown by Assyrians who, like the Egyptians, used the new chariots to defeat their old masters. Kassite rule in Babylon lin-gered until the Assyrians came south to "liber-ate" the rest of Mesopotamia from foreign rule; although, as it turned out, the Babylonians were not especially eager to be ruled by Assyrians either.

Religion, Writing and Art in the Chariot Age

The mixing of peoples and quickened communi-cation that resulted from the chariot invasions called older religious beliefs into question. Gods who could not protect their faithful worshipers hardly seemed worth much. Moreover, local tra-ditions about how the world had been made and how the gods ruled over it conflicted with each other. If one were true, others had to be false. And if one were false, might not all of them be false?

Traditional Faiths   When merchant cara-vans, armies, and diplomats regularly traveled to and fro across the Middle East, it became hard to believe that a local god, worshiped in some small town in Syria, for example, could call the Egyptians from one end of the civilized world and the Assyrians from the other in order to punish the local inhabitants for not offering him the proper sacrifices. Yet that was how disasters were traditionally explained.

Nonetheless, people could not readily bring themselves to reject established rituals and doc-trines. Instead they went through the motions of traditional worship, partly from habit and partly just to be sure that the gods would not strike back if they were neglected. But when what happened often depended on events far, far away, how could there not be one single divine power over the whole world? The world was ripe for monothe-ism, but old faiths cluttered the ground too much to permit a fresh start. All that could be done was to emphasize the greatness of one god at the ex-pense of all others. Accordingly, among the Baby-lonians, priests of Marduk praised their god so much as to make all but him—the great god of Babylon—quite unnecessary.

Seeds of Monotheism: Atonism

These problems hit the Egyptians particularly hard. Before the Hyksos invasion, they had smugly disregarded everything that happened

The Aton Revolution   These busts represent the Pharaoh Akhnaton and his wife, Nefrititi. Akhnaton wished to wipe out all the gods of Egypt and make everyone worship only Aton, the sun-disk. He used his rights and prerogatives as Divine Pharaoh to carry through this religious revolution. Akhnaton's version of Aton-worship was thus not strictly monotheistic, though it moved in that direction. One of the principles of the new faith was that truth and openness should prevail. In sculpture this meant allowing Nefrititi's unusual beauty to shine through, in contrast to her husband's facial deformity. But note how the strange, tense face of Akhnaton is framed with the traditional symbols of Pharaoh's headdress, beard, and crook.

outside the Nile Valley. But when the Pharaoh came to rule an empire in Palestine and Syria, the world beyond the borders of Egypt could no longer be neglected. Nor was it easy to apply Egyptian political and religious ideas to lands where there was no Nile and where the local peoples had never even heard of the Pharaoh's divinity.

But the sun was everywhere, and no one who had ever crossed the desert between Egypt and Palestine was likely to forget its mighty power. Accordingly, a group of Egyptian religious reformers came to the conclusion that the sun-disk, Aton, was the only true god in nature and that all other gods were false. A young Pharaoh who came to the throne in 1380 B.C.E. accepted this idea. He renamed himself Akhnaton,* to honor Aton, and proceeded to try to stamp out all other kinds of worship in Egypt. Since he claimed to be divine himself, Akhnaton's reform was not strictly monotheistic, that

---

*Several variant spellings of these Egyptian names exist in English: *Akhnaton* as Ikhnaton, Akhenaten, or Akhenaton: *Aton* as Aten; and *Amon-Re* as Amen-Ra or Amon-Ra.

The Temple of Amon-Re at Karnak After Akhnaton's death, religious reaction in Egypt brought Amon-Re and his priests back into power. The mighty Temple of Amon-Re at Karnak still survives to show how rich and powerful the temple and its priesthood then became. Pharaohs became puppets of the priests, or close to it. The rituals of the temple were what Akhnaton's revolution had tried to overthrow. Knowing the right words with which to invoke the power and good will of the supreme god, Amon-Re, was what gave the priests their power after Akhnaton's attack on them failed. The carvings on the columns combine scenes from religious myths and hieroglyphic writing to explain the myths.

is, acknowledging only one god. But it was radical. Stonemasons were sent up and down Egypt with instructions to chisel the names of other gods out of every inscription they could find. The god Amon-Re of Thebes, whose priests led the resistance to Akhnaton, was the special target of this purge. The Pharaoh set up a new capital near the village known today as Tell el-Amarna. There he tried to remake traditional Egyptian styles of art and architecture along lines pleasing to Aton. This meant an effort to be informal, true to the moment, and open in thought and deed. The contrast with the stiff postures and dignity of traditional Egyptian art could hardly be greater.

Akhnaton's revolutionary movement did not outlast him, however. Religious reaction set in immediately after his death. The capital was moved back to Thebes, and new bands of stonecutters were sent out to erase the name of Aton wherever they could find it. The priests of Amon-Re became more powerful and independent of the Pharaoh than they had been before. Nothing but a few broken fragments of the Aton

cult remained, until modern scholars began digging at Akhnaton's abandoned capital. They were able to piece together a number of very interesting hymns to Aton and discovered a detailed file of diplomatic correspondence between the Pharaoh and distant rulers in Syria and Anatolia.

The Puzzle of Egyptian-Israelite Relations

The relationship between Egypt in its imperial period and the Israelites is a puzzling and unsolved problem. The Bible tells how Abraham left the Sumerian city of Ur (perhaps about 1950 B.C.E., toward the end of the Ur III period) and then wandered with his sheep and his human followers until they reached the land of Canaan. After Abraham's death, first Isaac and then Jacob (renamed *Israel* after wrestling with an angel) led the people. When famine struck, the aged Jacob with his sons and their followers fled into Egypt, where grain was available. Meanwhile, according to the Bible story, Jacob's favorite son, Joseph, who years before had been sold into slavery by his jealous brothers, had become the Pharaoh's chief minister. He gave his father and brothers the grain they needed and then revealed himself to them. Great was Jacob's joy. He remained in Egypt until his death. His descendants also stayed on for many years until a Pharaoh "who knew not Joseph" began to oppress them. Then God raised up Moses to lead them back to the promised land. Moses obeyed but died before the "children of Israel" reached their goal and began to settle in Canaan, where Abraham had pastured his herds long before.

Scholars have not been able to find anything in Egyptian records that corresponds to the biblical account. Some have suggested that the story of Joseph and his brothers might be a folk memory of the Hyksos invasion and their expulsion. But the dates do not fit, and the Hyksos did not come to Egypt as refugees from famine but as conquerors. Some scholars have thought that Moses (whose name is Egyptian) got the idea of monotheism from the worshipers of Aton. But this does not seem very likely, since Atonism was not strictly monotheistic, and Yahweh,* the God whom Moses worshiped, was not in the least like Akhnaton's Aton. In short, the records we have from Egypt and the records in the Bible do not match up in any satisfactory way. The puzzles cannot be solved unless new archaeological discoveries fill vital gaps in our information.

Simpler Forms of Writing

The mingling of peoples from many different backgrounds during the age of the chariot empires provoked the invention of a simpler form of writing. In Egypt and in Mesopotamia, well-established school systems for training scribes in the complexities of hieroglyphic and cuneiform continued to exist. As long as that was the case, no important changes could occur. But

throughout the in-between zone, particularly in Syria and Palestine, confusion prevailed. In the town of Ugarit in Syria, for example, archaeologists found texts written in six different scripts. No school system could cope with the task of teaching so many complicated kinds of writing. As a result, intelligent but very badly trained scribes resorted to a radical simplification by inventing alphabetic writing.

The Earliest Alphabets   Sometime between 1700 and 1500 B.C.E., and somewhere between Sinai and northern Syria, someone discovered that fewer than thirty signs could represent all the sounds used in speech. The secret was to neglect differences in vowel sounds. For example, a single symbol "b" could stand for *ba, be, bi, bo,* and *bu.* Since the Semitic languages used in Syria and Palestine always alternated consonant and vowel, it was not too difficult for a reader to supply the right vowel sound to go with the consonant. For example, *b-n-n* may not look like "banana," but if you try to say it, you will soon see that it cannot be read as anything else. Thus, what the scribes invented was in effect an *alphabet* in which only the consonants were recorded.

Such an invention made learning to write comparatively simple. To learn fewer than thirty signs was much, much easier than memorizing the thousands of symbols required by the older scripts. Indeed, as early as 1300 B.C.E., snatches of writing scratched onto bits of pottery prove that ordinary people had learned how to write. They sometimes recorded very trifling matters in this way.

Eventually, simpler writing made it possible to spread knowledge from specialists to common folk. But this result was slow to appear. Priests were not anxious to write down their sacred songs and stories for ordinary people to read. Indeed, the Egyptian and Mesopotamian priests and scribes clung faithfully to the old, complicated ways of writing until shortly before the Christian Era, when both hieroglyphic and cuneiform writing finally died out. Other kinds of knowledge was also likely to belong to a special group who saw no advantage in putting it into general circulation. Consequently, the fact that more people could read and write did not of itself make very much difference until a body of

---

Yahweh is used in this book to designate the God of the ancient Hebrews. Another way of writing the Hebrew word is "Jehovah."

literature came into existence that opened new thought or made new types of information available. This occurred in a significant way only after 1000 B.C.E. (See Chapter 4.)

The Use of Papyrus and Parchment for Writing

A second change in ways of writing is worth noticing. Instead of using the Mesopotamian clay tablet, which when baked became hard and all but indestructible, and instead of carving inscriptions in stone, as the Egyptians did, people began to write with pen and ink on a prepared smooth surface made from papyrus reeds. Papyrus sheets were usually prepared in long strips and then rolled up at each end on a stick. Writing was done in columns, running across the roll. Instead of turning a page, readers rolled up what they had read on one stick and unrolled the next column from the other stick. Sheets of papyrus resembled paper, though they were thicker and not so smooth as writing paper is today. The papyrus reed grew only in Egypt, where production of papyri (the prepared sheets) became an important business.

Many centuries later, parchment was invented as a substitute for papyrus. It was made by splitting sheepskins into thin layers and rubbing down the surfaces until they became smooth. Parchment was especially important in places where Egyptian papyrus could not be had easily.

The Use of Pen and Ink

Pens were made by splitting the stem of a reed partway up, so as to control the flow of ink by capillary action. The use of pen and ink, however, required changes in the shapes of letters. A cursive (rounded, flowing) style of writing thus came in, related to more formal lettering just the way our written script is related to printed letters.

By 1200 B.C.E., therefore, when a fresh wave of invasion began a new period in Middle

---

A Potsherd from Syria, Near Where Alphabetic Writing Was Invented
This is a sort of receipted bill that a merchant used to record a private business transaction. Before about 1500 B.C.E., writing required scribes to memorize several thousand symbols for separate words. Learning to read and write became much easier when some genius discovered that words could be broken down into distinct sounds and that only about twenty signs were needed to represent all the sounds in all the words. This, of course, is still the way we read and write. Ordinary people soon began to exploit the possibilities of private record keeping and written discourse, as this potsherd shows.

Eastern history, people had all the devices needed for making written learning really important. But the critical breakthrough came long afterward when the ancient Jews compiled their sacred scriptures and built a new way of life around the study and observance of God's will as revealed in those written texts.

Art and Society

Other facets of human life in the Middle East were not much affected by the chariot invasions. No important new principles of government administration or law were introduced by the charioteers. The Egyptian, Hittite, and First Assyrian empires made no improvements on Hammurabi's system of government. Economic relations were not fundamentally altered either. The great majority remained peasants, excluded from active participation in all the higher aspects of civilization. Commercial and military links between distant regions multiplied. But militarization brought destruction to peaceable (perhaps priest-managed) civilizations, like those of Crete and the Indus Valley, and made unsafe the peaceable sort of seafaring upon which the megalithic priests relied to spread their doctrine. Strangers, instead of being received as honored guests, were likely to be robbed and killed. Small boats could therefore no longer put in at night along an unfamiliar shore. Long-distance travel by sea had to be organized like a military expedition. Sailors became part-time pirates, a fact Homer takes completely for granted.

No arresting new art styles arose either. Except for short-lived experiments under Akhnaton, Egyptian art remained almost unchanging. But Pharaohs like Ramses II were in a hurry to create vast new monuments. They therefore went in for shortcuts and preferred size and bulk to elegance and perfection. Yet the extraordinary splendor of Pharaoh Tutankhamon's grave furnishings shows how excellent Egyptian craftsmanship was and how rich the Pharaoh's court must have been. Tutankhamon was the son-in-law of Akhnaton. He died while still a boy, after a reign of only a few years. Yet, when archaeologists discovered his previously untouched grave in 1922, they found an entire room crammed with furniture and precious objects, abounding in gold—a profusion that had only been dreamed of before.

In other parts of the civilized world, art, as always, reflected the age. Styles mixed and mingled all around the Mesopotamian center but nowhere attained real distinction.

Conclusion

Between 2000 and 1200 B.C.E., people in the Middle East learned how to establish complicated, civilized societies on land that did not enjoy the special advantages of irrigation. Both trade and war tended to spread civilized complexity from the centers where such societies first arose into barbarian border lands. In addition, contacts by sea in the Mediterranean succeeded in stimulating the people of Crete to make a new civilization that was much more original than were any of the satellite civilizations that arose on the mainland.

The expansion of civilized societies suffered a setback after about 1700 B.C.E., when barbarians living on or near the steppe learned how to combine mobility and firepower by harnessing horses to light, maneuverable chariots. Protected by the speed of their horses, charioteers could attack any foe without much risk to themselves. The new style of warfare was therefore quite literally irresistible at first. Chariot conquerors overran all of the Middle East, and civilizations that had flourished in India and in Crete for centuries were destroyed. In the older and more deeply civilized regions of Egypt and Mesopotamia, however, the invaders merely set up new empires, and in time native peoples, having learned how to use chariots themselves, rose in revolt and overthrew them.

During and after the chariot invasions, widened contacts among distant and different peoples caused many Middle Easterners to doubt older religious ideas. Egypt, in particular, went through a religious revolution that tried to substitute the worship of Aton, the sun-disk, for all other gods. But reaction set in, and the old rituals and doctrines revived. Old, complicated ways of writing also were carefully preserved by the priests and scribes of Egypt and Mesopotamia; but in the regions in between, where schools for training scribes were not well established, a new, simplified alphabetic system for writing was invented by 1300 B.C.E. Our own alphabet and all the other alphabets used in the world today descend from this ancient invention.

The major importance of the Chariot Age and of the resulting rise and fall of empires lay not in any changes brought to the Middle East, for such changes were relatively modest. But during these same centuries, between 1700 and 1200 B.C.E., chariot conquerors in India, China, and Greece laid the basis for three new and distinct styles of civilization. Each of these civilizations was destined to play a great role in the world's history, and we will consider how each of them came into existence in later chapters. But first it seems best to continue with the history of the ancient Middle East until about 500 B.C.E., for both Greece and India drew important skills and knowledge from that part of the world during these centuries when they were shaping their own distinct styles of civilizations.

Bibliography

Many of the books listed in the bibliography of Chapter 2 also deal with the period of 2000 to 1200 B.C.E. Two books that embrace developments beyond the river floodplains in early times are Jack Finegan, *Archaeological History of the Ancient Middle East* (1979), and J. Mellaart, *Earliest Civilizations of the Near East* (1965).

O. R. Gurney, *The Hittites* (rev. ed., 1990); Sinclair Hood, *The Minoans: Crete in the Bronze Age* (1971); Emily T. Vermeule, *Greece in the Bronze Age* (1964); and Donald Harden, *The Phoenicians* (rev. ed., 1971), describe the earliest and best-known civilizations that arose on rain-watered lands. Philip K. Hitti, *History of Syria* (2nd ed., 1957), needs to be supplemented by Paolo Matthiae, *Ebla: An Empire Rediscovered* (1980), which describes the most spectacular recent archaeological discovery in Syria. For Palestine, Kathleen M. Kenyon, *The Archaeology in the Holy Land* (4th ed., 1967), and W. F. Albright, *From Stone Age to Christianity* (2nd ed., 1957), are standard authorities. For information on Iran, see John Curtis, *Ancient Persia* (1990).

Cyril Aldred, *Akhenaten, King of Egypt* (1988), and Donald B. Redford, *Akhenaten, the Heretic King* (1984), offer contrasting interpretations of one of the most intriguing personalities of ancient history. K. A. Kitchen, *Pharaoh Triumphant: The Life and Times of Ramesses II, King of Egypt* (1982), describes another famous Egyptian Pharaoh who left unusually detailed records of his career. John Romer, *Ancient Lives: Daily Life in Egypt of the Pharaohs* (1984), and Thomas G. H. James, *Pharoah's People: Scenes from Life in Imperial Egypt* (1984), look at Egyptian society from below in a way that is impossible elsewhere because Egyptian art and literature are so rich and well preserved.

On alphabetic writing, the most important innovation of the age, see David Diringer, *Writing* (1962), and Keith Gordon Irwin, *The Romance of Writing, from Egyptian Hieroglyphics to Modern Letters, Numbers and Signs* (1956).

As before, art offers direct access to the new varieties of civilization that arose on rain-watered lands. Ekrem Akurgal, *Art of the Hittites* (1962); Reynold Higgins, *Minoan and Mycenean Art* (1967); Roman Ghirshman, *The Art of Ancient Iran* (1964); and W. F. Albright, *The Archaeology of Palestine* (1949), are available for this sort of exploration.

The Use of Plants and Animals in Agriculture

SLASH AND BURN

For slash-and-burn farmers, leafy forests are the only kind of terrain suitable for farming. They slash the bark to kill the trees; a few years later they burn the dead tree trunks and branches and use the ashes as fertilizer. Slash-and-burn methods were first used in the Middle East before 7000 B.C.E.

1. For this kind of agriculture, farmers used land with thick and leafy forest growing on it. Such land produced a good grain crop.
2. To kill the trees, farmers slashed the bark all around the tree trunk. Sunlight reached the ground, filtering through the dead trunks.
3. Farmers raked away dried leaves to expose soft loam underneath. They scattered seeds on the loam and covered these with loose soil.
4. At first no competing plants existed in newly cleared forest patches, so only desired food-producing grasses could grow.

Slash and burn agriculture, Venezuela.

5. When the grain ripened, farmers harvested it with sickles and stored seeds in jars or baskets.
6. After a few years of cultivation in this way, farmers burned the dead tree trunks and scattered the ashes as fertilizer.
7. Each year more airborne seeds came onto the cleared land. These grew into plants that competed with planted seeds, until a satisfactory crop could no longer be raised.
8. Slash-and-burn farmers then moved on and found a new patch of forest land where they could repeat the whole cycle.

Crops   Wild grain reseeds itself by allowing the ripe kernels to break off from the spike and fall to the ground. When people began to harvest grain, only kernels with tougher spikes could reach the storage area without being shaken to the ground and lost. And only kernels that reached the storage area were available for seed next season. This meant a very rapid seed selection for kernels that had tough spikes. New types of grain arose with spikes to tough that they could not seed themselves without human help. People, too, soon came to depend on these kinds of grains for food.

Highlights   The significance of slash-and-burn agriculture is that

Human beings brought seed-bearing grasses into regions in which they did not naturally grow and eliminated the mixture of plants found in nature.

Slash-and-burn farmers created food for themselves instead of finding or killing what grew naturally, as hunters and gatherers did.

A new interdependence arose as human communities came to depend on plants while the plants in question came to depend on human action for their biological existence.

IRRIGATION

Irrigation is the process of channeling water onto dry land to make arid soil fertile. This was the basis for Middle Eastern river valley civilizations along the Tigris-Euphrates, Nile, and Indus rivers, beginning 3500–2500 B.C.E.

1. Rivers, like the Tigris and Euphrates, that start in high mountains and flow through plains cut into the land in their upper reaches but drop gravel, sand, and silt as they flow more slowly across the plains.
2. In spring the river floods; and as it rises above its normal banks, it widens out, flows more slowly, and leaves large deposits at the edges of its usual bed. This creates natural levees.
3. When the flood subsides, the river returns to its bed, trapped between the levees. It continues to deposit gravel and sand. In time, therefore, it flows above the level of the surrounding plain.
4. When the flood subsides, stagnant water lies in shallow pools and swamps outside the levee on both sides of the river. As the year passes, these swampy pools evaporate until the annual flood comes to fill them again.
5. When the swamp water gets low, a channel cut through the natural levee can allow river water to reach the lower land lying on each side of the stream.
6. With construction of bigger channels, diked on each side to direct the flow of water, wide regions can be irrigated by following the contour of the land downstream. This is known as arterial irrigation.
7. Irrigation along the Nile differs. The lower Nile carries only fine silt which sinks too slowly to form natural levees.
8. The Nile flood comes slowly and gently, so that dikes can channel the flow of water onto the land and from field to field. This is called basin irrigation.

Highlights   The use of irrigation is important because

As long as floods occurred, the same fields could be cultivated year after year. Comparatively large populations could then live in a relatively small space.

The operation of an arterial irrigation system required much human labor for construction and maintenance. Centralized control and planning were needed as canals became longer and deeper and irrigated more land.

Massed human labor, responding to centralized organization, created the material basis for the first civilizations.

FIELD AND FALLOW

Field and fallow is a method of farming in which a piece of land is plowed and sown with seed during one growing season, then plowed and allowed to remain idle during the next. It was probably first developed in Middle Eastern river valleys a little before 3000 B.C.E.

1. Field-and-fallow farmers used animals to pull a simple plow through the soil. This allowed them to cultivate more ground than when human muscles alone supplied digging power.
2. This method effectively kept down weeds by plowing the fallow field in summer time, killing competing plants before they formed seeds.
3. As a result, the former grain field, left fallow, was cleared of weeds by being plowed.
4. By plowing and planting the grain field at the start of the growing season, then plowing the fallow field, then harvesting the ripened grain, labor was spread more evenly through the year.

Crops and Draft Animals   The main crops of early field-and-fallow farming were the same as for slash-and-burn: wheat and barley. The big change was the use of animal power. Castrated bulls, called oxen, were used for plowing because of their strength and tameness.

The scratch plow had three essential parts: a beam or rope that attached the plow to the oxen, a share that dragged through the soil, and a handle which plowmen used to "steer" the share through the soil. The scratch plow had to be light enough for a man to steer, so it did not work well in heavy clay soil.

Highlights   The field-and-fallow style of farming meant that

Effective weed control and cultivation of more land allowed an ordinary farmer to harvest more grain than his family could eat.

This surplus grain could support people who did not produce their own food but worked at other things. Such specialists created the earliest civilizations.

Farming had been women's work until the invention of the plow brought men into the fields with their animals. This made men, as in the hunting days, the main providers of food within families and assured male dominance in society at large.

VEGETATIVE ROOT

In vegetative root farming, roots were cultivated for food, sometimes on flooded areas of land. Vegetative root agriculture probably began somewhere in the tropics of southeast Asia. The date of origin is quite uncertain. It may have begun as early as 13,000–9000 B.C.E., before slash-and-burn agriculture got started.

1. Vegetative root farming probably started near the edge of rivers or lakes where fishermen had settled in permanent villages.
2. A live shoot from the parent plant was partly buried in the moist or flooded ground so that it would take root.
3. In tropical climates all stages of growth may be found on a single patch of land at any given time.

Crops   Many different kinds of crops were grown in vegetative root agriculture. Taros, yams, and manioc were most important. They have large tuberous roots that store large amounts of starch. A single root can make a meal for two or three persons and can be fried, boiled, or baked.

Highlights   Vegetative root farming differs from grain farming because

Old habits of gathering wild plants did not need to change very much since roots can be made to ripen at all times of the year in the tropics.

Cultivaters met the weed problem simply by pulling out unwanted plants by hand from around individual large, transplanted shoots.

Once out of the ground, moist roots rot quickly. As a result, no one could accumulate a surplus of food much beyond everyday needs, and occupational specialists could not begin to depend on others to produce the food they needed.

For all these reasons, vegetative root farming did not alter older forms of human society as radically as grain farming did and failed to become the basis of complex civilized communities.

RICE PADDY

Rice paddy cultivation requires the land to be under water while the rice plants grow, but at harvest time fields are drained dry. This procedure causes competing plants to be either drowned or baked out, thus keeping weeds down. Rice paddy cultivation began somewhere in China or southeast Asia, perhaps about 3000–2500 B.C.E.

Rice cultivation in Java.

1. Since rice paddy land must be perfectly level, farmers have to cut down the higher portion and fill in lower parts of a field until water will stand at a uniform depth.
2. Only regulated amounts of water are wanted on the field. A rice paddy must therefore be surrounded by waterproof dikes with sluices and channels to control water flow.
3. After this preparation, fields are plowed and planted with seedlings sprouted in a special nursery. The water which flows gently into the fields prevents the growth of weeds that live on land, carries dissolved minerals, and supports a complex interaction of organisms that keep the soil fertile.
4. When the rice is ready to ripen, the farmer stops the water from flowing into the paddy, and it dries out. This kills weeds that flourish in water.
5. The rice is harvested with sickles; and if water remains available, a second crop of rice can be planted in the same growing season.

Fields   Rice has the enormous advantage of producing more food per acre than any other crop, particularly when double-cropping is possible. This allows a very dense population to come into existence. The high food yield from rice paddies, in turn, supports the abundant labor force needed to construct and maintain paddy fields with the elaborate conduit system that brings water into fields and keeps it there as long as it is needed. The rice plant requires a mean temperature of 70°F, a good deal warmer than wheat.

Highlights   The importance of the rice paddy is that

The alternation between flooding and draining achieves both weed control and fertilization of the soil.

The labor required to build rice paddies ties the farmers to the land permanently. Nowhere else can they hope to secure as much food for their labor.

Dense populations depending on rice paddy cultivation can be compelled to support distant governments, since farmers cannot leave the land nor hide the harvest from tax collectors. This makes state-building easy.

MOLDBOARD PLOW

The moldboard plow turns the soil over in furrows instead of merely breaking it up into loose bits as the scratch plow does. The moldboard plow came into existence in the moist climate of northwestern Europe about C.E. 100; but it came into general use slowly, between C.E. 500 and 1000.

1. **Construction of the Moldboard Plow.** The moldboard plow has a share and a beam essentially the same as the scratch plow.

The moldboard plow at work. An illumination from the Duc de Berry's *Book of Hours*.

Two new parts were added to this. A colter that slices vertically through the earth from above runs just ahead of the tip of the share. A moldboard, lying behind the share, turns the furrow, cut from the earth by the combined action of the colter and plowshare.

2. **Use of the Moldboard Plow.** Four to six oxen were needed to pull the moldboard plow, and such a team cannot turn quickly or easily. Long, narrow fields were, therefore, the only efficient shape for cultivation

The moldboard turns the furrow to one side only. As the plow comes and goes the length of the field, it turns the slices toward a center furrow, or ridge.

On a field plowed year after year in the same way, this builds up ridges in the centers and makes shallow ditches called balks on each side. The plow thus creates a drainage system on flat, water-logged fields.

Highlights   The moldboard plow changed farming methods because

Moldboard plow agriculture opened the flat, abundantly watered plains of northwestern Europe to cultivation on a large scale for the first time.

With the moldboard plow, a rotating three-field system with winter crop, spring crop, and fallow could be used. In northwestern Europe, the soil could be plowed with the moldboard plow at any time of the year. A single farmer could therefore cultivate more land and raise more food than in lands where plowing was seasonal. This helps to account for the rapid rise of Latin Christendom after 1000.

ELIMINATION OF FALLOW

Between 1600 and 1750, Dutch and English farmers discovered that they could plant certain valuable new crops on land previously left fallow, and still keep down weeds or even increase and improve the soil's fertility. These new crops were used mainly for animal feed.

1. One way to use the fallow productively was to plant a fast-sprouting cover crop, like clover, alfalfa, or vetch, that can get started early in the growing season and smother competing plants.
2. A second way of using fallow was to plant crops in rows, and then cultivate between the rows often enough to destroy weeds.
3. Agricultural "improvers" used manure and other materials to fertilize their fields: chalk, lime, seaweed, ashes, even soot and sometimes sand were tried with good results.

Crops   New crops came into use with the elimination of fallow. Nitrogen-fixing bacteria flourish in the roots of clover, alfalfa, and vetch. When the top part of these plants had been used for cattle food, the roots remained with extra nitrogen that the bacterial action had taken from the air. This assured a noticeable improvement in the field's fertility. Turnips were the most important row crop; cabbages, beets, and later potatoes were also raised in this way.

Highlights   The elimination of fallow meant that

The new crops, suitable for fields formerly left fallow, were mainly used for animal feed. This allowed a vast increase in pigs, cattle, and sheep and an improvement of the human diet.

The nitrogen-fixing crops incidentally improved fertility for grain raising, thus increasing cereal yields also.

With more and better fodder, farmers could develop specialized breeds of dairy, meat, and draft animals.

SCIENTIFIC AGRICULTURE

During the nineteenth century, the application of science and technology to agriculture became conscious and widespread. From western Europe and North America, scientific efforts to improve agriculture spread throughout the world.

Crops and Farming Methods   Fertilizers and food additives supply chemicals needed for plant and animal growth. A German professor, Justus von Liebig (1803–1873), was the first to analyze plants chemically and experiment with artificial fertilizers. Scientific study of animal nutrition began only in the twentieth century with the discovery of vitamins.

Geneticists can alter plants and animals to suit human uses. Mendelian theories of inheritance (named after Gregor Mendel, whose ideas were published in 1866 but forgotten until 1900) enabled experimenters to create strains of hybrid corn in the 1920s that greatly increased U.S. farm yields. In the 1960s, other experimenters invented new kinds of rice, giving Asians a chance to increase their food production very greatly.

Machinery allows farmers to plow, plant, and harvest large areas quickly. Farmers had always used simple machines, from the digging stick on up. But only with the industrial revolution could big, complicated, factory-made machinery come to the fields. The first practically successful factory-made farm machine was the McCormick reaper, patented in 1834.

Food storage and distribution were also altered by the application of science. Canning depends on heat to sterilize food and prevent decay. It was discovered in France in 1809, but came into common use in the United States only with the Civil War, 1861–1865. Freezing, another important method of preserving food, became common after World War II.

Highlights   The significance of scientific agriculture is that

Fewer hands can produce more food in less time. As a result, in the parts of the world where scientific agriculture has spread, most people eat food produced by others. Until about 100 years ago, most human beings worked as farmers. Now a majority live in cities and work at other tasks.

AMERICAN CROP MIGRATION

With the opening of the world's oceans to shipping (1500–1600), the Old World received several important new food crops from recently discovered lands.

Maize   The center for early domestication of maize was probably in Mexico and Central America. It was taken to Europe by Spanish explorers in the sixteenth century, and from there it reached the Middle East. The Portuguese are credited with introducing maize into Africa and India. Magellan is supposed to have brought it to the East Indies via the Pacific Ocean.

Potatoes   Potatoes were native to the Andes in South America and were first domesticated by the ancient Peruvians. They were introduced into Europe twice: first by Spanish sailors and a second time by Sir Fancis Drake after his circumnavigation of the glove in 1580. From western Europe, potatoes were introduced to the North American colonies, central and eastern Europe, and the Middle East. As was the case with corn, the potato came to Africa with the Portuguese and to southeast Asia and China by way of the Pacific.

Sweet Potatoes   Sweet potatoes probably originated as a cultivated crop in the Caribbean region. Spanish explorers brought them back to Europe before white potatoes arrived from the more distant coasts of Peru. Sweet potatoes never became very important in Europe. But in southern China, the sweet potato, introduced across the Pacific in the sixteenth century, became a crop of basic importance. In parts of Africa, too, sweet potatoes rivaled maize in importance.

EURASIAN CROP MIGRATION

As food crops were introduced into Europe, Asia, and Africa from the New World, the crops, domesticated animals and agricultural methods of the Old World also spread to the rest of the earth.

In many parts of the world, European settlers brought with them the equipment of agriculture that was familiar to them in their

The Harvesters, by Pieter Brueghel. *(Metropolitan Museum of Art, Rogers Fund, 1919)*

Modern harvesting done by machine.

homelands. They simply displaced the peoples they found living there, as in most of North America and in Australia.

In some parts of the world, however, older forms of agriculture were little affected by the skills and knowledge that opening the oceans diffused around the world. This was the case with rice paddy cultivation, which continued unchanged and spread slowly in southeast Asia and to some Pacific islands.

In between were regions where new crops or domesticated animals radically altered older lifestyles. An example was the rise of Plains Indian cultures in North America after they learned to use the horse, introduced by Spaniards.

The American And Eurasian crop migration had several effects:

Human food supplies increased in amount and in many places there was an improvement in quality as well.

The diffusion of agricultural techniques caused by regular oceanic movements of people, plants, and ideas tended to equalize food production within each climate zone all around the globe.

Empire and Religion in the Middle East

1200 to 500 B.C.E.

4

Officialdom at Work   This painting once decorated the walls of the
palace of the Assyrian governor of Syria. It shows how Assyrian styles
of art spread with the Assyrian Empire across the entire Middle East.
It also demonstrates that bureaucratic officials gathered resources
from diverse populations to build palaces, sustain armies of
unparalleled efficiency, and thus make empire possible.

Between 1200 and 500 B.C.E., the civilized regions of the Middle East went through a cycle of social and political change. At the beginning of this period, there were widespread invasions leading to the collapse of the old chariot empires. At first the newcomers divided into many small tribal groups, but rather rapidly large kingdoms and empires began to arise. By 750 B.C.E. most of the civilized parts of the Middle East had been united under a new Assyrian Empire. When the Assyrians in their turn suffered destruction, a Persian Empire soon took its place, uniting the whole Middle East and outlying regions into a single great state that lasted until 330 B.C.E. Arts of the government already known in the age of Ur III and Hammurabi were improved and refined by the Assyrian and Persian rulers.

This political experience was accompanied by two fundamental changes, one in economic relations and one in religion. In economics, the use of iron for agricultural tools made work in the fields easier and increased yields. In religion, the centuries between 1200 and 500 B.C.E. saw the rise of a new pattern of belief. Instead of thinking that the world was controlled by innumerable and often rival gods, some thoughtful individuals came to believe that a single God ruled the entire universe and ruled it justly. Such views are called *ethical monotheism*—"ethical" because God governs according to just or ethical principles, and "monotheism" (Greek: *mono*, one; *theos*, god) because a single God was believed to rule the world.

Older ideas lingered on but were discredited. People knew too much about the contradictions that existed among different religious myths. Only the Jews and a reforming sect among the Persians, led by the prophet Zoroaster, took the radical, logical step to monotheism. And only Jews fully developed the advantages that came from writing down sacred scriptures. By making sacred texts available to large numbers of quite ordinary folk, the whole Jewish people became able to shape their belief and behavior on models provided by the scriptures. A broadly based, popular religion, founded on extensive knowledge of sacred writings, was an entirely new phenomenon in human history.

This and the bureaucratic techniques for ruling empires constituted the two most important achievements of ancient Middle Eastern society and civilization. Both were passed on to later ages and still affect our lives profoundly, even though we live half a world away and three thousand years later.

The Iron Age— The Importance of Iron

The use of metals was characteristic of civilized peoples, though some primitive societies also knew how to smelt copper and other ores. Most metals were used mainly for jewelry; only bronze was hard and tough enough to serve as a tool or weapon. But bronze was expensive, since the copper and tin ores that had to be combined to make bronze were rather scarce.

For a long time no one could use iron effectively. When iron was melted and poured into a mold—the way other metals were treated—it crystallized as it cooled and so became both very hard and very brittle. Any sharp blow simply shattered anything made of it. In addition, cast iron rusted easily and was not particularly handsome. Hence, even though iron ore was by far the commonest metal in the earth's crust, early smiths had no use for it.

About 1400 B.C.E., however, an entirely new technique for treating iron was discovered somewhere in eastern Anatolia. For a long time the ironworkers and their Hittite rulers kept the new methods secret. But after about 1200 B.C.E., the Hittite Empire broke up and blacksmiths scattered in all directions. Knowledge of how to make useful tools and weapons out of common iron ore spread with them. As this happened, usable metal became vastly more abundant. New applications in ordinary everyday life became possible. Both farming and fighting were changed in fundamental ways. A new age dawned—the Iron Age. The Chariot Age, dominated by aristocratic warriors whose weapons were of bronze, faded into the past.

The secret of making iron into a useful metal was to mix small quantities of carbon into it. This changed the qualities of the metal in remarkable ways. Instead of the brittleness of cast iron, iron that had carbon mixed into it became flexible, yet hard and tough like bronze, and nearly as cheap as cast iron. Ancient smiths did not know that small quantities of carbon from the charcoal, on which they heated the iron, entered into the molten metal and changed its characteristics. What they knew was that if they took a piece of cast iron and heated it in a bed of burning charcoal until it became red hot and soft, it could then be hammered into any shape desired. Of course, this had to be done over and over again until the piece of metal had been beaten into what was needed—sword blade, helmet, plowshare, or whatever it might be. And if, after being hammered into shape, the metal was heated again and then suddenly plunged into a bath of cold water, a hard, tough, and strong end product would result. We call it wrought iron. The one disadvantage of the new metal was that it rusted. No cure could be found for this, but the abundance of iron more than made up for this inferiority to bronze.

Iron Age Migrations

Because iron weapons and tools were very much more abundant than bronze weapons had been, they became available to far larger numbers of people. This changed the balance of military strength between the civilized states of the Middle East and the peoples who lived in the deserts to the south and in the hills to the north. In the civilized part of the world, the political masters of the land did not dare to arm the rank and file of peasant farmers. They were subjects and rent-payers, not warriors, anyway. With weapons in their hands, they might attack their masters rather than fighting against invading barbarians. Among the nomads of the desert and the tribes of the hills, however, every grown man was a potential soldier, eager for plunder and ready to obey his chief.

The result was the rapid overthrow of the charioteers' empires. The chariot lost most of its terror when shields and helmets of iron guarded foot soldiers against the charioteers' arrows. Infantry, of course, could not compete with chariot mobility. But a well-armored raiding party of foot soldiers, if properly disciplined, could keep the field against even the most furious chariot charge. And by catching chariots in a narrow valley or at some other disadvantageous place, foot soldiers might even be able to destroy the sort of chariot army that had once been irresistible.

Invaders of the Iron Age came both by sea and by land. The people known as Philistines, for example, came by ship from somewhere in Asia Minor or the Aegean. Their fleet may even have included some ships' crews from the shores of the Black Sea. After trying several times to invade Egypt, the remnant of the Philistine host settled in Palestine (ca. 1190 B.C.E.). They conquered the Canaanite peasants of the land and ruled over them from fortified cities near the coast. At about the same time, Hebrews from the desert filtered in from the east and occupied the high ground overlooking the coastal plain of Palestine.

Farther north, along the Mediterranean coast, the Phoenicians remained little affected by the collapse of the Hittite Empire (1200 B.C.E.) and the decline of the Egyptian Empire, which began about 1100 B.C.E. They soon became the most active sea traders of the eastern Mediterranean, taking over the role formerly played by Cretan and then by Mycenaean ships. Inland, however, new tribes, from the desert, known as Aramaeans, occupied the land around Damascus, in Syria. They, too, became famous traders by operating caravans between Phoenicia on the coast and the cities of Mesopotamia. In southern Mesopotamia still a third group of tribesmen penetrated civilized ground, taking over the territory where Sumerian cities once had stood. These were the Chaldaeans, who, like the Hebrews and the Aramaeans, spoke a Semitic language.

In their native environment, these Semitic-speaking tribes from the north Arabian desert did not have easy access to iron or the fuel needed for smelting it. Iron weapons were therefore not an important factor when they first invaded civilized regions. All the same, their victories were made easier by the fact that the civilized empires were also being attacked by barbarians from the north—such as the Philistines—who did have iron. By and large, the invaders from the southern deserts learned about the new metal only after they had settled down in Palestine, Syria, and Mesopotamia.

The northern invaders spoke Indo-European languages. At least some of their ancestors had been warlike pastoral nomads on the steppelands between the Black Sea and the Aral Sea. Thus, nomadism and herding were still familiar to the Dorians who overran Greece between 1200 and 1000 B.C.E. The Medes, too, moved onto the plateau of Iran at about the same time and at first continued to depend on herds of cattle and horses. Between these two flanks, the most important new peoples who appeared in the Middle East when the Iron Age invasions got underway were the Phyrgians in Anatolia, who overthrew the Hittite Empire, and the Armenians, who settled south of the Caucasus Mountains around Lake Van.

Return to Civilized Patterns of Society

These movements of people tapered off after about 1000 B.C.E. Among the older states, only Egypt and Assyria survived as independent kingdoms, but they ceased to be empires because they lost control of all their outlying territories where subject peoples had once obeyed them. The Hittite and Mycenaean empires disappeared entirely. Yet the memory of how to rule a great state did not vanish, and the bureaucratic principle was not forgotten completely. In due course new empires arose on the ruins of the old.

During and after the Iron Age invasions, however, rough, independent farmer-herders established themselves in many parts of the Middle East. Among these peoples, tribal ties and a strong sense of the equality of all fighting men remained near the surface; but before long, differences began to appear. Some families became rich and powerful, others stayed poor and became dependent on the rich. Rulers discovered again the advantages of standing armies and learned how to collect taxes in order to maintain professional soldiers. All the features of civilized society, in other words, speedily started to develop again, even among the most old-fashioned, equality-minded newcomers.

Trade, war, and population growth combined to produce this result. As the invaders settled down and became more numerous, they soon had to give up most of their animals and become crop farmers. With further population growth, some farmers found themselves in possession of too little good farmland for comfort. After a bad season they might have to borrow seed grain from a more fortunate or more prudent neighbor. If the borrower could not repay, he would first lose his land and then might have to become a slave simply in order to eat.

The prudent and ruthless lender soon grew into a landowner. He might then begin to use his extra wealth to trade with distant parts for various luxuries that could not be produced at home. A more luxurious style of life thus became possible. This, in turn, made it worthwhile to get hold of more and more land. As the rich got richer and the poor got poorer, it became easier for those who had large holdings to increase their possessions.

War had the same effect. Local chieftains needed bodyguards to be able to impose their will on others. Bodyguards in time grew into regular standing armies because of danger from neighbors and, sometimes, disloyalty at home among those who regretted the loss of the old tribal traditions of freedom and equality.

Obviously, an army required taxes, and taxes had to be collected from ordinary farmers—by force, if necessary. The whole development from tribal simplicity to full-blown bureaucratic government went very fast. Models lay close at hand in both Egypt and Mesopotamia, where civilized techniques of government survived without interruption. As a result, by 900 B.C.E., even a rather backward kingdom like of that of the Hebrews in Palestine evolved all the features of civilized society.

The New Relation of Villagers and Townsfolk

At first glance, therefore, it appears that the invasions of the Iron Age made almost no difference. But in fact this was not so. Even after landlords and tax collectors, standing armies, and bureaucratic governments had once again established themselves all over the Middle East, the structure of society did not become exactly the same as in the Bronze Age. There were several reasons for this.

First of all, iron plowshares, sickles and scythes helped to extend cultivation. Heavy clay soils that a wooden plow was unable to penetrate could be plowed with iron plowshares, and the labor of the harvest was much reduced by the use of iron sickles and scythes. This meant that more food could be produced. It also meant that every farmer had to go to the market from time to time to get new tools or to have his old ones repaired. The work of the blacksmith was too specialized for an ordinary farmer to learn; hence, he had to have his ironwork done by a professional.

This was a true landmark in history. Peasant farmers of earlier civilized communities ordinarily made their own implements. But, with the coming of iron tools, peasant farmers for the first time began to get a direct, practical benefit from the specialization of labor and the enlargement of human skills that had begun more than 2000 years earlier with the rise of the first cities and civilization.

Previously, only privileged classes of society—priests, soldiers, rulers, landlords—had reaped the benefits of such skills. The peasants at the bottom of the social ladder had worked in the fields and been forced to pay over part of their crop to somebody else. Now, however, with the coming of iron, every farmer had to have some of his tools made for him. This meant buying and selling, saving a little extra grain to trade for a bit of iron or for a fine new sickle. Once the idea that even the poorest cultivators could buy and sell got to be accepted all round, farmers who happened to have something left over when the season came to an end might buy other artisans' products too: a useful pot to put things in or a pretty piece of cloth for a bride-to-be.

It is worth emphasizing the importance of this new relationship between artisans of the town and cultivators of the countryside. In ear-

lier ages, if some military action wiped a town from the face of the earth, the local farmers felt no loss. On the contrary, they would find themselves freed—at least for a while—from having to pay rents and taxes to the cityfolk. The townspeople, in other words, were their natural enemies, not their friends.

This ever-present, half-suppressed hostility between town and country dwellers had meant that town life had always been fragile, insecure, and liable to drastic setbacks. This is why civilized life was so easily wiped out in Greece and India when rude invaders, who did not know or care much about city life, overran the towns and plundered everything they could lay hands on. The invaders then moved on, looking for fresh plunder, new pasture for their cattle, and fertile farmland for themselves.

When peasants began to depend on town artisans for essential supplies, however, a bond of mutual interest began to link the two classes together. Smiths, after all, needed metal, and metal came only by trade—at least in most places where mines and fuel supplies were not immediately at hand. Trade, in turn, required some sort of public order, which, in turn, required government, armies, and priests, too, for the gods could not safely be neglected. Such experts could only be maintained by the payment of rents and taxes. In short, for the peasant majority of humankind, the price of iron was acceptance of the whole burden of civilization.

This does not mean that the peasants of the civilized world came to feel that paying rents and taxes was right or just. It does mean, though, that they began to have a stake in the survival of town life. When a town was destroyed, there were strong reasons for starting it up again, or for finding another town nearby where the services needed by the population could be provided.

Town life, therefore, became firmly rooted on rain-watered land in the Iron Age, not before. A new economic base level had been attained. Everybody, with the possible exception of nomad shepherds and herders, now had real interest in keeping town life—and therefore civilization—alive.

Restoration of Bureaucratic Government—the Hebrew Example

The speed with which the political structure of the Middle East returned to bureaucratic government between 1100 and 900 B.C.E. shows how stubborn the pressures toward civilized complexity were. We are particularly well informed about how this happened among the Hebrews because the historical parts of the Old Testament deal in some detail with the conquest of Canaan and the campaigns of the earliest Hebrew kings.

When they first moved into Canaan, the Hebrews were organized loosely into tribes. The twelve tribes cooperated only on special occasions. Local problems were settled by "judges" whose authority rested on personal prestige and holiness. However, war with the Philistines required better organization. One of the judges, Samuel, called all the tribes together and anointed

Saul, a young man of unusual strength and stature as king. This happened about 1020 B.C.E. For a while Saul was a successful war leader, but he quarreled with some of his best fighters, including David, son of Jesse. In the end, King Saul met defeat and death in battle against the Philistines. His rival, David, succeeded to the kingship, decisively defeated the Philistines, and seized Jerusalem from the Jebusites and made it his capital.

Under David, who ruled from about 1012 to 972 B.C.E., the kingdom became relatively stable. Taxes maintained a formidable standing army; diplomatic relations with neighboring kingdoms became important; commerce developed.

King Solomon, David's son, brought the Hebrew kingdom to its highest peak of prosperity. He imported workers from Phoenicia to build a temple to Yahweh in Jerusalem, and he was famous both for the number of his wives and for the wisdom of his administration.

After Solomon's death the kingdom split into two halves: Israel in the north and Judah in the

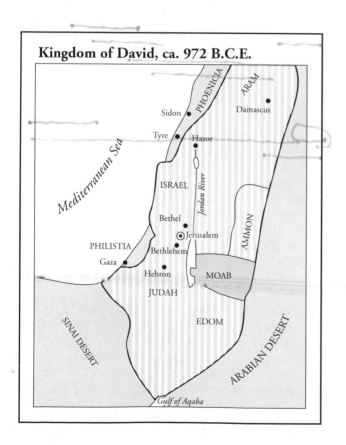

Kingdom of David, ca. 972 B.C.E.

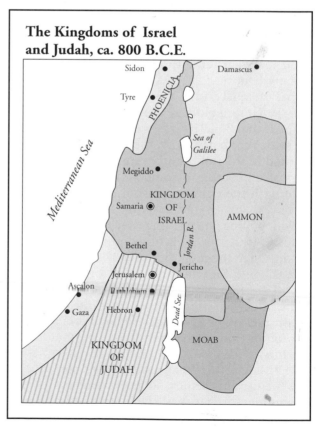

The Kingdoms of Israel and Judah, ca. 800 B.C.E.

south. Israel was ruled from Samaria, Judah from Jerusalem. For nearly 200 years the two kingdoms fought one another from time to time and played a minor part in diplomatic and military maneuvers with greater powers. Then in 722 B.C.E. the Assyrians conquered the kingdom of Israel. They carried all the cityfolk of the kingdom off into captivity in Babylonia. Only peasants remained behind, subject to alien tax collectors and to governors appointed by the distant monarch of Assyria.

The Israelite upper class never returned. They made up the "ten lost tribes" of the kingdom of Israel. Presumably they simple merged into the general population of the Middle East. The peasants of Israel remaining behind were known to later Jews as Samaritans (so-called after the capital city, Samaria). Their religion differed on some important points from later Jewish beliefs and ritual, a fact that horrified Jews who felt that the Samaritan religion was particularly dangerous because in most respects it was close to their own.

How to Rule an Empire: The Assyrian Example

The Assyrian kingdom that conquered Israel in 722 B.C.E. had barely survived the Iron Age invasions. The Assyrians were the cultural heirs of Babylonia located on an exposed frontier, where barbarism lapped up against the most northerly outpost of the ancient civilization of Mesopotamia. In such a position, the Assyrian kings were especially exposed to attack from the north but had the advantages of superior numbers and wealth that came from irrigation agriculture. After a slow start, therefore, Assyrian power began to expand more and more rapidly. All of Mesopotamia and Syria had been conquered before the Assyrian armies attacked Israel. Thereafter, other campaigns extended Assyrian power still further into Egypt, Armenia, and Iran. Such an empire was larger than any known before. It was also more systematically governed, but it proved brittle because all the subject peoples hated Assyrian ruthlessness.

The Assyrians' success depended upon some important advances they made in military organization and government. In particular, the Assyrians seem to have been the first to organize an entire army into regular units of uniform size—tens, hundreds, and thousands—each with standard equipment and under commanders who could be promoted for success and bravery or demoted if they failed to perform as expected of them. The Assyrian army also had specialist troops: engineers for siege works, and cavalry and chariotry for pursuit and reconnaissance. Its backbone was a hardy infantry spearmen and archers—commanded by a career officer corps.

All modern armies are built up on these principles. So were the later Persian and Roman imperial armies. The reason, of course, is that the system works. Ordinary men from very diverse backgrounds can be fitted into standardized army units and become effective and obedient soldiers, using the Assyrians' patterns of army administration. Promotion for demonstrated efficiency in the field made subordinate commanders into willing, even eager servants of the monarch. Anyone, if appointed by the king, could command any unit of the royal army. Because officers were often shifted around, their careers depended directly on the king. Their loyalty turned to him, too. No other ties—to locality, to a particular piece of property, or to a special body of troops—lasted more than a few years out of an officer's total career.

All of this permitted (and still permits) control from the center to a degree otherwise impossible. Thousands upon thousands of men could be made to act together and cooperate effectively to win a victory and conduct an entire campaign. When a regular chain of command came into existence and was accepted by all from top to bottom of the army, generalship on the grand scale, with planned encirclements, ambushes, cross-country marches and other surprises, became possible. Over and over again Assyrian victories demonstrated the advantage of such a system of military administration in an age when opponents could not, or did not, equal it.

The Assyrians also built roads to facilitate the march of their armies toward threatened frontiers. They were wide enough to carry wheeled vehicles through difficult passes and across rough country. Such roads cut down the time needed for the king to arrive with his armies at any threatened point. A messenger system, using relay horses to carry news of any important event to the capital, also allowed the central government to react quickly to danger.

The elaborate Assyrian military system was supported by taxes and by a draft of able-bodied young men. Taxes were collected by governors appointed to administer provinces in the same way that the king appointed his military commanders. The Assyrians also had a code of laws, which the governors seem to have applied throughout the area under their control. These principles were not new. Similar arrangements had prevailed under Hammurabi and earlier. Thus, the major breakthrough the Assyrians made was in military organization rather than in civil administration.

All the same, their victories did not produce obedient subjects. Both the Babylonians and the Egyptians found it difficult to submit to upstarts, as they felt the Assyrians to be. Repeated revolts therefore took place, and Assyrian efforts to terrorize their subjects never checked rebellion for long. Endless campaigning cost a lot of Assyrian lives. Toward the end, the ranks

of the Assyrian armies were filled with conscripts raised among their defeated enemies. Perhaps such soldiers did not fight as well as native Assyrians had once done.

Even so, it took attack from a new quarter and six years of war to overthrow the Assyrian Empire. Nineveh, the capital, was sacked in 612 B.C.E. Seven years later, the last organized Assyrian army had been destroyed, and the whole Assyrian nation with it. Three groups combined to destroy the Assyrians: Medes from the plateau of Iran to the east, Babylonian rebels from the south, and Scythians from the grasslands of southern Russia.

The Cavalry Revolution   The appearance of the Scythians marked an important new epoch in Middle Eastern and world history. They were cavalrymen who exploited the speed of their horses and the accuracy of their arrows much the way charioteers had done, but without the elaborate and expensive equipment charioteers had needed.

Using horses for cavalry seems obvious now, but when humans first began to associate with horses, the idea of riding into combat seemed

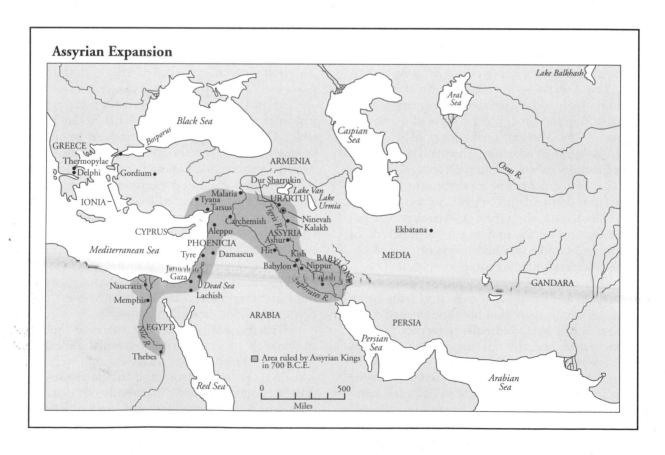

Assyrian Expansion

Assyrian Cavalry. This carving from an Assyrian palace wall shows a cavalryman in action. When it was carved, shooting from horseback was probably still quite new. To use his bow, a rider had to let go of the reins and keep his seat without the help of stirrups, invented only about a thousand years later.

The Assyrians may have been the first to use horses for war in this way, but the people who benefited most were nomads from the steppelands to the north. Once they learned to shoot from horseback, nomads could concentrate superior force almost at will. Consequently, from about 750 B.C.E. their raids and conquests increased in scale and frequency, and continued to dominate Eurasian political history for the next 2500 years.

foolhardy. To shoot from horseback with a bow, a rider must let go of the reins. This frees the horse to move as it pleases, and until the invention of stirrups about 200 C.E. any sudden change of motion was liable to pitch the rider off right in the face of the enemy. Only long and intimate association between horse and rider made shooting from horseback safe enough to risk.

Actually, the first records of the use of cavalry in battle came from the Assyrian army itself and date from about 875 B.C.E. Thus it appears that Assyrians paved the way for the eventual overthrow of their empire by learning how to ride horses into battle. For when the nomads of the steppe mastered this simple and cheap way to exploit the strength and speed of their horses, they gained an enormous military advantage. Raiding parties of horsemen could rove far and wide, and they could be gone before any defend-

ing infantry force could catch up with them. Only equally well-mounted defenders could hope to meet such raiders on more or less even terms. But, as pointed out earlier, horses were costly to keep where there was no natural grass for them to eat.

Steppe peoples living as they did, on grass-covered plains, had the permanent advantage of being able to raise horses cheaply so that every man could easily possess two or three mounts. Bow and arrows and hit-and-run tactics did the rest. If cavalry raiders met serious opposition, they simply galloped off over the horizon and tried again somewhere else, after a day or two to rest their horses.

The Assyrian army was not prepared to cope with this kind of threat. Accordingly, the combination of Scythian tactics with mass rebellion in the rear brought the empire down. To be sure, the

Scythians returned home after the sack of Nineveh in 612 B.C.E. Civilized lands did not have enough pasture for their horses, so they could not stay away from the steppe for very long. But neither the Medes nor the Babylonians—nor the Egyptians, who tried briefly once again to exert imperial power over Judah—were able to prevent renewed cavalry raids from the steppes.

Imperial Consolidation Under the Persians

The overthrow of the Assyrian Empire and the departure of the Scythians created a power vacuum in the Middle East. The victorious rebels divided the spoils between themselves but soon

quarreled. The Babylonians wanted to control Palestine and Syria as the Assyrians had done, but the Egyptians wished to keep them at a safe distance and began trying to exert influence over the little kingdom of Judah. This persuaded Nebuchadnezzar, the Chaldaean ruler of Babylon, to attack Judah. The Egyptians were no help, so Nebuchadnezzar captured Jerusalem in 586 B.C.E., destroyed Solomon's Temple, and carried the cityfolk of Judah back to Babylon with him.

The shock to worshipers of Yahweh was tremendous, for after the destruction of Israel in 722 B.C.E. priests and religious reformers in Jerusalem had drawn the conclusion that their sister kingdom to the north had been punished for failing to obey God faithfully. They therefore set out energetically to reform religion and government in Judah, only to have a similar disaster

The Pride and Glory of Babylon This winged bull, made of brightly colored glazed bricks, guarded one of the gates of the city of Babylon. It was constructed in the time of King Nebuchadnezzar, infamous in the Bible as an oppressor of the exiled Jews. This guardian figure symbolizes the pride and wealth of a city that dated back almost to the beginning of Mesopotamian history. It reached the peak of its political power under Nebuchadnezzar, only to succumb soon afterward to the Persians.

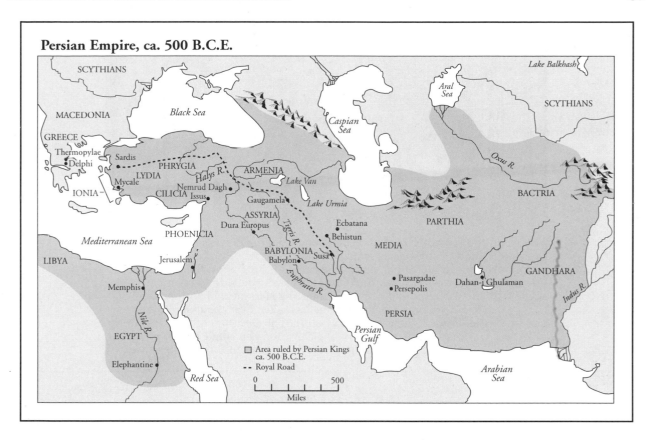

Persian Empire, ca. 500 B.C.E.

visited upon them. Yet, as we shall soon see, the dismay of the exiles from Judah led only to a renewed and deepened effort to understand God's will—an effort that made Judaism into an enduring world religion.

The Jews who "wept beside the waters of Babylon" when they remembered Jerusalem did not have long to wait before their Babylonian masters' power was itself overthrown. In 539 B.C.E. Cyrus the Persian entered Babylon as a conqueror. He began life as a vassal of the Medes, but when he entered Babylon he had already conquered both the Medes' empire and the smaller kingdom of Lydia in Asia Minor. By the time of his death (530 B.C.E.) Cyrus was master of all the lands between the Aegean Sea on the west and the Amu Darya (Oxus River) on the east.

These amazing successes resulted from the fact that Cyrus had a hardy and warlike people under his command—the Persians, who spoke an Indo-European language closely related to the language of the Aryans who had invaded India nearly a thousand years before his time. In addition, Cyrus was helped by popular revolts against his rivals for imperial power, which he encouraged by giving special rights and privileges to everyone who would support him. Thus, for example, he allowed the Jews, whom Nebuchadnezzar had carried off to Babylon, to return to Judah. A few did; most, however, stayed behind amid the riches and wonders of the great city on the Euphrates.

The Persian Empire went from strength to strength. Cambyses, Cyrus's son and successor, conquered Egypt in 525 B.C.E. Darius the Great, the next Persian king, campaigned against the Scythians in southern Russia (512 B.C.E.) and extended his eastern boundary to the Indus River. He adapted Assyrian patterns of civil and military administration and improved upon the Assyrian example by organizing a navy.

The Persians had considerable trouble along their northern frontier. Cyrus died fighting against a nomad tribe that lived near the Aral Sea, and Darius failed to win any kind of decisive victory when he invaded Scythia. The best

The Grandeur of King Darius   This scene from the Persian palace at Persepolis shows King Darius seated on his throne while ambassadors or suppliants appear before him humbly seeking his judgment. Behind stands his son and successor, Xerxes, and other lesser courtiers. If you compare this scene with the earlier monument showing King Hammurabi and the God Shamash, (p. 54) you will see how Darius has taken over the role played by a god in Mesopotamia a thousand years before. The elevation of the King above all others was matched in religion by the elevation of a single god to power over all the earth. The two ideas fitted together, each reinforcing the other.

solution Darius could find was to "hire a thief to catch a thief." By paying tribute to nomad tribes close by, others who lived farther off in the steppe could be kept away from the Persian frontiers.

The Persian Empire was also troubled by internal revolts, just as the Assyrian Empire had been. Nevertheless, even the pride of Egypt and of Babylonia gradually wore out in the face of repeated disasters. It took a fresh attack from outside, this time from Macedonia, to overthrow Persian power in 330 B.C.E. Until that time the vast Persian Empire kept all the Middle Eastern peoples under a single political roof. The sheer size of the empire shows what a remarkable achievement this was.

The Rise of Ethical Monotheism

In the age of the Assyrian and Persian empires, there was a great deal of mingling and borrowing among the peoples of the Middle East. Local peculiarities tended to wear away. Priests preserved ancient rituals and doctrines that had been inherited from Sumer and the Old Kingdom of Egypt. But much of that inheritance had become hollow and was no longer really believed in by anyone, not even by the priests who handed the old texts on from generation to generation. In secular life there had been great changes. The art of government and military administration had attained greater efficiency. Vast palaces and newly founded capital cities, like Nineveh in Assyria and Persepolis in Persia, allowed artists to express their rulers' greatness and glory. But in Egypt and Mesopotamia, religious thought and invention lagged. The weight of ancient tradition was too great.

In Palestine among the Hebrews and in eastern Iran among the Persians, conditions were different. In both these regions, prophets arose who taught that a single God ruled the entire universe, who was both good and just himself and required that human beings try to be good and just in all their dealings with others. In particular, two new religions took shape: Zoroastrianism in the east and Judaism

Judgment after Death   A new religious idea in the first millennium B.C.E. was that God or the gods expected people to be just and would reward or punish them after death according to how they had behaved while on earth. Egyptians had always emphasized life after death, and the idea of divine judgment took special root in Egypt. The scene reproduced here was painted on the walls of a tomb. It shows a man and his wife appearing before the seated god, awaiting judgment. According to Egyptian conceptions, even divine justice could be influenced by suitable gifts, like those piled in front of the two figures; and the texts inscribed on the walls likewise implored favorable judgment.

in the west. The ideas of Zoroaster and of the Hebrew prophets have shaped human lives ever since by changing human hopes and expectations. By comparison, the impact of governments and armies remained superficial as long as rulers only demanded outward obedience from most of their subjects and did not expect or get their active loyalty. Religion did; hence, its power.

Zoroastrianism

Zoroaster was a Persian, who probably lived only a short time before Darius (ruled 521–486 B.C.E.) became king. Zoroaster grew to manhood in the part of the Persian world bordering India. His ideas were radical, for he taught that Persia's old gods were devils and should not be worshiped. He also declared that traditional rituals—especially blood sacrifices—were wicked.

In Zoroaster's lifetime the Persians, who had once lived as herders, were still adjusting to settled life as farmers. This was troublesome enough, but in addition they found themselves suddenly become rulers of a vast empire. As rulers, the Persians had to deal with all kinds of people who told various stories about how the world was made and governed. Each claimed to tell the truth, but nevertheless they all contradicted one another. What could anyone believe?

Zoroaster found an answer in inspiration. He believed that a supreme god, Ahura Mazda, communicated directly with him through supernatural spirits or angels. And what they told him he then repeated to all who would listen. His sayings took the form of poetry. Followers, believing the truth of Zoroaster's messages, memo-

Old and New in Politics and Religion   This is an impression of a cylinder seal that once belonged to the Persian King Darius. He came to power only after a short civil war, and afterward had to prove his right to the throne in every way he could. This seal was part of that effort. On the right it says "Darius the Great King" in three different languages and scripts so everyone would know. The main scene was age-old. Mesopotamian art had shown kings hunting lions from chariots for centuries. But at the upper center something new appears: a symbol of the god Ahura Mazda, who had revealed himself to the Prophet Zoroaster as champion of law and right throughout the universe. This seal thus deliberately aimed at making Darius's rule legitimate by combining very ancient symbols of royal prowess with radically new religious ideal.

rized them. Later they were written down, but the *Gathas,* as Zoroaster's verses are called, are difficult for modern scholars to understand; and the modern Parsis of India, who still followed Zoroaster's religion and who believe the *Gathas* are divinely inspired scripture, do not entirely understand their meaning either.

All the same, the main ideas of Zoroaster's preaching are clear enough. Zoroaster taught that the world was the scene of a great struggle between Ahura Mazda, supreme god and champion of good, on the one hand, and Ahriman, the prince of darkness and of everything evil, on the other. Every human being had to choose sides in the struggle. Simple rituals built around the recitation of Zoroaster's poems, and good deeds based upon knowledge of the truth, were what Zoroaster asked of his followers. The good must join the fight, helping Ahura Mazda and the angels of light. They might have to face hardship, disappointment, and injustice but could do so without flinching because they knew, from Zoroaster's revelation, that Ahura Mazda would win the struggle in the end. Eventually the wicked would be burned in a vast fire, the world would

cease to exist in its present mixed form in which good and evil were everywhere intertwined, and the good would live on forever in eternal bliss. Zoroaster believed that Ahura Mazda could not be seen by human eyes; but, though immaterial, his power extended over the entire world. Other gods were all false. Existing temples and religions were forms of devil worship. Only reverent acceptance of Zoroaster's revelation could save each and every person from religious error and fiery destruction at the end of time.

Zoroaster made converts in important places. King Darius himself used Zoroastrian language in some of his inscriptions; so did his son and successor, Xerxes (ruled 486–465 B.C.E.). Presumably a good many other important Persians also believed the prophet's teachings. But before long some of the things he had forbidden crept back into the religious practice of the Persian court.

No other peoples ever accepted the message. Zoroastrianism remained a Persian religion, but some of Zoroaster's ideals lived on among other peoples in a different form. Some Jews, for example, found Zoroaster's picture of a fiery end of the world very persuasive; later, Christians and Moslems also accepted the idea. The concept of angels in both Judaism and Christianity owes a good deal to Zoroaster's doctrine. Certainly, the Christian idea of Satan, God's rival and enemy in trying to win human souls, was strongly influenced by Zoroastrianism.

Three other points are worth noticing. First, Zoroaster taught that the supreme god who controlled everything that happened in the whole universe cared very much what individuals did and how each person behaved. Those who believed Zoroaster's revelation and obeyed Ahura Mazda's rules of life would be saved, and those who rejected the prophet's message and instead "espoused the lie" would be burned to a crisp. Reward and punishment for human behavior were postponed until the end of the world—an event not necessarily far away. In the meanwhile, if the wicked prospered, so much the worse for them. Righteous persons knew that Ahura Mazda would sooner or later punish evildoers in a very painful way.

Such a doctrine made it easier to face the hardships and injustices of everyday life. With such beliefs, civilization became much easier to take, especially for those at the bottom of the social ladder, who often saw scant justice in the world around them but could count upon God to set things right in the not-too-distant future.

Second, Zoroaster addressed his message to individual human beings everywhere. Anyone who listened to his words and understood them could join the ranks of Ahura Mazda's followers. Religion thus became separable from other circumstances of life. Anyone could earn salvation anywhere in the world, by knowing the truth. Not the tribe or the city or some other social group, but the individual human soul became the unit of religious action—known to God, and, perhaps, to his fellow believers, whoever they might be and wherever they might find themselves. Zoroastrianism, in other words, was a universal faith, intended to appeal to everyone, even though in fact only Persians accepted the prophet's words.

Last, Zoroastrianism was prophetic. The founder claimed to speak with supernatural authority, inspired directly by Ahura Mazda. Truth was in his words, and true religion depended on getting the meaning of the words right. Ancient tradition was false and utterly misleading. Truth came new-minted from Zoroaster's lips, its authenticity vouched for only by the prophet's own conviction and the persuasiveness of the inspired words themselves.

Judaism

By 500 B.C.E. Judaism, too, had become prophetic as well as ethical and monotheistic and addressed its message to individual souls. The history of Judaism, however, was far more complicated than that of Zoroastrianism. The Hebrew prophets never rejected the past. They claimed always to be calling their hearers back to the original revelation God had made to Moses and to Abraham. Moreover, the prophets were counterbalanced by a priestly tradition based in Solomon's Temple at Jerusalem. This religious inheritance somehow had to be reconciled as far as possible with prophetic revelations, which were sometimes critical of priestly practices in the Temple.

The reconciliation of priestly and prophetic traditions was achieved by gathering various writings about law, religion, and history into a carefully edited sacred scripture. The books into which these writings were divided became the only authentic revelations of God's will, according to Jews. Christians, however, believe that these books are only part of God's revelation—the Old Testament—which was later supplemented, and in some important ways altered, by the further revelation recorded in the books of the New Testament.

Even after the Jewish scriptures had been carefully gathered together, many seeming contradictions remained. This offered an unending series of problems for commentators to try to solve. Nothing could be more important, since the scriptures offered the only sure way to find out what God wanted human beings to do under varying circumstances. It was, therefore, every pious man's duty to study the pages of revealed truth with utmost care. Generation after generation of Jews have been shaped by this kind of study, down to the present.

History According to the Old Testament
When the books of the Old Testament had all

been assembled and recognized as sacred (a process not entirely completed before about 150 C.E.), a magnificent panorama of world history unrolled itself before believers. The Bible story of creation, the Flood, and the repeopling of the earth after the Flood closely resembled Mesopotamian sacred stories. But beginning with the account of Abraham, Isaac, and Jacob, and the sojourn in Egypt, the biblical story becomes unique.

According to the Bible, the God of Abraham did not fully reveal his special character until after the Exodus or journey of the Israelites out of Egypt. Whether or not we believe in the divine inspiration of Scripture, we can understand that when the people of Israel, under Moses' leadership, escaped from Egypt and gathered at the foot of Mount Sinai in the desert, they needed rules to govern their everyday actions. For generations they had lived in Egypt and had forgotten desert customs. Now that they were returning to the old style of nomadic life again, they needed a written law because their traditional unwritten customs had been lost. This was the situation Moses confronted when he ascended Mount Sinai and, according to the Bible story, received the Ten Commandments from the hand of God. On returning Moses made the people promise to obey the Ten Commandments and accept the law of God. This Covenant (agreement) between the people and God was, at least as understood in later times, the real beginning of Judaism.

Nevertheless, there is some doubt as to the original meaning of the Covenant. Yahweh, the God whom Moses met on Mount Sinai, was certainly God of the Israelites. But it is not clear that the Israelites regarded him as supreme over all other peoples and all parts of the world. Some biblical passages speak as though God merely protected the Israelites, while other gods protected other peoples and fought against Yahweh, as Yahweh also fought against them.

The Prophetic Tradition

In the days when the Hebrews settled the land of Canaan (ca. 1300–1100 B.C.E.), they began to worship fertility gods—the baals—of the Canaanites. Yahweh was a god of the desert and of battle; what did he know about making grain grow in the fields? Yet there were always some among the Hebrews who felt

that honoring any god but Yahweh was wicked and would stir him to wrath against his people, sooner or later. These men sometimes gathered as bands of "prophets" and denounced the wickedness of baal worship and the greed of the rich.

The balance between baal worship and the religion of Yahweh tipped decisively during the wars against the Philistines that led to the establishment of the Hebrew monarchy (ca. 1028–973 B.C.E.). Yahweh was a god of battles. With his aid the Hebrews had conquered Canaan. Saul and David therefore again called on Yahweh's aid in fighting their wars and made him their special God. But later, both David and Solomon were willing to allow other forms of worship in their kingdom. Their successors followed a similar policy.

Nevertheless, the old prophetic tradition never died away. Elijah, for example, led a great revival movement about 865 B.C.E. and temporarily drove out the worship of foreign gods. Israel and Judah thus became Yahweh's. To please him became the religious duty of all the people. When the fate of the kingdoms began clearly to depend less on what happened within the borders of the state itself than on wars and diplomatic dealings with Egypt, Assyria, and all the other powers of the Middle East, Yahweh's worshipers concluded that their God controlled all the world. His plans raised up the Assyrians and threw down the Egyptians. His purposes guided the feet of every living thing; nothing was too small and nothing too great for Yahweh to care for and control.

These ideas found expression in the poetry of a series of great prophets, beginning with the shepherd Amos, who preached about 750 B.C.E. His words were written down at the time of or very soon after his death. Other prophets followed Amos' example and either wrote themselves or caused their words to be written down. In this way their thoughts and feelings were preserved for future generations. Like Zoroaster, the Hebrew prophets claimed to speak with the words of the only true God. Many of their hearers believed them. In time their poems were accepted as part of the sacred scripture, revealing the will of God for the benefit of everyone who was prepared to listen and understand.

The prophets' central message was simple. Unless his people stopped doing evil, God would punish them with some dreadful disaster. False

GOD'S HAND IN HISTORY
II KINGS 18:13; 19:9–36,
WITH ELISIONS

Now in the fourteenth year of king Hezekiah* did Sennacherib, king of Assyria, come up against all the walled cities of Judah and took them. And he sent messengers unto Hezekiah, saying: "Let not thy God deceive thee, saying, Jerusalem shall not be delivered into the hand of the king of Assyria. Behold, thou hast heard what the kings of Assyria have done to all lands, by destroying them utterly, and shalt thou be delivered? Have the gods of the nations which my father destroyed delivered them?"

And Hezekiah went up into the house of the Lord, and spread the letter from the hands of the messengers before the Lord. And Hezekiah prayed before the Lord: "Lord, bow down thine ear and hear; open, Lord, thine eyes and see; and hear the words of Sennacherib. Of a truth, Lord, the kings of Assyria have destroyed the nations and their lands, and have cast their gods into the fire, for they were no gods, but the work of men's hands, wood and stone. Now therefore, O Lord our God, save thou us out of his hand, that all the kingdoms of the earth may know that thou art the Lord God, even thou only."

The prophet Isaiah,† the son of Amoz, sent to Hezekiah saying: "Thus saith the Lord God of Israel: 'That which thou hast prayed to me against Sennacherib, king of Assyria, I have heard. Therefore he shall not come into this city, nor shoot an arrow there, nor come before it with shield, nor cast a bank against it. For I will defend this City, to save it, for mine own sake, for my servant David's sake.'"

And it came to pass that night, that the angel of the Lord went out and smote in the camp of the Assyrians a hundred four score and five thousand; and when they arose early in the morning, behold, they were all dead corpses. So Sennacherib, king of Assyria, departed and returned to the city of Nineveh.

_____

*In 701 B.C.E.

†Not the same Isaiah who prophesied in Babylon about 150 years later.

---

gods were to be put aside. Moral conduct toward others and reverence for God—these were the things that mattered. God would punish those who disregarded the prophets' warnings, in a terrible Day of Yahweh, when all the injustices of the world would be set right.

Against such a background, the fall of Israel to the Assyrians in 722 B.C.E. looked like a partial fulfillment of the prophets' warnings. A reform party in the kingdom of Judah therefore set out to escape a similar fate by purifying religion in every way they could. Old manuscripts were consulted. With their help pious scholars put the record of God's dealing with humankind into an authoritative form. In this way many of the books of the Old Testament took something like their present form. The busy scholars discovered the entire Book of Deuteronomy and made so much of it that the movement is often referred to as the Deuteronomic reform.

Yet as we have seen, their efforts to reform religion did not ward off disaster. Nebuchadnezzar came and conquered; like the Assyrians, he carried off the educated population of Judah into exile (586 B.C.E.). What could the reformers do now? Their hope in God's help seemed to have failed. What more could Yahweh want?

Two great prophets, Ezekiel and Isaiah, addressed this question. Ezekiel declared that God wanted an even more scrupulous personal holiness than the reformers of the Deuteronomic period had imagined. Precise rules for everyday conduct were required, and the Scripture lay ready for everyone to inquire into and find out exactly what God wanted him or her to do. If Jews would study the Word of God carefully and do exactly what it told them to do, then and only then would the kingdom be restored, glorious and united, as in the days of David and Solomon.

The second prophet, Isaiah, who was alive at the time when Cyrus conquered Babylon (539 B.C.E.), had an even grander vision of the future. Soon, he declared, God would come in glory and set the children of Israel in their rightful place at the head of all the nations. The humbled exiles in Babylon would become rulers and governors, entrusted with the supreme task of guiding all people to knowledge of God's truths. Thus, for Isaiah, the Day of Yahweh, which the older prophets had treated as a dreadful time when evildoers (and who was not an evildoer in some degree?) would be punished, became a time of hope and expectation.

From this point of view, the more wickedness and oppression prevailed in the world, the sooner the longed-for Day of Judgment could be expected. With this belief Jews could endure any

Cherubim in Ivory   These figures, carved in the ancient Kingdom of Israel, represent guardians known in the Bible as cherubim. Israel's location between Egypt and Mesopotamia is apparent. Egyptian models lay behind the hairdo and lifelike modeling of the creature's body on the left. On the right, a cruder carving reflects Mesopotamian art traditions. The two conflicting models of high culture available to the Hebrews helped to stimulate their religious creativity.

sort of disappointment or injustice and still keep alive the confident hope that relief was coming since the end of the world's wicked ways was not far off. Meanwhile, the task was to study carefully the sacred books so as to know God's will, and to wait in patience until His purpose might be fulfilled.

The Importance of the Synagogue   While they were in Babylon (or soon afterwards), the exiled Jews created a new pattern of worship to go with their renewed hope. This was the *synagogue*—a weekly gathering where the faithful read from Scripture, explained to one another the meaning of what they had read, and thus confirmed each other's faith. It was difficult for everyone to be expert in the Scriptures. In time it became customary for each synagogue to have a teacher or rabbi who was specially trained, so as to be able to settle difficult points of scriptural interpretation. In essence, these same practices continue among Jews to this day.

A synagogue could be set up wherever Jews lived. (The legal minimum was later set at ten adult men.) In this way even scattered Jewish communities could and did keep their consciousness of being a special people, in Covenant with God. Instead of merging into the general population, Jews henceforward were able to maintain their identity through good and bad times, among hostile and among hospitable peoples, and in almost every country of the world. The religion was no longer tied to the soil of Palestine, nor to the Temple in Jerusalem. It had become independent of all outward circumstances. It was a matter of belief and of learning, of obeying God's will as made known in the pages of Scripture, and of waiting in hope for final deliverance from the evils of the world.

To be sure, when Cyrus permitted the Jewish exiles to return to Palestine, some of them did so and tried to rebuild the Temple and restore the old rituals. Some even sought to restore the kingdom of David by finding a descendant of the royal line and putting him on the throne, but the Persians would not permit that. The returned Jews had therefore to settle for a community built around the Temple. This did not affect the life of the synagogues, however. The Jews who remained in Babylon and those who took up residence in other cities of the Middle East continued to build their religious life around weekly meetings in the synagogues.

Today we take very much for granted the idea that religion is personal and more or less private. It does not strike us as odd that groups of believers may worship God in any part of the world, each in its own way. Because these ideas seem so commonplace now, it is difficult to realize how surprising such ideas would have been before 600 B.C.E. Earlier peoples had always thought that their gods were tied to a particular place and had to be approached through a particular temple ritual. Zoroaster went part of the way by making sacred words the heart of his religion; but he did not invent a meeting place like the synagogue, where the faithful could hand on the truths and make them come alive each week by reading and reflecting and hearing others speak about them, the way the Jews did.

When Judaism emerged from the trial of exile, therefore, it was a more flexible, stronger faith than ever before. The worship of Yahweh had begun with the Covenant in the desert. It had rallied the Hebrews in their wars. It had inspired the prophets to denounce unrighteousness. It had even sustained the Jews during their Babylonian exile. Such a religion could flourish and survive almost anywhere.

Judaism was particularly helpful to people trapped in the recesses of great cities, where no one much knew or cared what happened to neighbors. In such an environment, the fellowship of the synagogue and scriptural promises of a bright future for those who studied and obeyed God's will comforted individual believers in time of hardship as other religions of that age could not do.

Finally, Judaism became a religion of the Book. The beauty and grandeur of many passages of the Bible entered profoundly not only into Judaism but into Christianity as well. Stories, metaphors, heroes, villains, symbols, phrases, and—not least—the central idea that God rules the world, and cares about each and every human soul, all became fundamental elements in Western civilization. No one foresaw such a history. Millions upon millions of Jews, Christians, and Moslems believe that God's will lies behind it.

Conclusion

With the full development of the techniques of empire and the matching development of ethical monotheism, the history of the ancient Middle East reached a logical fulfillment. No fundamental improvements have ever been made in the techniques of governing large numbers of people, living in different environments, and speaking different languages since the days of the Persian Empire. Modern means of communication and transportation, of course, make such government easier, shortening reaction time to threats and other challenges; but the principles of imperial rule remain the same.

Monotheism, as developed by Zoroaster and by the Jews, went through greater changes subsequently. Yet here, too, the fundamental idea and the basic institutions by means of which believers might give full expression to their faith had been invented by 500 B.C.E.

These were the two principal Middle Eastern contributions to the rest of the world. Other civilizations put their emphasis on other things, and it is time for us to turn to them now and see how the ancient Greeks, Indians, and Chinese worked out their own distinctive styles of civilized life.

Bibliography

As before, many of the books listed in the bibliographies of Chapters 2 and 3 also deal with this chapter's subject matter.

Scholarly accounts of the ancient empires of Egypt, Assyria, Babylonia, and Persia may be found in appropriate volumes of the *Cambridge Ancient History* (rev. ed., 1962–68). Assyrians, in particular, have a bad reputation, due to their portrayal in the Bible; but two books on ancient warfare treat them with respect: Y. Yadin, *The Art of Warfare in Biblical Lands in the Light of Archaeological Study* (2 vols., 1963), and Arthur Ferrill, *The Origins of War: From Stone Age to Alexander the Great* (1985). J. Oates, *Babylon* (1974), is a short introduction to that empire; and Richard N. Frye, *The Heritage of Persia* (2nd ed., 1976), has chapters on the Achamaenids and their predecessors.

For the rise of Jewish monotheism, the pages of the Bible are of course the principal and most accessible source. Students who are not familiar with the Old Testament, particularly Exodus, Samuel, and Kings, ought to have a look for themselves at what the Scriptures say. Since interpretation can be difficult, modern scholarly accounts, such as the early volumes of Salo W. Baron, *A Social and Religious History of the Jews* (2nd ed., 15 vols., 1952–73), will supplement and clarify the biblical texts. Other similar works include William F. Albright, *From Stone Age to Christianity: Monotheism and the Historical Process* (1957); Y. Kaufmann, *The Religion of Israel from Its Beginnings to the Babylonian Exile* (1960); Y. Kaufmann, *The Babylonian Captivity and Deutero-Isaiah* (1970); and Louis Finkelstein, ed., *The Jews: Their History, Culture and Religion* (4th ed., 3 vols., 1970–71). Briefer and more recent books on the subject include Michael Grant, *The History of Ancient Israel* (1984); Robert B. Coote and Keith Whitelam, *The Emergence of Early Israel in Historical Perspective* (1987); and Hershel Shanks, ed., *Ancient Israel: A Short History from Abraham to the Roman Destruction of the Temple* (1988).

On Zoroastrianism, Mary Boyce, *A History of Zoroastrianism* (2 vols., 1975–82), may be supplemented by translations of the *Gathas* available in S. Insler, *The Gathas of Zarathustra* (1975). The context for the rise of Zoroastrianism has been authoritatively set forth by two Russian scholars, Muhammad A. Dandamaev and Vladimir G. Lukonin, *The Culture and Social Institutions of Ancient Iran* (1989).

The Greek Style of Civilization
to 500 B.C.E.

5

The Charioteer of Delphi, ca. 470 B.C.E.   This life-sized statue commemorates victory in a chariot race. When it was made, the Greeks had long ceased to use chariots in war, but a few rich men, like yachtsmen today, raced them at sacred festivals where this and other forms of athletic competition honored the gods. Our modern Olympic Games are a revival (and adaptation) of the most famous of the ancient Greek athletic competitions that took place every four years at Olympia and lasted for more than a millennium from their beginning in 776 B.C.E.

In the mountainous land of Greece, the climate was much like that of the fertile parts of the Middle East. In summer the winds blew steadily from the northeast and the sun shone every day. In winter Greece came under the influence of westerly winds that brought in storms of rain or snow from the Atlantic. The Greek mountains were heavily wooded before slash-and-burn farmers cut the trees down; some of the flatter land had trees, too, and where less rain fell, there were some small grassy plains.

Neolithic farmers reached this land by about 4500 B.C.E., but for a long time the population remained too thin and scattered to make civilization possible. Shortly before 2000 B.C.E., Greek-speaking tribes began to filter into Greece from the northern Balkan Peninsula. Being warriors and herders, they soon made the earlier inhabitants submit to their rule. In time the Greek speech of the invaders became universal among the population as a whole, but some traces of pre-Greek life remained as late as 500 B.C.E.

With the rise of Minoan civilization (ca. 2100 B.C.E.) in Crete, familiarity with metal and other aspects of civilized accomplishments began to spread among the inhabitants of the Greek mainland. Mycenae and a few other strongholds became seats of civilization by about 1600 B.C.E. But local resources from surrounding farmland were never great enough to support the artisans, soldiers, servants, and courtiers that made Mycenae splendid. Instead, the king and his warriors depended on booty gathered through pirate raids to keep their courts and capital cities going.

Civilization based on piracy was bound to be insecure. After a few unsuccessful expeditions, the wealth and power of the king at Mycenae might simply evaporate. His followers would cease obeying if he led them to disaster. Something of the sort must have happened, but we do not know the details. We do know that, about 1100 B.C.E., Mycenae was burned and pillaged by a fresh wave of Greek-speaking invaders who came from the north. Thereafter, the great walls guarding the high king's palace remained a hollow shell. Yet the stones of which they were made were so large that later generations of Greeks told one another that they had been put in place by giants.

The Dark Age of Greece: 1100–600 B.C.E.

The tribes who destroyed the Mycenaean palace strongholds spoke a dialect of Greek called Dorian. They were herders and farmers, armed with iron weapons, and were more numerous and more primitive than the Greeks who had preceded them into Greece. With their arrival, courts and cities disappeared. By degrees, however, the newcomers settled down. Population began to increase; and because of a growing shortage of land, instead of cultivating a field for only a few years and then moving on, the Dorians began to plow the same fields year after year. All this paralleled what was happening at the same time in Palestine and other parts of the Middle East where Iron Age invaders had come in.

Aristocratic Government

The social consequences of settling down to fixed agriculture were also the same as in the Middle East. Chieftains and a few others became richer and richer, but many common folk became too poor to equip themselves as fighters, and, after losing their land, some even had to sell themselves as slaves.

In the days of the Iron Age migrations, Greek society was tribal. When it seemed a good time to move on and look for new and better land, all able-bodied men gathered together to hear what their leaders—clan chieftains by heredity—recommended. If a move required military action, as usually it did, every arm was needed and everyone had to know in a general way what the plan of campaign was going to be. Such plans were worked out in council meetings. The commander-in-chief or king consulted the clan chieftains first, and then the leaders informed all the male fighting force of the tribe what they proposed to do.

As the tribes settled down, there came to be fewer and fewer occasions on which the military strength of the entire community had to be mobilized. Families scattered over the land, and each chieftain's household conducted its affairs more or less as it pleased. Under such circumstances, the authority and power of the king weakened. He became just one among equals, not much stronger or better off than other chieftains.

Councils of the noble clan chieftains continued to meet from time to time, settling quarrels between families, arranging for worship of the gods, or planning defense against a hostile neighbor. But the common people were called in only in time of unusual emergency. Most matters could be handled by the nobles assembled together. Quite often, instead of trusting the king with too much authority, the council of nobles decided to assign special duties to one among themselves. The next step in dismantling the king's power was to appoint members of the noble council to handle public business for a year or for some other specified period of time. Kingship itself was sometimes made appointive. Authority thus fell into the hands of temporary appointees or magistrates, chosen annually by the council of nobles from among its members.

This privileged political position was backed up by the nobles' new economic power. As large landowners they found it easy to lend grain to hungry farmers who needed seed for the next harvest. Debtors either had to repay such loans with interest or else give up their land and become servants or slaves of the person from whom they had borrowed.

Concentration of power in the hands of a noble class was also furthered by a change in military tactics. For the cavalry revolution that had come to the Middle East between 975 and 600 B.C.E. affected Greece, too. When Greeks learned to fight from horseback, superior mobility gave the cavalry a decisive advantage over mere foot soldiers. In Greece, however, pasture was sparse at best, and only the rich could afford to feed horses with grain. But, after the cavalry revolution, it was precisely those few who really

counted in battle. The rest often became too poor to equip themselves with sword, spear, helmet, and shield.

The *Iliad* and the *Odyssey*

The ideas and values held dear by Greeks of the Dark Age found expression in poetry, some of which survived into later times. The greatest of the early poets, Homer, probably lived about 750 B.C.E., when life in mainland Greece was dominated by petty local clan chieftains. Homer took his themes from more ancient times, when the high king of Mycenae had ruled far and wide. The poet knew of these distant ages through an unbroken oral tradition. In Mycenaean times and later, warriors liked to listen to professional bards—poets and singers who recited tales of fighting and adventure. The Dorian invasions did not destroy the art, although perhaps it was only among those Greeks who claimed descent from the heroes of Mycenae that the bardic tradition survived.

In time new material crept into the songs, where it mingled with information about old genealogies, geography, battles, and feats of daring. Like other storytellers, the ancient Greek bards did not memorize their poems exactly. They had, however, a repertory of especially apt, fixed phrases that could be used to fill out a line or give the singer time to remember the next episode in his story.

From such materials the poet Homer fashioned the *Iliad*, one of the world's greatest literary masterpieces. Then a little later, the *Odyssey* was composed, either by the same man, as ancient tradition asserted, or by a different poet, as some modern scholars believe. The *Iliad* tells of the siege of Troy; the *Odyssey* is a tale of the strange adventures that one of the heroes of the siege of Troy experienced on his trip home to Ithaca in western Greece.

Actually, the *Iliad* tells only a tiny part of the whole story of the siege of Troy. Other poets, seeking to fill out the work of Homer, later wrote poems to explain how Agamemnon gathered his hosts to attack the Trojans because Paris, a prince of Troy, had run off with Helen, the wife

Death of a Hero   This jar was made in Athens about 750 B.C.E. to commemorate a hero like those Homer praised in his poems. The corpse of the hero is shown in the middle at the top, flanked by mourners; below, chariots and spearmen are shown ready for battle. The draftsmanship is awkward, as befitted the Dark Age of Greece when this pot was made, but the heroic values that would characterize Greek civilization were already taken for granted by the people who made and decorated this jar.

of Agamemnon's brother. Legend held that only after ten long years of siege did Troy fall, and then by deception.

According to the old tale, Odysseus, the hero of the *Odyssey*, advised the Greeks to pretend to sail away, leaving an enormous statue of a wooden horse behind with a few Greek soldiers hidden inside. As Odysseus had hoped, the Trojans believed the horse was an offering to the gods. They hauled the horse into their city, on the theory that the gods' goodwill for the offering would come to them if the horse entered the city. Then, after celebrating the end of the siege,

the Trojans went to sleep, only to be wakened by the noise of the returning Greeks storming in through the gate, which their companions— emerging from their hiding place inside the hollow wooden horse—had opened for them in the night.

None of this is in the *Iliad*. It tells only of the wrath of Achilles, the greatest of Greek warriors. Achilles quarreled with Agamemnon over the distribution of booty taken from the Trojans. He swore he would fight no more for such an unjust king. The gods, sympathizing with Achilles, decided to let the Trojans win, at least for a while. Soon, therefore, the Greeks found themselves driven back to their ships, which were beached on the shore some miles from the walls of Troy.

Disaster loomed. In the emergency Achilles agreed to let his followers join the battle. They were led by his favorite and friend, Patroclus, who disguised himself by putting on Achilles' armor. But Hector, the greatest champion among the Trojans, killed Patroclus. This roused Achilles to furious anger. After getting a new set of armor by supernatural means, he hunted Hector down and killed him. Then Achilles fastened the slain Trojan's body to his chariot and dragged the fallen hero back to the Greek camp to show to gods and men how he had avenged Patroclus' death.

So ends the *Iliad*, a savage tale of pride and bloodthirsty violence. Yet this unpromising material comes to life in Homer's hands. In particular, the scene between Hector and his wife Andromache, just before he goes out to be killed by Achilles, is as poignant as any passage in literature. Hector foresaw death and disaster yet went to meet his fate, brave and undaunted, because he was a hero, and heroes had to abide by the warrior code of conduct, come what might. Death was the end of it all; sooner or later it came to everyone. What mattered was to live heroically. Never quail; defend personal honor by always accepting battle, whatever the consequence; stand ready to meet death bravely when, decreed by fate, it finally arrived—these were the imperatives of the hero's career.

Measured against such an ideal, Homer's gods lacked heroic stature. They were immortal, by definition, and never had to pay the price of death for their escapades. Indeed, Homer's picture of the gods lacks all dignity. They quarreled over trifles and played favorites among the fighters in shameless fashion. Behind them all loomed Fate, something as much greater than the gods as the gods were greater than men and women. For no matter what a person or god might will and hope and plan, Fate caused things to happen, often in ways neither the immortal gods nor any mere human being had foreseen or wished.

The *Odyssey* is a tale of magic and adventure. The hero, Odysseus, met with all sorts of strange experiences on his way back from Troy. He was blown off course, shipwrecked, and encountered giants and magicians. When he returned home, he found that various noble suitors had been trying to persuade his faithful wife, Penelope, to marry one of them; so he appeared unannounced and slaughtered them all with his mighty bow in his own dining hall.

The travel tales woven into the *Odyssey* came from a much later time than the materials of the *Iliad*. Some scholars therefore think that the poem was composed later than the *Iliad* and by a different author. But ancient tradition always attributed both of the poems to Homer, and many modern students of the "Homeric question" think that the same man might have been able to produce a poem as different as the *Odyssey* is from the *Iliad* by turning to a new type of material.

The Influence of Homer   We can be sure that both the *Iliad* and the *Odyssey* were recognized as masterpieces from the time they were first created. Homer probably composed orally, like his predecessors. Tradition held that he was blind. But not long after Homer's time the Greeks learned from the Phoenicians how to write, and they put his poems into written form. Corrections and variations, of course, crept in. An official text was produced in Athens about 200 years after the time Homer lived, and it was carefully handed down thereafter.

The importance of Homer's poems for later Greek life is difficult to exaggerate. They have been called the Greek Bible, and with good reason. Boys memorized the poems in school. Everyone knew about Homer's heroes. Even today, references to Homer remain familiar in all Western lands.

In addition, Homer's ideas molded later Greek thought. Priests could not reinterpret theological doctrine when Homer's words fixed his particular view of divine behavior in every Greek mind. Very soon, thoughtful individuals therefore rejected traditional religion completely. This opened the door for Greek philosophy.

Abstract ideas appealed to only a few, but Homer's ideal of the hero reached deep into classical Greek society and affected nearly everybody. Violence and self-assertion, courage and craftiness, shrewd counsel and naive joy in material gain—all these were aspects of heroic life as Homer defined it. These attitudes, admired across the centuries, gave Greek civilization much of its special tone. Above all, the efforts to excel every rival took hold of Greek minds. Meekness, patience, and submission played no part in their catalog of virtues, and for this Homer was largely responsible.

Development of the Greek Polis

Homer had no counterpart in the Middle East; neither did the Greek city-state, or, to use the Greeks' word for it, the *polis*. The contrast with Middle Eastern developments was profound. Nothing like the bureaucratic, tax-collecting, royal government of Kings David and Solomon—much less the vast, imperial bureaucratic structure of the Assyrian and Persian empires—arose in Greece. Instead, Greek soil came to be divided among small city-states, in which a rather large proportion of the adult male population took a very active part in politics and in war.

In its fully developed form, each polis had a city and surrounding territory, within which its laws prevailed. Not everyone took part in governing the polis: Women, children, slaves, and foreigners were always excluded. In many times and places poor men also were excluded. Each polis had a center for public business. This was usually a particularly safe place, often on top of a hill, where a supply of water could allow defenders to survive days or weeks of siege. In time, such strong points became citadels with real cities spread beneath them. But in the beginning the polis was an administrative unit, not a center for artisans and traders.

The Ionian Example

Full-fledged *poleis* (plural for *polis*) arose first along the Aegean coast of Asia Minor among the so-called Ionians, who had fled from mainland Greece to escape invading Dorians. The tribal councils, dominated by nobles, that ruled in mainland Greece during the Dark Age joined together to form poleis, too, but only after a working model of the new political structure had been established across the Aegean.

Tribal and other traditional ties were disrupted in crossing the sea to Ionia. The refugees probably came from different parts of Greece and needed all the help they could get to survive on unfriendly shores. Hence, those who started the new settlements could not afford to be choosy about whom they made welcome.

Under these emergency conditions, the classical polis was born. The settlers agreed upon rules of law and procedures for choosing leaders, whom they promised to obey as long as the leaders acted according to the rules. The customary discipline of a war band was the model for this sort of arrangement. But in this case not just the fighting men but whole families joined up, and the rules were laid down not for a campaign but forever. Instead of merely accepting temporary rules, the settlers agreed to submit to permanent laws. As a result, the community that came into being was not merely a war band but a political association—a polis. (The English word "political" comes, of course, from *polis*.)

The Role of Law   Two or three centuries earlier, Moses and the Israelites had founded another political association. In their case, the basis of agreement was different. Instead of agreeing among themselves as the Greeks of Ionia did, the Israelites had entered into a Covenant with God and promised to obey the laws of God Moses brought down from Mount Sinai.

The early Greeks, too, did not think of their laws as something they made by themselves. Good laws, they believed, were eternal and could not be changed. But the Greeks could not find such laws by asking the gods to set them forth. Their gods were, after all, Homer's gods; and Homer's gods were spiteful, willful beings, quite ready to play dirty tricks on one another and on humans. Instead of falling back on the gods, therefore, the Greeks believed that wise and good men could discover the law by using their own powers. When truly discovered, law fitted the nature of things. It guided everyday thoughts and behavior and thus defined real or true human nature. Good law made everything prosper and go well. Good law prevented unjust quarrels. It created harmony and established cooperation, not only on the human plane but also upward to include the gods and downward to include natural objects and forces as well.

On the Greek mainland, polis law and government did not replace tribal organization until a later date. The traditional authority of local chieftains made written law unnecessary for a long time. But when the poor complained loudly enough against what they felt were injustices done by wealthy landowners, magistrates found it wise to write down the customs they proposed to enforce. In this way, by about 600 B.C.E., tribal communities on the Greek mainland began to catch up with the Ionian model. They turned into city-states, too, with magistrates, laws, and citizens who obeyed the laws—at least in principle—regardless of tribal and kinship connections or the personal whims of men in authority.

Not long thereafter, by about 560 B.C.E., the Ionian cities fell under the rule of Croesus, King of Lydia; and when Croesus was defeated by Cyrus the Persian, they became part of the vast Persian Empire. As such, the Greek cities of Asia Minor sent tribute to the Persian kings. Ionian workers helped make the sculptures for the palace of the Persian King Darius I at Persepolis, and a Greek ship captain explored the Indus River at the command of the same Darius. The Ionian Greeks, in other words, seemed about to

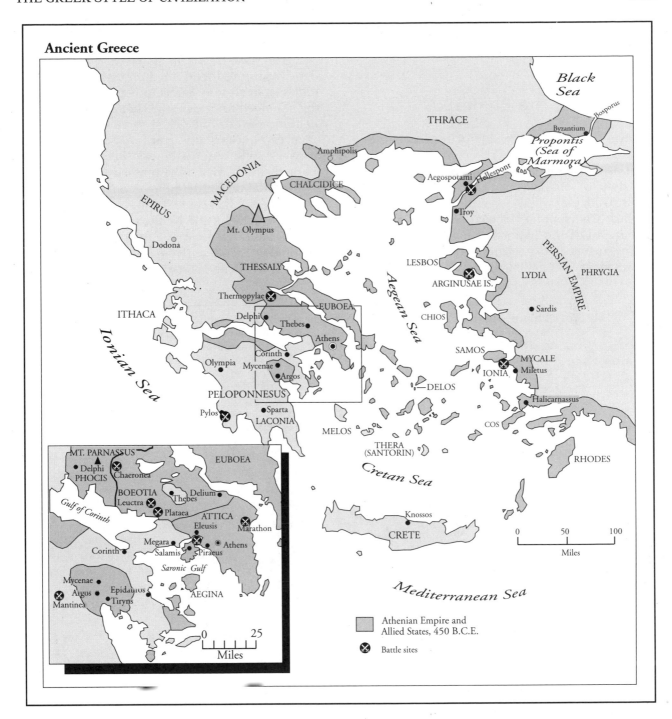

Ancient Greece

Black Sea

THRACE

Byzantium

Propontis
(Sea of
Marmora)

Bosporus

Amphipolis

CHALCIDICE

Aegospotami

Hellespont

Troy

MACEDONIA

Mt. Olympus

EPIRUS

Dodona

LESBOS

PERSIAN EMPIRE

THESSALY

ARGINUSAE IS.

LYDIA

PHRYGIA

Thermopylae

ITHACA

EUBOEA

Delphi

Thebes

Athens

CHIOS

Sardis

Aegean Sea

Ionian Sea

Olympia

Corinth

Mycenae

Argos

SAMOS

MYCALE

IONIA

Miletus

DELOS

PELOPONNESUS

Pylos

Sparta

LACONIA

MELOS

Halicarnassus

COS

THERA
(SANTORIN)

RHODES

Cretan Sea

Knossos

CRETE

Mediterranean Sea

MT. PARNASSUS

Delphi

PHOCIS

Chaeronea

EUBOEA

BOEOTIA

Leuctra

Thebes

Delium

Gulf of Corinth

Plataea

ATTICA

Eleusis

Marathon

Megara

Athens

Corinth

Salamis

Piraeus

Saronic Gulf

Mycenae

Argos

Epidaurus

Tiryns

Mantinea

AEGINA

0   25
Miles

0   50   100
Miles

Athenian Empire and
Allied States, 450 B.C.E.

Battle sites

become one more bit in the mosaic of peoples that constituted the Persian Empire.

The Role of the Phalanx

Yet events on the other side of the Aegean Sea checked and eventually reversed this drift toward assimilating Greeks into the Middle Eastern style of civilization. A critical turn came about 670 B.C.E. when two cities on the island of Euboea, Chalcis and Eretria, stated a long war for control of the plain that lay between them. During this war a new military formation was perfected. It was called the phalanx, and it had profound military as well as political consequences for the Greek world.

The idea of the phalanx was very simple. Heavily armored men lined up eight ranks deep, standing so close to one another that each man's shield helped to protect the right side of the man standing next to him. Then at the command signal everyone started to run forward, keeping the array as solid as possible so that the ranks remained closed. When the massed weight of such a formation encountered an enemy who was not organized in the same fashion, resistance was simply brushed aside by the sharp points of the spears each soldier carried and the momentum of the phalanx's charge. Horses could not penetrate an array of spear points backed by seven follow-

Phalanx Fighting   In ancient Greece, success in battle depended on how perfectly armored infantrymen kept ranks as they charged against the foe. Armies prepared for battle by lining up eight deep, each soldier close enough to his neighbor to form an unbroken shield wall. By learning to charge at a run, keeping time by shouting to the shrill sound of pipes, a whole army could dash up against an enemy with enormous force. If the foe did not crumble under the initial impact, each man had to keep his place in line and use his spear resolutely. Eventually, one side or the other was sure to break and run, and the battle would be won. Much practice was needed to be able to maintain the shield wall unbroken while running across open ground. In this vase painting you see the front ranks closing in for combat, while the second rank enters to the sound of pipes.

ing ranks of armored men. Since only a small area around the eyes was not protected by armor, arrows were almost harmless. If a fighter did fall, the man in the rank behind him was trained to move up at once to fill the vacant place.

When the Greeks discovered the superiority of a well-trained phalanx, the nature of their warfare changed. Nobles on horseback no longer dominated the battlefield. Cavalry could still chase a dispersed foe and turn a defeat into a catastrophe. And cavalry could also make trouble before and during a battle, if friendly horsemen were not on hand to guard the flanks and rear of the phalanx. But cavalry could no longer win battles nor hold a battlefield. That was the prerogative of the phalanx of heavily armored infantry.

When a well-drilled phalanx became decisive in war, every able-bodied citizen who could afford to buy body armor, shield, and spear—and this was not too difficult in the Iron Age—had to spend long hours in his youth practicing spear fighting and running alongside his fellows. This created a quite unreasoning but nevertheless profound sense of belonging together. To learn to keep the ranks closed and straight, young men had to go to a practice field, beginning at the age of eighteen. There the youths of the polis formed into a long line and began shouting in rhythm—the Greeks called this "raising the paean"—until everyone was keeping time together. Then, dressed in full armor, they would run, sometimes at top speed, sometimes more slowly keeping carefully in line.

Anyone who has ever tried to keep step while walking down an aisle knows how difficult it is to get a large number of persons to move in unison. Anyone who has danced with others to the sound of music will realize how strongly human beings respond to the experience of moving together in a common rhythm. Probably our first ancestors used to dance together after a successful hunt and shouted their joy after a good meal in good company. And because it rouses echoes of these very ancient capacities for fellow-feeling that lurk in all of us, massed rhythmic motion has an extremely powerful effect upon the participants' innermost emotions. Even in a modern army, close-order drill and the blare of marching bands create esprit de corps. When a man's life and the welfare

of his city depended on how well each and every individual kept his place in the phalanx, the emotional effects of rhythmic motion were, presumably, much stronger than they can be today when marching in step is irrelevant to modern combat.

Moreover, the most primitive levels of human experience were directly evoked by the fierce, sharp, sudden muscular effort of battle, when the accurate timing of a thrust with spear and sword made the difference between life and death, victory and defeat. This form of combat was the skill of the ancient hunters brought up to date. Men who shared the dangers of such battles bonded closely together. Everyone's safety, as well as the common victory, depended on each man's keeping his place and facing the foe valiantly until the enemy line broke and ran.

The emotional solidarity aroused by the phalanx soon overthrew the nobles' political power in all the leading cities of Greece. Soldiers could not be excluded from taking part in decisions affecting their lives. The rich could no longer be allowed, for example, to take a poor man's land if it meant that the impoverished citizen could no longer equip himself for the phalanx. A polis that let such things happen would soon have too small a phalanx to fight successfully against its neighbors, and that, plainly, was the way to disaster. The needs of defense thus created the strongest possible reason for checking the growth of inequality among the citizens. Such needs soon provoked drastic responses and gave Greek life a characteristic stamp of its own, very different from anything known in the Middle East.

Sparta

The most extreme example of making society over to fit the phalanx occurred in Sparta, a leading city of the Peloponnese (the peninsula forming the southern part of Greece). About 610 B.C.E., the Spartans found themselves engaged in a desperate war with their Messenian neighbors. In order to defeat the Messenians, the Spartans introduced new laws that made every Spartan an "Equal." These laws required all boys from the age of seven to leave home and submit to a rigorous training. At twenty years of age, males en-rolled in special barracks, where they lived and ate and trained for battle when they were not actually on campaign. At age thirty they could go home and live with their wives; but until the age of sixty, each man was subject to military service with the Spartan phalanx whenever called upon. These laws were later declared to be very ancient, the work of a mythical figure, Ly-curgus.

The system worked. Sparta not only de-feated the Messenians but quickly became the most powerful city-state in Greece. Its phalanx was never equaled by less professionally expert troops. But the cost was high, for Spartan citi-zens had no time for anything but war and preparation for war. To feed themselves, they compelled the defeated Messenians—now called helots—to cultivate the fields for them and hand over about half the harvest to their Spartan masters.

No further change in the Spartan constitu-tion took place for many centuries. The citizens, trained for success in battle, held down the helots at home and established governments sympathetic to themselves in neighboring city-states. Sparta also set up a league among nearly all of the cities of the Peloponnese which re-quired each member to send troops to fight alongside the Spartan phalanx when called upon to do so. Otherwise, each city was left to its own devices.

Even so, the Spartans never got over the fear of helot revolt. In fact, the "Equals" became a professional army of occupation stationed in their own land. The stern discipline of the Spar-tan system of training suppressed all discon-tent. Spartans could never afford to quarrel too sharply among themselves lest they weaken their position against the helots.

Athens

In Athens, the other Greek state about which we have substantial information, the reaction to the phalanx was not as drastic, but it still made a great difference. As in other cities, Athens' prob-lem was that poorer citizens, if they fell into debt, might lose their land or becomes slaves and so could no longer equip themselves for ser-vice in the phalanx. This was too dangerous to be tolerated.

In 594 B.C.E., therefore, Solon was ap-pointed *archon* (magistrate) with special powers to revise the laws. He canceled debts and made debt-slavery illegal. He classified the citizens ac-cording to the amount of grain and oil they har-vested each year, and he defined the duties and rights of each class in war and in peace. All but the poorest class of citizens were allowed to vote for the magistrates, who, however, had to come from the wealthier classes. In addition, large ju-ries of ordinary citizens were allowed to review and, if they wished, could reverse the judicial de-cisions made by magistrates.

Power within the Athenian polis thus shifted away from the nobles and men of wealth. Ordinary farmers, the soldiers of the phalanx, could now control the Athenian polis. These were the men upon whom the welfare and pros-perity of the city had come to depend, for with-out a strong phalanx there could be no security or prosperity for anyone.

But Solon's reforms did not stop the Athe-nians from quarreling violently among them-selves. The chief political figure in the next gen-eration was a great noble named Pisistratus. He first distinguished himself in a war with Megara that broke out over possession of the island of Salamis. The war ended (565 B.C.E) in an Athe-nian victory. Soon, thereafter Pisistratus took personal control of Athens. He kept Solon's laws in force—or pretended to. He was content to rule from behind the scenes by controlling elec-tions to office.

Pisistratus favored the poorer citizens, who supported him against rival noble families. He distributed land to some of his followers and en-couraged them to plant olive trees and grape-vines by giving them loans, at low interest rates, to tide them over the long period between the planting and the first harvest. Finally, he took an active part in founding colonies to relieve over-population in Athens and to develop trade in the Black Sea region.

The Spirit of the Polis

Greek city-states were able to tap human ener-gies to a degree seldom equaled before or since.

Herodotus on Freedom and Law among the Greeks

Herodotus tells us that as the Persian king, Xerxes, was about to invade Greece in 480 B.C.E., he sent for Demaratus, an exiled Spartan king who was living at the Persian court, and asked whether the Greeks would really dare to fight against his vast army. According to Herodotus, the following dialogue ensued:

"Come what may," Demaratus declared, "they will never accept thy terms, which would reduce Greece to slavery; and further, they are sure to battle with thee. . . . As for their numbers, do not ask how many they are, that their resistance should be a possible thing; for if a thousand of them should take the field, they will meet thee in battle, and so will any number, be it less than this, or more."

When Xerxes heard this answer of Demaratus, he laughed and answered "What wild words, Demaratus. A thousand men join battle with an army like this! . . . If, indeed, like our troops, they had a single master, their fear of them might make them courageous beyond their natural bent, or they might be urged on by lashes against as enemy which far outnumbered them. But left to their own free choice, assuredly they will act differently. . . ."

Demaratus answered him: "I knew, oh king, at the outset that if I told you the truth, my speech would displease thy ears. . . . The Spartans, when they fight singly, are as good as any men in the world, and when they fight in a body, are the bravest for all. For though they be freemen, they are not in all respects free; Law is the master whom they own; and this master they fear more than thy subjects fear thee. Whatever he commands, they do and his commandment is always the same: it forbids them to flee battle, whatever the number of their foes, and requires them to stand firm, and either to conquer or die."

This dialogue is surely fictitious, but it gave Herodotus a chance to explain to himself and his hearers why the outnumbered quarrelsome Greeks were able to resist the Persian imperial army successfully, obeying polis laws and fighting of their own free will.

Reproduced from *The History of Herodotus*, George Rawlinson trans., new ed., London: J. Murray, 1862.

An ordinary male citizen could and did feel that the polis was an extension of himself. He was part of it and it of him. Men have seldom felt such an identity between the political community and their individual person. Public affairs took precedence over private concerns because the state demanded so much of each citizen's time, wealth, and service. Men felt that, with good laws and by their own efforts, they could accomplish whatever they wished and still remain free.

Manners soon changed to fit this spirit. To be too rich was no longer good form. Personal display of any sort was soon judged to be worthy only of a barbarian. The rich could use their wealth to make public religious celebrations more splendid or to help with some other enterprise undertaken by the polis. But a rich person who used wealth for private purposes would be disgraced. For rich and poor alike, the sphere of private life was narrowed by the demands for personal participation in polis affairs. The phalanx, the assembly of citizens, religious celebrations, and everyday gossip about what was going on—all demanded the attention of every male citizen. Women, on the other hand, were strictly excluded from public affairs. So were foreign-born slaves and strangers of every kind who lacked citizenship rights.

Tyrants, Colonies, and Trade

However successful the phalanx training may have been in making farmers into enthusiastic citizens, Greeks still faced serious problems. Chief among these was a continued, rapid growth of population. A farmer with several children had no choice but to divide his land among his heirs; but a piece of land just large enough to support a family, and allow the head of the household to equip himself for the phalanx, obviously could not support three or four new families.

In Athens, as we saw, Pisistratus rose to power by rallying the support of the poorer citizens. Other cities, too, reacted by raising a single

man to power. The Greeks called such upstarts tyrants; later the term came to mean a wicked or oppressive ruler. The tyrants could not do much to solve the economic problem, even when they seized lands belonging to their political rivals and redistributed them among their own followers, as happened in several cities. Continued population growth soon caught up with all such efforts at redistribution.

Colonization   A second obvious response to the problem of too many mouths and not enough land was emigration. The cities of Ionia took the lead here, from about 750 B.C.E., by sending groups of colonists off to the Black Sea coast and to Sicily and southern Italy. Later on cities from the mainland did the same, until these coastal regions came to be lined with Greek colonies. Each colony became a new polis and kept only sentimental ties with the mother city. Each had its own laws and government. Such communities were usually established near good farmland, for it was land that the Greek colonists wanted.

The Growth of Trade   After a few years, if the settlement flourished, trade possibilities opened up. A prosperous colony could produce a

The Acropolis of Athens   In early Greece, farmers needed a safe place of refuge from piratical raids by sea and sudden attacks overland. As the Greeks settled down to farming, they chose such spots and improved them with artificial fortifications. Soon it became habitual to gather there for other purposes— religious, political, economic. In that way strongholds became the core around which the classical cities formed. Here you see the craggy hill the Athenians made into their place of refuge or Acropolis (literally "High City"). The main building was a temple to Athena, the city's patron goddess.

surplus of grain and other products to exchange for wine and oil and manufactured goods. Greek colonies were also able to act as middlemen between Greece and various barbarian peoples who lived inland.

A sizable class of artisans began to develop in cities that were situated favorably for this kind of trade. Greek merchants also began to sail their ships to and fro across the Aegean Sea, the Black Sea, and throughout the Mediterranean.

Farmers had a stake in the development of trade, for the most important commodities the Greek cities could offer for export were wines and oil. As long before, in Minoan times, these precious products of Greek soil commanded a brisk market along the shores of the Mediterranean and Black seas. Local chieftains and landowners were eager to supply grain, fish, metal, timber, or other raw materials in exchange for wine and oil. Imported grain and fish fed the growing populations of Greece, and imported timber and metals supplied Greek shipwrights and artisan shops with materials needed to keep the trade going.

Such a pattern of exchange differed fundamentally from the economic patterns that prevailed in the Middle East. There peasant farmers entered only slightly and occasionally into the market. Middle Eastern cities got their food by taking rents and taxes from the countryside, but sent almost no goods back in exchange.

Sparta's helots found themselves in the same economic position that Middle Eastern peasants endured, but no such oppressed rural class existed in the commercially active parts of ancient Greece. Quite the contrary. The small landowning farmer became and long remained the ideal kind of polis citizen, even in times and places where such individuals were a minority. To own no land and have to depend on trade or, worse still, on artisan labor was always looked down upon as beneath the true dignity of a citizen. Slaves did much of the hardest work; foreigners without rights of citizenship did most of the artisan tasks; citizens took such jobs only when poverty forced them to do so.

The Decline of Colonization   As trade in oil and wine and the export of manufactures

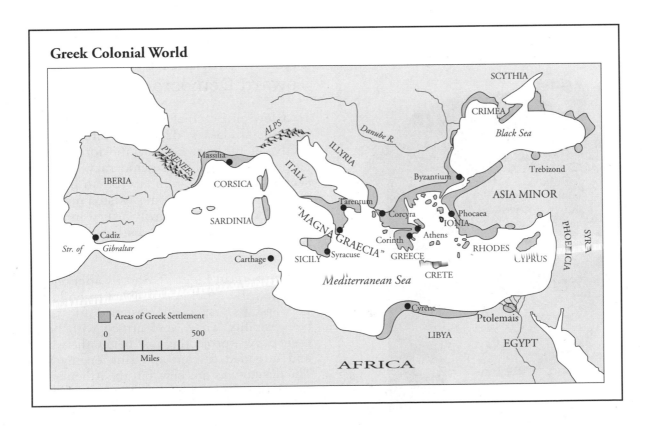

Greek Colonial World

took hold in Greece, the movement overseas to new colonies slackened. This was partly because it became difficult to find good farmland within easy reach of the sea, where local peoples were not well enough organized to resist Greek colonization. In the western Mediterranean, for example, the Carthaginians, who lived in north Africa, and the Etruscans, who lived in north-central Italy, joined forces in 535 B.C.E. to drive a newly established Greek colony out of Corsica. That defeat virtually stopped Greek colonization

---

Ships and Seafaring   The scene painted on the interior of this drinking cup shows dolphins gamboling around a ship in which the god of wine, Dionysus, is sailing across the Aegean to Greece from his home in Thrace. The square sail and steering oars are accurate enough, but the vines with their enormous bunches of grapes that entwine the mast are imaginary. The scene nevertheless records one of the central realities of Greek civilization. Athens and other cities prospered by exporting wine and olive oil to barbarian lands in return for grain and raw materials. Oil and wine were scarce, so Greeks could exchange an acre's production of wine or oil for the grain harvested from many acres. Greeks of the classical age could therefore enjoy a far higher standard of living than when their ancestors had raised all their own food locally. Cheap, reliable sea transport made it all possible.

in the west. The conquest of Asia Minor, first by Lydia and then by Persia, had a similar effect in the Black Sea region. Under Darius, Persian forces gained control of the Dardanelles (ancient Hellespont), the passage between the Aegean and Black seas. Greeks therefore could no longer be sure of free and easy access, except on terms agreeable to the new masters of the straits.

At the same time, the need for new land decreased. More people were needed to perform all the tasks connected with the growing export trade. Ships had to be built and manned; oil and wine had to be produced, graded, stored, and shipped. Sails, ropes, oars, and ships had to be manufactured. Pots to hold oil and wine were needed in enormous quantities. Metalwork also flourished with the growth of trade and population.

All in all, the new trade patterns opened important new economic opportunities in Greece. In the active seacoast towns, merchants, artisans, and sailors became numerous and politically important. These new social groups began to alter the older, sharp class division between rich and poor, which had been based on ownership of land.

The Development Toward Democracy

In a few cities, chief among them Athens, the new social classes, depending directly or indirectly on the sea, became the force behind a surge toward political democracy. As long as seafarers played no military role in political affairs, however, such groups existed more or less on sufferance of the heavily armed infantrymen of the phalanx, who won battles and protected the city.

The Athenian Fleet   Shortly after 500 B.C.E., however, the Athenians decided to build a fleet of warships, especially designed for fast maneuverability. They were armed with beaks at their prows, projecting just below the waterline and intended to ram and sink enemy vessels. The design was not new, but the Athenians built more vessels of this type than any Greek or

Phoenician city had ever built before. Citizen oarsmen manned the fleet. With practice, they learned how to maneuver their ships as skillfully as any phalanx. As a result, in 480 B.C.E. the Athenian fleet (with help from other Greek cities) was able to defeat the might of Persia. In the years that followed, the oarsmen of the fleet built up an empire and made Athens more wealthy and powerful than any other Greek city.

As the greatness of Athens came to depend mainly upon naval victories, the rowers of the fleet assumed a dominating role in Athenian political life, just as members of the phalanx had done in Athens and other Greek cities a hundred or more years earlier. This involved a shift of power to the poorer citizen classes. An oarsman needed nothing but a strong back; the ship and its equipment were provided by the richest citizens, who were assigned the task as a special honor each year. Any citizen, sound of wind and limb, qualified as a rower. A free man who owned no land at all, or such a tiny parcel as to be insufficient for his maintenance, could still take a full and active part in Athenian political life in his capacity as an oarsman.

Pulling an oar was hard, sweaty work, but the elements of rhythmic motion, shared danger, and shared excitement were similar to the experiences that welded men of the phalanx so strongly together. Hence the Athenian rowers, like the Athenian infantrymen, were schooled by their experience in war to become active, committed citizens. They developed a strong sense of their collective worth and dignity, and they stood ready to defend their stake in the polis against all comers.

The Special Case of Athenian Democracy

A thoroughgoing form of democracy, giving political power to the propertyless class of citizens, made sense for Athens because the fleet became the backbone of Athenian power. Other cities did not go the way of Athens, except when under Athenian influence. Most Greek cities limited full citizenship rights to the moderately well-to-do, who were able to buy arms and armor and take their place in the phalanx.

Even though it was so exceptional, the Athenian democratic adventure proved enormously successful and deeply impressive. Ordinary Athenians took part in deliberations of state. Every citizen was entitled to attend the assembly where all matters of importance were debated and decided by majority vote. Most Athenian citizens, in the course of a lifetime, must have served on one of the "committees of fifty" that took turns at presiding over public affairs. The members of these committees were chosen by lot. Each committee was charged with the conduct of state affairs for one month and then handed over responsibility to a new committee.

The intensity of such involvement still commands wonder and amazement. The success with which the Athenians conducted their affairs between 510 B.C.E., when changes in rules for voting made Athens definitely democratic for the first time, and 431 B.C.E., when a destructive and (for Athens) disastrous war with Sparta broke out, is equally surprising.

Yet it is worth reminding ourselves that, at its height, the Athenian democracy never allowed more than about half the adult males to take part in public affairs. The disfranchised half were slaves and foreigners. Many of these, especially the foreigners, were well treated and lived in Athens by choice. Some slaves, on the other hand, were miserably driven to work in the silver mines at Laurium—some thirty miles from Athens—under extremely harsh conditions.

The polis always remained, in Greek eyes, a privileged body of free men. Women were completely excluded from political affairs. And the only issue between a democratic polis, such as Athens, and an undemocratic polis, such as Sparta, was the proportion of the male population that had the right to take part in public affairs. The Greeks never thought that every man, regardless of where he had been born or who his parents were, should have full and equal part in the privileges of the polis. The right was almost always reserved for those born to citizenship.

The Culture of the Polis

The rights of citizenship were accompanied by duties, above all in war but also in peace. No citizen long escaped the tasks his status put upon him. It is not, therefore, surprising that the polis put its distinctive mark upon Greek religion, philosophy, and literature.

Greek Religion

The Greek inheritance in religion was confused. Gods whose origin extended back to Neolithic villagers, who spoke languages other than Greek, continued to be honored. Hades, Persephone, and Demeter were cases in point. Their special function was to assure the fertility of fields. But when Greek-speaking tribes first arrived in Greece, they brought their own quite different family of gods—Zeus, Poseidon, Hera, and others. These gods were said to inhabit the snowy heights of Mount Olympus in northern Greece, when not traveling abroad and making mischief among mortals. Finally, there arose a group of gods with mixed ancestry, including Apollo, Athena, and Dionysus.

Such a pantheon made no sense. The different gods' functions and powers overlapped hopelessly. Moreover, Homer's poems gave many of the leading gods an all-too-human character,

both spiteful and petty. Since every educated Greek learned Homer in school, no later generation of priests or poets was able to come along and tidy up the system by assigning powers and duties (and a more respectable character) to the different gods.

Another factor that created confusion was that no single body of experts had the job of preserving or elaborating religious truths. Tribal chieftains, local kings, and heads of families all had religious functions to perform on special occasions. There were also priests and ritual experts at a number of especially holy places. Of these, by far the most important was the Temple of Apollo at Delphi, where an oracle gave advice to petitioners who wanted divine guidance in their affairs. Then there were wandering poets and soothsayers, who claimed to be inspired and might give advice on almost any issue, whether anyone asked their opinions or not.

Lastly, there were secret societies into which individuals could be initiated and thereby acquire religious knowledge or some other sort of religious benefit. Of these cults, the most famous was the Eleusinian Mysteries; but the

The Parthenon   Athens' principal temple was the Parthenon, dedicated to the goddess Athena. In 480 B.C.E., invading Persians destroyed everything they found on the Acropolis, so the Athenians had to rebuild the temple between 447 and 432 B.C.E. In later times the Parthenon became first a church and then a mosque. When the city was beseiged by the Venetians in 1687, the Turkish defenders stored gunpowder in its interior. A cannon ball touched off an explosion that destroyed the roof and central parts of the building. Later, Lord Elgin removed most of the surviving sculptures and carried them off to England, leaving behind the beautifully proportioned shell shown here.

Poseidon the Earthshaker Like the ancient Sumerians, the Greeks imagined their gods in human form and believed that they lived on the top of Mount Olympus in northern Greece. But a god could move invisibly and at will, and might take up temporary residence in a statue if it looked attractive enough. Thus making sculptural images of the gods was important, since it could bring divine aid and protection close to those who needed it. Accordingly, the Greeks became expert sculptors. The photo shows a statue of Poseidon, god of earthquakes and of the sea. It was recovered in undamaged state from an ancient shipwreck off the coast of Greece. The muscular body, standing about seven feet tall, befitted the might of Poseidon, the earthshaker, while the serene and lofty expression of the face rises godlike above the trivia of everyday existence.

most widespread was Orphism, connected with the worship of Dionysus, the god of wine.

What could anyone make of such a jungle of confusion? Not very much; the Greeks certainly never reduced their religion to a logical system. They settled instead for rule of thumb. The polls became the frame within which most religious ceremonies took place. Worship of gods of diverse origins and with the most diverse rituals went forward under public control, with magistrates in charge.

In Athens, for example, the worship of Athena was tied in with the Eleusinian Mysteries through a great ceremonial procession, the Pan-

thenaea, which went from Eleusis to the Acropolis, where Athena's great temple stood. Similarly, the worship of Dionysus in Attica became the occasion for the presentation of dramas, sponsored by the state and paid for by private donors who were appointed to the job by state officials.

Other city-states made similar arrangements. No one tried to reconcile theoretical differences and contradictions. The persons in charge were politicians and magistrates, who could not get excited about such questions. Practical problems of getting the celebrations underway on time and as magnificently as possible, were what they cared about. This ap-

Greek Athletics   To be safe, a Greek polis needed to have a well-trained citizen army. Young men prepared themselves for war by going to special exercise grounds known as gymnasia, where they practiced infantry drills as well as engaging in boxing, running, and other sports, as this vase painting shows. Once every four years, the Greek cities suspended warfare and sent their best athletes to compete for prizes at Olympia. A crown of olive leaves awarded to the victors, though worthless in itself, was a trophy a whole city could be proud of. The modern Olympic Games started in 1896 in imitation of this ancient Greek custom. Modern athletes, however, wear clothes, whereas in ancient Greece the competitors stripped themselves naked—a practice that other people often found shocking.

proach worked very well. The great occasions and major festivals were managed by the polis. Older tribal and family rites could go on as before, but they tended to fade before the magnificence and ritual elaboration of public religious celebrations.

The Ceremonial Games   Among the more important religious ceremonies of ancient Greece were athletic contests. To honor the gods, naked young men ran races, wrestled, boxed, and competed in other tests of strength and skill. The winners were much admired; songs were composed in their honor; sometimes statues were erected to commemorate their success. Individual athletes from all over Greece came to the most famous of all these ceremonies, held in honor of Zeus at Olympia in the western part of the Peloponnese. The Olympic games were held every four years, beginning—if later records are correct—in 776 B.C.E. Other festivals, like that at Corinth, were almost as important for the ancients, but our modern international athletic competitions took the Olympic name when the tradition was revived in 1896.

Athletic games and the great oracles, like that at Delphi, helped to keep the Greeks to-

gether. Individuals from different cities could meet and talk freely at the important athletic festivals. The Greeks counted it a great crime to harm anyone on such occasions, even (or especially) an enemy. The Delphic oracle, by giving advice on important issues that arose between states, also played a large role in uniting the Greeks and keeping war and violence between cities within bounds.

Despite its logical flaws, Greek religion met practical needs quite adequately by providing for private and family ceremonies as well as public festivals in each city, along with all-Greek ceremonies and institutions like the Olympic games and the Delphic oracle.

Greek Philosophy

Nevertheless, a small number of individuals in ancient Greece could not be satisfied with the theological confusion they had inherited. In early days, poets tried to bring some sort of order to traditions about the gods. Hesiod, for example, wrote a long poem, *Theogony*, in which he tried to explain which of the gods was descended from whom, and in what fashion. He lived two or three generations after Homer, when Greek life was still rural. Later, when trade opened up contact with other peoples, Greeks became aware that their religious traditions were both similar to and oddly different from those of other peoples. When authorities disagreed, who was right? Who, indeed, really knew anything at all about the gods? Thoughts like these led a few Ionians to turn away from religious speculation. They tried instead to explain the natural world in terms of law. Law, after all, ruled the polis; perhaps it also ruled the heavens, the seas, and the earth. At any rate the idea seemed worth exploring. Those who did so were called *philosophers*, a word that means, literally, "lovers of knowledge."

The first philosopher, according to later tradition, was Thales of Miletus (the most im-portant Ionian city), who lived about 636–546 B.C.E. He declared that the world was made from water. Water condensed to become earth, and it turned into air and the fiery substance of sun, stars, and planets by becoming thinner. Thales had no proof for his theory; he just stated it. In choosing water as the originating substance, he borrowed an old Mesopotamian idea that creation had started with a primeval ocean. Indeed, from one point of view, all Thales did was omit the gods—whether those of Mesopotamia or those of Greece—from the old Mesopotamian account of how the world had come to be what it was.

But in another sense he broke fundamentally with all older ideas of how things happened in the world. For he suggested that the process

---

The Theater at Delphi   The rhythm of work on the land in ancient Greece left plenty of free time after grain had been harvested in May and before grapes and olives could be picked in October and November. The Greeks used this period of summer leisure for war, for sailing, and for civic celebrations. One such event, the festival of Dionysus, god of wine, developed into elaborate dramatic productions rather like modern operas. These became so popular that special seating to accommodate the citizens had to be built. A theater, like this one at Delphi, allowed the seated audience to watch and hear the chorus that danced and sang in the central circle, commenting upon stories of gods and heroes reenacted by individual performers from an elevated platform off to the right of this photo.

that changed water into other things followed a regular pattern and needed no miracle-working power to explain it. Condensation and rarefaction were ordinary enough and could be seen on a small scale every day. Thales had the bright idea that those processes, spread out over a long enough time and on a large enough scale, could explain how the world came to be.

Other philosophers, who came after Thales, tried to improve on his suggestion. One proposed that air was the primary substance; another preferred the theory of primacy of the infinite or the unlimited—something a little like our idea of outer space. Later still, the notion that there were four primary substances—earth, air, fire, and water—gained widespread acceptance. Everything, including animals and plants, was believed to arise from different mixtures of these substances. Nothing was too complicated for these optimistic thinkers to try to explain.

In leaving out the gods and attributing everything in nature to the operation of regular laws, Thales and his successors were, in a sense, trying to analyze the inscrutable Fate that, according to Homer, presided over both gods and human beings. If Fate worked regularly, then it ought to be possible to say how it did so. The result would then be a law of nature. But Thales also had the model of polis law before him. The actions of his fellow citizens in Miletus were controlled and directed by the invisible bonds of laws that were declared in public and known to all. Free men they were, yet slaves to law. Could not nature be the same? The philosophers answered yes. They therefore discarded the stories that poets told about the gods as mere fairy tales and boldly tried to explain things by discovering natural laws.

Over the centuries, this stab in the dark turned out to be incredibly fruitful. Modern science is based on the assumption that natural laws exist and can be formulated in words or in mathematical symbols. Modern life would be inconceivable without science; its underlying basis is still, as it was for the Greeks, a belief in natural law.

In later Greek times Thales' basic idea continued to dominate philosophy. Later philosophers turned attention to a much wider range of questions: about our minds, about language and how we know; how we ought to behave; and how the polis should be run. But in asking these and yet other questions, philosophers always kept to the assumption that if they tried hard enough, natural laws could be discovered to answer these questions too.

The Middle Eastern peoples had come to a different conclusion. For them the basic assumption always remained that one or several gods controlled both natural and human actions. God's will, not natural law, was the ruling principle of the universe for them.

These two world views remain vigorously alive to the present. The problem of reconciling or combining them in a satisfactory fashion continues to be the central intellectual problem of Western civilization.

Greek Literature

Greek literature came into its own before the rich and noble found it necessary to conform to the modest norms of behavior established by the farmer-footsoldiers of the phalanx. Homer's heroes were egoists, pure and simple. They had absolutely nothing to do with the polis. Later poets, too, concentrated on exploring personal pursuit of glory, love and honor.

To be sure, verse was used for all kinds of formal composition, because it was easier to remember. Thus Solon, the Athenian lawgiver, wrote poetry to set forth his political ideals, and the first philosophers wrote in verse too. In a long poem, *Works and Days*, Hesiod laid down rules for farming. Poems praising service in the phalanx have also survived. But in spite of these exceptions, it remains true that the major Greek poets stayed outside the polis framework and concentrated on exploring their own personal, private feelings.

Yet, paradoxically, the heroic ideal of conduct, so powerfully expressed in Homer's poems, entered the inmost fiber of Greek polis life. Citizens and soldiers, brought up on Homer, simply transferred to their city the heroic attributes that Homer and other poets had assigned to individual warriors. The Athenians felt about their city as Achilles or Hector felt about himself. The Spartans, Corinthians, Argives, and all the rest felt the same about their own particular city-state. Glory and greatness for the polis became ends in themselves, to be pursued at any cost. Cowardice was unforgivable; no human resource of strength or skill should be withheld, they felt, from the task of advancing the greatness of their particular polis.

It was not so much the polis that shaped Greek literature, therefore, as Greek literature that shaped the polis.

Greek Art

In art the relationship was reversed, for the polis gave rise to a distinctive art style and technique. Even though only a few damaged statues survive, early Greek sculpture offers us a very sensitive indicator of how public purposes affected the way statues were made.

The earliest examples of Greek sculpture betray strong Egyptian influence. Several statues reproduce a stiff Egyptian posture as exactly as the imperfect skill of the Greek stonecutters then allowed. Once started, however, Greek techniques improved rapidly. Between 600 and 500 B.C.E., noble patrons commissioned statues, many of which have been recovered from the Acropolis in Athens. They portray rich, well-dressed women who seem to breathe an aristocratic atmosphere of luxury and display that was very different from the polis ideal that came to prevail later. Another type of statue portrayed naked athletes—winners in the Olympics or at some other famous games.

Then, from about 500 B.C.E., sculptors more and more used their skill to decorate public buildings, especially temples. For such purposes, portrait art was out of place. Statues of the gods required a more abstract, idealized sort of beauty. Sculptors learned how to achieve such an effect and, in doing so, created a classical style that has been admired and praised ever since.

Among the lesser arts, vase painting found an enlarged scope with the development of the export trade in oil and wine, for these products were shipped from Greece in handsomely painted pots, many of which have been dug up all over the Mediterranean world.

Because so many painted pots have been discovered, it is possible to observe how styles changed. In the Dark Age, vase decorations took geometric shapes. Next came a period when Greek vase painters borrowed heavily from the Middle East. Processions of animals and similar designs predominated. Then, about 600 B.C.E., an independent, new "Greek" style emerged, featuring human figures, sometimes drawn with exquisite skill. Often the painter illustrated a story from Homer or another poet. Battle and hunting scenes or gymnastic contests were common subjects; but unlike the Egyptian wall paintings, themes from everyday life rarely appeared. Thus, even in their relatively humble art, the Greek vase painters remained true to the heroic vision of human life.

Conclusion

By 500 B.C.E. the Greeks had developed a style of civilization that was different in some important respects from anything known elsewhere. This style of life was attractive enough, strong enough, and persuasive enough to stand comparison with the most highly developed Middle Eastern culture. The master institution of the polis, with its extreme demands upon all citizens, dominated nearly all aspects of Greek life. The master idea of natural law, which a handful of philosophers had begun to explore, rose out of and took nourishment from the polis environment, where citizens did in fact run their affairs according to law. The idea that all forms of human association and loyalty should be subordinated to the territorial state, and that such a state should be governed by its citizens, is one of the fundamental inheritances we and all the world take from the ancient Greeks. The modern concept of natural law also descends from their speculations about how the world had come to be.

Middle Eastern administrative techniques and the idea of monotheism were different from, but just as vigorous as, the Greek polis and natural law. Therefore, when the Greeks began to build up their own distinctive way of life, it became inevitable that the new Greek way would both rival and interact with the older, more massive, and immensely deep-rooted civilization of the Middle East.

This enrichment of the human scene was matched by a similar development in India where, by 500 B.C.E., another great new civilization had taken an enduring form. We must see how it arose and study its characteristics in the next chapter.

Bibliography

The ancient Greeks, like the Jews, created literary monuments that constitute the best possible introduction to their world. Homer's two poems, the *Iliad* and the *Odyssey*, were fundamental guides to life for ancient Greeks. They are available in several excellent translations, and students who have not read them should hasten to do so. Two other classical authors will also repay attention: Herodotus, *Histories*, and Plutarch, *Parallel Lives of the Greeks and the Romans*. These, too, are readily available in several fine translations. Aristotle, *Constitution of the Athenians*, is a short, constitutional history, important for anyone trying to understand the evolution toward democracy. It, too, is available in several translations.

General accounts of early Greek civilization include Chester G. Starr, *The Origins of Greek Civilization 1100–650 B.C.,* (1961); A. M. Snodgrass, *The Dark Age of Greece* (1971); A. R. Burn, *The Lyric Age of Greece* (1960); M. I. Finley, *The World of Odysseus* (2nd ed., 1979); W. G. Forrest, *The Emergence of Greek Democracy, 800–400 B.C.* (1979); and a noteworthy revision of a famous older work, J. B. Bury and Russell Meiggs, *A History of Greece to the Death of Alexander the Great* (4th ed., 1975). Two briefer introductions are Edith Hamilton, *The Greek Way* (1930), and Antony Andrewes, Greek Society (4th ed., 1992). For overseas contacts and colonization, John Boardman, *The Greeks Overseas* (1974); T. J. Dunabin, *The Western Greeks* (1948); and M. M. Austin, *Greece and Egypt in the Archaic Age* (1970), are informative.

On the beginning of Greek philosophy, F. M. Cornford, *From Religion to Philosophy: A Study of the Origins of Western Speculation* (1912), is an opinionated and penetrating study. A more standard work is John Burnet, *Early Greek Philosophy* (4th ed., 1930); a more recent one is G. S. Kirk, J. E. Raven, and M. Schofield, *The Presocratic Philosophers* (2nd ed., 1983).

On early Greek art, Gisela M. A. Richter, *Archaic Greek Art against Its Historical Background* (1949), is standard. More specialized themes are treated by Pierre Demargne, *Aegean Art: The Origins of Greek Art* (1964), and Humfry Payne and G. M. Young, *Archaic Marble Sculpture from the Acropolis* (1936).

Classical Definition of Eurasian Civilizations; 1250 B.C.E. to 500 B.C.E.

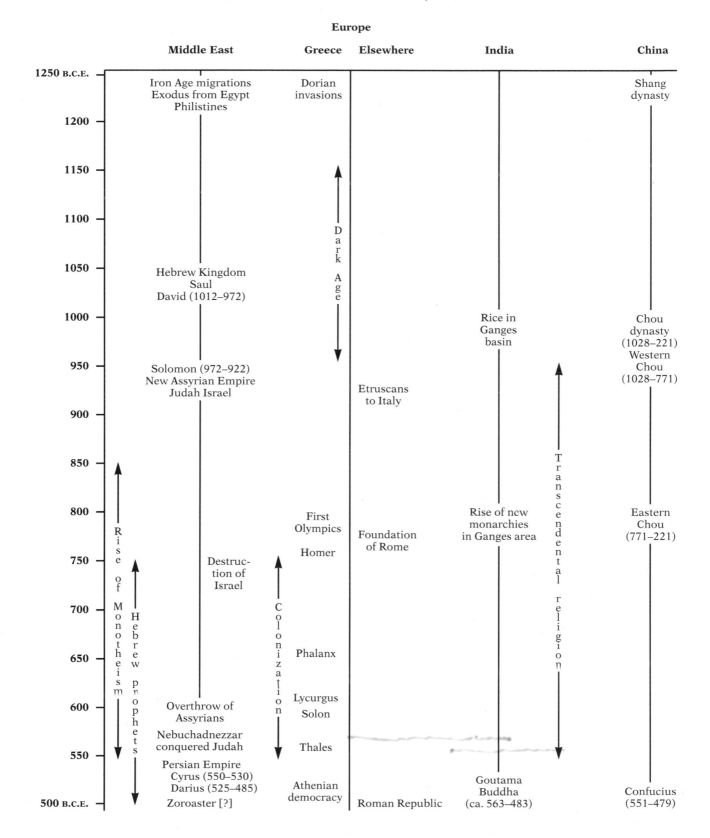

The Indian Style of Civilization

to 500 B.C.E.

6

Yakshi of Patna   This statue was discovered in the bed of the Ganges River in almost perfect condition. How it got there and when it was made remain mysteries, but it is among the very earliest known statues from classical India, and its fine workmanship shows how skillful artists had become. Figures like this, known to Hindus today as *yakshi*, are connected with fertility rituals.

The literature of ancient India that has come down to us is not much interested in wars and battles, nor in kings and empires. The authors wrote about what they felt were more important matters; for example, they believed that a hidden reality stood behind appearances and made all the pomp and ceremony of this world nothing but an empty show. It would be a mistake to assume that all Indians agreed with the people who composed the texts that have survived. There were plenty of kings and warriors in India, as well as merchants, dancing girls, and millions of peasants, for whom the ordinary everyday world surely mattered a great deal and whose interest in the world beyond may not have been particularly vivid. But we cannot know what they did and how they felt, because priests and holy men, who made the record, left out everything that did not interest them.

The fact that Indian literature was oral also makes things difficult for historians. Works survived by being memorized. A master who had memorized a particular work taught it to his pupils, and they to theirs. But texts passed on in this fashion changed with the generations. Passages that did not seem to make much sense were forgotten; new explanations or stories to illustrate a point were put in; and language changed as old words faded out and new ones came into use. When such works eventually came to be written down, therefore, there was no way of telling what parts were very old and what parts had been added later. The "Homeric question" that troubles students of Greek literature arises from the oral tradition that lay behind Homer's poems. But Homer stands alone in Greece, whereas almost all of early Indian literature is the deposit of uncounted generations of oral transmission. As a result, scholarly techniques for dating manuscripts, which proved very powerful in unscrambling the European historical record, simply will not work on Indian texts.

Archaeology is only beginning to fill some of the gaps. Moreover, the scraps and pieces of archaeological information that we have are hard to tie in with literary references. It is always difficult to learn much about ideas or social structures by picking through ruins and rubbish heaps, which is what archaeologists must do, and it is particularly awkward when the literary record itself says almost nothing about everyday tools and materials and seldom even mentions governments or rulers.

Historians therefore find themselves handicapped when trying to write about ancient India. Main lines of change can only be guessed at.

India's Dark Age

Before discussing what we know and can guess about India's early history, it is important to get a clear idea of the geographical conditions of India as they were before human activity did much to change the natural landscape. (See map, page 125.)

The Geography of Ancient India

The lower Indus Valley was a desert, quite like that surrounding the lower course of the Tigris-Euphrates rivers or the Nile. South and east of the Thar Desert, as it is called, increased rainfall supported grasslands like those north of Arabia, with woods on some hillsides and along watercourses. All this closely resembled the conditions of the Middle East and of Greece, with the difference that India was a little hotter and lacked any season in which temperatures plunged below freezing.

Eastern and southern India had a very different climate and natural vegetation. Everything in that part of the country depended on the monsoon, a wind that blows off the land in winter and onto the land in summer.

In winter, when the monsoon winds come out of central Asia and blow across India from the north, little rain falls and vegetation dries up. In summer, when the winds reverse themselves and begin to blow in over the land from the Indian Ocean, they bring heavy rainfall. Where the rain-rich winds encounter the Himalaya Mountains, in northern Assam and Bengal, the result is one of the heaviest rainfalls in the world. Hills and mountains in other parts of India also affect rainfall and patterns of vegetation. In southern

123

India, for example, the high central plateau—called the Deccan—is rather dry. Most of the moisture that comes in from the Arabian Sea and the Indian Ocean is squeezed out as the winds rise over the coastal ranges on either side. Lush, dense forests and swamplands therefore extend along the two coasts; but inland, thinner forest and grassland, or even semidesert, prevail.

The most fertile and important region of India is the Ganges Valley in the northeast. The Ganges River drains the towering Himalayas to the north; and though it is relatively short, it carries more water than does the other great river of India, the Indus. Also, the Ganges Valley gets the full benefit of the monsoon. Before men cleared the jungle away, it was heavily wooded and frequently swampy underfoot. Slash-and-burn cultivation did not work very well where the ground underneath was waterlogged. But on either side of the river floodplain, more lightly wooded and better-drained land offered primitive farmers really favorable ground, much like the hills where grain farming first started in the Middle East.

The Aryan Invasions

This, then, was the sort of country that the Aryan tribes found when they crossed the mountains and began to trickle into India about 1500 B.C.E. Except in the area where the Indus cities had organized irrigation farming, population was scant. As a result, after they had destroyed Harappa and Mohenjo-Daro, civilized skills disappeared from India for several centuries. Perhaps the irrigation works on which Indus civilization depended were destroyed, and no one put them in order fast enough to keep the people from either starving or fleeing into the forests to the south and east. In any event, the Indus cities were abandoned.

Various references in Aryan sacred hymns to cattle and to an open-air, migratory existence make it seem likely that the newcomers maintained, for a while, something like their old nomadic way of life after reaching India. Natural grasslands were not lacking in northwestern In-

dia. These regions, in and near the Indus Valley, remained the main center of Aryan population for a long time. But eventually, Aryan-speaking peoples filtered south and east into forested regions, where they found peaceable slash-and-burn cultivators living side by side with peoples who were still hunters and gatherers.

None of these communities could resist the Aryan warriors. Yet the Aryans could not force such peoples to pay rents or taxes. Slash-and-burn cultivators seldom had a food surplus. If strangers tried to collect rents from them, they could simply disappear into the forest and hide in some little clearing miles away, where it was difficult to find them again. Hunters had still less that a conqueror could take away from them, for they ate what they killed as soon as they could. Aryan military superiority, therefore, did not lead immediately to state-building.

If this reconstruction is correct, the Aryan and the pre-Aryan peoples had relatively little to do with each other in the first phases of the Aryan penetration of the forested parts of India. Hunters had to learn not to attack the Aryans' herds of cattle. We may be sure that sudden and violent reprisal would follow the slaughter of a cow. Perhaps the Aryans discovered that they could force hunters to make arrows for them or that some of the forest peoples had priests and sorcerers who could cure disease or ward off disaster. Since they were skilled warriors, Aryan tribesmen could demand such services under threat of violence—and probably got them.

Farming   The Aryans knew how to raise wheat and barley before they crossed the mountains into India. Little by little, as in Europe and the Middle East, the newcomers settled down to farming. But the forests of India were broad, and slash-and-burn cultivation was an effective and cheap way to exploit that sort of environment. Hence, when they turned to farming, the Aryans took up the same style of cultivation that the pre-Aryan farming people used.

The spread of Aryan speakers throughout nearly all of India (only in the extreme south did a different language, Tamil, become a carrier of literature) was a result of their search for new plots of forestland to be cropped and then abandoned.

Warfare   In parts of India the Aryans created an aristocratic, warlike society quite like that which prevailed, for example, in Mycenae. Noble charioteers fought one another in single combat. A few phrases in the Vedic hymns—almost certainly the oldest surviving Aryan literature—reflect this sort of violent, heroic life. If the stories of the *Mahabharata*—a long epic poem—are to be believed, they did not dismount, as did Homer's heroes, but shot arrows at one another from galloping chariots. The whole poem is built around the story of armed struggle between two tribal groups. But this heroic framework was crusted over with an enormous number of pious lessons and tales intended to point a moral or explain some local custom or religious practice. Religious experts apparently took over from secular bards and then added various other matter to the original core. Still, there is no reason to deny that the *Mahabharata*'s battle scenes probably reflect the kind of life that noble Aryans and chariot warriors did in fact know.

When iron became common, chariot warfare ceased to dominate battlefields, although chariots continued to have ceremonial importance for many centuries afterward. Cavalry was also introduced, but it seems never to have been

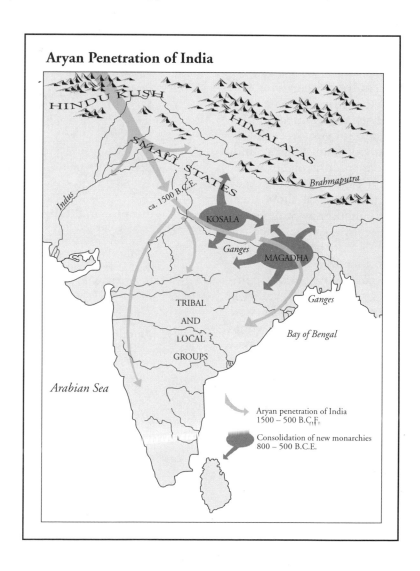

Aryan Penetration of India

HINDU KUSH

HIMALAYAS

Indus

SMALL STATES

ca. 1500 B.C.E.

Brahmaputra

KOSALA

Ganges

MAGADHA

TRIBAL

AND

LOCAL

GROUPS

Ganges

Bay of Bengal

Arabian Sea

Aryan penetration of India
1500 – 500 B.C.E.

Consolidation of new monarchies
800 – 500 B.C.E.

very important. Horses did not flourish in the hot Indian climate, and in later times they usually had to be imported. This restricted the number of mounted warriors who could be maintained in India, since the road over the mountains from the north was long and hard, and shipping horses by sea was difficult and expensive.

The Rise of Monarchies

The big change that came to India was the rise of large, centralized monarchies in the Ganges Valley. How this happened, or even when statebuilding began, remains unknown. We can guess that iron tools made the tasks of clearing the jungle easier and opened new land to cultivation. We know, too, that the staple crop of the Ganges Valley was rice rather than wheat and barley, as in the Indus region.

Rice cultivation required irrigation and elaborate preparation of the ground. To be sure, the Ganges floodplain was well suited to rice cultivation, being both flat and very wet. A skillful layout of canals and dikes in such a landscape allowed the farmers to control the water supply at will. While the rice was growing, they kept the fields or paddies under a shallow sheet of water. When the rice ripened, they drained the water away to make harvesting easier. Once the necessary dikes and canals had been built, two crops a year could be produced.

Exactly how this intensive type of rice cultivation established itself in the Ganges Valley is unknown. It cannot have been very old; otherwise some trace of ancient cities in the region would surely have been found. Of course, some new archaeological discovery may yet prove these guesses wrong; but in the absence of evidence it seems best to assume that rice cultivation established itself soon after 1000 B.C.E., only a few generations before the rise of the Ganges states.

About 800 B.C.E. big, powerful monarchies, ruled by Aryan speakers, started to thrive in the Ganges Valley. This, indeed, is the reason for supposing that rice farming had begun to take hold in that part of the world a few generations before we begin to hear of Magadha, Kosala, and similar kingdoms. Rice farmers could not afford to move away to escape tax collectors. Too

Empire and Religion in India
These carved lions once stood on top of a seventy-foot column in Sarnath, India. They symbolized royal power and celebrated the greatness of King Ashoka, who ruled over most of India between 274 and 236 B.C.E. But after winning hard-fought wars early in his reign, Ashoka became a Buddhist and gave up warfare as an evil. This monument proclaims his new faith by placing a wheel beneath the lions' paws; it symbolized the endless rebirths from which Buddha's teaching could free a weary soul. On top of Ashoka's column the elegance and pride of courtly culture affirmed the otherworldliness of Indian religion.

much work went into making the fields ready for planting, since the cultivators always had to build suitable canals, dikes, and water sluices. At the same time, rice farmers could afford to part with a large proportion of their harvest. Paddies yielded abundantly, so that a hardworking family could produce a lot more than it needed for its own nourishment. With such a sure source of tax income, rulers, soldiers, administrators, artisans, and all of the other specialists associated with cities and civilized life could, therefore, come quickly into existence. This is what seems to have happened in the Ganges Valley.

The rise of cities and states in this part of India brought civilized life into a physical and social environment that was significantly different from that of the Indus Valley, where the Aryan as well as the ancient Indus culture had centered earlier. Some of the peculiarities of later Indian civilization reflected the special character of the monsoon environment. For example, there was no ambiguity about when to plant, once the monsoon rains began. This probably encouraged the Indians to see the world as a theater for an endless return or repetition of fundamentally the same experience. Time and the particular moment seemed unimportant, whereas Middle Eastern farmers had always had to worry about just when to sow the precious seed grains, and needed accurate calendars to avoid making disastrous mistakes.

The Development of Bureaucratic Government   We can only assume that the new Ganges kingdoms gradually built up the apparatus of a bureaucratic state—administrators, tax collectors, soldiers, and a train of merchants and artisans necessary to equip and feed the ruling classes. Sea trade between western India and Mesopotamia opened up on a more or less regular basis about 800 B.C.E. If the Ganges kings needed any help in figuring out how to extend their power by bureaucratic government, perhaps helpful hints came from traders who had visited the Middle East and knew something of the workings of government among the Babylonians and Assyrians.

Magadha was the most successful of the Ganges states, and eventually it became an empire that embraced nearly all of northern India. But before that came about, several other states, Kosala among them, divided the river valley and spread into adjacent regions. They fought one another and expanded their territory at the expense of less well-organized peoples who could not defend themselves successfully against the professional soldiery of the Ganges kings.

The Slow Pace of Change in Other Regions

Elsewhere in India no comparably rapid changes in society or politics occurred. The Indus Valley remained in the hands of Aryan tribes or tribal groupings who depended on shifting agriculture and herding. Nothing really is known about southern India. No very dense populations or powerful political units arose until much later, presumably because there was still enough land to allow herding, hunting and gathering, and slash-and-burn cultivation to support whatever population there was in that part of the world.

Disease was a factor that may have delayed the peopling of India and kept back the level of development. In warm climates various disease organisms flourish, which cannot survive in regions where subfreezing temperatures prevail during part of the year. Animals and people moving from cooler to warmer climates are therefore always liable to meet diseases for which they have no immunity. If settlement becomes dense, new "tropical" diseases can wreak havoc with such populations. But as long as human communities remain very thin, infections are checked because there are fewer hosts in whose bodies infection can lodge and fewer contacts among human beings that would allow the disease to pass from one person to another.

If, in fact, diseases were important in keeping India thinly populated in early times, then it is obvious that the rise of the Ganges kingdoms depended on the development of a population that was relatively immune to local infections and that could, therefore, survive even when living in densely settled communities. Perhaps pre-Aryan peoples had an advantage here, having been exposed to the special conditions of a monsoon climate much longer than the invading Aryans had been. Certainly, some of the aspects of historic Indian culture seem surprisingly at odds with the attitudes expressed in the earliest

Aryan literature, and it is tempting to believe that these differences arose from the survival of pre-Aryan values and points of view in historic India. But since we do not know anything for sure about the pre-Aryans, we can only guess.

What we do know is that historic Indian society allowed numerous local groups to survive and maintain distinct ways of life. This was possible because Indian society as a whole was organized into castes, each marked off from the rest by special customs and rules. Since the whole notion of caste is strange to Westerners, we need to define the concept carefully.

Caste—The Master Institution of Ancient India

In modern times, and as far back as records can take us, Indian society has been organized into castes. A person's caste was and is the most important thing about him or her. In any face-to-face encounter, the first thing that has to be established is to which caste each person belongs. With that information, everybody more or less knows how to behave, and the business in hand can then go forward with minimal confusion or friction. By comparison, the question of what state or kingdom a person belonged to was trivial. Nobody cared very much about that, except for the kings and tax collectors, who, of course, constituted a separate caste of their own.

An Indian caste today is a group of people who will eat together and who intermarry. They usually also refuse to marry or eat with anyone from outside the caste. Membership is therefore hereditary; and in most situations, each member carries some mark (usually on the forehead) that tells everyone which caste he or she belongs to. Caste is an extremely flexible thing. If a group of strangers appears, and everyone refuses to eat with them or to marry them, this group too, becomes a caste whether the individuals concerned wish it or not.

Most modern caste distinctions are related to occupation. If a new kind of job develops, such as the tasks of driving and maintaining automobiles, a new caste is likely to form among those who work around cars and know how to repair them. This is because other occupational caste groups treat such persons as outsiders, who must, therefore, eat together and intermarry because no one else will eat with them or marry into their circle.

Another characteristic of the modern caste system is that rather exact rules define how the members of one caste are supposed to deal with the members of another. Thus, even indirect contact with a member of a lower caste "defiles" a member of an upper caste, who then has to wash, or perform some other ritual, to become "clean" again.

Some, but not all, castes have formal ways of disciplining their members. If a person disregards the caste rules, he or she can be excluded—lose caste—and have to face the world thereafter as an outcast, acceptable to nobody. This is a severe penalty in a village or small town, where everybody soon learns of what has happened. It is less meaningful in the impersonal environment of a big city, where many of the caste rules about defilement cannot be enforced anyway.

Early Records of Caste Society

Modern castes, of course, do not tell us anything about castes in the beginning of Indian history. The trouble is that nothing else tells us much about castes either, though a number of casual references make clear that something more or less like the modern caste system existed very long ago. About 300 B.C.E. a Greek ambassador to the court of Magadha, named Megasthenes, wrote a book about India in which he described seven hereditary classes into which, he said, Indian society was divided. And Buddhist stories and sermons, some of which were probably written earlier than 300 B.C.E., sometimes mention caste, taking it completely for granted.

Theoretical Basis for Caste

Even older than the Buddhist stories are texts called Brahmanas. These are commentaries on the most ancient and sacred Sanskrit writings, called Vedas. In the Brahmanas a theory of caste is set forth, according to which everyone is born either as Brahmans who pray, as warriors who fight, as farmers and artisans who work, or as Sudras, the lowest caste of all, who do ritually unclean jobs, like picking up the garbage or tanning leather. The first three castes, according to the Brahmanas, are Aryan; the fourth caste is reserved for non-Aryans. Later an additional group of "outcasts" or untouchables was added

Castes in India Today No one knows when caste took shape in India, nor exactly how it changed over time. These two photographs were taken in recent years and show a Brahman taking his ease in the shade of an umbrella with an attendant who seems to be preparing a meal for his superior. At the opposite end of the caste structure are the so-called untouchables. They are so humble that they have no caste whatever and must confine themselves to unclean tasks like sweeping streets. The status of untouchable was officially abolished by the Indian government soon after independence in 1947. But old habits die slowly, and the caste structure of Indian life still affects marriages and daily behavior, especially in rural communities.

to the fourfold classification of the Brahmanas. The outcasts occupy the lowest positions in modern Indian society.

The Brahmanas also developed a theory to account for the differences of caste. Human beings, they say, do not start life with a clean slate. The soul of every newborn infant formerly inhabited some other body. Sometimes the soul came from another human being, sometimes from an animal. Wherever it had been before, it accumulated *karma*. Karma is a little like dust: It collects on the soul just through the process of living. Only a very wise and good individual, aided by ritual purification, can avoid accumulating a lot of it. Souls that in former lives had gathered a heavy load of karma, then, were born into babies of the lowest castes. Those who in former lives had accumulated only a little karma earned the right to be born as Brahmans; and those in between, or course, acquired an in-between caste status. Persons who lived well in whatever caste they had been born to could hope for rebirth higher up the scale. By the same principle, anyone who abused his or her position or failed to observe caste and religious rules of behavior would be reborn in a lower caste or might even reappear as an animal or insect.

These ideas may seem strange, but one should never assume that something many millions of people have believed is absurd, however unfamiliar it may be on first acquaintance. Actually, the idea of reincarnation, as the doctrine of rebirth is called, explains sleep, birth, and death in a very convincing way—as long as one assumes that every living thing has a soul that can separate itself from the body at will. Since people had dreams and could "see" things in their sleep, remembering strange and distant scenes and extraordinary experiences upon awakening, it seemed only reasonable to believe in a soul that could leave the body in sleep and return whenever it wished to wake the person up again. What, then, of death? Obviously it was due to the permanent departure of the soul. And where would the soul of a dead person or animal go? Reincarnation in a newborn body seemed a very reasonable answer to such a question—particularly since it explained why every newborn creature had a soul.

Once such ideas had been accepted, the doctrine of reincarnation had an additional ad-

vantage. It explained the inevitable injustices of life in a very neat way. Reward and punishment for good and bad actions did not have to wait for the end of the world, as Zoroastrians and Jews believed. Death and reincarnation were always close at hand. The poor and abused could therefore look forward, if they were patient and kept their assigned place in the caste system, to rebirth higher up the scale. Since civilization involved injustice, this idea helped everyone to endure the pains and sorrows of life more calmly. Civilized life became more stable as a result.

The Brahmanas, however, do not really tell us when or how the caste principle established itself in India. In all probability, there never were only four castes, and a good deal of wishful thinking went into the classification of Brahman priests above warriors and rulers. In other words, we have here a priestly theory rather than a description of what really existed.

Social and Psychological Bases of Caste

A search of the Vedas themselves for signs of caste yields no definite results. There are phrases distinguishing the color of Aryans from the color of the older inhabitants of India. Probably, when they first came into the country, the Aryans were white-skinned and very conscious of the difference between themselves and the dark-skinned peoples they encountered. This color line may have been an important factor in creating caste.

It would be wrong, however, to think that the caste principle arose only, or even mainly, because a group of Aryan conquerors wished to draw a barrier between themselves and those they had conquered. On the contrary, the strongest factor in caste organization was probably the preference that members of any group feel for doing things without interference from outside. Groups of hunters and gatherers or slash-and-burn cultivators, finding themselves more and more closely surrounded by others who had different customs—and who, in many cases, spoke different languages—could get along by becoming a caste within Indian society. As a caste they could keep most of their own ways and preserve private family customs, while still spending their lives in close daily contact with all sorts of other people. Each such group occupied a niche in the larger society. Members of such groups could survive, more or less comfortably, as a part of Indian society as a whole, simply by finding out who stood above and who ranked below them in the caste system.

In point of fact it seems very likely that this was the way Indian society expanded. In modern times remote parts of Assam have been edging into Indian society in just this fashion. Hill tribes, some of them still very primitive, become castes when their members, having come into contact with the outside world, take on special roles—as fishers or porters or something of the sort. What brought these groups into Indian society was the steady advance of settled agriculture. This, as in the Middle East or Europe, was in turn the consequence of population growth, making older ways of using the resources of the soil insufficient.

If this process extended back to the beginning of Indian history, it is likely that when cities began to arise on Indian soil, after about 800 B.C.E., the caste structure of society faced a crisis. In a city new possibilities opened up. People no longer knew one another from birth, as they did in villages. Strangers were everywhere, and a person could change caste without anyone who mattered knowing a thing about it.

This sort of pulling up of roots was what happened in the Middle East when a peasant made his way to town and began a new life as an artisan or porter or soldier. Sooner or later the newcomer left village ways behind and acquired new habits and new ways of looking at the world. Similar shifts certainly occurred in early Indian history. Some Buddhist stories, as a matter of fact, tell of changes in caste—a thing theoretically impossible. Perhaps this happened quite often during the first centuries of city life in the Ganges kingdoms.

Nevertheless, in the long run, caste prevailed. The religious idea of defilement from contact with persons of the wrong caste may have helped to produce this result. Religious literature certainly suggests that this was a major consideration. The number and variety of subgroups of peoples who inhabited India prob-

ably was another reason why caste survived. Over 200 languages are still spoken in India, and in times past the number may have been much larger. Forest hunters and gatherers, who for all practical purposes are still in the Stone Age, survive today in a few secluded regions of India. In times past they were certainly more numerous.

When so many different people found themselves more and more closely entangled in the network of fields made by plowing farmers, what could they do? The Indian answer was simple: Become a caste. Cities and towns therefore, in attracting peoples from far and near to perform the varied functions a large center of population requires, drew upon groups so different from one another that they formed a series of separate castes. These castes learned how to maintain their separateness even in an urban environment. Thus, instead of assimilating citizens to a more or less common pattern of life, as the Greek city-states set out to do, Indian society allowed maximum variety and freedom for all its different subgroups and peoples.

The Political and Cultural Consequences of Caste Organization

The organization of society into castes had far-ranging consequences. As long as people owed first allegiance to their caste, politics and the state remained superficial. Rulers could not make ordinary persons identify themselves with the state in the manner of the Greeks. What the government did or failed to do was its affair. Defeat or victory only concerned soldiers and administrators, not ordinary folk in the field or in the shop. Life went on within the caste framework, while states and rulers might come and go, depending on who won the latest local battle. Ordinary people cared very little for such things, and writers did not even bother to record them. Enormous gaps in our knowledge of the political facts of India's history result. But then, politics and war, however complicated and full of sudden reversals and surprises, had little importance for most Indians.

In matters of culture, the caste organization of Indian society allowed very primitive ideas and magical practices to survive indefinitely. Any sort of ancestral religion (so far, at least, as it did not interfere with the lives of other groups of people) could be kept going generation after generation. Ideas and movements among an educated few had no particular impact on cult practices conducted within the privacy of the home, or in the semiprivacy of some humble caste gathering. On the other hand, these ideas and practices were always at hand, ready to be made use of by the educated classes if it suited their purposes to fall back on primitive magic.

For society as a whole, the division into castes meant a certain rigidity. The caste structure reinforced the normal human habit of sticking to familiar and well-tried ways of doing things. If a person were born to be a garbage collector, it was hard for him to do anything but collect garbage; and that put a limit on social mobility. Other civilized societies, however, were not really very different, for in the Middle East, Greece, and China nearly everyone also did what he or she was born to do. Still, Indian castes, and the religious theory that went with them, made changes in an individual's social position that much more difficult.

On the other hand, caste had positive values. First and foremost, it gave every person a definite group with which to identify. What the synagogue was for Jews living amid strangers, the caste was for any Indian who found himself also living among strangers, or, if not with strangers, at least with people whose habits and customs were very different from his own. In addition, the theory of reincarnation and of caste solved the problem of inequality in society more effectively than other doctrines were able to do. By doing what one was supposed to do, and staying in one's caste position, promotion in a future life could be counted on. The Assyrian kings had used the same sort of reward to create a body of loyal and efficient officers for their army.

It worked for the Assyrians, as it has for other armies that have tried the system since, and the prospect of promotion up a strictly graded scale of ranks in society worked with the same force among the Indian population as a whole. Taking reincarnation for granted, as something too obvious to be doubted, what else could a person do but conform to whatever local custom and caste rules prescribe in hope of future promotion?

On the negative side was the fact that caste weakened the military effectiveness of Indian society. States could not mobilize the emotions and loyalties of their subjects as Greek cities or even Middle Eastern empires could. India was, therefore, easily and repeatedly conquered by one wave of invaders after another. But as long as the invaders came as barbarians, they soon accepted Indian civilization and simply faded into the Indian social structure as one more caste.

Thus we can say that caste was India's master institution and molded Indian society the way bureaucratic empire molded Middle Eastern society and the way the polis molded Greek society.

Transcendental Religion

Emphasis upon a realm of reality behind or beyond the world of our senses became characteristic of Indian religions. This is called transcendentalism because it *transcends*—that is, goes beyond—what ordinary people experience. Sights and sounds and all the everyday contacts we have with one another and with ordinary things make up the world of the senses, of appearances, of material things—in short, make up the usual, common, average world people live in. But Indian sages all agreed that this world was an illusion; reality was something else—spiritual, pure, perfect, hidden. How could they reach such a conclusion? What can be real, except experience?

The answer is that people do sometimes have unusual and extraordinary experiences—trances, dreams, ecstasies. Indian holy men came to treasure such experiences and learned how to bring them on by various kinds of bodily exercises. One easy way to have such experiences is to take various drugs, but the Indians did not do this very much. Instead, they held back their breathing until the oxygen supply in the blood stream got very low, and sometimes they also starved themselves or went thirsty for long periods of time. Such bodily rigors produced visions and other extraordinary experiences, as of course drugs can also do.

These experiences aroused intense emotions and seemed to open the door upon a far more significant world than the world of everyday. Visions, in short, revealed a new level of reality—a spiritual truth—that lay behind and above ordinary experiences, or so many millions of Indians, as well as Christians, Moslems, and Buddhists of later ages, came to believe.

The bodily discipline that leads to such visions is called asceticism. The visionary experience itself is often called mystical, and those who have such visions are referred to as mystics.

We Americans may find it hard to take asceticism and mysticism seriously. It is all too easy to mock what other people hold dear simply because our own habits, values, and institutions make little room for such behavior or experience. The real task, though, is to try to understand the many different ways in which human beings have tried to cope with the world around them. Anyone who does so will soon realize that, however strange it may seem at first sight, Indian transcendentalism was and remains a very attractive way of looking at the world.

Transcendental Religion and Caste

As might be expected, caste and transcendental religion tended to support one another. Since religion taught that everyday things were mere illusion, the pursuit of wealth, power, fame, and

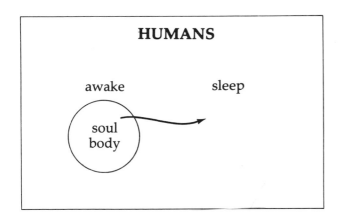

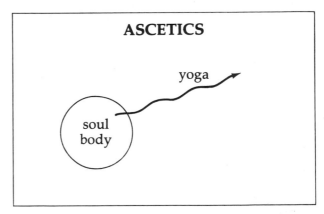

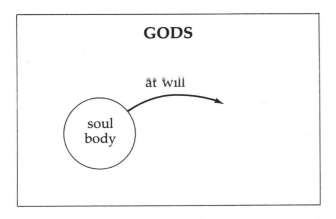

Body and Soul in Ancient India These diagrams suggest the way ancient Indians thought about the relationship between body and soul. The first diagram shows how human souls are firmly tied to the body while awake but can wander away in sleep. That explained how a person could see things in dreams far away and long ago while the body stayed behind and slept. The lower diagram shows how gods were supposed to be able to move their souls in or out of a body—often appearing in different bodies at different times—all just as they pleased. The third diagram shows how ascetics, by their special training or yoga, could also, like a god, separate soul from body deliberately by attaining a mystic state of consciousness.

glory was obviously silly as well as futile. This did not mean that some Indians did not struggle for such things. But most Indians agreed that those who did so were less wise, good, and noble than the poor ascetics who withdrew from ordinary society in order to pursue holiness and religious truth. Such attitudes tended to weaken military and political efforts, just as caste did.

In addition, the doctrine of reincarnation that justified caste distinctions fitted in well with transcendentalism. The realm of spiritual reality, approached through mystical visions, was the same as the world inhabited by souls when they were not tied to a particular body—for the mystic's soul, too, apparently left his body at the moment of visionary ecstasy. Thus, an overarching world view could and did arise that made everyday life seem trifling and unimportant when compared to the spiritual world that was inhabited by souls, some of which were pure and free of material entanglements, and some of which were tied temporarily and, so to speak, by accident, to a particular body living in the material world of mere appearances.

How Transcendentalism Developed

Indian religion did not arrive at its distinctive transcendentalism all at once. The Aryan invasion of India brought a kind of religion into the country that had little or nothing in common with the religions of the peoples already there. Aryan gods were like those of other Indo-European peoples. Sun, air, sky, thunder, flame, and other natural forces were vaguely personified. Worship took place out of doors, at specially prepared places. But these altars, as befitted the life of a nomadic people, were abandoned after a single use and so could not easily become temples. Religious rituals centered around the slaughter of animals, as an offering to the gods, and the drinking of an intoxicant called soma, made from the juice of a plant which cannot be identified today. Priests prepared the sacrifice, and by voice and gesture they called upon the gods to accept the offering.

These statements are based upon the hymns of the *Rig-Veda* and the three other Vedas. The four books of the Vedas were gathered together in their present form by priests, who recited the Vedic hymns while preparing the altar and conducting the sacrifice. What purpose the Vedic poems may have served when first composed is unclear. Some of the surviving texts seem to have little or no connection with the ritual of sacrifice for which they were, nevertheless, used. How old the hymns may be is likewise unknown. Some may descend from the age of invasion itself.

Pre-Aryan Religion

About the other main element in Indian religion we are far less informed. The religious ideas of the Indus civilization are simply unknown. The fact that two or three seal engravings from Indus sites closely resemble the great god Shiva of later Hinduism certainly suggests continuities between the Indus cult and later Hinduism. Such continuity is entirely probable because villages continued to exist after the overthrow of Harappa and Mohenjo-Daro, where worship of the old gods could continue. It is tempting to believe that the Indus priests claimed very great magical power—power, in fact, to create and sustain the world anew each time they made sacrifice. It is tempting also to suppose that mystic visions were important to the pre-Aryan religion of India. But in truth we do not know. When these traits crop up later in Indian religious practice, they may have been fresh inventions rather than reaffirmation of pre-Aryan ideas and customs.

Very likely the sharp departure from Vedic ideas, which shows up in later Indian religious texts, gathered headway when the Aryans abandoned their nomadic, warlike ways and became settled farmers.

Radical transformations were forwarded by special schools of religious learning. These were founded to pass on the sacred tradition from one generation of priests to another. Unless the right words were said at the right time, and the right gestures performed when the ritual of sacrifice called for them, the gods might be displeased and the whole ceremony fail. Worse than that, a badly performed sacrifice might anger the gods. It became, therefore, a matter of the utmost importance to have priests who knew exactly what to do and what words to say. This required taking instruction from a master who had committed the sacred texts to memory, letter-perfect.

It is not known when this sort of school system arose, but when it did the Vedas soon took a fixed form. Teachers who had mastered the exact pronunciation of old and unfamiliar words insisted that accuracy of that kind was the only way to please the gods. This, in turn, soon made systematic study of the sacred language—Sanskrit—necessary, since everyday speech continued to alter, so that the meaning of old words and grammatical forms ceased to be obvious. But the priests of India relied entirely upon oral memory for transmitting and preserving Sanskrit literature and learning. The gods did not want to be read to; the sacred words had to be memorized instead.

This bias against writing slowed the development of written texts. Even after writing became an everyday matter in government administration, books were not used for religious purposes. The school system was built around memorization, and anything else was judged inferior, second-rate, not worth serious attention. This, incidentally, meant that nearly all forms of literature had to be put into verse to facilitate memorization and to remind anyone reciting the work of what came next.

Mastery of Sanskrit grammar was not enough to make the sacred Vedic texts meaningful, particularly when verses that must have been composed for other purposes were recited as an accompaniment to the sacrifices. Some secret, inner meaning had to be extracted before such procedures made sense. This led learned priests and their pupils to invent explanations so as to get to the "real" meanings of old verses. These explanations were extremely fanciful and seem quite unconvincing to us. On the other hand, they allowed the priests to develop their own religious ideas freely by discarding the obvious, superficial meaning of the Vedas and treating their words as symbols or hints of a deeper meaning that only the expert and educated could understand.

The Brahmanas   The texts in which such ideas were elaborated are called Brahmanas. The general drift of the Brahmanas was to exalt the power of the priests. The importance of the gods faded. In fact, the old gods of the Vedas became little more than puppets. If the sacrifice were performed in exactly the right way, the god to whom it was offered had no choice but to grant long life, abundant cattle, or whatever else the priest had asked for on behalf of the person who paid for the sacrifice. In its extreme form, the doctrine of the Brahmanas stated that priests created the world and the gods afresh each time they performed sacrifice. Everything, in short, depended on them and their ability to make the sacrifice in exactly the right way. An ungenerous patron, who grudged paying the priests their full fee, might find that the priests turned a blessing into a curse simply by slipping a word or two into the ritual in the wrong way.

Asceticism   Not everyone in India was satisfied with this sort of priest-ridden religion. A handful of ascetics fled from human company into the forest and there sought escape from the pains and frustrations of ordinary life. Such persons often had little to eat, and they developed various bodily disciplines aimed at reducing all appetites to a minimum—or, ideally, extinguishing them entirely. Remarkable things can be achieved in this way. Ascetics have been able, for example, to control heartbeat and breathing and other "automatic" bodily processes, slowing them down until they almost come to a stop.

The basic idea behind Indian asceticism was that the body and its needs were bad, or at least troublesome, and interfered with the pursuit of truth, joy and beauty. These supreme values the ascetics discovered through mystic trances, when for varying periods of time they entered into rapturous communion with another, infinitely superior, reality. After a while, however, the rapture always faded and the mystic returned to the ordinary world of sense.

Mystics and holy men in India were much admired, so that groups of disciples often formed around a particularly holy man, even if he lived far away in the forest. Such disciples, of course, tried to imitate their master and hoped above all to learn from him how to achieve the mystic vision. Thus, the relationship was not unlike the relationship between master and pupil in the Vedic schools where priests acquired their sacred knowledge. Before long, the words of especially holy men also seemed worth learning by heart. Experiences and insights gained from a lifetime of asceticism could be put into literary form and memorized by admiring followers. In this way another body of literature, known as the Upanishads, came into existence.

The Upanishads   The Upanishads, as one would expect from their origin, had no use for priests and rituals and ceremonies. They thus contrast sharply with the Brahmanas, though the two may have been composed at more or less the same time. The central teaching of the Upanishads is expressed in the phrase "That art Thou." What this means is difficult to express in English, since our words do not carry the meanings of the Sanskrit very exactly. But, roughly, what was meant is this: Each human soul ("Thou") is really part of a universal Spirit ("That"). Spirit is the only true reality. Matter and the body are illusions that hide the facts from ordinary individuals. By learning how to subdue the body and thus free the soul, mystic union with the universal Spirit can be achieved. Those who have succeeded in entering into such a union can then come back and tell others about it; and this is what the Upanishads set out to do.

Once the mystics had established the meaning of their strange experiences by interpreting them along these lines, it was a matter of simple logic to extend their views to cover human life as a whole. No longer was it a good thing to try to secure the gift of wealth or long life from the gods—as the Vedas had assumed. Rather, the proper religious goal was to escape from life and allow one's soul to return to the great universal Spirit from which it had come.

The doctrine of rebirth and karma fitted into this framework very easily. A person could now hope to rise so high in the scale of being as to shed the burden of karma altogether. In such

a case a soul would no longer have to be reincarnated but might rejoin the universal Spirit, safely disentangled from connection with any sort of body, thus escaping all the pains and discomforts of life in the material world.

Eternal bliss, therefore, came to be thought of as an escape from selfhood. It might require many incarnations before a person could rise to such heights. The wicked might even slip downward in successive reincarnations and get farther from the ultimate goal of release from the pains of bodily existence. But the wise and good knew what to aim for, and knew how to get there faster—by imitating the ascetic practices and mystic trances of holy men.

Brahman priests soon agreed that this ideal was fitting for old age. Earlier in life, however, family duties and the rituals of sacrifice and purification had to be attended to. Such a compromise made a good deal of sense in a poverty-stricken peasant society, where those too old and infirm to do their share of the work could become a heavy burden on the family. By going off into the forest and seeking holiness and release, such persons could hasten their time of death and relieve their relatives of the burden of feeding and caring for them. They could also die in hope of a more blessed future—whether reincarnated, or, perchance, escaping reincarnation and the pains of life entirely. Eventually, these ideas were combined with Vedic rituals and with new ideas of personal devotion to a particular god to create the religion of Hinduism.

Buddhism   In the long run, this compromise prevailed in India, but it took many centuries for Hinduism to come clearly into focus, even though its elements were mostly present in India by 500 B.C.E. One reason for the gradualness with which Hinduism emerged was that another faith, Buddhism, came into existence in India just before 500 B.C.E. and seemed, for several centuries, to be destined to dominate India as well as most of the rest of Asia.

Buddhism arose because not everyone was willing to settle for a life divided between a period of ordinary activity and a period of ascetic withdrawal, as the Brahman priests recommended. There were young people who found the conditions of their everyday life so utterly

BUDDHA'S YOUTH

Siddhartha Gautama was born a prince, son of a king of the Sakya, close to Kapila. Kapila was located in the foothills of the Himalaya Mountains, between what is now the eastern end of Nepal and Sikkim. According to Buddhist legends, the young prince was very carefully raised. Servants supplied his every want, and since he had good health and was handsome and strong, he escaped all suffering. In due season he married a beautiful wife and began to look forward to becoming a king and father himself.

Then one day the young prince sallied forth from the palace gates and for the first time encountered the world of ordinary people. What he saw distressed him deeply. Other people did not enjoy the luxuries to which he had been accustomed. Many were sick and hungry. Animals and plants, too, suffered many injuries. Indeed, to live at all, people had to kill everything they ate; and even when they had killed enough to satisfy their hunger, they often went further, killing wantonly and even hurting and slaughtering one another. Suffering, in short, appeared to be the price of life. Being compassionate by nature, after such a revelation Prince Gautama could no longer enjoy his comfort as before. His knowledge of the world's suffering spoiled his joys. He was caught up in the pain of the world, whether he wanted to share in it or not.

As a result, the prince soon decided to abandon his former life. He left his wife, parents, and all the court behind, resolved to conquer suffering and free all living things from the pain of existence. He tried asceticism, but he found that punishing his body did not destroy pain but merely increased it. He lived as a wanderer, depending on others' gifts for his daily food. Then one day, sitting in meditation under a Bo Tree at Buddh Gaya (in northeastern India), he suddenly experienced Enlightenment and became Buddha— that is, the Enlightened One. As Buddha he saw and followed the Noble Eightfold Path and taught others how to overcome suffering by doing so too.

unsatisfactory that they wished escape right away. One such person was Prince Gautama, the Buddha. (*Buddha* is a title and means the "Enlightened One.") The Buddha was born well before 500 B.C.E. and probably died about 485 B.C.E.

Guatama's personality and the power of his example may account for the impact his teaching came to have. He had at least one mystic experience—the Enlightenment, as Buddhists call it. Sitting under a tree one day, he entered into a trance and saw in a flash all the fundamental truths of religion. Buddha's vision aimed at the same goal as the Upanishads: personal annihilation and escape from all the suffering due to in-

carnation. This was to be achieved by following the Noble Eightfold Path: Right Views, Right Aspirations, Right Speech, Right Conduct, Right Livelihood, Right Effort, Right Mindedness, and Right Rapture.

All schools of Buddhist thought agree upon these formulas, but difficulties multiply when we try to spell out what each heading means. Presumably, what Buddha meant by these phrases was the sort of life he led himself. As followers gathered around him, they asked his opinions about how they should behave, and he settled such questions as they came up, in a common-sense sort of fashion. By degrees, a set of rules for the good life emerged from such decisions—

but they applied only to those who took the pursuit of holiness very seriously and sought escape to Nirvana—as the Buddhists called the state of self-annihilation. Buddha's rules, therefore, applied only to religious devotees who wished to develop their spiritual power at the expense of everything else. We commonly call such persons monks, although the term is, of course, Christian, and the organization and rules to which Buddhist monks submit are quite different in detail from those that bind Christian monks.

Buddhist monks, for example, do not usually take definite vows, and there is no single head or ruler of a Buddhist community. For particular purposes one of the monks may, indeed, take special responsibility, but each man is supposed to be his own master and to regulate his activity according to his own will and judgment.

In Buddha's lifetime he had such prestige that everyone deferred to him in matters of importance. New members were admitted after an informal conversation designed to test their sincerity and purpose. Every so often the monks gathered to speak to one another about their spiritual experiences and to confess personal shortcomings.

Such an informal style of common life, with emphasis upon equality among all the members, may have been modeled on the aristocratic tribal community that Buddha had known in his youth. If so, one of the secrets of Buddha's success may have been that his community of monks preserved, in a new context, the personal freedom and independence which was becoming harder and harder to maintain in an age when great bureaucratic kingdoms like Magadha were growing more powerful every day.

Gautama Buddha, Savior   As Buddhism developed, the founder became a savior for the faithful, but artists had a difficult problem portraying a being that had entered Nirvana by escaping attachment to self and all the suffering that selfhood brought in its train. One solution shows adoring disciples surrounding Buddha's vacant seat, leaving behind only the wheel of the law and the imprint of his sandals on the footstool. But portraying a savior as mere emptiness was not very satisfying, and other Buddhist artists therefore adopted the practice of portraying Buddha in the way the Greeks portrayed their gods. This solution is shown on the right, where disciples are again bowing in reverence before the (headless) figure of Gautama Buddha, who stands taller than they, dressed like a Greek god.

For this reason, perhaps, and also because the daily round of religious life as Buddha outlined it had its own appeal, the company of followers who had gathered around him during his lifetime did not dissolve when Gautama died. Instead, the community continued to gather new members, and offshoots soon spread to other parts of India. As a result, about 200 years after Buddha's death, it looked as though India would become a Buddhist country.

As communities of monks separated, their interpretation of Buddha's words and doctrines diverged, and new emphases crept in. The enormous doctrinal variation that exists among Buddhists today may therefore have begun quite early. What kept the movement together and gave it consistency was the rule of life and community organization that Buddha had laid down. Monastic communities always remained the organizational form of Buddhism. Here, more than in details of doctrine, lay the secret of its success.

But here also lay the great defect of Buddhism. It was not a religion for all occasions, even though ordinary persons soon began to find a role for themselves, giving food and other gifts to the monks and making pilgrimages to places where the ashes of a great saint had been preserved or where some sacred event, such as Buddha's Enlightenment, had occurred. This was satisfactory to all concerned; what was not satisfactory was the lack of Buddhist rites and ceremonies with which to celebrate the ordinary crises of human life: birth, marriage, death. For these the Indian householder had to rely on Brahman priests. As a result, India could never become an entirely Buddhist land. The Brahmans with their Vedic learning continued to have a necessary place in everyday life, and they kept their schools alive, in competition with Buddhist monasteries and with other, more extreme ascetic communities.

There was room in India for all. Any religious group that made special demands on its members could fit into the caste system by being treated like another caste. From the point of view of other Indians, Buddhist communities of monks were exactly that: honored for their holiness, perhaps, or feared for their magical powers, but in other respects a group apart, and treated for all practical purposes like another caste.

And just as separate castes adjusted their habits and customs to fit one with another, so also the Brahman priests, the Buddhist monks, and the ascetics of the forest retreats borrowed

Buddhist Monument When Buddhists wanted to find public expression for their faith, they hit upon the practice of building monumental structures called *stupas* to house a portion of the ashes of Gautama Buddha and some of his especially holy followers. This photograph shows such a stupa from central India. It is in disrepair because Buddhism eventually faded away from the land of its birth, leaving no one to maintain the stupas. But when Buddhism was still flourishing in India, ordinary folk used to make pilgrimages to this place, walk around it in solemn ceremonies, and then return home with a feeling of satisfaction at having come to so holy a place.

from one another and adjusted their ways to one another. They adjusted not by any plan or design but bit by bit, as a result of on-the-spot encounters. Before long Brahmans also accepted the otherworldly goals of religion which Buddhists and ascetics proclaimed. All varieties of Indian religion thus became transcendental. Sacrifices and rituals were reinterpreted as devices to help souls on their way toward release from the round of rebirths. The old, practical, material rewards for piety were played down. Religious attention was shifted away from this world. Every kind of holy man, priest, and ritual expert agreed that the proper thing to work for was escape from it all.

Conclusion

When Indian religions came to agreement on this point, soon after 500 B.C.E., one of the characteristic aspects of all later Indian civilization came fully into focus. More than any other part of the world, India has ever since remained the home of spirituality and transcendental aspirations.

Yet this side of Indian life constitutes only half the story. Side by side with playing down the values of the senses and of material goods, there was a luxurious, indulgent court life, which did not get praised in books and about which we know very little. Artisan skills and administrative skills also achieved high development. Many Indians cared very much about this world, and some of them explored the extremes of sense indulgence with almost as much energy as ascetics explored the extremes of self-denial.

It is perhaps true that the two extremes tended to support one another. That is, ascetics and sensualists may have existed partly in reaction to one another. Whether this is true or not, the sensuality of Indian life made a smaller impression on strangers from other civilizations than the ascetic, transcendental extreme did. In this sense—and because it was the religious tradition, not the courtly one, that entered the literary record that has come down to us—we are justified, perhaps, in taking it as the primary, most distinctive, and characteristic aspect of Indian civilization.

By 500 B.C.E., when Buddha was in mid-career, the special qualities of Indian civilization had become clear. At the same time another great teacher of humankind, Confucius, was active in China. We must turn our attention to that part of the world in the next chapter, to see how still a fourth civilization, comparable to those we have studied already, came into existence in the valley of the Yellow River.

Bibliography

Ancient Indian writings often make difficult reading for us because we lack the appropriate background, but careful editing can diminish this obstacle by explaining obscurities. The oldest and holiest Sanskrit text may best be approached through Wendy D. O'Flaherty, ed. and trans., *The Rig Veda* (1981); and the first part of India's great epic has been translated and edited by J A. B. Van Buitenen, *The Mahabharata* (1973). India's other epic is available in Robert P. Goldman, ed. and trans., *The Ramayana of Valmiki* (3 vols. 1984–1991). Similarly, R. E. Hume, *The Thirteen Principal Upanishads* (2nd ed., 1931), and S. Radhakrishnan, trans., *The Bagavadgita* (1948), allow a firsthand approach to Indian transcendentalism. Ainslee T. Embree and Stephen N. Hay, eds., *Sources of Indian Tradition* (2 vols., 2nd ed., 1988), provide a carefully edited sampling of other texts.

An excellent general introduction to Indian civilization is Arthur L. Basham, *The Wonder That Was India* (rev. ed., 1985), while D. D. Kosambi and Romila Thapar, *A History of India*, I (1966), offer a fine distillation of Indian historical scholarship. J. H. Hutton, *Caste in India: Its Nature, Function and Origins* (1946), provides an instructive account of this master institution. N. R. Banerjee, *The Iron Age in India* (1965), explains advances in technology; while R. S. Sharma, *Aspects of Political Ideas and Institutions in Ancient India* (2nd ed., 1968), and Charles Drekmeier, *Kingship and Community in Early India* (1962), discuss the comparative fragility of Indian political institutions Narendra Wagle, *Society in the Time of the Buddha* (1966), embarks on social history with the help of Buddhist sources.

Indian religions have long been the center of attention for Western scholars. An impressive monument to this investigation is Charles Eliot, *Hinduism and Buddhism: An Historical Sketch* (3 vols., 1921). This and two other old books, T. W. Rhys Davids, *Buddhist India* (1903), and Arthur B. Keith, *A History of Sanscrit Literature* (1928), remain among the best scholarly books available on their subjects. More recent books include Arun Shourie, *Hinduism, Essence and Consequence: A Study of the Upanishads, the Gita and the Brahma Sutras* (1980); David R. Kinsley, *Hinduism, a Cultural Perspective* (1982); Etienne Lamotte, *History of Indian Buddhism* (1988); William R. Lafleur, *Buddhism: A Cultural Perspective* (1968); and Mircea Eliade, *Yoga: Immortality and Freedom* (2nd ed., 1969).

For ancient Indian art, Herman Goetz, *The Art of India* (2nd ed., 1964), and Benjamin Rowland, *Art and Architecture of India* (3rd ed., 1967), are standard. Another work is Heinrich Zimmer, *The Art of Indian Asia* (2 vols., 1955).

Music and dance were important features of ancient Indian religion and everyday life, but left few tangible traces behind. Herbert A. Popley, *The Music of India* (3rd ed., 1970), sketches what is known about the past and explores the living tradition of Indian music. A more technical work is Swami Prajnananda, *A History of Indian Music*, Vol. I (1963).

The Chinese Style of Civilization

to 200 B.C.E.

7

Chinese Imperial Dragon   Sacred and secular authority blended together in ancient China and were never separated. This union is symbolized by the fact that a supernatural beast, the dragon, here shown cast in bronze, remained the image of imperial power throughout China's long history, until 1911 C.E.

Chinese civilization began in the region where the Yellow River (Chinese name: Hwang Ho) breaks through the last range of hills and starts across its floodplain toward the sea. Upriver lies a semidesert, known as Inner Mongolia, beyond which rise the snow-capped peaks where the river begins. The Yellow River can be considered the easternmost and largest of a series of streams that flow northward from the high mountains of central Asia. Most of these streams quickly peter out in the desert lands that lie at the foot of the mountain ranges. But before each stream dies in the desert sands, it creates an oasis, large or small, where irrigation farming can be successfully carried on. Stronger streams form interior seas, of which the Aral Sea and Lake Balkhash are the most extensive. Only the Yellow River breaks through to the ocean.

The Landscape of China

The greater size and power of the Yellow River arise in part from the fact that its middle and lower course carry it through the northern fringes of the area of monsoon rains. In this part of the world rainfall is irregular. Often it comes in sudden, heavy downpours, but there are seasons when the rains are weak or fail to come at all. Just before reaching the floodplain, the Yellow River passes through a special kind of soil, called loess. This soil is made of finely powdered dust, deposited during the Ice Age by winds blowing from desert lands farther north. Loess, which also exists in smaller deposits elsewhere in the world, is a very fertile and easily worked soil, but liable to erosion. The Yellow River, in fact, gets its name because it carries such a heavy load of silt, picked up as it passes through the loess region.

On reaching the flat floodplain, the river's load of silt sinks to the bottom, with the result that the riverbed builds up until, from time to time, the whole stream shifts its course, just as the Euphrates River does. The waters from the melting snow of distant central Asian peaks sometimes reach the lower part of the river's length just as the first rains of the monsoon ar-

rive. Disastrous floods result. The Yellow River thus deserves its nickname, "China's Sorrow." But it was also China's cradle, and learning how to farm successfully in so uncertain a climate shaped Chinese society fundamentally. People who could tame the Yellow River found other river valleys to the south comparatively easy to manage, thanks to the habits of hard work that were necessary to overcome the difficulties of farming in a region where flood and drought were both frequent visitors.

When Chinese settlers began to move southward into the valley of China's other great river, the Yangtze, geographic differences made farming much less risky. The waters of the Yangtze are cleared by passing through lakes that lie immediately below the famous gorge. Consequently, the lower portion of the river carries very little silt and does not usually flood. The Yangtze Valley also receives regular rainfall from the monsoons, so drought, too, is seldom a problem. In its natural state, the Yangtze Valley was heavily wooded. The floodplains must have been very wet. Still farther south, the Chinese landscape becomes hilly and mountainous. Since they are well watered, the slopes of south China were covered with dense jungle growth before being cleared by human hands.

The Chinese Style of Farming

Archaeological work in China is still exploratory. For all practical purposes, nothing is known about the root and rice cultivators who must have been living along the riverbanks of south and central China by 2400 B.C.E. when rice was already a crop of some importance in the middle reaches of the Yellow River. But rice, which had to be grown in shallow freshwater ponds or swampy land flooded in spring by the river, was not what the early farmers of the Yellow River valley depended on. Their basic crop was millet, grown on loess soil without irrigation. In addition, they cultivated wheat and barley, the staple crops of western Asia. It looks, therefore, as through the Neolithic cultivators of northern China combined crops and techniques of farming that had originated far to the west (wheat and barley) with other crops and very different farming methods unique to China (millet and perhaps rice).

A fundamental difference between civilized society in the Middle East, Europe, and India, on the one hand, and China, on the other, arises from the fact that the use of the plow did not reach China until after a mature Chinese style of civilization had come into existence. The first definite records of the use of plows in China come very late indeed—after 400 B.C.E. Even if the plow was used somewhat earlier than that, which is possible, it never came to have the same importance for Chinese agriculture that it had in most other parts of Eurasia. A Chinese peasant, even today, can get on, if he must, without use of animal power. Some farms are so small that the owners do all the work themselves. Chinese farming, therefore, was, and is, akin to gardening; it depends on an enormous output of human labor and only secondarily upon animal power. By contrast, farming among the civilized peoples of the Middle East, Europe, and India depended on the plow, and on the exploitation of animal power, to allow farmers to cultivate enough land to support the various specialists upon whose skills civilization depended.

It is easy to see why the plow failed to reach China quickly. In the small, crowded oases that lay between the Middle East and the Yellow River valley, fertile land was limited in extent. Pioneer hoe-and-spade farmers had plenty of time to occupy all the available fertile land before they had ever heard of the plow. Once they had done so, they had absolutely no reason to start keeping big hungry animals, whose food could only be produced at the expense of food for humans. Hence plow agriculture could not easily spread across the oases of central Asia that lay between ancient China and the Middle East, where the plow was invented.

But how was it possible for the Chinese to create a civilization without the extra food production per capita that the plow permitted? For one thing, loess soil is unusually soft and easily dug. Therefore a hard-working peasant and his family could cultivate more square yards in the Yellow River valley than elsewhere. The loess soil was also unusually fertile when it got enough rain.

Another factor may also have been important. Because of the special geographical characteristics of the loess region of the Yellow River valley, early Chinese farmers may have been more easily taxed than farmers in most other regions. When farming first began in the Yellow River loess region, ground suitable for cultivation was quite limited in extent. Desert lay to the north and west, while the river floodplain was too wet to cultivate without first building elaborate drainage ditches. In between lay slopes and patches of well-drained loess soil, with enough rainfall, in most years, to raise a crop. Deeply eroded valleys separated one such area from another. Thus river swamps or slopes too steep to cultivate broke the landscape up into a series of "islands" of good farmland.

The farmers who established themselves on such islands found it difficult to disappear when tax collectors came around. There was no place to go, no vast forest as in Europe and India, where a new clearing could be made with only a few weeks' work. It took many years of labor to dike and drain the waters of the Yellow River so that fields could begin to creep out into the flat floodplain itself. In time this vast task was carried through, so that a great carpet of fields engulfed the separate islands of loess cultivation where Chinese agriculture began. But this enormous engineering enterprise was organized by rulers and officials, though the work itself fell, of course, upon the peasant farmers.

A garden style of cultivation, demanding intensive human labor, gave an enduring stamp to Chinese civilization. During most historic ages the occupation of new territory by Chinese peasants was slow because a great deal of labor had to be expended to tame new landscapes. But the human mass that was needed and could be sustained by the Chinese type of agriculture also meant that, when Chinese settlers moved into a new region, they—quite literally—dug themselves deeply into the landscape and utterly transformed earlier patterns of land use.

Chinese farmers have, in fact, moved across east Asia like a great glacier, beginning in a small way in the special environment of the loess regions of the Yellow River valley, about 2400 B.C.E., and spreading slowly but irresistibly

Topography of Central and East Asia

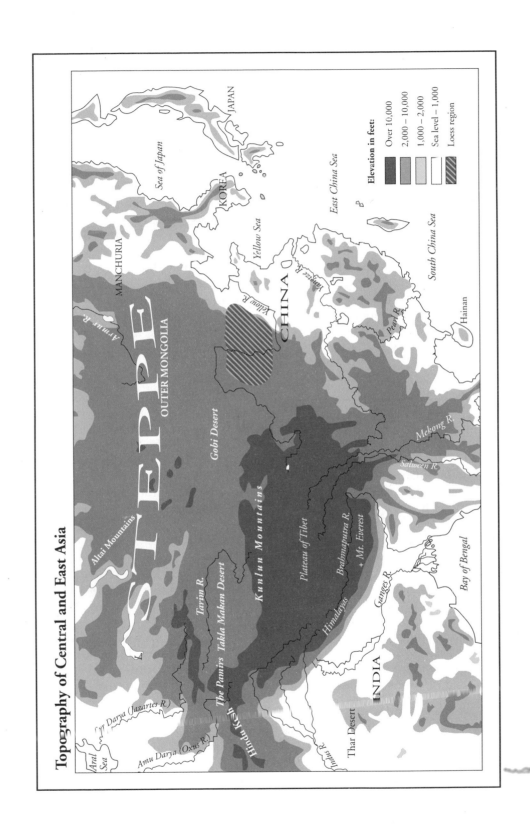

Elevation in feet:
Over 10,000
2,000 – 10,000
1,000 – 2,000
Sea level – 1,000
Loess region

JAPAN

Sea of Japan

MANCHURIA

KOREA

Yellow Sea

East China Sea

CHINA

South China Sea

Hainan

Pearl R.

Yangtze

Amur R.

OUTER MONGOLIA

Gobi Desert

Mekong R.

Salween R.

Altai Mountains

STEPPE

Yellow R.

Kunlun Mountains

Plateau of Tibet

Brahmaputra R.

+ Mt. Everest

Himalayas

Tarim R.

Takla Makan Desert

The Pamirs

Hindu Kush

Syr Darya (Jaxartes R.)

Amu Darya (Oxus R.)

Aral Sea

Indus R.

Thar Desert

INDIA

Ganges R.

Bay of Bengal

eastward, southward, and, in recent times, also northward into Manchuria. Throughout this vast expansion, Chinese garden cultivators took possession of the land in a far more intimate sense than farmers with plows ever did. Each valley and hillside they brought under cultivation required the use of human muscles to make the land over, yard by yard and foot by painful foot.

Enormous population density was one result. Relatively small surpluses from single families could become quite impressive when the number of families to be taxed was totaled. A civilization of a massive and extraordinarily stable character could and did arise on the basis of such surpluses. And at the bottom of the social scale, China's peasant farmers developed a capacity for work that no people dependent on animal power has ever equaled.

Empire and Family in Ancient China

Our knowledge of ancient China depends largely on written histories. Unlike the Indians, the early Chinese valued history and compiled lengthy and elaborate records of past events. These records were arranged according to reigns and dynasties, and it is still customary to divide Chinese history along these lines, even when, as sometimes happened, the change from one ruling family or dynasty to another was not particularly significant.

One result of studying Chinese history in this way is to concentrate attention on court life and administration. Fundamental changes in the provinces, or gradual transformation of the structure of Chinese society as a whole, are often difficult to detect from the traditional Chinese dynastic histories. Nevertheless, these accounts at least define China's political past. From as early as 841 B.C.E. dates for emperors' reigns seem amazingly accurate, according to all the tests modern scholars can apply. Nothing remotely similar exists for Greece or the Middle

East, much less for India, and we owe the scholars and historians of ancient China a great deal for keeping court records so carefully.

The Ruling Chinese Dynasties

According to the written tradition, China was first ruled by five Heavenly Emperors, who discovered or invented most of the useful arts. This story presumably, was invented to explain the beginnings of civilized life. Subsequently, the merely human rulers of the Hsia dynasty were succeeded by the Shang, who ruled from 1523 to 1028 B.C.E. Archaeologists have been unable to identify a capital city for the Hsia, but certain large Neolithic villages, distinguished by rather fine black pottery and stout earthen walls, may have flourished under that half-mythical dynasty.

When we come to the Shang dynasty, archaeology becomes far more helpful. Their third and last capital, Anyang, was located and excavated in the late 1920s. The city of Anyang was the capital of the Shang Empire from about 1300 B.C.E. to the end of the dynasty (1028 B.C.E.). It was laid out on a rectangular pattern, with entry gates in the middle of each side and two main streets that crossed in the center. This is the same pattern that charioteers in the Middle East used for their encampments. The Shang capital also had other characteristics that associate it with Middle Eastern charioteers: horses and chariots, bronze weapons, and a short reinforced bow suited for use in the cramped space of a chariot.

It therefore looks as though men who had somehow mastered the skills of chariot warfare overran China and founded the Shang dynasty. One difficulty with this theory is that no definite connecting links between the Middle East and China have been discovered. It is a long distance, to be sure, and if charioteers did in fact travel from oasis to oasis through central Asia, one would expect to find traces of their passage. On the other hand, only very hasty surveys have as yet been made of the oases of Central Asia. Further digging is needed to reveal what lies hid-

The Chariot in China This photograph shows how archaeologists unearthed a two-wheeled chariot and skeletons of the two horses that pulled it at Anyang, China in the 1920s. Chariots had been invented in the Middle East about four hundred years before this one was buried in the grave of a ruler of the Shang dynasty, so it is very likely that the techniques of chariot warfare spread eastward across Asia from the Middle East. How it happened is unknown, but we can guess that all across Asia rulers and warriors wanted battle-winning chariots very badly, and as soon as they heard of their effectiveness in war, they did everything they could to obtain them. Discovery of this chariot shows that Chinese civilization owed something to borrowings from the West and did not arise entirely in isolation from the more ancient centers of high skills in the Middle East.

den beneath the surface, before connecting links between China and western Asia can be expected to turn up.

Shang Writing Whatever connections with western Asia may have been, the civilization of Anyang was thoroughly Chinese. That is to say, styles of art and methods of writing, which continued to flourish in later Chinese times, were used by the Shang rulers of Anyang. Some Shang customs were later abandoned: human sacrifice, for example. The Chinese also gave up the Shang method of interrogating the spirits by heating a sheep's shoulder blade or a tortoise shell—on which questions had been written—until it cracked and then "reading" the cracks according to a special lore that gave yes or no answers to the questions. But Shang archaeological remains show a basic continuity with all subsequent Chinese culture. The amazing fact is that hundreds of cracked shoulder blades and tortoise shells were discovered at Anyang, with writing so like modern Chinese that scholars were able, without much difficulty, to read what ancient rulers of Anyang had asked the spirits.

Both modern Chinese and the ancient Anyang script are pictographic; that is, they are built upon hundreds of simplified little pictures. The pictures themselves, and the way several pictures may be put together to make a single "character," as each separate unit of the script is called, do not resemble any other known system

Oracle Bones from Anyang
Chinese rulers, worried about the future, would find what they needed to know by writing a question on a specially prepared bone or tortoise shell and then applying heat until it cracked. The path of the crack was interpreted as answering the question with a Yes or No. Many thousands of inscribed bones, like the one pictured here, were discovered at Anyang in the 1920s and, amazingly, the writing on them proved to be close enough to modern Chinese that scholars were able to read questions asked as much as 3400 years earlier such as "Will it rain?" or "Will barbarians attack?" No other literary tradition has so long a continuous history—proof of the remarkable continuity of Chinese civilization as a whole.

of writing. It must have been invented in China, perhaps by persons who had heard of the possibility of writing down words and sentences. The writing system discovered at Anyang was complete and could record any sentence or idea. No evidence of a gradual development, such as that which the Mesopotamians left behind, is known. But the archaeological record is so incomplete that we cannot be sure that Chinese writing was invented all at once, although it looks as though it might have been.

The discoveries at Anyang proved that the Yellow River valley had indeed become the site of a considerable empire by about 1300 B.C.E. The city was large and had special artisan quarters. Extraordinary skill was necessary to produce some of the objects found there. In particular, bronze pots, elaborately decorated with complex patterns, demonstrate a skill in bronze casting that has never been exceeded. Some of these pots, used for religious ceremonial, have shapes similar to earlier black pottery vessels. This suggests that there was some sort of religious continuity between the Hsia and Shang peoples, if, in fact, the Hsia are correctly identified with the black pottery sites archaeologists have discovered.

Shang Religion and Family Life   Reliable information about Shang religion comes to us only from the inscriptions used for interrogating the spirits. But the tortoise-shell and shoulder-blade inscriptions reveal only a fragment of the whole picture. Other practices and ideas simply escape our knowledge. From the inscriptions it is clear that the Shang peoples revered gods or spirits associated with various natural objects—hills, lakes, rivers and the like. Ancestral spirits also commanded much attention, for the ancient Chinese expected them to protect their descendants from natural disasters and barbarian raids.

The importance Shang rulers gave to ancestral spirits reflected the vitality of the family in Chinese life. Every society has some kind of family organization, of course; otherwise children could not survive. But Chinese families are unusual and seem to have exerted an enormous influence upon their members from very ancient times. A Chinese family is not just a group of parents and children. Instead, it extends to innumerable generations. The living are only a small part of a much larger and more powerful community; for the spirits of the ancestors instruct, reward, help, and protect their descendants as long as their descendants respect and honor them. Without the aid of the ancestors, nothing can be expected to go well; with their aid, however, comes prosperity and good fortune.

Among the living, too, Chinese families enforce a strict pattern of good manners and duties. Age carries prestige and demands deference; so does the male sex. Thus husbands are superior to wives; elder brothers to younger; and between cousins, careful rules have been worked out to define exact precedence, depending on the relative ages both of the children and of their parents. Proper patterns of deference and authority are clearly understood by everyone concerned. Youth obeys, age commands; and the psychological strain of having to do what one is told, when one is a child, is made up for later by the satisfactions that come with age and the right to command the respectful attention and obedience of those lower down in the family order.

Obviously, not all Chinese families conform to this pattern. Bad-tempered wives and disobedient sons existed in China, too. But the ideal was clear, and its force in molding the conduct of young and old was and is very great. Proof of this force can be observed among Chinese living outside of China in modern times. Family discipline and manners survive among most Chinese, even in the United States. Open rebellion against a father's authority is extremely rare. The old customs continue for generation after generation, sustained by family practice and tradition.

The question that cannot be answered is when and how this pattern of family life arose in China. Was it present from Shang or even pre-Shang times? Shang inscriptions that refer to spirits of the ancestors suggest such a possibility. On the other hand, the cult of the ancestors may have been limited to the upper classes. Peasants in historic times never lived in large households, as the wealthy generally did. Only the relatively well-to-do could afford time-consuming rituals of politeness that day after day reaffirmed family ties among an extended circle of relatives. In early times, perhaps only noble families were expected to have ancestors who mattered. We simply do not know.

The importance of the family was reinforced by the fact that there seems to have been no distinct class of priests in ancient China. On all ordinary occasions, the head of the family acted as his own priest and dealt with the spiritual world—ancestors in particular—by means of traditional rites and ceremonies he had learned from his own father and which he would, in due time, pass on to his eldest son. The ancient Chinese seem to have sought supernatural help and protection mainly through family channels, not, as in other civilized societies, outside them. This enormously increased the father's power, for his role as link between ancestral spirits and the living generation meant that any disobedience to him might result in the ill will of the entire spiritual world.

Their priestly duties made it almost necessary for heads of families to be able to write. The reason was that very early in their history, the Chinese decided that the best way to ask the ancestors questions was to write them a letter. As we have seen, in Shang times writing was done on tortoise shells and sheep shoulder blades. But this method was most likely reserved for royal or other high-ranking suppliants, since the supply of specially prepared bones and tortoise shells was not large enough to accommodate everyone. Later on, the usual method was to write out a question on a piece of paper and then burn it, thus "delivering" the letter to the spirit world by causing it to "die." Other perishable materials were probably used for writing such messages before the Chinese invented paper, but naturally nothing remains to show us how it was done.

Even today in China some heads of family cannot write, and in ancient times schooling was presumably much rarer. All the same, we know that as early as the Chou dynasty (1028–221 B.C.) the sons of the chief nobles of the empire went to school in the royal palace, where they learned archery, manners and ritual, and how to write. In this way they prepared themselves for their future roles as heads of families and vassals of the emperor.

Such a linkage between literacy, priestly functions, military leadership, and the headship of families was unique to China. Warriors who could write were rare in other civilized societies, until quite modern times. Warriors who were also priests and experts in the supernatural were difficult to find outside of China, and no other society ever developed a family system that required its heads to combine all of these roles as the Chinese pattern of family life did. This, more than anything else, shaped Chinese civilization from very early times almost to the present. The Chinese family, like caste in India and the polis in Greece, became a master institution.

Yet the available evidence does not really prove when or how the peculiar features of Chinese family organization came into existence. Unfortunately for historians, fundamental aspects of society are often taken so completely for granted that the persons who make records never bother to explain what everyone already knows. Yet despite gaps in the evidence, it seems probable that the family had an unusually wide range of functions in ancient China. If so, families must have shaped Chinese behavior more profoundly than families did in countries where religious and political affairs were carried on largely outside the frame of family life.

We can, perhaps, think of ancient Chinese society as a cluster of families, subordinated to the emperor who was himself, of course, the head of a family even larger and more important than that of any of his subjects because it embraced them all. In other words, family structure and the imperial structure were not really different. The emperor's relation to his subjects was like the relation of the family head to its living members. He was priest and father, leader, commander, protector—all of these at once. And just as everyone had a proper place within the family structure—above some and below others in rank and dignity—so also within the empire everyone had a proper place, and it was his or her duty to know what it was and then to fulfill it faithfully.

Nevertheless, the power of the emperor and his central government to some degree conflicted with the power of each separate family head; for the emperor's power was real only insofar as he could command obedience from the heads of families, who might not wish to obey him. But of course, similar tensions arose within a family when the head commanded obedience from some junior member who might not wish to obey him.

Interaction Between Imperial and Family Loyalties

We really know nothing of how the Shang Empire was held together, and we have no direct evidence of family structure from that long ago. Exactly how far the empire's boundaries extended is unknown, as are the names and locations of subordinate tribes, peoples, families, provinces, or whatever else made up the empire.

With the establishment of the Chou dynasty (1028–221 B.C.E.), more information becomes available. The Chou people came from the Wei Valley in the west, and when they first conquered Shang China they were classed as barbarians; that is, they were not Chinese. But the newcomers eagerly took on Chinese cultural traditions. Hence in art, literacy, and most other respects, the new dynasty did not bring any sharp break. Changes did come, however, and some important elaborations. The Chou, for example, brought the seven-day week to China, replacing a ten-day week used by the Shang. This change probably reflected some ultimate connection with Babylonia, where the seven-day week had its origin.

It may be worthwhile to pause a moment to ask why the seven-day week, which is so fundamental to our own life patterns, achieved such universal acceptance, since Greeks and Indians as well as Chinese all followed such a calendar. It had two advantages. First, a seven-day week fitted into the cycle of the moon fairly well, since the moon takes only a little more than twenty-eight days to complete its circuit round the earth. The phases of the moon were by far the most conspicuous measure of time available to ancient peoples, and a calendar that matched the changing shape of the moon seemed obviously better than one that did not. Secondly, there were seven wandering "lights" in the sky: sun, moon, Mercury, Mars, Venus, Jupiter, and

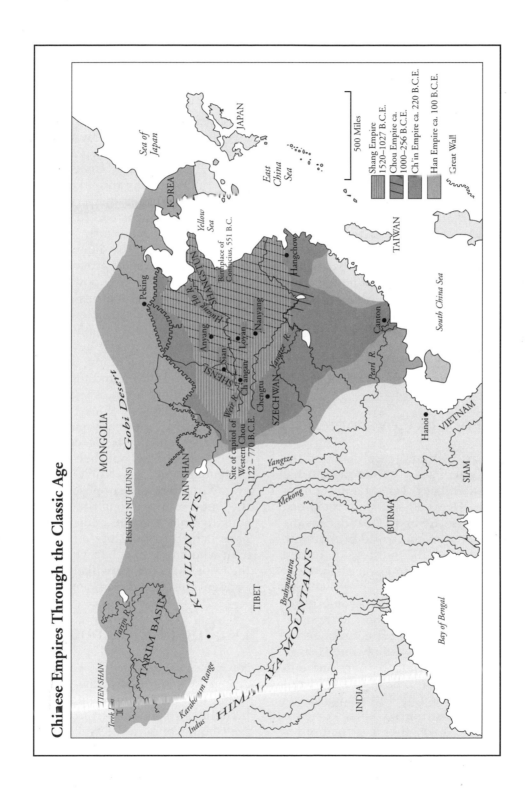

Chinese Empires Through the Classic Age

Sea of Japan

JAPAN

East China Sea

KOREA

Yellow Sea

Birthplace of Confucius, 551 B.C.

MONGOLIA

HSIUNG NU (HUNS)

Gobi Desert

NAN SHAN

TIEN SHAN

Tarim R.

Tarek Pass

TARIM BASIN

KUNLUN MTS.

Karakoram Range

TIBET

Brahmaputra

HIMALAYA MOUNTAINS

Indus

INDIA

Bay of Bengal

Mekong

Yangtze

BURMA

SIAM

VIETNAM

Hanoi

South China Sea

TAIWAN

Canton

Pearl R.

Hangchow

SHANTUNG

Huang Ho R. (Yellow R.)

Peking

Anyang

Sian

SHENSI

Ch'angan

Wei R.

Loyan

Nanyang

Yangtze R.

Chengtu

SZECHWAN

Site of capitol of Western Chou 1122 – 770 B.C.E.

500 Miles

Shang Empire 1520–1027 B.C.E.
Chou Empire ca. 1000–256 B.C.E.
Ch'in Empire ca. 220 B.C.E.
Han Empire ca. 100 B.C.E.
Great Wall

Saturn—one for each day of a seven-day week. Each of these bodies moved among the fixed stars in complicated ways. The planets, for example, seemed to advance and then go backward for a while before moving ahead again. Because of these irregular patterns, early observers of the sky concluded that the wandering lights must have special power or importance. A day dedicated to each seemed no more than prudent, and the fact that the result fitted the moon cycle seemed to prove the system.

In another and more important way, the Chou may have brought Babylonian ideas into China. The Babylonians believed that changes in the heavens were systematically related to changes on earth. Therefore, careful observation of the motions of the planets and sun and moon would enable men to forecast events and foresee dangers. The Chou, too, believed that events on earth corresponded to events in the skies. But instead of measuring and calculating the exact positions of the planets, as the Babylonians did, they contented themselves with a looser theory.

Chinese Theory of Government

Their central idea was that Heaven granted the right to rule on earth to a family of unusual merit. As long as members of that family continued to deserve it, Heaven's mandate remained with them. The emperor, Son of Heaven, was the connecting link between the world of men and the skies; and just as the entire sky turned around the polestar, so all things on earth ought to revolve around the emperor.

This theory of government became absolutely basic to all later Chinese political thought. It had several important logical consequences. For one thing, since there was only one Heaven and one polestar, there could be only one emperor. His authority ought to be universal, and if some distant barbarians failed to recognize his merit and submit to his rule, so much worse for them. By such ignorance, they cut themselves off from Heaven's good graces and from the benefits that resulted from conformity to the proper, constituted order of civilized life.

In the second place, the theory justified any successful revolt. The fact that a dynasty fell proved that Heaven had withdrawn its favor. Various signs could always be found to show, at least *after* the event, that the mandate of the old ruling family had expired. Bad crops, unusual events, like the impact of a meteorite or the birth of a two-headed calf, might be signs of Heaven's displeasure. So might invasions and revolt. And an emperor, surrounded by such possibilities, always had to watch his step and be careful not to offend Heaven. If perchance he did so, he had to know the right way to make amends as quickly as possible, lest his dynasty be overthrown. In practice this meant careful attention to traditional rituals of every sort.

One of the most dangerous things an emperor could do was to provoke the enmity of the ancestral spirits of any powerful and important family. Thus, the emperor's power over his chief nobles was severely restricted. Any punishment that involved, for example, taking land away from a powerful family automatically offended the ancestors, who might be expected to make trouble with Heaven and thus endanger the emperor's position. Perhaps such religious scruples mirrored military realities.

To offend too many powerful families was certainly dangerous to the central power, for the Chou had parceled out their empire into a series of feudal holdings. Noble families that were granted lands were supposed to serve and obey the emperor. For a long time they did send their sons to school at the court. This practice may have helped to hold the empire together, since men who had spent their youth being trained at the imperial court were likely to retain a sense of deference toward the emperor all their lives.

Decline of the Chou Empire

Nevertheless, in time, the Chou Empire disintegrated. A significant blow came in 771 B.C.E., when barbarians from afar—perhaps raiders breaking in suddenly from the steppe—sacked the Chou capital in the Wei Valley and killed the reigning emperor. After this disaster another member of the family set himself up as emperor and reigned from the city of Loyang, thus establishing an Eastern Chou dynasty (771–221 B.C.E.) in succession to the earlier Western Chou (1028–

771 B.C.E.). But the prestige and practical power of the emperor never recovered. Local nobles soon became princely rulers in their own right, owing only nominal obedience to the Chou Emperor. Princes struggled against one another and began to develop their own bureaucratic governments, standing armies, and tax systems to support their power.

This became possible, in part, through an increasingly rapid and successful reclamation of the river bottom lands. Availability of iron for tools may have helped to open the broad and fertile floodplains of the Yellow River to agriculture, though exactly when iron manufacture became important in China is not known. Large-scale diking and digging were needed to protect the bottom lands from flood. Noble or princely rulers organized the work. They then were able to get large rents from the land they had reclaimed from swamp. Before long the more successful landlords and princes began to seize weaker neighbors' lands, despite ancestral spirits and traditional rights and duties. War between neighboring princes hastened the consolidation of power in the hands of about a dozen rulers; and as the wealth and power of these rival princes increased, their wars became more ruthless. So severe did wars become that traditional Chinese historians called the last years of the Chou dynasty, 403 to 221 B.C.E., the "Period of the Warring States."

An important by-product of these struggles was the expansion of the area of Chinese civilization. Thousands of individuals, finding themselves in danger, fled from the crowded center of the Chinese world, carrying with them various skills that neighboring peoples were often ready and eager to put to use. In addition, princes whose territory happened to lie along the boundaries of the civilized areas of north China were able to push their frontiers outward onto barbarian ground, and then by degrees they brought the new lands to a fuller share in Chinese life. Systematic resettlement of peasant farmers was the most effective way of expanding Chinese territory; teaching former barbarians how to work and live like the Chinese was almost equally important.

Eastward this type of expansion extended to the peninsula of Shangtung and the coastal region immediately north of that peninsula—a region that has ever since remained an extremely important part of China. Expansion southward toward the Yangtze River was equally significant. Chinese settlement and civilization took root in that river valley during the Eastern Chou period. However, because of the vastness of the region and the enormous amount of work involved in constructing fields throughout the Yangtze Valley, it took centuries for this middle region of historic China to become fully occupied. Not until after the beginning of the Common Era, therefore, did the Yangtze Valley begin to rival and then surpass the Yellow River valley as a center of Chinese population and agricultural production.

Northward and westward the Chinese style of agriculture could not expand because the water supply in Mongolia and the Gobi Desert was insufficient. Human occupation of these regions must, indeed, have been very sparse until shortly before 300 B.C.E., when Chinese records first mention horse-riding nomads along China's northwestern border. Thereafter, the problem of guarding China's peasant masses from parties of raiding cavalrymen became acute.

The border state of Ch'in, located in the Wei Valley, where the Chou dynasty had originated, bore the first brunt of nomad attack. The princes of Ch'in finally solved the problem by developing a professional standing army of cavalrymen, who were equipped like the nomads with horses and bows and who were paid with taxes collected from the public at large. This cavalry army, tested and tempered by frequent campaigns against the nomads of Mongolia, proved itself superior to all other Chinese military forces. As a result, Shih Huang Ti, prince of Ch'in, conquered all China in 221 B.C.E. He declared himself Son of Heaven, thus bringing the Chou dynasty to an end.

The new rulers did not, however, last beyond the lifetime of Shih Huang Ti's son. Old loyalties to the princely states that the first Ch'in emperor had destroyed could not be rooted out all at once, and Shih Huang Ti's violent methods aroused general hostility. Hence, when he died (210 B.C.E.), revolts broke out all over China and a fresh round of warfare began that continued even after Shih Huang Ti's son died (206 B.C.E.).

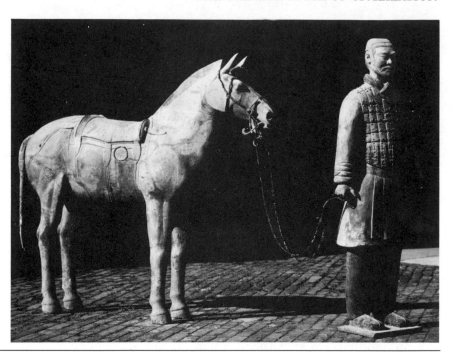

China's Cavalry Revolution   This clay model of a soldier and his mount was buried to guard the tomb of Shi Huangi-ti, the emperor who unified China in 221 B.C.E. Hundreds of such figures were uncovered in the 1970s, giving us a remarkable glimpse of the military might behind China's unification. The state of Ch'in from which Shih Huang-ti started his career was located next the steppelands of Mongolia, and the emperor's victory owed a good deal to cavalrymen like this one, who had learned his art by fighting off the steppe nomads.

Out of this confusion a new ruling family, the Han, emerged supreme over the whole of China in 202 B.C.E.

Under the Han dynasty, a more or less effective balance was struck between the competing requirements of imperial unity and family loyalty. To gain a better understanding of how this balance was achieved, we must consider the Chinese intellectual and moral reactions to the confused and troubled time between 771 and 221 B.C.E., when the nominal authority of the Chou emperor in Loyang was increasingly disregarded and a spiral of more and more ruthless wars kept the princely states in turmoil.

Three Schools of Chinese Thought

Respect for the spirits lay at the heart of Chinese family life, and this concept provided the ultimate explanation of why some persons should obey orders while others could rightfully issue commands. Refusal to conform would, or at least ought to provoke supernatural punishment. But the conduct of the more successful rulers in the time of the Eastern Chou dynasty (771–221 B.C.E.) flouted all such rules of conduct. They did not hesitate to dispossess a family from its ancestral lands if they were strong enough to do so. The wrath of ancestral spirits seemed ineffective. Moral conduct seemed only to lead to defeat and failure. The most deceitful double-crosser often won out, and a thoroughly pious and dutiful member of society might suffer all kinds of wrong without having the spirits come to the rescue.

Experiences of this sort were profoundly disturbing. What could and should a wise and good person do under the circumstances? Many different answers were suggested to this question, and the writings of some of the men who attempted to solve the problem were read and respected throughout later Chinese history. The troubled time of the Eastern Chou period was thus the golden age of Chinese thought, when the enduring lines of the classical Chinese world view were first worked out.

In later times, six different schools of thought were recognized, but it is enough here to describe three that were especially important later. Followers of these schools were known as Legalists, Taoists, and Confucians. Confucians predominated in later times, though not until after they had adjusted their doctrines to make room for elements of both Legalist and Taoist thought.

Legalists

The Legalists were closely associated with the state of Ch'in. They justified Shih Huang Ti's ruthlessness that allowed him to conquer the rest of China in 221 B.C.E. Their central doctrine was simple: The will of the ruler was law. Anything he commanded was morally right. Absolute obedience was a duty. The first and most important task was to create and maintain military strength. Only so could peace and security be attained, and from these prosperity would follow. Legalists paid no attention to the supernatural and left no room for the family. They had a low opinion of human character and argued that people had to be driven by force.

Legalists put no limit on the ruler's power. Censorship of books and close control of education were part of their program for making the state strong. Arbitrary conscription of labor for state projects was also taken for granted. Such ideas were not mere theories, for Shih Huang Ti conscripted Chinese peasants wholesale for his armies, for work on the famous Great Wall of China, and for building a no less remarkable system of military roads throughout the empire. He also censored books and suppressed all doctrines opposing his policies, including, among others, Confucianism.

In sum, according to Legalist principles, the state and its ruler were everything and the family—not to mention the private individual—was nothing. Between the two poles of Chinese society, the Legalists chose exclusively and emphatically in favor of the state.

Taoists

Taoists utterly rejected all such ideas. They claimed Lao-tzu as their founder, whereas the Legalists had no single founder nor any one preeminent writer who expressed their views. The most distinguished Legalists were men of action, who served as administrators and generals and scorned mere theorists, which they considered the Taoists to be. Lao-tzu, according to tradition, had also served as a minister in one of the smaller states of ancient China not long after 600 B.C.E. But this may be myth, invented to give Lao-tzu a career like that of Confucius. As a matter of fact, modern scholars are not even sure that such a man as Lao-tzu ever lived.

What is sure is that a book attributed to him survives. It taught the doctrine of ruling by "nonaction." A good ruler, the Taoists claimed, did nothing. He simply let the grass grow and allowed the people complete freedom to do what came naturally. The good life required complete freedom from any kind of outward compulsion. In a world where force and violence were all too common, a wise and good person would always live for each moment, without fear or dread, freely and quietly.

Only so could human life accord with Tao. The word *Tao* is difficult to translate: Literally, it means "the way," but this translation does not suggest the full range of its meanings. Tao was the way of the universe. It was not merely passive, for Tao could act. If people disregarded it, Tao eventually undid their deeds and destroyed their achievements. On the other hand, if people lived in accord with Tao, they prospered and things went well for them.

Tao, in other words, carried a supernatural as well as a natural meaning. It was the whole nature of things, and no one could ever escape it, however hard he or she might try. By understanding Tao, moreover, a person could acquire unusual powers. In particular, one could extend life, perhaps indefinitely, and move from place to place at will. These magical aspects of Taoism were much elaborated among the Chinese in later times, although they were not emphasized in Lao-tzu's little book.

Taoism was essentially a personal and private doctrine. It completely disregarded all the obligations ordinary persons owed to their families or to the state. But, perhaps just because so much of Chinese life was hedged in by such duties, the appeal of Taoist ideas proved to be enduring. Throughout Chinese history, Taoism remained a significant school of thought. Many found the effort to attune themselves to nature and the Tao a pleasant change of pace from the usual round of self-restraint and dutiful deference to superiors. On vacation Taoism was fine, though in ordinary human situations most Chinese found some more specific guide to conduct was necessary. But between Legalism, with its ruthless pursuit of state power as an end in itself, and Taoism, which denied the effectiveness of deliberate human interference with Tao, there could be no compromise.

Confucians   The third school, Confucianism, traced its doctrine to the sage Confucius, who lived from about 551 to 479 B.C.E. He was a native of the state of Lu, near the center of the Chinese world, and he came of noble family. As a young man, he was appointed minister but failed to persuade the prince of Lu to follow his principles, and so he left office to spend the rest of his life as a private citizen who "loved the ancients" and delighted to talk about them with anyone who shared his concerns. A group of admiring disciples gathered around Confucius. They recorded his sayings as well as stories about him in a book called the *Analects*.

Oddly enough, Confucius' reputation in later ages did not depend on anything he wrote or said himself. Instead, the Chinese revered him as the editor and compiler of the Five Classics, over which later generations of schoolboys were to labor. The Five Classics were a miscellaneous collection of poems, annals, histories, and handbooks of divination and of manners. When and for what purpose they were first gathered together is uncertain. Many modern scholars do not think that Confucius was the editor, though he may have been familiar with some or all of the books that later became the Five Classics.

In time these books, together with the *Analects* and some commentaries and independent works explaining the Confucian points of view, formed a body of literature that every educated Chinese studied long and carefully. By reading these works and committing many passages to memory, children learned to write and, at the same time, acquired an intimate familiarity with the code of values and manners that defined what it meant to be a fully civilized Chinese.

No events during the lifetime of Confucius made such an outcome seem likely. He felt his life to be a failure because he believed that a really good man could only exercise virtue to the full by ruling, or by serving as minister to one who rules. Indeed, Confucius claimed no originality. All he wanted was to reassert the ways of the ancestors, as he knew them through books. This required, of course, a united country, obedient to a single emperor, chosen properly by Heaven. It required also well-ordered families, with sons obedient to their fathers, and fathers respectful toward the spirits. This side of Confucian teaching can be summed up in a word: decorum. If everyone knew his or her place and kept it, then, said Confucius, all would be well.

The first task, therefore, was to know what was proper. That could best be found out by studying the ways of the ancients as recorded in the Classics. The second task was to behave properly in each situation as it arose. Confucius seems to have felt that this would follow more or less automatically if everyone knew what should be done in every human relationship. Knowledge, acquired by study, was therefore the key; and Confucians always put enormous value upon mastery of the Classics.

In emphasizing book learning in this fashion, Confucius altered older ideals without admitting or perhaps realizing it. At the court of the Western Chou, which Confucius took as his model, archery and military drill were part of the young nobleman's training. Confucius approved of archery. How could he do otherwise and be faithful to the ancients? But he abhorred war, thinking that the resort to violence was the result of a failure to observe decorum on someone's part—either a superior who had failed to secure obedience of an inferior who had refused to conform. Deliberate preparation for failure had few charms for the Confucians. They thought it better to avoid war by wisdom and good order. Hence, a soldier's skills had a very low place in the Confucian ordering of virtues; as a consequence, in later ages educated Chinese, though eager for bureaucratic office, usually left military command to barbarian hired hands.

Confucius did not consider that nobility or virtue was necessarily inherited. By training and study a person could become virtuous, whatever his origins. This concept, too, was a significant departure from ancient practice. It had the ef-

Confucius on How to Lead a Good Life

Soon after Confucius' death (479 B.C.E.), some of his disciples collected his memorable sayings into a book called the *Analects,* from which the following excerpts come. Most are surely authentic; but some of the sayings attributed to Confucius are later additions. In any case, in later times Chinese officials and landowners revered everything in the *Analects* as a guide to life, even if they never entirely lived up to its precepts.

Exerpts from the *Analects* of Confucius

II, 3. The Master said, "Govern the people by regulations, keep order among them by chastisements, and they will flee from you and lose all self-respect. Govern them by moral force, keep order among them by ritual, and they will keep their self-respect and come to you of their own accord."

[handwritten: v. legalism]

II, 13. Tzu-kung (a disciple) asked about the true gentleman. The Master said, "He does not preach what he practices till he has practiced what he preaches."

III, 7. The Master said, "Gentlemen never compete."

[handwritten: v merchants]

IV, 13. The Master said, "If it is really possible to govern countries by ritual and yielding, there is no more to be said. But if it is not really possible, of what use is ritual?"

V, 12. Tzu-kung (a disciple) said, "Our Master's views concerning culture and the outward insignia of goodness, we are permitted to hear; but about Man's nature and the ways of Heaven he will not tell us anything at all."

[handwritten: Heaven]

VI, 25. The Master said, "A gentleman who is widely versed in letters and at the same time knows to submit his learning to the restraints of ritual is not likely, I think, to go far wrong."

VII, 1. The Master said, "I have transmitted what was taught to me without making up anything of my own. I have been faithful to and loved the Ancients."

XII, 2. Jan Yung (a disciple) asked about Goodness. The Master said, "Behave when away from home as though you were in the presence of an honored guest. Deal with the common people as though you were officiating at an important sacrifice. Do not do to others what you would not like yourself. Then there will be no feelings of opposition to you, whether it is the affairs of a State that you are handling or the affairs of a Family."

[handwritten: Jen ?]

[handwritten: Golden rule — negative — Family State]

XII, 11. Duke Ching of Ch'i (a ruler) asked Master K'ung (Confucius) about government. Master K'ung replied saying, "Let the prince be a prince, the father a father, and the son a son."

XIII, 18. The Duke of She (a nobleman) addressed Master K'ung saying, "In my country there was a man called Upright Kung. His father appropriated a sheep, and Kung bore witness against him." Master K'ung said, "In my country the upright men are of quite a different sort. A father will screen his son, and a son his father—which incidentally does involve a sort of uprightness."

[handwritten: priority of family over "law"]

XV, 23. Tzu-kung (a disciple) asked saying, "Is there any single saying that one can act upon all day and everyday?" The Master said, "Perhaps the saying about consideration: Never do to others what you would not like them to do to you."

Reproduced from *The Analects of Confucius,* Arthur Waley, trans. London: George Allen and Unwin, Ltd., 1958.

fect, when Confucianism became official, of opening a career to talent. Any young man, having secured an education, who had been admitted to the bureaucracy, might rise as high as his abilities and the emperor's favor would carry him.

Finally, Confucius refused to speculate about supernatural forces. As long as it was so difficult to know how to conduct oneself among the living, Confucius considered it fruitless to wonder about the world of the spirits. Established old-fashioned ways of dealing with the supernatural had his complete support. But he did not think it useful to argue about details. Proper observance of ancestral rites was all that really mattered.

The central thrust of Confucius' thought was a refusal to make any distinction between public and private life. Virtue was one and the same, whether a person occupied high office in the government or lived as a private citizen. Decorum was one and the same for those high and low in the social scale. The emperor stood at the top; all others ranged in proper order beneath him. Relations up and down this social pyramid seemed, to Confucius, no different from relations within a family. They were more complex, no doubt, requiring more careful learning of roles than was required within the bosom of a family. But the essentials of good order were the same. The empire was the family writ large, and a state was well run insofar as it approached the patterns of family life. Ideally the ruler ruled without having to punish or threaten anyone, and all obeyed because each knew his or her proper place and accepted it.

If we compare the Confucian position with that of the Legalists and the Taoists, it is easy to understand why Confucianism prevailed in the end. For the Confucian way combined and reaffirmed the importance of both family and empire—the two central realities of ancient as well as of modern Chinese society. Confucians did not glorify tyranny as the Legalists did. The ruler had his duties and conventional role to play just as much as any of his subjects. But neither did Confucians despair of human society, as Taoists tended to do. The good life, for Confucius, could

be led only in society, by fulfilling exactly and graciously the roles that fell to each individual human being, day by day, hour by hour, and even minute by minute, throughout life.

The Establishment of Confucianism as an Official Philosophy

In Confucius' lifetime, his disciples were not particularly influential. Nevertheless, Confucius' ideals continued to live among those who read the Classics and mulled over the *Analects*. The growth of bureaucratic government played into the Confucians' hands, for princes needed literate administrators, and literate men who accepted the values of the Classics were likely to be reliable and faithful servants.

Another important change in the texture of Chinese society was even more important in bringing the final triumph of Confucianism. The violent upheavals of the Period of the Warring States (403–221 B.C.E.) eliminated most of the old landowning nobility. This development did not, however, mean that peasant villages escaped the authority of landlords. Instead, a new class of landowners arose, men who had no particular claim to noble birth or descent, but who nevertheless secured a right to collect rents and taxes from the peasants. Exactly how this "gentry" class arose is unclear. Moneylending and the amassing of landed property by richer and more prudent farmers may have raised some to the gentry. In other cases local tax collectors may have been allowed to keep part of what they gathered from the peasants for themselves, which then became a sort of rent.

The gentry were not as a rule military men. Posts in the administrative bureaucracy seemed to them the natural way to rise in the world. Such attitudes fitted Confucianism very well, or perhaps one should say that Confucianism expressed these attitudes, for Confucius himself and his first followers were mostly of gentry background.

Yet the unification of China by Shih Huang Ti in 221 B.C.E. at first seemed to be a serious setback for Confucianism. The new emperor was impatient with Confucian talk; he saw in the reverence for old ways, which constituted the core of Confucianism, an indirect expression of resistance to his rule. Accordingly, in 213 B.C.E., he ordered all Confucian books to be destroyed, except for a single set to be kept in the imperial archives, where only authorized persons could consult them. Extensive book burnings apparently did take place.

Even more disruptive to the continuity of old, learned traditions was a simplification of the script, which Shih Huang Ti also decreed. At nearly the same time, the habit of writing with a brush, instead of with a sharp-pointed pen or stylus, was introduced. This brought about rapid change in the form of characters, which had now to be shaped to suit the strokes natural to a brush. As a result, within a short time, as the new and simpler kinds of writing caught on, old texts became almost unintelligible. Any copies of the Classics that had escaped Shih Huang Ti's book burning, therefore, soon lost their meaning for any but a few specially learned scholars.

The Ch'in conqueror rode roughshod over the states he had conquered. Shih Huang Ti stationed troops at strategic places all over China and ruthlessly hunted down his enemies. He divided the land into provinces and districts and appointed officials over each unit. He standardized axle lengths so that carts would make only one set of ruts in his roads. He harassed members of the upper classes who failed to support him and ordered hundreds of thousands, if not millions, of peasants to work on roads and on the Great Wall. Only those members of the gentry class who were prepared to submit completely to his will, and who did not mind the military brutality of the Ch'in emperor, could serve him comfortably. Not many did, so when Shih Huang Ti died, resistance came out into the open and a fresh round of war broke out.

The new victor who emerged as emperor of all China and founded the Han dynasty in 202 B.C.E., owed part of his success to the courteous, open manner he had shown to all who crossed his path. A more or less conscious effort to woo the support of the gentry seems to have been part of his policy. And although many of the Ch'in practices were kept—the new script and the new provinces for example—the Han government allowed free circulation of books once more.

The tacit alliance between the gentry and the Han dynasty elevated Confucianism to the rank of official doctrine by 136 B.C.E., when one of the most successful of the Han rulers, Emperor Wu Ti, decreed that anything not within the Confucian school of learning "should not be allowed to progress further."

By that time, however, official Confucianism had made extensive adjustment to practices that had first been approved by the Legalists. An emperor who commanded great armies and organized campaigns across all of China's borders scarcely conformed to the Confucian pattern of a good ruler. Yet the emperor who made Confucianism official was nicknamed "The Martial Emperor" because he had done exactly these things. Only by accepting, therefore, some of the important changes brought by the Ch'in dynasty and by the Legalists did Confucianism achieve official status.

Taoism and related schools of thought did not disappear, nor were their followers persecuted by Confucians, despite the wording of Emperor Wu Ti's decree. Rather, Taoism was allowed to flourish in private, among men out of office. Those who sought to serve the emperor and rise to positions of authority in the government were expected to be familiar with the Classics, and they were expected to have schooled themselves in the good manners and self-restraint that went with such learning. Official Confucianism and unofficial Taoism thus came to complement each other very effectively. The ever-present formal restraints of Confucian decorum may even have required the alternative that Taoism offered—an escape from tightly organized society into private communion with nature.

Thus, by absorbing elements from Legalism and by making room for Taoism, Confucianism finally became the official ideology of imperial China. From the time of the Han dynasty until the twentieth century, Confucian scholars governed China. Generation after generation of schooling produced men remarkably uniform in outlook and style of life. They gave a conservative stability to China that no other civilization came close to equaling. Thousands of gentry families, scattered across the face of China, drawing rents and taxes from millions of peasants, aspired to serve the emperor in some appointive office. This became the human reality upon which Chinese civilization rested. The resulting reconciliation of family loyalty with the imperial ideal

was so effective that any further basic changes seemed entirely unnecessary.

Conclusion

Chinese civilization arose in comparative isolation from the civilizations of Greece, India, and

Wood and Bronze across the Pacific   The most distinctive art of early China was the casting of bronze bowls, vases, and boxes. They came in a great variety of shapes but all are decorated with complex raised relief patterns like the one on the left. A masklike design in which eyes and mouth are clearly recognizable was usual and may be seen on the front of this ancient Chinese bronze casting.

If you imagine the face on the totem pole from British Columbia flattened out to fit the surface of a bronze box, you can see the probable origin of the Chinese style of decoration. Of course all examples of the ancient east Asian style of wood carving, if it existed, rotted away long ago, leaving ancient Chinese bronzes on one side of the Pacific and the living tradition of totem pole carving on the other.

the Middle East. Labor-intensive garden agriculture gave Chinese society a different economic base from that familiar in other parts of the civilized world. Even more fundamental was the special character of the Chinese family structure that provided a model for public as well as for private life throughout most of China's history.

A distinctive style of art and method of writing arose in China under the Shang dynasty (traditional dates: 1523–1028 B.C.E.), but the classical definition of Chinese intellectual tradition occurred under the Chou dynasty (1028–221 B.C.E.). Rival Chinese schools of thought all tried to answer questions about how human beings ought to behave. Legalism glorified the state and ruler at the expense of private life and family ties. Taoism, on the contrary, was individualistic and had nothing to say about public and family duties. Confucianism occupied a kind of middle ground, finding rules for proper behavior both in public and in private through careful study of ancient books and records.

Important changes came to Chinese society during the last centuries of the Chou dynasty. After 771 B.C.E., the effective power of the emperor evaporated. Instead, rival princes built up bureaucratic governments and armies and fought one another until the state of Ch'in conquered all the rest and unified China once more. The Ch'in conqueror, Shih Huang Ti, reorganized Chinese government along Legalist lines and carried through many reforms. Although fresh revolts and wars broke out, when a new conqueror founded the Han dynasty in 202 B.C.E. he kept many of Shih Huang Ti's changes. Similarly, when a later Han emperor made Confucianism the official ideology of China, room was still found for Legalist and Taoist ideas within the official Confucian system.

The upshot of this evolution was to establish a conservative and stable style of civilization in China. The pattern of education that produced experts in Confucian learning also supplied the empire with loyal and capable officials. The landlords and peasants, who constituted the overwhelming majority of the population, found that the balance between imperial and family duties that the Confucians advocated fitted quite well with their own interests and needs. The result was a remarkable uniformity and stability across many centuries, even though China had become a vast and varied land by the time the Han Empire was founded and continued to extend contacts into new regions in the centuries that followed.

The secret of this stability and uniformity seems to have been the ability of Chinese families to mold their members to the roles tradition demanded of each of them, generation after generation, no matter where the family might find itself. The link between this "master institution" and the imperial system was close, for the whole empire was, ideally, a vast family that, at least in principle, ought to include all human beings.

Bibliography

Translation from Chinese into English is even more difficult than translation from Sanskrit and other Indian languages because of the profound gap separating the two languages in matters of grammar, terminology, and script. Nevertheless, Arthur Waley, *The Book of Songs* (1954) and *The Analects of Confucius* (1938), produced smooth and readable translations of two of the most important classics of early Chinese literature. Another famous translation, Richard Wilhelm, *The I Ching: or, Book of Changes* (3rd ed., 1967), presents the most impenetrable of Chinese classics in a way that makes this handbook for divination oddly attractive to American readers. On a far more sober note, selections from the work of Ssu-ma Chi'en, the first historian of China who fixed the form of dynastic histories for all subsequent generations, are available through Burton Watson, ed. and trans., *Records of the Grand Historian of China* (2 vols., 1961). Another dimension of China's literary heritage is available from Wu-chi Liu and Irving Yucheng Lo, eds., *Sunflower Splendor: Three Thousand Years of Chinese Poetry* (1975), which offers an anthology that runs across the entire span of Chinese history.

Archaeological discoveries allow modern scholars to supplement the portrait of the origins of Chinese civilization transmitted through China's literary tradition in some significant ways. Kwang-chih Chang, *The Archaeology of Ancient China* (3rd ed., 1977), and David N. Knightley, ed., *The Origins of Chinese Civilization* (1983), offer accounts of new discoveries and how they match traditional learning about China's earliest dynasties.

A general introductory account of Chinese history, aimed specifically at American college students, is John K. Fairbank and Edwin O. Reischauer, *China: Tradition and Transformation* (rev. ed., 1989). Other general histories include Wolfram Eberhard, *A History of China* (4th ed., 1977); Jacques Gernet, *A History of Chinese Civilization* (1982); and Charles O. Hucker, *China's Imperial Past: An Introduction to Chinese History and Culture* (1975). Franz Michael, *China through the Ages: History of a Civilization* (1986), is a brief, lively essay aimed at the general reader.

Books concentrating on the formative period of Chinese history include Ping-ti Ho, *The Cradle of the East,* (1975); Kwang-chih Chang, *Shang Civilization* (1980); and William Watson, *China before the Han Dynasty* (1961).

On agriculture, see E. N. Anderson, *The Food of China* (1988); for warfare, Frank A. Kiernan Jr. and John K. Fairbank, eds., *Chinese Ways in Warfare,* (1961); on the Chinese family, Patricia Buckley Ebrey and James L. Watson, eds., *Kinship Organization in Late Imperial China, 1000–1940* (1986), explores what is knowable about the master institution of Chinese society.

On Confucius and Confucianism, Kaizuka Shigaki, *Confucius* (1974), attempts a biography of the founder of the dominant strand of Chinese learning. Herlee G. Creel, *Confucius: The Man and the Myth* (1949); John K. Shryock, *The Origin and Development of the State Cult of Confucius* (1932); and Benjamin I. Schwartz, *The World of Thought in Ancient China* (1985), all try to set Confucius' life and thought into the general context of Chinese history. Other, rival intellectual traditions are assessed along with Confucianism in Yu-lan Fung, *A History of Chinese Philosophy* (2 vols., 2nd ed., re-issued 1983).

On the political plane, Derk Bodde, *China's First Unifier* (1938), deals with the career of Shih-huang Ti, the revolutionary shaper of China's imperial tradition. His account needs to be supplemented by Arthur Cottrell, *The First Emperor of China* (1981), who draws upon the remarkable and recent archaeological discoveries from Shih-huang Ti's tomb.

For Chinese art, Lawrence Sickman and Alexander Soper, *The Art and Architecture of China* (3rd ed., 1968), is standard. See also Jessica Rawson, *Ancient Chinese Art and Archaeology* (1980).

Epilogue: Part I
The State of the World

500 B.C.E.

The four civilizations that existed in 500 B.C.E. in the Middle East, Greece, India, and China occupied only a small part of the earth. Each was bordered by regions where barbarians had become aware of the charms of civilization, but there were still large parts of the world where the influence of civilizations had not been felt. Hunters and gatherers, whose way of life had not altered noticeably in thousands of years, occupied all of Australia. South Africa also was inhabited by hunters and gatherers, as were large regions of southeast Asia and the Indonesian islands. The same was true of the Arctic shores and of large areas in both North and South America.

The Spread of Agriculture

There was also a zone where agricultural or pastoral societies had come into existence but where full-scale civilizations had not yet emerged. It is difficult to see clearly what took place in this twilight zone because there are no written records, and archaeological study of such societies had only begun to scratch the surface. We may safely assume that agriculture continued to spread wherever suitable new ground could be found, but by 500 B.C.E. nearly all slash-and-burn cultivators had probably come up against various climatic obstacles. In Europe, for example, the wet climate of the Atlantic fringe made the great north European plain too waterlogged for wheat and barley. Only especially well-drained soils, on hill slopes, could be cultivated successfully with the methods known to these early farmers. The denser forests of the swampy plains were left to hunters, but along the shores of the Baltic Sea cattle raisers cleared wide areas to make pastures for their herds.

What, if anything, limited the advance of the root and rice growers of southeast Asia is altogether uncertain. Disease may have been a factor. Rice growing had caught on extensively in the Ganges and Yangtze floodplains before 500 B.C.E. Elsewhere we have no sign of the dense populations rice cultivation might be expected to maintain. We do know that Indonesian root crops reached Africa by the beginning of the Common Era. As yams, bananas, and taro from Indonesia became established in what is now Nigeria, Ghana, and nearby regions, a populous agricultural society arose in the grassland zone of west Africa.

Sea Voyaging and Migrations

This surprising plant migration underlines the importance of sea routes, even when ships were still very small and simple. About the beginning of the Common Era, for example, the island of Madagascar, off the southeastern coast of Africa, was settled by people speaking Malagasy, an Indonesian language closely related to languages spoken today in Borneo. The transfer of this language implies that large numbers of people crossed the breadth of the Indian Ocean. Since that ocean is relatively calm, such a voyage is not as surprising as at first it might seem. Monsoon winds blow half the year from one direction and half the year from a nearly opposite direction, making return voyages particularly easy. Moreover, coastal voyaging required only small, light boats that could be dragged ashore almost anywhere to cook a meal, to take on fresh water, or merely for a good night's sleep. As long as local populations did not attack the ships' crews— and the peoples living along the coast of the Indian Ocean appear to have been unwarlike— there was really no effective obstacle to traveling very long distances, once seaworthy boats, propelled by sails, had been invented.

There is strong reason to believe that seagoing vessels existed along the shores and rivers of southeast Asia from very ancient times. Chinese references to "longboats" coming from the south, and the undeniable fact of Indonesian settlement in Madagascar, are the principal evidence for this belief. Unfortunately, small wooden boats leave few archaeological traces.

The shore villages and river mouths, from which such vessels presumably sailed, also do not make particularly impressive ruins. Hence, in this instance, archaeology does not help much.

On the other hand, archaeological finds at Dongson, in North Vietnam, reveal a people who used bronze and had horses from about 750 B.C.E. Horses in such an environment are surprising enough, for the horse was native to the Eurasian steppelands, far to the north. Even more puzzling is the fact that the bridle bits and other cavalry accessories found at Dongson closely resemble similar materials found north of the Black Sea in Scythian graves. A speculative theory explaining how such a linkage between southeastern Asia and southeastern Europe might have arisen suggests that when cavalry tactics were new, Scythians living in and around the Altai Mountains of central Asia may have made a raid into China (the overthrow of the Western Chou, 771 B.C.E.). A party of the raiders may then have proceeded south until they reached Dongson, where they met a people who were already accustomed to sailing to and fro across the South China Sea and who had accumulated enough wealth to make it worthwhile for the raiding cavalrymen to set themselves up as rulers. Then, about a generation later, the main body of Scythians left their Altai homeland and migrated westward to the regions around the Black Sea. This meant breaking off further contacts with the Far East. The small party that had established itself at Dongson became isolated from the rest of the Scythian community. Migrations of such a kind are not impossible, but archaeological evidence is too sketchy to confirm the theory.

Whatever the truth about such early cavalry raiding across the breadth of Asia may be, there is no doubt that the Dongson peoples, whoever they were, regularly voyaged across long sea distances. Ships traveled from bases on the Asian mainland to the islands of Indonesia, and from island to island. It has even been suggested that Dongson boats (probably canoes hollowed out from big logs) may have crossed the vast expanse of the Pacific and made contact with Amerindian peoples in Mexico and Peru.

The reason for making such a surprising suggestion is that some of the bronze objects, which began to be manufactured in the Americas about 500 B.C.E., closely resemble objects manufactured along the south China coast. But most of the scholars who have studied American archaeology believe that the evolution of Amerindian cultures occurred in isolation from anything that was happening in Asia.

Speculation is really not very fruitful until more evidence has been discovered. For example, it seems obvious that the critical breakthrough for long-distance voyaging in the Pacific was the invention of outriggers to stabilize sailing canoes. With outriggers, there was small danger of tipping a canoe over, even in rough weather. Before these devices had been introduced, voyages across the open ocean probably occurred only by accident, when a canoe got blown off course and found itself out of sight of land. But with outriggers lashed firmly into place, trips of thousands of miles across open oceans became possible, as the Polynesians later proved. The difficulty is that no one has a clue as to when outriggers were first invented. Without such information, guesses about the range and importance of early navigation in the Pacific and Indian oceans are not very profitable.

Changes in the Continental Interiors

Practically nothing is known about the history of the world's continental interiors before 500 B.C.E., except in those regions where civilized peoples left written records. Yet changes were certainly afoot, and the pace of change probably tended to increase with time as the consequences of increasing control over the natural environment were felt in more and more parts of the earth.

In Africa, for instance, agriculture increased in importance. The simple hunting and gathering style of life retreated southward and into the recesses of the Congo rain forest. But details are unknown, and even such an important matter as the establishment of Indonesian crops in west Africa cannot be dated exactly, nor are the routes by which yams and the other roots reached west

Africa at all clear. Some think they were handed from one people to another across the interior of the continent, from east to west. Others believe that coastal voyaging may have carried the roots to western Africa by sea. We simply do not know. It does, however, seem sure that before 500 B.C.E. no African society south of the Sahara had yet attained a level of complexity to justify the term "civilized."

The same was not quite true of the Americas. Maize cultivation had become important there long before 500 B.C.E. and settled village life allowed the development of pottery and other new arts. Some impressive ceremonial centers arose both in Mexico and Peru, starting as early as 1150 B.C.E. The most remarkable traces were left by the Olmecs, who lived in the coastal lowland of Mexico, south of Vera Cruz, and created a number of strikingly realistic colossal helmeted heads. It is possible that ships' crews from west Africa crossed the Atlantic and founded the cults that left those monuments behind. Assuredly, some of the colossal heads have an African appearance, but because no writing survives from Olmec sites, next to nothing is known about the priests or priest-kings who organized the human effort that went into constructing the monumental walkways and other structures of the various ceremonial centers. Most experts think the development of American societies was not affected by contacts with Africa or any other part of the Old World.

In Asia, two interesting changes took place that altered human relationships in significant ways. After about 1000 B.C.E., the camel became important as a domesticated animal. By that date, or soon thereafter, the camel's ability to withstand desert conditions allowed men to organize packtrains that could cross previously impassable desert barriers in Arabia and nearby lands. Soon afterward the Bactrian, or two humped, camel was put to similar use in the cold deserts of central and eastern Asia. With camels, long-distance trade and movement throughout the desert zone of Asia became much easier than before. Gradually the use of camels also spread to north Africa. Caravans crossing the Sahara Desert were not organized on a regular basis until about the beginning of the Common Era.

Olmec Sculpture   This head has an African look to it and dates from before 900 B.C.E. The stone had to be transported about fifty miles from the place this head was discovered. Since it is nearly seven feet tall and weighed many tons, that was no small feat for a people who lacked wheeled vehicles and animal traction. It may be wearing a protective helmet used by players in a head-bashing ball game, perhaps ancestral to lacrosse, that seems to have been important in Olmec religious and cultural life. But in the absence of written records no one really knows how Olmec society functioned, why such statues were carved, or whether there was any actual connection with Africa.

We have already seen something of what happened farther north, on the grassy steppe, where not long before 700 B.C.E. men first learned to shoot arrows from the back of a galloping horse.

The art of riding horseback was very old in southern Russia, to judge by the discovery of horse bits dating as far back as 4000 B.C.E. But letting go of the reins and using both hands to shoot a bow came in much later, when riders and horses had become so used to one another that it became safe and practicable to do so. The first swarm of cavalry bowmen to appear in the historical record (690 B.C.E.) were called Cimmerians by the Greeks, but they were soon displaced from southern Russia by Scythians who came from Central Asia, near the Altai mountains. About 600 B.C.E. the Scythians set up a loose "empire" all around the north and west shores of the Black Sea. At almost the same time, another people, the Celts, living in southern Germany and Bohemia, also learned to ride but they preferred to wield extra long swords instead of shooting arrows from horseback. As mounted cavalrymen, they quickly conquered other peoples throughout most of northwest Europe, occupying northern Italy, all of France and much of Spain as well as the British Isles. In some of these places the Celtic horsemen encountered related peoples who had preceded them from the steppe. Elsewhere, in Spain, for example, they met quite different and linguistically unrelated populations, ancestors of the modern Basques.

The art of fighting from horseback also spread eastward along the grasslands of Asia, until, shortly before 300 B.C.E., mounted horsemen established themselves in Mongolia, the harshest part of the entire Eurasian steppe. Mongolia's cold winters and sparse rainfall made for poor pasture, and people who were used to living in that environment had to be as tough and hardy as their shaggy ponies. The farther west on the steppe one moved, the better the pasture and the milder the climate became. The richest part of the steppeland lay north and west of the Black Sea, in southern Russia and Romania.

As soon as the whole steppe came to be occupied by warlike horsemen, a tendency to migrate westward along the steppe asserted itself. No one wanted to go toward Mongolia; everyone wanted to move to better pastures. Hence, when there was any displacement, the conquerors or refugees usually headed west to see what they could find. Many must have met death and destruction at the hands of those already in possession of the pasturelands; but every so often the newcomers were victorious. The net effect, therefore, was to create a westward drift of languages and peoples throughout the length of the steppe.

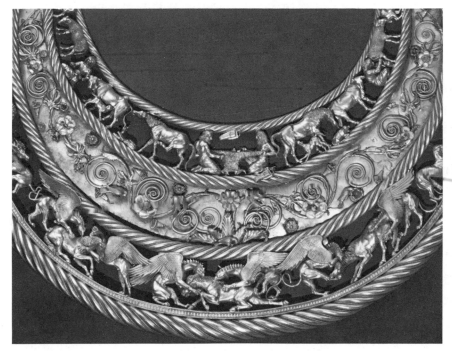

Nomad Art This handsome piece of jewelry came from a Scythian grave in southern Russia. It was made about 350 B.C.E. by goldsmiths who were in touch with art traditions of the Middle East and of the Aegean. The winged animals attacking horses resembles similarly fierce imaginary animals from Mesopotamian art, and the scroll work in the middle resembles a standard decorative motif of Greek art. But the artist also recorded scenes from Scythian pastoral life in the top row, where we see milking (both by humans and by young animals) and cheesemaking.

Forest hunters in the northern woods likewise tended to press southward into the grasslands, whenever a chance presented itself; and the steppe nomads, of course, were steadily attracted toward the rich lands of the civilized, agricultural peoples who lived south of them. Through most of recorded history, migration from the forest to the steppe and from the steppe to the cultivated land of China, the Middle East, India, and (less frequently) Europe competed with the movement from east to west along the steppe itself.

For the next 1500 years, this pattern of migration and conquest profoundly affected the political-military life of Eurasia. Steppe peoples, being nomads and dependent on their herds of horses and cattle, remained relatively few and lacked many of the skills that made civilized peoples wealthy and powerful. But they were mobile and could concentrate superior fighting power at a given point almost at will. Civilized states and rulers therefore had great difficulty countering them. Raids regularly turned into conquest whenever local defenses failed. Yet, seduced by city life, conquering nomads soon lost their military habits and hardihood, thus allowing new challengers for political power to overthrow them—either coming freshly from the steppes, or as a result of rebellion among their subjects.

The Exchange of Ideas

The net effect of all these migrations and conquests, and of improved communication, was to link all the parts of Asia and Europe more closely than at any previous time. South of the Sahara, Africa remained pretty well isolated from events in the north. The Americas remained separate, and Australia was unaffected. Yet by 500 B.C.E. most of Eurasia, inhabited by the great majority of humankind, had become a far more closely interacting whole than ever before. No important new invention or discovery could fail to affect the lives of people throughout this wide zone—sooner or later, directly or indirectly. Invention meant change, upheaval, danger, and discomfort. No people could stay put for very long without having some new thing come up that required them to alter their customary ways. Historic change could nowhere be resisted or, indeed, really controlled. No one foresaw the consequences of a new idea or of a new technique. Innovations spread from place to place and from group to group, sometimes slowly, sometimes very quickly; and each borrowing involved a new twist because of the way the novelty fitted, or failed to fit, with the other things that the borrowers were familiar with or accustomed to.

As we have seen in Part One, within this interacting *ecumene*—a Greek word that means "inhabited world"—four main styles of civilized life had been defined by 500 B.C.E. Each was complete and self-sufficient. Problems could be answered, both practically and theoretically, by calling upon the ideas and techniques already worked out by the bearers of each of these civilizations. For the following 2000 years, each of these major civilizations went its own way, within the basic guidelines that had been laid down by 500 B.C.E.

Contact and communication did not cease; on the contrary, they increased with the passage of time. More and more territory was brought into the circle of civilized society along every frontier. But this interaction among the separate civilizations, and between civilized and barbarian peoples, never upset the original fourfold balance of Old World cultures that had defined itself 500 years before the Common Era. This fundamental fact of human history is what Part I: Beginnings has tried to show.

The Classical Mediterranean World and Its Expansion

500 B.C.E. to 200 C.E.

8

Etruscan Portait ca. 150 B.C.E. Greek artistic skill was put to a slightly different use when it penetrated Italy. Greek sculptors portrayed gods and heroes as ideal types; in Italy their skills were used to portray individual persons with lifelike accuracy. This sort of mutation always happens when high skills cross cultural boundaries, as was the case when classical Greek civilization flooded west into Italy.

By 500 B.C.E. distinct and different styles of civilization had taken form in China, in India, in the Middle East, and in Europe. During the 2000 years that followed, each of these civilizations continued to flourish and, despite some setbacks, tended to expand its territory by incorporating neighboring barbarians. In addition to this kind of interaction between the civilized centers and barbarian fringe lands, the four civilizations also acted and reacted on one another in different ways at different times.

First one and then another of the Eurasian civilizations attained a particularly brilliant flowering, and each was then able to export to the rest of the world some aspects of its achievement. The other peoples of the continent accepted what impressed them favorably and rejected the rest.

The first Eurasian civilization to pass through a special period of bloom—and thereby to influence its neighbors, both civilized and barbarian—was the civilization of Greece. This chapter will therefore describe the Greek achievement and trace how other peoples reacted to what they learned about classical Greek culture.

The Persian and Peloponnesian Wars

In 499 B.C.E. the Greek cities of Ionia revolted against their Persian rulers. Since local Persian forces were few and weak, the Greeks met with initial success. The leagued rebellious cities even sent an expedition to capture Sardis, which was the former capital of Lydia and the provincial headquarters from which they had been governed.

The Great Persian War

It was not long, however, before the Persian monarch gathered his imperial armies and set out to punish the rebellious Greeks. One by one the cities were retaken, until Miletus alone remained. In 494 B.C.E., it, too, was captured and

sacked. The revolt had ended, but the wars between the Greeks and the Persians had only begun. During the revolt two obscure cities from across the Aegean Sea, Athens, and Eretria, ventured to send a few ships to aid the Ionians. The Persians resolved to punish them for having dared to interfere.

The Persian general Mardonius, son-in-law of Darius the Great (Darius I), led the avenging army. He first restored Persian authority along the north shore of the Aegean Sea. Then he sent a small expeditionary force across the Aegean to attack Eretria and Athens (490 B.C.E.). He captured Eretria, after a week's siege, and transported all of its citizens to Susa, one of the empire's distant capitals. Mardonius turned next to Athens.

Battle of Marathon   The Persians, guided by an exiled Athenian, landed on the plain of Marathon, about twenty miles north of Athens, and waited for a faction within the city to open the gates. The Athenian army marched out to block the overland approach to their city but did not dare to attack. Nothing happened. After a few days the Persians decided to board their ships in order to sail around the tip of Attica and land immediately in front of the city. When the Athenians saw what was happening, they formed their phalanx for the attack and charged across the plain of Marathon. The Persians were in confusion, trying to get on board their ships. The result was a great Athenian victory. The Persian army suffered heavy losses, while only 190 Athenians were killed. The Persian fleet finally got underway, but by the time it rounded the tip of Attica and approached the city, news of the battle had reached Athens. All chance of betrayal was gone, and Mardonius decided to withdraw his fleet. Athens had turned back the Persian forces singlehandedly. In later times the Athenians looked upon this as their finest hour.

Renewed Persian Attack   The death of King Darius in 486 B.C.E. and a revolt in Egypt and Babylonia prevented Xerxes, Darius' son and successor, from taking up the Greek question until ten years after the Battle of Marathon. But by 480 B.C.E. the Persian king was ready to invade Greece with the full force of his imperial army and navy: more than 600 ships and perhaps as many as 150,000 men. Xerxes made careful preparations to speed the Persian attack. Stores of food were gathered along the route of march from Sardis. A bridge of boats held in place by heavy cables, was flung across the Hellespont (modern name: Dardanelles). Envoys were sent to all the Greek cities, demanding that they submit to the Persians. So overwhelming did the Persian host appear that the oracle at Delphi, most respected of Greek shrines, advised all who consulted it to yield.

Nevertheless, a ragged coalition of thirty-two cities refused to submit to the Persians. All leagued together under the leadership of Sparta. Athens' role, although subordinate, was especially important because of the Athenian fleet.

Athens' fleet came into existence as a by-product of bitter political rivalries within the city. The decisive turn came in 483 B.C.E. when a politician named Themistocles came to power in Athens through a remarkable device known as ostracism. This was a procedure which called for a vote *against* a citizen rather than for him. It worked in the following way. Voters were asked to write the name of the person whom they considered most dangerous to the state on pieces of broken pottery, or *ostraka*, from which the term ostracism derives. The names were counted, and the man with the highest total vote was then exiled for ten years. Through two such votes Themistocles' rivals were banished from the city, leaving him in control. Aware of the need for a navy with which to oppose the Persians, he persuaded the Athenians to build a fleet of warships with income from newly discovered silver mines, located some thirty miles from the city. Thus two hundred new Athenian *triremes* (ships rowed by oars arranged in three banks) were ready to oppose the Persian attack. No other Greek city had more than a fraction of

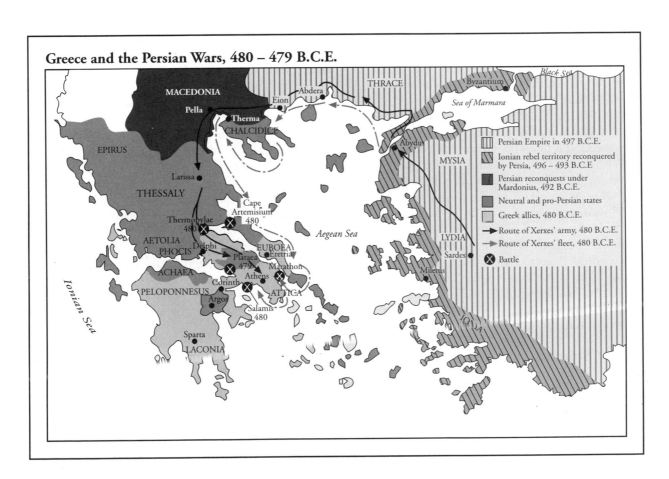

Greece and the Persian Wars, 480 – 479 B.C.E.

this number of ships to contribute to the allied fleet.

Battle of Thermopylae

When the Persian army invaded Greece in 480 B.C.E., the Spartans tried to check its advance at a narrow mountain pass known as Thermopylae. The name means "Hot Springs." The Persians sent a select force over the mountains to attack the Greeks from the rear. Leonidas I, the Spartan king and commander, ordered all of the allies to withdraw, and with 300 Spartan "Equals" he held the narrow pass until they were all killed.

The opposing fleets, meanwhile, had fought three battles near Thermopylae, in the straits between the island of Euboea and the mainland. Once the Spartans had been overwhelmed, there was no point in holding such an advanced position any longer. The Greek fleet therefore withdrew to the Bay of Salamis. This left Athens exposed. The city was evacuated. When the Persians arrived, they destroyed the empty city.

By this time, the season was growing late. The main Greek fleet and armies had not been defeated. The Persian army was too large to subsist very long on local supplies of food, and bringing what was needed from Persian soil could not be done safely in winter, when storms interrupted navigation on the Aegean Sea. So Xerxes needed a decisive victory at once.

Within the Greek camp, there was great disagreement about how to conduct the war. Some wanted to retire to the south and defend the Peloponnese from behind a wall that had already been partially constructed across the Isthmus of Corinth. Themistocles, on the other hand, wanted a naval battle. He figured that in a general fight the Greek ships could destroy a large part of the Persian fleet. Then Xerxes' supply line across the Aegean would be endangered and the Persians would have to withdraw.

Battle of Salamis

To trap both Xerxes and his fellow Greeks into accepting his plan, Themistocles resorted to stratagem. He sent a message to the Persian king saying that the Greek ships were planning to slip away from the Bay of Salamis in the night and suggested that if the Persian fleet were to attack, Greek resistance would crumble. Xerxes took the bait and ordered his ships to row in through the narrow straits between the island of Salamis and the mainland. He watched the fight from a throne specially set up on the steep bank. Great was Xerxes' dismay when the Persian ships ran afoul of one another in trying to crowd through the straits. This allowed the Greeks to ram and sink many vessels that were tangled, one with another, and unable to maneuver freely. As a result, the Greeks won a great victory. Nearly 200 Persian warships were sunk, while the Greeks lost only 40.

After the Battle of Salamis the Persian plan for subduing Greece became unworkable. Xerxes went home to Persia with most of his troops. Part of his army remained behind, however. The reduced Persian force, after spending the winter in Thessaly and Boeotia, once again moved south and devastated Attica, in the spring of 479 B.C.E.

Battle of Plataea

The Greek strategy this time was to take the offensive by sea. A fleet crossed the Aegean to Ionia. Meanwhile the Spartan army, with the Athenian phalanx and all the other troops the leagued Greek cities could put into the field, marched against the Persians. They met at Plataea, where the Greeks won the only major land battle of the war—not so much by superior generalship as by the superior steadiness of their heavy-armed infantry. At the same time, the Greek fleet won a victory at Cape Mycale in Asia Minor. As the news spread, Greek cities along the coast of Asia Minor revolted against their Persian governors once again. The Greek fleet headed north to besiege the main Persian base at the Hellespont, which controlled the straits between the Black Sea and the Aegean. With the capture of Sestos, late in the winter, the retreat of the Persian troops was cut off. Only tattered remnants of Xerxes' proud host ever made it back.

It was a famous victory won by a handful of Greek cities against the might of the vast Persian Empire. And it presented the victors with a series of critical new problems: Should war continue? Should the struggle be broken off? What should be done with the Greek cities that had submitted to the Persians? What about the league of cities that had so successfully resisted the invasion? What was Athens' relation to Sparta going to be?

The Peloponnesian War

All these and other issues were decided by each city for itself. The Spartans drew back; the Athenians, on the other hand, carried the war to the Persians by sending out naval expeditions year after year. Athens invited other Greek cities to send their fleets too, but the command always rested with an Athenian. Accordingly, until 448 B.C.E., the Athenians launched a naval expedition almost every year. In this way, they drove the Persians from the Aegean and Black Sea coasts entirely. They tangled indecisively with them along the south coast of Asia Minor. But they were badly defeated when they attacked the Persians in Egypt. Then, after an indecisive campaign on the island of Cyprus, peace was finally concluded (448 B.C.E.), leaving command of the seas firmly in Athenian hands.

The Rise of an Athenian Empire   In the course of all these years of fighting, the free association of Greek cities, which had first carried the war to the Persians, was gradually converted into an Athenian Empire. In 467 B.C.E., when the threat from the Persians had diminished, the people of the island of Naxos, feeling that they had done enough, refused to send ships to join in further offensive operations. The Athenians regarded this as treason. They therefore attacked Naxos and compelled the Naxians to pay money tribute, instead of manning ships as before. Other Greek communities, voluntarily or by force, also began to pay tribute to the Athenians. Athens used this income to pay its citizens for rowing in the fleet. The livelihood of thousands of poorer citizens came to depend on continual war, for if there were no enemy to fight, they could not count on rowers' wages and the booty that came from a successful expedition.

The peace of 448 B.C.E. consequently threatened disaster for poor Athenians. A solution was found by using the tribute money for restoring the damage done by the Persians when they had occupied Athens in 480 B.C.E. The Parthenon—the great temple to Athena of the Acropolis—was built in this way, giving employment to many of the Athenians who could no longer count on a job each summer with the fleet.

This policy solved a critical problem at home, but it only made Athens into a tyrant in the eyes of other Greeks. They, after all, had fought the Persians to preserve their freedom. But a city that had to pay tribute to Athens was not free. Moreover, the Athenians often interfered in the political struggles of other Greek cities, helping their friends and trying to prevent their enemies from coming to power.

Sparta's Reaction   At first the Spartans did nothing. They continued to direct the "Peloponnesian League" of cities in the southernmost part of Greece and to watch, with growing alarm, the rise of Athens' power. In 460 B.C.E. some of Sparta's allies went to war with Athens. Spartans eventually joined in, but only halfheartedly, and they made peace at the first opportunity. The Athenians did not remain quiet for very long, however. Soon they were busy extending their empire along the north shore of the Aegean; and they also began to reach out toward Sicily and southern Italy, where prosperous Greek cities, quarreling among themselves, were eager to invite the formidable Athenian fleet to join in their struggles.

Athens had already become supreme in the Aegean and Black Sea regions. The further possibility that Athenian naval power might fasten itself upon the western part of the Greek world threatened the economic prosperity of some of the Peloponnesian cities. In such case they would find their exports and imports completely at the mercy of the Athenian navy.

War Between Athens and Sparta   Such a threat stirred the reluctant Spartans into action. War broke out in 431 B.C.E. A long and bitter struggle lasted until 404 B.C.E.—this is usually called the Peloponnesian War, although from the Spartan point of view it was surely the *Athenian* war. Its history was written by Thucydides (ca. 471–400 B.C.E.), an Athenian who lived through it and personally took part in its beginning phases. At first the Athenians were able to prevail, even though they could not prevent the Spartan army from invading Attica and burning

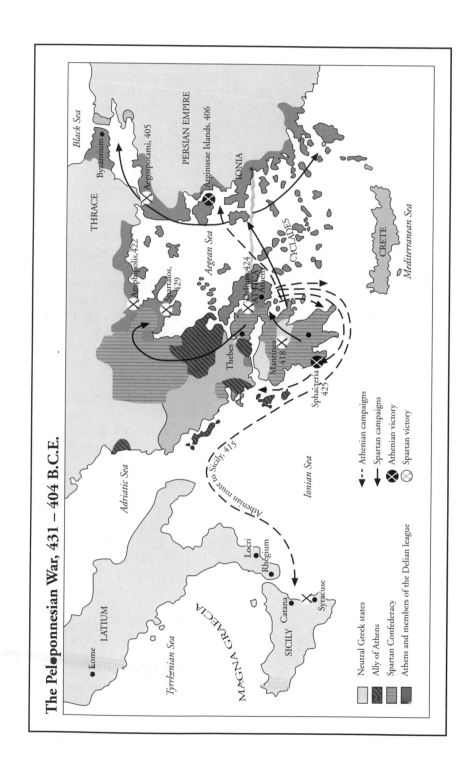

The Peloponnesian War, 431 – 404 B.C.E.

Rome

LATIUM

Adriatic Sea

Tyrrhenian Sea

MAGNA GRAECIA

SICILY Catana
Locri
Rhegium
Syracuse

Ionian Sea

Athenian route to Sicily, 415

Black Sea

Byzantium

THRACE

Aegospotami, 405

PERSIAN EMPIRE

Arginusae Islands, 406

IONIA

Amphipolis, 422

Spartalos, 429

Aegean Sea

CYCLADES

Delium, 424

ATTICA

Athens

Thebes

Mantinea, 418

Sphacteria, 425

CRETE

Mediterranean Sea

Neutral Greek states
Ally of Athens
Spartan Confederacy
Athens and members of the Delian league

Athenian campaigns
Spartan campaigns
Athenian victory
Spartan victory

Athenian Empire in Art   When the Athenian empire was at its peak, poor citizens made a living by rowing in the fleet each summer. After 448 B.C.E., peace was made with Persia, the citizens needed other employment and found it at home, reconstructing the Acropolis that had been devastated by Xerxes' invasion in 480 B.C.E. On the left is a view of the Parthenon as rebuilt, seen through the pillars of the entry gate. The grandiose entry was never completed because war broke out anew, this time with Sparta, in 431 B.C.E.. When peace returned (421–415 B.C.E.), the Athenians went to work on the Acropolis once more and built the Temple of Victory, shown on the right. It flanks the grand entryway on the south, proclaiming Athens's success against the Spartans and their allies. But when war resumed, Athens met defeat (404 B.C.E.). Work on the Acropolis halted permanently. Deprived of revenues from the empire, the city could not pay its poorer citizens either for rowing in the fleet or for building temples. Athens's political greatness swiftly faded into the past, leaving these famous and still impressive monuments to the city's imperial age.

their farms. But in 415 B.C.E. the restless Athenians overreached themselves by sending a large fleet to Sicily in hope of conquering that island. The whole expedition perished; then the Persians entered the war against Athens and supplied the Spartans with money for hiring rowers to man a fleet. Eventually, after several dramatic reversals on the sea, the Spartans destroyed

Athens' last fleet, whereupon the city was compelled to surrender.

Sparta's victory in 404 B.C.E. marked the end of the "Golden Age" of Greece; for amidst so much war and turmoil, the Athenians, with some help from other Greek cities, created classical Greek art and literature. Philosophy and science flourished also, though those branches of learning reached their high point later. Classical Greek culture became a model for later generations and still influences us today. It therefore deserves close consideration.

Classical Greek Society and Culture

Athenian Society

As Athens became an imperial city, the trade and tribute of the Aegean and Black Sea coasts began to flow toward the city's harbor, Piraeus. Strangers from all over the Greek world came, too. On the eve of the Peloponnesian War, the population of the city and its surrounding farmland was about 300,000, of whom nearly half were slaves and foreigners without political rights. Adult male Athenian citizens numbered not more than 50,000, yet they held an empire in their hands and governed themselves in a democratic way. Some 30,000 citizens were able to equip themselves to serve in the phalanx as heavy-armed infantry. Many of them were farmers, with small, family-sized plots of land in the countryside, who came into the city only on special occasions. Others had little or no land and depended on wages gained by rowing in the fleet. These citizens, when the fleet was idle, had lots of time to attend meetings of the assembly. They therefore tended to dominate its decisions, unless some unusual emergency called the farmers in from their fields.

Clearly, the citizens who depended on booty and on wages gained by rowing in the fleet could not afford to stop annual campaigns. This was the reason for Athens' aggressive foreign policy. As long as it brought victories and new

Pericles of Athens This portrait was made in Roman times and may or may not be entirely imaginary. It shows Pericles in his official capacity as a general of the city, helmeted but at rest. The reflective pose was surely meant to show the political and strategic foresight for which Pericles was famous.

wealth, the more conservative countrymen were willing enough to go along with this democratic-imperialist policy. Pericles, who dominated Athenian counsels from about 461 B.C.E. until his death in 429 B.C.E., was the main architect of this coalition between the rowers of the fleet and the soldiers of the Athenian phalanx.

After Pericles' death, under the pressure of the Peloponnesian War, the two parties found their interests diverging. For a while the landless, urban elements prevailed. Cleon was their chief spokesman in the assembly. Pericles' nephew, Alcibiades, attempted to revive the alliance of interests that had sustained his uncle's policy, but the conservative farmers distrusted Alcibiades' overweening personal ambition. He was driven from office just when his most dangerous project, the expedition to Sicily, got underway. Real trust and mutual collaboration between the two elements in Athenian society was never restored.

Similar social fissures opened among the citizens of most other Greek cities. By the time the Peloponnesian War had run its course, democrats who had been in alliance with Athens were discredited nearly everywhere. Thereafter oligarchies—government by the few, namely the richer citizens—prevailed. Even in Athens, where democracy was restored, the old energy evaporated. Poor citizens no longer rowed in the fleet. They preferred to collect fees, if possible, for sitting on juries or attending the meetings of the assembly and left soldiering to hired mercenaries from the poorer parts of the Greek world.

In this fashion the intense tie between citizens and the polis that had made Greece different from other civilized societies, began to wear out. Class division and private concerns took over. Greek society became more like that of the Middle East. The shared experience and risks of war that had bound all the citizens together dissolved into nostalgia for a glorious past that could never be equaled again.

Literature, Art, Science, and Philosophy

The fifty years between the defeat of the Persian invasion and the outbreak of the Peloponnesian War spanned a time when everything seemed possible to the Athenians. Dedicated to the greatness and glory of their polis, as almost all the citizens were, the Athenians constituted an unusually responsive, and at the same time critical, audience both for political speeches and for the public religious festivals that created Greek drama.

The Greek Drama   These festivals evolved from ceremonies honoring Dionysus, the god of wine. Rude songs and dances, performed by a chorus, first developed into a dialogue between a leader of the chorus and the rest of the dan-

cers. Then a story line was introduced; and soon the story line required two or three actors to appear at the same time, so that they could talk to one another as well as to the chorus. Thus tragedy and comedy were born from a common root.

At the yearly festivals, the Athenians awarded a prize for the best poet as well as for the best-equipped and best-trained chorus. Under the stimulus of popular acclaim, three great tragedians arose in succession to test their poetry against the taste of the Athenians: Aeschylus (524–456 B.C.E.), Sophocles (495–405 B.C.E.), and Euripides (480–406 B.C.E.). Each of them took old stories about gods and heroes—stories the Greeks thought of as ancient history—and put them in dramatic form. In addition to the magnificence of their verbal music—the poetry—the Greek tragedies were also serious efforts to express the truth, as each playwright saw it, about relations between human beings, the gods, fate, and the nature of things. Finally, song and dance, costumes, and painted scenery enhanced the emotional impact of the original performances in ways we can only imagine.

Though we cannot share nor accurately recreate these ancient spectacles, the dramatic texts that survive continue to command admiration. The ancients agreed; and next only to Homer, an apt quotation from one of the three Athenian tragedians became, throughout Greek and Roman antiquity, the mark of an educated man.

The Greek tragedians' view of the human condition was a modification of Homer's ideal. Their heroes were great and admirable, but too proud to submit to ordinary limitations upon human knowledge and power. Such pride brought its due punishment, either directly from the gods or through some natural and inevitable interlocking of cause and effect. Heroism, in other words, was treated as something admirable but dangerous. Wisdom required submission to the human norm. Such a conclusion nicely fitted the needs of a city that demanded so much from its citizens both in war and in peace.

The gods, however, presented the dramatists with unresolved problems. Traditional stories, such as those enshrined in Homer, could not be reconciled with the moral standards of the age. Thoughtful Athenians found it harder and harder to respect gods who behaved like spoiled children. Yet few were ready to doubt their existence. When so many things happened in defiance of human purposes, it seemed obvious that supernatural powers were at work in the world.

Comedy had a very different character. It was topical, funny, and bawdy. Aristophanes (448–385 B.C.E.), the only comedian whose works survive, wrote during the Peloponnesian War and made fun of everyone of note, with absolutely no holds barred.

Art and Architecture

Art also achieved a new perfection. The greatest monuments of the age were the buildings on the Athenian Acropolis, dominated by Athena's temple, the Parthenon. Simplicity of line and exquisite refinement of detail made it, and the other buildings of the Acropolis, a standard for all later ages. Their ruins still remain—solid evidence of how skillfully the ancient Greeks designed and constructed public ceremonial buildings.

The outside of the Parthenon was richly decorated with sculpture, but the admiration of the ancients was especially reserved for the great gold and ivory statue of Athena that stood inside the temple. Its creator, Phidias (500–431 B.C.E.), was also entrusted with the construction at Olympia of a similar and equally famous statue of Zeus, who was known as "father of all the gods." Both of these statues have long since disappeared, but some of the surviving Parthenon friezes suggest the calm, aloof dignity with which Phidias endowed the gods' images.

The Greek Historians

No less impressive was the work of the two great historians of ancient Greece, Herodotus (ca. 484–428 B.C.E.) and Thucydides (ca. 471–400 B.C.E.). Herodotus was born at Halicarnassus, in Asia Minor, and traveled widely in Egypt and Asia. He probably spent little time in Athens. Nevertheless, he made that city the hero of his story of the Persian Wars. Thucydides did so as well, though with a tragic sense, when telling the story of the Peloponnesian War. His skill in analyzing motives and the interplay of circumstance within the Greek world during the war set a standard

for historical writing that has seldom been equaled since. Both historians were also great writers. Indeed, it was their literary style that later generations of Greeks and Romans valued most of all.

The Practice of Medicine

Like the earliest Ionian philosophers, Herodotus and Thucydides kept the gods out of their histories. This same cast of mind, applied to the practice of medicine, created the Hippocratic school, named for Hippocrates of Cos, who lived about 400 B.C.E. Books attributed to Hippocrates or, more vaguely, to his school, carefully describe the symptoms and stages of various diseases. Hippocratic texts regarded diseases as natural and prescribed rest and quiet as cures.

Medical school graduates today often take the "Hippocratic oath." This oath requires doctors to use their skills only to help their patients. It thus established an ideal of professional conduct that still stands.

The Greek Philosophers

Even though Hippocrates and his school gave up the idea that disease was caused by some kind of alien "spirit" entering into a person's body, the ancient Greek doctors did not really get very far in their effort to understand natural bodily processes. The same was true of philosophers. Yet they did hit on some remarkably fertile ideas—for example, the atomic theory—and kept on bringing up new questions to wonder about. The philosopher Empedocles (ca. 444 B.C.E.) tried to explain physical and biological changes as the result of combinations and recombinations of elements. Another philosopher, Anaxagoras, was banished from Athens about 440 B.C.E. for trying to explain the nature of the heavenly bodies by comparing them with red-hot stones.

A second line of development made logic the key to solving all problems. The founder of this school was Parmenides (ca. 480 B.C.E.) He proved—at least to his own satisfaction—that all change was an illusion. He said that a thing either was or was not. If a thing really was—really had *being*—then it could never turn into its opposite, *nonbeing*. That would be a logical contradiction. Hence he concluded that whatever was, simply *was* and could not change.

Parmenides' logical puzzles provoked Democritus of Abdera (ca. 440 B.C.E.) to suggest that the world was made up of atoms, so small as to be invisible but each of them unchangeable in itself—just like the unchangeable *being* that Parmenides had described. Democritus explained growth and decay as the result of the coming together and breaking up of clusters of atoms. To account for their movement, he had, of course, to assume a void for them to move about in.

Other philosophers boldly set out to apply logic to human affairs. They were known as Sophists, and they undertook to instruct young men in all they should know to enter public life. This meant, in a democratic city like Athens, teaching their pupils how to speak and argue a case to the public in a way that would seem convincing. Some of the Sophists really thought that skillful manipulation of words could solve any problem. Like Parmenides, they assumed that words naturally or necessarily corresponded to things. Hence if a man got his words into order, so that one followed logically from the other, he would know all there was to know about the natural world and about human beings as well.

Other Sophists felt that truth did not really matter. Practical persons did not need to worry about whether words really corresponded to things in some ultimate sense. Words were merely tools for convincing other people. For the Sophists who thought in this way, right and justice and all the other moral standards to which politicians appealed were no more than useful devices for persuading the common people to accept one opinion or another.

Such ideas challenged the very basis of polis loyalty. If the world were nothing but a place where clever politicians attained power by deceiving their followers, then the willing dedication to common enterprises that had held Athenians together in war and peace was based on nothing but delusion. A real man would follow his own interests, regardless of others.

The disasters of the Peloponnesian War encouraged such attitudes. Sophistry, however, also provoked a powerful and important reaction. Socrates (469–399 B.C.E.) and his pupil Plato (427–347 B.C.E.) were the key figures. They sought to find a basis for truth and justice in the nature of things. Socrates never wrote anything,

and we know of his thought mainly through dialogues in which Plato later recorded his own version of what Socrates had stood for. Plato also wrote dialogues to explain his own ideas, and sometimes he put words in Socrates' mouth that the real Socrates probably would never have used.

We can be sure, nevertheless, that Socrates spent his time in the streets and public places of Athens, talking with all comers and asking them difficult questions about truth and knowledge, the good life, and how people ought to behave. Socrates' questions swiftly showed how flimsy most common opinions really were. For himself, he claimed only to be aware of his own ignorance.

Socrates performed the duties of a citizen, fighting as an ordinary soldier during the Peloponnesian War and serving on the council when elected to that post by lot. He never violated his own sense of justice and right. But some of the bright young men who listened with relish while Socrates deflated democratic politicians and would-be politicians took part in coups d'état against Athens' democratic government during the later stages of the Peloponnesian War. When democracy was restored after the war, therefore, Socrates was accused of corrupting the youth of the city. He was tried and condemned to die by drinking poison. Although his friends urged him to flee, he refused, arguing that he could not defy the laws of the city which had nourished him and protected him all his life. Before sorrowing friends, one of whom was Plato, Socrates drank the poison and died quietly in 399 B.C.E.

Plato became a philosopher through his association with Socrates. Like his teacher, Plato was always mainly concerned with how one ought to behave. To know how to behave properly, he felt, a person had to know what was good, true, and beautiful. All the different things commonly thought to be good or true or beautiful, he argued, must have something in common, just as all tables have something in common that makes them into tables. A philosopher, therefore, ought to be able to find out exactly what it was that all similar things had in common. With enough study, a person might catch a glimpse of the changeless and immaterial essences (Plato called them ideas) that lie behind every particular example of any class of objects. Then he would know how to behave. Anything less, Plato felt, was just an opinion, not necessarily better than its opposite.

Plato developed this theory in a famous dialogue, *The Republic.* Yet he was never altogether satisfied with such an answer to his main problem. How could he really prove the existence of pure and unchanging ideas? And even if they did exist, how did things "participate" in them to become good or true or whatever? Since he was unable to solve such problems, Plato left to later generations a series of questions rather than definite answers. But Plato's questions defined most of the issues about which Western philosophers still concern themselves. Above all, how do we know? And how do words and ideas connect with things? Plato's great pupil Aristotle (384–322 B.C.E.) had answers. He undertook to master all the knowledge of his day and classified it into neat, logical parts. Nothing escaped him—or almost nothing. He perfected a method for arguing according to rules of logic, and he applied those rules to all the questions Plato had asked as well as to matters we call science—physics, biology, and even the weather. In fact, many of the distinctions we still take for granted—for example, between politics and economics—were first formulated by Aristotle.

Plato founded a school, which Aristotle attended for many years before establishing his own separate lecture hall. After the two philosophers' deaths, their pupils kept the rival institutions going. Plato's Academy, in fact, lasted nearly 900 years, longer than any university yet has done. Other philosophic schools were set up later in Athens, and similar institutions arose in other cities. Athens, however, remained the most famous "university town" of the ancient world. There wealthy young men continued to come from all over the Greek and Roman world to sow their wild oats and learn enough philosophy to keep them out of mischief. As a result, little by little, philosophy as well as other aspects of Greek culture gradually turned into a code of conduct for well-to-do gentlemen.

Such a change could be carried through only after the city-state framework, which had raised Greek civilization so high, itself broke down. We must next consider how this happened.

The Rise of Macedon and the Expansion of Hellenism Eastward

Conquest from the north, at the hands of a semibarbarous kingdom of Macedon, ended Greek political independence in 338 B.C.E. But before the Macedonians were able to transform the political basis of Greek life in this way, far-reaching changes had first to occur within the kingdom of Macedon itself.

Macedonian Empire

When the Persians marched into Greece in 480 B.C.E., they passed through Macedonia without meeting any resistance. Later the Athenians treated the kings of Macedon as a kind of dependent ally. Then under King Philip, who reigned from 359 to 336 B.C.E., Macedonian power grew very rapidly. For the first time Philip was able to get the Macedonian nobles to stop weakening the country with bitter feuds.

The secret of his success was to bring young noblemen to court, where they became accustomed to the luxuries and refinements of the Greek style of life. After spending some years at court, few of them cared to return to the backwoods. Instead they stayed to serve the king as administrators and army officers. This quickly allowed King Philip to mobilize the full resources of his kingdom for war. By comparison with any of the Greek states, the kingdom of Macedon was enormous. Hence, when the Macedonians stopped fighting among themselves and learned how to put an efficient phalanx into the field, superior numbers began to tell.

As for the Greeks, they found it impossible to unite. After Athens' defeat in 404 B.C.E., for a while the Spartans were by far the strongest power in Greece. But they quickly antagonized all the other Greek cities and were overthrown by a coalition led by Thebes, a former Spartan ally. The Thebans, in turn, soon saw their allies against Sparta turn into enemies. They were, therefore, defeated easily enough by King Philip at the Battle of Chaeronea in 338 B.C.E.

Alexander's Dazzling Career   King Philip made himself president of a league of all the Greek cities. His plan was to lead the Greeks in a war of "revenge" against Persia. But Philip was assassinated in 336 B.C.E., before he could start. His son, Alexander, was then only twenty years of age. The Thebans rose in revolt; so did barbarian Thracians to the north who had also been conquered by King Philip's armies. The youthful Alexander proved his mettle by the speed with which he checked both of these threats to his power. Thebes having been captured and de-

stroyed, the rest of the Greek cities quickly submitted. Alexander then took up his father's project for an attack on Persia.

The great adventure began in 334 B.C.E. King Alexander won battle after battle as he moved deeper into Persian territory. In 333 B.C.E. he met and defeated the full muster of the Persian field army at Issus, in the southeast corner of Asia Minor. Then he marched his army into Egypt, where he founded the city of Alexandria before returning to face the Persian king Darius III again, defeating him this time at Gaugamela (331 B.C.E.) in northern Mesopotamia.

In the following year Darius III was murdered by his own followers. Alexander thereupon claimed to be the legitimate successor to the Persian throne. He had to campaign hard in the eastern parts of the Persian Empire to en-

---

Alexander the Great   The young Macedonian king who conquered the Persian empire between 334 and 323 B.C.E. is portrayed here leading a charge against the Persians in his first great victory at the Battle of Issus (333 B.C.E.). This mosaic comes from Pompeii, a southern Italian town buried in 79 C.E. by an eruption of Mount Vesuvius. The artist who created this image had never seen Alexander, and all surviving portraits of him are equally imaginary. But this is how he ought to have looked, as imagined by later generations. His armies spread Greek styles of life eastward to the Indus and beyond. His personal embodiment of the heroic ideal was so perfect that his reputation still lives in the oral traditions of remote villages of Afghanistan as well as in our schoolbooks.

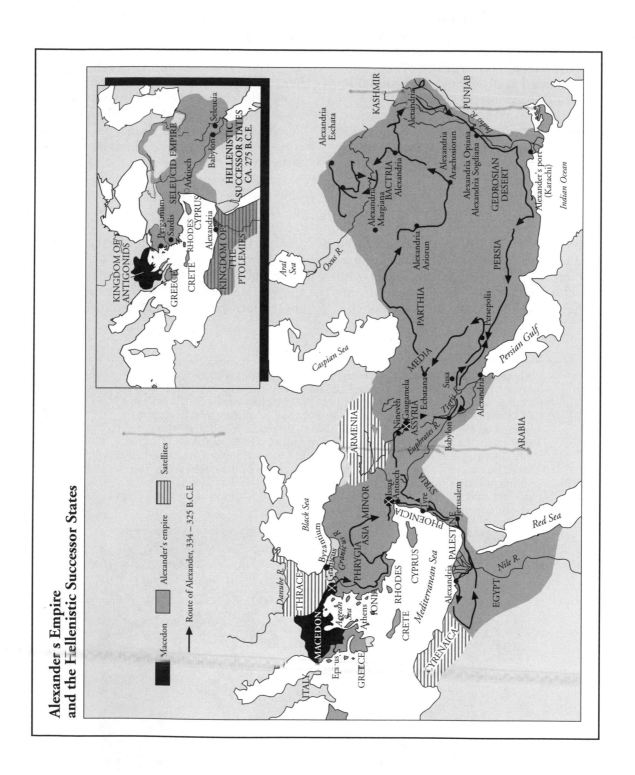

**Alexander's Empire
and the Hellenistic Successor States**

Macedon

Alexander's empire

Satellites

Route of Alexander, 334 – 325 B.C.E.

KINGDOM OF ANTIGONIDS

SELEUCID EMPIRE

KINGDOM OF THE PTOLEMIES

HELLENISTIC SUCCESSOR STATES CA. 275 B.C.E.

Pergamum
Sardis
GREECE
CRETE RHODES
CYPRUS
Alexandria
Antioch
Babylon Seleucia

Aral Sea
Oxus R.
Caspian Sea

KASHMIR
Alexandria Eschata
BACTRIA
Alexandria Margiana
Alexandria
Alexandria Opiana
Alexandria Arachosiorun
Alexandria Sogdiana
PUNJAB
Indus R.
Alexander's port (Karachi)
Indian Ocean
GEDROSIAN DESERT
PERSIA
Alexandria Ariorun
PARTHIA
Persepolis
MEDIA
Ecbatana
Persian Gulf
Nineveh Gaugamela
ASSYRIA
Susa
Tigris R.
Alexandria
Euphrates R.
Babylon
ARABIA

ARMENIA

THRACE
Byzantium
Granicus R.
ASIA MINOR
PHRYGIA
IONIA
Damube R.
Black Sea
CYPRUS
RHODES
CRETE
Mediterranean Sea
Alexandria
Antioch
Issus
Tyre
Jerusalem
PHOENICIA
SYRIA
PALESTINE
Red Sea
Nile R.
EGYPT
CYRENAICA

ITALY
MACEDON
Aegean Sea
Athens
Ep us
GREECE

force his claim. Then he crossed the mountains into India; but when he tried to press ahead into the Ganges Valley, his troops mutinied and he had to turn back. Alexander did not return by the way he had come. Instead he followed the Indus River to its mouth and then marched through a barren desert, along the shores of the Persian Gulf, until his weary troops finally arrived in Mesopotamia. Soon afterward, in 323 B.C.E., Alexander died of a fever in Babylon at the age of thirty-three.

Such a career dazzled everyone. The young Alexander had set out to rival Achilles, hero of the *Iliad;* he more than succeeded. While in Egypt, priests of Amon-Re greeted him as a god, as they had greeted every ruler of Egypt from the days of the Old Kingdom. Alexander himself may have half-believed it (and many of his new subjects certainly did), but the idea shocked most Greeks and Macedonians.

He left an empire in confusion. Nevertheless, his reckless daring and vast conquests, all crowded into the space of eleven years, had changed the course of history. Alexander's importance lay not so much in his astounding military exploits and personal actions as in the way he spread Hellenism (Greek culture) everywhere he went. He founded numerous cities in the conquered lands. These became centers of Greek and Macedonian population. And wherever they settled, the conquerors brought their customs and institutions with them. As a result, in the centuries that followed, local peoples of the Middle East, northern India, and central Asia had ample opportunity to take over whatever they felt was worthwhile in the Greek cultural inheritance. The blending of Greek and Middle Eastern civilization that resulted we call "Hellenistic" because, at least to begin with, the Hellenic element tended to dominate.

Alexander apparently wished to rule the empire he had conquered by uniting the Greek, Macedonian, and Persian peoples. He even arranged a mass marriage of his soldiers to Persian women, and he himself married a Persian princess. But when he died, this policy died with him.

Hellenistic Monarchies   His successors, hard-bitten Macedonian generals, despised both Greeks and Persians. They had to depend on the loyalty of their Macedonian soldiers to maintain power. Soon the generals quarreled, and the great empire split apart. Egypt passed to the family of Ptolemy. Most of Asia fell into the hands of Seleucus I and his heirs. Macedonia itself eventually passed to the family of Antigonus I.

Greece became independent again, but the separate cities were no more than playthings for the vast new Hellenistic monarchies. Efforts to form leagues that might withstand the new empires met with limited success, but Greece as a whole could never unite. The leading cities shifted back and forth between alliance with the Ptolemies, who had a powerful fleet, and with the Antigonids, who had a strong army. Never again did the Greek city-states really matter militarily. But the Greeks became very important to the new rulers of Asia and Egypt, who could not trust the native population and who badly needed well-trained soldiers and administrators. A great emigration therefore took place. Parts of Greece became depopulated. Farming passed into the hands of slaves or of poor strangers who had no voice in city politics.

Within Greek cities, political rights more and more were limited to the wealthy. In other words, the pattern of Greek society came to resemble the more ancient civilized society of the Middle East. At the same time, the Middle Eastern peoples eagerly took on many of the traits of Hellenic culture. Peoples farther east, in India and central Asia, also learned to admire and imitate aspects of the Greek achievement.

Cultural Blending in the Hellenistic East

The cultural interaction that resulted from Alexander's conquests was very complex. Babylonia and Egypt resisted Greek ways, as did the Jews. In Syria and Asia Minor, on the other hand, Greek dress, speech, and manners slowly seeped down the social scale until most city residents spoke, and in a certain sense were, Greek. Oddly enough, the Greek influence was also felt far to the east, where Alexander had founded a

Poor and Rich, Rural and Urban   In Hellenistic times, the ideal of equality among citizens, nourished by phalanx warfare, wore thin and eventually disappeared. Military service became mercenary and professional. Rich and poor went their separate ways in the great monarchies that inherited parts of Alexander's empire.

The two statues shown here reflect the sharp divisions of Hellenistic and later of Roman society. On the left, a poor shepherd woman; on the right, a goddess—the Victory of Samothrace. The fact that expert artists sometimes portrayed poor, rural folk perhaps reflects nostalgia for the old social bond that had once held Greek citizens together so tightly. Yet the Greeks, who migrated from their native places to occupy administrative and professional posts in the Hellenistic monarchies, also experienced the exhilaration of new worlds to conquer and enjoy, as may be sensed in the exaltation of victory that is expressed so skillfully in the swirling garments of the goddess on the right.

lot of garrison cities near the frontier. Persians and others living in those parts found Greek civilization more impressive than any they had known before. Even when a Parthian empire rose in Iran, the court and cities continued to prize Greek culture. Still farther to the east, Greek rulers of Bactria flourished from about 250 B.C.E. to about 50 B.C.E. Their kingdom strad-dled the mountain divide between India and central Asia.

From Bactria, in turn, Greek influences passed into India and also spread farther east along trade routes toward China. Sculptural style is the main surviving evidence of this encounter. But the sculptors of India and those of China were not copyists; they altered and transformed the Greek models, just as, long before, the Greek sculptors of the Archaic Age (650–500 B.C.E.) had borrowed and transformed Egyptian models while developing their own art style.

About other matters we know far less. Some ideas in astronomy seem to have traveled from the Aegean to India, and perhaps to China. The idea of world empire may have entered Indian political theory by imitation of Persian or Hellenistic examples, and Indians began to supplement their oral learning by writing books on the model of the Greek book trade. But Greek impact in such distant parts remained always fragmentary, weak, and superficial.

Westward, however, things were different. The peoples of Italy and western Europe were still barbarians when classical Greek civilization reached its height. As familiarity with Greek culture spread, those who could afford it eagerly absorbed all they could of the Greek style of life and luxury. We shall consider this great movement next.

The Rise of Rome and the Expansion of Hellenism Westward

Greece was conquered by the Romans but, as the Roman poet Horace expressed it, the captive Greeks revenged themselves by captivating their conquerors. But that is only part of the truth. Long before they allowed themselves to be captivated by Greek high culture, the Romans had a well-worked-out lifestyle of their own. This was a blending of native Latin ways with other cultural strands. In particular, the Etruscans contributed much to Roman life. The Etruscans were a semi-civilized people who invaded northern and central Italy about 900 B.C.E. They probably came from Asia Minor. Some of their skills and customs that became important in Rome—for example, the art of divination—seem closely connected with ancient Mesopotamian traditions. In addition, contact with both Greek and Phoenician traders, who carried goods up and down the coasts of Italy, added to the knowledge and skills of early Rome.

The Early Republic

According to legend, Rome was founded in 753 B.C.E. by two brothers, Romulus and Remus. The city began to grow into a center of some importance when a few Etruscans captured the place and made Rome their headquarters. Then about 509 B.C.E., through a revolt, the Etruscan king, Tarquin, was overthrown and a republic was established. The Romans now found themselves between two worlds: the world of city-state civilization—Etruscan, Greek, or Phoenician—on the one hand, and the old Latin world of loosely federated villages and tribes on the other. In the years that followed, the Romans managed to combine these two principles of political organization. For themselves they kept the city-state form they had inherited from the Etruscan kings, but they also maintained a "Latin league" uniting them with simpler rural communities living nearby.

Roman Society   Warfare broke out practically every summer as soon as the harvest was in. For a long time the Romans' simple rural life made it difficult for them to keep the better-equipped Etruscans at bay. Eventually, however, the Romans began to prevail. Rome's great advantage lay in numbers, for even the poorest Romans were ready to fight—especially when victory might mean new land for them to settle on and cultivate. The rulers of the Etruscan and Greek cities of Italy lived mostly on rents. They could not easily mobilize their rent-paying subjects, who often spoke a different language and were reluctant to fight in their masters' wars.

Roman society, too, was divided sharply between privileged patricians and the common folk, or plebs (plebeians). The plebs often quarreled with the patricians, demanding and in time securing a greater share of political power. But when outside danger threatened, the Romans managed to check their domestic strife and could therefore offer a united front to the outside world. No other city of Italy could do so. No other ruling clique could call upon the fighting manpower of the countryside in the way that Romans did. The result was first a slow and then a very rapid expansion of Roman power over Italy.

Roman manners long remained conservative. Traditional religious rites were strictly maintained; luxury and display of private wealth were frowned upon. Most citizens remained simple farmers. In the early days, even the patricians sometimes worked in the fields, as shown in the famous story of how Cincinnatus was called from a plow to become temporary dictator of Rome. As long as that pattern lasted, sympathy between the various social classes of Rome remained strong enough to allow them to overcome all rivals in Italy.

First Conquests

The first important success for Roman arms came in 396 B.C.E. with the capture of the Etruscan city of Veii. The Romans destroyed the town and divided up the conquered land among themselves. This policy gave the plebs a solid stake in military enterprise. Success in battle meant land for the poor. Yet scarcely had this victory been won when Roman power suffered a severe setback. A raiding band of Gauls came down from the north and sacked the city in 390 B.C.E. Only the fortified capitol held out. Nevertheless, when the raiders withdrew, Rome recovered quickly and in the next fifty years conquered much new territory, becoming one of the "Great Powers" of the Italian peninsula. Seventy-five years later, after still further warfare, the Romans became supreme in all of Italy south of the Apennines (265 B.C.E.).

The Constitution of the Republic

The Roman constitution was extremely complicated. Three different kinds of assemblies had different and at times overlapping powers. The *Comitia Curiata*, organized by "tribes," voted on laws. Election of magistrates, who exercised executive power, rested with the *Comitia centuriata*. This was a citizen body in military array; and those with better equipment had a larger number of votes than the poor and ill-equipped. To counterbalance this distribution of power by wealth, the plebs created their own assembly, called the *Concilium plebis*. This body of plebeians elected tribunes of the people who had the power to veto any action undertaken by any other magistrate.

In addition to the popular assemblies, there was a Senate. This body originally admitted only patricians, but in 367 B.C.E. (when plebs were permitted to stand for election as magistrates), ex-magistrates of plebeian birth also were admitted to the Senate. Its influence was very great, largely because nearly all of the most active and individually powerful citizens of the state were members of the Senate. They usually tried to settle things quietly among themselves before bringing any important question before one or other of the assemblies.

Roman Military Organization

Rome's military organization evolved away from the phalanx of the Greeks. In the course of difficult wars in the hill country of central and southern Italy, the Romans discovered that the long, unbroken line of the phalanx was ineffective. Instead, they divided their army into tactical units of 200 to 300 men, each of which could maneuver independently, suiting its line of march to the terrain. In flat open country the separate *maniples*, as these units were called, could form a solid battle line, like that which the Greeks worked so hard to maintain. In rough country each maniple could act on its own, keeping only loose contact with other units on its flanks. Maniples were grouped into larger units called legions, numbering, usually, about 6000 men. Special units of cavalry and light-armed troops supplemented the legions, but the strength of Roman armies rested always, as it had with the Greeks, on heavy-armed infantry. The great superiority of the Roman legions was their ability to fight in rough country as well as on open plains—a superiority which soon made them masters of the entire Mediterranean basin.

The Federal Principle

Another factor of critical importance was the use of the federal principle to bind subject allies to the Roman state. At strategic locations, the Romans established colonies of Roman citizens on conquered land. Such colonists continued to enjoy full citizens' rights, but they could vote only by coming to Rome. There were not nearly enough Roman citizens to occupy all of Italy, so in most cases the Romans simply concluded a treaty with a conquered town or tribe. Such treaties required the signatory "to have the same friends and enemies as the Roman people" and to send troops whenever and wherever called upon to do so.

Everything else was left to local custom and initiative. The net effect of these arrangements was to allow the Roman city-state to organize the male population of all Italy for common military enterprises. By 265 B.C.E. no other state in the entire Mediterranean area could call on such a large pool of military manpower.

Roman Conquest of the Western and Eastern Mediterranean

The Punic Wars   The greatest test the Roman Republic ever faced took the form of a long struggle with Carthage, a Phoenician colony in north Africa. The Romans referred to the conflict as the Punic Wars ("Punic" being derived from *Poeni,* which is Latin for Phoenicians).

While the Romans had been welding Italy together, the Carthaginians had also built an empire that in some ways resembled the Roman confederation. Carthaginian power, like Rome's, rested on collaboration between a city-state government and native manpower—in this case Numidian manpower in what is now Tunis and Algeria. Later, the Carthaginians added recruits from Spain (Iberia) and southern France to their armies. But Carthage differed from Rome in being first and foremost a naval and trading city. There was no great reservoir of countryfolk sharing the ideas and attitudes of the city leaders and backing up Carthaginian policy. Rome had such a reservoir; and in this, fundamentally, lay the Romans' decisive advantage.

War broke out in 264 B.C.E. when the rivals clashed over control of Sicily. To fight in Sicily required the Romans to create a fleet for the first time. Despite heavy losses, they persisted until Carthage ceded the island to them in 241 B.C.E. This victory presented the Romans with a new problem. How were they to govern an overseas territory that was inhabited by Phoenicians, Greeks, and various native peoples? Their decision was to put Sicily under a Roman governor, since it seemed impossible to trust the various local communities to govern themselves in alliance with Rome, as had been done so successfully in Italy.

The Carthaginians did not accept defeat passively. Instead, under the leadership of the Barca family, Carthage built a new empire along the coast of Spain. The Barcas created a formidable army by enlisting native Celts and Iberians under their personal command. They used this force to capture new territory and extend their power, much as the Romans had done in Italy. This aroused Roman fears. Hence, when Saguntum (modern name: Sagunto)—a small Greek city situated along the Spanish coast south of the Ebro River—asked Rome for an alliance against the Carthaginians, the Romans agreed. In effect this act said to Carthaginian empire-builders, "So far and no further."

Hannibal, who had just succeeded his father in command of Carthaginian forces in Spain, was not willing to submit to this kind of limitation. He therefore attacked and captured Saguntum in 219 B.C.E. The Romans declared war. Hannibal promptly marched from Iberia (Spain) through southern Gaul (France) and over the Alps, bringing his war elephants with him. In northern Italy he met and defeated Roman armies in two major battles. Victory seemed to be in his hands.

Yet the Romans stubbornly refused to make peace. After another costly defeat at Cannae in southern Italy (216 B.C.E.), they decided to fight no more battles against Hannibal. Instead, they sent out armies year after year to shadow Hannibal's every move, cut off stragglers, and in general make life difficult for the invaders. Cities that had broken their treaties with Rome and opened their gates to Hannibal, whether voluntarily or by force, were besieged by still other Roman armies. Hannibal could not match Roman numbers; little by little the balance in Italy turned against him.

Carthage and Rome spared no effort in this great war. It eventually turned into a general war involving the entire Mediterranean region. Carthage, for example, made an alliance with the king of Macedonia, who, however, contributed little to the struggle. Rome countered by sending an expeditionary force to Spain and making an alliance with the king of western Numidia (modern Algeria) against Carthage.

Carthage eventually broke under the strain. In 207 B.C.E. the Romans defeated reinforce-

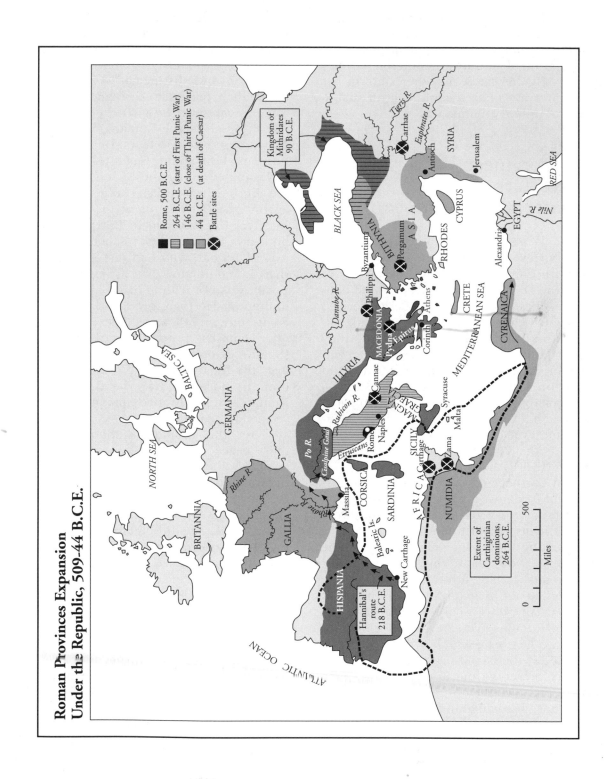

**Roman Provinces Expansion
Under the Republic, 509–44 B.C.E.**

Rome, 500 B.C.E.
264 B.C.E. (start of First Punic War)
146 B.C.E. (close of Third Punic War)
44 B.C.E. (at death of Caesar)
Battle sites

Kingdom of
Mithridates
90 B.C.E.

Extent of
Carthaginian
dominions,
264 B.C.E.

Hannibal's
route
218 B.C.E.

BLACK SEA

Carrhae
Tigris R.
Euphrates R.
SYRIA
Antioch
Jerusalem
RED SEA

Byzantium
BITHYNIA
Pergamum
ASIA
CYPRUS
RHODES
Nile R.
EGYPT
Alexandria

Philippi
MACEDONIA
Pydna
Epirus
Corinth
Athens
CRETE
MEDITERRANEAN SEA
CYRENAICA

ILLYRIA
Cannae
Rubicon R.
MAGNA
GRAECIA
Naples
Syracuse
Malta
SICILY
Zama
Carthage
AFRICA
NUMIDIA

Danube R.

Po R.
Cisalpine Gaul
Etruscans
Rome

Massilia
CORSICA
SARDINIA

Rhine R.
Rhône R.

GERMANIA

NORTH SEA

BALTIC SEA

BRITANNIA

GALLIA

HISPANIA
Balearic Is.
New Carthage

ATLANTIC OCEAN

0   500
Miles

ments which had come to Italy from Spain to help Hannibal. The next year, Scipio, a Roman general later nicknamed "Africanus," drove the Carthaginians out of Spain. Scipio also made a secret alliance with the king of eastern Numidia, who had formerly been an ally of Carthage. In 204 B.C.E., therefore, when Scipio led a Roman army into Africa, all the Numidians went over to his side. This threatened Carthage's position in north Africa even more seriously than Hannibal's presence in Italy threatened Roman power. The Carthaginians had to call their great general home. Accordingly, in 202 B.C.E. Hannibal fought the last battle of the war at Zama in north Africa, not far from Carthage itself. There, for the first time, he met defeat. Carthage had to sue for peace.

The Romans wanted to be sure that the Carthaginians could never again endanger them. Spain became a Roman province. The Numidians were declared free. The Carthaginians agreed to pay a war indemnity, to destroy their fleet of warships, and "to have the same friends and enemies as the Roman people," that is, to become Rome's subject allies.

Within a generation Carthaginian trade revived. This excited alarm in Rome, where the memory of Hannibal's invasion remained fresh. A party of old Romans kept demanding the utter destruction of their former rival. In 149 B.C.E. a quarrel arose between the Carthaginians and the Numidians. Rome sent an army. The Carthaginians tried to make peace again, but the Romans would not agree. Instead, they sacked and destroyed the city and, according to legend, sowed the area with salt so that Carthage could never rise again. The region around the former city was made into a province; the rest of north Africa was handed over to the Numidians. Rome was now absolute master of the western Mediterranean.

Hannibal's years in Italy led to great changes there. His soldiers lived off the country. Year after year the small farmers of Italy were called to serve in the Roman armies. The land became desolate. Many army veterans felt no wish to go back to the hard, quiet life of the farm. To start again without tools or animals, or even a house, was difficult at best. To loiter in the city and see what might turn up seemed far more attractive to a great many discharged vet-

erans. Supplies of grain coming from Sicily as tribute made such an existence possible. Add on the prospect of booty from new campaigns, and city life became far more attractive than rustic poverty. It also meant that many Roman citizens became eager for war in distant lands where rich booty could be had.

Rome's Conquest of the Eastern Mediterranean   Rome had reason enough to quarrel with the powers of the eastern Mediterranean. In 215 B.C.E., when Hannibal was at Rome's gates, the Macedonians had made an alliance with Carthage. After Carthage had been defeated, the Romans were therefore ready to respond when Greek cities appealed to them for aid against the Macedonian king. Rome sent an army into Greece in 197 B.C.E. and defeated the Macedonian phalanx at Cynoscephalae (Dog's Head). The Romans then demanded that the Macedonians pay an indemnity, reduce their army to 5000 men, and make war only with Roman approval. As for the Greeks, like the Numidians, they were declared free.

No such settlement could last. All sorts of quarrels among the Greeks were appealed to Rome, and though some Romans resisted involvement, others were very ready to intervene, since soldiers and commanders alike found the rich booty and easy victories of campaigning in the east too attractive to give up. In 148 B.C.E., therefore, after another campaign, Macedonia also was made into a province. Rome was now able to dominate the eastern as well as the western Mediterranean.

Changes in the Economic and Political Life of the Romans

By this time the old simplicity of Roman life had gone by the boards. Land-grabbing senators had taken possession of large estates in southern and central Italy, where Hannibal's devastation had emptied the countryside. Slaves cultivated those lands or tended sheep and cattle on them. A new class of traders and financiers had grown wealthy by organizing the collection of tribute from the provinces. Rome, in other words, evolved very rapidly into a society sharply divided between rich and poor, free and slave, citizen and noncitizen, soldier and civilian. A rash of civil wars and upheavals resulted, including a spectacular slave revolt led by Spartacus, a Thracian gladiator.

Efforts at reform got nowhere. Tiberius Gracchus in 133 B.C.E. tried to use his power as tribune of the people to break up the great estates and divide the land among the city poor. He was murdered in an election riot and when his brother, Gaius Gracchus, tried to renew and extend Tiberius' program in 123 B.C.E., he, too, was killed by his political opponents. Street gangs of thugs began to play an important part in electioneering, but this kind of violence was soon eclipsed by the soldiers, who in the end overturned the civilian game of politics.

Roman armies became increasingly professional, especially after property qualifications for serving in the ranks were waived in 106 B.C.E. This meant that the old idea of sending soldiers back home to the farm when a campaign was over could not work any longer. Veterans had no home to return to. If they could not be reenlisted for another war almost at once, land had to be found for them. The return of a victorious army thus created a crisis for Romans at home. This became painfully clear in 100 B.C.E., when Gaius Marius, after victories in northern Africa and in southern France, acquired land for his soldiers by executing his political opponents among the Senatorial party and seizing their possessions. His example was soon followed by Sulla (83–79 B.C.E.), who tried to restore the old government by violently suppressing the so-called Popular party that Marius had helped to establish.

Pompey and Caesar: Rivals for Political Power   The feud between rival cliques continued in the next generation. Pompey the Great (Gnaeus Pompeius Magnus) and Julius Caesar became the two chief figures. Pompey conquered the East, putting Syria and most of Asia Minor under Roman governors and setting up client kings in Palestine and elsewhere (65–62 B.C.E.). Caesar conquered Gaul as far as the Rhine (58–51 B.C.E.) and made a brief invasion of Britain. In 60 B.C.E. Caesar, Pompey and Marcus Licinius Crassus (a Roman financier

and politician) entered into a political alliance that allowed them to control the Roman state.

The First Triumvirate, as this arrangement was called, lasted until 53 B.C.E., when Crassus met his death in an attempt to conquer Parthia to the east.

Not long afterward Pompey and Caesar quarreled, and civil war broke out. Caesar prevailed, but not until 45 B.C.E. was he able to defeat all his rivals. Caesar thereupon returned to Rome, where he faced the task of somehow putting the government in order. Caesar probably wished to control Roman politics from behind the scenes, although his enemies accused him of wishing to be king. A clique of conspirators decided that the only way to preserve the Republic was to kill him. They therefore stabbed and killed Caesar on the steps of the Senate house in 44 B.C.E.

Civil war broke out again. Caesar's friends rallied to defeat the armies raised by his assassins. Then they set out to divide the Mediterranean world between them. Mark Antony, Caesar's most ambitious general, took the East. He expected to win great victories against the Parthians and to return, as Caesar had done, in triumph to Rome, where he could dictate his own terms to his rivals. Octavian, Caesar's adopted son and heir, was assigned the difficult task of trying to bring peace and order to Italy. He had to share power with another of Caesar's generals, Marcus Lepidus.

This so-called Second Triumvirate lasted from 43 B.C.E. until 32 B.C.E., when open war broke out between Antony and Octavian. Octavian's fleet won a great battle at Actium (31 B.C.E.) and Antony fled to his headquarters in Egypt. There he committed suicide. His ally and mistress, Cleopatra, did the same when it became clear that she could not captivate the victorious Octavian as she had captivated first Caesar himself and then Antony.

The Beginning of the Roman Empire

By 30 B.C.E. the entire Mediterranean basin was once again under the military control of a single man, Octavian, or, as he is more commonly called, "Augustus"—an honorific title meaning

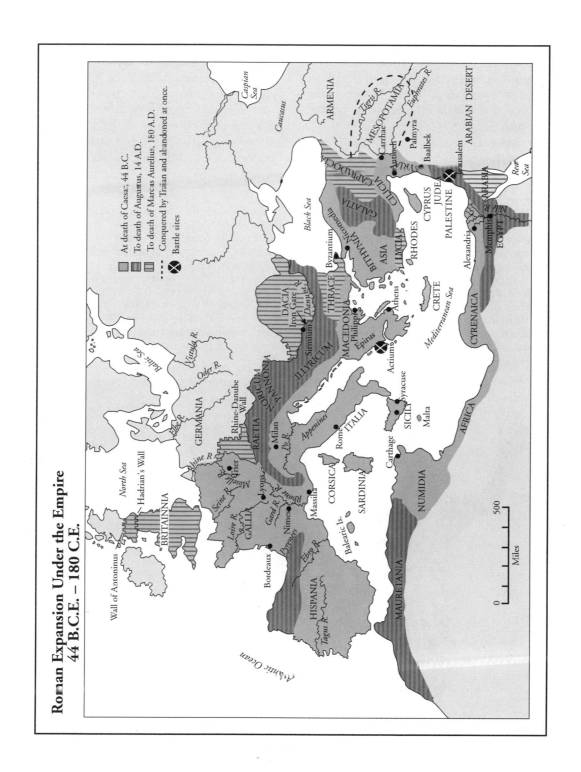

**Roman Expansion Under the Empire
44 B.C.E. – 180 C.E.**

At death of Caesar, 44 B.C.
To death of Augustus, 14 A.D.
To death of Marcus Aurelius, 180 A.D.
Conquered by Trajan and abandoned at once.
Battle sites

North Sea
Atlantic Ocean
Baltic Sea
Caspian Sea
Black Sea
Mediterranean Sea
Red Sea

BRITANNIA
Hadrian's Wall
Wall of Antoninus
GERMANIA
GALLIA
Trier
Lyons
Bordeaux
Nimes
Massilia
HISPANIA
CORSICA
SARDINIA
Balearic Is.
Elbe R.
Rhine R.
Moselle R.
Seine R.
Loire R.
Gard R.
Rhone R.
Pyrenees
Ebro R.
Tagus R.
Vistula R.
Oder R.
Rhine-Danube Wall
RAETIA
NORICUM
PANNONIA
ILLYRICUM
DACIA
Iron Gate
Danube
Sirmium
THRACE
Byzantium
MACEDONIA
Epirus
Actium
Athens
Philippi
Milan
Po R.
Apennines
ITALIA
Rome
SICILY
Syracuse
Malta
Carthage
NUMIDIA
MAURETANIA
AFRICA
CYRENAICA
CRETE
RHODES
ASIA
BITHYNIA
Nicomedia
GALATIA
CAPPADOCIA
CILICIA
CYPRUS
SYRIA
Antioch
Baalbek
Palmyra
ARMENIA
Caucasus
MESOPOTAMIA
Carrhae
Tigris R.
Euphrates R.
PALESTINE
JUDEA
Jerusalem
ARABIA
ARABIAN DESERT
EGYPT
Memphis
Alexandria
Nile R.

0   500
Miles

"great and holy one." The new ruler of the Roman world proceeded cautiously. He personally kept command of most of the Roman armies. He stationed the troops along the frontiers, where they could keep barbarians at bay and had less temptation to intervene in politics. As *imperator* (commander) of the soldiers, Augustus' power remained supreme.

Yet Augustus deliberately disguised the military basis of his power. In 27 B.C.E. he "restored the Republic"—at least in name. What he restored were the procedures of electing magistrates and of consulting the Senate on matters of importance. Augustus also organized police and fire services for the city of Rome and took charge of supplying the city with grain.

A far more orderly life set in, free from the fierce destructiveness of the period of civil wars. As *princeps* (first citizen) of the Senate and imperator of the soldiers, Augustus exercised firm

Peace and War in Ancient Rome   These statues look remarkably alike, yet the one on the left comes from an Etruscan city and shows an anonymous orator addressing his listeners on some matter of public concern. The one on the right is Emperor Augustus (reigned 30 B.C.E.–14 C.E.) dressed in armor and speaking, presumably, to his soldiers. Continuities between Etruscan and Roman urban tradition in central Italy were very real, as these statues suggest. The shift from civilian to military control of Roman society was also real and took place during and just before Augustus' time, when civil wars destroyed the Roman republic. Yet Augustus claimed to have restored the Republic in 27 B.C.E.—a pretense his pose in this statue both affirms and denies by portraying an orator in armor—a man seeking to persuade but in a position to compel obedience if anyone dared object.

control in the city and provinces, although in theory the Senate and people of Rome once more ruled themselves according to the old Republican constitution. The difference was that only men whom Augustus had approved could now expect to be elected to office. All the zest went out of politics. But few grumbled. Civil war and disorder were too high a price to pay for the old Republican liberties.

The Pax Romana   The principate, as the system of government Augustus established is usually called, lasted more than 200 years. During most of that period of time, the peoples of the Roman Empire enjoyed unbroken public peace. To be sure, there was plenty of fighting along the frontiers against barbarian tribes; two bitter Jewish revolts devastated Palestine, and twice the Roman legions deserted their posts on the frontiers to take part in civil war to determine who should succeed to the imperial office. But never before or afterward in European history did so many people—some 60 million according to one estimate—enjoy peace for so long a period of time. Memory of *Pax Romana*—the Roman peace—lasted for centuries.

A weakness of the principate was uncertainty over succession to the imperial position. In theory the office was freely conferred by the Senate and people of Rome. In practice each reigning emperor was at pains to choose his successor—often a son or other relative. Memories of the old Republican freedom, when elections were real and no single person controlled the state, lingered for a long time. Not until the Roman noble families died out, and new provincial landholders took their place as the principal supporters of the Roman Empire, did these memories fade away. This occurred by about 100 C.E. when a series of "good" emperors came to power, beginning with Nerva in 96 C.E. and ending with Marcus Aurelius, who died in 180 C.E.

Greco-Roman Culture

As long as Roman society was composed of small farmers and conservative patricians, Rome offered only a limited scope for the arts and refinements of civilization. With the very rapid change that came to Roman society dur-

ing and after the Punic Wars, however, a few wealthy Romans developed an interest in Greek art, literature, and thought. A far larger number of the Mediterranean world's new masters became interested in fancy cooking, popular music, and elegant living. The new wealth also allowed the Romans to develop their own customs in new ways. For example, gladiatorial combat, which had once been performed as a religious ritual at dead heroes' graves, was revived and made into a spectator sport. Men fought against men or were pitted against wild beasts, as the Roman people howled with excitement. One of the best ways for an aspiring politician to win votes was to put on a particularly lavish display of gladiatorial games. Later, under the principate, this became the responsibility of the emperor.

Cicero   Romans were not philosophic. They found suitable ideas ready and waiting among the Greeks, where philosophy had already become a school of good manners for the leisured class. But to be available to the Roman world, Greek ideas had to be translated into Latin. This task was vigorously undertaken by the famous orator, Cicero (Marcus Tullius Cicero, 106–43 B.C.E.). Cicero sometimes had to invent new words to carry new meanings into Latin, and in doing so he made it a more flexible, sophisticated tongue. His orations and private letters, published after his death, made it possible for us to know him, both as a private and public figure, more intimately than any other man of classical antiquity. His use of Latin became standard in Renaissance Europe and is still taught in our schools. His writings became the model for western Europe's medieval and early modern men of letters.

Playwrights and Historians   Plautus (ca. 254–104 B.C.E.) and Terence (ca. 190–159 B.C.E.) are the only significant Roman playwrights whose work survives. They wrote comedies of manners, borrowing heavily from Greek comedy writers of the Hellenistic period. The two greatest Roman historians were Livy and Tacitus. Livy (59 B.C.E.—17 C.E.) wrote a very long history of the Roman Republic, of which only a small part has survived. He was full of regret for the decay of the old Roman simplicity and virtue, which he held to be responsible for the breakdown of Republican government. Tacitus (55–118 C.E.) wrote of the empire, full of bitterness at the loss of liberty that Augustus and his successors had inflicted upon Rome.

The Roman Poets   Next to Cicero, the greatest literary figures of the Roman world were poets. Lyric whimsy, eager explanation of why there was nothing to fear from the gods, reflection on the joys of private life, and epic accounts of the foundation and destiny of Rome all found a place in Latin poetry. Vergil (70–19 B.C.E.) was the most famous and influential. He modeled his great epic poem, *The Aeneid*, on Homer, intending to give the Romans as respectable an origin as the Greeks could claim. Vergil traced the wanderings of Aeneas, a Trojan prince, from Troy to Italy, where his descendants, in due course, established the city of Rome. In his great poem, Vergil defined Rome's role; not to rival Greece as the home of art and literature but to rule the world and put down the proud.

Biographical, Philosophical, and Scientific Writings   About 100 C.E. Greek writing revived. Plutarch (46–120 C.E.) wrote a popular series of parallel lives of the Greeks and Romans. Marcus Aurelius, the Roman emperor (who reigned 161–180 C.E.), wrote his *Meditations* in Greek. Galen (ca. 130–200 C.E.), a doctor, and Ptolemy (ca. 85–165 C.E.), a mathematician, geographer, and astronomer, each wrote extremely influential handbooks of science. Galen's work became a standard for medical practitioners of both the Islamic and Christian worlds until after 1700. Ptolemy's authority was overthrown only by the great European explorations after 1500 and by the astronomical advances associated with the names of Copernicus and Galileo.

Roman Law   Roman law, the other great inheritance passed on from the ancient world to medieval Europe, matured later. Its development began in the early days of the Republic, when *Praetors* (the principal judicial magistrates) adopted the custom, at the beginning of their term of office, of publishing the laws they

intended to enforce. Under the empire this practice continued, and the praetors' edicts assumed a more or less standard form.

Changes came as Roman law had to be applied more and more widely to citizens who were scattered all over the empire. This caused jurists to wonder about the relationships between natural law, which some Hellenistic philosophers had emphasized, and the actual laws magistrates were supposed to enforce. Simple but radical principles, prevailed—for example, recognizing one—and only one—owner with full rights of use or sale for each piece of tangible property. Law so conceived could be applied to private affairs everywhere and anywhere in the world. Such laws made relationships among strangers far more predictable, flexible, and precise. Society became more capable of adjusting to new circumstances as a result.

Lasting formulations of the Roman law, however, came only after 200 C.E., and a definitive code was finally drawn up by command of the Emperor Justinian (who reigned 527–565 C.E.).

In 180 C.E. the law was still growing. Little else in the cultural world of upper-class Romans was. Great artists, writers, philosophers, or scientists failed to appear. Polite education and the luxuries of civilized life became very widely available to landlords in all the provinces of the Roman Empire. Everywhere the Greek model, as modified and adjusted to Latin tastes in the period of the later Republic and early empire, prevailed. But the trouble was that no one cared very much any longer.

Statues and handsome public buildings sprang up all over Spain, Gaul, and the other parts of western Europe that were brought under Roman rule. (Augustus had conquered the lands south of the Danube; his successors added Britain and Dacia; for a short time they also controlled Mesopotamia.) Orators delivered elaborate speeches about unimportant subjects, and provincial towns put on gladiatorial shows modeled on those that made Rome famous.

All the political commitments that had made life worthwhile in the times when Athens fought for survival, or when Rome first built the empire, had evaporated. The lower classes were not interested in their masters' philosophy and

Roman Architecture Romans improved on Greek technical achievements in architecture and public works, using arches and domes, as the Greeks never did, and using cement to hold building stones firmly together. Among the most impressive structures the Romans left behind them were the network of roads that ran through the empire and a number of aquaducts, like the one shown here, located near Nimes in southern France. Built to carry water across a valley, it has stood intact for more than 1800 years, thanks to the sound engineering of its arches and the quality of the cement binding it all together.

art; nor were the masters sure of themselves and their luxurious way of life. Human aspiration had turned away from the classical forms of expression, seeking instead a predominantly religious outlet. In the next chapter we shall try to see how this happened.

Conclusion

The classical civilization of ancient Greece and Rome attained an enormous success between 500 B.C.E. and 200 C.E. The Greeks, an unruly little people on the fringes of the great Persian Empire in 500 B.C.E., turned the tables completely. The whole Middle Eastern region felt the impact of their culture after Alexander's conquests; even distant India and China found aspects of the Greek achievement interesting. Westward, too, Greek ideas, art, and styles of life spread widely after the Romans had conquered Greece itself along with all the rest of the Mediterranean world.

What was the essence of this Greco-Roman classical civilization? In Athens' greatest days, active and eager participation by all citizens in the public life and culture of the city was a hallmark that later generations never forgot and never lived up to. Rome, too, in its early days involved its citizens in war and politics far more deeply than most rival states ever tried to do. The ancients themselves believed that political freedom—the right of every citizen to take part in public debate and decision making according to some recognized rules of law—was at the heart of their distinctiveness. Though power was, in fact, often concentrated in the hands of a few men or even of a single person, as in the days of the Roman Empire, the ideal of free participation in political affairs always remained a distinguishing mark of the ancient classical world.

Classical art and thought, too, had their own distinctive characteristics. Sculptors made their works more and more realistic, even down to such details as showing veins in arms and legs. Most classical thinkers relied on their powers of reason and argument and accepted nothing on the strength of sacred revelation. These ideals, too, were not fully maintained, especially in the eastern parts of the Greek world. But people never forgot them either, even when it was perfectly clear that reason and argument would not permit citizens to agree about very much.

Political liberty, naturalistic art, and rationalistic thought—these perhaps made up the essence of classical civilization. These values were enshrined in the pages of the great classical writers, and through them have continued to be a living force down to the present. The heights of heroism and despair described in the works of Aeschylus, Herodotus, Thucydides, Plato, Aristotle, Cicero, and Vergil—to name only the most illustrious—have provided models and examples for later generations of Europeans and their descendants overseas. In this fashion the influence of deeds done long ago at Marathon and Salamis, Zama and Actium, looms large even today. For the ancient Greeks and Romans are a pivotal part of our past; and like all human beings everywhere, we are both prisoners and beneficiaries of the part of the past we choose to remember.

Bibliography

The splendors of classical literature, all readily accessible in expert translations, are the best way to pursue further understanding of the era described in this chapter. In addition to Herodotus and Plutarch, previously mentioned, Thucydides, *History of the Peloponnesian War;* Plato, *The Apology;* Cicero's *Letters;* Vergil, *The Aeneid;* and Tacitus, *Annals* and *Histories;* are particularly telling, along with the plays of Aeschylus, Sophocles, and Euripides. The books of Maccabees, telling how Jews in Palestine won independence from their Greek rulers (often printed among the Apocrypha of the Bible) is another vivid and available source.

Michael Grant and Rachel Kitzinger, eds., *Civilization of the Ancient Mediterranean: Greece and Rome* (3 vols., 1988), offers a recent and authoritative collection of essays on main themes that classical historians have debated, thus constituting an encyclopedic introduction to the subject. In a way it rivals the *Cambridge Ancient History,* which has long provided a standard scholarly account in English of the history of the ancient world. This, too, is a collaborative work, with each chapter written by a recognized expert. Any search for detailed information and bibliographical guidance can profitably start with these two collections. Only a few famous or particularly readable books are listed here.

A. R. Burn, *Persia and the Greeks* (2nd ed., 1984), gives a modern account of Xerxes' invasion and the Greek victory that set classical Greece on its way toward dominating the Mediterranean. Russell Meiggs, *The Athenian Empire* (1972), describes the peak of Athenian power and its collapse. For Alexander of Macedon, Mary Renault, *The Nature of Alexander* (1975), offers a popularly written, well-informed fictional interpretation; A. B. Bosworth, *Conquest and Empire: The Reign of Alexander the Great* (1988), is a recent work of more formal scholarship.

A fine introduction to the Hellenistic age is provided by F. W. Walbank, *The Hellenistic World* (1987), and by W. W. Tarn and G. T. Griffith, *Hellenistic Civilization* (3rd ed., 1952). Moses Hadas, *Hellenistic Culture: Fusion and Diffusion* (1959), analyzes the interaction of Greek and Middle Eastern cultures with great sensitivity. W. W. Tarn, *Hellenistic Military and Naval Developments* (1930), and E. W. Marsden, *Greek and Roman Artillery: Historical Development* (1969), describe the transformation of warfare that occurred between 350 and 150 B.C.E.

For the rise of Rome, a general overview is provided by H. H. Scullard, *A History of the Roman World, 753 B.C. to 146 B.C.* (4th ed., 1980), and H. H. Scullard, *From the Gracchi to Nero* (5th ed., 1982). Peter Garmsey and Richard Saller, *The Roman Empire: Economy, Society and Culture* (1987), broaden the rather narrow political focus which the nature of most Latin literary sources tends to impose on modern scholars. Among the many books dealing with more specialized themes, a famous book by Ronald Syme, *The Roman Revolution* (1939), analyzes the breakdown of the Roman Republic; and Roman military organization is authoritatively described by H. M. D. Parker, *The Roman Legions* (new ed., 1958). Another famous book, A. H. M. Jones, *The Greek City from Alexander to Justinian* (1940), deals with urban life and social structure in the eastern Mediterranean lands. J. P. V. D. Balsdon, *Life and Leisure in Ancient Rome* (rev. ed., 1974), concentrates upon the city of Rome itself.

For classical art, Gisela M. A. Richter, *A Handbook of Greek Art* (2nd ed., 1960), Jocelyn M. C. Toynbee, *The Art of the Romans* (1965), and Diana E. E. Kleiner, *Roman Sculpture* (1992), are leading authorities.

For those who find it easier to read novels than histories, Mary Renault's series of novels portraying eras and famous personalities from Greek history may be recommended warmly. She is both learned and accurate, and her invention is consonant with all that scholars know about those distant times. Very few historical novels are as successful as hers.

Civilizations 500 B.C.E. to 100 B.C.E.

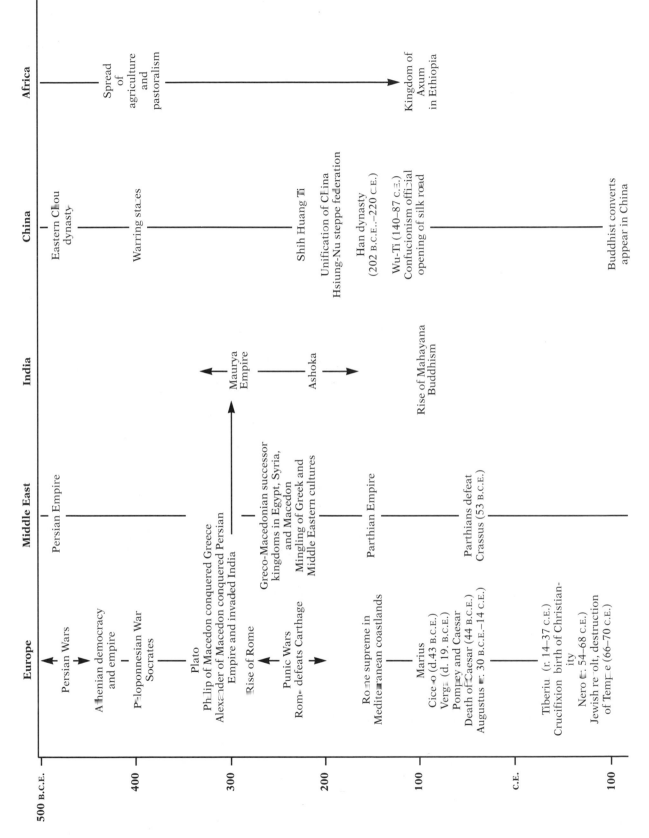

	Europe	Middle East	India	China	Africa
500 B.C.E.	Persian Wars	Persian Empire		Eastern Chou dynasty	
	Athenian democracy and empire				
	Peloponnesian War				Spread of agriculture and pastoralism
	Socrates				
400	Plato			Warring states	
	Philip of Macedon conquered Greece				
	Alexander of Macedon conquered Persian Empire and invaded India		Maurya Empire		
300	Rise of Rome	Greco-Macedonian successor kingdoms in Egypt, Syria, and Macedon	Ashoka		
	Punic Wars	Mingling of Greek and Middle Eastern cultures			
	Rome defeats Carthage			Shih Huang Ti	
200		Parthian Empire	Rise of Mahayana Buddhism	Unification of China	
				Hsiung-Nu steppe federation	
				Han dynasty (202 B.C.E.–220 C.E.)	
	Rome supreme in Mediterranean coastlands			Wu-Ti (140–87 C.E.)	
100	Marius			Confucianism official opening of silk road	Kingdom of Axum in Ethiopia
	Cicero (d.43 B.C.E.)	Parthians defeat Crassus (53 B.C.E.)			
	Vergil (d. 19. B.C.E.)				
	Pompey and Caesar				
	Death of Caesar (44 B.C.E.)				
	Augustus (r. 30 B.C.E.–14 C.E.)				
C.E.	Tiberius (r. 14–37 C.E.)				
	Crucifixion birth of Christianity				
	Nero (r. 54–68 C.E.)				Buddhist converts appear in China
	Jewish revolt, destruction of Temple (66–70 C.E.)				
100					

Civilized Religions
and Barbarian Invasions
200 B.C.E. to 600 C.E.

9

Galloping Across Eurasia   This spirited horse comes from Kansu in northwest China, where cultivated ground merges into grassy steppe. When it was made (ca. 200 C.E.), cavalry warfare was becoming dominant all across Asia. Animals like this carried barbarian conquerors into China and the eastern Roman Empire, India escaped, but only for a few centuries.

Between about 100 B.C.E. and 200 C.E., the civilized peoples of Eurasia organized caravan and sea trade far more effectively than ever before. The result was a mingling of goods, diseases, and ideas across the whole breadth of Eurasia, from the British islands on the west to the Japanese islands on the east, and embracing India and the islands of Indonesia as well as parts of east and west Africa.

Population losses, resulting in large part from the ravages of new and unfamiliar diseases, helped to break off regular and close contact across such long distances after 200 C.E. Subsequently, barbarian raiding and conquests, issuing mainly from the steppe regions of Eurasia, tended to break up peaceful long-distance trade.

But before the separate civilizations of Eurasia fell back upon their own local resources, the mixing and blending of traditions, which traders unintentionally provoked, stimulated the creation of three new world religions: Mahayana Buddhism, Christianity, and Hinduism. In later centuries, each of these faiths spread widely, in part through organized missionary efforts, and provided a lasting cultural mold for a large part of civilized humanity. The barbarian migrations that assumed a new scale after 200 C.E. established language and cultural boundaries that have lasted until the present in many parts of Europe and, to a lesser extent, also in Asia.

The rise of new faiths and the migration of peoples are thus the dominant themes of world history between 200 B.C.E. and 600 C.E.

Trade Routes and Empires of Eurasia

The rise of the Roman Empire around the Mediterranean Sea in the Eurasian Far West closely paralleled the establishment of a strong and reunited Chinese Empire in the Far East. Indeed, the foundation of the Han dynasty in 202 B.C.E. came in the year of Hannibal's defeat at Zama in north Africa—the event that established Rome's supremacy in the western Mediterranean. The fall of the Han dynasty in 220 C.E., more than 400 years later, came at a time when the Roman Empire was also suffering from serious barbarian invasions and seemed near collapse. These parallel events were not entirely unrelated. The two great empires were in contact with each other indirectly through trade. In addition, both of them bordered on the Eurasian steppe, where barbarian nomads acted and reacted upon each other and upon their civilized neighbors. In this chapter we shall first consider the influences that passed between the different civilizations of Europe and Asia along the trade routes and then see how the barbarians of the steppe, by their conquests and migrations, changed the course of civilized history between about 200 B.C.E. and 600 C.E.

When China was first united by Shih Huang Ti (221 B.C.E.), the Far East was still isolated from western Asia by the desert region of the Tarim basin. In 102 B.C.E., however, the Chinese emperor, Wu Ti, sent an army exploring westward. It reached an outpost of the Middle Eastern world in Fergana (modern Uzbekistan). Wu Ti's army thus opened regular contact between China and the civilized peoples of the Middle East for the first time. More than 200 years before, the conquests of Alexander of Macedonia in India had established a close connection between the Middle East and India. His successors in Asia, the Seleucids, maintained diplomatic and trade relations with India, where soon after Alexander's time the king of Magadha conquered all of the Ganges and Indus valleys and founded the Maurya Empire. The civilized region of the Middle East was therefore already in regular touch with both the Greek and Indian worlds when the Chinese showed up in Fergana and joined the circle of interacting Old World civilizations.

Increase of Trade

In the course of the next 100 years, regular caravan trade was organized between China and the eastern end of the Mediterranean Sea. This required a great deal of effort. To organize, supply, and protect a caravan was as complicated as equipping a ship for distant voyaging. Local authorities had to establish safe resting places (caravansaries). They also had to learn that they could not tax traveling merchants so heavily as to destroy their profit. Means of financing trade and methods of distributing goods at both ends of the caravan route also had to be found before trade could become important. In ways we know nothing about, all these things were done. As a result, what the Romans called the Silk Road came into existence by about 1 C.E. It ran from the Wei Valley in China through central Asia to Mesopotamia and ended at Antioch on the Orontes River in Syria. Thousands of men and animals began to move back and forth along nearly 4000 miles of tracks rubbed smooth by camels' feet. Goods and ideas, as well as diseases, traveled with the caravans. Their combined impact on the civilized societies along the way was very great.

At about the same time, the sea routes between the Mediterranean area and India gained new importance. About 120 B.C.E. a ship captain sailing from the Red Sea discovered that he could steer his ship by the stars, far from land, and travel directly from the Straits of Aden to southern India. Such a trip took a much shorter time than when vessels skirted the coast and stayed within sight of land. Moreover, there were no tolls to pay or pirates to fear far out at sea. And by waiting for the monsoon wind to reverse itself, the return voyage became just as easy. This discovery soon gave employment to a fleet of vessels sailing between Egypt and India. Venturesome captains went on to explore the Bay of Bengal; and not long after 180 C.E., at least one traveler portaged across the Isthmus of Kra, took ship again on the eastern side, and arrived in southern China, where he claimed to be an ambassador sent by the Roman emperor, Marcus Aurelius. In this fashion, therefore, the seafaring peoples of southeast Asia made firm contact with the seafarers of the Mediterranean. All the southern seas became a single trade network.

Many different sorts of things traveled along these trade routes. The first Chinese expedition to Fergana brought back grapevines, alfalfa, and warhorses. Later they imported metals, glass, and silver. The Romans wanted silk above all else, for this fabric became extremely fashionable.

Chinese silk cloth was actually unraveled in Antioch and then rewoven into a much thinner, semitransparent fabric. From India came perfumes and spices. Alexandria sent many sorts of manufactured goods, including mass-produced statuettes of Greek gods, to India. In addition, coined money was exported to India from Roman territory.

Other trade routes connected barbarian peoples, living both north and south, with the belt of civilized territory that had come into existence across the middle of Eurasia. An "amber route," for example, ran from the Baltic Sea to the Black Sea, following the river courses. Camel caravans also began to cross the Sahara, thereby linking West Africa with Roman North Africa. Along this route gold from the Niger River area was exchanged for salt and other products. India's trade relations with southeast Asia and Indonesia became quite important. China, similarly, traded with the nomads of Mongolia and opened up political and commercial relations with both Korea and Japan before 600 C.E. Altogether, the range of civilized influence was clearly expanding across every frontier.

Spread of Diseases

But with goods came new diseases, some of which proved very damaging to densely settled civilized populations. Exactly what kind of germs caused ancient plagues and epidemics cannot now be discovered. Records are incomplete and usually do not describe symptoms in a way that would permit modern doctors to know what the disease was. Yet we do know this: In modern times, childhood diseases—measles, mumps, small pox, and even the common cold—can be killers when they reach a population that has never before been exposed to them. At some time in history, civilized peoples must have acquired their present levels of immunity to these diseases. The centuries between 100 B.C.E. and 300 C.E. were probably the time when at least some of them first entered into general circulation in Eurasia. Long-distance trade in Eurasia and Africa was more regular than ever before; and diseases, too, could therefore spread farther and faster than ever before. We have references

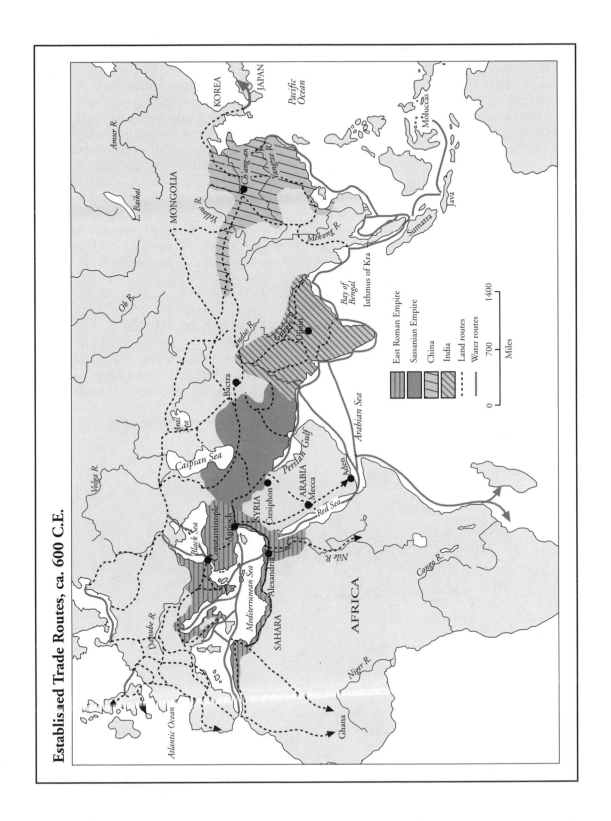

Established Trade Routes, ca. 600 C.E.

East Roman Empire
Sassanian Empire
China
India
Land routes
Water routes

0   700   1400
Miles

KOREA
JAPAN
Pacific Ocean
Moluccas
MONGOLIA
Amur R.
L. Baikal
Ob R.
Yellow R.
Ch'ang-an
Yangtze R.
Mekong R.
Sumatra
Java
Bay of Bengal
Isthmus of Kra
Ganges R.
Ujjain
Indus R.
Bactra
Aral Sea
Caspian Sea
Volga R.
Arabian Sea
Persian Gulf
Aden
ARABIA
Mecca
Red Sea
SYRIA
Cresiphon
Antioch
Black Sea
Constantinople
Mediterranean Sea
Alexandria
Nile R.
Danube R.
SAHARA
AFRICA
Congo R.
Niger R.
Ghana
Atlantic Ocean

to unusually severe epidemics, especially in Roman and Chinese sources; and much evidence shows that both the Roman and Han empires suffered from serious depopulation beginning soon after 100 C.E.

It is worth noting that when the ravages of a disease became sufficiently serious, the situation tended to correct itself. As population became thinner, infections passed less often from one person to another because close contacts became fewer. In addition, severe epidemics interrupted long-distance trade and travel. Depopulation meant less wealth; less wealth made trade unprofitable; and as trade became unprofitable, strangers who might accidentally bring in some new disease stopped coming. Moreover, those who survived developed various kinds of biological immunity to each disease. When enough people in a given population become immune, epidemics cease. The disease does not disappear entirely; instead it may become a childhood disease, attacking only persons who have not yet developed immunities. And even so, fewer people die because children inherit partial immunities from their parents.

A natural cycle of this kind probably took place in the ancient world. New diseases spread, especially in Europe and China, and at first killed off large numbers of people. Then, in the course of three or four centuries, rising immunities and greater isolation combined to check the spread of lethal infection. But before that occurred, both the Roman and the Chinese empires had collapsed. Depopulation due to disease probably played a part in weakening both these great empires. But with records as imperfect as they are, this explanation is no more than a good guess—not an established fact.

Exchange of Ideas

Exchange of ideas along the trade routes of the Old World was even more important for later history than the exchange of goods and diseases.

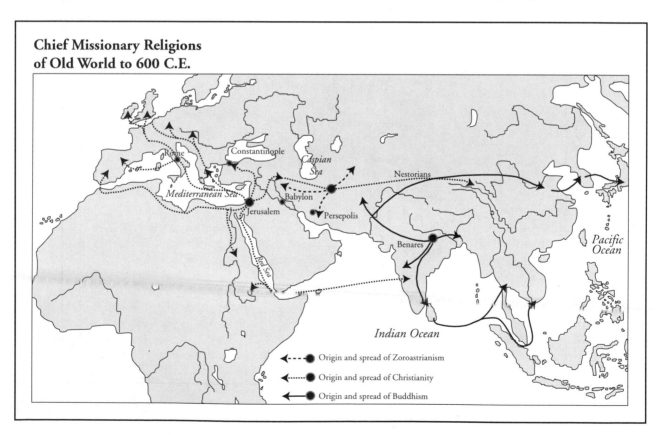

Chief Missionary Religions of Old World to 600 C.E.

◄---●   Origin and spread of Zoroastrianism

◄····●   Origin and spread of Christianity

◄——●   Origin and spread of Buddhism

The most significant of these ideas were religious, although some were (or were thought to be) scientific. Thus, for example, what Europe later knew as alchemy seems to have started among Chinese Taoists, who tried to concoct a magic drink to prolong life. As alchemy spread westward, its sister "science," astrology, traveled eastward to India and China from Alexandria in Egypt, where it originated from a combination of Greek and Babylonian ideas about the heavens.

Alchemy and astrology were always more or less secret sciences and much mixed with magic. New religious ideas, on the contrary, were public and affected everyone. Three new world religions—Mahayana Buddhism, Hinduism, and Christianity—arose between 200 B.C.E. and 200 C.E. And, in the next country, Manichaeism (founded in 241 C.E. by a Persian prophet named Mani) almost succeeded in becoming a fourth world faith. Each of these religions expressed a similar idea, namely that every believer could attain salvation through a close relationship with a savior who was at one and the same time both human and divine. For all of them, the world of eternity beyond the grave was more important than the ordinary, everyday world. Common to all three of the major religions was the belief that women, too, had souls to be saved, and they were therefore expected to take an equal part in religious observations with men. These are important resemblances, but the differences were also very great.

Mahayana Buddhism

Mahayana Buddhism shifted emphasis away from self-annihilation, which earlier Buddhism had declared to be the supreme religious goal. Instead, Mahayana Buddhists believed that the souls of good persons entered any of a number of "heavens" where they might live happily until, at last, every single soul in the universe was freed from the suffering of incarnation. At that far-off time, all the souls of the world would complete the cosmic cycle by entering Nirvana together. But until that time, it was the function

of saved souls to help others up the ladder of existence, until they too could escape reincarnation and enter heaven. Souls that had purified themselves and reached heaven were called "bodhisattvas." They resembled Christian saints.

From a practical point of view, an ordinary person might help his or her soul along by praying to a bodhisattva or by honoring him in some other way. The bodhisattva might then be expected to take particular care of the soul of the person who had called upon his aid. Buddha ceased to be a historical figure for the monks who speculated along these lines. They argued that there had been innumerable Buddhas who took on a visible body in order to explain salvation to souls who needed help; and since there had been innumerable worlds, created and destroyed over and over again, innumerable Buddhas were none too many to keep the true doctrine alive.

Fusion of Indian and Greek Ideas

Statues representing bodhisattvas and Buddhas were very much a part of the Mahayana faith. Making such a statue was a good thing in itself and might help others along the path to salvation. Caves and temples richly decorated with statues were built as centers of worship and prayer.

Mahayana art bears an unmistakable relation to Greco-Roman art. Some of the details of Buddha statues were borrowed from standard Greco-Roman statues of Apollo. To be sure, Buddhist art soon left the Greek model behind and developed along its own lines in India, in China, and in Japan.

The fusion of Greek and Indian ideas in Mahayana Buddhist art gives visible form to a more general mingling of Indian with Greek ideas. The bodhisattvas, who were both divine and human resemble Greek ideas as developed in the centuries after Alexander, when the monarchs of Egypt and Syria, though undoubtedly human, all claimed to be divine and sometimes called themselves "savior." At courts and caravansaries, people from the Greek world had

plenty of opportunity to argue about religion and reality with travelers from the Indian world. Just as the Buddhist sculptors borrowed some features from mass-produced Greek statues, it seems probable that the monks who developed the Mahayana doctrine may have accepted some of the ideas coming to them from the eastern Mediterranean through Greek-speaking traders. But, since no one kept records of such conversations, we can never be sure.

The Spread of Mahayana Buddhism

By 200 C.E. Mahayana doctrines began to spread along the trade routes of central Asia into China. Two centuries later, Buddhism in China had assumed a form of its own, derived mainly from the Mahayana. By 600 C.E. Chinese forms of Buddhism had been firmly planted in Korea and had made an initial impact upon Japan as well. In these two countries, conversion to Buddhism was a very important step toward civilization. Local courts and rulers welcomed the monks, who brought literacy and part of the learning of the Chinese world with them. Even when, during the T'ang Dynasty, the Chinese government began to persecute Buddhists, the Koreans and Japanese remained attached to the faith that had come to them through China from India.

The expansion of Buddhism north of the Himalaya Mountains is one of the tremendously significant facts of history. China, India, and Japan support more than half the human race; and insofar as they to this day share a common background, it is because of their common experience of Buddhism. To be sure, Buddhism did not remain the dominant faith in either India or China. It survived most strongly along the fringes of Asia, in Korea and Japan, and in Southeast Asia and Ceylon. Buddhist missionaries reached southeast Asia by sea some time before the time of Christ. Most of them taught the older form of Buddhism, so that Mahayana doctrines were (and are) unimportant in such countries as Ceylon, Burma, Thailand, and Vietnam.

Hinduism

The part of India where Mahayana Buddhism flourished most was in the extreme northwest, not far from where the routes leading across the mountains into India met the Silk Road. At almost the same time, however, another important religious development was taking place in southern India. There Brahmanism developed into Hinduism. Brahmanism is a name for the rules and rituals that were developed by Brahman priests. It was based partly on the old Vedas, partly on a great variety of local religious customs. Hinduism continued to honor the Vedas and accepted all of the rules and rituals that

How Buddhism Spread Across Asia   These four images of Buddha show how representing the founder of the Buddhist religion changed as the faith spread across Asia. On the upper left you see a statue that was carved on the frontier between India and Afghanistan before 300 C.E. The pattern of drapery and the knotted hairstyle are both modeled on Greco-Roman representations of Apollo, but the seated posture is characteristically Indian. On the upper right is a statue from central Asia that came from a caravan stop along the ancient Silk Road that ran between China and the Roman empire. The drapery and hairstyle are still recognizable, but facial details and the halo depart from the realism of the first statue.

Below are a statue from China and a standing Buddha from Japan. Both date from the seventh or eighth century C.E. and show how the figure of Buddha was adapted to suit the needs of converts in China and Japan. Thus, the hand gestures and the lotus pedestal on which the Japanese figure stands had special doctrinal significance for Buddhists, but the drapery and top knot still connect back to the original (borrowed) way of representing Buddha.

the Brahmans had devised. The difference was that Hinduism concentrated attention on two great gods, Vishnu and Shiva. Ordinary Hindus devoted their religious observances to one of these two deities, believing that, if properly worshiped, the god would assure them of reincarnation at a higher level on the ladder of souls. Indeed, if devotion to Vishnu or Shiva were intense enough, it might even permit the worshiper to merge his or her soul with the soul of the great god himself.

Once again, the idea of a savior god was central to the faith. The Hindu myths, however, treated the incarnation of Vishnu and of Shiva as something that happened over and over again. Indeed, it might occur at any moment and at any place. The god might appear in almost any form: as a magnificent animal, as a simple herdboy, or radiating a blinding splendor. Devout worshipers might meet him walking down the street or find him through mystic ecstasy; or they might never see the god at all. The important thing was to trust in Vishnu or Shiva. The god and his worshiper were lovers who had been separated by the accident of birth. Through love, expressed in private devotions and through public ceremonies, salvation could be attained.

The Changing Balance Between Hinduism and Buddhism

Elaborate temples, built around a statue of the god, became the centers of Hindu worship. Hindu art does not show Greek influence in the way Mahayana art does. Moreover, the adventures attributed to the two high gods seem closer to peasant life than to the city life of the traders who came to southern India, by sea, from Egypt. Hinduism, far more than Mahayana Buddhism, smacks of the soil. Perhaps it was for that reason that it prevailed over Buddhism in the end.

The changing balance between the two religions in India is difficult to trace. About 250 B.C.E., when the emperor Asoka ruled nearly all of India, it looked as though Buddhism were going to become the official religion of the entire

country. Asoka was an enthusiastic convert to Buddhism, and he tried to spread the doctrine throughout his domains and beyond. One way he chose to do this was to erect pillars in far-distant parts of his empire, on which he inscribed religious instruction for all to read. Several of these pillars still exist; they give us practically all of the definite information we have about Asoka's reign. After his time, information fades away again. The empire broke up; Indian life went on.

Hinduism was not a missionary religion. Some of the courts of Indonesia and Southeast Asia became Hindu, or at least took on Indian culture in a Hindu form. But the worship of Shiva, by far the most popular Hindu god in "Greater India," was probably built upon older cults that were practiced in those parts of the world before Indian courtly civilization ever reached Java, Cambodia, and regions located in between.

The Mixed Culture of the Gupta Dynasty

Five hundred years passed before northern India was once again united into an extensive empire. This new state was created by the Gupta dynasty that ruled from about 320 C.E. to about 535. The Gupta kings were Hindus, but so far as we can tell they did not take religion too seriously. Their court became the center of an unusually elegant and luxurious life. Kalidasa (ca. 400–455 C.E.), the greatest of Sanskrit poets, lived at the Gupta court. His plays and lyric poems reflect an exquisite refinement of life.

During this same period of time, India's two great epics, the *Mahabharata* and the *Ramayana*, reached something like their present form. The first of these, like the *Iliad*, is a story of heroic chariot combat, but priests later added so much other material that the original story was nearly buried. Folktales, religious instruction, incantations, philosophical discourses—all were put in. As a result, the entire poem is longer than the Bible, with which it should be compared, since the Hindus regard the *Mahabharata* as a book of religious instruction. The *Ramayana* is much shorter and better organized. It tells the story of the wonderful adventures of Rama. Once again religion became central, for Rama was an incarnation of Vishnu, one of the two great gods of Hinduism.

The Indian epics had a long evolution before the Gupta period, and a few additional passages may have been added later. But in the age of the Guptas, Indians adopted the practice of writing down works of literature instead of preserving texts by transmitting them orally. This was a borrowing from the Greeks, as we know from the fact that the technical terms connected with books are of Greek origin. Written literature required professional copyists who worked mechanically and were less likely to add new material or alter old passages, as those who memorized orally were tempted to do each time they recited. Hence, when book writing and copying spread to India in the Gupta Age, the two epics as well as such complicated texts are those from the pen of Kalidasa assumed a stable, lasting form.

Ever since then, the Gupta Age has been considered India's classical high point. We know it almost entirely through literature; and its surviving art is mostly Buddhist. This points out the fact that Hindus and Buddhists lived quite peacefully side by side, just as the different kinds of Buddhists did. No one in India thought that persecution over differences in religion made sense. The drift away from Buddhism toward Hinduism in India therefore left almost no traces. Buddhist monasteries continued to exist until Moslem raiders destroyed them after 1000 C.E. But once destroyed, nobody cared enough about the monks' way of holiness to restore them. The search for salvation had found new ways of expressing itself. Buddhist monasteries simply had become unnecessary.

Christianity

Christianity began in Palestine among the Jews. It later spread among Greek-speaking peoples of the eastern Mediterranean. From this center it then expanded rapidly in almost every direc-

tion—eastward along the Asian trade routes, south into India and Ethiopia, and west throughout the Roman Empire. Not until after 600 C.E. did Christianity win much of a foothold north of the old Roman borders. Between 600 and 1000 C.E., however, practically all of northern Europe was converted to the Christian faith. Despite such successes, Christianity, like Buddhism, was eventually pushed out of its land of origin. Islam, the faith of Mohammed, surged up from the Arabian desert, beginning in 634 C.E. Hence, while Christianity was winning converts among Slavs and Germans in the European north, Islam conquered Palestine and Syria—Christianity's cradleland—and all of the rest of the Middle East and north Africa.

Jewish Background

Christianity built upon Judaism. The later Hebrew prophets had proclaimed a Messiah, an anointed King and Savior, who would restore the Kingdom of David and remedy injustice. By the time of Christ, differences of opinion arose among pious Jews as to how to interpret the words of the prophets. Some expected a supernatural end of the world, when the skies would open to reveal God in splendor and the Messiah would come down from God's right hand to reward and punish individuals for their good and bad deeds. Others thought the Messiah would be a man like King David, sent by God to restore justice and defend true religion.

The Jews expected the Messiah with mounting intensity because times were very hard in Palestine. Wicked rulers and brutal taxgatherers seemed to be tempting God's forbearance and inviting his punishment. Nearly two centuries before the time of Christ, the Seleucid monarch Antiochus IV Epiphanes (reigned 175–163 B.C.E.) had tested the faith of the Jews by requiring them to honor him as a god. But the Jews refused to commit idolatry and rose in revolt. Under the leadership of Judas Maccabaeus, Jewish forces were victorious. This seemed clear proof of God's help; but to the distress of pious Jews, the kingdom that Judas Maccabaeus established soon fell into the hands of rulers who were more interested in pagan Greek culture and in getting along with the Romans than in observing God's law or governing justly.

In 64 B.C.E. the Romans established a protectorate over Palestine and put a new dynasty on the throne. Herod the Great (reigned 37–4 B.C.E.) was the last of the line to rule a sizable kingdom, for on his death the lands he had ruled were divided among his four sons. Then in 6 C.E. the eldest died and the two central provinces of Herod's kingdom, Judaea and Samaria, were put under direct Roman administration. About 30 C.E. a minor Roman official, Pontius Pilate, was in charge. As procurator of Judaea and representative of the emperor Tiberius, he authorized the crucifixion of Jesus of Nazareth because his followers recognized him as the long-awaited Messiah, God's Son, who had been sent to redeem the world. Crowds in Jerusalem had hailed him as "King of the Jews."

Most Jews were not convinced that Jesus was the Messiah. His career on earth did not correspond to their expectations. They therefore continued to wait. In 66 C.E. many Jews thought that the time for the Messiah's coming was finally at hand and revolted against Roman rule. Fighting lasted until 70 C.E. After a siege, the Romans captured Jerusalem and destroyed the Temple. It was never rebuilt. The war also scattered the little Christian community that had remained in Jerusalem after the crucifixion. From that time on, Christianity left its Jewish origin farther and farther behind. When still another revolt broke out in Palestine in 132 C.E., Christians were not directly affected. This time, however, the Romans took extreme action. They devastated the rebel territory and destroyed almost the entire Jewish community of Jerusalem and Judaea. Only Jews who lived in other places, mostly in cities among strangers, survived. The Jewish hope for the Messiah remained; but military uprisings of the sort that had occurred repeatedly from the time of Judas Maccabaeus ceased.

The Teachings of Jesus of Nazareth

This was the background for Jesus' ministry and teaching. He spent his active years in Galilee, far to the north of Jerusalem, where he preached among the poor peasants and fishermen of the region. His central theme was, "Repent, for the Kingdom of Heaven is at hand"; and he urged his listeners to observe a very strict moral discipline without, however, worrying too much about all the rules for ceremonial purification that had become important to Judaism. Jesus' preaching aroused great excitement. Acts of healing convinced many of those who gathered to listen to him that Jesus did indeed possess supernatural power. When he started toward Jerusalem for the Passover feast, his closest followers, the Twelve Apostles, expected that God would reveal the fact that Jesus was the long-awaited Messiah. Such talk frightened the leaders of the Jewish community in Jerusalem. They therefore arrested Jesus, convicted him for claiming to be "King of the Jews," and handed him over to the Roman authorities for punishment.

Jesus' death on the cross was a terrible shock to his disciples. Simon Peter, chief among the Apostles, three times denied any connection with Jesus. Yet soon afterward, gathered in an upstairs room, some of the Apostles suddenly felt their Master's presence. They sensed that the Holy Spirit had descended among them; joy and excitement replaced their disappointment and fear. In the next few days, several of his most devoted followers reported that Jesus had shown himself to them, still very much alive, despite his death on the cross. Here, they felt, was the final proof that Jesus was the Messiah. He had risen from the grave, victorious over death itself, and would soon come back in glory to establish the Kingdom of Heaven.

The good news could not be kept bottled up among the handful of disciples and their friends. They began to preach in the streets of Jerusalem. Soon missionaries appeared in other cities where Jewish synagogues existed. In some of these communities, the everyday language was Greek. The Hebrew word "Messiah"—the Anointed One— was translated into Greek as "Christ." Believers in Christ were first called "Christians" in Antioch, one of the great centers of Hellenistic culture and commerce and the former capital of the Seleucid Empire.

The first generations of Christians lived in daily expectation of the Second Coming of

Christ. They tried to prove to unbelieving Jews that Jesus was in fact the Messiah, by showing how his first appearance on earth had already fulfilled prophecy in many details. A series of questions soon arose: Were the provisions of the Jewish law, as they had been laid down in what Christians came to call the Old Testament, still binding? Or had Christ's authority repealed the old law? This question was important for the Jews; it was even more important for persons who were not Jews, but who, listening to the Christian message, were attracted to the faith. The man who gave a decisive answer to this question was Paul.

Born a Jew and a Roman citizen in the Greek-speaking city of Tarsus on the coast of Asia Minor, Paul was a highly educated man, unlike the simple Galileans who had first responded to Jesus' message. At first, Paul took an active part in persecuting the Christians in Jerusalem. Then he started for Damascus to warn the Jews there against the new doctrine. However, Paul met a strange experience on the road. He had a blinding vision of Christ. His blindness lasted only a few days; on recovery he became a fervent Christian.

On the basis of his personal experience of the risen Christ, St. Paul emphasized the idea that faith in Christ was what mattered. Whoever believed in the Resurrection and the Second Coming of Jesus Christ would be ready for the Last Judgment. For them death had no terrors; a blessed life beyond the grave in the presence of God himself was assured. Everything else was secondary, and in particular observing the rituals of Jewish law did not matter. Before Christ's coming, the law had been needed to lead people to God, but it was beyond human power to live up to the law in every detail. Salvation by the law was impossible. Therefore, Christ had come to show another way to eternal life. He would soon return; in the meanwhile, all that a Christian needed to assure salvation was faith in Christ and a warm, mutual, loving care for the welfare of every member of the community of the faithful.

Christianity as interpreted by St. Paul soon took root and flourished in the Greek-speaking cities of the eastern Mediterranean. When arguments broke out, he wrote letters to explain disputed points. These letters, together with the four Gospels—parallel accounts of Christ's life and ministry on earth—were later gathered together to form the core of the New Testament. A few other apostolic writings were also added; chief among them were the Revelations of St. John, which described in detail Christ's return and the expected end of the world.

St. Peter, the chief of the Apostles, and St. Paul both got into trouble with the Roman authorities. Preaching the end of the world sounded like revolution, and religious arguments between Jews and Christians provoked riots. The emperor Nero authorized the first organized persecution of Christians in 64 C.E. Both St. Peter and St. Paul were probably martyred at Rome in the course of this persecution.

Usually the Roman government paid little attention to Christians. Most of them were poor people who met, more or less secretly, to hear the gospel story once again and to share a ritual meal. Like the Jews, they refused to offer sacrifices to the emperor's statue, arguing that this was idolatry. But Roman authorities were usually willing to overlook this stiff-necked behavior as long as Christians offered no open threat to public order.

Another kind of problem arose for the Christians, however. What did Christian good news really mean? What was the true relationship between Jesus Christ and God? What was the Holy Spirit that had inspired the prophets of old and that sometimes descended upon Christian congregations, inspiring new (often very surprising) prophecies, excited and unintelligible speech, and other unusual behavior? Learned Greeks, trained in philosophical argument, were not satisfied with the simple text of the New Testament. What did Holy Scripture mean?

For a long time these matters could be left for the Second Coming to decide. But the urge to present a logical defense of Christian faith was difficult to resist, especially when critics began to argue against it. Between 200 and 300 C.E., therefore, Christian theologians began to define and defend a Trinitarian doctrine, according to which God the Father and Christ His Son shared a single and undivided Godhead with the Holy Spirit. By degrees, the method and much of the vocabulary of Greek philosophy

entered the Christian tradition through such discussion.

Christianity's Effect on Political and Social Life

After the death of Marcus Aurelius (180 C.E.), the Roman Empire met with hard times. Civil wars and barbarian attacks troubled the peace. Plagues depopulated many parts of the empire. Taxes were harder and harder to collect, and without taxes it was impossible to maintain a strong army to guard the frontiers. Many Christians believed these disasters proved that the end of the world was at hand. Increasing numbers of pagans agreed—and accepted the new faith. Others accused the Christians of being responsible for the bad times. Accordingly, a few of the emperors launched widespread persecutions. These reached their climax under the emperor Diocletian (reigned 284–305 C.E.), who reunited the empire after fifty years of confusion and then tried to root out and destroy what he viewed as the Christian conspiracy. However, in the end it was Christianity that prevailed.

This occurred when Constantine came to power after new civil wars. While marching toward Rome in 312 C.E., he saw a brilliant cross of light in the sky, which he interpreted as the first two letters of Christ's name. Constantine concluded that Christ was on his side. When, therefore, his troops won a victory at the Milvian Bridge just outside Rome, Constantine believed that he owed his success to Christ's help. Consequently, he stopped official persecution of the Christian communities in the territory he controlled and, instead, began to favor them. Imperial favor soon turned to support. By 395 C.E. the emperor Theodosius forbade all pagan worship. The Roman Empire thus became Christian exclusively, officially, and enduringly.

This great victory quickly created a new problem, however. As long as Christians had been a persecuted minority, they got along with one another in spite of differences of opinion about doctrine. To be sure, even in early days, extremes of behavior and belief had to be ruled out. Some of St. Paul's letters addressed themselves to such problems. There were always routine matters to be decided; for example, procedure at meetings or how to distribute gifts for the poor. From the very beginning the Apostles helped to decide such matters. When they died, successors, called bishops, inherited the responsibility of managing Christian affairs. In early times, each city where there was a Christian community or church had its own bishop. Bishops of larger cities, where richer and better-educated Christian communities arose, naturally had greater prestige. It was for these reasons that Alexandria in Egypt and, later, Constantinople on the Bosporus exercised religious leadership over wide territories. On the other hand, churches that had been personally founded by one of the Apostles claimed to have superior knowledge of true doctrine because of their origin. The Church of Rome had special prestige on both grounds. Rome, after

---

Changing Images of Christ   These four representations of the founder of Christianity show how variously the new faith was portrayed. On the upper left, when Christianity was still a persecuted religion, Christ appears as the Good Shepherd. But after Christianity became an official religion, a different aspect of Christ came to the fore, as is illustrated on the upper right. This Roman mosaic shows Christ as a lawgiver. Two adoring figures on either side and the sheep in the foreground echo other attributes; but the upraised right arm bespeaks power and authority. (Compare with p. 192.) Mingling of Christian and secular authority went a step further in the representation on the lower left, which comes from Ravenna about 500 C.E. It shows Christ in Roman military uniform, trampling a snake and lion underfoot; the open book says: "I am the way, the truth and the life." This stern image penetrated Germanic Europe, as you can see from the ivory carving of Christ that comes from a monastery near Essen and was made soon after 600 C.E..

all, was the traditional capital of the Roman Empire; in addition, the Roman Church traced its establishment to St. Peter, the chief of the Apostles.

These claims did not, in themselves, solve the problems that arose when rival theologians began to denounce one another as teachers of false doctrines. From time to time local bishops met and tried to settle disputes by common agreement. Then in 325 C.E., the emperor Constantine set out to define the true doctrine by summoning all Christian bishops to a meeting or council at Nicaea. It prepared the Nicene Creed. Creeds had been used for a long time among Christians in ordinary services of worship and especially at baptism, when new members were formally admitted to the Church. But the Nicene Creed was the first official effort to define the exact relationship between God the Father and God the Son, in a brief but authoritative way.

The Council of Nicaea, however, failed to end quarrels. Christians found it impossible to agree on the exact relationship among the persons of the Trinity. After more than a century of bitter debate, Christians of Syria and Egypt, most of whom spoke the local Syriac and Coptic languages, refused to accept the creed as defined by Greek-speaking Christians; and they set up their own independent churches.

Difficulties also arose between Latin-speaking and Greek-speaking Christians. The issue was not theological doctrine, however, so much as the question of how the Christian church should be governed. As successors to St. Peter, the bishops of Rome claimed authority over all Christian churches; but bishops of the Greek-speaking East refused to accept Roman authority in disputed matters of doctrine and discipline. They argued that the whole body of bishops inherited the authority over the Church that Christ had conferred upon the Apostles.

After 378 C.E., as we shall soon see, barbarian invasions destroyed Roman government in the Latin-speaking parts of the empire. This meant that most Latin-speaking Christians were no longer effectively under the control of the Roman emperor, who continued to reign from Constantinople. Each Christian community of the Latin West simply had to do the best it could under very uncertain conditions. This often meant

giving wider powers to bishops, who took over functions formerly reserved for local governors and judges. For example, the bishop of Rome, or pope, as he is usually called, became the effective ruler of the city and its immediate environs. But in the troubled and disturbed times that followed the barbarian invasions, the pope usually could not make his authority felt beyond the walls of the city, and often faced challenges within Rome itself.

The Teaching of St. Augustine of Hippo

The collapse of the Roman Empire in the West led some old-fashioned pagans to blame the disaster on Christianity. St. Augustine of Hippo (354–430 C.E.) set out to answer this accusation in a book called *The City of God*. Writing in Latin, Augustine developed a Christian view of history on the basis of the Old and New Testaments. According to his vision of humanity's experience on earth, the barbarian attack on Rome in 410 C.E. was a trifling event, of no significance when compared with God's plan for human salvation. God had begun to reveal his plan in the days of Abraham and Moses; it had been fully revealed by Christ and would be fulfilled by the Second Coming, when God would bring the great drama to its appointed close. In the meanwhile, the world was divided into two parts—or, as Augustine called them, cities: the City of God, or Heaven, and the City of Earth.

The Church was the great link between the two parts of creation. By means of the Church, people could hope to pass from the evils of earth to the glory of Heaven, for it was through the Church that God had chosen to dispense his grace to sinful humankind. This assigned a far more important role to the Church than early Christians had usually done. The end of the world and Christ's Second Coming, which had been so eagerly awaited by the first Christians, became, for Augustine, a matter that would come to pass when God willed, at the end of time. But for the present, and indefinitely into the future, Christ had established the Church to shepherd the souls God had chosen for salvation toward their eternal home, the City of God.

Augustine's vision of the human condition shaped all later Latin Christianity. His view of the Church, of sin and salvation, and his interpretations of biblical passages all played a central role in later theological discussion. In addition, our consciousness of time as a fundamental dimension of reality can in large part be attributed to Augustine.

After Augustine's death the heat of theological controversy slowly died down. The Greeks defined Orthodox doctrine, in a lasting way, at the Council of Chalcedon in 451 C.E. They accepted a creed formulated by Pope Leo the Great. This kept Latin and Greek Christians in agreement on doctrine for a while longer. After Chalcedon, the Copts in Egypt and the Syriac Christians in Asia defined their own creeds in opposition to the Greeks. When each of these major segments of the Christian community had defined its position with an official creed, further controversy was controlled by the care each church took to stay within its own particular definition of the truth.

By 600 C.E., therefore, when Christianity was about to face a fresh challenge from the followers of Mohammed, the Church had changed very much from its early days. Expectation of the Second Coming did not cease; but day-to-day prayer, rituals, and the routine of administration mattered more because this was what dominated everyday religious activity. And for those who were not content with such routines, special monastic communities developed. These started as loose gatherings of hermits and ascetics, who swarmed into the Egyptian and Syrian deserts after about 250 C.E.. Later on, more strictly organized communities were established. The most influential of these in the Greek church were governed by the rule of St. Basil (330–379 C.E.), while in the Latin-speaking world the rule of St. Benedict of Nursia (ca. 529 C.E.) became standard.

The Impact of Barbarian Invasions

The rise and spread of Mahayana Buddhism, Hinduism, and Christianity changed the aspect of civilized communities throughout Eurasia.

People expected more from an afterlife and less from life on earth. This is not so surprising, since most of them found little ease or comfort in their daily experience of the world. One reason was that wave after wave of destructive barbarian invasion inundated civilized lands. Even when the invaders did not conquer, they strained civilized defenses to the limit. This often meant heavier taxes.

If we try to view the military problem facing all the civilized states of Eurasia—from the Roman Empire in the west to the Chinese Empire in the east—a common factor at once appears. They all had to protect themselves against bands of raiders coming from the grassy steppes extending across almost the entire continent—from Hungary, Romania, and southern Russia in eastern Europe, to Mongolia and Manchuria in eastern Asia. Nomadic cavalry bowmen had first occupied the steppe regions (moving from west to east) between about 800 and 300 B.C.E. Raiding and trading were both important for these peoples. Successful raids on civilized populations never supplied exactly the assortment of goods the raiders needed, so trading surpluses for needed items afterwards at some safe haven was very much part of the nomad way of life. In addition, when long-range caravans began to cross Eurasia, nomads could and did supply animals and caravan personnel for the trade that had tied Eurasian civilizations together after about 100 B.C.E.

Although peaceful trade clearly became more regular and important, raiding remained more exciting. After all, the nomads' quickest way to wealth was to make a successful raid on someone else's herds. Success was greatly admired. Fighting, in short, was essential to the way nomads lived—and died. Their weapon was the bow; they rode to war on the backs of hardy ponies that could survive on the natural grasses of the steppe. Speed and surprise gave them an enormous advantage over slower-moving armies. On the other hand, steppe cavalry seldom could capture a fortified town. In particular, a long siege was almost always beyond their capacity. After a few weeks of staying in one place, pasture for their horses was sure to run short and then they would have to move on to keep their mounts in good condition.

Yet farms and villages exposed to nomad raiding suffered great damage. City dwellers, de-

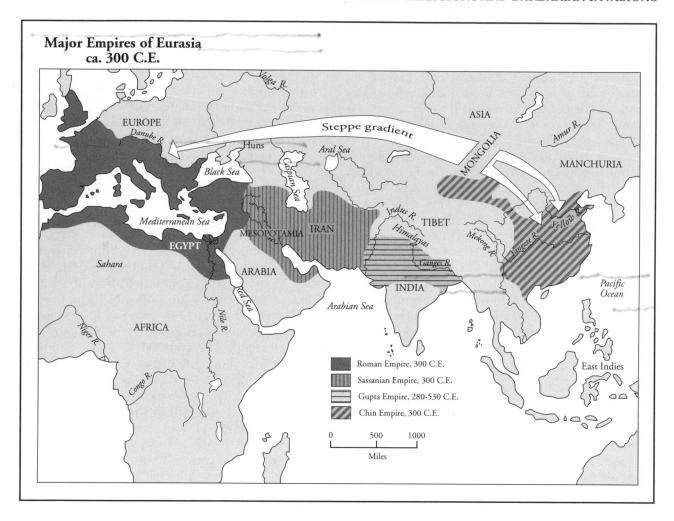

Major Empires of Eurasia ca. 300 C.E.

Steppe gradient

EUROPE · Danube R. · Huns · Black Sea · Mediterranean Sea · EGYPT · Sahara · AFRICA · Niger R. · Congo R. · Nile R. · Red Sea · ARABIA · MESOPOTAMIA · IRAN · Caspian Sea · Aral Sea · Volga R. · Arabian Sea · Indus R. · Himalayas · Ganges R. · INDIA · TIBET · Mekong R. · Yangtze R. · Yellow R. · ASIA · MONGOLIA · MANCHURIA · Amur R. · Pacific Ocean · East Indies

Roman Empire, 300 C.E.
Sassanian Empire, 300 C.E.
Gupta Empire, 280-530 C.E.
Chin Empire, 300 C.E.

0 · 500 · 1000
Miles

pending on the flow of food from the surrounding countryside, might suffer almost as much as the plundered farmers. How to stop nomad raids therefore became a critical problem for Eurasia's settled agricultural populations from the time when the steppe came to be occupied by tribes of nomad cavalrymen.

We have already seen some of the earliest consequences of this confrontation. The first massive raids by steppe cavalry accompanied the overthrow of the Assyrian Empire (605 B.C.E.). Nearly four centuries later, the unification of China (221 B.C.E.) was another example of the impact of steppe warfare on civilized society, for the Ch'in armies that conquered China had learned their skill through long border strife and had borrowed the nomads' style of cavalry warfare themselves.

As soon as the Eurasian steppe had been fully occupied by nomad warriors, major events in any region of the steppe echoed throughout its length. If one group of people were driven from traditional pasturelands by some neighboring tribe, they had either to find a new home by driving others away from their traditional pastures or else perish. Thus, for example, when the Hsiung-nu formed a powerful confederation in Mongolia about 200 B.C.E., they were able to drive away other people who had formerly lived on the borders of China. The defeated nomads fled westward along the steppe. One branch of these refugees later established the Kushan Empire in what is now Afghanistan. At about the same time, Parthian tribes left the central regions of the steppe and overran Iran and Mesopotamia.

A few generations later another people, the Sarmatians, pushed into southern Russia, the lower Danube region, and eventually reached Hungary, where they collided with the Roman defenses soon after 150 C.E. A domino effect thus ran all across Eurasia, from the borders of China westward to the Middle East and Europe.

Civilized Countermeasures

Shortly before the beginning of the Common Era, however, civilized peoples perfected a new style of warfare that went a long way toward stopping nomad raids and making the agricultural villages and fields of the countryside safe for farming. The Parthians, who controlled Iran and Mesopotamia from about 141 B.C.E. to 226 C.E. played a particularly important part in this development. They discovered that by feeding horses with alfalfa and hay during the winter when natural forage was scarce, a far bigger and stronger breed could be maintained. A stronger horse could carry heavy armor itself and bear the additional weight of an armored rider, without ceasing to be mobile. Such heavily armored cavalry could withstand nomad attacks very successfully, since nearly all the raiders' arrows would simply shatter or glance off harmlessly. At the same time, skilled horse archers, astride their great horses, could pick off a fair share of any unarmored steppe cavalrymen who dared to approach them. This meant that a body of properly equipped and trained cavalrymen could defend any locality against the hit-and-run tactics of steppe warfare. On the other hand, this type of warrior could not take the strategic offensive against nomad enemies because at most times of the year the big horses could not find adequate grazing on the open steppe.

The great problem with the new heavy cavalry was how to pay for it. It required years of practice to become a really effective horse archer. The rider had to be able to hit a target from a moving horse while also controlling his mount without holding the reins. Moreover, food and armor for the big horses were very expensive. The Parthian solution was to scatter the cavalrymen out among the villages and let them collect rents from local peasants. This

had the advantage of keeping skilled and effective defenders always at hand. Its disadvantage was that the central government could not control such warriors. When the king called on them for a campaign, he could never be sure how many would show up or, having shown up, whether they would follow him where he chose to lead.

The Chinese government was never willing to adopt the Parthian style of local self-defense against nomad raiding. The big horses proved too expensive. Instead, the Chinese preferred to hire light cavalrymen who rode and fought like the Hsiung-nu whom they opposed. Alternatively, by sending gifts (or tribute) to the Hsiung-nu, the Chinese could hope to keep them quiet. The Roman government, too, long refused to make use of the Parthian pattern of local self-defense. The Romans were therefore ill-prepared for the next wave of barbarian attacks that developed abruptly after 374 C.E., when a people known as Huns broke into southern Russia from the east, conquered the Ostrogoths, who had set themselves up there a short time before, and spread terror far and wide.

In the next year, the Visigoths fled before the Huns into Roman territory. There they soon quarreled with Roman officials. When an imperial army went to subdue them, they defeated the army and killed the Emperor Valens in the Battle of Adrianople (378 C.E.). The Visigoths were never driven from Roman soil again. They plundered the Balkans thoroughly before going to Italy, where they sacked Rome in 410 C.E., and then went on to Spain. Other German tribes soon followed, fleeing from the terrible Huns, who had meanwhile established their headquarters in Hungary and were raiding deep into Roman territory year after year.

Sassanian Persia

While devastation thus spread through much of the Roman world, the central portion of the civilized front against the steppe held firm. To be sure, in 226 C.E. the Parthian kings were replaced by a new Sassanian Dynasty. Their empire is often called the New Persian Empire (226–651 C.E.), because the Sassanians took the

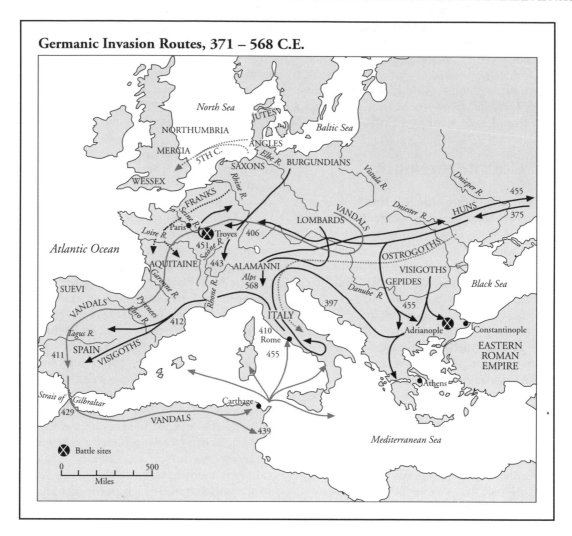

Germanic Invasion Routes, 371 – 568 C.E.

empires of Darius and Xerxes as their model. Realities, however, had changed, and the Sassanians depended even more completely than their predecessors upon heavy-armored cavalry dispersed among the villages of the Iranian countryside.

The Sassanian government tried a number of interesting religious experiments. One king patronized the prophet Mani (lived ca. 215–273 C.E.), who tried to create a new religion by bringing together the "true" teachings of Zoroastrianism, Judaism, and Christianity. But official favor did not last. When his royal protector died, Mani was arrested and actually died in prison. Nevertheless, his followers met with considerable missionary success. They penetrated both Roman and Chinese territory as well as regions along

the trade routes in between. In Roman lands, Mani's doctrines rivaled Christianity for a while. St. Augustine, for example, became a Manichaean in his youth, as he tells us in his *Confessions*. But when Christianity became the official faith of the Roman state. Manichaeism was outlawed and the combined forces of church and state soon eliminated it from Roman soil. The faith lasted much longer in central Asia and China; but there, too, Manichaeism ceased to have a numerically significant following after about 900 C.E.

The long-range failure of Mani's faith to establish itself among the great world religions did not affect the ability of the Sassanian Empire to hold neighboring barbarians at bay. On the contrary, rural landholders, trained from childhood to ride and shoot—and ready at a moment's notice to don their armor and ride forth to defend the locality from which they drew their rents—proved very effective in discouraging raiders from the steppe. Because of their geographical position, the Sassanian warriors also protected India, where, as we saw, the Gupta Empire flourished through a long period of peace.

China's Recovery

But the fact that the Sassanian frontier guard, in the middle portions of the steppe frontier, was so successful tended to concentrate nomad harassment of civilized peoples at the two extremes, east and west. China, for example, suffered a long series of raids as the Han dynasty approached its final collapse (220 C.E.). During the following three and a half centuries, China was divided into a varying number of rival states, many of which were ruled by barbarian invaders. This was also the time when Buddhism won its major successes in China. Then in 589 C.E. a new dynasty, the Sui, was able to unite the whole country once more, and launched vigorous military expansion into Korea and south toward Vietnam.

In 605 C.E. the Sui opened the Grand Canal that connected the Yangtze River with the Yellow River. This canal allowed cheap and easy transport between the two great river valleys of China for the first time. It became possible to deliver rice and other commodities produced near navigable water anywhere in the Yangtze basin to the imperial capital at Loyang, far in the north. The Grand Canal therefore doubled or more than doubled the income at the disposal of the imperial court. Always before, the Chinese emperors could expect to have only the tax yield from the Yellow River valley available for feeding the capital and supplying the armies needed to stand guard against the nomads in the north. But after the canal came into operation, the surplus products of the vast Yangtze Valley could be carried north and used for these same purposes. An enormous strengthening of the Chinese imperial government therefore resulted. Rapid development of the Yangtze region and a southward shift of China's center of wealth and population were other consequences of the opening of the Grand Canal.

China's reunification was long-lasting and launched the Chinese upon a new phase in their history. As long as China's vast resources were united under one command, it was not too difficult to keep the nomads at a safe distance from Chinese soil. Even when another powerful steppe confederation arose, the Juan-juan, China remained secure. Nomad peoples, defeated by the Juan-juan, started westward and headed toward the European steppe. There, as we shall see, new migrations of peoples broke through the frontiers of the East Roman or Byzantine Empire and changed the linguistic map of Europe in far-reaching ways.

Emergence of Byzantium

While these events were taking place in China, Europe went through a similar cycle of barbarian invasion and recovery. The barbarian invasions that followed the overthrow of the Han dynasty in 200 C.E. were like the Hunnic and German invasions that brought down the Roman Empire in the west after 375 C.E.. But in 454 C.E. the Huns' confederacy broke up after the death of their greatest leader, Attila. Thereafter, flights and migrations slacked off. Fairly stable governments, ruled by German tribal chieftains or kings, emerged on what had formerly been Roman soil. The Vandal kingdom in North Africa, the Visigothic kingdom in Spain and southern Gaul, and the Ostrogothic kingdom in Italy were the most important of these states (see map, p. 216).

As pressure from the steppe frontier decreased, Roman power in the eastern half of the empire recovered. Under the emperor Justinian (reigned 527–565 C.E.), the empire launched a systematic effort to regain control of the lost western provinces. Justinian was in fact able to recover north Africa from the Vandals and Italy from the Ostrogoths. He also won control of part of Spain from the Visigoths. The East Roman or Byzantine Empire won these victories with a combination of sea power and heavy-armored cavalry, equipped and trained on the Sassanian model but supported by the imperial treasury

The Empress Theodora

Theodora was an actress—slender, vivacious, popular. She was born into the theater, for her father exhibited trained bears in the circus at Constantinople. Yet from this disreputable origin, at the age of twenty-four Theodora became the reigning empress of Byzantium, sharing power with her husband, the famous emperor Justinian.

Before they could legally marry, an old law forbidding men of high rank to marry actresses had to be repealed. The bitter opposition of the imperial family also had to be overcome. Indeed, not until after the death of Justinian's aunt could the emperor Justin, who preceded Justinian on the throne, be persuaded to agree to the marriage.

As empress, Theodora took an active part in the government of the empire. Her most fateful act came in 532, when the populace of Byzantium broke out in fierce riots. For many years the Byzantines had been passionately interested in chariot racing. The races were held between two factions, the Greens and the Blues, and practically everyone in the city belonged to one or the other faction—betting on and hoping and praying for the victory of one side or the other.

Feeling ran so high in 532 that the rival factions came to blows in the great circus, where the people had gathered for the race. When Emperor Justinian tried to check the rioting by ordering his soldiers to clear the circus, the crowd turned against the imperial couple, then only five years on the throne. So fierce were the crowds and so uncertain the loyalty of Justinian's soldiers that after several days of wild rioting, the emperor decided to flee from the city in hope of saving his life by giving up the throne. But Theodora, who had risen so high so surprisingly, refused to flee. "The purple makes a handsome shroud," she said, as she persuaded her husband to renew the battle. Within a few hours the fighting spirit of the crowds melted away, the soldiers' discipline held, and peace returned to the capital. After 532 Justinian never forgot that he owed his throne to Theodora, as she had previously owed her throne to him.

and not by land grants, as was the custom among the Persians.

Only in remote Britain and along the Rhine and Danube frontiers of the Roman Empire, did German advances remain unchallenged. In Britain, Saxons and Angles, who had their homes near the German coast of the North Sea, invaded Britain, beginning about 420 C.E., and gradually drove back the older Celtic and Latin-speaking inhabitants. Similarly, along the Rhine and Danube frontiers, tribes of German farmers—Franks in the west and Bavarians, Burgundians,

and others along the upper Danube—steadily advanced their line of settlement by clearing new fields in the vast forests that covered these regions.

Toward the end of Justinian's reign, it looked, therefore, as though the reunification of at least the Mediterranean parts of the Roman Empire could be carried through successfully. On the surface, this recovery resembled the reunification of China by the Sui dynasty that occurred only a little afterward. In reality, there was a great difference. Thanks to the Grand

Canal, the Sui were able to tap new revenues that made the restored imperial government in China stable and secure. The East Roman or Byzantine government was not able to do anything of this sort. On the contrary, when dangers from the steppe frontier in the north once more became acute, the Byzantine authorities lacked the armies and material resources required to hold the invaders back. As a result, in Justinian's last days and throughout the half century that followed his death, a new avalanche of barbarian migration set in.

The driving force behind these movements was the appearance of a new steppe people, the Avars. Like the Huns before them, they set up their raiding headquarters on the grassy plain of Hungary and plundered far and wide. A German tribe known as Lombards ("Long Beards") fled from the Avars and invaded Italy. The Byzantine armies that had been able to overthrow the Ostrogoths were too few to hold the Lombards at bay. In the Balkans, Slavic tribes filtered southward in great numbers. Farther west, Franks and neighboring Germanic peoples continued to advance their settlements at the expense of Latin-speaking inhabitants; and across the English Channel, the Anglo-Saxons did the same. These movements permanently changed the language map of Europe. Franks and Anglo-Saxons in the west and Slavs in the east made the land their own by settling on it as farmers. The language boundaries that resulted from these migrations remain almost unchanged to the present day.

One reason the Byzantines failed to resist these barbarian pressures from the north was that their eastern frontier was also threatened. The Sassanian heavy cavalry, so effective against nomad raiders, could also be mobilized against the Byzantines. Byzantine armies, generally speaking, were too few in numbers to stop such attacks. On the other hand, the Byzantines always kept command of the sea. This allowed the emperors to use ships to outflank any force that raided so far into Asia Minor as to threaten the capital of Constantinople itself.

In 634 C.E., just after the conclusion of a long and costly struggle between the Sassanian and Byzantine empires, a new and revolutionary force appeared in the Middle East. In that year, Arabs from the southern desert, united by the new religion of Islam, attacked the exhausted Byzantine and Sassanian empires. In an amazingly short period of time, they overran Byzantium's richest provinces and utterly destroyed the Sassanian state. By doing so, the Arabs inaugurated a new period of world history, which we will consider in the next chapter.

The Fringes of the Civilized World

The rise of three new world religions and all these raids, invasions, and migrations of peoples had the overall effect of blurring the boundaries between civilized and barbarian territory. The Hsiung-nu and Juan-juan, in the periods of their strength, enjoyed a rich supply of goods sent from China as tribute. Obviously, the tastes of at least the upper classes among them came to be attuned to the Chinese style of living. The same was true of the Germans who invaded Roman territory. As Roman civilization coarsened with the destruction of the class of landowners who had shared the classical pagan culture, it became easier for the barbarians to take full part in what remained. Accordingly, the Ostrogoths of Italy and the Visigoths of Spain soon came fully abreast of the level of culture that existed among their Roman subjects. But the fact that these German tribes had accepted a form of Christianity that the Latin Christians viewed as heretical kept them and their subjects apart.

Beyond the old Roman frontiers, only by slow degrees did rude, rural, and warlike Slavs and Germans find anything of interest in the Greek or Roman brands of Christian civilization. In distant Ireland, however, Christianity was introduced about 430 C.E. by St. Patrick, a native of Wales. The Irish quickly agreed that Christianity was an improvement on druidry, which had existed there before. The druids were priests whose doctrines may have descended, at least in part, from the old megalithic religion. Irish Christian monasteries were probably influenced by druid practices. Thus, the special love of learning shown by the Irish monks may have been a Christian version of a pagan custom that required each generation of druids to memorize lengthy texts in order to perform traditional sacred ceremonies. Their apprenticeship to Christian learning was so successful that, by 600 C.E., Irish monks far surpassed anything known in England or anywhere else in western Europe.

Along the southern flank of the Roman world, new civilizations, or the beginnings of new civilizations, came into existence during these same centuries. In west Africa, for example, the first evidence of an organized state, known as the kingdom of Ghana, dates from about 300 C.E.. Farmers raising crops that had originated in distant Indonesia produced a surplus rulers could tax. In addition, they profited from caravan trade that crossed the Sahara and connected Ghana with Roman North Africa. Little is known of Ghana's court life or high culture, since no written documents from that ancient African Empire have survived.

Farther east in Africa, the kingdom of Abyssinia also rose to prominence and, for a short while, extended its power across the Straits of Aden into Arabia. The wealth of Abyssinia rested in large part on taxes levied upon the trade passing through the Red Sea. When the Abyssinians raised their tolls too high, overland caravan trade, up and down the length of Arabia, became a practicable way of bypassing the tolls. Sea trade between Egypt and India thus died away. It was partially counterbalanced by the rise of Arabian caravan trade upon which the city of Mecca, where Mohammed was born, prospered.

In Asia, also, new border states and regions attained a level of organization we recognize as civilized. Beginning about the start of the Common Era, a series of kingdoms in southeast Asia and Indonesia imported their court culture from India, in either a Buddhist or a Hindu form. Trade, missionary work, and peaceful penetration were the methods of Indian expansion. War and violence played a very small role. Tibet, to the north and such mountain regions as Kashmir also came within the circle of Indian culture between 200 and 600 C.E..

China added Korea and Japan to its sphere of influence in the same centuries. South and west, in Vietnam and in central Asia, just before 600 C.E., the Chinese began to penetrate regions that were already in touch with Indian culture. Thus, the expansion of the zones of influence around these two great Asian civilizations almost closed the geographical gap that had formerly separated them from one another. Pockets of wild country remained in southeast Asia, where primitive hunters and slash-and-burn cultivators lived as their ancestors had done for uncounted centuries; but along the rivers and wherever transport was easy, the impact of higher civilizations made itself felt.

Farther south, Australia and southern Africa as yet showed no signs of reacting to the changes underway in the civilized world. In the Congo rain forest, however, the arrival of Indonesian plants, suited to cultivation in such an environment, allowed the development of agricultural communities throughout central Africa. Exactly when this type of cultivation began to spread in Africa is not known; but it was probably well established by 300 C.E..

Across the ocean in the Americas, however, vigorous civilizations arose between 200 and 600 C.E. One principal center was in Guatemala and adjacent parts of Mexico, where the Mayans built a series of elaborate cult centers. They developed a way of writing that scholars have recently begun to decipher with growing certainty, and learned to assure abundant harvests of corn and other crops by creating raised fields in otherwise swampy land. Each Mayan center was governed by local rulers who were part priest, part warrior. They confirmed their powers by conducting public ceremonies in which self-inflicted wounds and the slaughter of defeated enemies involved a good deal of bloodletting. The Mayans also developed an elaborate calendar and dated many of their carved stone monuments, so that experts can say, with exactitude, that the earliest known date for a Mayan monument corresponds to April 9, 328 C.E..

Three hundred years later, their civilization was rising toward its highest levels of accomplishment as measured by the elegance of carving, the size of its pyramidal temples, and the scale of monumental construction. By that time, similar cult centers were also appearing far to the north in the central valley of Mexico where

Two Faces of Japan   The Japanese actively entered the civilized world of
Eurasia when Buddhism took root among them soon after 550 C.E. But the new
religion encountered a vigorous warlike society with traditions of its own. Old
and new are here embodied in the figure of the warrior on the left, made about
500 C.E., and the two weeping monks lamenting Buddha's entry into Nirvana
on the right, made about two hundred years later. The obvious gap between
these works of art reflects a tension within Japanese high culture that lasted to
modern times.

Aztec power was later based. Similarities in
their art suggests that the early civilized centers
of the central valley shared some of the Mayan
religious ideas, but the lack of readable texts
from that part of the Amerindian world makes
exact knowledge impossible.

The same is true of Peru, where other, independent, styles of civilization were flourishing
by and before 600 C.E. Peru offered two very
different environments in which monumental

building and other traces of complex societies
have been discovered. On the one hand, rain-watered lands high in the Andes allowed crops of
potatoes and other plants unique to the region to
support an abundant population. Rulers eventually learned, as in ancient Egypt, how to mobilize the labor power of most of the population by
gathering foodstuffs into storehouses and then
paying food out again to those who worked at
the rulers' command on various public tasks

during the season of the year when nothing would grow in the high altiplano.

Near the sea coast, a very different way of life came into being, for there streams tumble down from the mountains and flow across a desert where rain almost never falls until they reach the Pacific. Agriculture therefore depended on irrigation as in ancient Mesopotamia or Egypt; and the need to coordinate efforts to create and maintain canals and dikes required the same sort of political organization in lowland Peru as had prevailed in the ancient river valley civilizations of the Old World. But since no written texts survive from Peru, modern scholars cannot understand the ideas which undoubtedly supported the complex societies that built the surviving monuments, nor can we know exactly how different social groups fought and cooperated to create them. Exact dating is disputed also, as is the question of how closely Peru was in touch with the skilled peoples of Mexico. The fact that corn became an important crop in Peru as well as in Mexico, where it was first domesticated, means that some sort of contact between North and South America must have existed; but whether that played any part in stimulating the Peruvian peoples to begin their march toward civilization is simply unknown.

In general, the rise of societies with civilized skills and complexity in the Americas happened about 3000 years after comparable beginnings in the Middle East. The peoples of the Americas never really caught up, and as a result, when regular contacts were opened up across the ocean after 1492, the Amerindians were at a great disadvantage. Nevertheless, the emergence of several quite different styles of civilization in the Americas and the multiplication of civilized societies along the margins of Eurasia's four principal civilizations meant that simple communities of hunters and gatherers, on the one hand, and of subsistence cultivators, on the other, were in retreat across large parts of the earth. They gave ground before far more complicated and more highly skilled societies whose spread, at least in the Old World, was beginning to lap up against one another to create a more or less continuous zone of civilization.

The commercial links that had united the Mediterranean world with China and India after

100 B.C.E. tended to break off in the subsequent centuries of barbarian invasion. Each civilization was more inclined to fall back upon its own devices. A period of withdrawal and comparative isolation therefore succeeded the extensive exchanges and migrations of people and of ideas that had been so prominent in the centuries between 200 B.C.E. and 600 C.E. The clash of intolerant rival religions after 632 C.E. confirmed this trend, giving a new character to the next era of Eurasian history.

Conclusion

A cycle of advance, retreat, and partial recovery can be detected behind all the confusing detail of events dealt with in this chapter. First, the different civilized regions of Eurasia came closer together than ever before as a result of organizing regular trade connections. Caravans linked China with the Mediterranean shore and moved southward into India as well. Sea trade between the Mediterranean and India was equally or more important, and a few Roman merchants got as far as southern China.

These enlarged contacts allowed new religious ideas to spread widely among civilized populations. In particular, Mahayana Buddhism and Christianity won enormous numbers of adherents, and Hinduism was not far behind. All three of these faiths offered their followers a hope for salvation and a future heavenly existence. Moreover, salvation in each case was believed to be possible because of a special link between each individual believer, no matter how humble, and a divine yet manlike savior. In detail, of course, the teachings of each religion differed from the others, and each faith developed its own kind of religious organization—church, monastery, or temple, as the case might be.

The three new religions continued to prosper and spread even when, after about 200 C.E., the complicated arrangements needed to sustain long-distance caravan and sea trade began to break down. At the two extremes of the civilized world, in Europe and in China, local self-sufficiency became more common. Trade did not cease, but the scale and regularity of movement to and fro across long distances declined sharply as the wealth and political stability of both Rome and China suffered serious decay.

Exactly what caused the decline of the Roman Empire—and the no less disastrous decline of the Han Empire in China—has long been a theme for scholarly debate. Depopulation, resulting from exposure to unfamiliar diseases that had been spread throughout Eurasia and parts of Africa by traders, was probably one important factor. Weakened and impoverished governments, in turn, found it impossible to prevent barbarians from overrunning wide territories in Europe and China. China recovered after 589 C.E., when the Sui dynasty united the Yellow River valley and the Yangtze River valley under their sway and proceeded to link the two parts of China securely together by building the Grand Canal.

In the Far West, civilized government could not be restored so quickly. To be sure, the East Roman or Byzantine Empire did indeed regain much lost ground in the age of Justinian (527–565 C.E.). But no new resources like those that became available to the Chinese emperors allowed the rulers of Byzantium to fasten their power securely over the full extent of the old Roman Empire.

The decline and recovery of the Roman and Chinese empires at the two extremes of the civilized world of Eurasia had no parallel in Iran, Mesopotamia, and India. There, on the contrary, barbarian raiders were kept at bay by heavy-armored cavalry, perfected, apparently, by Parthians about 100 B.C.E. The solid success of the Parthians and of their Persian successors in keeping the steppe peoples from invading the Middle East also protected India, which reached its classical peak under the Gupta at a time when both China and Rome were in the throes of barbarian invasion and civil wars.

Thus the cycle of expansion, contraction, and then at least partial recovery made itself felt mainly at the extremes of the civilized world—that is, in Europe and in China. The Middle Eastern regions, where danger from the steppe was most immediate, suffered less because local institutions and defense establishments were better fitted for holding the steppe peoples at bay. Yet in the centuries that followed, the Middle East proved vulnerable to a new kind of nomad attack, issuing this time from the Arabian desert to the south and inspired by a new religious faith, Islam.

The surge of Islam, sudden and successful in surprising degree, sharply altered the pattern of relations among Eurasian civilizations and marked a new era in the history of the world. This will be the subject of the next chapter.

Bibliography

As always, direct approach to the past by reading what was written at the time is the first and most valuable supplement to any textbook. For this chapter, an understanding of the rise of Christianity and of Buddhism, especially its Mahayana form, is what matters most. For that purpose, the pages of the *New Testament* are available to everyone, and students ought to read one or more of the Gospels and the Book of Acts to know more about how Christianity started. Among later Christian books, Augustine, *Confessions*, is perhaps the most telling and, like the *New Testament*, is readily available in several different translations. Buddhist texts are far less accessible. Long ago, Henry Clarke Warren, *Buddhism in Translation* (1896), made a collection of Buddhist stories and pious writings; and the previously cited collection of readings by Ainslee T. Embree and Stephen N. Hay, *Sources of the Indian Tradition* (2nd ed., 1966), also reproduces a selection of Buddhist materials. But because Buddhist piety followed many diverse paths from the start, no single text has the importance for the religion as a whole that the *New Testament* does for Christianity.

The other key development with which this chapter dealt was the emergence of an elegant courtly culture in India. Another old translation, Arthur W. Ryder, *Shakuntala and Other Writings by Kalidasa* (1912), can introduce you to the work of India's most accomplished courtly poet, and Hari Prasad Shastri, trans., *The Ramayana* (3 vols. 1957), makes India's second famous and influential epic available to English readers. A. L. Basham, *The Wonder That Was India* (3rd ed., 1967), is a far more accessible book that reproduces excerpts from these and other ancient Indian writings.

This period of world history was distinguished by the collapse of imperial government in China and in the Far West. One reason was the onset of serious epidemics, discussed in William H. McNeill, *Plagues and Peoples* (1976). The increasing formidability of steppe nomads and other barbarian war bands was also a

224CIVILIZED RELIGIONS AND BARBARIAN INVASIONS

key factor, as is made clear by Rene Grousset, *The Empire of the Steppes: A History of Central Asia* (1970); Thomas Barfield, *The Perilous Frontier* (1989); Malcolm Todd, *The Northern Barbarians, 100 B.C.–A.D. 300.* (1987); and Herwig Wolfram, *History of the Goths* (1988).

The contrasting experience of China and Europe under these conditions may be followed by looking at Arthur F. Wright, *Buddhism in Chinese History* (1971), and Xinru Liu, *Ancient India and China A.D. 1–600* (1988), which describe how Buddhism penetrated a politically divided China; while in the Far West, Paul Johnson, *A History of Christianity* (1975); Peter Brown, *Power and Persuasion in Late Antiquity: Towards a Christian Empire* (1992); A. H. M. Jones, *The Later Roman Empire, 284–602* (2 vols., 1986); and Judith Herrin, *The Formation of Christendom* (1987),

describe how Christianity penetrated politically divided Roman lands. Meanwhile India attained its classical apogee as R. K. Mookerji, *The Gupta Empire* (4th ed., 1969), and Bardwell L. Smith, ed., *Essays on Gupta Culture* (1983), show.

Art as always is another way to understand what happens to human consciousness and feeling. For early Christian art, Andre Grabar, *The Beginnings of Christian Art, 200–395* (1967), and Andre Grabar, *The Golden Age of Justinian: From the Death of Theodosius to the Rise of Islam* (1967), are standard. I know of no comparable study of early Buddhist art as a whole, but Dietrich Seckel, *The Art of Buddhism* (1964), deals with its central Asian and Chinese manifestations, and Joanna Gottfried Williams, *The Art of Gupta India: Empire and Province* (1982), treats Indian art in the same age.

Civilizations; 1 C.E. to 600 C.E.

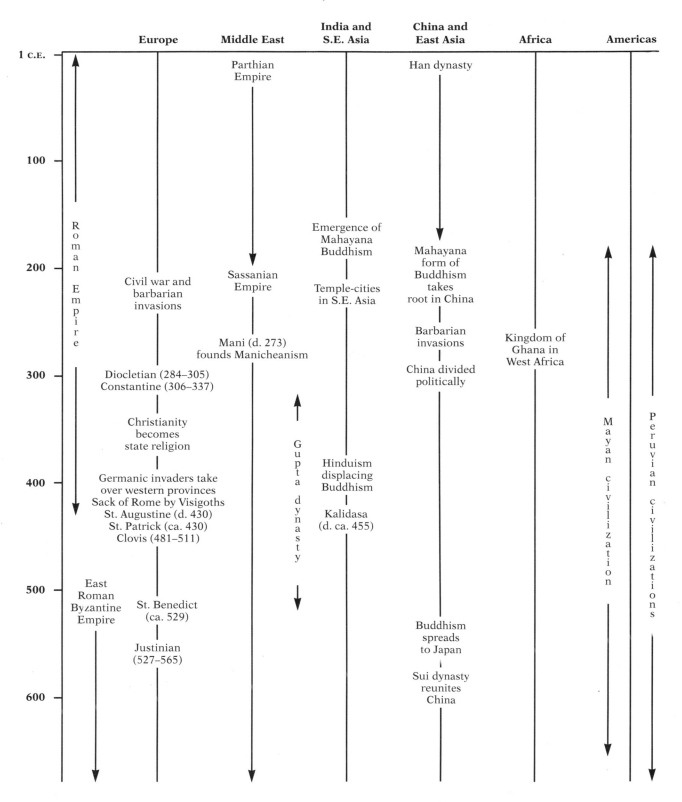

	Europe	Middle East	India and S.E. Asia	China and East Asia	Africa	Americas
1 C.E.		Parthian Empire		Han dynasty		
100						
200	Roman Empire — Civil war and barbarian invasions	Sassanian Empire	Emergence of Mahayana Buddhism — Temple-cities in S.E. Asia	Mahayana form of Buddhism takes root in China — Barbarian invasions — China divided politically	Kingdom of Ghana in West Africa	
300	Diocletian (284–305) Constantine (306–337) — Christianity becomes state religion	Mani (d. 273) founds Manicheanism	Gupta dynasty			Mayan civilization / Peruvian civilizations
400	Germanic invaders take over western provinces Sack of Rome by Visigoths St. Augustine (d. 430) St. Patrick (ca. 430) Clovis (481–511)		Hinduism displacing Buddhism — Kalidasa (d. ca. 455)			
500	East Roman Byzantine Empire — St. Benedict (ca. 529) — Justinian (527–565)			Buddhism spreads to Japan — Sui dynasty reunites China		
600						

Islam and India
600 to 1200

10

The Koran   Being the record of God's revelation to the Prophet Mohammed, pages like these were the most authoritative guide for human life and were absolutely vital to salvation for all Moslems. The care that went into writing so decoratively reflected the importance of the sacred text to the new civilization that arose in the Middle East after 634.

The prophet Mohammed (570–632 C.E.*) established a new world religion, Islam, that transformed relationships among the peoples of western Asia within an amazingly short period of time. Mohammed's new revelation united the Arabs as never before. They then set out to conquer and subdue the peoples of the world, beginning with those nearest at hand in Syria, Egypt, Mesopotamia, and Iran. Many of the inhabitants of these regions were quite willing to submit. Ever since the time of Alexander the Great (336–323 B.C.E.), Semitic-speaking peoples of the Middle East had been subjected to rulers who drew their culture from Greek sources. Just before Mohammed's time, Syrians and Egyptians had proved their growing self-consciousness by breaking away from the Greek form of Christianity. Farther east, in Mesopotamia, the successors to the ancient Babylonians had shown their dislike of Persian (Sassanian) rule by espousing still another form of Christianity—Nestorianism.

The Arab conquests brought all these peoples back under a single political roof for the first time since the overthrow of the old Persian Empire. By extending their power across North Africa and into Spain, the Moslems (as followers of Mohammed's faith are often called) added to their domains the territories that had once belonged to the empire of Carthage.

This was a remarkable achievement. Even more remarkable was the fact that the power of Islam quickly created a new civilization within this broad territory. The new Moslem civilization carried forward and developed some aspects of the Greek and ancient Near Eastern heritages. But in many ways it was unique, built around religion and the fresh revelation of God's will that, as all Moslems believed, had inspired the prophet Mohammed.

The rise of a strong and self-conscious civilization in the Middle East created new problems for neighboring peoples. Even the distant Chinese were affected by it, for the collapse of the T'ang Empire in central Asia began with military defeat suffered in 751 at Moslem hands. Living much nearer the centers of Moslem power,

Christian rulers of Europe found themselves hard pressed to hold back the Moslem advance. India, on the other flank of the Middle East, entirely lacked the military organization needed to resist the warriors of Islam successfully, particularly when Moslem armies were reinforced by Turks from the central portions of the Eurasian steppe. As a result, between 1000 and 1200, Islamic invaders conquered northern India, and Hindu religion and culture had to adjust to the loss of state support throughout the broad territories that passed under Moslem rule.

In a worldly sense, such a record was a tremendous success story. Throughout the first six centuries of their history, Moslems never stopped adding new territories to the realm of Islam. All rivals had to withdraw or submit. In a deeper sense, however, as military successes followed one after the other, the original aspiration of the community of the faithful failed dismally. To understand this seeming contradiction, we must look more closely at the faith Mohammed preached.

Mohammed's Life and His Message

Mohammed was born in the trading city of Mecca in the west-central part of Arabia. Until he was about forty years of age he led an ordinary, modestly successful life. In youth he traveled north with caravans carrying goods to Palestine, which was under Byzantine rule. Later on he married a wealthy woman and could afford to stay at home while others trudged with camels. By local standards, this was a successful career. However, Mohammed was troubled by voices and visions. After several years of distress and uncertainty he came to the conclusion that he, Mohammed, had been chosen to deliver new and compelling revelations from God.

With nothing but his conviction and eloquence to back him up, Mohammed therefore began to preach in the streets of Mecca. His message was direct and simple: The established local worship was abhorred by God. The idols

---

*Henceforth all dates are C.E. unless otherwise specified.

of the Ka'aba, as the local temple was called, should be destroyed at once and give way to the worship of the one true God, Allah. In addition, Mohammed threatened scoffers with the Day of Judgment, when God would raise the dead and judge everyone, condemning sinners and unbelievers to eternal torment in a fiery Hell and admitting the faithful to a cool and delicious Paradise.

Mohammed believed that the messages he received were dictated to him by the Angel Gabriel and came from God—the only true God—who had revealed himself to Abraham and to Moses and to the Hebrew prophets. Jesus, according to Mohammed, was also a prophet, a mere man like Mohammed himself. Here, according to Mohammed, lay the fundamental mistake of Christianity. Human error had ascribed divinity to Christ, whereas in fact there was no God but God—and Mohammed was his prophet, sent expressly to correct the errors of the Christians and Jews. As for the latter, their great error was the Law, which had come not from God but from human invention.

At first, few Meccans took Mohammed seriously. In particular, his denunciation of the traditional local religion aroused opposition. Nonetheless, the old faiths of Arabia were no longer able to inspire deep convictions. Bedouin tribes, who lived as nomads, could rest content with ill-defined local gods and observances that expressed reverence for unusual natural features, such as springs, rocks, or trees. But Arabs who had become city dwellers, living as oasis farmers or on the profits of the caravan trade, found these old faiths inadequate. Many became Jews, and some became Christians, but Mecca itself had remained a stronghold of the older paganism.

Mohammed was acquainted with stories from the Bible. Perhaps he had heard them around campfires when the caravan reached more settled country on the fringes of Palestine. At any rate, his inspired utterances repeat several of the episodes familiar to Jews and Christians from the Old Testament, with some variations. This was only to be expected, for Moslems believe that Mohammed's revelations corrected errors that had crept into Jewish and Christian scriptures through human carelessness and wickedness.

At first, Mohammed expected Jews and Christians to recognize their mistakes and accept the new revelation. Was he not a prophet sent by God—the same God who had inspired Jesus and all the other prophets of old? And had he not been chosen for the precise purpose of correcting and completing the record of God's dealings with humankind? Mohammed, in fact, did not think he was preaching a new religion, for God's will did not change. Rather, obedient to God, he set out to restore and perfect the old, corrupted faiths so that believers could once more know God's authentic will and obey Him faithfully once more.

In 622 Mohammed left Mecca and went to a nearby oasis city, Medina. He departed secretly, fearing that his enemies in Mecca might waylay him on the road. His withdrawal to Medina was afterward referred to as the Hegira (Arabic for "flight"), and it is from that event that the Moslems date the establishment of their religion. To this day in Moslem countries, dates are counted from the year of the Hegira, and according to a lunar calendar that does not exactly fit the solar year so that, for example, the Islamic year 1416 began on 30 May 1995.

In Medina, Mohammed entered upon a new life. The oasis in which Medina was situated was in the throes of civil strife. Some of the inhabitants were Jews, while others had remained pagan. Tribal relationships had weakened and the community badly needed a lawgiver to declare and enforce rules that would fit the conditions of agricultural and urban life. A faction among the people of Medina had invited Mohammed to play this role. On his arrival he energetically took up the new task. With God's help, Mohammed prescribed a set of rules for everyday behavior.

A handful of followers accompanied Mohammed to Medina. Soon the Prophet's lawgiving won over most of the pagans of Medina, but the Jews stubbornly refused to admit the truth of Mohammed's revelations. A trickle of new recruits drifted in from Mecca and elsewhere, as news of the new faith spread.

This created a serious economic problem, for the fertile land of the oasis of Medina was limited, and the newcomers had no means of support. Mohammed met this problem by taking the offensive. He sent out war parties to intercept Meccan caravans; and when the angry Meccans attempted to revenge themselves by attacking Medina, the little army Mohammed sent against them won a victory. Mohammed hailed this success as a miracle, a clear sign of God's will. His critics had long demanded a miracle to prove the genuineness of his mission. Now God had given them a miracle—or so Mohammed and his supporters believed.

In addition, Mohammed drove the Jews from Medina and seized their property. He promptly divided their fields among his followers; but the size of the community continued to grow, so that the oasis of Medina soon became insufficient to support them all. Mohammed therefore launched an attack upon another oasis, some distance away, which was also inhabited by Jews. This time he did not drive them out but instead required that they pay a head tax as a sign of their submission to the community of the faithful.

Perhaps Mohammed made this arrangement because he did not want to split up his followers. It was to have enormous importance later, for Mohammed's policy toward these Arabian Jews set the pattern for all subsequent Moslem policy toward "People of the Book," as Mohammed termed both Christians and Jews. Mohammed's view of the proper relation between his own followers and their Jewish and Christian contemporaries was simple. Those who were too stubborn to accept the truth revealed to Mohammed ought not to be forced to change their religion, but ought to pay a head tax to the Moslem community as a price for such toleration.

In the immediate situation at Medina, this policy brought in much needed material support for the Community of the Faithful. Later on it became binding on every Moslem government. As a result, although Christian governments usually tried to make sure that everyone under their control accepted the official doctrine and often persecuted dissenters, Moslem governments always tolerated Jews and Christians, even though they sometimes persecuted heretical Moslem sects.

As the Community of the Faithful grew, Mohammed defined what was expected of a Moslem believer, partly through revealed utterances and partly by quite casual acts and everyday decisions. These too, in later time, became binding upon Moslems. The fundamental aim of everything Mohammed did was to try to obey God completely. He called his faith *Islam*, which means "submission"—submission, that is, to God's will.

As interpreted by Mohammed, God's will did not impose very complicated obligations. The faithful prayed together five times daily. That was the chief ritual. It consisted of the repetition of set phrases of praise and of bowing down on the ground before God's majesty. As long as it was possible for the entire community to assemble in one place, Mohammed led them in prayer. When a portion of the community was sent off on some military expedition however, their commander took over the role of prayer leader in the absence of Mohammed.

In other words, civil and religious authority were one and the same. Nothing like an organized church, distinct from society as a whole ever grew up within Islam. The idea of separating religious duty from other affairs would have seemed absolutely incomprehensible to Mohammed and his early followers. God's will was just as important in deciding how to eat or fight or marry as it was in choosing how to pray.

In addition to daily prayer and public acknowledgment of God's unity and his own prophethood, Mohammed imposed three other religious duties. Good Moslems should give aid to the poor when they could afford it; they should fast from sunrise to sunset during the month of Ramadan each year; and, after his triumphal return to Mecca (630), Mohammed also required Moslems to make a pilgrimage to Mecca. Other rules, such as how to divide booty taken from the Meccan caravans or how many wives a man could marry (the answer was four), became of importance later, but they did not rank as religious duties in the same way as the five "pillars of Islam."

During his years in Medina, Mohammed gathered a tightly knit and extremely well-disciplined community around himself. Believing as they did that Mohammed spoke the word of God, everyone obeyed him unquestioningly. Daily prayers had a psychological effect similar to that which had been achieved among the soldiers of the phalanx during the classical age of Greece. Hundreds and soon thousands of men, praying

Mohammed's Prophetic Predecessors

Moslems recognized Jesus, as well as Abraham and Moses, as true prophets who had revealed God's will to those who would listen, only to have their messages distorted and misunderstood by succeeding generations. The following excerpt from the Koran tells how Jesus was born and how he made known his role as prophet while still an infant.

Excerpt from Sura XIX of the Koran

And mention in the Book of Mary when she withdrew from her people to an eastern place, and she took a veil apart from them; then We sent unto her Our Spirit that presented himself to her a man without fault.

She said: "I take refuge in the All-merciful from thee! If thou fearest God . . ."

He said: "I am but a messenger come from thy Lord, to give thee a boy most pure."

She said: "How shall I have a son whom no mortal has touched, neither have I been unchaste?"

He said: "Even so thy Lord has said: "Easy is that for Me; and that we may appoint him a sign unto men and a mercy from Us, it is a thing decreed."

So she conceived him, and withdrew with him to a distant place, and the birthpangs surprised her by the trunk of a palm tree. She said: "Would that I had died ere this, and become a thing forgotten!"

But one that was below her called to her, "Nay, do not sorrow; see thy Lord has set below thee a rivulet. Shake also to thee the palm tree-trunk, and there shall come tumbling upon thee dates fresh and ripe. Eat therefore, and drink and be comforted; and if thou shouldst see any mortal say, "I have vowed to the All-merciful a fast, and today will not speak to any man.' "

Then she brought the child to her folk carrying him; and they said, "Mary thou hast surely committed a monstrous thing! Sister of Aaron, thy father was not a wicked man, nor was thy mother a woman unchaste."

Mary pointed to the child then; but they said, "How shall we speak to one who is still in the cradle, a little child?"

He said, "Lo, I am God's servant; God has given me the Book, and made me a Prophet. Blessed He has made me, wherever I may be; and He has enjoined me to pray, and to give alms, so long as I live, and likewise to cherish my mother; He has not made me arrogant, unprosperous. Peace be upon me, the day I was born, and the day I die, and the day I am raised up alive!"

That is Jesus, son of Mary, in word of truth, concerning which they are doubting. It is not for God to take a son unto Him. Glory be to Him! When He desires a thing, He but says to it "Be," and it is.

Surely God is my Lord and your Lord, so serve you Him. This is the straight path.

_____

Reproduced from *The Koran Interpreted*. Arthur J. Arberry, trans., London: George Allen and Unwin Ltd., 1955.

The Great Mosque at Mecca   This aerial view of the holiest sanctuary of Islam shows a rectangular structure, the Ka'aba, in the midst of a large, irregularly shaped enclosure. Inside the Ka'aba is a sacred stone from heaven that made Mecca an important religious center even before the time of Mohammed. After the Prophet returned to Mecca in 630, new Moslem rituals maintained the importance of the Ka'aba. In particular, every mosque throughout the realm of Islam is oriented so that the faithful face the Ka'aba when they pray. And the climax of the pilgrimage to Mecca, which every pious Moslem aspires to make at least once in a lifetime, is a visit to this mosque and a ritual circling of the Ka'aba. This spot therefore binds Moslems together in a unique and powerful way, for persons from all over the Moslem world meet here every year, and every week hundreds of millions think of it when they pray.

together and making the same ritual motions together, learned to think and feel together. This in turn allowed them to act together with an energy and conviction that made Moslem raiding parties extremely successful.

From the beginning, many Meccans were not sure that it was right to oppose Mohammed. Every success he won seemed to prove that God was really on his side. Opposition therefore crumbled, and in 630 the Prophet was able to return in triumph to his native city. Other Arab tribes then had the choice of either recognizing the religion of Islam and accepting Mohammed's leadership or facing Moslem attack. One by one the Arab chieftains came to terms with Mohammed and joined the Moslem community by publicly reciting the creed of Islam: "There is no God but God and Mohammed is his Prophet."

The First Caliphs

The unification of Arabia was barely complete when Mohammed died (632). Many of the Arab chieftains assumed that their only obligation was to Mohammed himself; they therefore withdrew from the Islamic community. This presented Mohammed's closest associates and followers with a difficult choice. How, first of all, could the community continue without the Prophet to instruct them in God's will? And what should be done to prevent the community from breaking up, now that Mohammed was no longer there to lead them?

Abu-Bakr   Mohammed's closest followers met soon after his death and decided to recognize Abu-Bakr as caliph. The term *caliph* means "successor"—successor, that is, to the Prophet. Abu-Bakr was one of Mohammed's earliest converts and came from a prominent Meccan family. He was also older than most of the other important Moslems. As Mohammed's successor, however, Abu-Bakr did not claim to be a prophet himself. The community would have to get along on the basis of the revelations already received. But pious Moslems consoled themselves with the thought that God, being just, would not take the Prophet away until all the truths they needed had been revealed.

Abu-Bakr also decided that anyone who had accepted Islam could not withdraw from the community. So he attacked the tribes that had fallen away from the faith. After two hard campaigns, the Moslems were victorious everywhere. At the time Abu-Bakr died (634), Arabia was therefore united once again.

Omar   The next caliph was Omar, a much younger man, who possessed both unusual energy and an absolute religious conviction. As caliph, Omar launched the fighting manpower of all Arabia against the Byzantine and Persian empires. Success came at once. In 636 a Byzantine army was defeated near the river Jordan (Battle of Yarmuk). The emperors in Constantinople never reasserted their power in Palestine and Syria. The next year Omar turned the Arab army against Mesopotamia and captured that rich province from the Persians. Egypt fell in 642 and the Sassanian Empire collapsed entirely in 651, opening all of Iran and the borderlands north and east of Iran to the Moslems.

Thus, in fifteen years the Moslems overran the entire Middle East, with the exception of Asia Minor, which remained in Byzantine hands. Nothing in Moslem military equipment or tactics can account for this success. The heavy-armored cavalry of the Persian and Byzantine armies should have been as effective against Arab troops as they had always been against steppe nomads from the north. The new factor

was religious; the conviction that God was with the Moslems gained force with every victory. Friend and foe alike could scarcely doubt that God's hand lay behind the Moslem's amazing successes. Moreover, years of campaigning, the habit of victory, and the discipline of Islam all reinforced one another to make the Arabs irresistible.

Omar had to decide how to manage the wide lands that fell into his hands. He had only Mohammed's precepts to follow, and follow them he did. He preferred to keep the Moslems together in communities, so that the pattern of life Mohammed had prescribed for them might continue. This meant that the new conquerors could not follow the Sassanian pattern of stationing warriors on country estates for local defense. Instead, Omar set up special garrison cities to control each important new province. Whenever possible, these were located on the edge of the desert, so that the Arabs stationed there could remain in touch with their old form of life. The conquered peoples paid taxes as always. Omar simply kept the Byzantine and Persian tax system in force. He even kept the same officials as tax collectors. The yield from the taxes was distributed among the garrisons, so that each Moslem soldier received something similar to a dividend each year, representing his share of the booty and of tax income that Moslem victories had made available for distribution to the faithful.

The Arabs continued to belong to tribes. A chief and his followers simply settled down in one of the new garrison cities where other tribes were also quartered. Except for conduct prescribed by Islam, tribal manners and customs remained in force. Islam made a difference, of course; Mohammed's rules for settling quarrels prohibited the old blood feud, for example. But the different tribes remembered past enmities among themselves as well as their more recent victories over their new Christian, Zoroastrian, and Jewish subjects.

Othman   Omar did not live to see the final victory over Persia, since he was assassinated in 644. His successor in the office of caliph was Othman, head of another important Meccan family, the Omayyad. Othman did not command

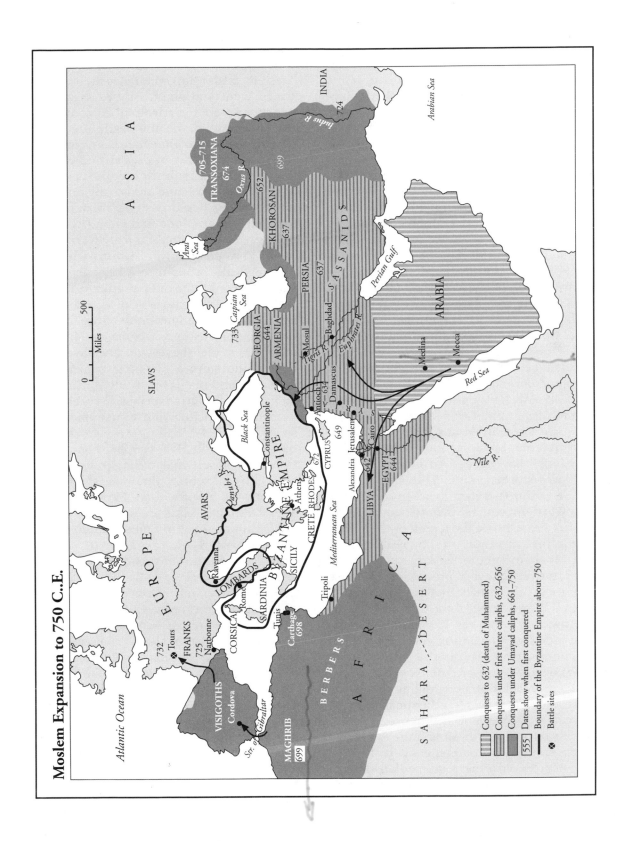

Moslem Expansion to 750 C.E.

Atlantic Ocean

EUROPE

ASIA

A S I A

Aral Sea

INDIA
724

Arabian Sea

TRANSOXIANA
705–715
674
Oxus R.
652

Indus R.

SLAVS

Caspian Sea

KHOROSAN
637

(699)

AVARS

GEORGIA
644
733

ARMENIA

PERSIA
637

S A S S A N I D S

Danube

Black Sea

Constantinople

Athens

Mosul

Baghdad

Tigris R.

Euphrates R.

Persian Gulf

ARABIA

Medina

Mecca

Antioch
Damascus
634

BYZANTINE EMPIRE

Ravenna

LOMBARDS

Rome

SARDINIA

CORSICA

SICILY

CRETE

RHODES

672

CYPRUS
649

Jerusalem

Alexandria

Cairo
642

Red Sea

Nile R.

Mediterranean Sea

Tripoli

Tunis

Carthage
698

EGYPT
644

LIBYA

B E R B E R S

A F R I C A

S A H A R A D E S E R T

FRANKS
732 ⊗ Tours
725 Narbonne

VISIGOTHS
Cordova

MAGHRIB
699

Str. of Gibraltar

500
Miles
0

Conquests to 632 (death of Muhammed)
Conquests under first three caliphs, 632–656
Conquests under Umayad caliphs, 661–750
555 Dates show when first conquered
Boundary of the Byzantine Empire about 750
⊗ Battle sites

233

universal respect among Moslems as Abu-Bakr and Omar had done. Naturally, he tried to reinforce his position by appointing members of his own family to key positions, making them commanders of the principal Arab armies and favoring them in other ways as well. Other families, not unnaturally, were jealous.

The Koran   Othman also faced opposition from those who felt that he was not a strict and reliable guardian of Mohammed's revelation. Since it no longer seemed enough to trust the memory and judgment of the caliph, a group of those who had known Mohammed closely went to great pains during Othman's lifetime to establish the correct text of the Prophet's inspired utterances. They did this by comparing their personal memories of what Mohammed had said. They wrote down each separate revelation, thus defining 117 distinct chapters or *suras*, and then arranged them according to length, starting with the longest and ending with the shortest.

This carefully authenticated text of God's revelation to Mohammed was known as the Koran. It has since remained absolutely central to Islam. In principle, Moslems took it for granted that everything they needed to know of God's purposes was recorded there. The beginning of piety and wisdom, therefore, was to memorize the Koran word for word. Since the entire book is only about a quarter of the length of the Christian Bible, this was not an impossible task. Nearly all Moslems memorize large parts of it; scholars pore over its every phrase with utmost reverence, for to them it is the Word of God in the exact and literal sense of the term.

The importance of the Koran was magnified by the fact that Moslems rejected the Jewish and Christian scriptures on the ground that careless, ignorant, or unscrupulous persons had confused God's revelation by mingling their own words with those that were authentically God's. Special precautions were needed to prevent anything similar happening to Mohammed's revelation. As a result, an overriding concern for the exact text of the Koran has remained absolutely central to all later Moslem learning.

The Problem of Succession to the Caliphate
The Koran, recited aloud before gatherings of

true believers, and the discipline of prayer, five times each day, standardized and defined the Moslem faith. But when Arabs from different tribes were stationed for years at a time in widely scattered garrison cities, it was impossible to maintain the unquestioning subordination to the caliph that had been possible when the whole company of the faithful constituted a single community in the small oasis of Medina. This situation became all too obvious when Othman was murdered in 656. Omar had been assassinated by a lone individual; Othman was murdered by a group of unruly warriors who accused him, justifiably, of favoring his own family. His death brought to a head the problem of succession. With armies scattered far and wide there was, in fact, no way of agreeing on a suitable caliph. The community of the faithful could not assemble in any one place; and if the attempt had been made, they could not have agreed. No one of the stature of Omar or Abu-Bakr was known to and respected by all Moslems.

Two conflicting principles were advanced to meet this crisis. Some argued that the rightful succession must belong to members of Mohammed's family. The Prophet had no surviving sons. His closest male relative was Ali (Ali ibn-abi-Tālib), son of Mohammed's uncle and the husband of his daughter Fatima. Accordingly, after Othman's assassination Ali claimed to be the legitimate caliph. Some Moslems, especially the garrison of Mesopotamia (or Iraq, as the Arabs called that land), supported him. On the other hand, members of Othman's family argued that the succession belonged to them by virtue of tribal custom that defined how chieftainship should pass from one generation to the next.

Only force could decide between these rival claims. But the Moslem rank and file were not eager to fight a civil war. Preliminary maneuvers, therefore, did not lead to much bloodshed. The problem seemed solved when Ali was murdered by one of his followers. Muawiyah, head of the Omayyad family, defeated Ali's son, Husain, who attempted to take command of the forces stationed in Iraq. The military base for Muawiyah's strength lay in Syria; part of the struggle between the rivals, therefore, was a contest for leadership between forces based on ex-Byzantine territory and those stationed on ex-

Persian territory. Tribal differences also entered into the struggle for power.

The lasting importance of this strife was that it provoked the first irremediable split in Islam. Some of Ali's supporters were religious enthusiasts who held that only a perfectly pious man could be a true caliph. This created an impossible standard against which to measure any ruler; and as long as Ali and his son, Husain, lived, the doctrine did not take firm hold. But after Husain had been killed in battle while trying to make good his claim to leadership over the Moslem community, the situation altered. A group of pious and enthusiastic Moslems then asserted that the true caliph was in fact hiding because the times were too corrupt for him to take his rightful place as head of the community of the faithful. At some future time, they believed, the "Hidden Imam"—the secret true head of God's faithful servants—would emerge; and until then it was necessary to wait patiently, mourn Husain's death, and be ready for the Imam's eventual appearance.

This represented one sectarian extreme. There were those who believed that, after Husain's death, legitimate succession to the Prophet passed to other descendants of Ali. One group recognized a line that ran for seven generations; another group preferred a line that ran for twelve. But all these groups agreed that the actual leaders of the Islamic community were usurpers, who should not be honored as true successors to the Prophet. Such dissenters were known as Shi'a, in contrast to the majority who came to be known as Sunni Moslems.

The Omayyad Caliphate

From 661, when Muawiyah made good his claim to be the caliph, until 750, the realm of Islam was governed by the Omayyad family. It was a time of continued territorial expansion. Moslem armies moved across north Africa and entered Spain in 711, where they speedily overthrew the Visigothic kingdom and made themselves masters of that country. By 705, on the opposite flank, other Moslem armies reached India and overran the province of Sind, along the lower Indus River. In central Asia, north of the Hi-

malayas, still other Moslem troops collided with the Chinese and defeated them in a battle at the river Talas in 751. As a result of such successes, the caliph controlled a territory that covered almost exactly the same ground that the old Persian and Carthaginian empires once had governed.

On one front, however, the Moslems met with failure. After several minor thrusts against Byzantium, the caliph sent his brother to lead an assault upon the capital of the East Roman or Byzantine Empire in 717. The siege lasted a year, and both sides used naval as well as land forces. The siege failed. This was a serious setback to the Moslems, materially as well as psychologically. For the first time, when large forces had been engaged, God had not crowned Moslem arms with victory.

The failure before the walls of Byzantium put other strains upon Moslem society. As long as new territories opened up rapidly, any individual or group that found itself defeated or snubbed at the seat of power in Damascus, where the Omayyads established their capital, could drift toward the frontier and there carve out a satisfying career. When, however, expansion came to a halt, discontented tribesmen were tempted to fight things out near the center of the caliph's domain and try to seize by main force what the caliph's administrators had awarded to someone else.

Armed clashes had not been wanting in the first years of Omayyad rule; but after the failure before the walls of Constantinople in 718, the scale of fighting among Arab tribes and factions increased markedly. Radical sects rose in revolt; tribal intrigues flourished. The upshot was the overthrow of the Omayyads in 750 and the transfer of the caliphate to the Abbasid family, which held that office until 1258.

Another important source of discontent that weakened the Omayyads was the rising friction between Arab and non-Arab Moslems. The Arab conquerors were not very eager to spread Islam among their subjects. First of all, conversion to Islam excused a convert from paying taxes, and that reduced the revenues upon which so many Arabs had come to depend. In the second place, as long as tribal organization survived among the Arabs, there was no way to fit a convert into the Islamic community without undermining the traditional tribal structure of Arab society. Converts could, indeed, be classed as "wanderers." This status, inherited from desert days, meant that the person in question was under the protection of the tribe but was not a member, since a tribe by definition was supposed to be based on common descent and blood relationship.

Nothing in Mohammed's revelations, however, said anything about tribes. Believers were all equal, animated by an immortal soul entrusted to him or her by God. And if someone accepted the truths of Islam and professed them in public, then the convert became a Moslem and should, in logic at least, have the same rights and status as any other Moslem. Naturally, converts were inclined to take Mohammed's revelation seriously and wished to be treated like other Moslems, not as inferiors. They therefore reinforced the groups among the Arabs who felt that the Omayyad caliphs were unworthy of their position.

The Hadith   The underlying fact was that, as the size of the Moslem community increased, the original identity between secular and religious leadership could not be maintained. Mohammed, Abu-Bakr, and Omar had been able to fill both roles, but the Omayyads were more like tribal chiefs presiding over an uneasy confederation of other tribal chiefs. Nevertheless, pious Moslems kept to the original idea of living a life pleasing to God in every detail. They studied the Koran, of course. And when questions arose that were not covered by any passage of the Koran, they fell back upon the memories of what the Prophet and his close companions had done in similar circumstances. These memories were carefully gathered and then checked, as far as possible, by listing who had heard the story from whom, all the way back to an eyewitness. The Hadith, as these records were called, became second only to the Koran as authoritative guides to conduct.

The Sharia   Yet in the environment of the Middle Eastern cities, amid alien peoples, Moslems encountered new situations to which nei-

ther the Koran nor the Hadith applied. Experts in Islam worked from analogy to answer such problems; and if analogy failed, they fell back on the general opinion of the faithful, arguing that God would not in fact permit the community to err on any important question.

On the basis of these four kinds of authority, a group of learned Moslems busily set out to create a complete set of rules for conduct according to God's declared will. The result was the Moslem Sacred Law or Sharia. The religious experts who worked it out were called ulama. (The word *ulama* means "learned" in Arabic.) At first, the ulama gathered mainly in Medina, where memories of Mohammed's life were most vivid. Later, experts in the Sacred Law scattered all over the Moslem world, ready to give advice to ordinary persons about how to obey God's will in any unusual or difficult case.

Religious Exercises   Conduct of the common prayer also passed into the hands of specialists, whose main qualifications were a loud, clear voice and good standing as a Moslem. At each of the appointed hours of the day, these men called the faithful to prayer. The summons caused all to interrupt whatever they were doing in order to kneel on the ground and pray, their faces turned toward Mecca. On Fridays, special services took place at specially designated spots— an open square, for example. There, prayer and recitation from the Koran reminded the faithful of their obligations to God. Sometimes the Moslems took possession of a Christian church for these services. That was the case in Damascus, for example, where the Omayyad caliphs seized the largest Christian church for Moslem use. In other cases, new structures were built, usually leaving the interior wide open to the sky. The enclosed mosque, with slender minarets and a high-domed roof, remained quite unknown until much later than the time we are considering here.

Cultural Relations Between Moslems and Their Subject Peoples   The first Moslem generations generally tried to hold themselves apart from the peoples they had conquered. Secretly and in private an Omayyad caliph might hire a painter to decorate his bedroom walls in Hellenistic style. Several such damaged frescoes survive from the period. In addition, the bureaucratic machine remained in Christian and Zoroastrian hands. The Omayyad caliphs were more concerned with adjusting frictions among tribal leaders of the Arab community than with details of how taxes were collected.

As for the Christians, they regarded Islam as a form of heresy. Most of the inhabitants of Syria and Egypt felt no loyalty to Byzantium. They had quarreled with the Byzantine authorities over the proper definition of the relation between the divine and human natures of Christ and had formed their own churches—Syriac in Syria and Coptic in Egypt. Hence when the Moslems first arrived, most Christians in Syria and Egypt felt that they were simply exchanging one kind of heretical rule for another. This, of course, aided the Moslem conquest enormously. In many cities the Arabs were welcomed as liberators; nowhere were they vigorously opposed.

Through the centuries, the inhabitants of Syria, Egypt, and Mesopotamia had become used to Roman, Greek, Parthian, or Persian domination. Foreigners of one sort or another had ruled for nearly a thousand years when the Arabs appeared on the scene. Passive withdrawal and careful preservation of what they valued worked just as well under the Arabs as under their predecessors. As a result, in the first Moslem centuries far less cultural interchange occurred than the geographical mixing of Arabs and Christians would lead one to expect.

In Persia proper this was less true. The Persians accepted Islam with some enthusiasm; their ancestral Zoroastrianism and the Manichaean effort to update Zoroastrianism somehow failed to hold their affection. As a warrior people—and the Persian gentry of the eastern frontier lands were above all warriors—they respected the Moslems. Clearly God was with them and sensible people did not fight against God. Hence the Persian nation, as a whole, rapidly went over to Islam, keeping its own language intact. Persians studied the Koran and Hadith with the enthusiasm of converts, but this did not erase the knowledge that their ancestors had once ruled the entire Middle East.

The Abbasid Caliphate

The Abbasid family, another Meccan clan, claimed distant relationship to Ali. This lineage attracted the Shi'a groups in the population. In 750 the head of the family, Abu-al-Abbas, was governor of Khorasan, one of the easternmost of the Persian provinces, and the troops that carried him to power were nearly all Persian. Persian Moslems did not really mind fighting the Arabs upon whose military supremacy the Omayyad caliphs had based their power. Moreover, when the Arab troops had been defeated, the victors took away the tax revenue that had supported the Arab garrisons ever since Omar's day. Loss of this privileged status had the effect of rapidly breaking up the old tribal structure. In the settled environment of the Middle East, tribal ties had already weakened. Many Arabs had married local women; some had acquired land. When the tribe members lost the privilege of sharing the tax income of the state, chiefs lost their power. Individuals simply scattered out among the rest of the population and soon forgot their tribal identity.

Separation of Sacred from Civil Authority
As a result, the former barrier between Arab Moslems and other Moslems disappeared, and a much more widespread and intimate interaction between Arab and non-Arab peoples set in. The Koran tied Islam to the Arabic language absolutely. This assured the ultimate linguistic dominance of the Arabs. On the other hand, the superior sophistication of the Syrian and Persian populations meant that many aspects of the new Moslem civilization emerging under the Abbasids were more Syrian and Persian than Arabic.

This was particularly evident in the pattern of Abbasid administration. The new rulers established their capital at Baghdad in Mesopotamia on the Tigris River. The manners of the court were modeled on Persian royal etiquette. The sovereign lived in private and seldom appeared before the eyes of his subjects. Day-by-day power rested in the hands of a minister, the *vizier* (literal meaning, "burden bearer"), appointed by the caliph. Military force was represented by a royal bodyguard; but when a major campaign had to be fought, landholders from the country were required to join the royal army. All this corresponded exactly to the way the Sassanian kings had ruled.

Obviously such a government did not satisfy the pious Moslems who wanted to see the original purity of the community of the faithful revived. The Abbasid family's claim to rule was no better than that of the Omayyads. Instead of being more than life-sized Arab chiefs, as the Omayyad caliphs had been, the Abbasid caliphs behaved like Persian kings who happened to be Moslems.

Such a failure to restore the original purity of Islam caused some of those who had supported Abu-al-Abbas in his struggle against the Omayyads to turn against him when he came to power. On the other hand, most Moslems were prepared to accept the informal compromise that the Abbasid government offered to the learned and pious by inviting experts who had memorized the Koran and mastered the Sacred Law to instruct ordinary Moslems in what they should do to please God. All that the Abbasids reserved for themselves was the collection of taxes and the defense of the community of the faithful from foreign or domestic enemies.

Four Mosques Moslems were uncomfortable with the traditions of Greco-Roman and Sassanian art, since Christian portrayals of God in human form were classed as idolatry. But mosques for Friday prayer were a religious necessity. Religious architecture therefore became the main artistic expression of early Moslem civilization. To begin with, borrowing prevailed, as the Great Mosque at Damascus (top) and the Mosque at Samarra (bottom), built near Baghdad about 830, clearly show. The mosque at Damascus began as a church, but it was cleansed of Christian symbols immediately after the Moslem conquest of the city in 636. The prayer tower at Samarra recalls the ziggurats of ancient Mesopotamia, even in respect to the seven levels of its ascending staircase.

Clearly such an arrangement fell short of the high hopes of religious fanatics. The caliph was not a model of piety. His fitness for office rested on descent, not on his religious perfection. But most serious Moslems were willing to accept half a loaf. After all, the Abbasid religious compromise allowed pious men to lead the community in everything that mattered most. The ulama, sitting in the marketplace, could pass judgment on all points of conscience brought

Pictured here are more innovative designs. On top is the octagonal Mosque of Omar, built ca. 640 in Jerusalem which used new Roman architectural principles to enclose a sacred place under the great dome; on the bottom is the Mosque of Ibn Tulun in Cairo, built 877–79, which combined the open air design of Mecca, with a domed fountain in the center (resembling Omar's Mosque in miniature), while the prayer tower echoes that of Samarra and the ziggurats. This mosque gives visual form to the three traditions that together formed the new Moslem civilization of the Near East. The fact that the three traditions were juxtaposed, not mingled, also suggests the incompatibilities of the three heritages that challenged Moslem minds in their early centuries.

before them. Private life could therefore be thoroughly Moslem, conducted in perfect conformity to the will of God as defined by the Sacred Law. And if public life fell short of such perfection, then it was the rulers and their ministers that would suffer the consequences when God's Day of Judgment came.

The Role of Science   A similar compromise allowed limited scope for science and even for philosophy. The Abbasids needed doctors to look after their health and astrologers to foretell the future. Experts able to serve in these capacities had to know Galen, who had summarized Greek medicine, and Ptolemy, who had summarized astronomy. As Arabic became more and more firmly established as the common tongue of all the peoples inhabiting the Middle East, such Greek texts had to be translated. And, of course, not all useful knowledge was to be found within the pages of Galen and Ptolemy. The caliph al-Mamun (reigned 813–833) therefore organized a "house of wisdom," where translations from Greek, Persian, and Indian languages were systematically made. Much of what we know of Greek science today was preserved through these translations, since in the Christian world of the time no one was interested in such pagan notions.

Among the Moslems, however, translations soon stimulated original work. Commentaries upon the ancient Greek texts were a first step; presently Moslem authors began to confront Greek learning with ideas and data that reached them from India and China. The best example of how important this could be is the history of what Europeans later learned to call Arabic numbers. The Greeks had used the letters of the alphabet to symbolize numbers, and the Romans had used an even more clumsy system of tally marks and letters. Such methods of notation made ordinary arithmetic very difficult and prevented calculations involving large numbers.

The ancient Babylonians sometimes used a place value notation for numbers, but without any sign for zero. This defect deprived the system of its main usefulness. In India, however, religious speculation about the reality of nonexistence may have made it easier to treat zero as something real. At any rate, Indian mathematicians invented a place value notation with a

symbol for zero. The system was in use as early as 269, but since nearly all early Indian writings have perished, we cannot tell how much use Indians made of this perfected notation for a decimal number system. Moslems picked up the idea from India in Caliph al-Mansur's time (reigned 745–775). Less than a generation later a famous mathematician, al-Khwarizmi (from Khiva, in central Asia, now a city in Uzbekistan), began to use the new notation to solve the problems called, from his name, algorithms—a form of algebra. Thereafter, the idea spread throughout Eurasia, carried mainly by traders, who needed to figure prices easily and rapidly.

The Abbasid example made patronage of scholars part of rulership. Hence, when the political unity of the Moslem world began to break up after about 950, the effect at first was only to increase the number of places at which scholars could find employment. The height of Arab science therefore came after the greatest days of the Abbasid caliphate had passed. Special scientific centers of activity tended to arise at the extremes of the Moslem world. Independent rulers in Spain, far to the west, and in Bokhara, in central Asia, were particularly anxious to prove their sophistication by patronizing men of science.

In general, the Moslem scientists kept within the framework of knowledge they had inherited from the Greeks. Galen's medicine and Ptolemy's astronomy always remained fundamental. In due time the Moslems produced famous summaries and handbooks of their own. In medicine the greatest textbook writer was ibn-Sina (980–1037), known as Avicenna by the doctors of the Latin West. His work did not so much replace Galen as add new cures and additional information to the body of observation and theory that Galen had offered. Such filling out of detail, rather than any fundamentally new theories, characterized nearly all Arabic sciences.

Philosophy and Religion   Study of the material world did not strike most Moslems as particularly worthwhile. Those who interested themselves in such things were religiously suspect because they studied pagan books, whereas the Koran, according to pious Moslems, contained everything anyone needed to know.

Some who were attracted to Greek philosophy became so entangled in the charms of logic that they, perhaps, deserved the reproaches that pious Moslems made against them. Al-Farabi (d. ca. 950), for example, had little use for revealed truth of any sort and thought it more important to try to combine Plato's doctrines with those of Aristotle into a perfect, rational system that would owe nothing to revelation. Later on, another famous philosopher, ibn-Rushd—or, as the Christians called him, Averröes (1126–1198)—argued that revealed truth and the truth knowable by reasoning were two quite separate realms. Rational and revealed knowledge might even be contradictory on such a question as whether the world was created or whether it had existed from the beginning of time. Most Moslems felt that this kind of speculation was plainly contrary to religion because it set up another kind of authority—mere human logic—against the Koran and God's revelation. Arabic philosophers, in short, were too much like Greeks to fit easily into the Moslem scheme of things.

On the other hand, the elaboration of the Sacred Law did not satisfy religious aspiration for long. By 800 or so, four orthodox schools of law had defined themselves. Thereafter, application of established rules to new cases became a more and more mechanical affair, requiring the expert only to find a suitable precedent or parallel case. How could that sort of dry-as-dust legal reasoning satisfy personal yearnings for God?

Islam prohibited monasteries, so this refuge for religiously troubled souls was not available. Mohammed had also denounced unauthorized prophets who pretended to converse with God. This meant that mystical religion was deeply suspect, since mystics claimed to see God, or to merge themselves in God, or in some other way to experience the presence of God. Yet in spite of the emphatic disapproval of the experts in Moslem law, mystical religion could not be held back. Moslems, too, began to experience God directly bypassing the Koran and the Sacred Law.

At first, all mystics were regarded as heretics. Moslem mystics therefore remained underground. Mystical sects and brotherhoods became channels for the expression of social and political resentments. Many artisans joined these underground societies, which served some of the same functions that guilds did in western Europe. But official disapproval and occasional persecutions could not prevent mystics from following their own way. So, eventually, the upholders of the Sacred Law reconciled themselves to allowing Moslems to seek God along this unorthodox path.

The Collapse of Political Unity   Before mysticism achieved general respectability, however, the Abbasid caliphate had become a hollow shell. The decay resulted from its military policy. The caliph al-Mutasim (ruled 833–842) surrounded himself with a bodyguard of Turkish slave soldiers. At first, these barbarians may have been more obedient and dependable than the Persian bodyguard his predecessors had relied on. But the Turks soon realized how easy it was to take advantage of their position and began to treat the caliph as a puppet.

Such abuse of the caliph's power provoked some outlying regions of the empire to break away. As a matter of fact, Spain had never recognized Abbasid rule because members of the Omayyad family continued to govern there after the rest of the dynasty had been overthrown. As the Turkish soldiery at the Abbasid court in Baghdad became oppressive, other families asserted independent authority in other regions. Until 909, however, no one had claimed the title of caliph—successor to the Prophet—except the Abbasids. Then a family descended from Mohammed's daughter, Fatima, took power in north Africa and Egypt. According to Shi'a doctrine, they claimed to be the only rightful caliphs. Soon afterward the Omayyads in Spain made the same claim. Thus the political unity of Islam was broken forever, not only in practice (that had been common enough even in the Omayyad period) but also in theory.

The Impact of Islam on India

Moslems regarded Hindus and Buddhists as idolaters because they made images of their gods and built temples to worship them in. Of all crimes against the majesty of God, this, according to Moslem ideas, was the most serious. The toleration accorded to Jews and Christians, "People of the Book," was therefore not extended to Hindus and Buddhists—at least, not in theory. But in practice, when Moslem conquerors brought substantial numbers of Indians under their rule, they found ways to get along without compelling Hindus to accept Islam.

The rise of Islam, however, did put the Indian world on the defensive. Moslems cut off the road to China north of the mountains almost at once. Moslem ships began to sail from the Persian Gulf and from the Red Sea into the Indian Ocean and soon cut Indians off from regular contact with southeast Asia and Indonesia, where flourishing courts had previously imported Indian culture wholesale. Only on the northeast did the Moslems leave India an open frontier. Here the old patterns of expansion continued. The royal courts of Nepal and Tibet became Indianized before 1000, and the slow process of taming the jungles in eastern Bengal and Assam continued as peasants laboriously built new fields.

Between 600 and 1000, India was divided among many rulers. Dynasties rose and fell, apparently without making much difference. Hinduism developed in two seemingly contradictory directions. On the one hand, a school of philosophers tried to reduce Hindu belief to a system. They explained that all of the different gods and rituals that had found a place in Hindu worship were mere images and suggestions of abstract truth. Their function was to lead simple and uneducated people toward a level of holiness that would permit them eventually to penetrate the veil of illusion. But this would require many incarnations. At any one time, only a few souls could be expected to rise above the world of ordinary appearances and know that God— infinite, eternal, impersonal—alone was real. Shankara, who lived about 800, was the most famous Hindu philosopher who argued in this way.

At the same time, other Hindus came to the conclusion that magic rites could give them supernatural powers. Instead of studying sacred texts or subjecting the body to painful ascetic discipline, as India's holy men had previously

Hindu Temple   This temple in north central India was built soon after 1000 by rulers of the Chandela dynasty. The central purpose of a Hindu temple, like this one, was the same as in ancient Sumer: It was a house for a god. Moreover, the god was expected to inhabit a special cult statue located in the interior under the highest part of the structure, at least part of the time, so as to be accessible to worshippers. But Hinduism recognized innumerable deities and spirits, and the sculptors who decorated this temple were eager to honor them as well; hence they included crowds of figures that adorn the exterior, barely discernible on the left of this photograph. The lion in the foreground may have been intended as a guardian, but the significance of its encounter with the humanlike figure is unclear.

Elegance and Sensuality in India   The ascetic ideal of Indian religions coexisted with an uninhibited acknowledgment of the sensual side of life. Dancing was an important art in India, as these sculptures show. Above, a Yakshi, whose dance celebrated fertility in all its manifestations; below, the god Shiva, whose dance created and sustained the world, according to Hindu tradition.

done, a school of Tantrism arose that offered the same results by means of magic. Buddhists as well as Hindus were attracted to this idea; but insofar as people believed such promises, there was no longer any reason for becoming a monk. Tantric magical rites emerged from the villages and among the submerged castes, where very primitive religious practices had survived. Tantric speculation centered much upon sex. Rites that may once have been expected to assure the fertility of crops were freely reinterpreted as means for securing enhanced personal vigor.

Beginning in the year 1000 Moslem raiders began to penetrate more deeply into India. The raiders systematically destroyed temples and monasteries, which to them were seats of idolatry and also offered rich plunder. Soon the Buddhist monasteries of northern India were all destroyed and no one cared to rebuild them. Hinduism proved more durable. Even without great state-supported temples, private rites and village observances continued. Temple services were replaced by open-air ceremonies at which singing and dancing prevailed. These rituals reinforced the fellow-feeling of all the participants and made them uninterested in the legal formalism of Islam.

All the same, the destruction of Hindu temples and the overthrow of Hindu rulers in northern India hurt Hindu civilization. Secular culture, which had reached such a high level at the Gupta court, faded away. The Moslem newcomers brought with them a Persian style of courtly life that accepted almost nothing from Indian tradition. Secular learning withered, too, for the Moslems also brought their own languages (Arabic, Persian, and Turkish), literature, and professional experts with them.

As partial compensation, in the southern parts of India the Tamil language achieved literary form between 600 and 1000. Tamil is not an Aryan language and is, therefore, not related to either ancient Sanskrit or modern Hindi, the popular speech of northern India that descends from Sanskrit.

The most important forms of Tamil literature were short religious poems or hymns and romantic epics that emphasized love more than war, and piety more than heroism. Many Hindu temples in the south escaped Moslem destruc-

tion, so temple rituals survived and flourished in Tamil country. This, together with the profound difference of language, gave the cultural scene of southern India a very different character from that created by the Hindu-Moslem encounter in northern India.

The Transformation of Islam, 1000–1200

When even the pretense of political unity had to be abandoned, Moslems confronted a new crisis. The Abbasid compromise, which left military affairs and taxes to the government and religious matters to the learned ulama, had broken down. Moreover, the political history of the centuries that followed made it harder and harder to believe that rulers could possibly be instruments chosen by God. Swarms of Turkish adventurers overran the heartland of Islam. Sometimes they kept their tribal organization and were able to create relatively stable states. This was the case with the Seljuk Sultanate, for example, which lasted from 1037 to 1092. But often the Turks came to power only after breaking away from their tribal order. In such cases, they became rootless, ruthless predators who owed loyalty to no one but themselves and served only those who paid them well or promised richer booty than the next man.

The Role of the Turks

The Turks, as they drifted in from the Asian steppes, were willing enough to accept Islam, but they took it lightly. Seeking God's will through careful study of the Koran never seemed really vital to them. The Turks did not abandon their own language, which a really energetic search for religious truth would have required. Instead they remained soldiers—Moslems in outward things but, above all else, eager to make their fortunes.

These tough and greedy warriors kept the political life of Islam in uproar. Abbasid rulers continued to sit on the throne at Baghdad, but they were only insignificant figureheads. Utter confusion prevailed. Yet by allowing Turkish fighters to crowd into Islamic lands, the Moslems acquired new and effective, if also disorderly, troops. Like Arabs in the first decades of the Omayyad caliphate, those who failed to rise to the top in the old centers of Islamic life tended to drift toward the frontiers, where fighting against unbelievers was an honorable duty.

Conquest of India   This situation fed the raiding armies that began to overrun India after 1000. By 1200 all of northern India had been conquered, and in 1206 a relatively stable Moslem government emerged. It lasted until 1526 and is referred to as the Slave Sultanate of Delhi, because Turkish slaves were the rulers and their capital was at Delhi. Since Turkish (and Persian) recruits from the north were always relatively few in number, the slave kings had to come to terms with the various local Hindu rulers and landlords, admitting them to military service and, in general, softening the official dividing line that Islam drew between idolaters and true believers. The fact that most Turks were usually not deeply religious made such accommodation easier.

This in turn allowed extensive interaction and interchange between Indian and Moslem elements in the population. Some Indians became Moslem, particularly those who stood near the bottom of the caste system. The equality of all believers, preached by Islam, had an obvious appeal to such persons. As a result, the Moslem community in India came to be sharply divided between an upper class of rulers and warriors and a poor class of people at or near the very bottom of society. Relatively few Hindus from the middle and upper castes were attracted by Islam, although the courtly culture of the Moslem rulers did make some impact upon the Hindu princes who served under the Moslem slave sultans.

Conflicts with Christendom   Along the frontier between Islam and Christendom, the arrival of the Turks also had important consequences. In 1071, at the Battle of Manzikert, the Seljuk sultans defeated a Byzantine army and captured the emperor himself. In the following period, the whole central part of Asia Minor passed into Turkish hands. Danger from the Turks persuaded the emperor of Byzantium to appeal to the pope in Rome for help in pushing them back.

Accordingly, in 1096, Pope Urban II proclaimed a crusade. The goal Pope Urban set was liberation of Jerusalem and the Holy Land from the Moslems. The response in western Europe surprised both Byzantines and Turks. Armies from France, Germany, and Italy made their way through the Balkans to Constantinople and then crossed into Asia Minor. After many difficulties, the crusaders captured the great city of Antioch on the Orontes River and then continued south to take Jerusalem in 1099. The victorious crusaders set up a series of little states along the eastern coast of the Mediterranean, leaving the hinterland to the Moslems.

The success of the First Crusade depended in large part on Moslem political disarray. When stronger Moslem rulers emerged, the Second Crusade was organized (1147–1149), but this time the crusaders never reached the Holy Land, meeting defeat in Asia Minor instead. The situation became more critical for the Christians when Saladin (ruled 1169–1193) built up a strong kingdom in Syria and Egypt. In 1187 he captured Jerusalem and wiped out what remained of the crusading states, except for the city of Acre on the coast. The pope responded by proclaiming the Third Crusade. But even though the kings of England, France, and Germany joined forces, this effort also failed. Saladin and the Moslems remained in control of the Holy Land, and nearly all of Asia Minor also remained under Turkish rule.

Expansion on Other Fronts   Along other fronts, too, Islam demonstrated a new expansive energy in the centuries after 1000. Moslem towns and traders spread far down the east coast of Africa. In west Africa, Moslems from north of the Sahara destroyed the pagan kingdom of Ghana in 1076. Thereafter, various Moslem states and empires dominated the farming peoples of West Africa.

Throughout the western and central steppes of Eurasia, Moslem missionaries also met with widespread success. Turks and other nomadic or

Sohrab and Rustum Made Visible
Moslems were initially prohibited from painting human figures, but this rule was disregarded by the Persians after about 1000, when they started to illustrate books with brightly colored miniature paintings like this one. It was prepared for a copy of Firdausi's *Book of Kings* and shows Rustum at the moment when he recognized his son, Sohrab, whom he had just killed in single combat. Flowers and other details have a brilliant jewel-like color in the original, which is just about the same size as this photograph.

partially nomadic peoples accepted Islam at various times, tribe by tribe, not because they were conquered, but because traveling holy men and merchants from the cities of the Middle East converted them. Even in distant China, substantial Moslem communities came into existence in the western borderlands of that country.

As a result, the territory of Islam almost doubled between 1000 and 1200. This tremendous success was less dramatic than the first burst of Moslem expansion had been, but it was scarcely less significant for world history.

Only in Spain did Moslem power retreat. Frontier fighting between Moslems and Christians in the Iberian Peninsula never stopped for long. At first the advantage lay with the Moslems, who reached their high point in 732 when a raiding party advanced as far as Tours in central France before meeting defeat. Later, the Moslems withdrew behind the Pyrenees, and their domain kept on shrinking southward as Christian knights pressed the attack. In 1212 the Christians won a great victory at the Battle of Las Navas de Tolosa. Thereafter Moslem power was restricted to the principality of Granada in the extreme south of Spain. But on a world scale, retreat in Spain seemed trifling in the overall balance between Islam and its rivals.

The Role of Sufism

The secret of Islam's new energy was not entirely military. The strong arm of Turkish adventurers was powerfully assisted by the preaching and example of enthusiastic missionaries. These missionaries were often merchants or wandering artisans, humble people who had no particular claim to knowledge of the Moslem Sacred Law. But they were mystics who experienced God or knew others who had done so and were eager to talk about it. Moslem mystics were referred to generally as Sufi.

All levels of involvement were possible. Some Sufi were full-time holy men, who lived only for God and communion with Him, but most were ordinary folk. An unusually holy mystic often gathered disciples and admirers. His followers might go their separate ways on their master's death, but sometimes they chose to remain together and continued to follow their founder's rules of holiness. Men who followed such a way of life were called dervishes. Their ways of entering into communion with God varied widely. Some danced and chanted; some smoked hashish (a drug that induces a trance); some suppressed normal breathing; some simply lived a quiet, regular life of meditation and prayer.

Sufis played a role in Islam much like that which friars played in Christendom. But there was one important difference. Mohammed had expressly prohibited monasteries, and he set up no separate clergy to minister to the religious needs of his followers. Hence Moslem mystics could not withdraw so sharply from ordinary life as was customary in Christian communities. Instead, Sufi holy men normally continued to earn a living like everyone else. Lay and religious organizations, therefore, tended to merge. Dervish associations became particularly important in towns and developed most strongly among artisan groups.

The contrast between Sufi mysticism and the legal approach to holiness, which had dominated the first centuries of Islam, is startling. Like some vast tide, Sufism seeped up around the older form of Moslem piety. The Sacred Law and the Koran were not rejected. Rather, a compromise was reached whereby Sufis agreed to honor experts in the Sacred Law while the ulama somewhat grudgingly accepted the direct experience of God through mystical experience as part of orthodox Islam.

The key figure in arriving at this compromise was a learned and religiously intense man named al-Ghazali (1058–1111). He started his career by becoming a professor at Baghdad, teaching the Sacred Law. But the brilliant young professor began to suffer doubts about religion. He left his position and for several years led an agonized life. Then he found relief in mysticism. Having seen God, his doubts were stilled. He returned to writing and teaching but preached the Sufi message. Argument and reasoning were in vain; only faith and mystic communion with God mattered.

After the time of al-Ghazali, a bulky Sufi literature developed, describing in great detail the steps and stages of the path to God. This literature supplemented the old commentaries on the Koran and the Sacred Law; between them, they came to define Islamic learning.

The new energy and respectability of Sufism meant that strangers did not have to subscribe to the entire code of the Sacred Law before they could become Moslems. Instead, reverence for a holy man, participation in mystical exercises, and listening respectfully to stories about the heroes of Islam—from Mohammed on down—was enough to start a person along the path to becoming a Moslem. Later, the Sacred

Law and the more formal apparatus of Moslem life might follow.

Conclusion

Islam, then, passed through two phases between 622, when the faith was founded, and about 1200. The first phase spread Arab power across the map of Asia, Africa, and Europe, from Spain and Morocco in the west to the Indus and Oxus rivers in the east. Within this vast domain a new Moslem civilization came quickly into existence, centered around the effort to follow in every detail the revelation of God's will that had been given to all humanity through Mohammed. Compromises proved necessary, but as long as the political unity of the realm of Islam could be maintained—at least in form—the effort to make human life and society match the ideal of the early Moslem community at Medina seemed worthwhile.

After about 1000, the inroads of Turkish adventurers and the political chaos they brought to the Moslem heartland inaugurated a second phase of Moslem history. Islam both suffered and profited from the Turkish invasions. The military energy of the Turks carried Islamic power deep into the Hindu and Christian lands. Simultaneously, the inner patterns of the faith were altered in such a way as to make the spread of Islam among barbarous peoples of Asia and Africa much easier than before. The result was to double or more than double the realm of Islam within about two centuries.

Yet, in another sense, Islam suffered a crippling defeat. The hope of the first days—to make a community totally pleasing to God—had to be abandoned. The political ideal of the early caliphate, when all Moslems were supposed to stand together against the infidels, had become a farce. By accepting mysticism, Islamic thinkers turned their backs upon science and philosophy. Instead of following up new experiments and theories, Moslem doctors more and more felt satisfied with manuals already available. Astronomy became astrology again, as suitable handbooks simplified the casting of horoscopes. Phi-losophy and abstract reasoning fell under too much suspicion to flourish.

Moslem intellectual energy, in short, turned almost entirely to mystical exercises at the very time when the universities of western Europe were beginning to foster an eager interest in their intellectual heritages from Latin, Greek, and Moslem writers. By contrast, Moslem scholars almost ceased to concern themselves with anything foreign, fearing that novelty would upset the faith. Even when the Mongols brought them into much closer contact with the Chinese than before, Moslems took little interest in Chinese knowledge and skills. The Europeans, on the other hand, felt no compunction about seizing upon anything that interested them and might be useful. Printing, for example, had almost no impact in the Moslem lands because the ulama forbade the use of that great Chinese invention for anything more intellectual than the manufacture of playing cards. They feared that God's Word would be defiled if reproduced by machine.

Yet we should not scoff. Their wisdom was, perhaps, demonstrated by the fact that in Europe the religious upheaval of the Reformation was largely created by the use of printing presses to spread new doctrines and controversies. That sort of upheaval, challenging fundamental convictions, was exactly what learned Moslems wished to avoid; and avoid it they did, but at the cost of falling behind their Chinese and Christian contemporaries.

But before that could happen, western Europe and China had to recover from the barbarian invasions that had overthrown both the Roman and the Han empires. China recovered before Europe was able to do so and, after about 1000, began to outstrip the realm of Islam in some important respects. How that happened will be the theme of the next chapter.

Bibliography

The first resort of anyone seeking to understand more about Islam should be to read all or part of the Koran, which is available in several different translations. Eric Schroeder, *Muhammad's People* (1955), weaves together excerpts from pre-Islamic poetry and other Arabic sources to present a vivid portrait of Arab life in Mohammed's age. W. H. McNeill and Marilyn Waldman, *The Islamic World* (1983), is a more general collection of excerpts from Moslem writings extending to modern times. Very much worth consulting is a slender autobiography of the man who, next to Mohammed, shaped the way Islam developed: W. Montgomery Watt, trans., *The Faith and Practice of al-Ghazali* (1953).

Marshall G. S. Hodgson, *The Venture of Islam, Vol. I: The Classical Age of Islam* (1974), is the best general book on the rise of Islam; his two subsequent volumes follow the history of Islamic peoples down to the twentieth century. Ira M. Lapidus, *A History of Islamic Society* (1988), is another, more recent general synthesis. As a place to look up information on any and all aspects of Islamic civilization, *The Encyclopedia of Islam* (new ed., 5 vols., 1960–88), is unexcelled.

Two fine books examine Mohammed's life and the beginning of the Islamic community: Tor Andrae, *Mohammed: The Man and His Faith* (1936), and W. Montgomery Watt, *Muhammad: Prophet and Statesman* (1974). For a Moslem view, see Muhammad Husayn Haykal, *The Life of Muhammad* (1983). For women's roles the sidelight offered by Nadia Abbott, *Aishah, the Beloved of Mohammed* (1942), may be supplemented by Lois Beck and Nikki Keddie, eds., *Women in the Muslim World* (1978).

For continuities and disjunctions with Greek thought and theology, Richard Walzer, *Greek and Arabic: Essays on Islamic Philosophy (1962);* W. Montgomery Watt, *The Formative Period of Islamic Thought* (1973); and George F. Hourani, ed., *Essays on Islamic Philosophy and Science* (1975), are instructive.

On the Sacred Law, try Noel J. Coulson, *History of Islamic Law* (1979); for Sufism and the transformation it brought to Moslem religion and society, Anne Marie Schimmel, *Mystical Dimensions of Islam,* (1975); J. S. Trimingham, *The Sufi Orders in Islam* (1971); Arthur J. Arberry, *Sufism: An Account of the Mystics of Islam* (1979); and Robert C. Zaehner, *Hindu and Muslim Mysticism* (1960), are all worth consulting. H. A. R. Gibb, *Studies in the Civilization of Islam* (1962), and Gustav von Grunebaum, *Medieval Islam: A Study in Cultural Orientation* (2nd ed., 1953), offer ripe reflections of two famous scholars on these and related themes.

T. W. Arnold, *The Caliphate* (1924), though old, is a good account of the problems of succession to the Prophet. On Islam in India, S. M. Ikram, *Muslim Rule in India and Pakistan, 711–1858* (rev ed., 1966), may be useful. For Islamic trade in the Indian Ocean and elsewhere, S. D. Goitein, *Studies in Islamic History and Institutions* (1968), may be recommended.

From early Islamic art, Oleg Grabar, *The Formation of Islamic Art* (1987), and K. A. C. Creswell, *Early Muslim Architecture* (2 vols., 2nd ed., 1969–79), are authoritative. Richard W. Bulliet, *The Camel and the Wheel* (1975), explores the transport revolution of the early Islamic age.

The Far East and the Americas
600 to 1200

11

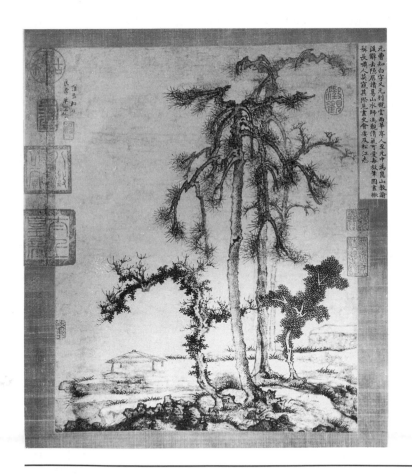

元載知白字文元刻歸畫西華亭人至元中萬龍山教諭
後辭去隱諸篤山水師馮覲清氣愛蘇故華圖畫概
梔長嗍人英蹟其際見畫史會要及松江志

Less Is More   Painting and writing became kindred arts in China. Both were pursued by gentlemen, and were often combined, as you see on the upper right of this painting. Such works of art became collectors' items. The marks on the margins are imprints of personal seals made by successive owners to prove their possession. An array of suitably distinguished owners added to a painting's value.

The establishment of Islam in the Middle East encouraged trade, for the Arabs were accustomed to caravans and respected merchants. But Islam was a dogmatic religion, like Judaism and Christianity. Very quickly, Mohammed's followers worked out a Sacred Law that, like the Jewish law, told the faithful followers of Islam how to conduct themselves in most situations. This, in turn, meant that everyone either had to conform to the Sacred Law, and be a Moslem, or else reject it. No halfway house was acceptable. Mingling and compromise of different cultural traditions under these circumstances still could occur but only in matters that did not come within the scope of religion. In everything concerned with faith and revelation, the boundary lines between cultures became sharp and clear.

The rise of Islam in the Middle East put the Moslems astride the lines of communication between the civilizations of Eurasia. By 750 they had reached the frontiers of India and China and had rolled back the boundaries of Christendom to the Taurus Mountains in Asia Minor and the Pyrenees in Spain. Across each of these frontiers, believers in Islam confronted enemies of the faith of Mohammed. A far more sharply divided world resulted.

Of the separate compartments into which the civilized world broke up, the Far Eastern area was by far the most populous. Between 600 and 1200 it also became the seat of a commercial transformation that increased China's wealth enormously by permitting more efficient use of resources. Artisan skills soon surpassed the level of other civilizations, and cities flourished as never before. Expansion of agriculture kept pace with the elaboration of urban life, however, so that the dominance of the rural landowners, or gentry, which had begun in Han times, was never seriously questioned. This gave a fundamental stability to Chinese civilization and set a limit to its growth. Nothing that really disturbed the interests or ideals of the bureaucracy and gentry could get very far without provoking official action to check the disturbance.

In the same centuries between about 600 and 1200 Chinese artists and writers filled out the older cultural framework. Confucian political and moral ideas were never repudiated, but

Buddhism added important new strands to Chinese art and thought. Even after the imperial government officially repudiated Buddhism, its influence continued. So-called Neo-Confucian thinkers asked new and, in part, Buddhist-inspired questions of the old classic texts—and consequently came up with new answers.

The style of life suitable to a Chinese gentleman also enlarged its scope. Painting and poetry became gentlemanly accomplishments; and where thousands dabbled, scores of truly great masters emerged. Life was also enriched by the development of public restaurants, featuring fine food and professional entertainers.

The lower classes were, of course, too poor to share in such elegance, but the Chinese gentry always accepted newcomers without question. A really bright young man, with aptitude for literary study, could rise as far on the ladder of imperial office as luck and his own talents allowed. Wealth that could be passed on to his sons and other relatives came with high office, and there were no hereditary bars to this kind of personal advancement. Humble peasant families sometimes pooled resources to send an unusually promising boy to school, hoping to profit from his later successes.

The people within the reach of Chinese culture all tried to acquire for themselves as much of the Chinese way of life as they could; and at the very beginning of the period we are considering, both Korea and Japan entered the Far Eastern circle of civilized nations with a rush. In later centuries, both nations modified the borrowed Chinese skills and ideas to suit local tastes and circumstances.

This Far Eastern circle of nations was relatively self-sufficient and indifferent to things happening far away. As educated Chinese saw the world, everything that mattered was concentrated in the "Middle Kingdom," as they called their own country. Round the imposing bulk of China proper were ranged various sorts of barbarians, each of whom shared to some degree the benefits of subordination to, and communication with, the "Son of Heaven"—who sat on the imperial throne of China and kept peace and order at home while holding barbarians in awe. This, of course, was exactly as things should be, according to Confucian principles.

Nevertheless, across the Pacific, far beyond the ken of Confucian sages, new civilizations—Mayan, Mexican, and Peruvian—entered their classic phases in Central and South America about the year 600. They then gave way to a more militarized age of empires some 300 or 400 years later.

The civilizations of the Americas were not related directly to the civilization of China. Yet we can be almost certain that accidental voyaging sometimes carried boats all the way across the Pacific, allowing occasional contact between Asia and America. The distribution of certain useful plants among Pacific islands, as noted by the first European explorers of that ocean, can only be explained by assuming that both Asian and American plants had arrived, from time to time, in different assortments on different islands. Certain striking resemblances between Chinese and Amerindian art also suggest that bits of Chinese pottery or bronze work had somehow crossed the ocean, giving Amerindian

stonecutters and metalworkers a model for some of their own designs.

The Growth of Chinese Civilization

China's Political History

Three major dynasties ruled China in the centuries with which we are now concerned: the Sui, 589–618; the T'ang, 618–907; and the Sung, 960–1279. This traditional organization of Chinese history hides more than it reveals. The Sui dynasty, which reunited China for the first time since the fall of the Han in 220, followed an aggressive military policy on every border. The first T'ang emperors followed the same policy. The change of ruling family that took place in

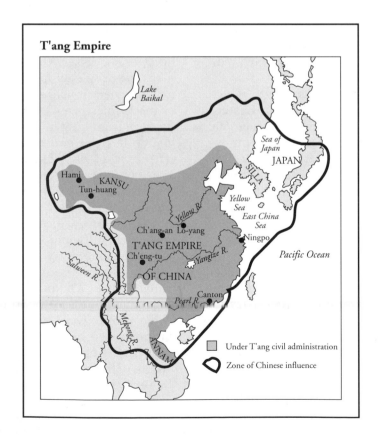

618 was therefore not important. But from 751 onward a series of military disasters struck the Chinese Empire. Defeat at the hands of the Moslems in central Asia was followed by defeat in Korea. Far more serious was a widespread revolt in 755 that paralyzed imperial power. The dynasty was rescued by barbarian intervention, but from that time on the T'ang emperors depended on foreign protectors and paid heavily in the form of tribute.

The remaining centuries of T'ang dynastic rule, consequently, were politically very different from the dynasty's first century of vigorous expansion and military success. Instead, the emperor's real power eroded bit by bit because he lacked an army capable of imposing the will of the central government. Local warlords sprang up, often fighting among themselves and paying scant obedience to the distant T'ang ruler. The end of the dynasty in 907 therefore made no real difference.

The rise of the Sung, on the other hand, did mark a return to centralized and effective bureaucratic government within the part of China which the dynasty was able to control. But the Sung never ruled the whole country. A tier of northern provinces remained in the hands of various barbarian rulers; Sung administration was never secure north of the Yellow River, and after 1127 the area it controlled shrank back toward the Yangtze.

The Sui, T'ang, and Sung Dynasties

Under the Sui and early T'ang dynasties, when China's government was strong and aggressive, Chinese armies were recruited from the sons of free peasants who had established themselves throughout most of north China during the barbarian invasions and the wars that followed the collapse of the Han dynasty. These troops were both hardy and numerous, and they carried T'ang arms deep into central Asia. Tribes located as far away as the Caspian Sea recognized Chinese authority, and for a brief moment the Chinese even claimed control over Kashmir on the southern slopes of the Himalaya Mountains.

But campaigns on distant frontiers required professional soldiers. Peasants could not leave their farms for long periods of time and remain taxpayers. But barbarians from China's borderlands were excellent fighters and eager for pay. By 750 the T'ang armies were therefore recruited almost entirely among barbarians and were even commanded by barbarian generals. The change in army recruitment had dramatic consequences when a series of defeats in the field set off a large-scale revolt in 755. The troops attempted to seize power on behalf of their commander, who was a barbarian. They were defeated only after many years of warfare, when a more cohesive barbarian force, led by Turkish-speaking Uighurs, rode in from the west and propped the helpless T'ang emperors up on their ancestral throne once more.

Thenceforward, the relation between the Chinese and the barbarians was reversed. Instead of trying to rule over the wide borderlands lying north and west of China, the emperors abandoned these regions to local tribes and kingdoms. Judicious distribution of tribute "gifts," and diplomatic intrigues among the rival chieftains, allowed considerable room for maneuver as long as the Chinese government was able to gather large resources through its tax-collecting system. But little by little the tax system broke down, too. Local upstarts intercepted the central government's tax income and built small domains for themselves. Barbarian intervention and raiding naturally increased under these conditions.

The decay of imperial government and the threat of barbarian conquest ran against the grain of Chinese feeling. By appealing to the ancient traditions and standards of the past, and by arousing anti-foreign feeling that was never far from Chinese consciousness, the Sung emperors were able to rebuild an effective central administration. A standing professional army, recruited from within China, was an indispensable instrument for the Sung rulers. But what held things together was a reformed bureaucracy. The reform was thoroughly conservative in spirit. Sung emperors consciously harked back to Confucius and the good old days. New men, recruited mainly from the southern provinces, came to office. They managed the Sung government more nearly on Confucius' principles than had ever been done before.

At the Top of Chinese Society   On the left we see a painting of the Emperor
Wu-ti (reigned 561–70) in the company of two high officials. According to
Confucian ideas, the Emperor was to earth what the pole star was to the
Heavens—the center around which all else turned. But on a local level,
landowners and gentlemen, like the personage portrayed on the right,
controlled those beneath them by their dignity and virtue more than by
physical force. Or so Confucian teaching held. Reality always fell short, but
Confucian ideals still helped to unite China under a long succession of
emperors and also helped to define and cushion landlord–peasant relations.

Yet Confucian principles failed to unite all
of China. The provinces north of the Yellow
River, including territory where Chinese civilization had originated, were ruled by various
barbarians—Turks, Mongols, and Manchus. The
most notable such state, known as the Chin dynasty to the Chinese, came from Manchuria and
ruled a large part of northern China between
1122 and 1234, when the advancing Mongols destroyed it.

Foreign Relations   As long as the Sui and
T'ang armies were strong, the Chinese kept their
doors wide open to strangers. Traders and merchants from the West brought new religions with
them. Christianity, Islam, Manichaeism, Zoroastrianism, and various forms of Buddhism all
mingled with one another in China's busy caravan cities. Buddhism soon gained official support, and Buddhist monasteries grew wealthy
through the gifts of pious or repentant individuals. With these foreign religions came other
things as well: art styles, ideas pertaining to astrology and astronomy, and the decimal system of numerical notation. But some of these
innovations did not take hold and flourish permanently. Instead, mounting anti-foreign sen-
timent persuaded the government to try to re-
press barbarian innovations and borrowings from
abroad.

The most dramatic turning point came in the period 843–846, when the emperor prohibited foreign religions. This policy was triggered by the collapse of Uighur power in 840. The Uighurs had made Manichaeism their official faith after 763, and they became the special protectors of that religion in China. Since the Chinese disliked paying tribute to the Uighurs, Manichaeans who accepted the Uighur protection also became the objects of widespread popular and official dislike. Therefore, when the Uighur Empire was attacked and destroyed by a new steppe confederation in 840, the Chinese revenged themselves on the Manichaeans dwelling in their midst by prohibiting their faith and seizing all their property.

This whetted the government's appetite. One by one the other foreign faiths suffered the same fate, including Buddhism, which by this time had many wealthy monasteries in various parts of China. The official T'ang history, in fact, records that 44,600 monasteries and nunneries were suppressed, and more than 400,000 monks and nuns were either enslaved or put back on the tax lists.

From that time onward, the Chinese allowed their distrust of all things foreign to blind them to foreign accomplishments. This set a ceiling upon the development of Chinese civilization that turned out to be very costly in the long run; but at the time and for centuries to follow, Chinese attainments were in fact so high that they had ample excuse for believing that there was nothing of value or importance they could learn from outsiders.

Social and Economic Evolution of China

The Spread of Rice Farming   The basic fact about Chinese society was the massiveness and density of the population. Hard-working peasants, tilling small plots of land with skills that had been perfected through generations, constituted the solid base of Chinese civilization. Tiny farms, having high yields per acre but relatively small surpluses per agricultural worker, made Chinese farming different from that of Europe and western Asia, where animal power allowed peasants to till more land and raise a larger surplus per head, but at the expense of a lower yield per acre. Year by year and generation after generation, the area under cultivation in China increased. New fields were built farther and farther up hill slopes, where more and more labor was required to carve out a level patch of cultivable ground.

A change in the center of gravity of Chinese rural life took place as the Yangtze Valley came under intense cultivation. This process began very early, long before the time of the Han dynasty; but it was not until the Sui dynasty opened the Grand Canal in 605 that the full economic and political importance of the agricultural exploitation of the Yangtze Valley was felt. Doubling and more than doubling the tax income at the disposal of the Chinese imperial court was important enough; but in addition, the climatic conditions of the Yangtze basin encouraged a shift toward rice farming and away from the cultivation of wheat, barley, millet, and other dryland crops that had been the staples of early Chinese cultivation in the Yellow River valley.

Rice had one enormous advantage. Far more calories could be harvested from a well-cultivated rice field than any other crop could produce on the same amount of land. There was a corresponding disadvantage since the labor of preparing the fields and of planting and harvesting rice was enormous. First of all, the soil had to be leveled and channels prepared through which water might flow onto the field. Dikes or low walls had to be built to retain this water, since rice plants prosper only when a few inches of standing water keep their roots well soaked. When the field was ready, rice seed had to be set out to sprout in special beds. Then each seedling had to be transplanted by hand into the field where it would grow. Only when the rice began to ripen could the water be allowed to drain off the fields, so that at harvest time the reapers might have the convenience of dry land beneath their feet.

It requires a stretch of the imagination to conceive how much human labor is required for successful paddy rice growing, as this kind of cultivation is called. The agricultural year con-

Rice Paddy Farming   As this photograph shows, when enough labor is available, rice paddies can transform natural landscapes. But the spread of rice paddies like these also transformed human society throughout central and southern China, creating an abundant source of food that sustained very dense populations.

sists of innumerable hours spent digging and diking the fields, followed by backbreaking days required to transplant the seedlings and the scarcely less difficult task of harvesting the ripe rice with sickles.

No one knows exactly when and where rice paddy cultivation first developed. Rice growing was already part of China's agricultural practice in Shang times, but it was only when the fertile, well-watered, and vast expanses of the Yangtze Valley came under cultivation that the rice paddy style of farming became *the* standard form of Chinese agriculture.

No records allow us to follow exactly the steps of the process whereby innumerable carpets of paddy fields spread from river edges and the margins of lakes up the slopes of valleys and along the contour lines of the hills, until almost every available patch of land that human labor and ingenious water engineering could make productive had been brought under cultivation.

The entire process may be compared to the way a glacier moves across the earth's surface, altering the landscape profoundly as it advances and engulfing all the obstacles that it may meet.

The numerical mass of the Chinese peasantry throughout historic time advanced like a glacier, taking over new regions, enfolding the remnants of other peoples, absorbing conquerors, and changing the natural landscape far more thoroughly than most other human communities have done. Only in Korea, Japan, Java, and some parts of southeast Asia—where rice paddy cultivation also became the dominant form of agriculture—have equally dense, disciplined, and hard-working rural populations ever arisen.

An important improvement came to Chinese farming during the centuries with which we are concerned. About 1000 a new kind of early-ripening rice was discovered or, perhaps, imported from southeast Asia. This kind of rice allowed peasants to harvest two crops a year on well-watered land. In addition, places where water was not available for more than a few weeks of the year became potential paddy land, since with the early-ripening rice it was not necessary to keep standing water on the ground for more than thirty to forty days. The result was a very substantial increase in total food production, for in many parts of China, especially inland, the spring run-off left dry, empty stream beds through most of the year. Such land could now grow rice. Accordingly, many interior regions that had previously lacked enough water were opened up to the Chinese style of agriculture for the first time.

The Growth of Trade   But it was not the indefinite multiplication of peasant village communities that made Chinese civilization prosper. The village surpluses had to be concentrated and used to support artisans, scholars, soldiers, and other specialists. Here, too, important improvements came into play during the Sui and T'ang periods. First of all, the opening of the Grand Canal meant that bulky and comparatively cheap commodities could move back and forth between the Yangtze basin and the valley of the Yellow River. A single barge, hauled by human muscles or by an animal, could easily carry a cargo of several tons. Long-distance overland transport thus became cheap enough to tie the richest and most productive lands of central and northern China into a single network.

By about 750, the construction of feeder canals and connecting waterways had advanced so far that the court no longer needed all of the produce that could be delivered. Instructions were therefore sent to local tax officials to sell portions of the foodstuffs and other coarse goods they had collected in their warehouses and buy fine artisan products instead. These were more valuable, and the court quickly developed an insatiable appetite for fine lacquerware, porcelain, or embroidered cloth—whatever it might be that local skills or resources could produce. The effect of such a policy was to stimulate local artisan trades. Regional specialization became possible on a substantial scale. Wealth increased, population grew, and China's skills began to surpass anything known elsewhere.

At the Bottom of Chinese Society   Whatever the virtues of the emperor, China was held together in another way by the Grand Canal, which linked the Yangtze River with the Yellow River after 605. Boats could carry goods quite cheaply along this canal and up and down the two rivers, whose natural courses were supplemented by innumerable other canals built to bring water to rice paddies. The photograph shows traffic on the Grand Canal in the twentieth century. The boatmen's clothing was different in T'ang and Sung times when the canal was still new, but the size of the barges and some of the cheap goods the canal carried were not very different then from what they are now.

The court and capital were the main beneficiaries of the new wealth, but others shared in it, too. Private trading grew up beside and around official transactions. The development of private trade meant a much wider use of money than had formerly been common in China. This, in turn, allowed the government to collect more of its income in cash and to rely upon purchases from private suppliers to provide many of the goods the government needed or wanted. Scattered statistics show, for example, that in 749 only 3.9 percent of the imperial tax income took the form of coined money, whereas in 1065 the proportion had risen to 51.6 percent.

The flexibility of a market economy thus came to China. Wider use of money and improved and cheaper transportation, together with enlarged scope for private trade, all combined to allow the Chinese to distribute and develop their resources more efficiently than had been possible before, when taxes in kind were liable to yield too much of one kind of commodity and not enough of another.

The rise of local warlords in the later T'ang period did not seriously check these developments. If anything, it spurred them on. For instead of having a single great capital to which tax monies flowed, the rise of independent provincial rulers meant that their residence cities began to attract tax income that had previously gone to the distant imperial capital in the north. This stimulated the development of provincial cities, particularly in the south.

Under the Sung dynasty, the commercialization of Chinese society went into high gear. Even poor peasants began to enter the market, buying and selling food and other commodities. By specializing on raising whatever sold best, they could increase their productivity, just as urban populations had done for centuries. But as the peasant majority began to respond to market prices by increasing the output of whatever could be produced most efficiently in each different locality, the wealth of the country as a whole shot upward.

Everything depended on cheap and reliable transport, provided by canal boats. These could

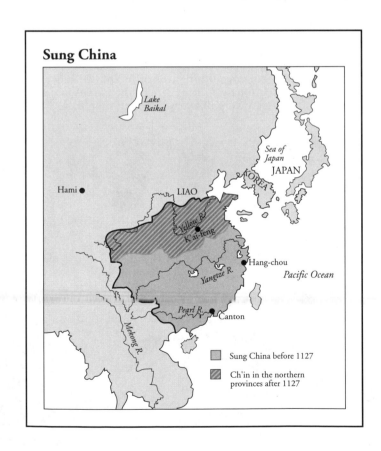

Sung China

move to and fro along the canal network that the Chinese had constructed initially to make sure their rice paddies got enough water each year.

Intensified trade within China and rising productivity soon spread beyond the limits of the two great river valleys where the canal system already existed. In particular, seafaring began to play a more significant role than before. Coastal cities in the extreme south began to trade with southeast Asian and Indonesian ports, thus opening another source of wealth. Important improvements in the design of ships made this development possible. Cotton sails instead of bamboo slats that had been used earlier, a centerboard keel that could be raised in shallow waters, and a large, sturdier hull were key inventions. In addition, by 1100 Chinese sailors began to use the magnetic compass for navigation at sea.

The value of the compass may need a little explanation. What it did was allow a ship to travel long distances across the sea without losing a sense of direction, even in cloudy weather when the stars could not be seen. Distant ports were comparatively easy to find if the ship's captain could steer along a compass line and know that he would fetch up within a few miles of the expected landfall. But in the monsoon climate that dominated the seas adjacent to the south China coast, the compass was not usually necessary. Clear weather prevailed most of the time, and sighting the stars could always provide a practiced mariner with the necessary sense of direction. In northern seas, where clouds might linger for weeks on end, the magnetic compass was of far greater importance, as European navigators discovered some three centuries after Chinese sailors first learned the advantages of having a compass on board ship.

The commercialization of the Chinese economy meant the rise of large, busy cities. The largest of them far surpassed anything known elsewhere. The hardheaded Venetian merchant and traveler, Marco Polo, left an account of his experiences in China (1275–1292), in which he explained with awe exactly how vast the Chinese capital was and how large and prosperous other Chinese cities appeared when compared with those of other parts of the earth.

By Marco Polo's time, China's lead over the rest of the world was unquestionable. Yet there were limitations built into China's economic and social system that eventually allowed western Europeans to catch up and surpass Chinese accomplishments. First of all, the social leadership of the landed gentry class was never seriously challenged by any of the new groups called into being by the commercial transformation of the country. Confucian doctrine viewed merchants as social parasites, who marked up the price of what they sold but added nothing to the value of the goods they handled. Together with soldiers, they were classed as necessary evils. Individuals who gained a fortune in trade were therefore strongly tempted to become respectable by buying land, sending their sons to school, and making them into gentlemen or even into officials. Merchants, in other words, lacked any sort of independent spirit. How could they challenge the gentry when each of them had the ambition of becoming a man of property, leisure, and education, if possible?

The predominant position of landlords in Chinese society was, of course, sustained by the growth in agricultural production referred to previously. In addition, the artisan trades were devoted largely to meeting the needs and pleasing the tastes of the gentry, since they were the class with money to spare for such purchases. Since they were naturally eager to please their best customers, artisans, too, found it impossible to challenge the gentry in any effective way.

The Development of Technical Skills   The tastes of the gentry of the court put a premium on luxury craftsmanship. Chinese artisans, consequently, developed unexcelled skills. Only a few examples of their handicraft survive from T'ang and Sung times—mainly porcelains and other kinds of pottery. But literary records make clear that more perishable objects of silk, wood, and metal were also produced with the greatest refinement of detail and workmanship. In Sung times, north China also developed a large-scale iron industry, using coke as fuel. Not until the eighteenth century did Europe began to likewise. Yet, oddly enough, when barbarian invaders sacked the capital and overran the region where

The Worthless Classes: Foreign Intruders According to Confucian ideas, merchants and soldiers were idlers who lived as parasites on others and did not belong in a well-managed society. This attitude was reinforced in T'ang China by the fact that foreigners played an especially prominent role as soldiers and merchants in that age. On the top you see a clay figurine of a merchant fondling his money bags and advertising his foreign, origin by the exaggerated size and curvature of his nose. The artist clearly shared Confucian dislike of merchants. On the other hand, the soldier and his horse on the bottom are portrayed in more sympathetic fashion, though most soldiers who served as cavalrymen in the Chinese army were foreigners recruited from among the nomad peoples of the steppe. The artist seems especially interested in details of cavalry equipment, for the saddle, stirrups, and quiver of arrows are very clearly represented. Yet, oddly, the bow is missing.

the iron furnaces were located, the industry was not revived.

Perhaps the most instructive example of how Chinese social structure and ideas channeled technical development along certain lines and checked its progress in other directions is the history of gunpowder—a Chinese invention. From about the year 1000 Chinese armies experimented with "fire arrows" and "fire lances" whose flammable substance was a form of gunpowder. They soon got the idea of putting the new explosive into a vase-like gun and firing a heavy arrow planted across its mouth. But the Chinese were not interested in developing this primitive form of artillery into wall-destroying cannon, as Europeans did soon after they learned from the Chinese how to make gunpowder. From a Chinese point of view it was foolish to develop weapons that could destroy fortifications. Their enemies were steppe horsemen who lived in the open, whereas the Chinese needed to be able to take refuge behind strong walls. Anything that made walled towns and forts along the frontier more vulnerable was exactly what the Chinese did not want. Therefore, quite rationally, they did not make big guns.

The policy worked well for more than five hundred years. Only after 1550, when European ships with large numbers of relatively enormous guns began to show up on the China coast, did the Chinese begin to experience the cost of having failed to develop weapons that could knock down fortifications at a distance. Before then, Sung rulers and their successors made only marginal use of gunpowder and met the challenge of nomad warriors on their northwest frontier in traditional ways—sending tribute, arranging alliances, and, when all else failed, defending walled towns and villages against raiding horsemen as best they could using crossbows more than guns.

The Flowering of China's Cultural Life

The T'ang and Sung dynasties saw China's greatest flowering in thought, art, and literature. Chinese in later centuries took the writings and paintings of this age as models for their own work and felt themselves inferior to the old masters whom they so admired. Modern scholars agree with this judgment, even though many famous masterpieces of Sung painting are known only through copies made by later generations of artists.

Perhaps the reason T'ang and Sung art and literature attained such heights was that under those two dynasties the Chinese absorbed and made their own the mass of foreign ideas that had flooded into the country during the troubled centuries after the fall of the Han, when the divided land of China was repeatedly overrun by barbarians. This meant, first and foremost, coming to terms with the art and thought of Buddhism, which itself combined Indian, Greek, and central Asian cultural strands.

T'ang and Sung China and Gupta India occupy a similar place in the cultural history of their respective civilizations. Each was an age of synthesis, richer and more complex than anything known in earlier centuries; each was luxurious, courtly, and refined. Each developed a school of poetry that concerned itself with the complexities of love and the ebb and flow of feeling that make up individual inner consciousness. Each has been greatly admired ever since.

Resemblances do not stop there, for both in India and China the high development of abstract thought came several centuries after artistic expression achieved its most admired perfection. Thus, Neo-Confucian philosophy flowered in the Sung period, especially toward its close; whereas in India, Hindu philosophy reached its full development three or four centuries after the court poetry of Kalidasa had scaled the heights of Hindu imaginative literature at the Gupta court (fifth century C.E.).

These parallels, like the parallels between the early river valley civilizations in the Old World and the development of the American civilizations in the Americas, may prove that there are norms in human history resulting from some kind of natural pattern of development that people fall into if left undisturbed for a sufficient length of time. On the other hand, these parallels may only be the result of paying attention to some aspects of the human past while overlooking others. The study of society is so inexact and the historical record is so patchy that we cannot really be certain.

The Buddhist Influence

Whatever the truth may be about resemblances in the histories of different civilizations, the manner in which the Chinese reacted to the Buddhist stimulus is easy to understand in a general way, even if the details were far from simple.

The first thing to understand is that even when they were in highest favor at court, Buddhists never tried to persecute Confucian scholars or others whose views differed from their own. This attitude was not shared by conservative Confucians. They looked upon the Buddhists with active distrust. The otherworldly Buddhist ideal, after all, took people away from their duties to family and ruler; of this a good Confucian could never approve. On the other hand, Buddhist writing raised many questions with which Confucians had never dealt. To refute all the elaborate doctrines Buddhist monks brought from India required Confucian scholars to work out their own views on these questions. Confucius' refusal to talk about the spirit world was no longer enough.

Yet a well-trained Confucian scholar could not feel comfortable with arguments that rested on nothing but their own merits. This was the way of the Greeks, the way of philosophy. Confucius had claimed that he invented nothing and merely passed on what the ancients had taught. A good Confucian had to do the same. The solution scholars found to this dilemma was to borrow from Buddhist thinkers a new way of reading the old classic texts. Buddhists were accustomed to finding hidden truths in old writings and stories by interpreting them symbolically. A person or a thing, they believed, might stand for something else—often an abstract idea. Thus, for example, the actual human being Gautama Buddha stood for a whole host of Buddha traits. He had become a symbol for cosmic principles, and the symbol was obviously more important than the actual man.

This method of reading and interpreting texts made it easy to discover new meanings in the Chinese classics. The men who developed Confucian thought in these ways are known as Neo-Confucians. The greatest of them was Chu Hsi (1130–1200), whose teachings offered convincing answers to all the questions that had been raised by the discussions between Buddhists and Confucians during the preceding 300 to 400 years.

Taoists also learned something from the Buddhists. Taoist doctrine borrowed little, so far as we can tell; but the Buddhist monastic pattern of organization did show Taoists how to pass their ideas on to larger numbers of persons in a more coherent fashion. Presently Taoists organized a monastic way of life similar to that of the Buddhists. From that time onward, as experts in dealing with the spirit world, Taoist monks offered their services to ordinary Chinese peasants and townspeople who needed to find out how the spiritual forces would react to the building of a new house, or why a child was sick, or whether a particular marriage offer should be accepted.

With the destruction of Buddhist monasteries after 845, surviving Buddhists competed with Taoists in performing services of this sort. Buddhism tended to benefit as well as suffer from falling out of favor with officialdom. Peasants and unsuccessful scholars, if they felt rebellious, were likely to find Buddhism especially attractive just because it was outlawed. This, in turn, powerfully affected the further development of Buddhism in China. It became an unofficial, intellectual opposition to prevailing Confucian and Neo-Confucian ideals. For example, the Chan sect, which became the principal Buddhist group in China, emphasized the futility of study and relied entirely on instantaneous "enlightenment." The challenge to Confucian emphasis upon study and perpetual self-control could not have been more direct. This sort of Buddhism had little in common with Indian ideas. In the Chinese environment, in other words, what had begun as an alien faith and pattern of life survived by coming thoroughly Chinese.

The Increase of Literacy

A balance between official Confucianism, private Taoism, and suspect Buddhism emerged in China by 1200 and remained quite stable thereafter, though the doctrines of each group continued to alter in detail. The invention of paper and printing (first recorded in 756) confirmed and strengthened this balance. Books became common. Cheaper books allowed a larger proportion of the population to read. City dwellers thus became able to share the literary heritage of the past more fully than before. Gentlemen scholars were no longer the sole guardians of book learning, as had tended to be the case in Han times, when books were expensive and had to be copied by hand.

Printing may have developed from Buddhist efforts to waft innumerable prayers to the countless array of bodhisattvas (Buddhist saints). Very ancient Chinese custom had known how to communicate with the spirit world by writing a question on some perishable material and then burning it. Buddhists in China adopted this method of delivering prayers to the bodhisattvas. Shortly before 756, it occurred to someone that if he first painted the characters of his prayer on a flat piece of wood—and chiseled out all the spaces in between—he could then reproduce the prayer over and over again by inking the smooth wood surface that remained and then pressing silk or paper (invented in the time of the Han dynasty) against the wood block. This seems to have been the first use to which printing was put in China. Later the same technique, using either stone or wood blocks, was used to print texts for human consumption. In particular, the Buddhist and Confucian classics were reproduced in large numbers. The first official printing of the classics took place at the T'ang capital between 932 and 953. Printed paper currency was also put into circulation, to the utter amazement of foreign visitors like Marco Polo.

The Chinese long continued to use block printing even when the possibility of printing with movable type had become thoroughly familiar to them. This was not due to mere conservatism, for the number of separate characters needed to write Chinese made it almost as easy to carve a whole page at a time as to assemble a page from thousands of different pieces of precast type. Only when printing passed to Korea, where an alphabetic script already existed, did movable type come into its own. Korean movable type was in use by about 1400. European printing with movable type began in 1456.

Printing made many kinds of Chinese literature available to far more people than could be reached with handwritten manuscripts. Histories, encyclopedias, essays, and poetry circulated widely. Each of these forms of literature flourished vigorously in T'ang and Sung times. The sheer bulk of Chinese literary output far exceeded anything known from other civilizations; and despite extensive losses that have since occurred, an impressive amount of T'ang and Sung writing still survives.

The Refinement of Poetry and Art In China, painting and poetry overlapped. Both were the work of the brush and both became genteel accomplishments. A painting might include a few words that added to the painting's effect, in much the same way that skillful brushwork in writing the characters added to the impact of a poem by giving it a pleasing appearance on the page. The poems of Li Po (701–762) and Tu Fu (712–770) provided the main model for later poets. Li Po in particular took verse forms from the popular songs of the streets; indeed, if his autobiographical references are to be believed, he led a semi-disreputable life by the standards of a Confucian scholar. But he expressed new feelings: love, longing, despair, self-disgust. Always he was acutely self-conscious in a way that earlier Chinese writers seem not to have been. So powerful was the impact of his poetry that the styles and verse forms he used were later made part of the imperial examinations. As a result, every scholar who wanted official position in the government had to learn to write passable verse in Li Po's manner. An enormous outpouring of polished but uninspired verse resulted.

Painting reached its peak under the Sung dynasty, when several famous masters developed the styles we think of as typically Chinese. It was an art of ink and paper, with little reliance on color. The Buddhist technique of using figures and scenes to tell a story became part of this style of art; in addition, the great Sung masters learned to portray three-dimensional space in their landscapes. Long vistas and mighty mountains sprang from the paper as the results of a few brushstrokes.

Despite the limits inherent in brush and ink, great variations of techniques proved possible, and quite different effects could be produced. Painters learned how to present haziness and mist, but they could also command clarity of line. Some went in for detail—there were painters who painted nothing but bamboo leaves; others painted panoramic views stretching toward infinity on a scroll only a few inches wide. The simplicity of their materials did not prevent endless variation. Because the variables were few, the greatest attention and skill could be concentrated upon making much out of little. The Sung painters succeeded as few artists have ever succeeded. They created Chinese styles of painting that lasted almost unaltered until the twentieth century.

China's Asian Neighbors

China moved south with the Sung. Chinese painting reflects the Yangtze rather than the Yellow River scenery. The northern tier of provinces that had been ruled by Han and T'ang emperors were never brought under the Sung dynasty's regular administration, although various barbarian rulers and chieftains who controlled these regions sometimes recognized the Sung imperial title in return for an appropriate gift or tribute payment.

Chinese records disguise the barbarian element in these northern states. Writers gave barbarian rulers and peoples Chinese names and tried to fit the facts to Confucian ideals as much as possible. Any trader or ambassador was described, therefore, as a bringer of tribute, eager to honor the Son of Heaven. Desperate efforts to buy off some threatened attack entered the records as gracious imperial gifts, delivered as a gesture of courtesy in return for the barbarians' deferential and polite behavior toward the emperor.

In reality, not all the barbarians who had important dealings with China were eager to become Chinese. The Uighurs, for example, became Manichaeans a few years after they assumed a dominant role in Chinese imperial politics. The effect was to mark themselves off from the Chinese more sharply than before. Tibetans, too, built up a considerable empire in central Asia af-

ter 751. But they did not hurry to become Chinese. Instead, they took their religion, a form of Buddhism, from India and combined it with local rites to produce a faith called Lamaism.

Farther east, China's neighbors could not so easily draw upon another civilized tradition to bolster their cultural independence. Inhabitants of Manchuria and nearby regions lived too far away from the central Asian trade routes to be able to acquire any foreign style of civilized religion to pit against Chinese ideas. Yet some of these peoples, when they conquered China's northern fringes, resisted assimilation into the Chinese body politic by setting up special political arrangements, leaving civil administration to the Chinese and keeping military affairs strictly in their own hands. The system worked for a few generations. But in time even the proudest barbarians found the attractions of Chinese civilization too much to resist.

The Koreans

Korea had a similar problem. Independent organized kingdoms arose there about 300 B.C.E.; but the great Han emperor, Wu Ti, conquered most of the Korean peninsula about two centuries later. Similar events had led to the incorporation of one province after another into China. Yet Korea, in the end, remained separate, in spite of the immediate presence of China to the west. Exactly why this happened is difficult to say. Fresh barbarian invaders came to Korea, as well as to China, with the end of the Han Dynasty; all the new Korean kingdoms that emerged in T'ang times were tougher and far more militarized than earlier Korean states had been. The Sui emperors tried vainly to replicate Wu Ti's accomplishment by conquering Korea. The T'ang, too, fought hard to subdue the peninsula. But in the end, when the Koreans admitted Chinese overlordship in 668, it was only nominal.

Two features of Korean life kept the country separate from China thereafter. One was the Korean language, which differed completely from Chinese and could not easily be written in Chinese characters. Soon after 600, Koreans began to write little marks in the margins beside Chinese characters to stand for grammatical endings and other parts of speech that were needed to make the meaning clear. In time this system evolved into a Korean script that differed from Chinese. Korea therefore developed a literary tradition of its own and preserved its separate language.

The other great distinguishing feature between Chinese and Korean civilization was Buddhism. When the Chinese turned against Buddhism, the Koreans clung to it all the more strongly. Korea thus became a Buddhist land. This meant that the study of Confucian classics and the eager imitation of the latest Chinese styles of dress or manners could never turn Korea into a mere province of China. To be sure, the Chinese chose to regard trade missions as tribute missions; in fact, however, Korea remained independent, though often divided into rival kingdoms.

The Japanese

Japan was far enough away from China not to have to fear cultural absorption. Japanese tradition holds that the emperor who reigns today descends in an unbroken line from the first emperor, Jimmu; and that Jimmu, in turn, descended from the Sun Goddess, who created the Japanese islands first and then went on to make all the other lands of the earth. Jimmu's traditional date, 660 B.C.E., does not have much greater claim to accuracy than the Japanese story of creation.

Chinese and Korean records show that, in the early centuries of the Common Era, the Japanese islands were divided among warlike clans or tribal groups, of which the imperial clan was only one. Not until 552, when Buddhism was first introduced into Japan, did the country come closely into touch with the civilization of China. In 607 the first of several official missions went from Japan to the Chinese court. These Japanese missions carefully studied Chinese ways in order to take home useful information. Each mission involved several score of persons, who remained in China for months or even years at a time. Hence, the Japanese—as later in the nineteenth century when they set out to learn about European civilization—were nothing if not systematic.

The result was spectacular. The Japanese court found Chinese ways attractive, if only because the Chinese attributed so great a role to the emperor—a role the emperor of Japan was eager to play among the warlike and insubordinate clans of his native land. A wholesale importation of T'ang courtly culture, therefore, took place. This era is known as the Nara period of Japanese history because the imperial court was then located at Nara (710–784). Literature, art, and manners were brought in from China and developed brilliantly. In 838 the twelfth and last official embassy went to China. Thereafter, the Japanese decided that they had nothing more to learn from the decadent T'ang court. Official relations were accordingly broken off.

The realities of Japanese clan life never fitted smoothly into the forms of bureaucratic imperial administration imported from China. Instead, rival clans continued to struggle for power and influence, much as before. The imperial court appointed successful warriors as provincial governors with due Confucian rituals; but the effective authority of such governors rested on fighting clansmen, who obeyed not because the emperor had appointed their leaders to office (as bureaucratic theory required) but because they were born to chieftainship or had risen to clan leadership in some other traditional fashion.

The hold of clan organization on Japan was steadily reinforced by the fact that the northern and eastern parts of the Japanese islands were a wild frontier region, where warrior clans steadily carved out new territories for themselves at the expense of earlier inhabitants known as Ainu. As a matter of fact, the military clans remained so important in Japan that one or more of them were often able to control the imperial court from behind the scenes, manipulating appointments and the award of dignities to suit the clan's interests.

In 794 the capital of Japan shifted to Kyoto, inaugurating the so-called Heian period (794–1185). Life at the new imperial capital was less completely modeled on Chinese patterns. Distinctive Japanese art and literature made their appearance. In particular, about 1020, a lady-in-waiting at the court, Murasaki Shikibu, wrote a

China's Neighbors   Between 600 and 1200 China's impressive cultural
accomplishments attracted attention among all neighboring peoples.
The painting on the left shows a Uigher prince from Central Asia, whose
headdress and silken robe came from China, as did the idea of royal
portraiture. The Uighurs were warriors who held China for ransom in late
T'ang times but, like so many other barbarians, were captivated by Chinese
culture. Japan's relation to China was different. Beginning in 605, the Japanese
imperial court began consciously to borrow Chinese skills. A trace of this
policy survives in the pagoda, located in Nara, the seat of the Japanese
emperor in the eighth century. Made of wood, it has been repaired more than
once, but still preserves the appearance of the original structure, modeled
faithfully on Chinese prototypes.

delightful prose romance, *The Tale of Genji*. A
lively love story and one of the masterpieces of
world literature, it owes little or nothing to Chinese literary models and everything to Lady
Murasaki's keen observation of human nature
and the manners of court life in Japan.

Buddhism, rather than the official Confucianism of the imperial court, took root among
the rough warrior clans of the Japanese countryside. So close was their association with the
rural and military classes that Japanese Buddhist monks often took sword in hand to defend

the interests of their monastery in a fashion that
other Buddhist communities never thought of
doing. Successful monasteries, in fact, behaved
very much like successful clans. Monastic discipline had its counterparts in clan discipline that
marked off the way of the warrior or *samurai*
class from peasant ways of life. And just as a
man could become a monk by accepting the prescribed pattern of monastic life, so too at least
some of the Japanese military clans admitted
promising warriors to their ranks. This happened most freely in the zone of the frontier,

where additional fighters were often much in demand.

At the bottom of society, of course, were peasants who learned to cultivate the soil as skillfully as Chinese peasants did. How and by what steps paddy rice fields spread through the mountainous landscape of Japan is not known. We may assume that the laborious leveling of fields and the channeling of water occurred slowly, advancing into new districts as the Ainu were forced back, step by step, toward the harsh and forbidding climate of the northernmost island, Hokkaido, where rice would not grow.

The imperial court appointed officials to collect taxes from the peasants. Obviously, taxes were collected; otherwise the luxury of the Nara and Heian periods could not have been achieved. Yet perhaps from the beginning and increasingly as time went on, military clans gained control of tax-free lands. Such warrior groups had the right to collect rice for their own support directly from the villagers. As this became more and more common, a feudal system arose in Japan that resembled the contemporary feudalism of western Europe quite closely. The emperor's theoretical supremacy was never called into question. But with the consolidation of Japanese feudalism, the imperial court's power and wealth decayed rapidly. Indeed, during the so-called Kamakura period (1185–1333), the emperor became no more than a puppet figure. Real power was concentrated instead in the hands of one particular clan that controlled the emperor and his court. As the imperial court became poorer, the courtly level of learning, art, and manners—modeled on the Chinese—decayed. Instead, a cruder, more popular style of thought and feeling began to emerge.

Thus Japan, too, by 1200 or so, had discarded the borrowed finery of Chinese civilization in favor of a simpler and more authentically Japanese style of culture and politics. Yet the civilizations of Japan, Korea, Tibet, and the less stable cultural styles of Uighurs and other central Asian peoples, would have been unthinkable had they not had the Chinese model against which to react and from which to borrow. China remained the Middle Kingdom, the central lodestone of the entire Far Eastern scene. Nothing could really rival the dignity, wealth, splendor, and power of imperial China.

The Pacific and the Americas

The Polynesians

Beyond the outermost fringes of China's sphere of influence, Polynesians began their extraordinary spread sometime about 600. Perhaps the key invention that allowed them to move across the wide Pacific was the outrigger canoe. By attaching buoyant outriggers to the gunwales, a canoe hollowed out from a single tree trunk became able to travel on the ocean with safety. Such vessels, driven by sails and guided by a steering paddle, allowed the Polynesians to establish themselves on isolated Pacific islands separated from one another by many thousands of miles. Hawaii and New Zealand represent extremes of their expansion north and south; Easter Island, which lies not very far from the coast of South America, became the Polynesians' easternmost outpost.

The Polynesians were root growers and did not know about rice. They may have had some connection with the Indonesian seafarers who settled on Madagascar some 600 or 700 years before the Polynesians began moving eastward through the Pacific. Both may, in turn, have been related to seagoing peoples of the southeast Asian mainland. But origins are unclear, and for that matter the stages and dates of the Polynesian migration through the central Pacific cannot be reconstructed with certainty.

Occasional boatloads of Polynesian voyagers must have arrived on the shores of the American continent. Some of them (or perhaps other voyagers) also returned to the islands of the Pacific. The evidence for these voyages is that various plants native to the Americas were growing in Hawaii and other islands when Europeans first visited them. These plants must have been carried there by human travelers.

The Amerindians

Such contacts may account for otherwise surprising resemblances that occasionally crop up between Asian art forms and some Amerindian artifacts. But accidental drifting across the Pacific probably made little difference to the way the inhabitants of Mexico and Peru developed their civilizations. About 600, the so-called classical period began in the Mayan region of Guatemala and Mexico; soon thereafter, or perhaps at the same time, Peruvian cultures and the civilization of central Mexico also entered their classical phase. The word *classic* in this connection simply means that, about 600, temples and other monumental works of art attained a scale and excellence of workmanship that surpassed anything that had been done before and was not equaled later. (See Chapter 9.)

Dense populations of farmers built the Mayan temples and sustained a rather bloodthirsty noble class of warriors and rulers. Maize and other crops were grown on swampy ground, made fertile by digging drainage ditches around a little plot, and piling the dug-up soil on top of it. Such fields were like rice paddy fields in reverse: artificially drained instead of being artificially flooded. But the social result was the same. When it took so much work to make fields fertile, the peasants could not run away from taxes. Hence, rulers found it possible to collect food from them to support themselves and all the specialized craftspeople who carved the stone monuments archaeologists have uncovered in the jungle.

But, beginning about 850, Mayan cult centers were abandoned, one after another. No sign of violence suggests conquest. Perhaps some sort of ecological collapse made the swamp plots infertile. At any rate, when Spaniards arrived in the region in the sixteenth century, Mayans lived in simple villages and used slash-and-burn methods for making fields on dry land. They had forgotten the old temples, hidden in the jungle, and had lost all the other specialized skills of their civilized past.

Farther north, in central Mexico, temple centers seem to have been overrun by warrior peoples at about the same time that the Mayan temples were abandoned. New and far more bloodthirsty religious ceremonies were introduced by these conquerors. Human sacrifice, sometimes on a mass scale, became central to temple rituals. In Yucatan a new center arose at Chichen Itza. The temple carvings there show a

mingling of the older Mayan styles with motifs derived from the warrior cults of central Mexico. It looks as though conquerors had come down from the north, overrun some of the Mayans, and set up a new religious center in Yucatan, several hundred miles away from the older Mayan cult centers in Guatemala and nearby parts of southern Mexico.

In South America, also, the classic period was followed by an age of empire. At any rate, this is a good way to interpret the fact that after each separate river valley of the coast had developed its local art style to a peak of refinement, a new and uniform type of art spread throughout the area. This "imperial" art style is associated particularly with Tiahuanaco, a great temple complex situated high in the Andes. Perhaps it was only a new religious cult that spread throughout Peru, but military conquest seems likely.

The civilizations of Mexico and Peru affected neighboring peoples just as the rise of Sumerian civilization touched the lives of people living within range of ancient Mesopotamia. Before 1200, for example, elaborate cult centers were beginning to develop in what is now the southeastern part of the United States. Amerindians of Colombia, in the northernmost part of South America, living between the Mayan and Peruvian area, had also acquired many of the skills of their civilized neighbors. They had, for instance, begun to manufacture fine gold ornaments. We can safely assume that agriculture was spreading through the woodlands of North America and into the southern parts of South America as well. But, as in the Old World, the rain forest was a difficult environment for primitive farmers, so that no noteworthy development seems to have occurred in the vast Amazon basin.

The Amerindians lacked several elementary devices that were of basic importance to Eurasian civilizations. They never used wheeled vehicles, for example, and knew nothing of iron metallurgy. Except for the dog, they also lacked the domestic animals of the Old World—and the llama of the high Andes was a poor substitute for cattle, sheep, horses, camels, donkeys, goats, chickens, and pigs of Eurasia.

Finally, Amerindian civilization got started late in comparison to the civilizations of Asia—about 3500 years late, if we take Sumerian tem-

Mexican Temples   These vast temples illustrate the geographical spread and intermingling of high cultures in Mexico during the so-called postclassical period of Amerindian history (900–1200). Earlier, the main ceremonial centers were located in southern Mexico and Guatemala, where the Mayans who built them, created a system of writing that has been deciphered by modern experts. The temples pictured here, however, come from Teotihuacan in the valley of Central Mexico, far to the north of the Mayans (top), and from Chichen-Itza in Yucatan, far to the southeast (bottom). Yet the general plan of the two structures resembles that of Mayan temples: an elevated high place for worship and sacrifice to the gods. Details of style and construction differ, however. Teotihuacan seems to have been more a rival than an heir of Mayan civilization, whereas Chichen-Itza, although clearly an heir, also inherited art motifs originating in Teotihuacan.

ple communities as roughly equivalent to the Mayan temple centers of the New World. This was a handicap the Amerindians never overcame. By comparison with the developments of Asia and Europe, they remained far behind—weaker and vulnerable to the superior skills, knowledge and disease resistance that Spanish conquerors brought from Europe after 1500.

Conclusion

This survey of the Far Eastern, Pacific, and American parts of the world between about 600 and 1200 reveals the very great contrasts that had developed within this vast region. Primitive hunters and gatherers continued to populate Australia, large portions of America, and the northern parts of Asia. A few regions of southeast Asia also harbored similarly simple peoples. At the other extreme was the rice paddy style of cultivation that remodeled the landscape of China, Japan, Korea, and some parts of southeast Asia and provided the principal economic basis for Chinese civilization and for the related high cultures of surrounding lands.

As compared to the situation in Europe, India, and the Middle East, what stands out about the Far Eastern and Pacific area is the sharpness of the contrast that resulted from such different ways of exploiting the geographical environment. The wealth, skill, cultivation, and learning of China were immense. By any quantitative standard China surpassed the achievements of all other civilizations of the age. Population was greater; cities larger; more goods were exchanged and carried longer distances; more books were printed, read, and discussed; education was better organized and more energetically pursued; more people painted pictures and wrote more poems. In these respects and in many others, China stood preeminent in all the world. The Middle Kingdom was even more overpowering within the circle of the Far East itself, where the achievements of the other great civilizations of the world remained almost unknown. China was like a vast sun, radiating skill, knowledge, and power. Other east Asian peoples were like planets, revolving around the Chinese sun. Beyond their planetary orbits, where Chinese influence was not felt directly, the achievements of the more distant peoples of the Americas and Oceania could not begin to compare with what the Chinese had accomplished.

The sharpness of the contrasts between the civilized and uncivilized regions of the Far East arose from the special nature of rice paddy agriculture. Where that kind of cultivation dug into the landscape, dense populations, intensive agri-

cultural production, and the human basis for high civilization existed. Where paddies were absent, it was simply impossible to approach, much less to achieve, Chinese levels of skill and organization. The best proof of this is the fact that the nomads of Mongolia and Manchuria, although they maintained close relations with the Chinese from 300 B.C.E., if not before, only knew Chinese civilization through the silk and other luxuries sent as tribute. They could not make Chinese artisan skills their own and never even tried to do so.

In the western half of Asia and in Europe, no such sharp boundaries arose. Civilized agriculture was not so intensive. Social skills shaded off more gradually from regions of the highest complexity toward the fringes of the habitable world. In short, in Europe and western Asia the gap between civilization and barbarism was smaller, cultural boundaries were fuzzier, and sharply contrasting ways of life less often existed side by side than in the Far Eastern and Pacific regions, where the geographic limits of civilizations built upon rice paddies were as clear and definite as the dikes that enclosed the rice fields to keep the water from running off.

Bibliography

The Japanese courtier, Lady Murasaki, ranks as one of the greatest writers of the world. The formalities of the court she inhabited and her private feelings are poignantly accessible by reading her masterpiece, *The Tale of Genji* (Arthur Waley, trans., 1935), and Murasaki Shikibu, *Her Diary and Poetic Memoirs* (Richard Bowring, trans., 1982). Donald Keene, ed., *Anthology of Japanese Literature to the Nineteenth Century* (rev. ed., 1978), provides a more general introduction to Japanese writings, and the previously cited Wu-chi Liu and Irving Yucheng Lo, eds., *Sunflower Splendor: Three Thousand Years of Chinese Poetry* (1975), does the same for China.

A good many of the books listed in Chapter 7's bibliography also deal with Chinese civilization in the centuries this chapter discusses. Other books of special interest for this later period are Mark Elvin, *The Pattern of the Chinese Past* (1973), who argues for the extraordinary significance of Sung economic changes; Joseph Needham, *Science and Civilization in China, Vol 7: The Gunpowder Epic* (1987), which examines the origin of gunpowder in China and its spread to

Moslem and Christian lands; and Jacques Gernet, *Daily Life in China on the Eve of the Mongol Invasion, 1250–1276* (1962).

For Japan, G. B. Sansom, *Japan: A Short Cultural History* (rev. ed., 1987), is a lucid and elegant introduction. H. Paul Varley, *Japanese Culture* (3rd ed., 1984), and John W. Hall, *Japan from Prehistory to Modern Times* (1970), give similarly valuable general accounts of Japanese history and culture. A more specialized work is Ivan W. Morris, *The World of the Shining Prince: Court Life in Ancient Japan* (1964), which provides a useful context for anyone studying Lady Murasaki's writings. For the Japanese form of militarism, see William W. Farris, *Heavenly Warriors. The Evolution of Japan's Military, 500–1300* (1992). For Japanese visual art, Robert T. Paine and Alexander Soper, *The Art and Architecture of Japan* (2nd ed., 1960), is a good place to start.

Recent archaeological discoveries combined with breakthroughs in deciphering of Mayan writing make older books on Amerindian civilizations obsolete. A recent collaborative survey, taking the new discoveries into account, may be found in Jesse D. Jennings, ed., *Ancient North America* (1983), and his companion volume, *Ancient South America* (1983). Muriel P. Weaver, *The Aztecs, Mayas and Their Predecessors: The Archaeology of Mesoamerica* (2nd ed., 1981), and Richard E. W. Adams, *Prehistoric Mesoamerica* (1977), deal with the Mexican heartlands. More narrowly focused books worth consulting are Roman Pina Chan, *The Olmec: Mother Culture of Mesoamerica* (1989); Norman Hammond, *Ancient Maya Civilization* (1982); and Richard W. Keatinge, ed., *Peruvian Prehistory* (1988). These works all rely heavily on artistic and archaeological evidence; but the photographs of an art book like S. K. Lothrop, W. E. Foshag, and J. Mahler, *Pre-Columbian Art* (1957), are worth looking at, too.

For proto-civilizations in what is now the United States, see Lynda N. Shaffer, *Native Americans before 1492: The Moundbuilding Centers of the Eastern Woodlands* (1992).

Civilizations; 600 to 1200

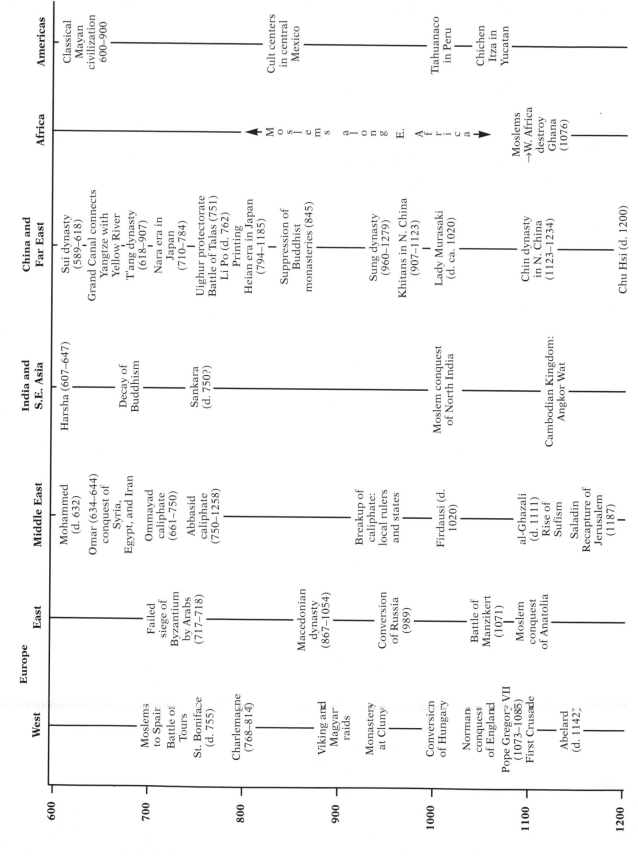

	Europe					
	West	East	Middle East	India and S.E. Asia	China and Far East	Africa	Americas

600

Sui dynasty (589–618) — China and Far East

Classical Mayan civilization 600–900 — Americas

Harsha (607–647) — India and S.E. Asia

Mohammed (d. 632) — Middle East

Moslems to Spain Battle of Tours St. Boniface (d. 755) — West

Grand Canal connects Yangtze with Yellow River — China and Far East

700

Omar (634–644) conquest of Syria, Egypt, and Iran — Middle East

Failed siege of Byzantium by Arabs (717–718) — East

T'ang dynasty (618–907) — China and Far East

Ommayad caliphate (661–750) — Middle East

Nara era in Japan (710–784) — China and Far East

Charlemagne (768–814) — West

Decay of Buddhism — India and S.E. Asia

Abbasid caliphate (750–1258) — Middle East

Uighur protectorate Battle of Talas (751) Li Po (d. 762) Printing Heian era in Japan (794–1185) — China and Far East

Sankara (d. 750?) — India and S.E. Asia

800

Viking and Magyar raids — West

Suppression of Buddhist monasteries (845) — China and Far East

Moslems a l o n g E. A f r i c a — Africa

Macedonian dynasty (867–1054) — East

Monastery at Cluny — West

Cult centers in central Mexico — Americas

900

Breakup of caliphate: local rulers and states — Middle East

Sung dynasty (960–1279) — China and Far East

Conversion of Russia (989) — East

Conversion of Hungary — West

1000

Firdausi (d. 1020) — Middle East

Lady Murasaki (d. ca. 1020) — China and Far East

Khitans in N. China (907–1123) — China and Far East

Moslem conquest of North India — India and S.E. Asia

Tiahuanaco in Peru — Americas

Battle of Manzikert (1071) — East

Norman conquest of England Pope Gregory VII (1073–1085) First Crusade — West

al-Ghazali (d. 1111) Rise of Sufism — Middle East

Moslems →W. Africa destroy Ghana (1076) — Africa

Chichen Itza in Yucatan — Americas

1100

Moslem conquest of Anatolia — East

Chin dynasty in N. China (1123–1234) — China and Far East

Cambodian Kingdom: Angkor Wat — India and S.E. Asia

Abelard (d. 1142) — West

Saladin Recapture of Jerusalem (1187) — Middle East

Chu Hsi (d. 1200) — China and Far East

1200

Europe
500 to 1200

12

Europe's Dark Age   This page from a manuscript
copy of the Bible made in Ireland about 800 shows
how barbarian and Roman traditions blended in
the Christian Dark Ages. The awkward figures
imitate Roman art, the geometric decorations are
barbarian, and together they became something new.

In Greek and Roman times, the civilized life of Europe centered on the Mediterranean; but between 500 and 1000, Europeans learned how to exploit the resources of regions farther north far more effectively than before. As a result, Europe's medieval civilization extended into parts of Europe that had always before been desolate forest and swampy wilderness. To understand how this happened requires a grasp of Europe's geography and of how the natural regions of that continent limited early agriculture.

The Mediterranean zone of Europe is defined by the annual shift of the trade winds, moving north in summer and south in winter. In summer, when the Mediterranean lands fall within the tradewind zone, no rain falls. In winter, when the tradewinds shift southward, the Mediterranean lands come under the influence of the cyclonic storms that move from west to east all round the globe. With these storms come clouds and rain and snow. The limiting factor in such a climate is moisture. Crops must be planted in the fall with the first rains. Grain sprouts in the fall and ripens in the spring after the last rains have fallen. Only deep-rooted plants, like olives and vines, can survive the summer drought by tapping groundwater that runs far below the surface of the soil. The Mediterranean type of climate exists in southern California but nowhere else in the United States.

To the north of a line drawn approximately along the Loire River in the west and just south of Constantinople in the east, the desiccating influence of the tradewinds is never felt. Instead, the zone of prevailing westerlies lasts all through the year, so that rain may fall at any season; and storms occur every few days, more severe in winter and somewhat less frequent in summer. This is the climate that prevails over most of the United States.

Surprising as it may seem, this type of climate was not favorable to early farming. Grain, after all, was a plant naturally adopted to semi-arid conditions like those of the Mediterranean lands. If standing water remains on the surface of the land for any length of time, grain plants drown. This is exactly what happened every spring in the flat plains of northwestern Europe. Especially in March and April, when the rainfall was at its highest point in the year, the flat landscape got thoroughly waterlogged and could therefore not be used for grainfields.

Only hill slopes, especially those with chalk or loess underneath—where drainage was especially good—made suitable fields for Europe's early farmers. Obviously, as long as farming had to be concentrated in these relatively small regions, there was little possibility of establishing a flourishing civilization in northwestern Europe. As a result, all through Roman times and until after 500 most of this region remained forested, with some open areas of pasture for cattle.

Wetness was greatest near the Atlantic. As the storms moved across Europe, from west to east, dropping their rain as they went, precipitation gradually diminished. In addition, the mild winter temperature resulting from the warming of the Atlantic waters by the Gulf Stream—a phenomenon so strong that dwarf palm trees grow in western Scotland—faded out as distance from the Atlantic increased. Eastward of the Elbe River, the oak and beech forests that grew luxuriantly in northwestern Europe gave way to birch and conifers, and sandy soils became more common. This region extended all the way to the Urals, fading off in northern Russia into tundra—a zone where the subsoil remains perpetually frozen and only scrub trees and mosses can grow.

Waterlogged soil was not usually a problem in this eastern forest zone. What limited early farmers there was the shortness of the growing season. Wheat and barley often could not ripen before frosts came to cut them down. Rye, a plant that probably originated as a weed in wheat fields, matured faster and became the staple crop of this region. It produced less grain per acre than wheat—yet required about the same amount of seed. As a result, farmers who raised rye had a smaller margin between what they harvested and what they needed for next year's seed than was usual in regions where wheat and barley could be raised. This, in turn, meant that rye cultivators could support fewer landlords and townspeople.

Civilization, in other words, could not flourish easily on such poor agricultural land. In fact, it did not spread to the northeastern forest zone of Europe until after 900.

Another factor that delayed the development of civilized patterns of life in northeastern

Europe was that the grasslands of the western steppe separated it from the Mediterranean centers of civilization. As we have seen, this landscape came to be occupied by warlike cavalrymen, beginning about 700 B.C.E.; and long before then it had supported nomads who depended on herds of cattle and horses for their livelihood and looked upon farmers as fair game for robbery and plunder. For many centuries, the fact that barbarian nomads separated the northern forests of eastern Europe from the Mediterranean lands hindered the spread of civilization northward.

By 1000 Europeans had worked a fundamental change in the way they farmed. New techniques, suited to the wet conditions of the northwestern parts of Europe, had spread across the formerly waterlogged plain between the Loire and Elbe rivers. As this occurred, the fertility of the soil, the abundance of rainfall, and the ease with which boats could move along the slow-moving rivers of northwestern Europe created conditions for the rapid and spectacular rise of medieval European civilization.

To understand how this happened, we need to look at the political history and migrations of peoples that came to Europe during the first part of the Middle Ages, between 450 and 900. This period is often called the Dark Ages because so little was written during this time. Yet however low the level to which literacy sank (and in that age very few people in western Europe could read or write), and however dangerous life became when one barbarian invader after another swarmed across the country—burning and looting as they went—these same Dark Ages were also a time of fundamental agricultural advance, when northern Europe's farmers laid the basis for the rapid development of western European civilization after 1000.

Barbarian Invasions and Migrations

The German tribes that fled before the Huns (375) to Roman soil were only the first of a long line of invaders who, in the course of the following 600 years, profoundly changed Europe's ethnic patterns. We have already seen how the Visigoths, Ostrogoths, and Vandals set up kingdoms in Spain, Italy, and North Africa, and how Justinian, emperor of Byzantium* (527–565), restored imperial administration in Italy and north Africa.

While these changes were taking place in the Mediterranean parts of western Europe, less spectacular but more important migrations also occurred in the north. Large numbers of German settlers crossed the Rhine into northern Gaul and pushed back the Latin-speaking population to about the line that still divides French and German speakers today. Britain also became English as Angles, from what is now Denmark, and Saxons, from the North Sea coastlands of Germany, started to settle the southern and eastern parts of what we can now begin to call England (that is, Angle-land).

These movements may seem trifling compared to the migrations of the Visigoths and Vandals, who traveled thousands of miles before settling down in their respective kingdoms. But the Anglo-Saxons in England and the Germans in the Rhinelands, who called themselves Franks (that is, the Free), took possession of their new lands in a way the Visigoths, Vandals, and Ostrogoths never did. As conquerors had done innumerable times before, the Visigoths, Vandals, and Ostrogoths set themselves up as landlords and rulers but left the hard work of the fields to the people already on the spot, most of whom spoke Latin or languages derived from Latin. Not so in the north, where the newcomers came in as settlers who cleared the forests and set up their fields in land which, for the most part, had not been cultivated before.

---

*Byzantium is the Greek name for the ancient city that was renamed Constantinople in 330, when Constantine made it his capital. The Turks, after capturing Constantinople in 1453, called it Istanbul. Oddly enough, scholars commonly use the term "Byzantine" for the period from about 527 to 1453, though the rulers called themselves Roman emperors and their subjects (most of whom spoke Greek) called themselves Romans. During all this period the official name of the capital city was Constantinople.

New Techniques of Farming

Obviously, the Franks and Anglo-Saxons knew how to farm land that had before been too wet to produce a crop. Their secret was a new kind of plow, called the moldboard plow to distinguish it from the scratch plow, which had been used by Middle Eastern and Mediterranean farmers from the time when plows were first invented. A scratch plow, as the name implies, simply scratches through the soil, breaking the surface into loose clods. A moldboard plow is more elaborate. In addition to the horizontal plowshare, which goes through the ground just like the share of a scratch plow, there was a colter to cut the soil vertically and an "ear" or moldboard attached on one side of the plow. This moldboard was curved in such a fashion that it turned the soil over in a long furrow as the plow drove through the earth.

In itself this may not seem like an important change. Turning the soil all the way over, instead of just breaking it up, took extra force so that plow teams pulling a moldboard plow had to have four, six, or even eight oxen instead of the pair of animals that sufficed for a scratch plow. The plow itself also had to be much bigger and stronger; it used more metal and was in every way more expensive. To make up for these disadvantages, such a plow could be dragged through heavier soils—that is, soils with more clay in them—than a light scratch plow could penetrate. Many of the soils of northwestern Europe are clayey; so this at once made it possible to cultivate wide areas of low-lying plain that before had been useless for farming.

But there was a second and less obvious advantage to the moldboard plow. The plow turned the furrow to one side only. To plow a field, it was necessary to go first, in one direction and then back again in the opposite direction, throwing the furrow to the opposite side as one did so. If fields were laid out in the same way each year, the effect of such cultivation was to pile the soil in toward the center of each "plowland" and to create shallow trenches between one plowland and the next. This made an efficient drainage system for flat, waterlogged land. Plowlands were laid out to take advantage of whatever natural slope there might be. Furrows all running parallel to one another down even a very slight slope and grouped into raised plowlands—with shallow trenches or "balks" every sixteen yards or so separating one plowland from the next—sufficed to make most of the flat, waterlogged plainlands of western Europe fit for farming.

No one knows when and where the moldboard plow and the Long Acre system of cultivation, as it is called, were first invented. It must have developed some time before 450, when the Frankish and Anglo-Saxon migrations got started. Pioneer German settlers used this kind of cultivation from the time of their arrival on formerly Roman soil. Obviously they brought the moldboard plow with them.

Heavy plows with "ears" may have been known for a considerable time in the flatlands between the Rhine and Elbe rivers. But it was not easy to assemble a plow team to pull such a heavy instrument through the soil. Possibly the most stubborn obstacle to the spread of the moldboard plow was the difficulty of establishing a workable pattern of cooperative tillage. Unless a group of farmers were ready to pool the oxen at their disposal to make up a single plow team, and then could agree on how to divide up rights to the land they had plowed, the heavy plow was not much good. No one family was likely to own the necessary four, six, or eight oxen and such an expensive piece of machinery as a moldboard plow—at least not among the free barbarians of the forests, where social inequality had yet to establish itself.

The way in which this problem was eventually solved seems to have been this: A group of six or more cultivators got together and each contributed an ox to the plow team. At the end of each day's work in the fields, the soil that been made ready for planting on that day was assigned to one of the partners who then had to wait for his *next* piece of land until everybody else had his turn. Eventually a day's plowing was standardized as an acre, 220 yards long and 16 yards wide, which was in fact about what a team could get done by working from dawn to dark. But before any kind of written records were made, which would allow us to understand how moldboard cultivation worked, permanent property rights to particular areas of cultivated land had been assigned to individual families, so that

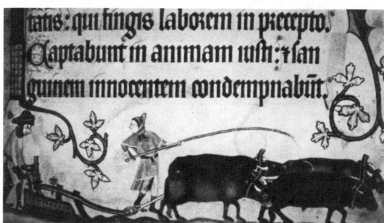

The Plow that Fed Medieval and Modern Europe When plows were first invented, they looked much like the scratch plow (top) shown here. A spade, attached to an animal with a rope, could be dragged through the ground, uprooting weeds and breaking up the soil to receive the grain. This sort of cultivation required cross plowing for maximum effect and squarish field shapes naturally resulted. On the bottom is a painting of the moldboard plow that changed European farming fundamentally between 500 and 1000. Such a plow was larger, heavier, and turned the soil over in a furrow. Being large and clumsy, and hard to turn around it needed long, narrow fields for efficient use. More importantly, the moldboard plow created artificial drainage in waterlogged soil because the furrows were turned over to one side when the plow went one way and to the opposite side as it returned, thus piling the soil into lands that were slightly raised above the balks from which the furrow had been lifted. This allowed medieval farmers to raise grain, naturally adapted to semi-arid climates of the Middle East, even on the flat, waterlogged plains of northwestern Europe.

only traces can be found of the system that may have allowed cooperative tillage to get started.

The whole history of how cooperative tillage started and spread among the West Germans is therefore speculative. Perhaps this kind of cultivation was easiest to establish in a new settlement, where there were no preexisting property rights to land and where the pioneers had to help one another anyway to make a go of their venture. It is not unlikely, therefore, that the moldboard plow and cooperative tillage really got started on a large and significant scale only at the time when the Franks and Anglo-Saxons began to colonize former Roman territory along the Rhine and in Britain. At any rate, the field layouts of these settlements are the earliest known examples of the typical Long Acre field,

which the moldboard plow made necessary because it was so awkward to turn.

The Frankish and Anglo-Saxon Kingdoms

As we might expect, the establishment of a new and productive style of agriculture in northwestern Europe soon resulted in the rise of new and more powerful states. At first, the Franks, as their name implied, were free from obligations to any sort of central authority. They did, however, recognize traditional clan or tribal leaders. Scattered about through their forest clearings, they lacked any sort of common government until the time of Clovis (reigned 481–511). Clovis started life as a petty chieftain of one of the Frankish tribes, but very early in his career he eliminated all rival chieftains among the so-called Salian (that is, "salty," living near the sea) Franks. He then began to use the fighting capability of his comparatively numerous subjects to extend Frankish power in every direction. By the end of his life, the Frankish kingdom extended over almost all of Gaul, and his sons conquered additional territory to the east, in the valleys of the Rhone and upper Rhine.

Frankish power in these conquered regions was like that exercised earlier by Visigoths and Vandals. A thin layer of landowners and military governors represented the Frankish king, but the work of cultivating the soil was performed, as before, by people who as yet knew nothing of the moldboard plow and spoke a language derived from Latin and ancestral to French. But relations between the Frankish ruling class and the "Roman" population were more cordial than in the Visigothic kingdom of Spain. This was because in 496 Clovis accepted the papal form of Christianity and thus ranked as orthodox in the eyes of his new subjects, whereas the Visigoths and Ostrogoths had both accepted what their subjects rejected as a heretical form of the Christian faith, known as Arianism.

Across the channel in England, the Anglo-Saxon settlers did not unite into a single kingdom until after 900, when raiding Danes forced them to do so. Instead, seven small kingdoms divided control over southern and eastern England, and by degrees they pushed the Britons back into Cornwall, Wales, and the highlands of Scotland. Christianity reached England from Ireland, where St. Patrick had established a flourishing church about 432. In 597, however, a missionary from Rome, named St. Augustine (not the famous author of *The City of God*), arrived in Kent and converted the kingdom of the Angles to Christianity. He made Canterbury, the Kentish capital, his headquarters.

Irish Christianity differed from the practices of the Roman church in several respects. Controversy centered around the question of how the date of Easter ought to be calculated. In 664 a meeting of leading representatives of the English churches took place at Whitby, and it was decided that the papal method of setting the date of Easter was correct. This decision led to the withdrawal of Irish missionaries from England and brought the Anglo-Saxons firmly within the circle of Latin Christendom.

Renewed Barbarian Invasions

The rise of the Frankish kingdom on the continent and the conversion of England to Christianity, together with the resurgence of Byzantine power in Mediterranean Europe in Justinian's time (527–565), did nothing to stabilize the situation in eastern Europe. In Justinian's last years, the arrival in Hungary of a new steppe people, the Avars, led to widespread raids climaxing in an unsuccessful siege of Constantinople in 626. Half a century later still another steppe people, the Bulgars, set up headquarters along the lower Danube and added their depredations to those of the Avars.

Balkan farmers could not survive such harassment. Land fell vacant, and the Avars and Bulgars allowed (or sometimes may have driven) Slavic-speaking tribes to move southward from the spruce and pine forests of the north into the richer farmlands of the Balkan Peninsula. The Bulgars, in fact, soon became Slavs themselves by intermarrying with Slavic women and taking the language of their subjects. When Slavic manpower was combined with the Bulgar war band organization, a strong new state came into existence that several times threatened to overwhelm Byzantium.

Arab, Avar, and Bulgar Assaults on Christendom

The Avar and Bulgar attack on Byzantium came at the same time that the Arab Moslems were threatening from the south. As we have seen, the emperors of Constantinople lost Syria, Egypt, and North Africa to the Arabs and had to fight hard to keep command of the sea. After the great siege of 717–718, however, the Moslems, for the time being, ceased trying to rival the Byzantine fleet. Indeed, after 750 the Abbasids were entirely willing to leave the Mediterranean and Black seas to the Byzantines and developed a flourishing trade with Constantinople.

Farther west, the Avars drove the Lombards into Italy, where those rough German barbarians divided control of the countryside with Byzantine garrisons still stationed in important cities. In Frankland, too, a new wave of Germanic invasion took place. Clovis' descendants, known as Merovingians, had divided the old Frankish kingdom into two separate halves: Austrasia in the east, where Germanic-speaking peoples lived, and Neustria (New Lands) in the west and south, where the former subjects of the Roman Empire still spoke a form of Latin. Effective power, however, had shifted from the Merovingian kings to officials known as "mayors of the palace" who conducted the actual tasks of government.

Pepin II of Heristal inherited the post of mayor of the palace in Austrasia from his father. In 687 he led his followers into Neustria and made himself mayor of the palace in that kingdom, too, thus in effect reuniting the two parts of the Frankish state. To secure his power in Neustria, Pepin then granted Neustrian lands to his Austrasian followers. The result was a new Germanic invasion, for the rude Austrasians had little use for the somewhat more civilized Latin-speaking Neustrians.

Then another invasion came from the south, for in 711 Moslems swarmed into Spain from North Africa, crossing at the Strait of Gibraltar. The Visigothic kingdom quickly collapsed, and the Moslems drove northward across the Pyrenees and along the Mediterranean coast of what is now France. This brought them into direct contact with the Frankish state. At first the advantage lay with the Moslems, but in 732 Charles Martel, Pepin's son and successor as Frankish mayor of the palace, met and defeated a Moslem raiding party near Tours. In the border wars that continued thereafter, the Franks usually had the upper hand. The Moslem frontier therefore shrank back southward toward the Ebro River, south of the Pyrenees, where a more nearly stable border defined itself by about 800.

Byzantine Recovery

We have seen how the Byzantine capital survived the Arab siege of 717–718. The emperor, Leo the Isaurian (reigned 717–741), who came to the throne at the moment of crisis, was able to push the Moslems back to the Taurus Mountains in eastern Asia Minor, thus regaining important territories for his empire.

After his victory, Emperor Leo tried to change his religious habits of his subjects by prohibiting the use of images in churches. Perhaps he felt that ignorant people were worshiping statues and paintings of the saints instead of God. But many monks resisted the emperor's effort to alter Christian custom, and the common people objected to having their holy images destroyed. Who besides the emperor supported the destruction of images is not known for sure; perhaps his soldiers attributed Moslem victories to Mohammed's rejection of images and so favored the reform.

In the end, the iconoclasts (as the people who wanted to destroy images were called) failed. Decoration of Christian churches with paintings of the saints became again an important part of Greek Orthodox culture. Statues, however, never really came back to favor, being too much like pagan statues of the gods. The result of the quarrel over images was to restore Christian customs nearly to what they had been before. The monks and the people had prevailed against the emperor and his armies.

The Rise of the Carolingian Monarchy

In the West, however, the iconoclastic controversy provoked fundamental realignments. First of all, the pope in Rome was among those who resisted the Byzantine emperor's efforts to remove images from Christian churches, and Rome was, at least in theory, still part of the Byzantine Empire. The pope felt the need of a new protector. He looked northward where Pepin III, known as Pepin the Short—a grandson of Pepin of Heristal—had succeeded Charles Martel as mayor of the palace. Pepin the Short wished to displace the figurehead Merovingian rulers and become king himself. But overthrowing Clovis' heirs was risky. The upstart Carolingians, as Pepin's family is called, needed papal blessing and support to get away with their usurpation. In return, the pope needed Pepin's military aid in Italy against both Lombards and Byzantines.

The alliance was sealed in 754 when Pope Stephen II traveled north to anoint Pepin as king of the Franks. In return, Pepin marched into Italy and rescued Rome from the Lombards. A second campaign in Italy was necessary before the Lombards, at Pepin's dictation, handed control over a belt of territory in central Italy to the papacy. In this way the "papal states" came into existence. They lasted, with many shifts of boundary, from 756 to 1870.

Charlemagne   The alliance between the Carolingian rulers of Frankland and the popes was of the greatest importance for European history. Under Pepin's son and successor, Charles the Great, or Charlemagne (reigned 768–814), the military strength of the Frankish state and the moral and religious prestige of the papacy worked hand in hand to unify most of western Europe. The geographical base for all later western European civilization emerged for the first time as a result of this collaboration.

On the military side, Charlemagne led his armies nearly every year to fight against some enemy. He annexed the Lombard kingdom of Italy in 774. Later he conquered German tribes and dukedoms that lay to the east of Frankish territory. The Bavarians in the south submitted without too much resistance, but the Saxons in the north proved extremely stubborn foes. No sooner were they defeated in one campaign than they revolted again. Thirty years of fighting were required to break their resistance. Still farther east, in 796 Charlemagne destroyed the Avar power, based in Hungary, and forced a fringe of Slavic tribes and kingdoms to recognize his authority.

On the religious side, Pepin and Charlemagne supported and encouraged Christian efforts to convert those Germans and Slavs who were still pagan. The most successful missionary was St. Boniface (d. 755). Boniface was born in England, where Christianity had made rapid progress. There the stimulus of Irish learning had created a much better educated clergy than survived anywhere in Frankland. St. Boniface and others, therefore, went among the pagan Germans, establishing monasteries, bishoprics, and schools for training priests.

Everywhere they destroyed idols, forbade heathen sacrifice, and tried to persuade the chiefs and warriors of the truth of Christianity. Except among the Saxons, who clung to paganism as part of their struggle against the Franks, resistance to Christianity was small. The prestige of Rome and of the pope, as well as the prestige and military strength of the Franks, backed up the missionary efforts. In addition, German chiefs and rulers could see the usefulness of literacy and law; and only the Church could bring them these advantages, for there was no educated class except the clergy.

The alliance between the Carolingian kings and the pope achieved its final form in Rome on Christmas Day, 800, when Charlemagne crowned himself emperor of the Romans in the pope's presence and with his blessing. The title of emperor had not been used in the West since 476, when Romulus Augustulus had been forced to abdicate and send the badges of supreme office back to Constantinople. The Byzantine rulers, of course, continued to call themselves Roman emperors and at first refused to recognize Charlemagne's new title. Later, however, in return for some territory in the western Balkans, Constantinople recognized Charlemagne's imperial rank.

The First Medieval Knights   Two other changes occurred during the Carolingian Age that were fundamental for later European history. The first of these was the emergence of a new kind of cavalry warrior: the European knight. Knights were protected by helmets, shields, and chain mail to begin with; later plate armor, cunningly fitted to the contours of the body, replaced the leather jerkins covered with overlapping rings of iron that protected the first knights. Armored cavalrymen were nothing new: Byzantine and Persian armies had introduced the big horses needed to carry armored men into battle centuries before. What was new in western Europe after 732 was the way heavy-armored cavalrymen fought. Earlier, their principal weapon

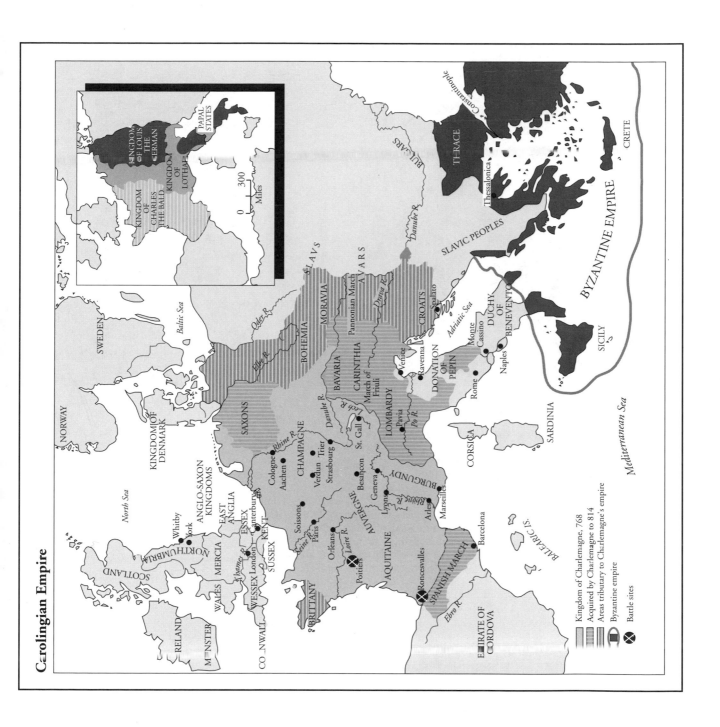

Carolingian Empire

Inset map

PAPAL STATES

KINGDOM OF LOUIS THE GERMAN

KINGDOM OF LOTHAIR

KINGDOM OF CHARLES THE BALD

0   300
Miles

Main map

NORWAY

SWEDEN

Baltic Sea

KINGDOM OF DENMARK

Oder R.

SLAVs

MORAVIA

BOHEMIA

Elbe R.

SAXONS

Rhine R.

Danube R.

AVARS

Pannonian March

CARINTHIA

BAVARIA

Lech R.

Drava R.

Danube R.

Danube R.

BULGARS

SLAVIC PEOPLES

THRACE

Constantinople

BYZANTINE EMPIRE

CRETE

CROATS

Spalato

Adriatic Sea

Venice

Ravenna

March of Friuli

DONATION OF PEPIN

LOMBARDY

Pavia

Po R.

Rome

Monte Cassino

DUCHY OF BENEVENTO

Naples

SICILY

SARDINIA

CORSICA

Mediterranean Sea

BALEARIC IS.

Barcelona

Ebro R.

SPANISH MARCH

Roncesvalles

AQUITAINE

AUVERGNE

Loire R.

Orléans

Poitiers

Paris

Seine R.

Soissons

BRITTANY

CHAMPAGNE

Cologne

Aachen

Verdun   Trier

Strasbourg

Besançon

St. Gall

BURGUNDY

Geneva

Lyons

Rhône R.

Arles

Marseilles

NORTH SEA

North Sea

IRELAND

MUNSTER

SCOTLAND

WALES

CORNWALL

NORTHUMBRIA

Whitby

York

MERCIA

EAST ANGLIA

Thames R.

London

Canterbury

ESSEX

KENT

SUSSEX

WESSEX

ANGLO-SAXON KINGDOMS

EMIRATE OF CORDOVA

Thessalonica

Legend

Kingdom of Charlemagne, 768

Acquired by Charlemagne to 814

Areas tributary to Charlemagne's empire

Byzantine empire

Battle sites

281

Rulers of Heaven and Earth   Medieval Christians believed that God decided
who should rule and who should obey. Memories of Roman imperial unity
were still strong, and most theories held that since one God ruled from Heaven,
a single person ought to rule on earth—or at least throughout the Christian
world. But the Roman Empire had been divided into Latin-speaking western
and Greek-speaking eastern parts since the fourth century. On Christmas day,
800, Charlemagne crowned himself emperor in Rome. Subsequently, the
Roman emperor in the east recognized Charlemagne's imperial title. Thenceforth
there were two Roman emperors again, one in Constantinople, the other in the
Latin-German west. On the left you see a mosaic of Christ, the Universal Ruler,
as portrayed about 1100 on the dome of a church in Daphni, Greece. The
statue on the right comes from the Latin half of Christendom and portrays
Charlemagne, whose imperial crown is surmounted by a cross to indicate
subordination to the Heavenly ruler, Christ.

had been the bow, European knights preferred
the lance. Instead of attacking the foe with arrows at a distance, European knights charged at
a gallop, with heavy lances fixed under their
arms and using stirrups to brace themselves
against the shock of contact. In this way the momentum of horse and man could be put behind
the lance head, producing an immense penetrating power. Nothing could stand against such a

force except another mounted man riding at
equal speed in the opposite direction, in which
case one or both of the charging knights might
be knocked completely out of the saddle. Sometimes the lance shafts shattered instead. This
simple tactic gave charging knights enough
shock power to overwhelm any and all opposition on ground where it was flat enough for
horses to gallop safely. Eventually, infantry tac-

tics were invented that proved capable of checking charging knights. But that took a long time. For about 300 years, therefore, European knights dominated the battlefields of western Europe and exercised social and political as well as military leadership over the whole of western Christendom.

At first, the number of knights that could be maintained in the Carolingian lands remained very small. A knight's warhorse, weapons, and armor were expensive, and it took years of special training to learn to exploit the possibilities of lance warfare to the full. But the need for knights to guard local communities against raiding strangers was very great. The second great invention of Carolingian times, the manorial system of agriculture, eventually solved that problem by providing the means for supporting relatively large numbers of knights. As a result, after about 1000, western Europe ceased to suffer invasion and began instead to expand its frontiers in every direction.

The Manorial System   The second important change that occurred in the Carolingian Age was the growth of the manorial system. A manor was a big farm, cultivated by the inhabitants of a village partly for themselves and partly on behalf of a lord or owner. Exact arrangements differed: Sometimes the lord held part of the land "in demesne." This meant that he owned part of the land personally and had the legal right to require the peasants to cultivate it for him. The peasants lived on what they could produce from what remained. In other cases, the lord got part of what every peasant raised and did not keep any part of the land under his own direct management.

This was nothing particularly new in the parts of the Frankish kingdom that had formerly been Roman territory. In those regions landlords had for centuries divided the produce of the soil with peasants who did the actual tillage. Among the Germans, however, no such inequality prevailed; as a result, during Carolingian times there were only a few manors in purely German lands.

But, as we have seen, the Germans already had the moldboard plow and knew how to cultivate low-lying land. When the German technique of plowing was joined with the Roman system of making peasants work for a lord, the

medieval manorial system came fully into existence. All the elements were present in Carolingian times, but deep resistances had to be overcome before the combination of German and Roman elements could be welded together into a new system of society.

Landlords of the former Roman lands were not always eager to serve as knights, preferring to live an easier kind of life. And German farmers, even more definitely, disliked the thought of submitting to a lord, even if he were a very good knight. Not until 900, when still another round of barbarian invasions had made it clear to all concerned that Europe vitally needed a numerous body of knights—ready at a moment's notice to ride off in any direction to drive invaders away—did these resistances collapse so that a new, enormously successful pattern of European society could finally emerge.

The Magyar and Viking Assaults

Fleeing from a defeat they had suffered on the Russian steppe, Magyar horsemen crossed into Hungary in 895. From this base they soon began to raid western Europe, just as the Huns and Avars had done before them. German foot soldiers could not oppose the mobile Magyar riders effectively. It became painfully obvious that to drive them off the Germanic peoples would have to find ways of maintaining cavalry themselves. Raids from the sea matched these new attacks from the steppe. In the eastern Mediterranean, Arab seapower revived soon after 800. Not long afterward, a new danger appeared, this time from the north. River pirates, coming from Scandinavia, having traveled along the Russian rivers, appeared before Constantinople in 860. The Black Sea, where Byzantine vessels had sailed unhindered, was no longer safe.

The appearance of Scandinavian river pirates before the walls of Constantinople was one extreme wing of a general Viking assault upon civilized Europe. Even in Charlemagne's lifetime, a few Viking ships appeared off the coasts of his domain; but there were easier pickings for these pagan warriors farther west in Ireland and Scotland, where undefended monasteries had accumulated considerable wealth. A few successful raids of this sort encouraged other Scandinavians to build ships and go looking for a fortune too. Hence the number of Viking boats increased rapidly; and since the boats could travel much faster than any opposing land forces, it was easy for them to coast along until they found an undefended place, then go ashore and seize anything that seemed worth taking. The Viking ships had a shallow draft—about three feet—and so could be rowed long distances up the rivers that flowed slowly across the north European plain. Thus a large part of the continent came within their reach. Where the Vikings did not penetrate, the Magyars usually did.

Viking Ship   This ship in a Norwegian museum is an authentic remnant from the Viking age. Vessels like this once sailed from the fjords of Norway and Sweden to raid and trade along the coast of Europe. They were quite seaworthy, being small and light enough to ride atop the waves, and the shallow draft meant that Viking ships could penetrate far inland along the rivers of northern Europe. A dozen or more of such ships, each carrying about fifty fighting men, could raid almost with impunity. Defenders could not concentrate comparable force at short notice as long as they had to walk to battle, since ships moved faster than they could travel on land.

The foot soldiers of the Carolingian army were utterly unable to cope with these new threats. They could not move fast enough. The emperor had to wait weeks on end before his troops assembled; and by the time they were ready, the raiders were gone.

The Peak of Byzantine Power

The Byzantines did better. A new dynasty, the Macedonian, came to power in 867 and remained in control of the Byzantine Empire until 1054. Most of the Macedonian emperors were energetic and capable generals. Basil I, who founded the dynasty, built up the navy and was able to push back Arab and Scandinavian marauders. He and his successors also created a strong army by allowing local magnates to create large households of professional cavalrymen. Of course, the emperor's household was greatest of them all, and when they all joined together, the Byzantine state was able to field a strong army.

The result was rapid territorial expansion. By now the Moslems were divided and politically weak. Hence the Macedonian emperors were able to recover Armenia and other lands to the east. But the most strenuous fighting and the greatest territorial gains came in Europe, where after long wars with the Bulgarians Emperor Basil II (reigned 976–1025), destroyed the Bulgarian state entirely and annexed its territory as far as the Danube. The Byzantines were also able to recover possession of southern and eastern Italy. Never since the days of Justinian had the Eastern Roman Empire extended so far.

Byzantium's reach was reinforced by missionary activity. In 865 the Bulgarians accepted Christianity in its Orthodox form. Long before Basil II destroyed their kingdom, the Bulgarians translated prayer books and other religious books into Slavic. A new literary language, Church Slavonic, thus came into existence. When in due course the Russians also became Christian, they took over their ritual language from the Bulgarians. This happened after 989, when Vladimir, Prince (and later saint), of Kiev, ordered his warriors to throw the old pagan idols into the Dnieper River and accept Christian baptism.

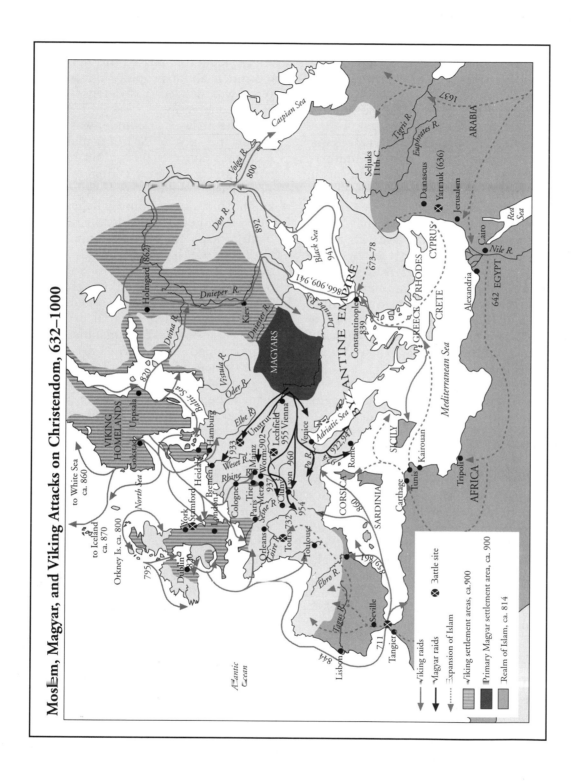

Moslem, Magyar, and Viking Attacks on Christendom, 632–1000

The Russian state, like the Bulgarian, combined Slavic manpower with foreign political organization. In the case of the Bulgarians, the military framework had been provided by steppe nomads. In the Russian case, it was river pirates, moving down from Scandinavia, who created the political umbrella under which the Russian peoples first united.

There is a reason why the Slavs entered history without forming large political units of their own. As we saw, agricultural conditions in the eastern spruce and pine forests, where they lived, were not nearly as favorable as elsewhere in Europe. Rye was the only grain that would grow well, and the yield from rye was much lower than from wheat. Hence, only a poor, thinly scattered population could exist in the eastern forestlands of Europe. Such communities could not support great states or large war federations like those familiar among the steppe peoples, or those possible among the Germans when the spread of the moldboard plow allowed their wealth and numbers to increase.

The Germans, too, had lived as poor and scattered tribes until the moldboard plow came into use. As wealth and population density increased, we have seen how new German war federations—like the Franks (meaning "free men") or the Alemanni (meaning "all men"), for example—took form. Comparable political federations established themselves among the Slavs, not through their own action but as a by-product of conquest or invasion by strangers. This did not mean that the Slavs were any less warlike. It did mean that they had not time and wealth enough to develop large military units of their own before foreign conquerors—the Bulgars and Rus, as the Scandinavian pirates were called—did it for them.

The Decline of the Carolingian Empire

While the Byzantine Empire was responding victoriously to barbarian and Moslem pressures, the Carolingian Empire fell to pieces. Viking and Magyar raids, year after year, met with no effective response from Charlemagne's successors. The western European rulers were helpless. Local authorities and self-made men had to do the best they could to pick up the pieces left behind after raiders had passed through. Nobody cared too much about property rights or formal law. What was needed was defense—local, dependable, and effective.

The answer, of course, was the knight, living on the spot as lord of a manor—ready at a moment's notice to put on his armor, mount his horse, and go off after Viking or Magyar raiders, as the case might be. If every village could have a knight in residence (and villages could flourish close together on the fertile north European plain), then a considerable number of extremely effective fighting men could gather, literally overnight, from a radius of only a few miles to attack dismounted Viking ships' crews with devastating effect. Instead of being nearly a sure thing, raiding then became extremely dangerous. Under these circumstances Viking ships soon stopped coming. The barbarian attack had been turned back, not as in the east by a reinvigorated central government, but by a host of armed men whose roots were local and whose obedience to any theoretical political superior was, to say the least, unpredictable.

Northern France was the center for the development of knighthood and of the manorial system that made it possible to maintain large numbers of knights. In Germany society changed more slowly. After the Carolingians had been thoroughly discredited by their ineffectiveness, a new ruler, Otto I, the Great, claimed the imperial title in 962. He did so after defeating the Magyars in a great battle at Lechfeld in 955. His army was partly composed of old-fashioned foot soldiers like those Charlemagne had commanded. But Otto and his successors also had increasing numbers of knights under their command. They were mostly supported, on the Byzantine pattern, as the rulers' own household followers rather than as lords of manors in the French fashion.

Nevertheless, the spread of knighthood, both in its French and in its German forms, not only turned back the last wave of barbarian attack but soon allowed European knights to take the offensive. As a result, from about 900, western Europeans began to expand their domain in every direction. The conversion of Poland in

Local Self-Protection in Medieval Europe   These two photographs show how medieval Europeans stopped the Viking raids. Fortified places in which to take refuge were part of the answer. The castle shown above is far more elaborate than the first rude fortifications, which were built of earth and wood; but the principle of concentric walled enclosures was the same. A few defenders, safe behind such walls, could hold off superior numbers of raiders long enough for help to come or for the invaders to run out of food and other supplies and have to give up the siege. But medieval Europeans were not content with passive defense; they also invented a very effective form of offense, as illustrated by the scene below from the Bayeux tapestry, woven in Normandy about 1077 to commemorate William the Conqueror's victory over the English at the battle of Hastings in 1066. It shows Norman knights on horseback attacking and defeating King Harold's foot soldiers. Knights like these, residing in villages as lords of the manor, could meet and repulse Viking attack far more efficiently than infantry forces had been able to—and soon did, with the result that raiding ceased after 1000.

966, and of both Hungary and Scandinavia in the year 1000, to the papal form of Christianity showed how attractive the new style of life emerging in western Europe had become.

Costs, of course, were real. Barbarian freedom and equality ceased to distinguish German society from that of more civilized parts of Europe. Moreover, Irish civilization, which had blossomed for a few centuries, had been killed off by the Vikings. The Anglo-Saxons also suffered severely from raiding Northmen. The monas-

teries, in which scholars such as the Venerable Bede (d. 735) had lived, were all destroyed.

The effort of fighting off the Vikings had, however, created a single kingdom of England. Alfred the Great (ruled 871–901) was the hero of this struggle. But when his heirs proved ineffective, the Saxons handed the crown to the Danish king, Canute II (1016). It looked for a while as though England might become part of a Scandinavian empire of the north, of which Scotland, Norway, Ireland, and Denmark would all

Expansion of Latin Christendom, 1100–1300

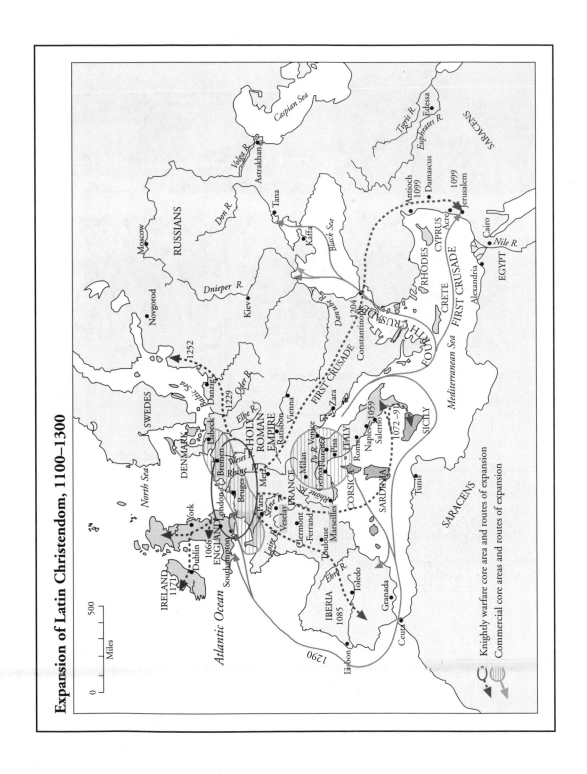

Knightly warfare core area and routes of expansion

Commercial core areas and routes of expansion

be part. But when King Canute died in 1035, the separate parts of his empire-in-the making broke apart again.

The net effect of all the barbarian invasions and Christendom's recovery from each assault was to bring the northern parts of Europe fully into the circle of civilization for the first time. The Russian rivers and Scandinavia as far as the Arctic Circle became active participants in the military, political, commercial, and religious life of Europe. The westernmost portion of the steppe in Hungary had been Christianized too. The center of gravity of the continent for the first time shifted north of the Alps to the fertile plains of northern Europe, where new methods of farming supported a new military class of knights and, before long, also made it possible to feed a growing population of townspeople.

The Rise of Towns and Trade

Until after the year 1000, Byzantium remained by far the biggest and richest city of Christendom. The splendors of the capital on the Bosporus dazzled the crusaders who passed through in 1097 on their way to Jerusalem. Nothing in the West came close to rivaling the seat of the Byzantine emperors. For 500 years, ever since the time of Justinian, the Byzantine state had profited from the geographical advantages of its capital city. The people of the city ran the empire. Trade brought goods from all the coastlands of the Black and Aegean seas to the city wharves. The interiors of the Balkan Peninsula and of Asia Minor were only sometimes controlled by Byzantium; but coastal Italy, especially in the south, was usually under Byzantine control. The empire of Byzantium, in other words, was built around a network of port cities connected with one another by the sea. In this, as in so many other respects, the Byzantine Empire was more the heir of the Greeks than of the Romans.

Under the Macedonian emperors, however, power shifted away from cities by the sea. Great landed estates in the interior of Asia Minor became important military units. Frontier defense

far inland became necessary to hold what Basil II and his predecessors had conquered. Cities and seaborne commerce took second place to the rough military men, who now ruled the empire. Simultaneously, Byzantine trade passed into the hands of upstart Italians. Circulation of money and goods between Constantinople and the provinces weakened as Italian merchants skimmed off the profits from the carrying trade. A period of commercial weakness set in, exactly when the commercial energies of western Europe were rising to new heights.

Mediterranean versus Northern Towns

In the west there was a basic contrast between the Mediterranean zone, where towns had been thickly established in Roman times, and the more northern regions, where Roman towns were few and where, beyond the Rhine and Danube, they did not exist at all. Revival of trade and town activity began in Italy and southern France even before 900. Venice, for example, was founded about 500, when refugees from the mainland fled to a cluster of mudbanks located at the head of the Adriatic Sea. The city became an important trade center after about 800 by distributing salt, produced by saltpans on the Adriatic coast, to the Italian mainland. Then, in 1082 the Venetian Republic won special trading rights in Byzantine ports and soon captured a large part of Byzantine trade. The Venetians also helped the First Crusade and got special privileges in all the cities the crusaders captured. Soon the only rivals that the Venetians had to fear in the eastern Mediterranean were other Italian cities, chief among them Genoa, located on the western side of the peninsula.

The climax of Italian commercial dominance over the Byzantine lands came in 1204. Knights who set out from Venice to go to the Holy Land on a Fourth Crusade stopped off at Constantinople and, after quarreling with the Byzantine emperor, besieged and captured his capital. A Latin empire was then established in which the Venetians—who had been the financial and diplomatic wirepullers behind the whole assault on Constantinople—enjoyed an even more privileged position than before.

The crusading idea was widely discredited by this attack on fellow Christians. Many efforts to revive the ideal were made, but none of them met with much success. The commercial spirit, so clearly expressed by the Venetians and other Italian trading cities, did not fit well with the crusaders' naive, aggressive faith.

North of the Alps, in Germanic territory, towns were mostly new foundations. Even when the Romans had built a town at a place that later became important—London or Paris, for example—urban society almost disappeared during the Dark Ages. Yet even in the Viking age, trade continued. The raiders never found just the booty they needed, and so they had to exchange their plunder for swords and sails, or for the raw material to make them. Typically, a ship's company started out in the spring—ready for either raiding or trading, depending on what they met. When raiding became unsafe, because there were too many knights scattered about the landscape, even the most bloodthirsty pirates had to settle for trading.

Before long, ships' companies found it expedient to settle down at a convenient place and set up a permanent headquarters. Often they clustered near a fortress, controlled by a bishop or some other lord. The relations between the merchants and the lord were usually cool. The merchants, with their hangers-on, were accustomed to defending themselves and did not wish to be treated like peasants or made to pay tributes or perform labor services. But the local lord did not like to have other people running their own affairs in a place that belonged to him.

Compromise was possible, though, if the trading community would agree to pay a lump sum to the lord in return for the right to be left alone. As trade and artisan production increased in volume, the sums a lord could acquire from a flourishing town became quite large. By 1200, when they saw how profitable such a town could be for them, local lords even began to found new towns, offering generous "liberties" to merchants and artisans who would settle there.

In the Mediterranean zone, towns also had some difficulty fitting themselves into the political pattern of the countryside. Often the townspeople admitted or invited local noble landowners to come into the city and become citizens. This, after all, was the ancient, classical pattern. But merchants and artisans maintained a more important place in town affairs than such groups had ever had in ancient times. They organized guilds for each particular trade or business, to protect their interests. Town politics therefore became a struggle for power among rival guilds and a struggle conducted by all the guilds against nearby territorial lords.

The Decay of Serfdom

Peasants soon began to benefit from the rise of towns. From late Roman times, peasants had been legally enserfed, that is, fixed to the land, so that a peasant could not leave the place where he or she was born without breaking the law. Towns, however, welcomed newcomers from wherever they came. No questions were asked; and serf owners had to accept the rule, "town air makes free." This was generally interpreted to mean that if a runaway lived for a year and a day without being challenged, he or she could stay forever. Serfs sometimes did run away, and those who stayed behind soon found themselves in a good position to improve their status. They could buy freedom from traditional services owned to the lord, since they could now earn money by selling foodstuffs in town. They could also demand better treatment, and the lord might think it well to agree, lest he lose his labor force.

By 1200, as a result, in the parts of Europe where town life had developed most strongly—in northern France and the Rhinelands, southeastern England and northern Italy—most peasants were free, in the sense that they did not owe compulsory services to their lord. The economic level of life in the countryside had quite perceptibly improved. Towns prospered by supplying ordinary peasants with such things as iron tools, smoked herring, and coarse wool cloth, as well as by selling luxuries to nobles and other wealthy persons. Lords prospered on rents and tolls charged on trade. Peasants prospered from selling extra foodstuffs and raw material to the towns. In short, northwestern Europe entered upon a boom period that reached a peak between 1200 and 1300. Military expansion across every frontier was matched by rapid economic expansion. New fields were cleared until forest land became scant. Trade intensified; population grew, and skills improved as western Europe caught up with the more anciently civilized lands of the Middle East.

Structure of Medieval Towns

Medieval town life organized in this way differed fundamentally from the town life of Greek and Roman times. In early Greece and Rome, citizens had been farmers. Traders and artisans were marginal people who had been squeezed off the land and had to make a living somehow. In later classical times, citizen rights in towns of the Roman Empire were nearly always limited to landowners whose income depended on rents paid by those who tilled the fields. But in northern Europe, knightly landlords remained modestly in the country.

The commercial and artisan classes of western Europe that began to flourish shortly before 1000 were used to defending themselves and made alliances and fought wars more or less at their own discretion. The local lord was a natural enemy. A distant lord, especially when he was a king or some other kind of superior to the local lord, was a natural ally. And if the townspeople became powerful enough to defend themselves against all comers, then complete independence could be, and often was, attained.

No other part of the world (except Japan) gave birth to a merchant and artisan class like this. Among other civilized peoples, merchants and artisans knew their place, they catered to the tastes and submitted to the control of their social betters, which meant soldiers, officials, and landlords. Self-government and aggressive self-assertion were not part of the merchants' stock-in-trade anywhere except in Europe and, a little later, also in Japan. The whole character and growth pattern of western European civi-

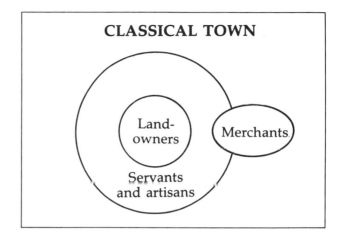

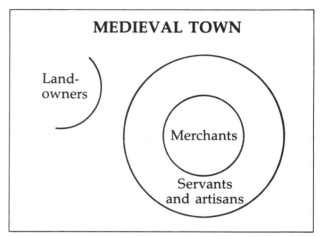

Town and Country in Ancient and Medieval Europe   These two diagrams point out a fundamental difference between ancient and medieval European society. In ancient times, the ideal citizen was a landowner, and merchants and artisans occupied a humbler, dependent place. In medieval and early modern times in Europe, however, towns were established initially by merchants, who attended to their own defense. They looked on local landowners as rivals and often as enemies, to be kept at arms' length. The self-confidence and even aggressiveness of European bourgeois classes made them different from merchants in other civilizations, who (except in Japan) remained subordinate to landowning classes.

lization depended on this fact. For towns became the primary seat of civilized activity in Europe, as they were elsewhere. The habits and expectations of the townspeople therefore played a particularly important part in defining the spirit of all later European civilization.

Church and State

The importance of towns in medieval Europe after about 1000 showed up at once in politics. The comparative simplicity of the Carolingian Age was gone. Instead of one great empire, cooperating with the Church to extend and defend Christendom, western Europe divided up into an extremely large number of more or less independent political units.

In theory, imperial unity lingered on. In 1000, Otto III of Germany prided himself on his imperial title, but his actual power was very limited. Charlemagne's empire had been divided among three grandsons in 843. Separate kingdoms of France and of Germany emerged from this division; and the middle zone, containing Italy and the Rhinelands, became a bone of contention between Germany and France—a bone of contention that remained critical as recently as World War I. When the pope conferred the imperial title Holy Roman Emperor on the German king, the rulers of France never admitted his superiority. The kings of England, Scotland, Denmark, Norway, Sweden, Poland, and Hungary also asserted independence (although some of them at times entered into special relations with the German emperor and admitted his claim to be supreme ruler of Christendom—or at least of its western half).

The papacy also claimed to have superior authority over all bishops, monasteries, and other church establishments. But the papacy was as unable as the emperor to enforce its claims to universal power.

Feudalism

In theory, Europe was organized according to the feudal system. This meant that every nobleman had a lord to whom he owed certain duties and from whom he received a fief in return. A fief was any kind of income-producing property, usually, of course, land. According to legal theory, God granted sovereign power to his chosen agent, the king. The king in turn granted large fiefs to his principal men, or vassals. They granted smaller fiefs to their subvassals, and their subvassals might in turn grant still smaller fiefs to sub-subvassals. At the bottom of the system was the single knight, lord of a manor whose peasants had to work for him, while he was supposed to protect them and serve his lord in battle or in council when called upon to do so.

At each level of the feudal system, duties and obligations bound superior and inferior one to another. A formal oath of homage sealed the contract between lord and vassal. The vassal who had taken an oath of homage to his lord was then honor-bound to come when called, bringing his fighting men with him. If a vassal failed to fulfill his duties, he could be judged guilty by his peers, that is, by his fellow vassals at the lord's court, and they would take steps to punish him. If a lord violated his duties, the vassals could band together to resist him. Everywhere, political relations were looked upon as contracts willingly entered into by men of honor and of war.

In practice things were never so tidy. First of all, a single knight might find himself the vassal of more than one lord; and if the two lords should quarrel, he could not obey them both. Moreover, many lords refused to obey the king. Indeed, in the year 1000, the king of France was only one of a dozen equally powerful men in the kingdom of France. His claims to sovereignty over such a mighty vassal as the duke of Normandy, for example, were entirely empty. Sometimes counts and dukes could not control their vassals either, in which case effective public administration broke up into very small units indeed.

Rise of Papal Power   In this confusion, towns fitted awkwardly. So did the Church. In all parts of Europe, the Church owned considerable amounts of land. Bishops and abbots controlled most of it; but unlike other great vassals, they could not pass their lands on to their sons, for the clergy did not marry. From the point of view of the German emperor, therefore, the most important power he had was to appoint most of the bishops and many of the abbots of his kingdom. He could put his own men in such posts and could count on their aid in his struggles with other lords, whose positions were hereditary. In France the king had no such power. Appointment to the key offices of the Church had fallen for the most part into the hands of counts and dukes.

According to the law of the Church, bishops were supposed to be chosen by the people and the clergy of their dioceses, not by a king or secular lord. Abbots were supposed to be chosen by the monks of the monastery. The Church, in short, was supposed to be independent of secular government. But these rules were seldom followed. Ever since Constantine had made Christianity an official religion, the emperor of Byzantium had claimed extensive powers over the Church. Charlemagne, too, had taken his right to appoint a new pope more or less for granted. On the other hand, Pope Stephen presided at his coronation in 800, and so it became possible to claim that the imperial power was a gift of God conferred on the emperor by the pope.

Such problems became acute after 1054, because a vigorous reform movement won control of the papacy. The reform began in 910, when the duke of Aquitaine founded a new monastery at Cluny. Cluny quickly became a center of piety and learning; and soon daughter monasteries, established by monks from Cluny, spread widely through Latin Christendom. The principle upon which the Cluniac monasteries insisted, above all else, was complete independence from control by lay rulers. To help protect each separate monastery, new ones remained in close association with the monastery of Cluny. Soon the monks began to claim that the rest of the Church should have the same independence from outside interference. In particular, they felt, the appointment of the pope should no longer depend on the whim of a few powerful Roman families.

In 1054 Cluniac reformers captured the papacy. Five years later the proper way to choose a pope was spelled out by listing the clergymen of Rome who had the right to elect the next pope. These were the cardinals, and each pope had the right to appoint new cardinals to keep the electorate at a proper size. Since the pope was bishop of Rome, each cardinal had to have charge of a parish in Rome—a custom that continues to this day whenever a new cardinal is appointed.

Struggles Between Empire and Papacy

At first the emperor (Henry IV at the time) sympathized with the Cluniac reformers. But the cardinals interpreted their power to mean that they ought to elect a pope without consulting the emperor, and this provoked quarrels. When a simple peasant's son, the monk Hildebrand, became Pope Gregory VII in 1073, dispute flared up fiercely. Gregory demanded that the German bishops should be chosen, as he had been, without lay interference.

Pope Gregory's reform required Emperor Henry IV to confront the prospect of seeing the strongest support of his government crumble away. He denounced Gregory; Gregory denounced him. After excommunicating Henry (1076), Gregory made an alliance with Norman adventurers in southern Italy and with towns in northern Italy that resented the efforts that the imperial government was making to bring them under control. Gregory also allied himself with the nobles of Germany who feared the emperor's power.

In 1077 Emperor Henry IV found himself so weakened by the foes the papacy had raised against him that he had to come to Canossa, in northern Italy, and there submit to all of Pope Gregory's demands. But when Henry's German opponents elected another "king" to oppose him, Henry attacked them and was again excommunicated (1080). He then marched on Rome and imprisoned the pope in Castle Sant'Angelo. Pope Gregory's Norman allies rescued him, but they sacked Rome so thoroughly that Gregory dared not return to the city. He therefore died—an exile from Rome—with the struggle undecided.

A compromise was reached between the papal and the imperial claims in 1122. According to this agreement, if a bishop were properly

Pope Gregory VII on the Scope of Papal Authority

The following document was filed with the private correspondence of Pope Gregory VII (1073–1085). It is probably an index to a compilation of quotations from Church Fathers and Canon Law defining the powers of the papacy that Gregory made before he became pope. When Pope Gregory set out to act on the claims set forth in this document, he provoked a controversy that convulsed Latin Christendom, for no pope had formerly exercised most of the powers set forth below.

The Dictate of the Pope

That the Roman church was founded by God alone.

That the Roman pontiff alone can with right be called universal.

That he alone can depose or reinstate bishops.

That, in a council, his legate, even if a lower grade, is above all bishops, and can pass sentence of deposition against them.

That the pope may depose the absent.

That, among other things, we ought not to remain in the same house with those excommunicated by him.

That for him alone it is lawful, according to the needs of the time, to make new laws, to assemble together new congregations, to make an abbey of a canonry; and, on the other hand, to divide a rich bishopric and unite poor ones.

That he alone may use the imperial insignia.

That of the pope alone all princes shall kiss the feet.

That his name alone shall be spoken in churches. . . .

That it may be permitted to him to depose emperors. . . .

That he himself may be judged by no one.

That no one shall dare to condemn one who appeals to the apostolic chair.

That to the latter shall be referred the more important cases of every church.

That the Roman church has never erred; not will it err to all eternity, the Scripture bearing witness.

That the Roman pontiff, if he have been canonically ordained, is undoubtedly made a saint. . . .

That he who is not at peace with the Roman church shall not be considered catholic.

That he may absolve subjects from their fealty to wicked men.

Reproduced from E. F. Henderson, ed., *Select Historical Documents of the Middle Ages.* London: George Bell and Sons, 1905.

chosen by the clergy of his diocese and approved by the people, then the emperor might give him power over the lands assigned to the bishopric (the so-called regalia) in a separate ceremony. But it proved impossible to make this plan work. Further struggles ended only when the imperial power north of the Alps had been utterly destroyed. Germany came to be divided into a

The Church in Town and Country As effective local defense created conditions for rapid growth of Europe's agricultural wealth, Christian piety and local pride found expression in large and impressive churches, like the two pictured here. At the top is the Church of St. Ambrose in Milan. It is an early example of Romanesque architecture, having been completed by about 900. The townspeople of Milan assembled here for Sunday worship, and since Milan was protected by city walls, the church itself did not need to be fortified. In the open countryside, however, monasteries, like the one pictured below, had both to provide monks with a place to worship and also be able to protect them from hostile attack. Hence the fortress-like design of this abbey in southern France, built soon after 1100.

large number of princely states and city-states, some of them ruled by bishops or abbots. The imperial title remained nominally in existence until 1254, but after 1197 the emperor had no real power in Germany.

Church Reform in France and England
Papal efforts at Church reform in France and England had no such disruptive effects. Reform in France mainly meant taking control over the appointment of bishops and abbots out of the hands of the great feudal lords, who were not usually obedient to the French king. The king was glad enough to see this change occur, and

the papacy was glad to have royal help in carrying through the reform.

In England the situation was still different. There, in 1066, William the Conqueror, duke of Normandy, made good a very dubious claim to the English throne by invading with a force of about 5000 knights. He distributed the land of England among his principal followers. William and his successors kept a tight control over the kingdom. Because of this, from 1066 onward England was a far more united kingdom than France or Germany.

With royal control of the nobles of England as secure as it was under the first Norman kings, control over Church appointments could be lodged in the hands of the Archbishop of Canterbury without in the least endangering royal power. Hence, so long as the archbishop checked with the king on all important matters before taking action, the Norman kings found it fairly easy to get along with the reform movement that was running so strongly in the Church.

The strength of that movement and the enhanced authority it brought to the papacy were influenced directly by the growth of towns. Townsmen served in various capacities in the Church. A man of ability could rise through the Church all the way to the top, as the career of Hildebrand (Pope Gregory VII) showed. Restless and ambitious men of lowly birth therefore found a career in the Church particularly attractive.

Such men systematized and extended Church law on the principle that anything affecting a sacrament—baptism, confirmation, marriage, ordination, mass, confession, extreme unction—came within the scope of Church courts. They organized the collection of Church revenues. They preached to and fed the poor. They taught law and theology to aspiring clergy. They built cathedrals, developed Church music, put on plays, and wrote histories. They constituted, in short, an active and adventurous segment of society—and completely dominated medieval artistic, literary, and intellectual culture.

Lagging Development of Eastern Europe
Farther east in Europe, the new life and energy pouring into the Church—and to a lesser degree into civil governments and other secular activities—did not show itself so strongly. Moldboard plow agriculture did not extend much beyond the frontier of German settlement. This meant that the countryside was less productive so that town life failed to develop as rapidly as in the western parts of Europe. In 1054 the last powerful ruler of Kiev died, and the Russian state broke up into a dozen or so smaller principalities. When a new wave of Turkish-speaking steppe invaders came from the east, the Russian princes were not able to drive them back or to convert them to Christianity. Instead, the newcomers became Moslem and so cut Russia off from easy communication with Byzantium.

Byzantium also fell on hard times. Seljuk Turks filtered into Asia Minor and, after the Battle of Manzikert (1071), pushed the Byzantine frontier back nearly to Constantinople. At almost the same time, a small company of freelance adventurers from Normandy seized control of the Byzantine portions of Italy, founding the Norman kingdom of Italy and Sicily that played such a key role in the struggle between pope and emperor. In 1054, also, a final quarrel between the patriarch of Constantinople and the pope led to a lasting estrangement between the Greek Orthodox and the Roman Catholic churches. Bad feeling was not reduced when Italian traders took over most of the Byzantine trade or when crusading knights captured Constantinople in 1204.

Inland in the Balkan Peninsula, an independent Serbia and a second Bulgarian Empire came into existence on the territory Emperor Basil II had once controlled. Only fragments of the Byzantine Empire remained. Thus the relationship between eastern and western Europe had been startlingly reversed. By 1200 the once backward and barbarous Latin West had become richer, stronger, and infinitely more venturesome in art and thought, as well as in war and trade, than the Greek East.

Cultural Life

In Europe's Dark Ages, Byzantium preserved far greater knowledge of ancient learning than did the Latin West. Byzantine scholars never entirely forgot pagan Greek writings. Roman law continued to live in Byzantium when it had been forgotten to the West. And early Christian literature counted for even more among the Byzantines. Anything they were able to make anew for themselves seemed poor and weak by comparison.

In art, however, the Byzantines were remarkably creative. In Justinian's day a great new church, St. Sophia, was erected in Constantinople. It embodied new principles of construction which made it possible to build a great central dome over a square space in the middle of the church. This type of construction may have been borrowed from the Persians or Armenians, but the Byzantines brought it to mature perfection. Mosaics, composed of many small fragments of stone or glass, sometimes coated with a thin layer of gold, shimmered on the walls. So successful was St. Sophia that, ever since, most Byzantine and other Orthodox churches have been modeled after it. No art style has had a stronger or more distinguished history.

The Dark Age and the Revival of Learning in the Latin West

At the time when Justinian's architects were building his famous church, the West was poverty-stricken and ignorant. Monasteries dotted the landscape, and in some of them monks spent part of their time reading books or teaching boys to read. In Ireland and England a higher level of knowledge and literacy existed; but on the continent, even in Italy itself, the Dark Age was very dark indeed. In Charlemagne's time a few scholars and teachers gathered at his court, many of them coming over from England. They made one very important change in European learning by introducing a tidier way of shaping letters. Our familiar small letters descend directly from the "Carolingian minuscule," as this style of handwriting is called.

After the breakup of the Carolingian Empire, learning once more fell upon hard times. Then the reform of the Church, beginning with the establishment of Cluny in 910 and reaching full force 150 years later, promoted scholarly and literary revival all over western Europe. Bishops developed schools to train clergymen; from these the medieval universities evolved after about 1150.

The universities of southern Europe formed around schools of law or, in some cases, of medicine. The University of Paris, which became the model for universities in northern Europe, formed around schools of theology. Law and theology remained overwhelmingly important for the Church. Church law was based on decisions at councils, on writings of the Church Fathers, and on the Bible. Papal decisions and decrees also added to it. It never became a closed system like the Sacred Law of Islam. Things changed

too fast. New problems continued to appear. And the bases of Church law were too complex and full of contradiction to allow anyone to create a single code that could harden into permanent form, as had happened among the Moslems.

Interest in Church law soon led to the discovery of the Roman law, which had remained continuously alive in Byzantium. Study of Justinian's Code offered a way of strengthening civil government. It made relations among strangers more predictable and flexible, easing transfer of property and defining all sorts of contract rights more clearly than the different kinds of local customary law could ever do. Roman law therefore found vigorous application within the Church and at every level of secular government, from the emperor downward.

Theological learning took on new life when men began to ask what some of the old books, which had been handed down in monastic libraries from ancient times, really meant. One famous teacher, Abelard (d. 1142), systematically listed the many points on which established authorities disagreed. He called his book *Sic et Non*—"Yes and No."

How could men solve such questions? The answer Abelard and others gave was to use human reason. Some 1800 years earlier, the Ionian philosophers of Greece had arrived at the same answer when they saw how traditional stories about the power of the gods contradicted one another. Shortly before 1200, keen-minded men in and around Paris, having come to the same conclusion, were therefore eager and ready to welcome Greek philosophy, which opened to them the answers pagan thinking had arrived at centuries before.

But to be useful to them, pagan science and philosophy had to be translated from Arabic or Greek into Latin. When scholars of the Latin West became aware of what treasures of ancient knowledge the Greeks and Arabs had preserved they therefore organized systematic translation centers in Spain and Italy. As a result, the Latin-speaking world soon had at its disposal almost all of the science, philosophy, and miscellaneous learning of the ancients that the Arabs and the Greeks could pass on to them. The recovery of this store of learning set the stage for the monumental task of thirteenth-century Scholastic philosophy—the reconciliation of pagan thought with Christian theology in such a way as not to sacrifice either human reason or Christian faith.

Art and Architecture

In art, western Europe proved equally creative. The best Charlemagne could do when he wanted to build a fine church was to imitate the Byzantine style on a much reduced scale. Viking and Magyar raiders soon compelled western Europeans to learn how to build with stone. By 1000, therefore, Europe was studded with stone castles. Towns, too, needed and got stout stone walls for their protection. Then as wealth increased, men were able to use their skills in stonemasonry to build monumental churches. The earliest of them were built in a style called Romanesque. It is distinguished by the use of round arches. Walls were mostly of solid masonry and, as a consequence, the interiors were dark.

About 1150 a new "Gothic" style of architecture was invented. By using pointed arches and ribs, it became possible to concentrate the weight of the roof on stone piers that could then support the whole structure. This allowed spaces between the piers to become great windows, and when the windows were filled with colored glass, a new and even more glowing sort of mosaic decoration became possible. Stained-glass windows, together with the lofty roofs and slender curved ribbing, made the interior of a Gothic church equal to anything the Byzantines had achieved. Sculptural decoration over church doors and on the outside of the edifice added another dimension to the Gothic structures, whereas, after the iconoclastic controversy, the Byzantines stayed away from sculpture as being too close to idolatry.

Conclusion

The long succession of barbarian invasions that brought Germans and Slavs into territory formerly part of the Roman Empire had the result of equalizing conditions between Mediterranean Europe and the northern forest regions in both eastern and western Europe. The gap that once existed between Roman civilization and barbarian backwardness was reduced, both by lowering the level of culture within Roman boundaries (the Dark Ages) and by Christian missionaries who established the first glimmerings of literate culture among the Slavs and Germans of the north. In this fashion, a boundary that had always before limited the northern range of civilized life in Europe was broken through. Consequently, by the year 1000, the groundwork for the rise of northern and especially of northwestern European civilization had been laid.

These same Dark Ages also saw the establishment and spread of a new type of agriculture built around the moldboard plow, which was well suited to the wet conditions of the north European plain. In addition, by 1000 Europeans established a new pattern for rural society—the manorial system—which allowed European peasants to make effective use of the new type of plow. Thus, the agricultural basis for western Europe's very rapid development in the following centuries was well and truly laid during the first turbulent centuries of the medieval period.

Finally, from 732 onward, European fighting men developed a knightly style of warfare that made both horse and rider into a single missile. Knights' violent shock tactics made defense of western Europe secure as soon as means were found to support enough of them. The manorial system served this purpose admirably by concentrating the rents from each village in the hands of a resident knight, whose function was to protect the community from raiding strangers.

As soon as these elements had been brought together, western Europe became too dangerous for barbarians to attack successfully Raiding stopped and was replaced by trade. Towns sprang into existence. In northern Europe they began as temporary settlements around some strong place where ship's crews—part traders, part pirates—spent the winter season. From such beginnings, self-governing and self-assertive town corporations speedily developed, ready to defend themselves against all comers and capable of effective self-government.

After about 900, the new forms of wealth that agricultural progress and the rise of trade and towns brought to western Europe allowed the development of more stable and effective government. The papacy was the first to take advantage of the new possibilities. Beginning in 1054, a series of reforming popes created a regularly administered Church government that extended all across western Europe and imparted a new level of religious and legal cohesion to Latin Christendom. Within the framework of the Church a new artistic and intellectual life also began to flourish, rising toward a peak of energy and perfection by 1200, when what is often called the High Middle Ages may be said to have started.

Eastern Europe failed to share in these developments. The moldboard plow did not exist there; manorial arrangements were uncommon; knighthood failed to take root. Until 1200, however, Byzantium remained by far the biggest city of Europe and it was, by most standards, still the seat of a more sophisticated civilization than anything known in the Latin West. Yet Byzantium's great days were already past, whereas the flowering of western European civilization was only beginning.

Nothing in the history of Europe itself really justifies breaking off our story at this point in time. Only when one considers the state of the entire civilized world does the date 1200 have much significance, for it represents the horizon at which the Mongol Empire, uniting China, most of the Middle East, and eastern Europe into a single vast state, burst upon the world's scene, starting a new round of interaction between China and the rest of Eurasia.

It seems best, therefore, to break off the story of Europe's development at this point to pay some attention to the remarkable career of the Mongol conquerors and the consequences of their extraordinary victories for world history.

Bibliography

Notable works of literature from this age of European history include two epic poems: *The Song of Roland*, which tells of how one of Charlemagne's warriors fought a suicidal rear guard action against the Saracens of Spain; and *Beowulf*, which tells of a no less suicidal struggle with a monster named Grendel. Both are available in several translations. A sampling of shorter medieval texts is conveniently assembled in J. B. Ross and M. M. McLaughlin, *The Portable Medieval Reader* (1949).

General accounts of special distinction include Robert Lopez, *The Birth of Europe* (1966); R. W. Southern, *The Making of the Middle Ages* (1992); Christopher Dawson, *The Making of Europe* (1932); and Judith Herrin, *The Formation of Christendom* (1989). For treatment of varying parts of the whole, the following are particularly incisive: Edward James, *The Franks* (1991); Dimitri Obelensky, *The Byzantine Commonwealth* (1971); R. W. Southern, *Western Society and the Church in the Middle Ages* (1970); Myles Dillon and Nora K. Chadwick, *The Celtic Realms* (1967); P. H. Sawyer, *Kings and Vikings: Scandinavia and Europe A.D. 700–1100* (1982); and George Vernadsky, *Kievan Russia* (1948).

On the material conditions of everyday life, George Duby, *Rural Economy and Country Life in the Medieval West* (1990); B. H. Slicher van Bath, *The Agrarian History of Western Europe A.D. 500–1850* (1966); C. S. and C. S. Orwin, *The Open Fields* (1938); and Eileen Power, *Medieval People* (1963), are particularly informative. On advances in maritime affairs, Archibald Lewis and Timothy J. Runyan, *European Naval and Maritime History, 300–1500* (1985), is recent and authoritative. On knighthood and the rise of cavalry warfare, Lynn White, *Medieval Technology and Social Change* (1980), and R. E. Smail, *Crusading Warfare 1097–1193* (1956), are no less authoritative.

Two recent books sketch the Frankish heartland of Latin Christendom: Patrick J. Geary, *Before France and Germany: The Creation and Transformation of the Merovingian World* (1988); and Donald A. Bullough, *The Age of Charlemagne* (2nd ed., 1973). For the Crusades, Steven Runciman, *A History of the Crusades* (3 vols., 1951–54), and Donald E. Queller, *The Fourth Crusade: The Conquest of Constantinople, 1201–1204* (1977), are good places to start. On the church, Geoffrey Barraclough, *The Medieval Papacy* (1979); Rosalind B. Brooke and Christopher Brooke, *Popular Religion in the Middle Ages* (1984); Walter Ullmann, *The Growth of Papal Government in the Middle Ages: A Study in the Ideological Relation of Clerical to Lay Power* (3rd ed., 1970); and David Knowles and Dimitri Obolensky, *The Middle Ages* (1968), are helpful.

Works of art, as always, reflected the age. Marilyn Stokstad, *Medieval Art* (1986), and David Talbot Rice, *Art of the Byzantine Era* (1963), more or less cover the ground between them. On a more specialized note, F. Henry, *Irish Art in the Early Christian Period to 800* (1965), illustrates for us a monastic culture that after flourishing remarkably for a few centuries was snuffed out by Viking raids.

Diseases and Their Effects on Human Societies

Disease has played a very big part in human history. In all modern wars, more soldiers died of disease than from enemy action until World War II. Whole societies have sometimes been destroyed by epidemics. Unfamiliar diseases prevented successful European settlement in many tropical lands. Elsewhere European diseases, spreading like wildfire among local peoples, often cleared the way for settlers.

This essay explores the way people and diseases have altered their relationships across the ages. Lack of exact information means that we have to guess details; but there are some general principles—for example, the difference between endemic and epidemic disease—that go far to explain what happened.

THE CASE OF THE VANISHING AMERICAN: 1519–1650

When Cortes invaded Mexico, the inhabitants of Montezuma's empire numbered 11 to 25 million persons. They lived close together in villages wherever good land for cornfields existed. They had never been exposed to Europe's "childhood" diseases: smallpox, chicken pox, measles, mumps, and whooping cough. One after another, these diseases spread among the Indians, killing adults as well as children. But the Spaniards, having almost always been exposed in childhood, did not suffer. By 1650 the population of central Mexico, where Montezuma had once ruled, was about 1.5 million; at least 10 million persons had disappeared.

Why did so many Indians die of diseases the Spaniards and other Europeans did not find so very serious? The answer lies in the different disease history of the two populations. In Europe, smallpox, measles, and the rest had become *endemic*. This means that the

disease was always around so that in the first years of life nearly everyone caught it. Natural immunities inherited from the parents made recovery more likely. Many children died all the same, but they were quickly replaced by new births. In Mexico and the rest of the Americas, the new diseases became *epidemic*. This means that old and young alike fell ill. Because they lacked any sort of inherited immunities, many died. When a large proportion of adults died, all activity began to fail.

Highlights The consequences of this disease pattern in the Americas were vast.

A handful of Spanish conquistadors and missionaries easily controlled large populations. Their resistance to diseases that killed so many Indians seemed to prove that God was with them.

In Massachusetts and Virginia, weaker Indian communities simply disappeared almost entirely, leaving empty land for English settlers.

Similar disease patterns arose regularly elsewhere. A population among whom a particular disease was endemic always had an advantage in any new encounter with another population among whom the disease was unknown.

HOW EUROPEANS ACQUIRED THEIR CHILDHOOD DISEASES

Medical records are too vague to allow us to know exactly what disease hit when. But general considerations tell us a good deal. We assume that different diseases first broke out in different parts of the earth and among separate human communities. In any one area, a new disease begins as an *epidemic*. Either it kills everybody, and the disease germ itself disappears, or enough people survive the first epidemic to raise children who inherit some immunity to the disease. If enough of them survive childhood exposure to be able to reproduce themselves, after four or five generations the new disease will become *endemic*.

The spread of disease endemic in one human community to another where it is not endemic depends on how far and how often people travel between the two communities. Most major changes in disease distribution ought, therefore, to take place when people change the pattern of their travel and communication in some important way. (The arrival of the Spaniards in Mexico was such a case.)

Our question then becomes: When did people *first* venture upon important new kinds of travel and communication? About 100 B.C.E. to 200 C.E., caravans regularly traveled across Asia along what Europeans called the Silk Road. During this period ships also sailed the southern seas, connecting the east Mediterranean lands with south China via India and Malaya.

The disease consequences are clear. Severe epidemics hit both the Han Empire of China and the Roman Empire of Europe in the first Christian centuries. Serious depopulation resulted. Depopulation eventually made trade unprofitable, until regular movement along the caravan routes almost petered out. This was probably the time when most of our familiar childhood diseases became endemic among all the civilized populations of Eurasia.

Highlights

The distribution of infectious diseases depends on the patterns of movement and contact among human populations.

Important changes in human travel are likely to trigger new patterns of disease distribution.

The epidemic impact of new diseases upon a dense population without immunities may destroy the conditions needed to sustain the trade and travel that triggered the epidemic in the first place.

This natural cycle had much to do with the decline and fall of classical civilization of the Han and Roman empires, though military and other factors also played a part in the collapse.

THE BLACK DEATH: A DIFFERENT DISEASE PATTERN

When infection passes direct from person to person, the transition from epidemic to en-

demic requires from four to five human generations. The pattern differs when there is another carrier for the disease. For example, the infectious organism for bubonic plague is carried by rats and is spread from host to host by fleas. It is endemic among wild rats in parts of India and China. From time to time, the disease takes hold as an epidemic among the dense rat populations of cities. When enough rats die off, their fleas may try to feed on humans, thus spreading the epidemic to humankind, too. Immunities do not build up, for the disease disappears among humans when an epidemic is over, only to emerge again from the regions where it is endemic among wild rats.

Why, then, did bubonic plague cease in western Europe after 1718? Probably because changes in the ways Europeans got along with rats and fleas checked the spread of the disease. First, public quarantine of ships, houses, or whole cities where plague broke out made it illegal for anyone to leave the quarantined area until after a fixed time—usually forty days—had elapsed without fresh outbreaks of the disease. Second, improved cleanliness made it harder for fleas to take up residence on human bodies. Third, with better housing people encountered rats less often. What really stopped bubonic plague were the changes in European habits that made contacts between human beings on the one hand and rats and fleas on the other less common than before. In Asia and other parts of the world where no such changes took place, bubonic plague continues to threaten fresh epidemics.

Highlights

Some epidemic human diseases are endemic among animal population.

In such cases, the natural shift from epidemic to endemic forms of disease does not occur as far as humans are concerned.

One method of protecting ourselves from the diseases carried by animals is to reduce human contacts with the animal carrier.

The Bubonic Plague in Europe, ca. 14th century.

An Aztec warrior stricken with smallpox.

THE IMPACT OF SCIENTIFIC MEDICINE

During the past 150 years, scientists discovered how infectious diseases spread. With the identification of disease-causing bacteria and viruses, new methods of preventing disease became possible. Chief among them is inoculation with a weakened form of the disease-causing organism. This induces the human body to build up antibodies in the blood that make infection unlikely. In this way a long list of former killers, like infantile paralysis, have become unimportant.

In other cases, chemicals and antibiotic medicines derived from moulds check the disease within the human body. In this way bubonic plague, malaria, pneumonia, syphilis, and other diseases have been brought under control. These artificial immunities have extended humankind's freedom from infectious disease enormously, increasing the average length of life by many years.

Today scientific medicine allows control of most infectious diseases. An enormous improvement in the quality and dependability of human life results. But there is a catch. Germs, exposed to new chemicals and antibiotics, quickly evolved resistances to their effects. As a result, human diseases, once seemingly conquered, have begun to regain their power to infect human bodies.

Even more dramatic was the way new viruses proved able to transfer from animal to human hosts. Most such transfers do not spread very far or last very long, but one of them, identified only in the 1980s, has defeated the efforts of the medical profession ever since, allowing the AIDS (Acquired Immune Deficiency Syndrome) epidemic to take hold in all parts of the world.

Highlights

Since the 1880s scientific medicine brought the main endemic diseases under control.

Sustained population growth (about .1% per year) began about 1750 when epidemic diseases has been largely checked. Galloping population growth (up to 1.5% per year) took over as many of the important endemic diseases were also brought under control.

But diseases came back (at least partially) when a new AIDS infection defeated medical countermeasures, and when some old infections developed resistances to the new medicines.

Because the causes of the bubonic plague were not fully understood, a variety of folk remedies were developed in an attempt to prevent infection.

Smallpox vaccination in 1870.

Steppe Peoples
and the Civilizations
of Eurasia
1200 to 1500

13

Cultural Blending   Here you see the Angel
Gabriel carrying the Prophet Mohammed to
Heaven, as portrayed by a Turkish miniaturist
about 1320. The theme may derive from
Christian art, but the way it is painted shows
that the artist was also familiar with Chinese
and Persian art traditions.

Between 1200 and 1500 two main developments altered the balance among the civilizations of Eurasia. Neither of these developments was exactly new, but each of them attained a scale and force much greater than in any earlier age. It therefore seems wise to treat 1200 as a benchmark in the history of Eurasia, even though (or just because) it intersects European history at the point when medieval civilization was rising to its most brilliant peak.

The two developments in question were (1) the Mongol conquest of China, central Asia, eastern Europe, and most of the Middle East; and (2) the maturation of independent, vigorous civilizations in the easternmost temperate part of Asia (that is, in Japan) and in the westernmost part of Europe (that is, in Italy, Spain, France, Germany, and England).

We will study these developments in turn, first taking up the Mongol explosion and its consequences for the old, established high cultures of Eurasia because it was so sudden and dramatic and because it defined a new era in Asian history. In this connection, we will also touch upon the rise of the Japanese version of civilization in the Far East. Then, in the next chapter, we will return to the story of medieval Europe to see how the brilliant first phase of western European civilization laid the groundwork for the expansion of European influence all round the world—the expansion that began with the great explorations just before and just after 1500.

The Great Mongol Conquests

While Turks from the central steppe were filtering into Islam in evergrowing numbers after 1000 and changing the political leadership of that civilization fundamentally, China, too, had constant trouble with its nomad neighbors. The Sung dynasty (ruled 960–1279) was never able to control the northern provinces of China. Instead, these lands were ruled by nomad confederations that collected taxes from the Chinese peasants with the help of Chinese officials. In other respects these nomad rulers generally left their Chinese subjects alone.

The reason for such a policy was that the nomads wanted to keep their own political-military organization separate from the Chinese tax-collecting bureaucracy. In practice the barbarian rulers had to try to maintain their traditional way of life, even when living among Chinese peasants. If they failed to maintain military habits and an abundant supply of horses, they became easy prey for new tribes of conquerors, fresh from the rigors of life on the steppes.

Nomad Rulers of China Before the Mongols

The first lasting empire built on this dual system was ruled by Khitans, known in Chinese history as the Liao dynasty. This dynasty ruled northernmost China and a broad stretch of steppe country in Mongolia and Manchuria from 907 to 1123. What the Liao rulers commanded was a tribal confederation, including peoples of several different language groups. The secret of their leadership, to a large degree, depended on receiving tax income from their Chinese subjects, which allowed them to distribute gifts and favors among lesser nomad chiefs in suitably generous fashion. As long as handsome gifts kept coming from the court, most local chiefs remained loyal, and their Khitan overlords had nothing to fear.

A leading principle of Khitan government was to keep the nomads separated from the Chinese. If they came too close, local nomad chiefs might discover that they could extort taxes and gifts from the Chinese directly, without having to depend on gifts from the Khitan ruler. Moreover, if nomad warriors were allowed to spread over the Chinese countryside and make particular villages tributary, the ruler would find it difficult to get them to assemble when he wanted them to rally for a campaign. It was much better, the Khitan rulers decided, to keep the nomads as *nomads*, ready to follow their chiefs into battle on short notice—leaving women, children, and animals behind to await their return.

The capital of the Khitan Empire was Peking, close to the zone where the grasslands of the steppe abutted on cultivated fields. Such a location was strategic, as Peking's later history proved. Canals connected the city with the Yellow River and with the system of waterways that had been constructed since the days of the T'ang dynasty (618–907) to allow rulers to bring tax income from all China to their place of residence. Yet at the same time, Peking lay within easy reach of the open steppe to the north and west, whence came Khitan military strength.

It was not too difficult to keep the Chinese and Mongol peoples apart. Most of the Mongols lived north of the Gobi Desert, in what is today Outer Mongolia. The desert region separating them from China could not be cultivated and, therefore, provided a form of natural insulation between the two communities. Moreover, the Mongols were in touch with the oases peoples of central Asia and with tribes living on the open steppe to the westward. Here they learned of civilizations other than the Chinese; in particular they had contact with the Uighur Turks, who kept Manichaeism alive in some of the oases of the Tarim River basin. Buddhism, Tibetan Lamaism, and Nestorian Christianity had followers in central Asia, too. Hence Chinese civilization was not the only kind of high culture the Mongols knew; and they were less eager, therefore, to accept Chinese models than they might have been if no alternatives had existed.

In Manchuria, to the east, however, geographical circumstances were different. In that direction no desert barrier separated the grasslands from Chinese fields. The soil was better watered; farming was possible. The tribes who lived in this region spoke a group of languages called Tungusic, and they knew only Chinese civilization. These conditions paved the way for a much closer and more intimate interaction between Chinese and Tungusic peoples than ever took place between Chinese and Mongols.

This difference became important when the Khitan Empire was overthrown in 1123 by a new ruling tribe, the Jurchens. They came from Manchuria and were not content to remain on the northern fringes of the Chinese lands as the Khitans had done. Instead the Jurchens drove on south approximately to the line of the Yangtze River. Nearly half of China thus came under their rule, together with much of Manchuria. The Jurchens, or Chin dynasty to give them their Chinese name, ruled until 1234. They allowed a more extensive intermingling between their own people and the Chinese than the Khitan rulers had done, and the Jurchens became thoroughly Chinese in culture.

Mongol Life

Meanwhile, the Mongols were thrown back on the meager resources of their homeland. Hunting and herding in the harsh climate of Mongolia offered a hard life at best, and it was made harder by constant struggles among rival clans and tribes for rights to the scant pastures of the region. Nevertheless, people (and horses) capable of surviving in such an environment were unusually hardy. They made excellent soldiers, being accustomed to outdoor living; but as long as the Mongols continued to be divided into small kinship groups, energies were spent fighting among themselves.

Yet in a sense, they already knew better. The Mongols had centuries of contact with China behind them, and in the days of the Khitan control of north China they had shared in the wealth that came from Chinese taxpayers. The trouble was that Mongolian pastures were so thin that the Mongols had to break up into very small groups—often as few as fifteen or twenty families—in order to find enough forage for their herds; and such scattered groups regularly quarreled with their neighbors over possession of animals and pasture rights.

About 1162, however, a son was born to a petty Mongol chieftain who was destined to unite all the Mongols and most of the Eurasian steppe into a vast new empire. His name was Temujin, but he is usually known by the honorific title he assumed when his victories had made him famous: Genghis Khan, that is, "Ruler of all within the seas."

The Secret of Genghis Khan's Success

What Genghis Khan did was simple but radical. He entirely disregarded clan and kinship ties in building the army that made his name so widely feared. Instead of relying on traditional kinship groupings, he organized his followers bureaucratically. In the early days when his forces were still small, each squad of ten men was put under the command of a leader personally chosen by Temujin for his abilities, and without regard for family ties or traditional social rank. Ten squads were in turn grouped into a company, commanded by a man who had demonstrated his capacities in battle. Later, when larger units of 1000 and of 10,000 men were organized on the same lines, senior officers had the authority to appoint squad and company commanders. But the bureaucratic principle, according to which a man's rank depended not on birth but on appointment to office, always remained in force.

By choosing his commanders shrewdly and promoting those who did well, Temujin quickly created a formidable fighting force. His followers soon overcame all opposition among the Mongols. Each victory meant new recruits for Temujin's army, since he promptly folded the manpower of his defeated enemies into the command structure he had created. This had the additional advantage of guaranteeing rapid promotion among his own followers, so that capable men found ample scope for their ambitions within the army Temujin had created.

When all the fighting manpower of the Mongol people had been organized in this way, they were in a position to strike with devastating

The Eurasian Steppe   This modern photograph shows a part of the open grasslands that extend across Eurasia, all the way from Hungary in the west to Manchuria in the east. The herds grazing in the distance are the same as those that supported the nomadic populations who united under the leadership of Genghis Khan to conquer the largest empire that the world has ever known.

effect against other steppe peoples. This soon brought Turkish and Tungusic-speaking peoples into the Mongol army. But they were treated in the same way as the Mongols themselves. Since the number of nomad Turks was far greater than the number of Mongols, the so-called Mongol armies, especially those operating in western Asia and eastern Europe, were in fact composed mainly of Turkish-speaking personnel. Topmost command, however, remained in Mongol hands.

Genghis' nomad army could also turn its energies against the settled agricultural peoples who lived southward of the steppe. In central Asia, his troops found it relatively easy to overrun the isolated oases with their mixed population of Uighurs, Persians, and other peoples. From these cities Genghis recruited a class of scribes and record keepers, who began to be needed as the size of the Mongol forces grew.

Expansion southward into China was a tougher proposition. The Jurchens were good fighters and had the vast resources of all north China at their disposal. New military problems arose when the Mongol cavalry came up against city walls and had to face sophisticated weaponry—including gunpowder. But the Mongol cavalry was able to overpower the Jurchens in open country. Genghis could therefore raid deeply into China, more or less at will. Moreover, the Mongols soon learned how to break through city walls with the aid of catapults and gunpowder bombs. These weapons were designed and produced by Chinese artisans, who were as willing to serve the Mongols as they were to work for the Jurchens. When, therefore, Mongol armies encountered walled cities in western Asia and eastern Europe, they were already equipped with all the skills of Chinese siegecraft and, as a matter of fact, were probably responsible for bringing gunpowder to the attention of Europeans for the first time.

As long as Genghis Khan lived, he alternated the main thrust of his campaigns at will. Some years he went southward into China; other years he turned his horses' heads westward along the steppe. Everywhere his armies proved victorious, but they behaved as raiders and plunderers rather than as rulers. By 1227, when Genghis Khan died, his forces had raided as far west as

Steppe Dancing   In the age of the Mongol empire, the steppe peoples reached the apex of their influence on Asia and Europe. One sign of this is that they developed an art tradition of their own, related to, but distinct from, that of neighboring civilized peoples. This painting, probably made somewhat close to the Volga River about 1450, shows that the Turkish peoples of that region danced as Russian cossacks did later, kicking their heels from a squatting position. Steppe populations met disaster in the fourteenth century, when bubonic plague became endemic in the grasslands, and their cultural independence and political power never recovered.

southern Russia and had almost destroyed the Jurchen Empire in north China. Central Asia oases were firmly tributary also. But the fundamental new fact was that for the first and last time in history, the fighting manpower of the entire Asian steppe, all the way from Manchuria to the Urals, stood ready and organized for further campaigns under the capable and experienced command of the Mongol generals that Genghis Khan had created around himself.

Alexander the Great of Macedon is the only man who can rank beside Genghis Khan as a conqueror. Both died undefeated, and through their victories both of them altered preexisting relationships among the civilized populations of Europe and Asia in lasting and significant ways.

Genghis Khan's Successors   According to Mongol custom, Genghis divided his possessions among his four sons. One of them died before Genghis did, so his share passed directly to Genghis' grandson, Batu. To keep effective unity among the separate "hordes"—as each part of the Mongol domain was called—Genghis arranged to transfer the Mongol part of the army to one of his sons, Ogadai (ruled 1229–1241). This made the others dependent on Ogadai, for even a son of Genghis Khan was helpless without Mongol officers and a Mongol bodyguard to overawe the Turkish, Chinese, and other peoples who had been portioned out to them. In this way, then, the unity of the Mongol Empire was maintained for a century.

Under Ogadai's leadership, Mongol victories continued as before. In 1234 the last of the Jurchen rulers was hunted down. The Mongols now had all of north China to exploit. They decided to restore the Chinese style of administration, using officials trained in the Confucian mold to collect taxes and run local affairs. Thereafter, Mongol rule made little difference to ordinary Chinese peasants or townspeople. Raiding horsemen from the steppe continued to travel across China from time to time, since the southern part of the country was not finally subdued until 1279. Even after that date, the Mongols organized expeditions against Burma (1287) and Siam (1289) by marching their forces across China. Nevertheless, on a day-to-day basis the Mongol overlords were not much in evidence. The availability of competent Confucians to staff the administrative machine meant that China continued to be governed, except at the highest levels, by Chinese.

Expansion westward matched the continued Mongol expansion southward. Between 1237 and 1241 all the Russian princes and cities, except Novgorod, in the far northwest, were subdued. The rich steppe country of southern Russia became the base for the "Golden Horde" that ruled from a headquarters at Kazan on the Volga.

The Mongols demanded tribute payments from the Russians just as they did from the Chinese. Indeed, it seems clear that the Mongols took their experience in China as the pattern for their government of the rest of the empire. To begin with, the Russians had no ready-made sys-

tem for collecting tribute. The Mongols, therefore, entrusted the task to merchant firms of central Asians—the same sort of people who kept Genghis' records for him. This did not produce very good results, however; so when the Russian princes offered their services as tax collectors, the Mongol overlords agreed. This required (or allowed) the Russian princes to build up a body of tax-collecting officials whose loyalty and obedience was to the prince who appointed them rather than to the distant and alien Mongol khan. The germs of the later Russian state thus came into existence.

A third great territory came into the Mongol orbit after 1256, when Mongol armies overran Persia, Mesopotamia, and Syria—the heartland of Islam. Baghdad was sacked (1258) and the last Abbasid caliph perished in the confusion. Moslems could no longer even pretend that the Prophet Mohammed had a worthy successor on earth to lead the Community of the Faithful. The original basis of Moslem political life had finally been swept away—a fact later Moslems never forgot.

In the Moslem world the Mongols applied the same pattern of administration as in China and in Russia. The trouble was that most Moslems were unwilling to cooperate by taxing themselves for the benefit of the Mongols. Christians who had lived for centuries under Moslem rule did not mind working for the new masters of the Middle East. But these formerly oppressed peoples were a weak reed for the Mongols to lean upon. The Moslems hated them as traitors, and the Christians had been submissive for so long that they could not easily become effective administrators.

Another weakness of the Mongol position in the Middle East was that most of the soldiers available to the Il-khans, as this branch of the Mongol ruling dynasty was called, were Turks. They had much in common with the Moslemized Turks who had preceded them from the steppe into that part of the world. Accordingly, in 1295 the Il-khans chose to become Moslem themselves and to conform to age-old patterns of Moslem, Turkish, and Middle Eastern imperial government. More than a generation earlier, in 1257, the rulers of the Golden Horde in Russia had taken the same step and, by converting to Islam, distanced themselves from their Russian and Christian subjects.

Mongol Power and Unity Under Kublai Khan

As both these western khanates became Moslem, the Turkish element in the Mongol armies and ruling class came to the surface. Correspondingly, the influence of the Far East receded. Yet before that happened, the Mongol Empire reached a peak of power and unity under Kublai Khan (ruled 1260–1294). Kublai succeeded his brother who had been in supreme charge of the empire from 1251 to 1259. Between them they ruled for nearly half a century over an empire that extended from the Pacific Ocean to Poland, combining eastern Europe, most of the Middle East, all of China, and the intervening territory in a single great empire.

The Great Khan's power rested on command of the Mongol army proper. Only small detachments of Mongols were assigned to the other khanates. A remarkably efficient postal system maintained communication between the Great Khan's headquarters and the other khans' courts. Horses and riders were kept ready at stations some twenty to thirty miles apart. When a message came through, it was carried at a gallop from station to station until it reached its destination. The same method had been used by the ancient Assyrians and Persians, but the distances traversed by the Mongol postal system had never been equaled before.

The Mongols were also good at spying. Sometimes they used merchants and other seemingly innocent agents to get information; sometimes they sent scouts as much as 200 miles ahead of the main force. When the Mongol army advanced, messengers, dispatched daily, kept separate columns in touch with each other. This allowed the columns to come together in time to attack an enemy or, as the case might be, to go around some defended place and take their foes in the flank and rear.

Traders and merchants enjoyed a high standing among the Mongols. The Venetian Marco Polo, for example, served Kublai Khan in a number of important posts, although at home he was only a trader in jewels. Indeed, skilled strangers of all kinds were welcome at the Great

The Mongol Ruler, Kublai Khan, Hunting When the Mongols ruled China (1234–1368) and most of Asia, they wished to maintain their nomad traditions while simultaneously enjoying civilized comforts. Of the civilizations they encountered, the Chinese impressed them most, as this painting, executed by a Chinese artist to appeal to Mongol taste, attests. The hunt and the steppe scenery reaffirmed the Mongols' nomad past. Yet the artist's style is fundamentally Chinese, even though his use of a few spots of high color betray the influence of Persian miniature painting. The Mongol empire made movement to and fro across the breadth of Asia easy and frequent; intermingling of skills and ideas from different civilized traditions resulted, as this painting illustrates.

Khan's court. The Mongol rulers always needed people with civilized skills—reading and writing, if nothing else—whom they could trust. Outsiders assigned a responsible job and a high salary were unlikely to disobey, if only because they owed their position entirely to the khan who had appointed them. This was the same principle that had made the army so effective; it worked when applied to civil administration too. Local tax collecting could be left to local leaders; but central records and positions around the person of the ruler, where high policy had to be decided, were entrusted to outsiders. Mongols were illiterate soldiers, incapable of keeping records. Men from nowhere, like Marco Polo, had to be used instead.

At court, there was a great commingling. Individuals from all parts of Europe and Asia drifted first to Karakorum, Genghis' capital, and later to Cambaluc, just outside Peking, the capital that Kublai built for himself in 1264. Practi-

cally every religion was represented among the crowd that assembled around these imperial capitals. This fitted Mongol policy perfectly. Genghis and his heirs took the line that there must be something true in every religion—or at least there might be. Therefore, it seemed sound policy to have experts from every faith on hand to help guard the khan against divine anger.

The Christians of Europe entirely misunderstood Mongol religious attitudes. When they discovered that the Great Khan admitted Christians to his court and sometimes entrusted them with important tasks, the pope and all Christendom assumed that the Mongol khan was about to become Christian. Repeated efforts were, in fact, made to send missionaries to make sure of his conversion. Two of them actually reached the

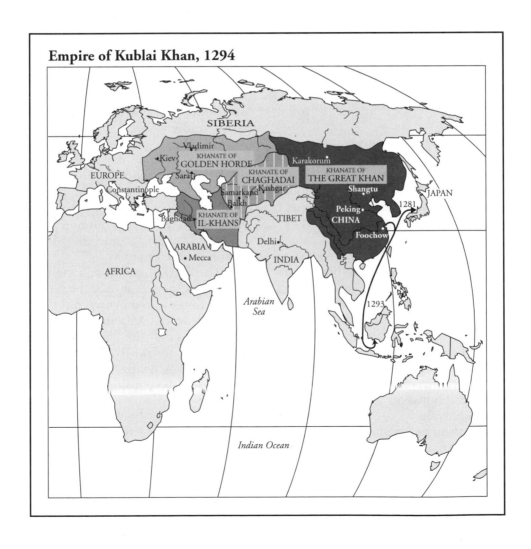

Empire of Kublai Khan, 1294

Great Khan's court. They were listened to politely—and the khan continued the same religious policy as before. Kublai perhaps favored Lamaism over other faiths as a matter of personal observance, but the religious intolerance that Moslems and Christians took for granted had no place in his world view.

The Breakup of the Mongol Empire

Mere distance set limits to the Mongol armies' triumphs. In 1241, for example, after subduing Russia, the Mongols started toward central Europe, where they defeated a Polish and German force in Silesia and overran all of Hungary. But the death of Ogadai called them home to Mongolia to take part in the choice of a successor. By the time the quarrels that this stirred up had been settled, there were other campaigns to be fought, and the Mongols never returned to Hungary.

Much the same was true in Syria and India. The main Mongol field army was called back from the Middle East by another succession crisis in 1259 and never returned. Egypt therefore remained unconquered. After Saladin's dynasty died out in 1250, that country was ruled by slaves, called Mamlukes. These slaves came mostly from the Caucasus Mountains at the east end of the Black Sea. As young men they were shipped to Egypt by slave traders, and served there as soldiers. A few were promoted to positions of command and ruled Egypt until 1798. The Mamlukes were formidable fighters and recovered Syria from the Il-khans in 1260.

As for India, the main Mongol armies never tried to invade. The Il-khans did launch several small raids into India between 1285 and 1303, but the Himalayan barrier was formidable, and the Il-khans needed their troops nearer home.

These setbacks in central Europe, Syria, and India were trifling, since the Mongols did not really try to send big armies so far away. On the other hand, their failure to conquer Japan in 1281 was a serious check—the first the Mongols had ever met. Kublai sent a large invading force, but the Japanese prepared special defenses, and a typhoon destroyed much of the shipping upon which the Mongol army depended for its supplies. The remnant of the invading host, therefore, had to withdraw in disarray. Kublai never gave up planning to do something about this failure; but other naval expeditions—undertaken in part to practice the art of landing on a hostile shore (one went as far as Java in 1292–1293)—never had sufficiently brilliant results to make another attempt on Japan seem feasible. After his death, in 1294, Kublai's heirs gave up the project, having enough to do trying to keep peace within the empire already under their control.

Three factors combined, after Kublai's death, to weaken and, in the end, to destroy the Mongol Empire. One was the wearing out of the Mongol manpower. Losses in battle and from disease must have been severe; moreover, the victors enjoyed an easier, more luxurious life than their ancestors had known on the harsh Mongolian steppes. As a result, the supply of hardy soldiery became too small to keep the Mongol armies at their original strength. Men who could not ride day and night for a week or longer, scarcely stopping for food or sleep, were not like the Mongols that Genghis Khan had led across the world. Without the ability to endure extreme hardship and fatigue, the extraordinary mobility that had made the Mongol conquests possible ceased to exist.

The second factor was the weakening of effective central power over the empire as a whole. If the Mongol field army could no longer come streaking across Asia in a matter of weeks, then the Il-khans and the khans of the Golden Horde had nothing to fear from the distant Great Khan. After Kublai's death, this became obvious and the unity of the empire evaporated.

The third factor was the growing divergences between the Mongol forces stationed in each of the three main agricultural areas that the Mongols had overrun. As the soldiers and administrators around Kublai Khan became more familiar with Chinese things, they lost touch with central Asian and Moslem civilization. The

Golden Horde and the Il-khans moved in the opposite direction, becoming more and more part of the Moslem world and being less and less in touch with the Chinese style of life that was seeping into the Great Khan's court.

By 1300, therefore, the administrative and military unity of the empire had disappeared, although close diplomatic and commercial ties continued to operate across all of Asia for another half century. The rulers of China, for example, usually cooperated with the Golden Horde against the two intervening khanates. As late as 1332 a bodyguard of Russians existed at Peking, specially recruited by the Golden Horde for the protection of the Great Khan's person. Not until 1368, when the Mongols were driven out of China by a new Chinese dynasty, the Ming (ruled 1368–1644), did the memory of Mongol unity fade.

Before that time, the Il-khans had lost control of Persia to a swarm of quarreling upstarts, most of whom claimed descent from Genghis Khan—although they were Turks in language, Moslem in religion, and resembled Genghis only in their ruthlessness. The Golden Horde lasted longer. Indeed, its last fragment was wiped from the map of Europe only in 1783, when Catherine II of Russia annexed the Crimea. But the power of the Golden Horde over the Russian lands had been broken by 1480.

Crowded back into Mongolia itself, the surviving Mongols remembered the great Genghis but were quite unable to equal his deeds. This was the case largely because the Chinese viewed every move toward unification among the Mongolian tribes with the most intense suspicion and took prompt steps to break up any new center of power by every means they could command—bribery, diplomacy, trade boycott, and in case of necessity, direct military action. Chinese diplomats and rulers had learned their lesson well and resolved never to permit the Mongols to unite again. Indeed, they were so concerned with the danger from the steppe that the Chinese court utterly failed to recognize the new opportunities and dangers that came in the following centuries by way of the sea.

Measured against the whole span of human history, the Mongol Empire was a short-lived affair. But its influence and impact lingered on long after it had broken up. Memories of the Mongol assault affected the behavior and policy of both the Chinese and Japanese governments very strongly. The Mongol Empire also had an impact, although less important, upon Islam and Europe. In the rest of this chapter we shall, therefore, look at each of these regions to see the different ways in which these peoples reacted to their collision with the Mongol conquerors.

The Ming Reaction in China

After the death of Kublai Khan in 1294, the Mongol control of China began to falter, but it was not until 1368 that the Chinese succeeded in uniting behind an ex-Buddhist monk who was able to drive the hated foreigners out of the country. The Ming dynasty, which he founded, ruled China from 1368 to 1644.

The overriding thought behind everything the Ming rulers did was to keep China free from another nomad conquest. They moved their capital to Peking in 1421 to be able to guard against any renewal of invasion from the steppe. Systematically the Ming officials set out to erase all signs of the Mongol period. Faithful and exact imitation of the old ways was the obvious path and they did their best to follow it. Merchants, who had enjoyed unaccustomed prestige in the time of the Mongols, were once again put firmly in their place near the bottom of the social scale. The old social order of China was restored as exactly as human will and intention could restore the past.

Some changes remained in spite of everything. For example, the use of gunpowder in war had become a lot more important under the Mongols. As a result, Ming armies knew a lot about big guns capable of launching projectiles against fortifications with devastating effect. The Ming navy also used guns "with muzzles the size of rice bowls," to quote instructions from the court addressed to ships about to explore the Indian Ocean in 1393.

Such weapons made it much more difficult than before for a local governor or upstart warlord to defy the central government. Even if it took several months to bring artillery from imperial headquarters to the scene, a few such guns could destroy the walls of any rebel stronghold in short order. The effect of gunpowder and heavy artillery was therefore to strengthen the central authority. In other words, the new weapons had the effect of reinforcing the old imperial ideal. The Ming regime accepted and approved of that novelty.

Ming Voyages of Discovery   When, however, new developments did not serve to strengthen old ways and values, the Ming emperors set out to check the source of disturbance. One of the strangest "might have beens" of history turns upon what the Ming court did with the navy they inherited from the Mongols. Kublai had repeatedly experimented with combined sea and land operations. The invasion of Japan in 1281 was the most famous of these, as well as the least successful. To support such ventures overseas, Chinese shipbuilders and merchants created a large and seaworthy merchant fleet. In doing so they had the full support of the imperial court. Kublai, after all, never gave up his intention of conquering Japan, and for that he required a very large fleet indeed.

The Ming policy was to put officials in charge of Chinese seafaring. Seven times between 1403 and 1433 a court official, named Cheng Ho, gathered a great fleet in south China and sailed into the Indian Ocean. He returned successfully, bringing with him the king of Ceylon, the prince of Sumatra, and tribute (including a giraffe from east Africa) from no fewer than sixteen rulers at whose ports the Chinese ships had put in. The Ming emperors were in a position to create a naval empire in the Indian Ocean, like the one that the Portuguese actually established a century later. But the court decided to draw back. In 1424 further voyages were forbidden; and although that order was later modified to permit Cheng Ho to undertake a final voyage in 1431–1433, the Chinese never followed up their initial exploration. Instead, the Ming emperors actually prohibited the construction of large ships for travel on the oceans and made it illegal for any Chinese to leave the country by sea.

Exactly why the Ming emperors made this decision is unknown. Perhaps it was mainly the result of a court intrigue, pitting one group of advisers against another. Cheng Ho, after all, was a eunuch, and this made him suspect in the eyes of Confucian scholars. Moreover, fitting out naval expeditions took manpower and resources that could be used to strengthen defenses against the Mongols. This was no mere theoretical problem, for in 1449 the reigning Ming emperor was actually taken prisoner when he took the field against a new confederation of Mongol tribes.

But what made the policy stick was surely the fact that the only people who seemed to benefit from such enterprises were merchants and other riffraff, for whom Confucian scholars had only the greatest contempt. Or, to put it another way, the merchants and other social groups who profited from seafaring were quite unable to make their interests felt at court. Classified as social parasites by Confucian doctrine, Chinese merchants lacked habits of self-assertion against their betters, the scholar-officials. Hence what the court decreed was in fact enforced. China deliberately threw away the strategic position in the Indian Ocean which Cheng Ho's voyages had won.

This was only the most dramatic example of China's overall course. For by settling back toward tried-and-true patterns of behavior, the Ming emperors and officials allowed the rest of the world to catch up with China. In 1400, as in 1200, China outclassed the rest of the world in numbers, skills, and habits of hard work. Chinese learning and art were exquisitely refined. A strong army and a vigilant emperor with well-trained officials kept the country secure, even against the Mongol danger. When the emperor was captured in 1449, for instance, his brother took the throne, and the government went on as before. Holding fast to the way of the ancients was exactly what Confucius had recommended. It was what the Ming dynasty did. It worked.

In the long run, to be sure, such a reactionary policy allowed Europeans to catch up and eventually leave the Chinese behind. But it is quite unfair to judge Ming policy by what happened 400 years later. At the time and within the world they knew, they did well. Order, security, and civilization were maintained; the hateful barbarian lordship had been overcome. What more could any reasonable person ask or expect?

Japan's Coming of Age

Until 1200, Japan's civilization had copied China's, always falling short of the model because Japanese society differed from Chinese society in some important ways. The most obvious differences were that Japanese warriors and landowners were organized into clans and maintained habits of violence that the Chinese upper classes entirely lacked. The warlike clans of Japan fought one another frequently and turned their practice in war to good use when the Mongols landed and tried to conquer the country in 1281.

The fact that they defeated the mighty Kublai Khan, when everyone else in the whole world had been unable to stand against the Mongol assault, gave a great fillip to Japanese self-confidence and pride. China did not seem so impressive to warriors who had turned back China's rulers.

Japanese Towns and the Samurai Class
This independent spirit was fed by the increasing importance of towns and of sea-roving in Japanese life. As long as the Japanese court was the only place where people had the leisure or the wealth for civilized pursuits, it was natural to imitate China. The rough border barons and feudal lords, who had taken nearly all practical power away from the court, were too busy fighting to bother much with culture. But as towns became larger and wealthier after about 1200, they began to provide a new setting in which a privileged few could read, paint, and amuse themselves in other ways. In such an environment Japanese culture took on the color of the local scene and ceased to be a mere copy of Chinese achievements.

Japanese towns housed artisans who made things for the warrior, or samurai, class. In particular, Japanese smiths learned to produce sword blades of specially treated steel that were the best in the entire world. Japanese towns also served as headquarters for merchant-pirates who operated overseas. Many of these men were of samurai origin. Driven away from control over rice-producing villages by some stronger clan, defeated groups of samurai took to the sea—and soon discovered that their military skills paid off handsomely in dealings with less warlike peoples of southeast Asia. New wealth, derived from piracy supplemented by trade, began to pour into Japanese ports, especially in the southern and western parts of the islands. Population grew, and an urban upper class that was ready and able to support a more distinctly Japanese form of high culture began to emerge.

The importance of seafaring for Japanese town life made the urban classes largely independent of the masters of the countryside. Readiness to resort to violence in pursuit of their own interests prevailed in the towns, just as it did among the samurai. Instead of catering politely to the demands of the warrior class, Japanese townspeople tended to deal with them sometimes as rivals, sometimes as allies, and always as equals.

To be sure, by far the majority of the Japanese population remained on the land and lived in rice-growing villages, controlled by the members of a samurai clan. This remained the norm. Towns began to grow to a new size and importance only by becoming havens for those who had failed to make good in the countryside—that is, for poor runaway peasants as well as for defeated samurai. But when these refugees began to prosper on the proceeds of their overseas ventures, the lords of the rural villages had to confront a new kind of rival for dominance within Japanese society as a whole.

Buddhist monasteries created a third center of power and wealth in Japan. These monasteries owned important rice lands, and the monks defended them—when need be, sword in hand—against samurai clans that tried to take over rights the monks claimed as their own. Some monasteries (mainly of the Zen sect) accepted monks primarily from the samurai class. Such communities simply maintained their warlike habits despite their monkish robes. Some, however (the so-called Pure Land sect), seem to have opened their doors to ordinary peasants and therefore represented a more democratic ele-

Kamikaze in 1281   After conquering China and most of Asia, the
Mongols sent a great expedition against Japan in 1281, but a typhoon
destroyed most of the invading ships, and the Japanese easily defeated
the shattered remnant that made it ashore. The Kamikaze, or Divine
Wind, that protected Japan in 1281 became a patriotic theme for later
generations. This print dating from the nineteenth or twentieth century,
shows how the Japanese continued to remember and celebrate the
Mongols' defeat down to and including the World War II years, when
many expected the divine help that had come so marvelously in 1281 to
return if the Americans ever tried to invade. The sea fighting shown here
is entirely misleading. The Japanese in fact fought only on shore against
the invaders, but sea fighting and Japanese piratical activity did flourish
between about 1400 and 1636. This print thus mixes and confuses popular
memories of that era with the Kamikaze of 1281.

ment in Japanese political and social life. Little
armies of monks from both of these sects entered into the armed struggles for power among
the samurai clans from time to time and held
their own quite successfully.

Presiding over this unruly political scene
was the emperor. The imperial office remained
hereditary in a single family. According to myth,
the imperial family descended directly from the
Sun Goddess through Emperor Jimmu. But the
emperor was powerless, despite the fact that all
Japanese clans accepted the fiction of subordination to his authority. Central control—so far
as it existed at all—was in the hands of an official known as the *shogun*.

The shogun was himself head of a clan and
leader of a coalition of clans sufficiently strong
to control the emperor, who was the only person
who could appoint a shogun. This made control of the imperial court worth fighting over.
Rivalries among the different clans never ceased
to alter the lineup of groups supporting the
shogun. To maintain his position, the shogun always had to maneuver among his friends and
enemies, seeking support and sometimes fighting regular campaigns against rival coalitions.
Occasionally, a shogun met defeat and had to
yield to a rival. One such overturn took place in
1338, when the Ashikaga clan seized the shogu-
nate (that is, the office of the shogun). Members
of this clan remained in office until 1568 and
gave their name to the entire epoch of Japanese
history.

Cultural Life   In matters cultural, the Japanese continued to be able to imitate Chinese

THE DIVINE WIND

Early in his reign Kublai Khan sent a message to the Japanese demanding that they should recognize his greatness with appropriate submission. The Japanese authorities refused to reply. Six years later, in 1274, Kublai sent an expedition of about 15,000 Mongol soldiers to enforce his demands. But the Japanese met force with force, and after a single day's battle, the Mongols reembarked and returned home. For the next five years, Kublai was busy in southern China, snuffing out the last traces of the Sung dynasty. He completed this task in 1279. The Great Khan was now free to turn his full forces against the rude and warlike Japanese.

The shogun of Japan and his followers kept themselves informed of what was afoot in China and made elaborate preparations for resistance. They built a wall around the harbor where they expected the Mongol fleet to land; they mustered all the fighters of the islands; they prayed to all the gods of Japan. Even the sacred person of the emperor was mobilized: He vowed to launch 300,000 prayers heavenward and did so by dividing the task among his courtiers, each undertaking his numerical share.

In June 1281, the test came. A Mongol army of about 50,000 men headed toward Japan from Korean ports, and a much larger expedition (about 100,000) sailed from southern China. The landing took place on June 23, and hard fighting lasted about fifty days. The Mongols had superior discipline, superior missiles (both arrows and gunpowder projectiles), and the habit of victory. The Japanese had superior swords and home ground beneath their feet.

Details of the struggle cannot be reconstructed. Desperate courage was plentiful on both sides. But the Mongols never were able to get their cavalry loose to launch long-distance raids across country, as they were accustomed to doing. Instead they remained cooped up in a narrow bridgehead through the summer, until the season of typhoons came on.

Early in August 1281, the first typhoon of the season struck and came with unusual force. Trees were uprooted on land, and on the sea the Mongol fleet suffered destruction. The Japanese claimed that of 4000 ships only 200 escaped, and that of the invading forces less than a fifth ever got back to the Chinese mainland.

It was a stunning victory. The whole affair paralleled the story of the Persian invasions of Greece that preceded Athens' Golden Age. But there was one great difference. The Greeks won the Battle of Salamis through human guile and their own seamanship; the Japanese attributed their victory to the gods who had so clearly demonstrated their special attachment to Japan by sending a "Divine Wind" when the human defenders of the islands were hardest pressed.

Memories of the Mongol invasions and their failures revived in World War II, especially when another August typhoon delayed the ceremony of surrender until September 1945 and postponed the arrival of the first American troops in Japan by several days.

painting and literature very skillfully. The court circles, where this had been done for centuries, continued to foster such activity. Sometimes the Japanese attained great excellence, particularly in painting. But in addition, new traditions emerged in the Ashikaga period. Cartoons and caricatures, for example, would have been beneath the dignity of a Chinese scholar-painter. In Japan, however, painters had a lower social status and often belonged to the artisan class. This allowed them not only to copy Chinese styles with utmost skill but also, when they felt like it, to express their own points of view.

Japanese literature also developed new forms. Noh drama was the most important. This was a ritualized performance by masked actors and a chorus, in which music played a large part. Great precision of movement and refinement of voice and posture made Noh performances into a dance and song recital as well as a drama. It appealed especially to the samurai. Other arts for which Japan is famous seem to date from the same period; for example, flower arrangement and the so-called tea ceremony. The tea ceremony was another ritual art. Every step in the making and drinking of tea had to be done in a particular way so that those who took part could admire the grace and beauty, the taste and rhythms, with which the host and his guests carried through the performance.

Japanese priests of the Sun Goddess, from whom the imperial family claimed descent, began to make their worship into an organized cult. This religion is known as Shinto. Shinto did not become generally important in Japan until later. In the beginning it was more like the Confucian cult of the ancestors, conducted by the imperial family for its own benefit and the benefit of the imperial household. But the religious practices that were later thrown open to the Japanese public at large took form in this period, as Shinto priests borrowed rituals and ideas from Buddhism as well as from Confucianism.

The rise of towns in Japan, the samurai lordship over villages, and the militaristic spirit of the country all resembled western Europe of the same age. The parallels were indeed real and important; yet there were two differences that are worth emphasizing.

First, the Japanese did not build their society upon any radically new technique, as did the Europeans. Moldboard plow agriculture and the manorial system provided western Europe with something new that changed daily experience at the very bottom of society. The Japanese had only rice paddies, familiar for centuries. With enough hard work, more and more land could be brought under paddy cultivation; and with Japan's abundant rainfall, it was possible to push the paddy fields quite high up the mountain slopes. But the routine of life for the peasant majority remained fixed as before. In medieval Europe, on the contrary, from about 900, peasants had new techniques to exploit and new horizons of the possible to explore. This made European society more changeable, even at the bottom of the social scale, than Japanese society.

In the second place, the Japanese, like the Chinese, were handicapped by shortages of metal, at least as compared to the supply available to western Europe. Why this was so is not easy to say. Shortage of ores may have been a factor, but the weak development of mining and prospecting techniques is more likely explanation for Japan's and China's restricted supply of metals. Whatever the reasons, the fact remained that in some key respects—particularly the casting of heavy artillery pieces—the Japanese (and Chinese) could not keep up with Europeans when the two peoples finally came into touch with each other.

Such differences between medieval Japan and medieval Europe were matched, of course, by the complete difference of cultural forms and social tradition that made the two civilizations what they were. Each was unique; each had recently played second fiddle to an older and more sophisticated civilization. And by about 1200, the world as a whole was richer both for western Europe's rise and for Japan's coming of age as an independent civilization.

The Response of Islam

The Mongol conquest was a great disaster for Moslems. The caliphate collapsed. God seemed to have deserted the Moslem cause, and many of their Christian subjects soon proved disloyal. Yet a half century later Islam had recovered its balance and self-confidence. The Mongol-Turkish conquerors had been converted to the faith of Mohammed; and as soon as they found themselves back in the driver's seat, the Moslems made life so uncomfortable for their Christian subjects that nearly all of them accepted Islam in order to escape persecution. For the first time, therefore, the overwhelming majority of the inhabitants of Syria, Mesopotamia, and Persia became Moslem. In Egypt and Asia Minor, where the Mongols never established their power, important Christian subject populations remained in existence. In India the great majority remained Hindu. Only where the Mongols had threatened Moslem political and social dominance did the religious minorities subsequently wither away.

To be sure, the old question of how the Moslem community ought to find a worthy successor to the Prophet was not solved. Political life in the heartland of Islam remained chaotic and violent. Turkish-speaking war captains, claiming descent from Genghis Khan, struggled against one another. The most successful of them was Timur the Lame, sometimes called Tamerlane (ruled 1360–1405). Timur built a vast empire along the lines of the empire of Genghis Khan. From his capital at Samarkand, he led victorious raids in every direction throughout central Asia and the middle steppe—to Persia and Mesopotamia, Asia Minor and southern Russia, and into northern India. At the moment of his death, he was preparing a great expedition against China. But after he died, the empire fell apart, for Timur had no solid core of fellow tribesmen upon whom to build, in the way Genghis Khan's successors could depend on the Mongol hordes.

Continual disorders and sudden reversals of fortune kept a stream of Turkish adventurers moving toward the frontiers of Islam. If unsuccessful in the center of the realm, a warrior might still hope to find fortune in India, or fighting against Christendom in the West. Accordingly, a flow of Turkish fighting men kept moving in from the central steppe and then either south into India or westward into Asia Minor. The state that benefited most from this sort of fortune hunting was the Ottoman Empire.

The Ottoman Empire started in obscurity, along the borderland between Christian and Moslem territory in Asia Minor. It got its name from Osman, or Othman (1290–1326), a Turkish warrior who carved out a small principality in northwestern Asia Minor at the expense of the Byzantine Empire. His heirs and successors enlarged the state steadily. In 1354 they crossed into Europe and took possession of the Gallipoli Peninsula. From there they spread rapidly through the Balkans. After defeating the Serbian army in a famous battle at Kosovo in 1389, the Ottoman sultan, as the head of the state was called, emerged as by far the most powerful ruler in the Balkans.

Constantinople remained in the hands of a Greek ruler who claimed to carry on the ancient Byzantine tradition, although continuity had been broken by the Fourth Crusade, when knights from the west captured the city (1204). Greek power was restored at Constantinople in 1261, but the tax income that had made Byzantium great could never be restored. Instead, the Turks took control of the Balkan interior and seemed about to close in on the old capital. Then Tamerlane appeared from the east, defeated the sultan in a battle near Ankara, and took him prisoner (1402). The great city therefore enjoyed a respite from Ottoman pressure until the Turks recovered themselves. This took until in 1453, when Sultan Mohammed II, the Conqueror, besieged it both by land and by sea. After a three-month struggle, he captured Constantinople, which then became the Ottoman capital.

The Ottoman state was, first and foremost, the creation of religiously dedicated warriors who believed God had sent them to extend the realm of Islam at the expense of Christendom. The rise of the Ottoman Empire was thus the Moslem equivalent of a crusade, lasting hundreds of years. Many of the most fanatical fighters for the Turks were themselves converted Christians, but the Turkish element in the empire was also steadily reinforced by the arrival of newcomers from the east.

But a stable empire could not be built upon religious enthusiasm alone. Heresies easily took root among the rude warriors of the Moslem

Spread of Islam, 850–1500

Legend:
Islam
Christianity
Hinduism
Buddhism
Confucianism
Lamaism
Ottoman empire: 1307–1481
Tamerlane's empire: 1360–1405
Areas with Moslem communities in China

Kansu
Yunnan

frontier. They particularly favored Sufi mystical teachers. But personal experience of God in moments of ecstasy made Sufis quite unwilling to obey any lesser authority—such as a mere sultan—in case of any conflict between their religious experience and their secular obligations.

Hence the Ottoman sultans fell back upon the learned experts in the Sacred Law of Islam to bring greater order and regularity into the religious life of their subjects. They chose the Sunni form of legality and soon made the Ottoman Empire the strongest supporter of that form of Islam.

The sultans also used their personal household, staffed by slaves, to conduct much of the business of government. Like other Moslem rulers, they organized a corps of slave soldiers, the Janissaries, who acted as a vast bodyguard and elite corps, always ready to obey any command the sultan might issue. With such troops at his disposal, the Ottoman sultan could counterbalance and control the disorderliness of the frontier warriors, upon whose religious enthusiasm and individual prowess the state still fundamentally depended for its continued victories against the Christians.

The sultan also used slaves to govern provinces and to run the central offices of his administration. Promising candidates attended palace schools for training young slaves in the necessary literary and administrative skills. The result was a career open to talent. A simple village boy, seized as a slave in his youth, might end up as grand vizier—the real ruler, on a day-to-day basis, of the Ottoman Empire. For many years, this slave system produced efficient and hard-working administrators who made the sultan's will effective throughout Ottoman territory. The unruliness of Turkish warriors and the strength of the unnumerable local ties and interests among the sultan's subjects were counterbalanced by the absolute dependence of all the members of the slave household upon the sultan—for their posts, promotion, income, and for life itself.

At first the sultan's slave household was recruited mainly through capture in war. When the supply of captives proved too small to staff the Janissary corps and all the posts in the sultan's administration, the Turks began to seize children from remote mountain villages of the western Balkans. These villages were generally too poor to be able to pay much in the way of taxes. But strong and healthy village boys, taken between the ages of twelve and twenty, could, with appropriate training, be made into splendid Janissaries and even more splendid grand viziers.

Thus, by a remarkable reversal of roles, the Ottoman Empire came to be governed by ex-Christian village boys, aided by freeborn Moslem experts in the Sacred Law of Islam. Turkish warriors continued to provide the bulk of the army. Each of them was assigned a village or two for his maintenance; but throughout the summer months these Turkish soldiers had to serve in the sultan's army, usually by fighting on some distant frontier.

This meant, in practice, that the Turks demanded less from the Christian peasants of the Balkans than Christian lords had formerly been accustomed to squeeze out of them. Hence the Turks were popular among the peasants and could afford to leave each village to run its own affairs while the Turkish armed forces were far away, fighting under the sultan's command. Security in the rear allowed the Turks to concentrate their whole fighting force on the frontier, with the result that victories continued to come, almost every year, and Ottoman territory continued to increase until long after 1500.

Islamic Expansion Elsewhere   On other fronts, too, Islam regained the initiative after 1300. In China important Moslem communities arose in Yunnan, to the southwest, and in Kansu to the northwest of China proper. Missionaries also won new successes in southeast Asia. Moslem communities arose in all important trading cities and gradually extended control inland. Java, for example, became a Moslem land by 1526, when coastal princes combined to overthrow the Hindu Empire of the interior. Mindanao, in the Philippines and Borneo in Indonesia, also became Moslem outposts by 1500 or before; while along the east coast of Africa, Moslem towns extended as far south as the mouth of the Zambezi River.

In Africa the Moslems won an important strategic victory when they overwhelmed the Christian kingdom of Nubia (ca. 1400). This al-

New Tensions Within Islam   Renewed expansion of the realm of Islam into India and Europe after 1000 was accompanied by important internal changes. The painting reproduced on top shows the most important novelty, for it portrays a company of dervishes dancing together to induce the trance through which they sought to encounter God. Many dervish orders arose. Not all of them danced; but all did seek direct experience of God, consequently bypassing the Koran and the rules of the Sacred Law. This was a drastic change indeed, and since dervish enthusiasm often threatened to get out of hand, many Moslem rulers set out to reinforce religious orthodoxy by building schools, like the one pictured on the bottom, for students of the Sacred Law. This madrassah, as such schools were called, was built in Samarkand, Tamerlane's capital, in the fifteenth century.

lowed nomadic Moslem tribes to move westward through Africa from the region near the Red Sea all the way to the Niger River. The arrival of these nomads in west Africa actually caused some retreat of agricultural settlement in that region, for the newcomers were accustomed to rob and plunder. But they brought west Africa more fully into contact with the rest of the world

Expansion of Islam These architectural monuments attest to the piety and luxury of two rulers who flourished along opposite frontiers of the Moslem world in the thirteenth and fourteenth centuries. On the left is a mosque built in Delhi in 1199 by the founder of the Slave dynasty that ruled northern India for the next century. It was constructed on the site of a newly destroyed Hindu temple, a fact that symbolized the way the new Moslem rulers of India dominated the Hindu majority with the help of enslaved Turkish soldiers recruited from beyond the Himalayas. On the right is a courtyard in the Alhambra—the palace of the Moslem ruler of Granada, Spain. It was built in the fourteenth century at the other end of the Moslem world and still exhibits the elegance that once prevailed within its walls.

than before, when caravans across the Sahara had been the main link.

Moslem Culture

With such a record of success on every front, the Mongol setback soon ceased to seem important. As Islam expanded into one new region after another, however, the rather narrow mold into which religious ideals had pressed early Islamic culture broke apart. A wide variety of new, or newly perfected, art forms arose. The principal surviving works of Moslem architecture, for example, mostly date from the period after 1300. Handsome mosques for public worship made the dome and slender minaret standard architecture throughout the Persian, Arab, and Turkish lands. In addition, vast and handsome palaces and pleasure gardens were constructed according to a more distinctively Persian architectural tradition. Fewer of these survive for modern inspection.

Persian miniature painting was another high art that began to flourish after the Mongol period. The Persian painters owed a great deal to the Chinese, whose art had come west with the Mongols. But their use of bright colors was entirely different. From Persia the art of miniature painting spread into India, where instead of illustrating Persian books of poetry and romance, artists often represented episodes from Hindu myths.

Persian miniature painting was, in fact, developed to illustrate books of poetry. And throughout the Moslem world Persian poetry became, next only to the Koran, the most important part of genteel education. Turks, Persians, and Arabs alike, if they wished to count as cultivated, had to learn at least a few tags from the great Persian poets.

Firdausi (d. 1020) started the revival of Persian as a language for poetry by writing an epic account of Persian history. But Persia's supreme poetic achievement took the form of lyrical verses in praise of love. Three great poets rang the changes on this theme. The earliest of them, named Rumi (d. 1273), was a Sufi mystic. His poems celebrated God's love for human beings in very sensuous terms. The slightly shocking effect of comparing human love with the relation between believers and their God was carried much further by the other two great Persian poets, Sadi (d. 1291) and Hafiz (d. 1390). By hovering on the edge of sacrilege, they achieved a particularly powerful effect. The poems of Rumi, Sadi, and Hafiz gave the Sufi mystical movement within Islam a suitably ambiguous body of inspired texts, for the Sufi holy men, like the poets, hovered always on the edge of heresy—at least in the opinion of orthodox Sunni Moslems.

In the realm of thought, Islam did not return to philosophy or science. But geographers and travelers described the widening world with gusto and considerable accuracy. And a North African, ibn-Khaldun (d. 1406), wrote a remarkable history of the world. He saw a repetitive pattern in politics based upon persistent differences between nomads and cultivators. Herder-conquerors, he said, always lost their military strength and discipline after three generations of ruling over cultivators, thus preparing the way for a repetition of the cycle of conquest and decay.

Islam was thus in a flourishing condition between 1200 and 1500, having recovered successfully from the Mongol disaster. To be sure, economic life in the old centers of the Moslem world did not thrive. In both Egypt and Mesopotamia, the irrigated area decreased and population declined. In Spain, too, the last Moslem ruler was overthrown by the Spaniards in 1492. But Asia Minor and the Balkans prospered under the Ottoman government, and cities grew up in the region of the central steppe and in eastern Iran where there had not been cities before.

If anyone had been able to survey the world in 1475, before the European voyages of discovery changed world relationships, it would have seemed obvious that the future belonged to Islam (since traders, holy men, and warriors fresh from the central steppes were spreading the faith of Mohammed at a rapid rate in Europe, Africa, and Asia). World affairs took a different turn after 1500, but pious Moslems still remember the times when God's will so obviously favored the Community of the Faithful, and many of them find it hard to understand why success in conflict with unbelievers started suddenly to elude them in modern centuries.

Balkan and Russian Christians

Whenever they were offered a choice, Balkan Christians preferred to submit to the Turks rather than to their fellow Christians from the west. The reason was twofold. As we just saw, Christian rulers squeezed the Balkan peasants and artisans harder than the Turks did. Then, in the second place, whenever western Christians achieved political power in the Balkans, they forced their subjects to change their religion to make it conform to their own kind of papal Christianity. Greek Orthodox populations resented this policy deeply, for they felt that theirs was the only true and correct form of the Christian faith.

The Greek Orthodox church underwent a vital rebirth about 1350. Monkish enthusiasts and mystics, supported by mobs in the streets, made it a rule that only monks could become bishops or archbishops. This was designed to overthrow a party in the Greek church which had tried to negotiate an agreement with the pope in the hope of getting military and financial help from the west. The anti-papal movement did not prevent representatives of the Orthodox patriarch from agreeing to accept a papal definition of Christian doctrine at the Council of Florence in 1439. But this decision was extremely unpopular in Constantinople and was repudiated even before the Ottoman conquest of 1453.

When Mohammed II entered the city, he promptly appointed a new Orthodox patriarch and entrusted him with responsibility for looking after the Christians in the whole of the Ottoman Empire. Armenian Christians and Jews were given a similar organization; so was the Moslem community, a little bit later. In this way the church became for Orthodox Balkan Christians a sort of state within a state. Lawsuits between Christians could not come before Moslem judges, who applied the Sacred Law of Islam. Disputes were therefore settled by church officials, or else by informal agreement and custom of the local Christian community.

Conversion from Christianity to Islam never entirely stopped, but it became much less common when the Moslem missionary enthusiasm of the earliest Ottoman times wore itself out. Only in frontier regions, where prolonged warfare between Moslems and Christians continued, did conversions occur on a mass scale after 1400. Thus, the Balkans remained overwhelmingly Christian. The Turks were only a ruling stratum, except in a few towns where an artisan population of Moslems also came into existence.

Far to the north, amid the Russian forests, another group of Orthodox Christians also found itself under Moslem rule after the khan of the Golden Horde accepted Islam (1257). Under the Mongols, however, both the native Russian princes and the Russian Orthodox church were allowed to conduct their affairs with no day-to-day interference from their distant overlords—so long, that is, as tribute payments were made regularly. The demands for tribute may have forced Russians to produce more; at any rate, agriculture and trade both increased in the Mongol period, and a powerful new administrative machine gradually took form under the control of the grand duke of Moscow. The grand duke owed his position to the fact that he became chief tribute collector for the khan of the Golden Horde. Anything extra he kept for himself; and in some years it even seemed safe to keep back all of the tribute, since the Mongols began to suffer from dynastic quarrels and internal splits after 1419.

The decay of the Golden Horde's power was dramatically demonstrated in 1480, when Grand Duke Ivan III (reigned 1462–1505) announced that he was not going to pay tribute any longer. The only response was an ineffectual raid. Thereafter Muscovy (the territory ruled from Moscow), which comprised most, but not yet all, of the Russian lands, was independent again. It emerged from the Mongol domination as a strongly centralized state supported by a tough-minded tax-collecting bureaucracy and a pious, obedient church.

If they had to choose between foreign overlords, the Russians—like their fellow Christians of the Balkans—clearly preferred the Moslem khans to western Christians. The choice often presented itself because after the crusading states in Palestine collapsed, crusading orders of German knights set themselves up along the coast of the Baltic Sea. From this base they pushed inland, subjugating Latvian and Estonian peasants and completely destroying a stubbornly pagan community of Prussians. (Prussia was then resettled by Germans who, however, kept the Prussian name.) When these Christian crusading orders came up against the borders of the Russian lands, they tried to force the Russians to accept the Latin form of Christianity. Russian princes and peasants agreed in rejecting this course and fought effectively, on several occasions, against the threat to their own faith and way of life that the western (mostly German) knights presented.

The widespread Russian distrust and dislike of the West found expression in the doctrine of the Third Rome. The idea was this: Rome had fallen to the barbarians because of its paganism. Constantine's New Rome on the Bosporus, Constantinople, also had fallen to the Moslem Turks because the Byzantine government had betrayed true Christian doctrine at the Council of Florence by accepting papal errors. Thus there remained only one haven of true Christianity: Moscow, the Third and last Rome, which would never betray Orthodox religion and would therefore endure until Judgment Day. The belief that they guarded a precious truth, destined to save the whole world, remained a deep conviction among the Russian people from that time almost until the present—although under Lenin, Russia began to guard a very different materialist faith.

Indian Inaction

Since the Mongols failed to penetrate India, Indian life and society were not directly affected by the great political storm that raged north of the Himalayas. Nevertheless, the centuries from 1200 to 1500 were full of political upheaval in India. Moslem rulers controlled most of the land, although a large Hindu kingdom of Vijayanagar arose in the south about 1335 and lasted until 1565. But Vijayanagar employed Moslem soldiers sometimes, just as Moslem rulers often employed Hindus as soldiers and administrators. Religious hostility was not important. The old zeal against idolatry that had inspired the first Moslem invaders, or at least had given them a good excuse for plundering Hindu temples and Buddhist monasteries, was gone.

With time, however, interaction between Islam and Hinduism began to make a difference to both communities. Among Hindus, some religious teachers began to argue that Hinduism and Islam had fundamentally the same message—a simple, monotheistic, and basically mystic faith. The most influential person who talked in this way was Kabir (lived about 1450), whom the Sikhs today regard as the founder of their religion.

Among Indian Moslems, the Indian environment encouraged the rise of a great variety of holy men, some of whom developed wildly heretical views. One sect, for example, held that Mohammed's son-in-law, Ali, was an incarnation of the Hindu god Vishnu. Moslem rulers were usually too insecure on their thrones to try to enforce any sort of religious uniformity. Even in the heartland of Islam all sorts of sects taught different doctrines and yet got along with one another somehow. The range of toleration in India was even wider, for the Moslems could not usually afford to offend Hindu feeling too sharply, and in Hinduism almost anything was possible.

India, therefore, saw no great changes. Life went on, while holy men, as they had done for centuries, looked beyond the varied everyday scene to the real world of transcendent truth—where suffering and luxury, victory and defeat, shrank to nothingness.

Conclusion

The dramatic rise of the Mongol Empire and its later breakup made less difference to the peoples of Asia than might be expected. This was because the Mongols, after an initial period of paganism, accepted the different cultural and religious traditions of the people they had conquered. Some mingling occurred as a result of the improved communications that held the Mongol Empire together. But they were limited to matters of little importance—Chinese motifs in Persian miniature paintings, for example. Each of the great Asian civilizations—Chinese, Moslem, and Indian—had worked out traditions and techniques of its own so well that even when attractive novelties appeared, they were marginal.

Deliberate rejection of new techniques and ideas went very far. The Moslems, for example, repudiated printing, although they learned of it from contacts with China long before Europeans did. The reason was that Moslem teachers felt it would be irreverent, even sacrilegious, to reproduce the Koran, God's own Word, by mechanical means. To prevent such a possibility, they prohibited printing entirely.

Such conservatism was fully matched elsewhere. When people felt that all important problems had already been solved, new ideas or methods of making things met with great resistance. Novelties from foreign lands were usually not worth the trouble they caused. As a result, the Mongol unification of northern Asia left few lasting traces behind. Ming rulers of China, where the Mongol imprint had been by far the strongest, tried systematically to erase everything they felt to be of foreign origin. Hindus and Moslems behaved in an essentially similar fashion, preferring to develop and carry forward—within their own civilizations—trends that had already been underway before the Mongol conquests.

Japan, however, reacted to victory over the Mongols by cutting loose from the Chinese leading strings that had previously dominated Japanese higher culture. At the other extreme of the Eurasian continent, western Europeans found themselves in a similar position. They never had to face the Mongol army, yet they took advantage of what they could learn from distant China, as well as from nearer regions and places, with reckless energy. And because Europeans were able to respond to new possibilities more successfully than others, they laid the basis for their later expansion around the world during the centuries 1200–1500, when the rest of the civilized world (except in the Americas) suffered from and reacted against the Mongol conquests.

In the next chapter we will therefore describe the changes that came to western Europe in these years.

Bibliography

Two famous travelogues constitute by far the best introduction from contemporary sources to the subject matter of this chapter: Marco Polo, *Travels*, available in many editions and with varying titles; and H. A. R. Gibb, trans., *Ibn Batuta, Travels in Asia and Africa* (1929). These two men, one from Venice and the other from Morocco, crossed the whole of Asia and reported what they saw with remarkable accuracy. The Mongol Empire did much to facilitate such travel, and Francis Woodman Cleaves, *The Secret History of the Mongols* (1982), allows us to read a contemporary Mongol account. A very different literary monument of the time was the work of Persian poets and mystics. These may be sampled in the translations sprinkled through Edward G. Browne, *A Literary History of Persia* (Vol. 2, 1956). Edward Fitzgerald, *The Rubáiyát of Omar Khayyám* (1859), is a free translation of one such poem. It is often reprinted in anthologies of English literature because of its extraordinary impact on Victorian England.

The Mongol Empire united northern Asia and eastern Europe as never before. Three recent books deal with these remarkable conquerors: David O. Morgan, *The Mongols* (1986); Thomas T. Allsen, *Mongol Imperialism: The Policies of the Grand Qan Mongke in China, Russia and the Islamic Lands, 1251–1259* (1987); and John J. Saunders, *The History of the Mongol Conquest* (1971). A readable biography of Genghis Khan, founder of the empire, is Rene Grousset, *Conqueror of the World* (1966). Paul Ratchnevsky, *Genghis Khan: His Life and Legacy* (1992), is more scholarly. Leonardo Olschki, *Marco Polo's Asia* (1960), offers an excellent survey of what the Mongols did with what they conquered.

Christopher Dawson, *The Mongol Mission* (1955), describes papal efforts to win the new world conquerors over to the Christian side. In addition to consulting appropriate general books listed in Chapter 10's bibliography, the Moslem response to the Mongols' assault may be examined with the help of P. M. Holt, *The Age of the Crusades: The Near East from the Eleventh Century to 1517* (1986); and John J. Saunders, ed., *The Muslim World on the Eve of Europe's Expansion* (1966). The main new political growth in the realm of Islam was the work of Ottoman Turks, incisively analyzed by Paul Witteck, *The Rise of the Ottoman Empire* (1957), and treated more at length in Halil Inalcik, *The Ottoman Empire: The Classical Age, 1300–1600* (1989), and Colin Imber, *The Ottoman Empire, 1300–1481* (1990). Two other books deal with important changes that altered Islamic society in these centuries: Patricia Crone, *Slaves on Horses: The Evolution of the Islamic Polity* (1980), which discusses how slave soldiers rose to political power in many Moslem lands; and Ira Lapidus, *Muslim Cities in the Later Middle Ages* (1967), which analyzes social changes within the great cities of Islam that facilitated the rise of slave regimes.

The Mongol impact on Russia is dealt with by George Vernadsky, *The Mongols and Russia* (1969), and Charles J. Halperin, *Russia and the Golden Horde: The Mongol Impact on Medieval Russian History* (1987). The Muscovite counter-thrust is the theme of

Robert Crummey, *The Formation of Muscovy, 1304–1613* (1987).

For Chinese developments, the following books are helpful: John D. Langlois, ed., *China under Mongol Rule* (1981); Herbert Franke, *From Tribal Chieftain to Universal Emperor and God: The Legitimation of the Yuan Dynasty* (1978); Theodore De Bary, *Neo-Confucian Orthodoxy and the Learning of the Mind and Heart* (1981); and Charles O. Hucker, *The Ming Dynasty: Its Origins and Evolving Institutions* (1978). The extraordinary story of Chinese exploration in the Indian Ocean is told by J. J. L. Duyvendak, *China's Discovery of Africa* (1949).

Books listed previously deal adequately with the art history of different parts of Asia in these centuries; but one specialized book may be added here: Sherman E. Lee and Wai-kam Ho, *Chinese Art under the Mongols: The Yuan Dynasty 1279–1368* (1968).

Civilizations; 1200 to 1500

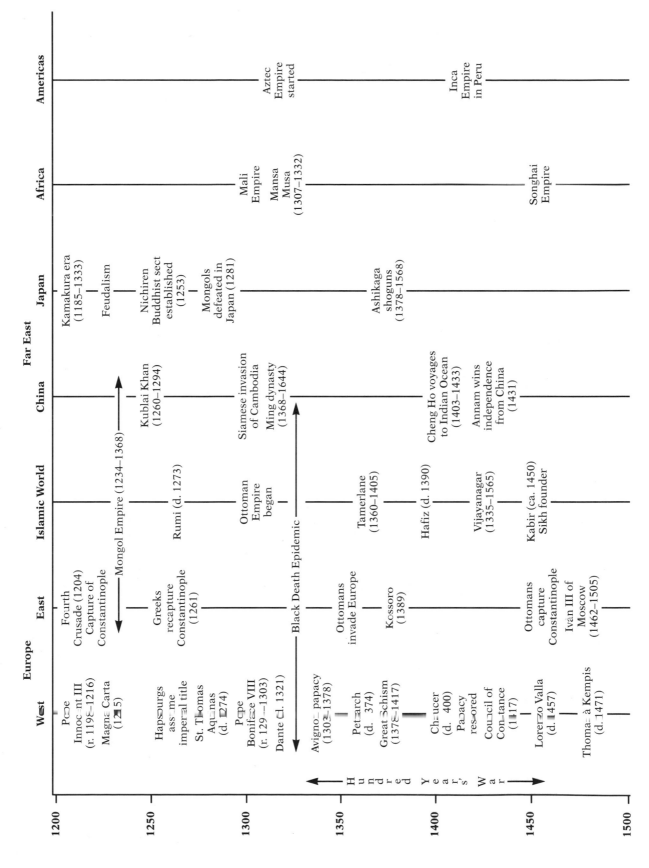

Western Europe
1200 to 1500

14

Gothic Art and Merchant Wealth   The Venetian merchant who built this Gothic
palace about 1430 used it as a place in which to live and do business. His
uninhibited pursuit of wealth, and equally uninhibited pursuit of truth and holiness
by others, coexisted uneasily in European cities during the Middle Ages.

Western Europe, between 1200 and 1500, went through a period when all the diverse elements of the western inheritance seemed to come together into a balanced, internally coherent pattern, and then found that balance toppling over as new ideas and techniques called into question various aspects of the earlier synthesis.

During the initial period of bloom, the Church played a central part throughout Latin Christendom. Church officials controlled most art and nearly all learning as well as many aspects of daily life. Secular rulers, landlords, craft guilds, and village communities also had their place; but the special and peculiar stamp of medieval civilization came always from the Church.

The breakup of this "medieval synthesis" therefore meant a weakening of the power of the Church. Royal governments, for example, clearly proved superior to the international administration of the papacy when matters came to a head in 1303. On the level of theory, critics arose who challenged the clergy's right to worldly power. Others undermined the position of the Church by turning to the study of ancient pagan authors with a new enthusiasm that left less room for Christian teaching. Art also ceased to be so wholly in the service of the Church.

The Church was, of course, not the only victim of Europe's continuing upheaval. Knighthood suffered from the rise of disciplined infantry and the multiplication of walled towns. Craft guilds and even the manorial system, upon which the economic upswing of medieval Europe had rested, also began to alter in fundamental ways when a class of cotters—who were part-time artisans, part-time cultivators—became numerous in the most developed parts of the European countryside.

What was challenged and in doubt could be defined easily enough by 1500. Not until long after that time did anything like a new pattern promising some sort of stability begin to emerge in western Europe. Nevertheless, 1500 is a good date at which to break off the story of how Europe changed and kept on changing, because it marks the approximate time when European ship captains opened all the oceans of the earth to regular voyaging and inaugurated a new era of world history.

The Medieval Synthesis

Between about 1200 and 1275, the medieval Church brought the entire civilization of western Europe into unusually sharp focus. Christian and pagan, as well as Roman and barbarian inheritances from the past, blended into a new whole. The different groups and classes of society quarreled often enough, yet the energies of townspeople, clergy, great lords, and common peasants nevertheless combined more effectively in these decades than they did earlier or later. Historians often refer to this period as the High Middle Ages. Another name, which draws attention to the way in which quite different elements were brought together harmoniously during this time, is the medieval synthesis.

By 1200 the poverty, ignorance, and local self-sufficiency of Europe's Dark Ages already lay behind. The rise of towns, the increase of communication through trade and travel, the crusades and pilgrimages to especially holy shrines, all meant that people knew a lot more about the world and about what others did and thought than had been possible before. This offered a challenge to the Church and to Christianity, since local variations in religion and many new thoughts could (and did) spread. It was not enough to say, "It is so because it is so." But priests and teachers met the challenge successfully and so were able to balance religious and secular ideas and ideals for about a century.

The Meaning of the Medieval Church

To understand medieval civilization, it is important to have a clear idea of what the Church was and how it affected ordinary people's lives. According to medieval theologians, the Church was the "channel of grace" through which God made salvation available to human beings. *Grace* was forgiveness of sins. Only God could grant that, and He did it through the sacraments of the Church.

There were seven sacraments. Four of them were usually administered only once in a person's life: baptism, which came soon after birth and wiped away the child's original sin; confirmation, which came in youth and signified the individual's conscious acceptance of membership in the community of Christians that had already been symbolized by baptism; marriage, which needs no explanation here; and extreme unction, administered on the deathbed, which erased any remaining sins.

Two of the sacraments could be repeated as often as needed. They were the Eucharist or sacrifice of the Mass that constituted the central act of Christian worship; and penance (or confession) which, in conjunction with the Eucharist, wiped away sins committed since the prior confession. The last of the sacraments was ordination, which made priests different from ordinary people by conferring upon them the power to administer the other sacraments. Without the sacraments, administered by a properly ordained priest, natural impulses were sure to lead human beings into sin; and sin, if not forgiven by God's grace, caused the soul's damnation to eternal suffering in Hell.

Careful attention to religious duties as defined by the Church was, therefore, the only way a person could expect to attain salvation. This meant obedience to priests, and priests were supposed to obey the bishops who ordained them. The authority of bishops, in turn, descended directly from the Apostles (whose successors they were); and the Apostles received their authority from Christ himself. Among the bishops, the bishop of Rome, or pope, was preeminent. Papal power rested on the doctrine that the bishop of Rome was successor to St. Peter, the chief of the Apostles. An old and probably correct tradition held that St. Peter had been martyred in Rome under the emperor Nero. This gave the popes ground for claiming to be his successor, endowed with all the powers that Christ had assigned to Peter.

But the popes also claimed to have superior authority to all secular rulers in matters of ordinary government. This claim was based in part upon a document known as the Donation of Constantine. According to this text, when the Emperor Constantine moved his capital to Constantinople, he transferred the government of the western provinces of the Roman Empire to

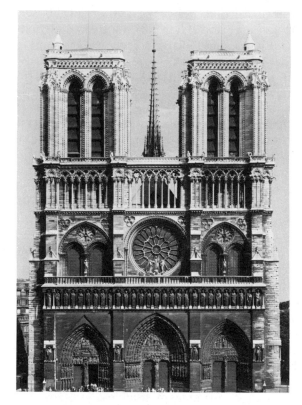

Notre Dame Cathedral, Paris   The foundation stone of this cathedral was laid by Pope Alexander III in 1163 on behalf of the bishop of Paris, who had conceived the ambition of building a new church for himself and the city of Paris. The architect used radically new methods of construction that permitted him to lift the roof 157 feet above the floor, while flooding the interior with colored light from rows of stained glass windows. The effect was (and is) gorgeous. Yet taste changed, and in the eighteenth century this style of architecture was disdainfully labeled "Gothic." Still later, in the nineteenth century, art historians began to admire the aesthetic and engineering triumphs of Gothic architecture, and it is still much admired today. The facade, shown in this photograph, was completed in 1240. Original plans called for slender spires on the top of each tower, but they were never built. Work on porches along the sides of the building and other ornamental details went on for a full century after 1240. Rising wealth and local pride combined to erect dozens of similar cathedrals in other towns of Latin Christendom between 1200 and 1500.

the pope. As early as 1450, a famous scholar, Lorenzo Valla, proved that this was a forgery; but in the Middle Ages, the text was believed to be authentic.

The pope's claims to superior authority over secular rulers did not rest entirely on the Donation of Constantine, however. There was also the Bible, which tells that, when Roman soldiers arrested Christ in the Garden of Gethsemane, Peter drew a sword, only to sheathe it again at Christ's command. This, medieval commentators argued, showed that St. Peter had the rightful power to inflict death on others; and this power, they asserted, descended to his successors, the popes of Rome, and gave them supreme secular as well as supreme religious authority on earth.

Church Government

Such arguments, of course, could only be meaningful if the popes were, in fact, able to build up a system of government that could make papal decisions hold, even when some local ruler opposed them. This had been the real issue in the great struggle with the German emperors that began in 1076, for if the emperors controlled the bishops and abbots of Germany and Italy, then the pope could not make his government effective. By 1200, as we have seen, the power of the emperor had been thoroughly broken and the bishops and abbots of Germany and Italy were, more or less, ready to obey the pope. Elsewhere the popes achieved nearly the same results without quarreling openly with kings and princes.

The whole of western Europe, wherever the pope's power was recognized, was divided into archdioceses, with an archbishop in charge of each. Archdioceses were divided into dioceses, each with its bishop; and the dioceses were in turn divided into parishes, where a priest had charge of all the souls living there. Parish priests might be appointed in various ways. Usually some local landowner had the right to choose a candidate. But only a bishop could ordain a priest. This usually allowed bishops to veto any bad appointment.

Much the same system prevailed in appointing bishops. Nomination had to come from the clergy of the cathedral, but the archbishop and pope both had the right to examine the way in which the election had been made, and they were in fact often consulted in advance. The pope, ever since the reform of 1059, was chosen by the cardinal clergy of Rome; and a reigning pope had the right to appoint cardinals.

Bishops were the key administrators of the Church. Building cathedrals and arranging for religious services constituted only a small part of their duties. Collecting rents and other income and administering Church properties took much attention. In addition, Church law covered any dispute in which the sacraments played a part. This meant, in effect, that practically any lawsuit could be brought before a Church court and tried according to Church law. However, local rulers never accepted this broad interpretation of the Church's power. Various deals were made, according to which some types of cases went to Church courts and other kinds of cases came before the king's or some lesser nobles' courts.

The question of which courts should have the right to try particular cases was of the highest importance in medieval government. Fees and fines brought income to the court that tried the cases; moreover, when possession of property was at stake, as was often the case, who it was that judged the case often affected the verdict. The Church, for example, often acquired property as gifts from repentant individuals on the point of death. The dying did not always have time to complete all legal formalities. Even when the intention of the deceased person was clear, heirs might not accept proofs offered by Church officials who were also beneficiaries of the will. In such a case, it mattered a good deal whether the quarrel came before the king's court or a bishop's court.

The Enforcement of Papal Authority   The pope tried to make all the bishops cooperate. Letters and more formal instructions were fundamental means for doing so. In addition, when something important was in the wind, the pope might appoint a legate with special authority to act in his place. The pope might also call a council, either of all bishops or of those in a selected part of Christendom, and give them instructions or ask their support and advice about particular problems. Thus, for example, when Pope Innocent III (reigned 1198–1216) called the Fourth Lateran Council in 1215, it settled various questions of doctrine and declared that every Christian ought to accept the sacrament of confession and do penance as prescribed by his or her parish priest at least once a year.

The magnificence of church services, the force of Christian doctrine as preached and taught by the learned men of Europe, and the threat of hellfire caused most people to honor and obey the Church, in principle at least. The great majority, of course, fell short and failed to live up to Christian virtues in some degree or other. But the sacraments were always available to wash away sins.

Some pious souls were not content with such an easy way of assuring salvation. For them, the regulated life of monks in monasteries offered a stricter life of worship and an opportunity to do holy works. The monks lived according to rules—in Latin, *regula*—and so are called regular clergy, whereas priests and bishops are called secular clergy. Because the regular clergy were particularly holy, they often became wealthy. Elderly people who felt the weight of their sins frequently gave property to a monastery, in return for which the monks promised to pray for the donor's soul even after he or she had died. Such gifts, of course, made the monks rich, and rich monasteries tended to relax the pursuit of holiness. This situation called for reform; but reformed monasteries, by their fierce dedication to holiness, regularly became wealthy, too, and so prepared the way for a new wave of reform.

Challenges Before the Church   From the time of the First Crusade (1096–1099) onward, the Church made considerable progress in Christianizing knighthood. The fighters who answered Pope Urban II's call for the crusade were serving the Church and Christendom, as well as looking for new lands to conquer for themselves. The idea that a knight should fight only in good causes, should protect the weak, and should remedy injustices became a theme of poetry. Courts and castles began to echo to the tales of King Arthur and his knights, Charlemagne and Roland, Parsifal, the Nibelungs, and others. These stories illustrated Christian ideals of *noblesse oblige*, that is, the duty of the strong to help others. Boys of noble and knightly rank, brought up to familiarity with these stories, acquired a code of manners softened, though by no means completely controlled, by Christian ideals.

The towns offered a more complicated challenge to the Church. Urban populations often opposed the bishop who, as chief local landlord, wanted to rule the town, or at least tried to restrict local self-government. In addition, townspeople often criticized ignorant, greedy, or immoral priests. Heresies began to spread, especially in northern Italy and southern France. The most radical was a form of Manichaeism, commonly called the Albigensian heresy because the town of Albi in southern France became a hotbed of the faith. The Albigensians, like most other heretics, were looking for more rigorous moral and religious leadership than ordinary parish priests were able to give.

Pope Innocent III found a solution to the challenge of disaffection in the towns when he authorized an informal brotherhood that St. Francis of Assisi (1182–1226) had already gathered around himself. St. Francis was a layman, a mystic, and a man totally given over to religion. He preached, helped the sick and the poor, and set an example of joyous selflessness. He and his followers strove to imitate Christ and the Apostles in a simple, literal fashion. Giving up all possessions, they lived from hand-to-mouth on charity and did good in every way they knew how.

Here were people whose practical example came up to the demands of even the most critical towndwellers. But from the point of view of priests and bishops, the friars—from Latin *fratres*, meaning "brothers"—offered an embarrassing kind of competition. Bishops, after all, were the official successors to the apostles. What right had mere laymen to imitate Christ and the apostles, especially when their mode of life, modeled on the Gospel account, differed so much from the pomp and wealth that surrounded the pope and other rulers of the Church?

Pope Innocent III, therefore, hesitated before approving St. Francis' order and insisted that the friars must have a definite organiza-

Authority and Innovation in the Church
Buying and selling and working for wages—
and above all lending money at interest—did
not fit in with the way Christ and the Apostles
had lived. Many pious souls were bothered by
the obvious contradiction between town life
and the Biblical ideal. St. Francis of Assisi was
one such soul. He therefore gave away all his
possessions and proceeded to imitate Christ
quite literally, going about doing good and
living on gifts from well-wishers. This style of
life contrasted with the wealth and dignity
enjoyed by the rulers of the church. When
Francis attracted a body of followers who
strove to live as he did, some of them started to
criticize the bishops, who claimed to be the
successors of the Apostles, for failing to
imitate Christ as they were doing. The
Franciscan movement thus teetered on the
verge of heresy; but in 1215 Pope Innocent III
set out to reconcile St. Francis's innovative
piety with the traditional authority of the
church by approving a rule that would govern
Francis's followers, St. Francis rather
reluctantly agreed. This painting, made by
Giotto more than a century after the event,
portrays St. Francis receiving the rule from
Pope Innocent, seated on his throne. Giotto's
art conveys the rival authority of Pope and
Saint—balanced, opposed, yet ultimately
reconciled.

tion. St. Francis was troubled by the Pope's efforts to regulate his followers. Accordingly, he
retired from the headship of the order shortly
before his death, because Church authorities
wanted his followers to set up houses, each with
its duly appointed head. This meant acquiring
property, which St. Francis thought would spoil
the whole idea behind his order. On the other
hand, he always emphasized obedience to the
pope; and on this issue, as on others, he submitted reluctantly.

St. Francis' obedience and Pope Innocent
III's statesmanship thus allowed the explosive
energy that gathered around the Franciscan
movement to operate within the framework of
the Church. Franciscan friars tapped feelings
that had previously poured into heretical channels, and they made Christian idealism a living
reality in the towns of western Europe.

St. Dominic (1170–1221) also organized a
brotherhood of friars. He wanted to make his
followers into popular preachers who would convert Albigensians and other heretics by arguing
the truths of Christian doctrine with greater
knowledge and conviction than parish priests
were usually able to muster. This required special training, and almost at once the Dominicans
became prominent in university life. It also required organization, and the representative system that St. Dominic invented for the government of the Dominican order became a model
for the reorganization of the Franciscan order
after St. Francis' death. It also influenced later
development of parliamentary representation in
royal governments.

The Church's Influence on Culture

The influence of the Church was strong on all
forms of cultural life. The music, hymns, and
splendid robes of church services, together with
the vaulted architecture of the new Gothic
churches that arose all over Europe, were great
achievements in themselves. An abundant literature of saints' lives reinforced Christian teachings. "Miracle plays" reenacted sacred stories.

Even the most irreverent tales, especially popular among townsfolk, often paid priests the backhanded compliment of expecting them to be better than other men by holding their failings up to ridicule.

The Church controlled almost all formal education. Elementary schools taught Latin—not the language of Cicero, but a living Church Latin that was used in everyday speech by the learned of all western Europe. It contained many words unknown to the ancients and used simplified grammar. In addition, schoolboys got a smattering of the liberal arts as handed down from antiquity. These were classified as grammar, rhetoric, logic, arithmetic, geometry, music, and astronomy. Above that level came university work for those who wished to qualify for professional careers. Medieval universities offered training in law, medicine, and theology. Medicine was studied with the help of the works of Galen and the Moslem Avicenna, both translated into Latin. Law meant study of Justinian's Code of the ancient Roman law or study of contemporary Church law. When, as in England, a body of royal law came into existence, it was not studied at universities, which were Church organizations, but in separate institutions, the so-called Inns of Court.

Scholasticism

Theology held first place among the subjects studied at medieval universities. Theologians undertook to explain Christian teachings about God's plan for saving human souls from their sins. They sought above all to make Christian doctrine logical and consistent, so when, soon after 1200, Aristotle's works were translated into Latin, they found his sort of clear logic exactly what they were looking for.

To be sure, some felt that Aristotle's writings should be left strictly alone because they were pagan. But unlike the Moslems, most of whom took this position, leading Christian theologians boldly set out to use Aristotle's logical method to show how the doctrines of the Church fitted in with truths knowable by human reasoning. The university of Paris became the main center of this enterprise. Those who carried it through are known as Scholastics because they taught in schools, and their ideas and method of arguing are called Scholasticism.

The greatest of the Scholastics was St. Thomas Aquinas (1225–1274). His main work is entitled *Summa Theologica*, that is, *Summary of Theology*. It consists of a series of questions, each answered by presenting various opinions pro and con, followed by Aquinas' own answer, with reasons for it, and ending with a refutation or reinterpretation of the opinions disagreeing with the position Aquinas had taken. In this book St. Thomas Aquinas took up almost every dispute that had been raised among theologians in his time, and he provided reasonable and moderate answers to all of them. He was both admired and attacked in his lifetime—for he trusted reason very far, believing that it could demonstrate all but a very few of the revealed truths upon which human salvation depended.

Dante's Divine Comedy

A second great literary expression of the medieval world view was created by the poet Dante Alighieri (1265–1321). Dante was born in Florence, Italy, but in 1302 his political enemies exiled him. These enemies were allies of the pope. This made Dante fiercely antipapal. Yet he was also profoundly Christian.

His great poem, the *Divine Comedy,* put everyone and everything in its proper place. He did this by sending his soul on an imaginary trip through Hell, Purgatory, and Heaven and describing what he encountered. Pope Boniface VIII, for example, Dante assigned to Hell; others found their places in Purgatory and Heaven. The poet also made clear in each case *why* each soul was in bliss or torment. The result, therefore, was a vivid poetic statement of the medieval conception of the human condition, teetering precariously on earth between an eternal home in Heaven or in Hell.

Dante was one of the earliest poets to write in Italian. He used the dialect of Florence, which through his work, and that of others, became standard for all of Italy. In other parts of western Europe, other vernaculars began to emerge as literary languages a bit later. Geoffrey Chaucer (1340–1400), for example, wrote his *Canterbury Tales* in London dialect and thereby helped to shape the mixture of Anglo-Saxon, French, and Latin spoken in London into the language we know as English.

The Rise of National Monarchies

The importance of the papacy between 1200 and 1275 and the unity in diversity that the Church was able to create in western Europe depended in part on the weakness of other political units.

Central and Eastern Europe

Emperor Frederick II (reigned 1212–1250) gave up trying to rule Germany and concentrated only on making his power over Sicily and southern Italy secure. This decision aroused papal opposition. Soon after Frederick's death in 1250, the imperial office became vacant. Not until 1273 did a new emperor take office. He was Rudolph of Hapsburg, a minor German nobleman, chosen largely because he had no hope of dominating Germany and Italy on the strength of his personal power or private possessions. Rudolph did not try. Instead, he founded his family's fortunes by taking for himself the first attractive landholding that became vacant, which happened to be Austria. His descendants remained rulers there until 1918.

All of central Europe, therefore, from the Baltic to Sicily, broke up into small states of various kinds. There were city-states, such as Florence, run by a republican government. There were princely states; states governed by bishops; and minor kingdoms, such as Sicily or Bohemia. In addition, a swarm of "imperial knights" who recognized no superior except the distant and powerless emperor were also effectively sovereign—at least in their own backyard.

Around Europe's rim, however, larger kingdoms took form. In the east, Poland and Hungary stood guard against the steppe. Like the Scandinavian kingdoms, they were relatively poor and thinly inhabited. The Polish kings saw the need for towns and trade, and they thus encouraged Jews from Germany to come to their kingdom in order to build up these activities. The Jews, living in small communities in many European towns, suffered serious persecutions during the crusades. Christian soldiers, en route to their wars against the Moslems, often attacked them as unbelievers. This made many Jews glad to flee eastward, with the result that Poland became the main center of Jewish population in Europe by about 1400. Most of the functions carried out by townsfolk in the west were performed by Jews in Poland. The Poles thus acquired a relatively well-developed town life and began to export grain, timber, and other raw materials to the more crowded lands of western Europe.

The Scandinavian kingdoms in the north were barely strong enough to resist the German trading cities of the Baltic, for with the end of Viking raids, the kings of Denmark and Sweden (Norway was usually combined with one or the other) had little income with which to maintain any kind of strong government.

The Kingdoms of France and England

The kingdom of France to the west was far more important, for it was the main center of knighthood, of manorial agriculture, of the Gothic style of architecture, of Scholasticism—in short, of everything most distinctive in Europe's civilization. But France was divided into dozens of feudal states, and the king of France was only first among equals.

From the time of Hugh Capet (reigned 987–996) the kings of France ruled the Île-de-France, that is, a territory lying between the Seine and Loire rivers, including both Paris, in the north, and Orléans, in the south. But this principality was no greater in extent or wealth than half a dozen others in France. Such states as the duchy of Normandy, established in 911 by Northmen or Normans who settled in the lower valley of the Seine, or the county of Flanders, where the cloth trade developed early, were nominally part of France. Their rulers held their land, in theory, as fiefs from the king of France. In fact, however, the duke of Normandy and the count of Flanders drew a good deal more income from their lands than the king enjoyed from the Île-de-France. They were correspondingly more powerful than their nominal sovereign.

This gap between theory and practice increased after 1066, when the duke of Normandy (William the Conqueror) seized England and became king of England as well as duke of Normandy. During the next century a series of marriages produced an even more lopsided situation, for Henry II, king of England (reigned 1154–1189), was also count of Anjou, duke of Aquitaine, duke of Normandy, and lord of still other French fiefs. He, in fact, controlled more than half of France and was a far more powerful ruler than the French king.

Nevertheless, legal forms sometimes mattered. In 1202 Henry's youngest son, John, was king of England. The king of France, Philip Augustus (reigned 1180–1223), stirred up trouble between John and some of his subordinate vassals and then summoned King John to come to court in order to try the case. This was entirely in accord with feudal law; and when King John refused to attend the court of his liege lord, the king of France, Philip Augustus, declared all his fiefs forfeit. This, too, was perfectly legal. The surprising thing was that King Philip was able to enforce the legal decision. He was helped by the fact that King John was also in trouble with the pope because of a dispute over the election of the archbishop of Canterbury. Philip was, therefore, able to march in and take over John's French fiefs, adding them to his own domain.

King John then decided to divide his enemies by making peace with the pope. Pope Innocent III required him to surrender his kingdom to the papacy, and then granted it back to him as a fief. From John's point of view, this maneuver was intended to assure papal support against Philip; but John's effort to get revenge failed in 1214, when his troops were defeated at the Battle of Bouvines.

This failure, in turn, encouraged the barons of England to revolt and demand that King John stop trying to wring more taxes from them and the whole kingdom, without their consent. John, once again, was helpless and had to submit to his vassals' demands by signing the Magna Carta at Runnymede, outside of London, in 1215. Magna Carta listed things King John and his agents had done against the will or interests of the barons and promised that the king would stop all such practices. The pope later declared that John did not have to obey an oath taken under threat of violence; but John's son, Henry III (reigned 1216–1272), reaffirmed Magna Carta early in his reign. It thus became a basic charter of English liberties to which opponents of royal power frequently appealed.

After this great success, the French monarchy went from strength to strength. The son of Philip Augustus led a crusade against the Albigensians and annexed the county of Toulouse, where heresy had been particularly widespread. The result was that between 1202 and 1216 the territory directly under royal administration in France increased about eight times. The French king had suddenly become the strongest ruler in Christendom.

Kingship and sainthood usually did not mix, but between 1226 and 1270 France was ruled by a man, Louis IX, who combined the two roles very successfully. Louis was a good and pious man. As such, he defended the Church and died on crusade against the Moslems in Egypt. He also made peace with the English, and allowed the separate duchies and counties of France to remain as they were when his predecessors annexed them. That is to say, separate administrations with different tax systems and local variations in law continued to operate as before. The difference was that the French king now received the income formerly collected by local counts or dukes. The king appointed bailiffs to make sure that the proper revenues were paid on time. This created the beginnings of a central administration—but only the beginnings.

In England, from the time of the Viking invasions, a far more systematic central administration existed. William the Conqueror kept the division of the kingdom into shires, each headed by a sheriff appointed by the king. In addition, a national system of royal justice developed. The king sent traveling judges on circuit (that is, on trips to certain places) to hear cases brought before them by aggrieved persons who were willing and able to pay the fees required before the royal judges would hear a case. The decisions of the king's traveling judges soon built up what came to be called the common law, that

Royal Power and Dignity   This painting shows Philip VI of France (reigned 1328–1350) presiding over a meeting of the Royal Council. The bishops on the right are just as much his subjects as are the noblemen on the left, while commoners, at the bottom, made royal power increasingly effective by carrying out the decisions of the king and council.

is, a body of law common to the whole kingdom. The procedure had the advantage of allowing low-ranking people to get justice against even a great nobleman, if they had both a good case and enough money to pay the necessary fees.

When the king of England lost his French possessions, the two kingdoms started to grow apart. Norman French gradually ceased to be the language of the English court, and a new language—English—developed from a merger between the Anglo-Saxon speech of the common people and the French and Latin formerly spoken by the governing class. A new nation likewise arose, as the nobility lost its French connections. In France, unification was much slower.

Differences between the old feudal principalities usually seemed more important than anything shared by all the subjects of the French king.

The Spanish Kingdoms

The Spanish peninsula was divided into five separate Christian kingdoms, of which Portugal, Castile, and Aragon were the most important. Aragon closely resembled southern France, but elsewhere in Spain there were important differences. For example, Moslems and Jews played a large role in the towns. This drove a wedge between the kings and the townspeople, for the Spanish rulers kept alive the crusading idea as long as part of the peninsula remained under Moslem control. The crusading outlook, in turn, tended to maintain close ties between the class of noble fighting men and the various kings of the Spanish peninsula, whereas in other parts of western Europe, kings usually aligned themselves with the towns and against the nobles. Spanish politics and society therefore differed from that of the rest of Latin Christendom in fundamental ways even before the discovery of America (1492) gave Spain a unique new role in world affairs.

The Breakdown of the Medieval Synthesis

St. Louis of France died in 1270; Henry III of England followed him to the grave two years later. They were succeeded by less pious and more aggressive kings who were not content to leave the pope with such wide powers as Louis and Henry had done. At about the same time, the growth of towns slowed down. Friction between the poor and the rich became serious; guilds split between masters and wageworkers, and political power in the towns tended to concentrate in the hands of a relatively small number of influential men and powerful guilds, squeezing out the poorer classes. The open flexibility of the years between 1200 and 1275, when townspeople, rulers, and clergy all worked together without sharp conflict, came to an end.

The Decline of Papal Power

The most dramatic sign of the new age was the disruption of papal leadership. Pope Boniface VIII (reigned 1294–1303) quarreled with Philip IV, king of France (reigned 1285–1314), over the question of whether the king had the right to tax the clergy who lived in France. Boniface prohibited such taxation; but King Philip defied the pope and felt the issue was so important that he called together representatives of all the influential classes of France—clergy, nobility, and townspeople—in order to explain to them what the quarrel was about and to seek their help. This was the first meeting of the Estates-General, which later French kings summoned from time to time when they wanted special taxes or some other kind of support from the country at large. It corresponded closely to the English Parliament that had emerged as a regular feature of English government a generation earlier.

Having assured himself of support at home, Philip sent a small detachment of troops into Italy and kidnapped the pope, who was staying in the little town of Anagni. Pope Boniface was outraged; Christendom was aghast; and Philip himself scarcely knew what to do with the pope once he had seized him. The French soon released their captive; but the events at Anagni in 1303 quickly became a symbol of the papacy's fall, just as the humiliation of Emperor Henry IV at Canossa in 1077 had symbolized the dawn of papal ascendancy over secular rulers.

Pope Boniface died a few months after his release. The cardinals then selected a Frenchman, Clement V, as pope. He promptly made peace with King Philip by giving in on all disputed points. The new pope did not go to Rome, but set up headquarters at Avignon, a town on the Rhone River just outside the borders of the kingdom of France. For more than seventy years the popes remained at Avignon and governed the Church by working closely in harmony with the kings of France. King and pope, in effect, agreed to tax the lower clergy more and more heavily—

and to divide the proceeds between themselves. A similar deal was made with the king of England, though cooperation was never so close. Elsewhere in Europe, too, the Avignon popes developed more and more ways of increasing papal income. Their methods often dismayed pious persons.

Some Franciscans felt that this kind of Church betrayed Christ's teaching and example. They remembered St. Francis' praise of poverty and declared that the only way to follow Christ and the Apostles was to give up income-producing property and depend on charity. These Franciscans were called "Spirituals." Their praise of poverty implied criticism of the pope and of all other rich clergy. The popes responded by declaring the doctrine that the Apostles had not owned any property to be heretical. When some of the Spiritual Franciscans refused to change their opinions, they were burned.

But no sooner did one heresy disappear under threat of persecution than another appeared. John Wycliffe (d. 1384), a professor at Oxford, for example, began to develop radical views that won wide following in England. From England, Wycliffe's movement passed to Bohemia, where John Hus (burned at the stake in 1415) found himself in sympathy with some of Wycliffe's ideas.

Obviously, the link that Pope Innocent III and St. Francis had established between the official Church, with all its pomp, ceremony, riches, and splendor on the one hand, and the intense religious enthusiasm of those who sought holiness, at any cost, on the other, was seriously strained. Both sides suffered from the break, for neither hunted heretics nor harassed administrators could do what they really wanted to do as long as each was fighting endlessly against the other.

The Hundred Years' War

The French monarchy, which had seemed so strong and victorious in collision with the papacy, also fell on evil days later in the century. In 1328 the last of the Capetian kings of France died; succession passed to a new family, the Valois. Ten years later, however, Edward III of England chose to challenge the legal principle according to which the Valois had claimed the French throne, and he sent an invading army to enforce his own claims to the French crown. This began the misnamed Hundred Years' War, for the ensuing struggle between France and England lasted on and off, with long periods of truce and military inactivity, from 1338 until 1453, a total of 115 years.

Long years of warfare brought severe devastation to France. The English king had to hire mercenaries to fight in France. The French king also found it useful to hire professional archers and other specialized troops to support the by now old-fashioned knights, who at the beginning of this long war constituted the main force at the king's command. Both kings found it difficult to pay their soldiers and discharged them at the end of each campaigning season, often withholding part of their promised wages. The discharged soldiers stuck together and lived by plundering until someone offered to hire them to fight once again.

As aggressors, through most of the Hundred Years' War the English had the advantage of being able to choose the time and place for attack. They also profited from deep and longstanding divisions among the different provinces of France. In particular, the dukes of Burgundy often collaborated with the English against the French king, for they hoped to build an independent kingdom of their own along the length of the Rhine between France and Germany. Yet in time, the presence of English troops on French soil roused a sense of common identity among the French. Provincial differences began to seem less important than their common hatred of the invaders.

The French cause reached a low point when a youthful English king, Henry V (reigned 1413–1422), put fresh energies into attacking France. Recovery began with the remarkable career of Joan of Arc. Initial successes were quickly followed by her capture and execution (1431); nevertheless, the tide of battle continued to favor the French thereafter. In 1439 the Estates-General granted the French king the right to collect taxes at his discretion and without time limit, in order to get enough money to pay an army that could drive the English finally and forever from French soil. When peace came in 1453, the French had all but achieved this goal; only the town of Calais remained in English hands. Moreover, the French king emerged from the struggle with a tax-collecting machine at his disposal that made him far richer and stronger than any other ruler in Christendom.

The Black Death

Early in the Hundred Years' War, western Europe was ravaged by the Black Death, a form of bubonic plague. For two years, 1347–1349, the plague raged in city and town. About a third of the entire population died. The infection probably came overland from China, but ship's rats spread it through Europe, for the lice that transmitted the infection to humans were carried by rats. At the time, of course, people did not know how the disease spread and felt sure it was a divine judgment for their sins.

The Black Death had long-lasting effects on Europe's economy. The disease reappeared at intervals after its first arrival in Europe. Each time the plague broke out, as many as a quarter or a fifth of the people living in the locality where it was raging would die. Exact figures are beyond recovery, but it is probable that the total population of western Europe did not recover to the level it had reached in 1346 until after 1480. This represented a serious setback to Europe's prosperity. Economic life slowed down, wages rose, and all traditional economic relationships were thrown askew. The boom that had prevailed from about 900 until 1270 gave way to much harder and more uncertain times, worsened by conflicts between rich and poor in the towns, and by the long-drawn-out agony of the Hundred Years' War.

New Forms of Economic Organization

Yet hard times had the effect of forwarding some new kinds of economic organization that were to play an important part in later ages. For example, in the manufacture of woolen cloth, guilds were supplemented by the "domestic" or "putting out" system. According to this system, spinners and weavers lived in cottages out in the country where town guilds had no jurisdiction. They sometimes worked at farming part-time, and the rest of the time spun or wove materials provided to them by a capitalist or middleman. The spinners and weavers did not own the wool they worked with; sometimes they did not even own the spinning wheels and looms they used but had these provided to them also by their employer. They were paid piece rates, so much for each yard of cloth or hank of yarn they produced.

Moreover, the middlemen who put the wool out to be processed were themselves only small cogs in a bigger machine. However rich and powerful in the eyes of poor spinners and weavers, such persons were usually mere agents for some big businessman operating from Flanders or Florence, buying and selling raw materials and the finished cloth in wholesale quantities across all of Europe. Greater efficiency and specialization could be achieved by such a system. But when the livelihood of poor weavers depended on market conditions in cities hundreds of miles away, there was also a new element of risk and uncertainty. Hard times hit hard, for the poor had no cushion against unemployment.

Mining also became big business in the late Middle Ages. In central and southern Germany, miners learned how to dig deeper and how to pump water out of mines. Prospectors opened up new bodies of ore in Bohemia and Hungary. Silver was most sought after, but with mining skills as highly developed as they were, Europe never suffered serious shortage of any metal and at all times had an abundant and comparatively cheap supply of iron.

Great financiers, operating from Italy and southern Germany, managed most of Europe's mining enterprises. This was a by-product of dealings with kings and emperors, who always needed loans. One of the best kinds of security for a loan that a ruler could give was the right to exploit subsoil minerals. Roman law made subsoil rights the property of the sovereign; and Europe's rulers gladly took over that right, since it allowed them to borrow larger sums from moneylenders. When, as often happened, the loan was not repaid, mining rights passed to the lender, who had to try to get his money back by organizing efficient, large-scale mining.

Other industries that remained within the older guild organization often stagnated or even

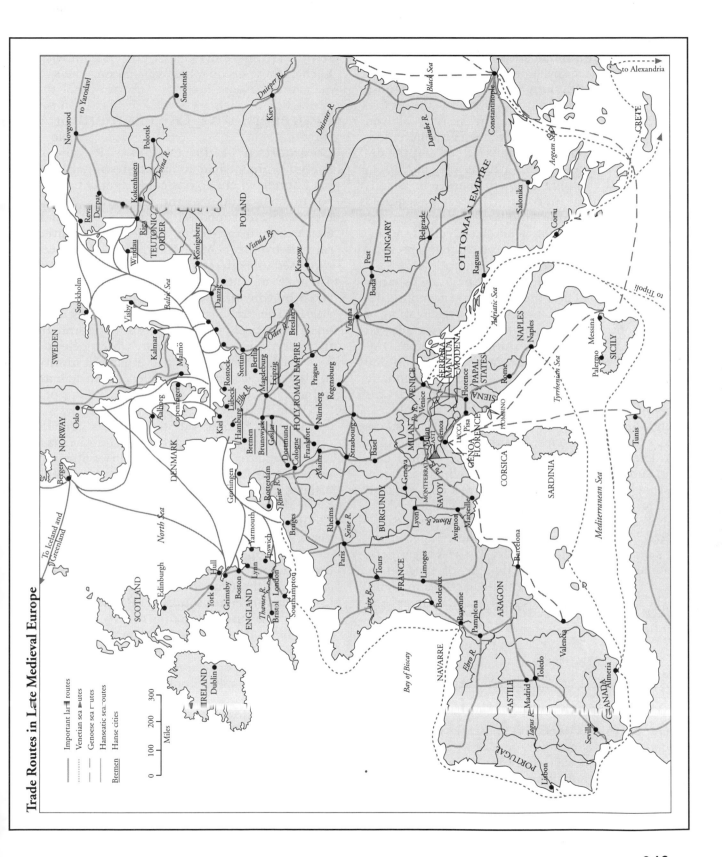

Trade Routes in Late Medieval Europe

Legend:
- Important land routes
- Venetian sea routes
- Genoese sea routes
- Hanseatic sea routes
- <u>Bremen</u> Hanse cities

Miles: 0 100 200 300

went downhill. Along the Baltic coast, however, prosperity continued to prevail. In that region German towns developed commercial relations with Swedes, Russians, and Poles, bringing those northern regions into close touch with western Europe for the first time. The herring catch in the North Sea and the Baltic Sea also increased. Better fishing boats and nets helped, but the development of a system for preserving herring in brine and shipping them to market in barrels was the critical innovation. This, too, required comparatively large amounts of capital for the salt (mostly brought from the Mediterranean), barrels, and ships needed for catching, preserving, and distributing the fish.

The difficulties in Europe's towns after about 1300 did not, therefore, stop economic development entirely. Capitalistic organization of the wool, food, and mining industries allowed greater regional specialization than before. But this tended to widen the gap between rich and poor and made the Church's rules for economic behavior more and more irrelevant to what was going on. The Church, for example, forbade taking interest on loans. Yet Europe's big business rested on such loans; and nearly all of Europe's rulers, including the pope, were up to their ears in debt to the same bankers who financed large-scale industry and charged interest on every loan they made—regardless of what the Bible said.

Such wickedness fed the anger of the Spiritual Franciscans and other heretics against the rulers of Church and state. Those same rulers, sometimes not without twinges of conscience, felt compelled to suppress their critics by force. The medieval synthesis of earlier times had clearly broken apart.

Responses to the Breakup of the Medieval Synthesis

People, of course, did not merely sit idly by and complain, although many did complain loud and long. Three different responses had a more positive ring to them and became important enough to alter the life of Europe. These were (1) an effort to develop representative government as a way of checking abuses in both Church and state, (2) religious mysticism, and (3) humanism. Each of these needs some explanation.

Representative Government

Conciliarism in the Church   Representative government had its greatest stronghold in the Church, where no one could simply inherit a position. According to the law of the Church, bishops were supposed to be elected by the clergy of their cathedrals and the selection then ratified by the people. Similarly, abbots were supposed to be elected by the monks of the monastery. Many other important decisions were taken by vote at meetings of bishops and other clerics. The Franciscans and Dominicans developed a precisely defined system of representative government, according to which delegates from each friary gathered in a general meeting to discuss overall policy and elect the head of the order.

The tradition of papal monarchy was, of course, very strong. But there was a conciliar tradition, too. In the emperor Constantine's time (d. 337) and for two or three centuries after, major issues had been settled at a council of all the bishops; and in those days the pope had been no more than bishop of Rome, even though his claim to be the successor to St. Peter assured him a degree of deference.

The pope's enemies had long been accustomed to emphasize the authority of a general council of the Church. Philip IV of France, in tangling with Pope Boniface VIII, had done so, for example. Such thinking gathered headway throughout the years when the popes stayed at Avignon (1305–1378). In 1326 Marsiglio of Padua, a professor at the University of Paris, published a famous book, *Defensor Pacis (Defender of the Peace)*, in which he argued that all legitimate political power came from the people and that the Church should be governed by councils and have nothing to do with the affairs of secular government.

Others criticized the popes for staying away from their proper post at Rome. Finally, one of the Avignon popes did return to Rome and died there in 1378. The cardinals met and elected a new pope under pressure from angry mobs who wanted the pope to stay in Rome. Then the cardinals withdrew and met again, choosing a second pope who took up his residence at Avignon. Each promptly denounced the other as a false pope. Europe was presented with the spectacle of two angry rivals, each claiming to be the earthly head of the Church. The Great Schism, as it is known, lasted until 1417.

It seemed obvious that the only way the quarrel could be solved was to call a general council. The professors of the University of Paris championed this solution, but the first effort misfired. Cardinals from each of the rival camps called a council at Pisa in 1409 and elected still a third claimant to the papal office; but the two others continued to exist. Finally, in 1414 another council met at Constance. Emperor Sigismund (1410–1437) joined forces with the pope chosen at Pisa to summon this council, and it was well attended.

The Council of Constance set out to reform the Church, combat heresy, and end the schism. Fortunately the assembled bishops succeeded in persuading two of the three popes to resign. The third lost all support, so that when a new pope was chosen by the council in 1417, all of Latin Christendom recognized him. The council combated heresy by declaring some of John Wycliffe's views to be false and by burning the Bohemian heretic John Hus, who made the mistake of attending the council on the strength of Emperor Sigismund's promise of safe conduct.

Church reform was more difficult. The University of Paris professors hoped that councils would be called regularly in the future to deal with important issues as they arose. They arranged for a new council that met at Basel in 1431. But the pope was unwilling to allow councils to cut into his authority, and the leaders of the Council of Basel, having quarreled with the pope, made the mistake of proposing to elect a rival pope. This roused general revulsion. The prospect of dividing the Church once again between two popes seemed too much of a risk.

The pope took advantage of this situation by calling a rival council at Florence in 1439, which won what seemed like a great victory: acceptance by representatives from Constantinople of the pope's definition of Christian faith. Thereafter, the Council of Basel simply petered out, meeting for the last time in 1449.

With its failure to reform the Church in any important way, the conciliar movement ended in defeat. Papal monarchy had been restored; and in the ensuing years the popes plunged eagerly into the busy world of Italian politics, where they were merely one among other princes and rulers. Less and less attention was paid by the popes to the religious concerns of anxious Christians who were not willing to settle for routine administration of the sacraments by a Church that was preoccupied with raising and spending money for wars and diplomacy, erecting churches, and maintaining hospitals, schools, monasteries, and bishops' palaces.

Parliamentarianism in Secular Government

The idea and ideal of representative government had smaller scope in most royal governments. In France, for example, the Estates-General ceased to be important after 1439, when it voted to give the king the right to assess and collect taxes as needed. Nevertheless, it did meet occasionally, at the king's command, until 1614.

In England, however, the Hundred Years' War had just the opposite effect. The king was always in need of more money for the wars in France, but the lords and commons of England were none too eager to give it to him. They made their feelings known through Parliament. Parliament developed from the custom of calling vassals to the lord's court for consultation, feasting, and the settlement of any judicial business that might have arisen since the last meeting. In the time of Henry III, who reigned from 1216 to 1272, the circle of men whom the king of England consulted on such occasions was enlarged to include representatives of the towns and of smaller landholders from the shires.

In 1295 a parliament met that became the model for later ones. Its membership was made up of two representatives from each shire and the same number from each town that had a royal charter. These made up the House of Commons, which met separately from the House of Lords, where the great nobles, bishops, and abbots of the kingdom gathered, each invited individually by the king.

Throughout the Hundred Years' War, parliaments continued to meet. The House of Commons began to go slow in approving new taxes or renewing old ones until after the king had promised to "redress grievances." These were listed in bills that the king had to agree to before the Commons would approve new taxes. The effect of such a procedure was to limit the powers of the of the king, especially in matters of taxation, at a time when the French king's powers were being enlarged. It also meant that the royal government had to pay close attention to the wishes and interests of the propertied men of the kingdom represented in Parliament.

The House of Commons, however, was by no means proof against control by great landed nobles. During the Wars of the Roses (1455–1485), for example, Parliament almost ceased to function. Rival cliques of nobles fought one another in an effort to put their candidate on the throne. Many noble families were killed off in these wars before Henry Tudor emerged victorious in 1485. After he was crowned as Henry VII, he was able to establish a nearly absolute monarchy in England. Parliament nevertheless continued to meet, even though it usually obeyed Henry's orders.

In other parts of Europe, representative government also suffered setbacks. Generally speaking, princes and kings got stronger, and checks upon their power from representative assemblies—called Estates or Diets—became weaker. In Germany, however, it was not the central administration of the empire but princes of the second rank—dukes, margraves, and bishops—that consolidated their authority. Each emperor's power depended on the family possessions he happened to have. This put the emperors more or less on the same level as other German princes, although they never entirely gave up the effort to revive some of the old imperial rights.

In northern and central Italy, town governments controlled most of the countryside. Until 1250 or later, these towns were governed by some sort of coalition among the guilds; but as time passed, republican forms of government broke down more and more often. Harsh conflicts between rich and poor were part of the problem. A growing unwillingness of citizens to drop their other activities and fight as common soldiers created an even more critical weakness. For when military affairs came to be entrusted to hired bands of professional soldiers, sudden coups d'état could put the commander of such

a band in charge of the city he was supposed to defend. But what one coup created, another could undo. Hence plot and counterplot produced innumerable sudden political shifts. Complicated alliances and factions racked the political life of almost all the cities of Italy.

The three most important cities (except for Rome, where the popes remained political masters) were Venice, Milan, and Florence. Each followed a different political path. Venice came into the hands of a small group of patrician families after 1297. Milan, on the other hand, fell under the despotic rule of the Visconti (1277–1447) and then of the Sforza (1450–1535) families. Florence was at first more democratic, permitting lesser guilds to take part in city government; but from 1434, a wealthy banking family, the Medici, took control by becoming political bosses from behind the scenes while leaving the republican forms of government outwardly unchanged.

In some remote and backward parts of Europe, monarchies remained weak, and local chieftains, of whatever kind, retained correspondingly greater importance. This was true in such lands as Scotland and Poland, for example. Free villages and associations of villages also survived in the Alps and in parts of Sweden and Norway. Taking western Europe as a whole, however, one must conclude that the effort to reform Church and state through representative forms of government clearly failed. The idea took fresh life in later times, to be sure, but in 1500 representative institutions looked like no more than outworn forms from a disorderly, half-barbarous past.

Religious Mysticism

Religious mysticism and doubt about the powers of human reason tended to replace the optimistic effort of the earlier age to fuse Aristotle and Christianity into a single, logical whole. William of Ockham (1300–1349), for example, was not convinced that Thomas Aquinas had really proved so much of Christian doctrine by reasoning. Ockham argued that faith and reason really had little to do with one another.

The more positive side of this kind of doubt was seen in personalities like Meister Eckhart (ca. 1260–1327) and Thomas à Kempis (ca. 1380–1471), who, as mystics, withdrew from the world of everyday in an effort to find God. *The Imitation of Christ*, a book of private devotions compiled by Thomas à Kempis, became and still remains a best seller. By searching within the individual soul and cultivating private virtues, this school of piety simply bypassed the tangled problem of how to reform the Church and human society. Instead of bothering with public problems, individuals could achieve salvation by private religious exercises and private, personal encounters with God. These ideas found their main response in the Low Countries near the mouth of the Rhine.

Humanism and the Renaissance

Humanism looked to ancient Greek and Roman authors for inspiration in somewhat the same way that the mystics looked for God within themselves. The term "humanism" was invented to distinguish the study of humankind and humanity's affairs from the theological study of God and God's relation to humanity. First Latin and then Greek authors were eagerly seized upon by scholars who found the moral code of Cicero and Livy helpful in defining an ideal of conduct for themselves. Some scholars, especially in Florence, hoped to create a kind of public virtue that would sustain republican government; but most humanists were hangers-on at princely courts or attached themselves to the papacy. Their humanism provided a pattern for private life and gentility.

The poet and essayist Francesco Petrarch (1304–1374), a Florentine who served in a minor capacity at the papal court in Avignon for most of his life, was one of the first to express the humanist ideal. Others after him became great scholars. They combed through monastery libraries in search of forgotten classical texts. They discovered how to correct errors that had crept into ancient books as one copyist after another made blunders, and they found excitement and value in the labors of scholarship, which became an end in itself. A limited circle of wealthy patrons shared their enthusiasm and supported them.

When these scholarly skills were turned upon sacred texts and medieval charters, problems arose. Lorenzo Valla (1406–1457), you will remember, took a careful look at the Donation of Constantine and was able to prove beyond all reasonable doubt that it was a forgery. This did not help the papal cause. The text of the Bible itself offered interesting problems also. But Italian humanists were too busy with pagan texts (and perhaps also too prudent) to try tampering with Holy Scripture. The first great scholar who attempted to purge errors from the Latin text of the Bible was a Dutchman, Desiderius Erasmus (1466–1536).

Still another result of humanist activity was to discredit the living Latin of the Church. Cicero's diction and style were so extravagantly admired that some scholars felt no Latin word should be used that Cicero had not employed. This ruled out a vast vocabulary that had grown up in European learned circles. Not everyone accepted Ciceronian Latin as the only proper standard; but in proportion as this ideal did take hold, it choked off Latin as a living language.

Humanists believed they were reviving the glory of ancient literature and thought. They viewed their age as a kind of rebirth, or renaissance, of Latin literature, and invented the term "Middle Ages" to mark their own new age off from the darkness of earlier centuries. Their choice of terms still dominates our view of Europe's history, even though we no longer think that the earlier years of the Middle Ages were so dark—and historians have applied the term "Renaissance" not simply to the rebirth of Latin literature but to a whole age, starting in Italy sometime about 1300, and spreading north of the Alps mainly after 1500.

Humanism and mysticism therefore, each in its own way, changed the texture of European thought and feeling; yet neither was entirely successful in coping with the problems of the age. The two movements represented opposite poles within the spectrum of European thought and feeling—the one emphasizing God almost to the exclusion of everything else and the other reversing matters by almost forgetting about God. Neither extreme could win general consent; the tension between them expressed the restlessness and dissatisfaction of the age.

PETRARCH ON MOUNT VENTOUX

The Italian poet and scholar Francesco Petrarch (1304–1374) has been called the first modern man. What this means is that his enthusiasm for classical Latin authors and for some of the pagan values—a desire for fame, above all—offers the earliest clear example of an intellectual movement known as *humanism*. But Petrarch was also a priest, and he looked back toward the Middle Ages as much as he looked forward to anything new or modern.

His own account of how he climbed Mount Ventoux, near Avignon in France, symbolizes the doubleness of Petrarch's life. He tells us that after some hours of climbing he reached the top and looked around to enjoy the view spread out magnificently below. The bridge across the Rhone River and the city of Avignon lay spread out before his eyes. Around and beyond these works of human hands stretched the surrounding hills and mountains, with glimpses of the Rhone sparkling in between.

But while contemplating how the grand works of humanity were dwarfed by the still grander works of God in the landscape below, Petrarch's mind suddenly turned inward. Overwhelmed with a sense of his folly at climbing a mountain simply to look at the view, he drew a copy of St. Augustine's *The City of God* from his pocket and began to read and meditate upon his own sinfulness. After a while he started down, careful to watch where he put his feet, but never raising his eyes to the view lest he lose sight of the state of his soul by enjoying the sights of the world.

The Mirror of the Age in Art

The two centuries from 1300 to 1500 were the time when western Europeans discovered a style of painting as powerful and original as the Gothic architecture of the period from 1150 to 1300 had been. The main centers of artistic development were Italy, especially Florence, and Flanders. Flemish art grew out of medieval manuscript illustration and always retained the rich colors and minute detail appropriate to illustrations. The greatest master was Jan van Eyck (1370–1440), whose realistic portraits and harmonious composition reflected the comfort and taste of the urban upper classes.

Italian painting developed out of Byzantine art styles. The need to decorate the walls of churches and other religious buildings gave a painter like Giotto (1276–1337) his main employment. A strain toward realism and accuracy of detail was apparent in Italian painting, just as in painting north of the Alps. The otherworldly effect attained by Byzantine elongation and other distortions of human figures did not satisfy western European tastes.

Methods for suggesting the roundness of limbs by skillful shading, for example, were invented by Masaccio (about 1401–1428); a few years later Leon Battista Alberti (1404–1472) discovered the geometrical rules for linear perspective. The trick was to make all parallel lines converge upon a disappearing point, located anywhere on the surface of the painting or, as was discovered later, even off the painting. By drawing figures and buildings to fit the differing scale thus established, an illusion of three-dimensional space could be created.

When painters first learned to construct their works of art on these principles, the effect was entrancing and delightful. It all looked "real," as though the viewer could walk in among the figures and scenes of the picture. We are so accustomed to photographs that we can hardly imagine how exciting the new art was to eyes that had never before seen three dimensions accurately plotted on a two-dimensional surface.

The effort to achieve perfect accuracy and realism called forth further refinements: so-called aerial perspective, which changes colors with distance; and the use of living models for figures of saints and mythological figures. The subject matter of painting broadened to include pagan and historical themes. Sandro Botticelli's (1444–1510) *Birth of Venus* shows how far painting could go in a secular direction. Leonardo da Vinci's (1452–1519) *Virgin of the Rocks* shows how far a religious theme could be humanized.

Renaissance painting was matched by changes in sculpture and architecture. Roman remains were plentiful in Italy, and the humanist enthusiasm for things ancient spread also among architects and sculptors, who assumed that what the Romans had done must be superior. Accordingly, Donatello (1386–1466) introduced free-standing nude statues again in imitation of classical works. Michelangelo (1475–1564) brought the Renaissance sculptural tradition to its climax just a century later.

Architecture was too closely tied to everyday wants and to the requirements of church services to imitate the ancient models exactly. But Renaissance architecture freely borrowed decorative details, such as columns and "egg and dart" design moldings. Grand and harmonious effects were sometimes achieved, the most famous example being St. Peter's Church in Rome, built between 1445 and 1626.

In painting and sculpture, as well as in architecture, tension between sacred and secular attitudes can be seen almost everywhere. Realism and interest in visual detail suggest the joys of ordinary human existence; yet the subject matter was more often than not religious. How to keep the two in harness was the great unsolved question people faced all over western Europe. It remained critical throughout the following century.

Bourgeois Wealth and Pride   This painting by Jan van Eyck was made in 1434 in Flanders. It portrays an Italian merchant, Giovanni Arnolfino, and his wife, Giovanna Cenami, as the inscription over the mirror tells us. Italians dominated large-scale long-distance trade in the fifteenth century, so it is not surprising to find an Italian residing in Flanders and prospering there. He probably dealt in cloth, which was the principal Flemish export. Arnolfino apparently commissioned this portrait by the most famous Flemish painter of the day to commemorate his married bliss and worldly wealth. Such a celebration of private life was unusual in the fifteenth century; but it allows us to glimpse the domestic comforts available to a man rich enough to own such luxuries as a mirror, chandelier, and richly textured robes of fur and wool. The innovative and essentially private theme of this painting was matched by the technical fact that Jan van Eyck pioneered the use of oil paints, applying them to a small, flat surface. He thus created a portable work of art suitable for hanging on the wall of a private house. This sort of painting became common in later centuries, but in 1434 it was radically new.

Conclusion

About 1450 western Europe seemed to be in real trouble. Yet, in fact, Europe was on the verge of its most dramatic expansion. After the event, it is possible to see some of the things at work in European society that made possible the extraordinary age of exploration and self-transformation that came to Europe between 1500 and 1650.

First, Europe's economy activated a larger proportion of the whole population than commonly happened elsewhere. Coarse and common articles came regularly into the market for sale and purchase: wool, fish, timber, plowshares. This meant that relatively large numbers

---

How to Sail the High Seas   European technology improved rapidly in the late Middle Ages, as illustrated here by views of two ships, one (left) dating from the 1440s and the other (right) from about fifty years later. In the earlier representation, notice such novelties as the stern post rudder, the pulleys for raising and lowering the sail, and the crow's nest atop the mast. By climbing up the rope ladders, crossbowmen could reach the crow's nest and then shoot downward at hostile boarders, while enjoying near immunity from those beneath them. Such a ship was safe from most attackers and could carry goods along the coasts of Europe quite safely, despite stormy seas and high tides. Fifty years later improvements made European vessels capable of sailing confidently across the oceans of the earth through any sea. Key advances were the multiple masts, which allowed the crew to adjust the extent of exposed sail to the force of the wind far more accurately than before, and use of guns on shipboard. Guns provided a potent offensive form of armament for European ships, supplementing the older defensive capability of the crow's nest. They remain hidden inside the ship in this woodcut, but their presence is indicated by the square gunports that appear alongside and in the rear.

of people benefited and suffered from the ups and downs of the business cycle. Responses to price changes drove workers into some lines of activity and out of others. This made Europe's economy flexible. Even fixed agricultural routines were less unchanging than elsewhere in the civilized world. When opportunity offered, labor and resources could be mobilized for new projects on a greater scale than was possible in more custom-bound societies.

This was Europe's first strength. It was the reverse side of the economic frictions and uncertainty that fomented struggles between rich and poor. The absence of any single, controlling center meant, also, that no distant imperial order could turn off sea ventures, for example, as had happened in China when the Ming emperors prohibited seafaring for reasons of their own.

A second element in Europe's life that proved advantageous in the long run, though also very costly, was the warlikeness that ran all the way through European society. Peasants and townspeople were in the habit of defending themselves; they did not meekly submit to their social superiors. And the nobles of Europe were specialists in war. Only the Japanese were as ready to resort to violence, or as dedicated to a code of personal heroism. In China the rulers of society were more pacific. In Islam peasants and townspeople knew their place and usually did not try to fight back against the specialists in violence who ruled over them.

Printing Shop Printing, gunpowder, and the compass were, according to Francis Bacon, the three inventions that made Europe superior to other civilizations. Bacon did not know that all three reached Europe from China, though it remains true that Europeans used them in new ways. This woodcut shows an early European print shop. On the left, compositors are setting type by taking individual letters from the frame in which they were stored and placing them in a hand-held frame. In the foreground a boy is taking a proof, while the man with eyeglasses in the left background is reading proof to make sure no wrong letters were put in the text. In the right rear a pressman is inking the type with two round pads; in the right foreground another pressman is turning the screw to make the imprinted letters uniform and clear on the page. Such shops could produce hundreds of identical sheets a day. This made communication cheaper and more accurate than ever before and allowed an enormous increase in what Europeans knew.

A third element was Europe's acquaintance with three new techniques whose potentialities had only begun to be explored in 1500. These were (1) printing with movable type and the more rapid and exact diffusion of knowledge that printing permitted, (2) the compass and other improvements in shipbuilding and navigation that made it reasonably safe to sail across even the roughest oceans of the world, and (3) gunpowder and artillery techniques that made it easy to breach even the strongest castle walls.

For all these reasons, and perhaps for others we are not wise enough to recognize, the fraying out of Europe's medieval synthesis did not lead to deadlock. Instead, it proved to be the preface to new and world-shaking changes within Europe and among the peoples of the entire world. Exploration of these changes, the province of modern history, will require a separate volume.

Bibliography

Three major monuments of European literature from this era deserve attention: Dante Alighieri, *The Divine Comedy;* Geoffrey Chaucer, *The Canterbury Tales;* and John Langland, *Piers Plowman.* Dante is readily available in several translations and editions, but the medieval English used by Chaucer and Langland is hard for us to understand in the original form. Fortunately, some editions ease this problem by modernizing spelling and providing notes to explain unfamiliar words.

Three general histories are especially worth your attention: Johan Huizinga, *The Waning of the Middle Ages* (1954); Steven Ozment, *The Age of Reform (1250–1550): An Intellectual and Religious History of Late Me-* *dieval and Reformation Europe* (1980); and Jacques Le Goff, *Medieval Civilization 400–1500* (1989).

On more specialized themes, the following are noteworthy: Henri Pirenne, *Medieval Cities* (1925); Daniel P. Waley, *The Italian City Republics* (1969); Philip Ziegler, *The Black Death* (1969); Christopher Allemand, *The Hundred Years' War* (1988); and Francis Oakley, *The Western Church in the Late Middle Ages* (1979). On friars and heresy see John H. Moorman, *A History of the Franciscan Order from Its Origin to the Year 1517* (1968); Lester K. Little, *Religious Poverty and the Profit Economy in Medieval Europe* (1978); and Malcolm D. Lambert, *Medieval Heresy* (2nd ed., 1992).

On the Renaissance, the classic work is Jacob Burckhardt, *The Civilization of the Renaissance in Italy* (1878, and often reprinted). More modern books worth checking out include Denys Hay, *The Italian Renaissance in Its Historical Background* (1961); Myron P. Gilmore, *The World of Humanism, 1453–1517* (1952); Garrett Mattingly, *Renaissance Diplomacy* (1953); Michael E. Mallett, *Mercenaries and Their Masters: Warfare in Renaissance Italy* (1974); Gene A. Brucker, *Renaissance Florence* (1969); and D. S. Chambers, *The Imperial Age of Venice, 1380–1580* (1970).

On the three great technological innovations of the age (printing, gunpowder, and the compass), all imported from China but put to new uses in Europe, see P. Butler, *The Origin of Printing in Europe* (1966); O. F. G. Hogg, *Artillery: Its Origin, Heyday and Decline* (1970); and Carolo M. Cipolla, *Guns, Sails and Empire: Technological Innovation and the Early Phases of European Expansion, 1400–1700* (1965).

For the history of art, Leon Battista Alberti, *On Painting* (J. R. Spencer, trans., 1956), offers us the record of how he invented geometrically accurate linear perspective in 1435—an accomplishment that became the hallmark of European painting for the ensuing 450 years. Standard modern authorities on Renaissance art include Bernard Berenson, *Italian Painters of the Renaissance* (rev. ed., 1957); Erwin Panofsky, *Renaissance and Renascences in Western Art* (2nd ed., 1965); Ernest T. Dewald, *Italian Painting 1200–1600* (1961); and Peter Murray, *The Architecture of the Italian Renaissance* (1966).

Epilogue: Part II
The State of the World

1500

Let us pause now to survey the world on the eve of Europe's oceanic discoveries and compare it with the state of the world 2000 years before. The four styles of civilization that had appeared by 500 B.C.E. were still much in evidence in 1500. China, India, the Middle East, and Europe each continued to support a civilization of its own; and in many ways the basic structures of each civilization were unchanged from what had been there 2000 years before in each of the areas concerned. Innumerable changes had come in detail. Ideas and skills had passed from one end of the civilized world to another. But still the European emphasis upon territorial states, the Middle Eastern concern with monotheism, the Indian caste system, and the Chinese familial form of government and social order continued to shape the lives of everyone belonging to each of these civilizations.

The territory on which civilized life flourished had increased so much that by 1500 an almost continuous belt of civilized land ran across Europe and Asia from the Atlantic to the Pacific Ocean; and important new offshoots had developed to the north and south of the four main civilizations. The rise of medieval Europe meant a shift northward from the Mediterranean Sea to a focus in the drainage area of the North Sea and English Channel. The conversion of Russia involved an even greater northward displacement of the center of gravity for the Orthodox Christian world from Constantinople to Moscow.

Moreover, in 500 B.C.E, Greek civilization had been a very new, small, and sharply focused pattern of life, planted around the Aegean Sea. By 1500 its heirs and successors had taken in so much from the barbarian world of the north, and from the Middle and Far Eastern civilizations, that the sharp definition of the early days was gone. Instead, the Greeks' European heirs had created two branches of Christendom—Greek

Orthodox and Roman Catholic—that were so different from each other as to justify counting them as separate civilizations.

Asian Civilizations

A similar development had taken place among China's northeastern borderlands; for, as we have seen, by 1500 Japanese civilization had become quite different from Chinese. It should, therefore, be counted as a separate civilization, too. Finally, the Moslem world had penetrated all of the western and central steppe region of Asia. It would not be wise to count the culture of the Golden Horde or of the other nomadic confederations as new civilizations, for nomads could never sustain the range of specialisms we expect of a civilization. Yet the steppe peoples were deeply tinged with Islamic civilization and distinct in their ways of life from their settled neighbors. Let us say, therefore, that a semi-civilization or high barbarism had arisen on the western and central steppes, related to Islam in the way that the new northern civilizations of Japan and Europe were related to ancient Chinese and ancient Mediterranean civilizations.

To the south, the expansion of civilization created a more diverse pattern. In southeast Asia, for example, those living in Sumatra and Java and mainland peoples living in what is today Thailand (formerly Siam), Cambodia, and Vietnam had come into touch with Indian civilization about the time of Christ; but by 600 they all began to develop independent art styles of their own. Fusion between local fertility cults and Buddhist and Hindu ideas produced a series of court cultures of great splendor. They are known to us mainly through the ruins of massive temples and palaces. But creating the social and political organization required to build such monuments was itself a great feat; and these cultures deserve the term "civilization" just as much as do the achievements of the Sumerian, Inca, or Aztec peoples. The comparison is, in-

Angkor Wat, Cambodia   This vast temple was built about 1150 by a Khmer ruler, King Suryavarum II. It celebrated the power and beneficence of the god Vishnu, whose worship had come to Cambodia from India centuries before. But at the same time it was designed to become a tomb for the King, so that after his death Suryavarum could become one with Vishnu and enjoy a blissful immortality. The temple was also an image of the world as Hindu teaching described it. The highest tower corresponded to—and in some sense was identified with—Mount Meru, which was believed to rise at the center of a flat and rectangular earth. The ground plan of the temple was therefore rectangular, surrounded by artificial ponds just as the earth was supposed to be surrounded by water. The greatness of Vishnu and of the King, as expressed inside the temple, affirmed and established their greatness in the world as a whole outside the temple. That was why Khmer rulers put so much effort into building this and other similar temples.

deed, difficult to avoid. Like the ancient river valley civilizations and the Amerindian civilizations, each of the civilizations of southeast Asia consisted of a great temple-palace and court set in the midst of simple peasant villages, with very little in between.

In Java and Sumatra, civilization was sustained by shipping; on the mainland, big river valleys provided the setting for local court civilizations. Each river valley was more or less self-contained, with fertile rice fields and only limited trade or other contacts with the outside world. The Indian imprint was strong everywhere, but it always mingled with differing native customs. After about 800 the region was also influenced by Moslems, who dominated the sea trade and eventually (1520s) conquered Java and Sumatra. The inland valleys, however, escaped Moslem control. Their rulers simply cut off most contact with the outside by preventing strangers from coming upriver. This policy left the landward, northern borders unguarded.

Thus, for example, the Khmers in the Mekong Valley built enormous temple-palaces at Angkor Wat and Angkor Thom. But by 1431 invaders from the north—the Thais—broke up their empire and established a more warlike state of their own based on the neighboring Menam Valley. The Burmese came down from the north at about the same time as the Thais. Both of these groups were dislodged by Chinese expansion. The newcomers preferred Buddhism to the mixed Hindu-Buddhism of the earlier empires; they were more military, less withdrawn, but did not create such vast and impressive architectural monuments as the Khmers had done.

African Civilizations

In Africa, too, a cluster of court civilizations came into existence, not only in the Islamic portions of east and west Africa but also much deeper in the continent. In the Congo basin, for example, a pagan kingdom of Kongo existed when the Portuguese first appeared along the coast. Farther south a similar empire of Monomotapa centered on the east coast between the Zambezi and Limpopo rivers.

These relatively large states were created by Bantu-speaking peoples who had begun to spread through central and southern Africa soon after the start of the Common Era, spreading out from a region around the Bight of Benin, where the west African coast turns southward toward the Cape of Good Hope. The spread of the Bantu peoples probably started when Indonesian food crops, suited to cultivation in the heavy rain forest of the Congo basin, reached them. They were skilled iron workers, too, so that they had tools suitable for clearing the forest and cultivating the ground afterward. At an unknown later date some Bantu tribes acquired cattle, perhaps from Nubia. A much more rapid movement down the highland spine of east Africa then began, as cattle herders and farmers drifted south looking for new pastures for their animals. Khoi and San hunters and gatherers retreated south before the advancing Bantus, while Pygmies withdrew into the shadows of the dense Congo rain forests.

Trade with Moslems brought a large part of Africa into touch with the rest of Eurasia. Caravans regularly crossed the Sahara, connecting the cities and kingdoms of west Africa with the Mediterranean. In addition, traders and raiders moved east-west through the grassy savanna country that lay south of the Sahara.

By both these routes, west Africa came into close touch with Islam. After the overthrow of Ghana (1076), a series of imperial states arose that united large areas of west Africa under a single monarch. The rulers and their courts all professed Islam and drew a major part of their income from trade. The most important of these states were the Mali Empire, which reached its peak soon after 1300, and the Songhai Empire, which ruled most of the Niger River region (and beyond) by 1500.

The fact that rulers and traders were Moslem did not make the common people into followers of Mohammed. Many villages in west Africa remained loyal to older, "pagan" forms of religion. They were little affected by the rise of the new empires, except when someone came from the capital and made the villagers perform some labor service (for example, carrying heavy goods to market) or forced them to give up part of their crop as a form of tax.

MANSA MUSA

In 1307 Mansa Musa came to the throne of Mali in west Africa. He inherited a great kingdom, centered on the upwaters of the Niger River but extending westward to the Atlantic coast and eastward below the place where the river bends southward and heads toward the sea. Many different peoples lived in this part of Africa, but the rulers were Mandinka, who specialized as traders. Caravans across the Sahara kept them in touch with the Moslems of North Africa, and the Mandinka people had themselves become Moslem several centuries before their kingdom reached its peak of prosperity under Mansa Musa.

He reigned for twenty-five years, during which time he conducted several successful military campaigns. But his reign was principally famous for the general prosperity that prevailed and for the development of new skills that brought Mali more fully into the circle of the Moslem world. Thus, Mansa Musa devoted considerable attention to building new and larger mosques, importing architects who taught his people to use brick instead of the pounded clay they had previously used for building purposes. He also brought in teachers of the Sacred Law and founded madrassas that made the cities of Timbuctu and Jenne into famous centers of Islamic learning and teaching. The government began to keep written records, thus giving employment to graduates of the new madrassas and making the law and practice of the land more thoroughly Moslem than before.

In 1324 Mansa Musa decided that he should make the pilgrimage to Mecca, as all pious Moslems were supposed to do if they could afford it. He could certainly afford it, for he traveled with a large retinue and carried an enormous quantity of gold dust gathered from the upwaters of the Niger River by placer mining. When he reached Cairo in Egypt, he stayed for several months, waiting for the season of pilgrimage. During that time he purchased all sorts of Egyptian goods and handed out gold dust so lavishly that for years afterward, the exchange rate between gold and silver in Cairo was upset by the abundance of gold that Mansa Musa left behind him.

The whole Moslem world marveled at such wealth and magnificence. West Africa remained an important source of gold for centuries afterward, until the placer mines ran out. But the Mandinka of Mali traded in many things besides gold, including salt, slaves, ivory, textiles, and food. The wealth and prosperity of the country depended on production and exchange of these commodities far more than on the gold that made it so famous abroad.

The imperial courts, however, like those of southeast Asia, were splendid indeed. Gold dust was abundant in the Niger and its tributaries. Rulers organized the search for gold and took possession of what was found. This made the monarchs of Mali and Songhai very rich. Merchants from all parts of the Moslem world were eager to exchange luxuries of every sort for African gold and ivory.

A trade in slaves also existed in parts of Africa, mainly along the east coast. But this way of exploiting African labor was not nearly as important as it became later, after the discovery of America.

African Sculpture This delicate head was carved in Zaire, though whether it was made before or after European sailors first encountered the Kingdom of Kongo in the 1480s is unknown. It exemplifies one style of African art, but different styles existed in different parts of the continent. That diversity attests to the wide-ranging cultural diversity of Africa, which remains a distinctive feature of the continent to the present. Local peoples had different modes of life, varying from small bands of hunters and gatherers who lived in much the same way as the earliest known humans, to powerful kingdoms with all the hallmarks of civilization—that is, a rural tax-paying majority subordinated to rulers, tax-gatherers, professional warriors, and merchants. These urban classes in turn patronized skilled artisans like the person who made this statue.

All in all, Africa remained on the margins of the civilized world up to 1500. Powerful states and grand courts had come into existence in several parts of the continent, agriculture and herd-ing were expanding quite fast, and a large part of the entire continent had entered into trade relations with the outside world. But due to tropical diseases and to the fact that all the African rivers (except the Nile) have falls near their mouths, it was difficult for strangers to penetrate deeply; and most Africans lived in small, self-sufficient villages and had only a few contacts with anyone outside their own immediate community.

Specialized skills, elaborate social organization, and other hallmarks of civilized life were definitely present in Africa. But they were concentrated at a few courtly centers. Moreover, these centers were vulnerable, like the temple-palaces of southeast Asia and of the Americas, because the common people scarcely shared in the benefits of civilization. Instead, they had to pay taxes and perform labor services for the rulers, and we may assume they did not like it. The early civilizations of the Middle East and of all other parts of the world had been just the same and suffered from the same basic weakness. Africa, like the Americas and southeast Asia, was simply at an earlier stage of development at the time when the opening of the world's oceans to European shipping changed relations among all the world's civilizations.

New World Civilizations

Across the ocean in the Americas, the "imperial" period, which seems to have begun about 1000, moved toward recorded history when the Aztecs began to build an empire in Mexico (ca. 1400) and the Incas extended their power over all of Peru (ca. 1438) and Ecuador (ca. 1500). The Inca Empire was a tightly administered, bureaucratic regime. The Aztec state, by contrast, exerted only a loose control over surrounding peoples. The Aztecs, in fact, spent much effort on raids required to round up the large numbers of captives that were needed to appease the Aztec gods, who fed on human hearts. No strong and stable empire could arise on the basis of such a relation between the Aztecs and their neighbors.

Tenochtitlán, the Aztec capital, was nonetheless a large and splendid city. It was situated on islands in a shallow lake, connected to the mainland by narrow causeways.

Aztec, Inca Empires on Eve of the Spanish Conquest

Vast temples, great marketplaces thronged by buyers and sellers, and stately palace rituals disguised the inherent fragility of Aztec society. Elsewhere in Mexico other palace and temple centers had evolved into genuine cities as well. To the north, in what is now the United States and Canada, many different agricultural and hunting peoples existed. Some of them were organized to support large ceremonial centers, vaguely modeled on the more splendid civilizations of Mexico. The Mayans, on the other hand, who had once supported temples and priests, relapsed toward simple peasant village life after about 1400, when their last imperial center in Yucatan somehow lost its hold on the surrounding countryside.

Peru, too, supported a series of impressive cities, some of them defended by enormous walls of stone. Roads and irrigation works were more elaborate than anything known in Mexico, and Inca rulers kept records by means of an ingenious arrangement of knots in fringed leather. Forms of picture writing also existed among the Aztecs; and calendrical calculations continued to play an important part in religious ceremonies, as they had among the ancient Maya.

Altogether, then, Amerindian civilizations, like those of Africa and southeast Asia, were in a flourishing condition in 1500, even though their skills and level of organization never caught up with the major centers of the Old World.

The Balance of World Civilizations

Obviously, the civilizations of southeast Asia, of sub-Saharan Africa, and of America were of a different magnitude from the four great "main stems" of Europe and Asia. Far more people shared Chinese, Indian, Islamic, and European styles of civilization than took part in any of these temple-palace civilizations. No single blow could disrupt one of the great civilizations. Devastation of a single center was not enough to destroy the tradition of skill, learning, and taste that made Chinese, Indian, Moslem, and European civilizations what they were. By contrast, devastation of a single center or of a few separate centers could easily destroy the weaker civilizations of the Americas, as the Spaniards soon proved. Southeast Asian civilizations were nearly as fragile. Moslem conquest of Java, for example, exterminated the Hindu court culture of that island after 1525, and the Thais did the same to the Khmers in Cambodia a little earlier.

If temple-palace civilizations were fragile when exposed to sudden, brutal contact with the

Inca Fortress from Peru   Civilized societies arose in the high Andes soon after the beginning of the Common Era, and others flourished just as early on the Pacific coastal plain. After about 1400, from their capital at Cuzco (elevation 11,132 feet), the Incas launched a career of conquest that carried their power to the northern border of modern Ecuador and about half way through modern Chile to the south. Elaborate engineering helped to hold this vast empire together. Remarkable roads and suspension bridges were supplemented by fortresses at strategic locations. This wall was built to defend Cuzco itself. The enormous size of some of the rocks and the fact that they were shaped and put into place without the help of wheeled transport are testimony to the ingenuity and organizing capability of the Inca engineers, handicapped through they were by having only simple tools at their disposal.

outside world, how much more defenseless were the remaining peoples of the earth! All the warlike populations of Eurasia had shouldered their way into the circle of recorded history by the time of the Mongol Empire. But farther from the centers of civilized life, simple hunters and gatherers still survived. Such tribes occupied Australia and southern Africa; and Eskimo hunters had recently spread all the way round the Arctic coastline, preying upon seals and walrus that lived on the ice. But, by and large, only refuge zones remained for hunters and gatherers. Their style of life was being pushed to the far corners of the earth.

In 1500 the four main civilizations of Europe and Asia were still more or less equal to one another in their skills and attainments. Europe had metals, ships, and guns, but was far behind the other great civilizations in refinement of artisan skills. China was by far the most populous, but after the experience of the Mongol conquest the Chinese deliberately decided to retire from the sea in order to concentrate on defense against the threat from the steppes. Islam, of all the great civilizations, seemed the strongest and most successful in expanding its frontiers. In particular, a majority of the steppe nomads had been won over to the service of Islam. This imparted a tremendous military drive to the Moslem world, for it was the steppe nomads who had harassed and invaded civilized lands of Eurasia, time after time after time, for a full 2000 years. India, of the four civilizations, seemed the weakest, having fallen, for the most part, under Moslem political domination. But India's greatest successes in influencing other peoples had never depended on military or economic strength; and one can argue that the rise of Sufi mysticism within Islam was yet another demonstration of the quiet, subtle power of Indian influences. Certainly the

Sufi path and the piety of Indian holy men had much in common; and in suffering Moslem conquest, Hindus had by no means lost the ability to convert their conquerors to traditional Indian ways of thinking.

Western Europe, therefore, was only one of four civilizations and, at least on the surface, not the most promising, strongest, or most successful of the four. Yet Europe's readiness to learn and experiment, to change its own habits in the light of new experiences, and, above all, never to flinch from the next confrontation meant that in three and a half centuries, between 1500 and 1850, a fundamental reversal of balance took place. Europe ceased, in that time, to be one among equals. It became instead the center of by far the strongest and most skilled civilization in the world. How that happened is the theme of the second volume of this book.

Bibliography

Two important parts of the world have been almost entirely omitted from the chapter bibliographies, and this is the place to repair that omission.

For the early history of Africa, five books are good starting points: David W. Phillipson, *African Archaeology* (1985); Paul Bohannan and Philip Curtin, *Africa and the Africans* (3rd ed., 1988); Peter S. Garlake, *The Kingdoms of Africa* (1990); Roland Oliver, *The African Experience* (1991); and Spencer Trimingham, *The Influence of Islam upon Africa* (2nd ed., 1980).

For southeast Asia, D. G. E. Hall, *A History of South-East Asia* (4th ed., 1981); Lawrence P. Briggs, *The Ancient Khmer Empire* (1951); Paul Wheatley, *The Golden Kheronese: Studies in the Historical Geography of the Malay Peninsula before 1507 A.D.* (1961); and Kenneth R. Hall, *Maritime Trade and State Development in Early Southeast Asia* (1985), are up to date and informative.

Index